Politics and Transcendent Wisdom: The *Scripture for Humane Kings* in the Creation of Chinese Buddhism

HERMENEUTICS: STUDIES IN THE HISTORY OF RELIGIONS

Kees W. Bolle, Editor

Richard G. Marks, The Image of Bar Kokhba in Traditional Jewish Literature: False Messiah and National Hero

Joanne Punzo Waghorne, The Raja's Magic Clothes: Re-visioning Kingship and Divinity in England's India

Devin DeWeese, Islamization and Native Religion in the Golden Horde: Baba Tükles and Conversion to Islam in Historical and Epic Tradition

Gregory D. Alles, The *Iliad*, the *Rāmāyaṇa*, and the Work of Religion: Failed Persuasion and Religious Mystification

Arvind Sharma, The Philosophy of Religion and Advaita Vedānta: A Comparative Study in Religion and Reason

Gregory Shaw, Theurgy and the Soul: The Neoplatonism of Iamblichus

Jess Byron Hollenback, Mysticism: Experience, Response, and Empowerment

Charles D. Orzech, Politics and Transcendent Wisdom: The *Scripture for Humane Kings* in the Creation of Chinese Buddhism

Charles D. Orzech

Politics and Transcendent Wisdom: The *Scripture for Humane Kings* in the Creation of Chinese Buddhism

The Pennsylvania State University Press
University Park, Pennsylvania

Library of Congress Cataloging-in-Publication Data

Orzech, Charles D., 1952–
Politics and transcendent wisdom : the Scripture for humane kings in the creation of Chinese Buddhism / Charles D. Orzech.
p. cm.
Includes bibliographical references and indexes.
ISBN 0-271-01715-5 (alk. paper)
1. Jen wang po je ching—Criticism, interpretation, etc. I. Title.
BQ1937.079 1998 96-52407
294.3'377—dc21 CIP

Printed in the United States of America
Published by The Pennsylvania State University Press,
University Park, PA 16802-1003

It is the policy of The Pennsylvania State University Press to use acid-free paper for the first printing of all clothbound books. Publications on uncoated stock satisfy the minimum requirements of American National Standard for Information Sciences—Permanence of Paper for Printed Library Materials, ANSI Z39.48-1992.

Contents

Part Three: The Transcendent Wisdom Scripture for Humane Kings
  Who Wish to Protect Their States (T 246)

Figures and Tables

Figures

Tables

In memory of Joseph M. Kitagawa

Acknowledgments

It is a cliché that books are the Olympian efforts of solitary scholars. Though individual effort is certainly a part of the recipe, the support, encouragement, and criticism offered by individuals and institutions comprise the other half of the conversation a book imperfectly records.

Research for this book took place over a number of years and under various auspices. I originally became interested in the *Scripture for Humane Kings* while writing a dissertation on Esoteric Buddhism at the Divinity School of the University of Chicago. The generous help of that institution, both intellectual and financial, has left its mark here. Some of the first, formative conversations on the role of the scripture in the history of Chinese Buddhism were the product of the National Endowment for the Humanities Summer Seminar on Buddhism in 1989. The National Endowment for the Humanities also funded a summer of intensive research in 1990, and one of their grants for travel to collections made it possible for me to use the library and databases at the University of Washington in 1992. Ms. Wu Yeen-mei, assistant head of the East Asia Library, took time to orient me to that university's excellent collections and to the arcana of using the database of Chinese dynastic histories. The University of North Carolina at Greensboro enabled me to spend spring of 1991 in Taiwan on research leave, and the Excellence Foundation supported the initial draft translation with a summer grant in 1993. Finally, the Graduate School at the University of North Carolina at Greensboro and the American Council of Learned Societies provided me an opportunity to discuss Buddhism and politics more broadly by underwriting my participation in the Conference on State and Ritual in East Asia held in Paris in June of 1995.

My colleagues and students at the University of North Carolina at Greensboro have provided both concrete help and intellectual inspiration. Special thanks are due to Paul Courtright (now of Emory University), Henry S. Levinson, Derek Kreuger, Ben Ramsey, John Sopper, Mary K. Wakeman, and

Pat Bowden. My assistant Jeff Richey made many suggestions for improving the style of the manuscript, and Howard Rhodes provided help with the bibliography. Jeff Mortimore, Budd Wilkins, and Mandy Wall helped to prepare the copyedited manuscript.

Various parts of the manuscript have benefited from comments by Robert Campany, Robert Duquenne, Hubert Durt, Dan Lusthaus, Victor Mair, Jan Nattier, Frank Reynolds, Robert Sharf, and John Strong. Tony K. Stewart made numerous stylistic suggestions on the translation and double-checked my Sanskrit. Stephen F. Teiser read and commented on the entire manuscript and saved me from many an error or infelicity. Kees Bolle, the series editor, steadfastly supported the project, and the final shape of the argument owes much to his insightful criticism. Over some fifteen years Jim Sanford has provided encouragement, intellectual companionship, and probing criticism. Philip Winsor, senior editor of Penn State Press, showed infinite patience with what at times must have seemed glacial progress, and Andrew Lewis did a superb job of copyediting. Mary Ellis Gibson read and commented on all the drafts. Over the years she has profoundly shaped both my style and my thinking. Emily Orzech has been a continual reminder that life and scholarship are not separate endeavors.

Earlier versions of portions of this book first appeared in a variety of venues and appear here with permission of the presses and journals involved. Part of Chapter 3 first appeared in "A Buddhist Image of (Im)Perfect Rule in Fifth-Century China." *Cahiers d'extrême-asie* 8 *Memorial Anna Seidel I* (1995): 139–53. A portion of Chapter 4 appeared as "Puns on the Humane King: Analogy and Application in an East Asian Apocryphon," *Journal of the American Oriental Society* 109.1 (1989): 17–24, while parts of Chapter 5 appeared in "Seeing Chen-yen Buddhism: Traditional Scholarship and the Vajrayāna in China," *History of Religions* 29.2 (1989): 87–114, © 1989 by The University of Chicago. All rights reserved. An earlier version of the translation of *Methods* found in Chapter 6 appeared in "Mandalas on the Move: Reflections from Chinese Esoteric Buddhism Circa 800 C.E." *Journal of the International Association of Buddhist Studies* 19.2 (1997): 209–44. Finally, brief excerpts appeared in "The Scripture on Perfect Wisdom for Humane Kings Who Wish to Protect their States," *Religions of China in Practice* (Princeton: Princeton University Press, 1996), 372–80; and in "Buddhism's Assimilation to Chinese Political Culture," *Sources of Chinese Tradition*, vols. 1 and 2, edited by William Theodore de Bary and Irene Bloom (New York: Columbia University Press, 1998), reprinted with permission of the publisher.

Abbreviations

Collected Documents	*Tai-tsung-ch'ao ssu-k'ung ta-pien-cheng kuang-chih san-tsang ho-shang piao-chih-chi*. Yüan-chao (d. 800). T 2120.
CTS	*Chiu t'ang shu*. Liu Hsü (887–946) et al. Peking: Chung-hua shu-chü, 1971.
Instructions	*Jen-wang huo-kuo po-jo-po-lo-mi-to t'o-lo-ni nien-sung i-kuei*. Pu-k'ung (705–74). T 994.
Method	*Jen-wang po-jo nien-sung fa*. Pu-k'ung (705–74). T 995.
MVS	*Ta p'i-lu-ch'e-na ch'eng fo shen-pien chia-chih ching* (*Mahāvairocānabhisambodhi Sūtra*). Translated by Śubhakarasiṃha (637–735) with aid of I-hsing (683–727). T 848.
New Recension	*Chen-yüan hsin-ting shih-chiao mu-lu*. Yüan-chao (d. 800). T 2157.
STTS	*Chin-kang-ting i-ch'ieh ju-lai chen-shih she ta-ch'eng hsien-ti ta chiao-wang ching* (*Sarvatathāgatatattvasaṃgraha*), translated by Pu-k'ung (705–74), T 865; *Chin-kang-ting yü-ch'ieh chung lüeh ch'u nien-sung ching* (*Sarvatathāgatatattvasaṃgraha*), translated by Vajrabodhi (671–741), T 866; *Fo shuo i-ch'ieh ju-lai chen-shih she ta-ch'eng hsien ti san-mei ta chiao-wang ching* (*Sarvatathāgatatattvasaṃgraha*), translated by Shih-hu (Dānapāla, fl. 980s), T 882. I specify which translation is intended.
Supplement	*Ta-t'ang chen-yüan hsu-k'ai-yüan shih-chiao lu*. Yüan-chao (d. 800). T 2156.

T	*Taishō shinshū daizō-kyō*. Takakusu Junjirō and Watanabe Kaigyoku, eds. and comps. 85 vols. Tokyo: Taishō issaikyō kankō-kai, 1924–34. Reprint. Taipei: Hsin-wen feng ch'u-pan she, 1974. References take the format T followed by Taishō number, volume, page, range, and line(s). For example, T 246 8.843b24–26.
T supplement or T supp.	*Taishō Zuzo* or Taishō Iconographic Supplement. 12 vols. Tokyo: Taishō issaikyō kankō-kai, 1924–34. Reprint. Taipei: Hsin-wen feng ch'u-pan she, 1974.

Note on Orthography, Conventions, and Translation Selection

Typical Western buddhological usage tends to falsify the Chinese Buddhist tradition in a number of ways. It is common, for instance, to take South Asian Buddhism and South Asian languages as the norm for the translation of Buddhist terminology wherever it appears. Thus the Chinese term for the name of the Bodhisattva whose vehicle is a white elephant is rendered in Sanskrit as Samantabhadra rather than in Chinese as P'u-hsien. One result of this practice is to make a single vocabulary—that of South Asian Buddhism—the only one with which a nonspecialist reader need be acquainted. Another, more negative result is that the reader gets a seriously distorted picture of the spread and familiarity of Sanskrit and Pali in East Asia.

In my translations I stick as close to the Chinese orthography as possible. Thus where Chinese *transliterates* to approximate the "sound" of a South Asian language, I have used the appropriate Sanskrit term. Where Chinese *translates* the South Asian term, I either transliterate using modern Mandarin or use the English equivalent. Some might object that the use of Mandarin constitutes as much a falsification as does the inappropriate use of Sanskrit. I disagree. First, the task of accurately representing the various late antique and medieval Chinese dialects (assuming, of course, that the dialect can be identified) is nearly impossible. Second, a Mandarin transliteration of Sanskrit accurately alerts the reader to the way in which foreign sounds had an obvious ring of the exotic to Chinese readers and avoids exoticizing terms that had achieved domestication by translation directly into Chinese. This constitutes far less falsification than the common practice, which emphasizes unduly the universals, which transcend culture, rather than the cultural specificity of Buddhism wherever it (or any other religion) is found.[1]

1. This sort of falsification is pervasive, and even penetrates archaeology. See Gregory Schopen, "Archaeology and Protestant Presuppositions in the Study of Indian Buddhism," *History of Religions*

Since Buddhist scriptures produced in China have become a topic for scholarly investigation in Western circles, the practice has been to call these productions "apocryphal" on the model of the biblical Apocrypha. In the past I have used this term.[2] However, several scholars have pointed out the shortcomings of this unfortunate usage and some are now discontinuing it.[3] In biblical scholarship an apocrypha is a text that misrepresents itself as the writing or pronouncement of another (such as the apocryphal Gospel of Thomas) or is circulated under the name of another (such as the pseudepigraphal letters of Paul). Yet modern biblical scholarship has shown the problems with such usage, problems which have grown more acute as scholars have become more aware of the nature of the biblical texts and their problematic authorship. Most New Testament texts are, in fact, pseudepigrapha. Obviously, biblical scholarship was led down this road through a notion of authorship and textual transmission enshrined in the biblical texts themselves. God, one way or another, is supposed to have written them.

By analogy, Buddhology has represented Buddhist texts originating in South Asia as "authentic" and those originating elsewhere as "apocryphal." This is silly, since we have not even a single word we can definitively point to as being from the Buddha! Thus, all Buddhist texts are apocryphal and the category is at best meaningless and at worst mischievous. A simple remedy to this confusion is to discard the analogy to biblical categories and designate texts as South Asian, Chinese, and so on, to the degree we can determine their provenance. This is not to say that Buddhists in South Asia, or in China, Korea, and Japan, did not argue over which texts were true Buddha *vaccana* and which were nefarious forgeries; they indeed were quite concerned about these things. But how they discussed and deployed their textual criticism must not get mixed up with how we discuss and deploy our textual criticism. The *Scripture for Humane Kings* is a scripture of Chinese Buddhism.

The third segment of this book contains a complete translation of the second recension of the *Scripture for Humane Kings*. This is the version produced by Pu-k'ung at the behest of the T'ang emperor Tai-tsung in the mid-eighth cen-

31.1 (1991): 1–23, and my own "Seeing Chen-yen Buddhism: Traditional Scholarship and the Vajrayāna in China," *History of Religions* 29.2 (1989): 87–114.

2. See my "Puns on the Humane King: Analogy and Application in an East Asian Apocryphon," *Journal of the American Oriental Society* 109.1 (1989): 17–24.

3. See Robert E. Buswell, ed., *Chinese Buddhist Apocrypha* (Honolulu: University of Hawaii Press, 1990); especially essays by Buswell, "Prolegomena to the Study of Buddhist Apocryphal Scriptures"; Kyoko Tokuno, "The Evaluation of Indigenous Scriptures in Chinese Buddhist Bibliographical Catalogues"; and Ronald M. Davidson, "An Introduction to the Standards of Scriptural Authenticity in Indian Buddhism." For a criticism of this usage, see Randall Nadeau's review of *Chinese Buddhist Apocrypha*, in *Journal of Chinese Religions* 20 (Fall 1992): 230–32.

tury. I have translated only those parts of the earlier fifth-century version of the scripture which differed from Pu-k'ung's version in significant ways. There are a number of reasons for this approach. First, a full translation of both texts would be repetitive and bulky. Second, the two versions are more alike than they are different. Third, in most places the two texts differ only in style; the earlier version is almost always tight and terse, while the latter version is explicit and verbose. Fourth, for ritual purposes the eighth-century scripture almost completely replaced the fifth-century scripture. Finally, this project grew out of my researches on T'ang dynasty Esoteric Buddhism, and I found myself working from that period back into the Sui, Ch'en, and Wei dynasties.

Introduction

On a clear winter day early in 1982 a friend and I visited a small Buddhist monastery in the New Territories of Hong Kong. We were warmly greeted and spent an hour or so drinking tea and discussing a range of Buddhist topics partly in English, partly in my less-than-perfect Mandarin. As we were about to leave, our host presented us with a parting gift of a few volumes from the monastery library. I glanced at the titles and gave them little thought until long after I had returned to the States. Like the proverbial karmic "seed," the volumes have borne fruit in this book. Among the scriptures I had been given were two recensions of the *Transcendent Wisdom Scripture for Humane Kings Who Wish to Protect Their States* (T 246 and 245, vol. 8): one an edition attributed to Kumārajīva in the fifth century; the other, with copious notations in an unknown hand, the work of the eighth-century Esoteric master Pu-k'ung (Sanskrit, Amoghavajra). The latter volume bore a seal indicating that it had been in a monastic library in Shanghai, and it had no doubt accompanied one of the many Buddhist monks who fled the communist takeover of the mainland. The colophon of this text was dated 1871, and it recorded a not-uncommon work of filial piety by a group of Chinese laymen:

> The faithful scholar Wang Wei-hsien has distributed five taels of silver to seek increased fortune and felicity on behalf of his mother of the Mei clan and his wife of the Ch'en clan; the faithful scholar Huan Pin of Chiang-tu[1] has distributed three silver dollars; *upāsikā* Sai-huang, Miao-in, and the others from Kuei-chu[2] distributed two silver dollars to engrave [the blocks for] this *chüan*, which altogether amounts to seven thousand four hundred and seventy-two characters. Recorded at

1. Chiang-tu is in the present-day Kiangsu-Anwei area.
2. Kuei-chu province is the Ch'ing Dynasty name for present-day Kueichow province.

the scripture engraving office of Chin-ling,[3] first month of T'ung-chih, ninth year.

This dedication seems little in keeping with the exalted notion of "transcendent" or "perfect wisdom" (Sanskrit *prajñapāramitā*) indicated by the title of the scripture.[4] Contrary to expectations that a discourse on transcendent wisdom should eschew worldly concerns, the *Scripture for Humane Kings* has long been employed in the pursuit of worldly ends. In this regard the *Scripture for Humane Kings* has much in common with other transcendent wisdom scriptures.

Yet unlike other such scriptures the *Scripture for Humane Kings* has features that insured its widespread popularity in East Asia, often to the chagrin of staunch anti-Buddhists. For example, the Confucian scholar Chang Chiu-ch'eng (1092–1159), in his *Commentary on the Doctrine of the Mean* (*Chung-yung chieh*), ridiculed the common practice of reciting texts to avert disasters: "This problem has reached the point where people want to recite the *Classic of Filial Piety* to ward off bandits and they recite the [Scripture for] *Humane Kings* to avert disasters such as that of Hou Ching."[5] Chu Hsi (1130–1200), not satisfied with Chang's lumping together of Confucian and Buddhist examples of this practice, excoriated those who recited the texts and even Chang himself: "In my view . . . those who recite the *Scripture for Humane Kings* are even more profoundly sunk in heterodoxy and vulgarity; one should not put these in the same category with those who recite the *Classic of Filial Piety*."[6] Chu Hsi's special loathing for the *Scripture for Humane Kings* probably stems not from its Buddhist provenance, but from its equating the cardinal Confucian virtue of humaneness (*jen*[a]) with the Buddhist perfection of forbearance (*jen*[b]).[7] The conflation of Buddhist and Confucian ideology had more than

3. This is in present-day Kiangsu province.

4. The scripture is a *prajñapāramitā*, a discourse on the "wisdom which has gone beyond" or "transcended" the world. Works on the *prajñapāramitā* sometimes translate the term as "Perfect Wisdom," which unfortunately misses some of its most important connotations. I translate *prajñapāramitā* as "perfection" only when used in the sense of the "six perfections."

5. As we shall see, recitation is a major dimension of the use of the text. The anecdote is from *Chang Chuang-yüan Meng-tzu chuan*, chuan 15, p. 8, *Ssu-pu tsung-kan*, Shanghai: Commercial Press, 1919–1937. My thanks to Thomas Wilson of Hamilton College for bringing this exchange to my attention. Hou Ching's (d. 552) rebellion against the Liang (548–52) caused great devastation throughout South China. This part of Chang's commentary concerns *Mencius* 4.1.12 and *The Doctrine of the Mean* 20.17, which the *Mencius* closely resembles. For the Mencius passage, see James Legge, trans., *The Works of Mencius* (New York: Dover Publications, 1970), pp. 302–3. For *The Doctrine of the Mean*, see Legge, trans., *Confucius: Confucian Analects, the Great Learning, and the Doctrine of the Mean* (New York: Dover Publications, 1971), pp. 412–13.

6. Chu Hsi's comments are from "Tsa-hsüeh pien," in *Hui-an hsien-sheng wen-kung wen-chi*, chuan 72, p. 376, *Ssu-pu pei-yao* (Shanghai: Chung-hua shu-chu, 1927–37).

7. For a discussion of the double entendre in the text, see my "Puns on the Humane King," and Chapters 3 and 4.

ethical or religious significance; it was also of great political consequence. This equation distinguished the *Scripture for Humane Kings* from a host of other Buddhist scriptures offering relief from calamities. No other Buddhist scripture advanced so bold a claim, a claim which was heeded both by common people and by their rulers.

While Wang Wei-hsien and the others who had the scripture carved sought to ease the afterlives of their relatives, others employed the scripture for national defense. The role of the scripture in Buddhist state cults is still evident in the Lecture Hall of the great Eastern Temple (Tōji) in Kyoto. For over a thousand years Tōji was the urban center of Japan's imperial Buddhist state cult, paired with the great mountain temple on Kōyasan. The Lecture Hall contains one of Japan's national treasures: the *Ninnōkyō mandara*, the Mandala of the Humane Kings. Said to have been designed by Kūkai, founder of the Esoteric School of Japanese Buddhism on his return from the Chinese court at the beginning of the ninth century, some of its statues stand more than ten feet high.[8] In the center is the Great "Sun" Buddha, Mahāvairocana, Lord of the Cosmos. To his left stand beneficent bodhisattvas, salvific manifestations of Mahāvairocana's compassion. To his right are the fierce, chastising Lords of Light (Japanese *Myōō*, Chinese *Ming-wang*, Sanskrit *Vidyārāja*), who stand ready to defend Buddhist rulers (and others) from invasions, bandits, and meteorological disasters. The *Ninnōkyō mandara* is a striking reminder of the imperial Buddhism that dominated China, Korea, and Japan for a millennium and which contributed much to the present political dispositions of all three nations. It is also a reminder of the power of religion to transform the political world.

Here I study and offer the first complete English translation of the *Scripture for Humane Kings*, the charter for a Buddhism of national protection in China, Korea, and Japan.[9] In Part One I investigate the political implications of religious experience, first more broadly, then with regard to Buddhism. In Part Two I probe the creation of the *Scripture for Humane Kings*, first in fifth-century north China, then in its new "translation" by the eighth-century Esoteric Buddhist master Pu-k'ung. In Part Three I present the translation itself.[10]

8. See Figure 3, page 158.

9. Korean Buddhism is often associated with the term "National Protection Buddhism" (*hoguk pulgyo*), though the designation is a bit of an oversimplification. Conversely, little is ever said of Buddhist cults of national protection in China and Japan, even though one can make a convincing argument that national protection and the care of ancestors were the primary functions of Buddhism throughout East Asia. For a recent reevaluation of the blanket use of national protection as a designation for Korean Buddhism, see Jong Myung Kim, "Chajang (fl. 636–650) and 'Buddhism as National Protector' in Korea: A Reconsideration" in Henrik H. Sørensen, ed., *Religions in Traditional Korea*, SBS Monographs no. 3 (Copenhagen: Seminar for Buddhist Studies, 1995), pp. 23–55.

10. The translation in Part Three of the eighth-century version of the text is by far the more important version. Passages from the fifth-century text that differ significantly from those in the eighth-century version appear in Appendix A.

The *Scripture for Humane Kings* poses an interpretive challenge. It does not configure the world, the path to salvation, and religious authority as we do today, or as they were in the world into which it came and which it forever altered. To understand the *Scripture for Humane Kings* we must treat Buddhist notions of polity and kingship not as mere appendages or compromises necessary for the survival of the faith in the world, but as integral parts of Buddhism.

Such an endeavor is by no means easy, for the world of kings and kingship has been replaced by our world of republics, democracies, or secular authoritarian states, which separate the "sacred" from the "profane." The problem is not one of taking a "humanistic" or "positivist" historical view as opposed to a "religious" one. Nor is it a problem of illuminating the "sacred" and its difference from the "profane," for these differences are artifacts of our world. Despite this fundamental difference in worldview we find studies of Buddhism which deal almost exclusively with its "philosophical," "sacred," or "transcendent" aspects to the exclusion of its "profane" politics or *vice versa* as though the former have no relationship to the latter. My aim in this book is to demonstrate how the two recensions of the *Scripture for Humane Kings* constitute a fulfillment of the political and religious implications of "transcendent wisdom."

In Part One I begin this process through an extended consideration of cosmologies; I demonstrate how careful attention to notions about the world, about authority, and about the path to salvation can help us understand the politics of Buddhism. In Part Two I examine the creation of the *Scripture for Humane Kings* in the heated political and religious atmosphere of the assimilation debates of fifth-century north China. Fifth-century Buddhists were struggling to understand how Buddhism and the "foreign" rulers of North China fit in with Chinese religious and political culture. The *Scripture for Humane Kings* was one answer to these problems. I then move on to the production of a new "translation" of the text in the eighth-century T'ang court, where the Esoteric master Pu-k'ung used it as the centerpiece for his Buddhist-state polity.[11]

At present there are two models for approaching religion and politics, each with its strengths and weaknesses. The first model, well articulated in the works of Max Weber, begins with the supposition of an original religious experience, an ontic seizure which bursts forth in a charismatic leader or founder.[12] Over

11. Like many of the new Buddhist revelations in fourth- through sixth-century China, the *Scripture for Humane Kings* presents itself as a translation from Sanskrit when in fact it was written in Chinese. The process of "re-translating" it in the eighth century raises some very interesting questions, which I treat in Chapters 5 and 6. Until quite recently, these "apocrypha" have been largely ignored.

12. This is a theme through much of Weber's large corpus. See, for instance, "The Nature of Charismatic Authority and Its Routinization," in *Max Weber on Charisma and Institution Building,* ed. S. N. Eisenstadt (Chicago: University of Chicago Press, 1968), pp. 48–65, and *The Sociology of Religion*, trans. Ephraim Fischoff (Boston: Beacon Press, 1964), pp. 262–74.

time this charisma is routinized in the creation of religious institutions. Religious experience must accommodate to the world of politics, and the history of religion is the history of "tension" between otherworldly transcendence and this-worldly politics. Religion then consists of a back-and-forth movement between resurgent charismatic experience and the demands of political and social acculturation. The second model is based on the notion of "traces" introduced by Jacques Derrida. For Derrida, "the trace is not only the disappearance of origin . . . it means that the origin did not even disappear, that it was never constituted except reciprocally by a nonorigin, the trace, which thus becomes the origin of the origin."[13] Rather than privilege an original experience that must accommodate to the world, and then attempt to access that primordial experience, Derrida proposes a dialectic of experience and routinization that is *already* in process at the beginning. Thus a Derridian approach has some similarities to the Weberian approach, but it denies a quest for the origin and its privileged place in interpretation. Bernard Faure has used this approach radically to reinterpret the history of early Ch'an Buddhism.[14]

As I see it, the Weberian and Derridian approaches—if we may term them such—are complementary. The Weberian approach alerts us to the power of religious experience radically to reshape culture. The Derridian approach reminds us that searching for a primordial experience may lead to our extracting of a "transcendent" religion from culture with a consequent emptying of meaning from "worldly" politics. This does not mean, as Rudolf Bultmann and others would have it, that we must strip religion of its otherworldly trappings and reduce it to the social and the political. Rather, I think we must recognize that religious experience—transcendence—is articulated in and through the world and that it involves power in the broadest sense of that term.[15]

Like many other branches of religious studies, Buddhist studies has been fixated on primordial experience, often to the point of ignoring the contexts of experience. This is a bit quixotic, since the earliest documentary evidence concerning Buddhism dates to some four centuries after its founder. If we accept that the Aśokan pillar edicts refer to the Buddhist dharma, our evidence goes back another two centuries.[16] While it may well be that early, pre-Aśokan Bud-

13. Jacques Derrida, *Of Grammatology*, trans. Gayatri C. Spivak (Baltimore: Johns Hopkins University Press, 1974), p. 61.

14. Bernard Faure, *The Rhetoric of Immediacy: A Cultural Critique of Chan/Zen Buddhism* (Princeton: Princeton University Press, 1991), esp. pp. 25ff.

15. The importance of power in religion was noted long ago by G. Van der Leeuw in his *Religion in Essence and Manifestation: A Study in Phenomenology*, 2 vols., trans. J. E. Turner (New York: Harper & Row, 1963). Mircea Eliade also moves in this direction in his discussions of yoga. See Eliade, *Yoga: Immortality and Freedom*, trans. Willard R. Trask, 2d edition enlarged, Bollingen Series no. 56 (Princeton: Princeton University Press, 1970).

16. For the thorny issue of what the Aśokan pillar edicts tell us about early Buddhism, see John S. Strong, *The Legend of King Aśoka: A Study and Translation of the Aśokāvadāna* (Princeton: Princeton Uni-

dhism was to some degree a reaction against new, more imperial forms of polity sweeping eastern India in the sixth century B.C.E., all forms of Buddhism which stand in the full light of history are already linked to the imperial state and are permeated with the terminology of kingship and preoccupied by its aims, its discourses, and its iconography. Patronized by local rulers and great monarchs, such as Prasenajit and Aśoka, Buddhism flourished in an imperial world. Notions such as the "Two Wheels of Teaching," wherein Buddha and *cakravartin* ("wheel ruler" or cosmic sovereign) divided responsibility for "spiritual" and "political" realms, were common. Whether we like it or not, the original content of Śākyamuni's enlightenment experience is, in Derridian terms, a "trace."

Although one might protest at this point, saying that Buddhism's aim is the attainment of enlightenment—that transcendent otherworldly goal—I would agree only in part. Certainly the aim of Buddhist practice is enlightenment. What I object to is the characterization of Buddhism as merely otherworldly and transcendent, a characterization that has too often led to the underestimation of the importance of Buddhist notions of political power which flow from the experience of nirvana. Although the ascetic rejection of the world is important in Buddhism, even this rejection of the world is often couched in the idiom of rulership and dominion. Aśvaghoṣa's (first century C.E.) great poetic biography of the founder begins "That Arhat is here saluted, who has no counterpart,—who, as bestowing the supreme happiness, surpasses (Brahman) the Creator,—who, as driving away darkness, vanquishes the sun,—and, as dispelling all burning heat, surpasses the beautiful moon."[17]

I do not want to argue that the quest for enlightenment in some dualistic sense has been pitted against and contrasted with the world; rather, insofar as Buddhism is a practice and ideology of people who live in this world, Buddhism has always been and remains to this day "worldly" and political. The mistaken impression that Buddhism is defined by "forest monks" (and even worse that these forest monks have nothing to do with the world) who are somehow kindred to the "desert fathers" of the early Christian centuries (or at least a misperception of them) is a serious distortion. One need only look where the vast majority of monastic establishments are or where the vast majority of Buddhists live: in or immediately around cities. Buddhism, particularly Mahāyāna Buddhism, is an urban, imperial religion and would be unrecognizable apart from the city and the empire. Its great fastnesses (Ajanta, Wu-t'ai, Hiei, and so

versity Press, 1983), pp. 3–15. On the historical problems of the study of early Buddhism, see Étienne Lamotte, *Histoire du bouddhisme indien des origines à l'ere Śaka* (Louvain: Bibliothèque du Muséon, 1958; reprint, Louvain: Institut Orientaliste, 1976).

17. E. B. Cowell, trans., *The Buddha-carita of Aśvaghoṣa*, in Cowell, ed., *Buddhist Mahāyāna Texts* (New York: Dover, 1969), p. 1, translating *Buddhacarita* 1.1.

on) only serve to underscore a polity that needs the world to be thinkable. For all practical and historical purposes, nirvana and Buddhist polity are reciprocally constituted. Buddhism—especially the Mahāyāna and the Buddhist tantras—viewed salvific accomplishment in a dialectic of world transcendence and world conquest, and it was this Buddhism that spread throughout Asia.[18]

The notion that "religion," even a foreign religion with radically different presuppositions, has everything to do with power has been and is even now resisted in European and American scholarly circles. This is particularly so in those cultures and disciplines formed in the womb of Judaism and Christianity as well as in many that have come under their influence. A foundational principle of these cultures and disciplines (including virtually all of modern sciences and humanities tracing their roots to the Enlightenment) is clearly enunciated in *Genesis* where the principle of an ontological gulf between creator and created is set as the cornerstone of orthodoxy and heresy. The serpent's sin—and that of Adam and Eve—is his proud assumption of divine status. In the centuries since the Enlightenment this gulf has been enshrined in the doctrine of the separation of church and state. The world and the divine are constituted by their difference.[19]

Even a cursory glance at Indian, Chinese, or Japanese religion reveals quite different presuppositions in which there is continuity between this and unseen worlds and forces, between "divine" and human agency. This is not to say that for these religions "it's all one," but rather that the assertion of oneness is made in the face of a perception of distinctions. The difference of presupposition is so fundamental that centuries of puzzlement have accompanied European evaluations of Asian culture: "They" are, at worst, heathen idolaters; they confuse what is properly "God's" with what is humanly created. Indeed, Western scholars still argue whether Confucianism and Shinto are "religions" at all.

Our presuppositions have spawned a host of binary categories: religion and science, religion and magic, and so on. When these are applied to premodern Asian cultures without regard to the indigenous worldviews, the result, while it may be interesting, is all too often a distortion adjunct to the appropriation and revisioning of those cultures.[20] Transcendent dimensions are shorn of the political cultures of which they are a part; in short, new "religions" are created.

18. For a discussion of this dialectic, see Stanley J. Tambiah, *World Conqueror and World Renouncer* (Cambridge: Cambridge University Press, 1976).

19. Medieval Christianity (and, for instance, present-day Islamic "fundamentalism") construed society as within the church. For the origins of these developments, see Walter Ullmann, *A History of Political Thought: The Middle Ages* (Baltimore: Penguin Books, 1970), esp. pp. 38–44.

20. Jordan Paper documents this problem with regard to Western sinology in *The Spirits Are Drunk: Comparative Approaches to Chinese Religion* (Albany: State University of New York Press, 1995), pp. 1–22.

This is nowhere more apparent than in treatments of "magic" or of religious activity aimed at "worldly benefit." Such misreadings are an obstacle in any interpretation of the fifth-century *Scripture for Humane Kings*, for in it worldly power and benefit are presented as the unmistakable signs of salvific accomplishment.

While such presuppositions present obstacles to interpreting the fifth-century text, they present even greater obstacles to interpreting the eighth-century text. The eighth-century recension of the *Scripture for Humane Kings*, which I examine in Chapters 5 and 6, was a key element in the creation of Chinese Esoteric Buddhism (*Mi-chiao*); and Esoteric Buddhism as developed and practiced throughout East and South Asia has often been the object of misunderstanding. Esoteric Buddhism (Buddhist Tantra, Vajrayāna), with its insistence on the salvific nature of the world, was seen as the last, "decadent" form of Buddhism. Only recently have such appraisals been questioned, and they are still widely accepted. In the case of Esoteric Buddhism (and also Taoism) in China the result of such Eurocentrism was the disappearance of the tradition from the Western disciplines of history of religions, buddhology, and sinology.

Yet Esoteric Buddhism in its various forms was one of the major religions of much of South, East, Central, and Southeast Asia from the seventh through the fourteenth centuries, and in East and Central Asia it was dominant into the twentieth century. This popularity was not accidental, and it is no exaggeration to say that the Buddhist tantras were among the most important vehicles for the spread of Indian political and religious ideas throughout East, Central, and Southeast Asia. The literal English rendering of its common East Asian name (*Mi-chiao*, "esoteric teaching") gives the misleading impression that it is practiced only in secret, occult groups. While access to the most profound of its "mysteries" is indeed given through initiation, most of these initiations are quite public in character, and its mysteries are of the same sort as those found in Catholic or Orthodox sacramental theology. Like the Catholic traditions of Europe, Esoteric Buddhism was patronized by kings, courtiers, and aristocrats in grand temples with elaborate public ceremony.

Indeed, it was in East Asian Esoteric Buddhism and Tibetan Vajrayāna that the full political implications of the Mahāyāna insistence upon the identity of this world and nirvana were developed and deployed in a comprehensive rhetoric and practice of "National Protection" (*hu-kuo*). As David Snellgrove notes, "Only in the tantras do we learn of new practices, which were able to turn the notion of kingship to practical account."[21] The attainment of tran-

21. David L. Snellgrove was one of the first to point out the importance of polity in the Buddhist tantras. For his argument, see "The Notion of Divine Kingship in Tantric Buddhism," in *The Sacral Kingship: Contributions to the Central Theme of the Eighth International Congress for the History of Religions* (Leiden: E. J. Brill, 1959), pp. 204–18. The quotation is from p. 204.

scendent wisdom was seen as inseparable from the attainment of worldly power. The *Scripture for Humane Kings*, in its fifth-century recension and even more in its eighth-century Esoteric version, expressed this salvific power and became the vehicle for a Buddhism of National Protection in China, Korea, and Japan.

PART ONE

Cosmology, Authority, and the Politics of Transcendence

1

Locating Authority

Cosmology and Complex Systems

Truth is one; the cosmos is one; hence knowledge also must be one.
—Joachim Wach

Everything is profoundly cracked.
—Georges Bataille

The Edge of Reality

Like many Mahāyāna Buddhist scriptures, the *Transcendent Wisdom Scripture for Humane Kings Who Wish to Protect Their States* opens with a stunning vision of the cosmos.[1] The great assembly gathered to hear the Buddha preach—humans, gods, asuras, and so forth—had been drawn from all levels of the universe, constituting a "cosmic" congregation. As a sign of authoritative revelation, Śākyamuni "arranged his seat and entered the ***samādhi*** of the great quiescent abode and his mindfulness caused a great brilliance which illuminated everything in the triple-world" (T 245 8.825b10–11). In response, the beings

1. For comparison, see the opening of the *Pañcavimśatisāhasrikā prajñāpāramitā* translated in Edward Conze, *The Large Sūtra on Perfect Wisdom* (Berkeley and Los Angeles: University of California Press, 1975), pp. 38–39, and Leon Hurvitz, trans., *The Scripture of the Lotus Blossom of the Fine Dharma* (New York: Columbia University Press, 1976), pp. 4–5.

in the congregation led by King Prasenajit used their spiritual powers to make an offering of music which "shook the three-thousand [worlds] and even the ***asaṅkhyeya*** [*innumerable, infinite*] Buddha-lands of the ten directions." This musical offering called forth the bodhisattvas of these other worlds, who appeared with their retinues to join the great assembly (825b29–c10).[2]

Such cosmological vision notwithstanding, the same scripture—again like many other Mahāyāna scriptures—denigrates cosmological inquiry, saying, "If a ***bodhisattva*** perceives a realm, perceives knowledge, perceives a doctrine, or perceives sensation, this is not the perception of a sage but the perverse view of a common person" (826b4–5).[3] Here all views about reality are repeatedly deconstructed by a series of paradoxes. The real nature of things (*dharma*-nature, *fa-hsing*) "resides neither in form nor in the formless." It "neither comes nor goes, it is not born and is not extinguished. Identical with the edge of reality (Chinese *chen-chi*, Sanskrit *bhūtakoṭi*), the nature of things is nondual and undifferentiated like emptiness."[4] This "edge" at once inscribes a totality and something more. Thus the deployment of all-encompassing cosmological vision somehow signifies its own inadequacies, and yet the transcendent realization of the Buddha in nirvana lays claim to unsurpassed cosmocratic authority.

Buddhism commonly uses paradox to eliminate, confound, and transcend dualistic thinking, including the sort of thinking that characterizes the construction of cosmological systems. To point beyond this world to the singularity of nirvana was certainly the intent of this "edge," this "emptiness."[5] Yet we cannot ignore the fact that the *Scripture for Humane Kings* inscribes paradox in an elaborate cosmic hierarchy and that this hierarchy is an indication of reli-

2. The eighth-century recension of the scripture cites the Buddha's brilliant light as the only cause of the appearance of the Buddha-lands of the ten directions. See T 246 8.835a25–26, my translation in Part three, Chapter 1, and Part three, Chapter 1, note 2.

3. The eighth-century text puts it more bluntly: "If a bodhisattva perceives a realm, perceives knowledge, perceives a doctrine, or perceives sensation, this is not the perception of a sage but the perception of a dunce" (T 246 8.836a10–12).

4. T 245 8.825c28–29 and 825c22–24. The term *bhūtakoṭi*, which literally means "the limit beings can reach" or their "culmination point," shows up in a variety of Mahāyāna texts and plays an important role in the *Scripture for Humane Kings*. Compare this passage with that of the eighth-century text (T 246 8.836a–b), which couches the paradoxes as Prasenajit's answer to the question of how he visualizes the Buddha: "At that time the World-honored One asked King Prasenajit, 'by what signs do you visualize the Thus-come One?' King Prasenajit answered, 'I contemplate his body's real signs; . . . [it is] not pure, not foul; not existent nor nonexistent; without signs of self or signs of another. . . . It is identical with the edge of reality and equal to the [real] nature of things. I use these signs to visualize the Thus-come One.'" Both texts are replete with other examples. *Bhūtakoṭi* is oddly reminiscent of Heidegger's "horizon" and of the paradox of the asymptotic limit in mathematics. Asymptotic limits are ever approachable but never reachable. For these limits, see Michael Guillen, *Bridges to Infinity: The Human Side of Mathematics* (Los Angeles: Jeremy P. Tarcher, 1983), pp. 23–30.

5. This position and the conundrums associated with it are well articulated by C. W. Huntington Jr. and Geshe Namgyal Wangchen, *The Emptiness of Emptiness: An Introduction to Early Indian Mādhyamika* (Honolulu: University of Hawaii Press, 1989), esp. "Methodological Considerations," pp. 5–15.

gious and political power.[6] Although paradoxical formulations—such as "the edge of reality," the "Two Truths," "emptiness," and the notion of the *tathāgatagarbha* (womb/embryo of the Thus-come One)—indicate a transcendent Buddhist soteriology, these apparently a-cosmological and a-political terms have frequently been an opening for highly sophisticated Buddhist cosmologies and polities.[7]

How can notions like the "edge of reality," which are intended to deconstruct the world, be employed in the construction of a world? Or, to put it another way, how does transcendence structure religious authority? To answer this question I first examine how authority, cosmology, and paths to salvation can and have been viewed as functions of one another. To this end I outline a simple typology of cosmologies, and then, building upon this typology, I examine the role of paradox and transcendence in what I term complex recursive cosmologies. This approach provides a way to understand the relationships between religious achievement and political power, first in Buddhism generally and then with regard to the content and contexts of the *Scripture for Humane Kings*.

Cosmology, Authority, and Salvation

"Truth is one; the cosmos is one; hence knowledge also must be one. This insight is all important."[8] This simple statement by Joachim Wach, made in what

6. The term "worldview" is often used interchangeably with the word "cosmology." Throughout this book I have chosen to use the words "cosmology" or "world," which seem to me more precise. My definition of cosmology is similar to the "inclusive" definition of cosmogony expounded by Frank Reynolds in his "Multiple Cosmogonies and Ethics: The Case of Theravāda Buddhism," in Robin W. Lovin and Frank E. Reynolds, eds., *Cosmogony and Ethical Order: New Studies in Comparative Ethics* (Chicago: University of Chicago Press, 1985), pp. 203–5. Ninian Smart has broken with this usage in favor of the term "worldview" in his recent book, *Worldviews: Crosscultural Explorations of Human Beliefs*, 2d ed. (Englewood Cliffs, N.J.: Prentice Hall, 1995). Cosmologies are closely related to taxonomy, typology, and classification, and here my thoughts have been influenced by the work of Bruce Lincoln, especially by his *Discourse and the Construction of Society: Comparative Studies of Myth, Ritual, and Classification* (New York: Oxford University Press, 1989).

7. Paul Mus has pointed out that although nirvana appears to be a-cosmological in early Mahāyāna texts, what is really the case is a reversal of cosmology, not a denial of it. This reversal was intimately connected with the relics of the Buddha (*śarīradhātu*), which came to occupy a plane that was neither transcendent nor immanent. I will discuss the role of the body of the Buddha in Chapter 2. See Paul Mus, *Barabudur: Esquisse d'une histoire du bouddhisme fondée sur la critique archéologique des textes*, 2 vols. (Hanoi: Imprimerie d'Extrême-Orient, 1935, reprinted as two vols. in one, New York: Arno Press, 1978), 1:60–84.

8. Joachim Wach, *The Comparative Study of Religions*, ed. Joseph M. Kitagawa (New York: Columbia University Press, 1958), p. 14.

is now a seldom-read work on method in the history of religions, calls attention to one of the most important and perplexing issues in the study of religions. It seems to many quite obvious that truth and the cosmos must be one, unified, whole. But is this really the case? If it were, at least in the most simple-minded understanding of this statement, then heaven and the world would be identical. In the Buddhist tradition, all would be a nirvanic realm and salvific action would be unnecessary. Indeed, at one level of understanding this is precisely what Mahāyāna Buddhism claims. The transcendent world of nirvana is here if we could but realize it.[9] But most do not realize it. And so truth is at minimum dual, and realities begin to multiply. Unity, wholeness, or as I shall refer to it, *continuity* is affirmed in the same breath as *discontinuity*. Cosmos is one and yet many, truth is one and yet two or three.[10] Religions or ideologies may try to enforce a single coherent weltanschauung, but in reality cosmologies are limited, plural, and complex.[11] Hermeneutics is necessary precisely because there is no big picture, only many individual, changing "pictures."[12]

From the perspective of the Buddhist tradition this problem is none other than the problem of "the place" of nirvana. Ironically, coming to grips with the place of nirvana has motivated—we might even say necessitated—the elaboration of Buddhist cosmologies. The interpretive task is effectively the same,

9. This is, of course, what Nāgārjuna is telling us when he says that "there is no difference at all between this world [and] nirvana." Nāgārjuna, *Mulamādhyamakakarika*, trans. Stephan Beyer (Beyer cites it as *Mādhyamaka-śāstra*), in Beyer, *The Buddhist Experience: Sources and Interpretations* (Belmont, Calif.: Wadsworth, 1974), p. 214. Compare Frederick J. Streng, *Emptiness: A Study in Religious Meaning* (New York: Abingdon Press, 1967), p. 216.

10. And thus we face the problem of "the two and the one." For the classic treatment see Mircea Eliade, "Mephistopheles and the Androgyne or the Mystery of the Whole," in *The Two and the One*, trans. J. M. Cohen (London: Harvill Press, 1965).

11. Pluralistic or complex cosmologies have often been labeled syncretic. The term actually has roots in late antiquity, but only gained currency in describing religions or cultures in the nineteenth century. Unfortunately it usually has been used to distinguish so-called pure religions, cultures, and so on, from "mixed" ones, with the explicit notion that syncretic religions were inferior and that pure religion (usually that of the person doing the labeling) exists. Carsten Colpe has documented the history of the term and its uses and argues for its principled application in "Syncretism," *Encyclopedia of Religion*, 14:218b–227b. While I agree with Colpe, my purpose is to force us to rethink the notion of cosmology as a totally unified and homogeneous worldview, so I have avoided the term altogether.

12. We should be aware and skeptical of the totalitarian ideology inscribed in our words "universe" and "cosmos" (both terms imply a single, overarching worldview). While individual cosmologies may seek hegemony over thought and practice, they do so because culture is pluralistic. Richard Rorty is only the most recent proponent of this more pluralistic viewpoint. Rorty's basic argument is that, ontologically speaking, there is no big picture; there are only an endless variety of epistemologically based contextual pictures. For Rorty, the pragmatists ultimately "abandon the idea that the aim of thought is the attainment of a God's-eye view." Rorty has detailed his position in a variety of works. For the problem of the God's-eye view, see *Essays on Heidegger and Others*, Philosophical Papers Volume 2 (Cambridge: Cambridge University Press, 1991), p. 12, and for a fuller treatment *Contingency, Irony, and Solidarity* (Cambridge: Cambridge University Press, 1989).

whether for members of the Buddhist community in fifth-century North China or for a late-twentieth-century scholar in North America.[13] Indeed, before we can come to grips with the social and political dimensions of Buddhism we need a systematic way of understanding the role of transcendence in alien and very complex worlds.

Unfortunately, discussions of cosmology have tended to be either narrowly descriptive or abstract, totalistic, and structural. Individual cosmological descriptions provide us only "snapshots" of complex, dynamic social constructions oriented by multiple perspectives. Understanding these complex systems, however, requires one to take into account more than one snapshot. In contrast to descriptive approaches to cosmologies, structural approaches are often so abstract and totalistic that they seem to float over historical and cultural specificity. Like totalitarian ideologies they attempt to impose on life a procrustean scheme that empties analysis of all specificity, plurality, and dynamics. If we are to understand successfully the impact of nirvana on Buddhist politics, we must examine the interaction of cosmological ideals *and* historical circumstances. Such an examination must take into account the dynamics of the complex and open-ended systems we call religions, systems that include the possibility of multiple and even mutually incompatible cosmologies, and of their evolution, deconstruction, and reconstruction.

Modeling the World

A common shortcoming of typologies or taxonomies originates in the construction of a type by generalizing from an idiosyncratic list of features derived from too narrow a sample of phenomena.[14] This was clearly the case with typologies of "sacred kingship," the features of which (dying and rising again, and so on) were inspired by the singular example set forth in Christian theology.[15] Such an approach merely replicates an indigenous taxonomy tied to one text or context and results in little analytical leverage.

13. For some of the issues in Buddhist hermeneutics, both from within the tradition and from without, see Donald S. Lopez Jr., ed., *Buddhist Hermeneutics* (Honolulu: University of Hawaii Press, 1988).

14. Throughout the study I use "taxonomy" and "typology" interchangeably. Taxonomies are by their nature models of the world, schematic outlines we use to understand complex systems. The works that have been most influential in the costruction of the model presented in the next few pages are Mary Douglas, *Natural Symbols: Explorations in Cosmology* (New York: Vintage Books, 1973); Stephen C. Pepper, *World Hypotheses: A Study in Evidence* (Berkeley and Los Angeles: University of California Press, 1966); and Claude Lévi-Strauss, *The Savage Mind*, The Nature of the Human Series (London: George Weidenfeld & Nicolson, 1966; reprint, Chicago: University of Chicago Press, 1969).

15. The amount of literature on the topic is vast. A good place to start is *The Sacral Kingship: Contributions to the Central Theme of the Eighth International Congress for the History of Religions* (Leiden: E. J.

An alternative to this "laundry-list" inductive approach begins by articulating a set of rules or abstract properties "and then, following an injunction by Durkheim in his rules of sociological method, we should include in our investigation any social facts . . . that exhibit the properties in question."[16] Of course, induction still plays a role here but a larger "sample" lends more credibility and greater utility to the resulting typology. Thus we can arrive at a set of features that exhibit what Wittgenstein called a family resemblance.

We should keep in mind that a typology is a tool, it is a model we use to solve a problem that is principally our own. However well crafted a typology might be, it is of little use if it becomes the end of, rather than the means to understanding. Too often typologies are little more than pigeon holes into which we tuck data, thus overlooking the dynamic dimensions of religious and social life we seek to understand. It is helpful in this regard to consider recent cross-disciplinary work on complex adaptive systems. Such an approach posits some very broad "rules" bounding but not directly dictating what happens. That emerges in the complex interactions of individuals over generations in specific times and places. One intriguing example is a computer-simulated evolution of a flock of "boids." The rules for each boid are simple:

1. It is to maintain a minimum distance from other objects in the environment, including other boids.
2. It is to match velocities with other boids in its neighborhood.
3. It is to move toward the perceived center of mass of boids in its neighborhood.[17]

Nowhere does the program prescribe how the boids should flock. Indeed, it doesn't even say they should form flocks. But after a number of simulated evo-

---

Brill, 1959). One of the most insightful contributions was made by the British anthropologist A. M. Hocart, who observed that "the bare proposition that 'kings are divine' could evidently not have sufficed to gain such an ascendancy on the human mind; an institution to take root so deeply must have wide ramifications, it must be a whole system." A. M. Hocart, *Kingship* (Oxford: Oxford University Press, 1927; reprint, 1969), p. 17. In other words, Hocart realized that he was dealing with taxonomic systems and that issues of cosmology were very likely issues of sociology, authority, soteriology, and so on.

16. Rodney Needham, *Reconnaissances* (Toronto: University of Toronto Press, 1980), p. 69. For Durkheim's full argument, see Emile Durkheim, *The Rules of Sociological Method*, trans. S. Solovay and J. Mueller (New York: The Free Press, 1938). The classic Durkheimian approach thus works deductively to construct a typology from foundational "rules." When examining data on the ground, we work from the opposite direction, inductively, to ascertain what Bruce Lincoln calls the "taxonomizers" of the system. See Lincoln, *Discourse and the Construction of Society*, esp. pp. 131–41.

17. The example is from M. Mitchell Waldrop, *Complexity: The Emerging Science at the Edge of Order and Chaos* (New York: Touchstone, 1992), p. 241. If we were to come upon this program without prior knowledge of its rules, it would not be too difficult to deduce its "taxonomizers" as related to mass, velocity, and distance.

lutionary generations that is exactly what happens. The boids begin to flock as real birds do. In other words, the creators of boids have crafted a model of the world that closely approximates its open-ended complexity while retaining a simple and analytically useful theoretical structure.

Similar models are used in computer predictions of weather, where the sampling of data and the formulation of hypotheses by induction serve as the basis for deductive computer models which in turn are tested and refined over and over again in specific circumstances. The result is models that better approximate the complex realities of weather and which enable us better to understand these realities.[18] Of course, models never can produce totally accurate predictions, and the accuracy drops off as more variables (longer periods of forecast time, for example) are added. Moreover, a variety of hypotheses originating in changing conditions may lead to new models for prediction, and some of these models may be incompatible.[19]

In the following pages I develop a model or typology to facilitate our understanding of the relationships among transcendence, the world, and authority in the complex open-ended adaptive systems we call religions. My model divides religious traditions according to their notions about the shape of the cosmos and the deployment of beings in it. Thus some religions presume a *continuous* universe, while others focus on *discontinuity*. So too, some religions analyze the social world in terms of the *position* a being occupies with respect to other beings, while other religions focus on the *personal* qualities of particular beings or groups of beings. Thus a tradition might emphasize that the really real is *continuous*, either obviously or in an underlying hidden continuity that is obscured through faults in epistemology or by sin. Other traditions place their primary focus on *discontinuity* and on a struggle to move from one realm to another. The central fact of the cosmos, then, can be its continuity or its discontinuity. When continuity is the key factor, discontinuity is regarded as an

18. This process has been neatly articulated by Clifford Geertz's formulation of religion as a "model of" as well as a "model for" reality. See "Religion as a Cultural System," in William A. Lessa and Evon Z. Vogt, eds., *Reader in Comparative Religion: An Anthropological Approach*, 3d ed. (New York: Harper & Row, 1972). That Geertz's method bears more than passing resemblance to cosmological thinking has been brought out by Catherine Bell's cogent criticism in her *Ritual Theory, Ritual Practice* (Oxford: Oxford University Press, 1992), pp. 25–27.

19. The examples given by Waldrop are the variety of more or less compatible models used in astrophysical explanations. Astrophysicists use one model to explain the behavior of quasars, another to discuss stellar evolution. One might also point to the incompatible theories about light as a wave phenomenon and as a particle phenomenon. Which is used depends on what problem we wish to tackle. Similarly, both religions and those who study them often involve a plurality of incompatible beliefs, practices, and theories. The Hindu householder, for instance, might go to Benares to perform the *piṇḍapradāna* to insure the transformation of a dead relative from a ghost (*preta*) to an "ancestor" (*pitṛ*), while still believing in reincarnation. It is not a matter of concern that the state of ancestor which involves a permanent abode with the other *pitṛ* is logically incompatible with the doctrine of reincarnation.

anomaly, an illusion, or a temporary state. Discontinuous cosmologies, in turn, see continuity as anomaly, illusion, or as a future state to be achieved.[20]

Concerning this second issue, some religions are obsessed with the place or position of the individual as part of an overall *structural* scheme of things. The worth of the individual, of his or her achievements, and so on, is defined in terms of role and *position* in the universal structure and whether that role or position is fulfilled. Other traditions focus on the special inborn qualities of *persons*, rather than their positions. In such traditions one finds a preoccupation with *substance*. Having "the right stuff," rather than the fulfillment of some role, is the measure of a person.[21]

To illustrate this typology of religious worlds in graphic form, we can set out two axes, the vertical axis running from those cosmologies which emphasize continuity to those that focus on discontinuity. The horizontal axis is based on the distinction between those cosmologies which emphasize innate or *personal* qualities of individuals—*substance*—and those which emphasize the role or *position* of an individual in the cosmos—*structure*. I refer to this horizontal axis sometimes in terms of structure and substance, sometimes in terms of position and person, depending on the context.

Each axis of this typology represents a spectrum of values, from total continuity to total discontinuity and from exclusive preoccupation with substance to exclusive preoccupation with structure, yielding four broad types of cosmology. Later in this discussion I use this typology to model the relationships among cosmology, authority, and paths to salvation. But for now, let us focus simply on the cosmological aspects of the scheme.[22] The following graph

20. Max Weber's notion of "tension" caused by perceived and unwanted discontinuity in a religious tradition is an attempt to articulate this distinction. See for instance, his "Soteriology and Types of Salvation" and "Theodicy Salvation and Rebirth," in *The Sociology of Religion*, in Weber's "Religious Rejections of the World and Their Directions." *From Max Weber: Essays in Sociology*, trans. and ed. H. H. Gerth and C. Wright Mills (New York: Oxford University Press, 1958), pp. 323–35, goes over similar ground. The works of Levinas and of Derrida on "otherness" and "difference" take a fresh look at discontinuity. See note 36.

21. The distinction between stuff and structure has a long and honorable pedigree in European and American academic discourse. See, for instance, Weber's distinction between the charisma of a person and the charisma of office in *Max Weber on Charisma and Institution Building*, pp. 46–77; James Frazer's distinction between contagious and homeopathic magic in *The New Golden Bough: A New Abridgement of Sir James Frazer's Classic Work*, ed. Theodor H. Gaster (New York: Criterion Books, 1959), p. 35; and Lévi-Strauss's distinction between sacrifice and totemism in *Savage Mind*, pp. 224–25.

22. I am using "soteriology" broadly speaking. The definitions of the Greek words *sōzō* or *sōtēria* include the idea of preserving or maintaining one's natural health or wholeness, and they seem to imply the "absence of any sharp distinction between the divine and the human world in the Grk. sphere." This definition is suggestive of the range of meaning of the word "soteriology." See the *Theological Dictionary of the New Testament* (1971), s.v. "sōzō," "sōtēria."

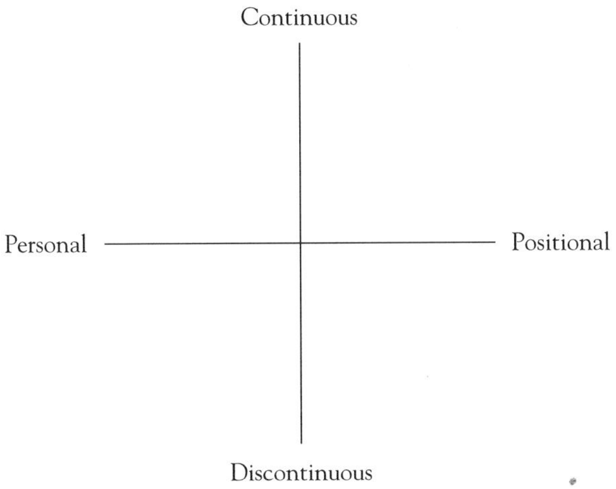

Fig. 1. Basic cosmological choices

represents four basic types of cosmology: continuous-personal, continuous-positional, discontinuous-personal, and discontinuous-positional.

The resulting typology, it must be stressed, is not descriptive in any straightforward sense. It depicts relationships between themes and motifs which are "ideal-typical" and which help us to conceptualize the evolution and dynamics underlying a variety of religious worlds. This in turn allows us to construct a more nuanced picture of the relationships among nirvana, the world, and authority in Buddhism and particularly in the *Scripture for Humane Kings*.

Continuous Personal Cosmology: The Great Family

The two types of cosmology defined by the upper half of the chart are marked by a fundamental notion of cosmic continuity. Discontinuities in the universe are considered secondary to the wholeness and connectedness of the cosmos.

Where *continuity* is further marked by a concern with *substance* or a *personal* view of the world, where the cosubstantiality of the various elements of the cosmos is affirmed, the system falls in the upper left corner of the chart. In such a system, the world is perceived to be an ordered continuum of related substances, and the origins of and relationship among these substances are often traced to a cosmogonic beginning. The universe is a collection of individuals more or less closely related. Kinship is often important, and discontinuity in such a system is sometimes viewed as disobedience to family, unfiliality, and the contamination or dilution of substance. The dynamics of this sort of cosmology are based on the mediation and transformation of one substance into another, the accumulation of important substances, the gradual purification of a substance, or the enhancement of personal qualities. Time is a function of substance, reckoned by the deeds of ancestors and generations. One might term such a worldview "aristocratic."

Continuous Positional Cosmology: The Great Chain of Being, or Grid

Continuous religious worlds that emphasize *structure* or *position* are located in the top right of the chart. Whereas discontinuity in the Great Family type of cosmos is considered in terms of divisions between generations or degrees of relatedness, here we have complementary structures or substructures. In some forms these systems are constituted by a hierarchy of structures, positions, and statuses like blocks of a great tower or parts of an organism or machine. In other forms it may be represented as a single structure replicated and mirrored over and over again at all levels of the system. Time in such systems is reduced to a cyclical function of some spatial archetype.

Discontinuous Personal Cosmology: The Heroic Cosmos

Both cosmologies represented by the lower half of the chart focus on fundamental discontinuities. In the lower left quadrant of the chart we find traditions in which *discontinuity* is coupled with the notion that each *person* is endowed with a special *substance*, whether inborn or developed. But that substance is opposed by other substances and persons, and notions of struggle and conquest, of triumph and defeat, are prominent. There is an ontological difference between parties in the struggle, between hero and villain, between spirit and matter, between good and evil. The universe is split between two or more competing substances or natures. Such an outlook is often found in a dualistic world in which time is seen as linked to great individuals and as rushing headlong toward an apocalyptic climax.

Discontinuous Positional Cosmology: Competing Orders

As we move across the bottom half of the chart to the right, we move from a discontinuous personal type of religious tradition to one which is *discontinuous* but *structural* or *positional*. Once again, the cosmos is marked by overriding discontinuities. But in such systems the discontinuities are seen as matters of order, position, or structure rather than of personal will and substance. Such a world might be formed of opposing orders or structures, alternative worlds which are defined in opposition to one another. In extreme cases the universe might be totally fragmented, as in the Abhidharma Buddhist system. Time in such systems may be regarded as a convenient illusion, a mask of structural continuity covering real discontinuity.[23]

Cosmological Types and Cosmological Strategies

Each type of religious world may be said to have a corresponding strategy for coping with challenges to its coherence. Further, each may be a part of a recursive transrational cosmology, which I will discuss shortly. First, let us look at the four basic cosmological strategies for dealing with pluralistic realities.

Whether they are oriented toward substance or structure, cosmologies based on continuity must find ways to assimilate or encompass other cosmologies and the discontinuity that these cosmologies might imply. Continuous personal traditions deal with the problem of the unity and multiplicity of reality as a problem of relatedness and lineage, of the mediation and transformation of substances. If the cosmos is the family writ large, then discontinuities are family disputes, lineage segments, subclans, and so on. They demarcate discontinuities in the substance of reality or between the qualities of persons. Any synthesis with new cosmological ideas will follow this line of reasoning. The newcomer must be ritually, ideologically, and socially initiated into the family. A transformation of substance must be carried out so that the "foreign" substance becomes family substance. Similarly, other substances may be viewed as impure and be reassimilated through mediation and transformation. Continuous personal traditions assimilate competing traditions through a process of substantial transformation.[24]

Religions based on continuity and position, on the other hand, define discontinuities as breaks in structure, as dividing lines between structural parts of a whole, or as matters of scale or distortions of structure.[25] Accommodation with new cosmological ideas proceeds through the placing of competing cos-

23. For a convenient synopsis of this theory, see Junjirō Takakusu's treatment in his *Essentials of Buddhist Philosophy* (Honolulu: University of Hawaii, 1947; reprint, Delhi: Motilal Banarsidass, 1978), pp. 55–80. For a more detailed analysis of the theory of instantaneous *dharmas*, see Th. Stcherbatsky, *Buddhist Logic* (Leningrad: Academy of Sciences of the U.S.S.R., ca. 1930; reprint, New York: Dover, 1962), pp. 79–118, or his *Central Conception of Buddhism and the Meaning of the Word "Dharma"* (London: Royal Asiatic Society, 1923; reprint, Delhi: Motilal Banarsidass, 1974).

24. Claude Lévi-Strauss's discussion of sacrifice on pages 224–25 of *The Savage Mind* is germane here.

25. By "matters of scale" I mean that the discontinuities are perceived simply as a difference in scale. The essential structure remains intact.

mologies in the dominant cosmological scheme and through formal analogy with some part of the structure. Foreign cosmologies are homologized to the continuous structural world rather than undergoing a transformation of substance as in continuous personal cosmologies.[26]

In discontinuous systems the centrality of discontinuity obviates the need to suppress or assimilate new visions of the cosmos. Since such traditions are based on fundamental notions of discontinuity or difference, they can easily categorize new cosmological visions without having to assimilate them fully. Thus partisans of a religious system based on discontinuity and substance will tend to interpret a structural system in terms of substance. These new cosmologies may be seen as entirely new competitors led by new wills or as versions of already recognized regimes. In the same manner, discontinuous positional systems are easily assimilated to old competitors or categorized as new competing cosmological orders.

But we cannot simply analyze cosmologies in isolation from their historical matrices. Religions are complex open-ended systems that call for nuanced analysis. By way of illustration, let us look at an example from Chinese religious history. There is a long-standing dispute concerning the controlling presupposition of Chinese religio-political culture. One side in this debate has championed a personal and substance-oriented interpretation of virtue (*te*), while others note that merit and virtue should be seen as the correct order of things and as fundamentally structural or positional. Confucian works produced in the late Chou period excoriate aristocratic culture for equating virtue with blood. The rule of the sage kings of the mythic past is portrayed as one in which virtue was a function of merit in the public service of the order of heaven.[27] The argument continued throughout Chinese history and can be summed up by two phrases: *tien-hsia wei chia*, "the world constitutes a family," and *tien-hsia chih kung*, "the world constitutes a public [domain]."[28] Usually the two interpretations coexisted, but occasionally, as in the "Great Ming Ritual Controversy," they resulted in outright battle.

26. Lévi-Strauss's discussion of totemism as an analogical process is a good example of this process. See *Savage Mind*, pp. 224–25. Another example is Mircea Eliade's use of homology as explained in *The Sacred and the Profane: The Nature of Religion*, trans. Willard R. Trask (New York: Harcourt, Brace & World, 1959), pp. 168–70.

27. For a discussion of this, see Donald J. Munro, *The Concept of Man in Early China* (Stanford: Stanford University Press, 1969), pp. 58–65. Victor Mair has argued persuasively that *te* ought to be translated as "integrity." See Victor H. Mair, trans., *Tao Te Ching: The Classic Book of Integrity and the Way* (New York: Bantam Books, 1990), pp. 133–35.

28. Howard J. Wechsler provides an analysis of these concepts and their interaction in early T'ang dynasty ritual in his *Offerings of Jade and Silk: Ritual and Symbol in the Legitimation of the T'ang Dynasty* (New Haven: Yale University Press, 1985), pp. ix–x, 94, 102–4.

Public controversy was touched off when the Ming Emperor Wu-tsung (r. 1050–21) died without an heir.[29] Wu-tsung's cousin acceded to the throne as the Emperor Shih-tsung (r. 1521–66). The question was whether the new sovereign should ritually worship or confer the honors of an imperial predecessor on his biological father or whether he should worship as the son of his uncle and predecessor on the throne, Hsiao-tsung (r. 1487–1505). Was Shih-tsung to take the position as the adopted son of his uncle or was he ritually to remain the son of his biological father, and thus retroactively change the dynastic bloodline by designating his biological father as a posthumous emperor?

Unfortunately the prescriptions in the *Huang ming tsu-hsün* (Ancestral Instructions) were mute on the point, and the new emperor was intent on designating his own father as his predecessor. The bureaucracy, led by Yang T'ing-ho, the Senior Grand Secretary, advanced a series of historical precedents to try to convince the young emperor to designate his uncle as *k'ao*, "imperial father," while naming his father *huang po*, "imperial uncle." Shih-tsung would have none of this, even though his bureaucracy was dead set against his position. A series of compromises ensued which delayed any showdown between the emperor and the bureaucracy until 1524.

That year, the controversy reemerged when Shih-tsung promoted his supporters to high positions in the central government and issued an order that the Ministry of Rites was to designate a day on which he would accept his father as *k'ao*. The following day thirteen memorials of dissent were presented, signed by approximately 252 officials. The next day the officials went in a body to the gates of the palace, prostrated themselves, and shouted the names of the dynastic founder and of the emperor Hsien-tsung. They resisted orders to disperse and finally 134 leading officials were taken into custody. Many were publicly flogged and sent into exile for life. Shih-tsung had his way through brute force.

One might initially regard this as a struggle between two bloodlines, a struggle taking place within the framework of a single cosmological presupposition but with competing allegiances. Indeed, the officials used the idiom of blood and lineage, invoking the progenitor of the dynastic line in their protest. Closer examination, however, reveals that the bureaucracy's opposition to Shih-tsung was based on the precedence of "public position" over "personal relationships."[30] In other words, the bureaucracy upheld the original dynastic

29. My account of the controversy is summarized from Carney T. Fisher, "The Great Ritual Controversy in the Age of Ming Shih-tsung," *Bulletin: Society for the Study of Chinese Religions* 7 (Fall 1979): 71–87.

30. Ibid., pp. 74–75. Thomas Wilson's recent work adds further support for this analysis. The deeper context of the Ming ritual controversy involved arguments for and against the use of images in Con-

line not because of the personal substance of the bloodline but because it was the correct public order of things. Position, not person, was crucial. In the eyes of these bureaucrats the world was indeed a public domain, while for the emperor, the world was his family domain.

This example demonstrates how any attempt to pigeonhole the Chinese or "Confucian" cosmology as monolithically personal or positional does not do justice to the complexity of Chinese history and culture. The struggle between Shih-tsung and his bureaucracy underlines this complexity and alerts us to the possibility that a religious tradition is likely a compound of forces, interests, and presuppositions that need not be easily assumable under a single cosmological description. A more profitable approach involves examining cosmological descriptions and political and religious phenomena with an eye to the underlying rules and strategies that both shape events and are shaped by them.

The case of the Ming ritual controversy was settled by the strategy of brute force, and at least in the area of rituals concerning the imperial ancestors, the principle of blood relations subsumed positional concerns about the correct order of things. Yet there is a limit to how comprehensive a given cosmological system can be. There are circumstances in which a cohesive vision of the cosmos, based on one of the strategies described above, is no longer tenable. Some things in life transcend rational systematic constructs. Such transcendence poses a challenge to religious worlds based on continuity, which, in attempting to provide a total account of reality, must account for any discontinuity. Under certain conditions this challenge is met by the development of a more discontinuous vision of the cosmos or by a recursive or even a multimodal cosmology that places transcendence at the heart of reality.

Transcendence and Recursion: Paradoxical Worlds

None of the four basic cosmological types I have discussed can account for everything. Indeed, historical circumstances constantly push the limits of any cosmological system. While discontinuous cosmologies can easily accommodate radical otherness or transcendence, cosmologies based on continuity have no ready place for what is beyond totality. Thus the rational coherence of continuous cosmologies tends to shade off into incoherence and anomaly. To put it another way, beyond the confines of "normative" reality is a world of com-

fucian temples. In this case (with the exception of Confucius's family temple in Ch'u fu), the positional outlook prevailed, leading to the removal of images from state Confucian temples. See Thomas A. Wilson, *Genealogy of the Way: The Construction and Uses of the Confucian Tradition in Late Imperial China* (Stanford: Stanford University Press, 1995).

plex, ambiguous, or paradoxical realities. The limits of a system are sometimes noticed in paradoxes, such as the simple sentence, "This statement is not true." Given the rules of English grammar it is impossible to determine whether this statement is true or false, both true and false, or neither true nor false.[31] If we try to analyze such statements we are pushed back and forth in a vicious circle of indeterminacy and are faced with the same predicament as the man who asks the Buddha where the arhat goes after death.[32]

The "edge" of the rational is valued differently in different cultures and situations. The total fragmentation of the universe into causally discontinuous *dharmas* is said to be the ultimate mystery of reality in the Abhidharma and Mādhyamika Buddhist systems. Yet the same fragmentation of causality is, from the standpoint of modern cosmology, a vexing problem that has engendered a search for the unity of all phenomena.[33]

No cosmology can account for everything in human experience or imagination. Given a set of cosmological assumptions, there will always be certain problems that defy rational determination or assimilation. Coherence always fails; there are always limits to the system. As mathematician Kurt Gödel demonstrated, a perfect formal number system must include its own imperfection to be complete.[34] Ultimately, incoherence and paradox seem built into human systems. For most of us such unanalyzable paradoxes or anomalies are unimportant. But disruptions in society can bring them to the fore where they become the ground over which other conflicts are fought.[35] At other times a sort of cosmological playfulness or a reflexive self-criticism and self-transcendence assumes a key role.[36] In its most radical form a continuous "totalistic" cosmology

31. See Douglas R. Hofstader, *Gödel, Escher, Bach: An Eternal Golden Braid* (New York: Basic Books, 1979; reprint, New York: Vintage Books, 1980), p. 17. This example is a transmutation of Epimenides' "liar" paradox, where Epimenides the Cretan says, "All Cretans are liars."

32. "The question would not fit the case." See "Questions which tend not to edification," *Majjhimanīkaya*, sutta 63, as translated in Henry Clarke Warren, *Buddhism in Translations* (1896; reprint, New York: Atheneum, 1963), p. 127.

33. For a lucid account of "grand unified field theories," see Robert P. Crease and Charles C. Mann, "How the Universe Works," in *The Atlantic Monthly*, August 1984, pp. 66–93. More challenging is Steven Hawking's "Is the End in Sight for Theoretical Physics?" which was his inaugural lecture as Lucasian Professor of Mathematics at Cambridge University, in *Black Holes and Baby Universes and Other Essays* (New York: Bantam, 1994), pp. 49–68.

34. Gödel's aim, of course, was a reason that could even figure out its own weaknesses. For a lucid introduction to Gödel's theorem, see Guillen, "Gödel's Theorem: An Article of Faith," in *Bridges to Infinity*, pp. 117–25. For a deeper probing of the issue, see Hofstader, *Gödel, Escher, Bach*, pp. 15–19. As is obvious from the title, Hofstader's entire work is ultimately a meditation on Gödel's theorem.

35. Bruce Lincoln analyzes such instances in *Discourse and the Construction of Society*, esp. in "The Uses of Anomaly," pp. 160–70.

36. A number of thinkers have tackled this issue under the guise of the notion of infinity. Emmanuel Levinas, in his *Totality and Infinity: An Essay on Exteriority*, trans. Alphonso Lingis (Pittsburgh: Duquesne University Press, 1969), p. 49, links the notion of infinity with that of transcendence and total

may deliberately deconstruct itself through appeal to a singularity, to the transrational or transcendent. This process of deconstruction constitutes a sophisticated form of religious and political thinking.

Cosmologically, Christian traditions—with the firm help of Aristotle—pushed the limits of coherent system in the consideration of a prime mover. God as creator provides a cosmological strategy of encompassment. Thus the cosmos, which may be regarded as continuous and substantial, operates on an encompassing strategy whereby a single personal continuity (God) is able to assimilate or take responsibility for the existence of all possible realities except one. Who created God? One might write a history of Western philosophy based on proofs of a prime mover, but the question of who "moved" the prime mover has always aroused suspicion, since it leads to what is usually regarded as an unacceptable infinite regress—a singularity.[37]

We meet with similar conundrums in the Hindu tradition, where for instance, in the Bṛihadāranyaka Upanishad the sage Yajñavalkya is questioned by his disciple Gārgī concerning the ultimate ground of being. A *regressus* takes place until the disciple asks of the origin of Brahman, at which point Yajñavalkya retorts, "Gārgī, do not question too much, lest your head fall off."[38] It is precisely at this point where religions which appeal to faith and grace come to the rescue of faltering rationality.[39]

But not all religious thinkers abandon rationality in their efforts to comprehend transcendence. Indeed, transcendence can and has been probed intellectually. One very important way of conceiving the issue is through appeal to

---

otherness: "Infinity is characteristic of a transcendent being as transcendent; the infinite is the absolutely other." By incorporating the notion of infinity into a cosmology, one engages in a strategy whereby a rational system can include what necessarily lies beyond its boundaries. Maurice Merleau-Ponty terms such strategies "hyperreflection" (*surrér-flexion*), which *implies* what is transcendent, other, or transrational through the use of the rational. As we shall see, recursive strategies do something similar. For a discussion of Merleau-Ponty on this issue, see Mark C. Taylor, *Altarity* (Chicago: University of Chicago Press, 1987), pp. 77–81.

37. See, for instance, Richard Taylor, "A Reformulation of the Argument for Contingency," in Keith E. Yandell, ed., *God, Man, and Religion: Readings in the Philosophy of Religion* (New York: McGraw-Hill, 1973), pp. 421–26.

38. The story is in the Bṛihadāranyaka Upanishad 3.6 and is quoted from Robert Ernest Hume, trans., *The Thirteen Principal Upanishads*, 2d rev. ed. (Oxford: Oxford University Press, 1931; reprint, 1971), pp. 113–14.

39. The religious appeal to faith in the face of the transrational has an exact parallel in modern mathematical responses to Gödel's theorem and other such paradoxes. When faced with "unprovable verities," mathematicians resort to various extralogical tactics. "Secular" tactics may be summed up under the heading of simplicity and are commonly referred to as Occam's razor. "Mystical" tactics judge a hypothesis "not only by how well it explains the evidence but also by whether it is consistent with a philosophy that assigns a purpose to everything." It is no accident that William Paley's faith-oriented "argument from design" has become a common religious counter to Darwinian theory. See Guillen, *Bridges to Infinity*, pp. 121–25.

some sort of recursion. In Hindu mythology, for instance, gods create themselves or one another.[40] The paradox of mutual creation signals that we are at the limits of a standard cosmology, just as the inability to confront the question of god's creator does. Where paradox becomes the focus of a cosmology, we encounter what is no longer a boundary of paradoxes around a normal cosmology. Rather, we have entered the realm of recursive cosmology in which the "paradox" is aggressively pursued either as a challenge to the accepted view or as the central organizing factor of a more sophisticated cosmology. Douglas Hofstader, Wendy Donniger O'Flaherty, and Bruce Lincoln have, in their own ways, explored this question. O'Flaherty's focus on mutual and paradoxical creation, as in the story of "The Monk Who Met People in his Dream," Hofstader's wonderfully engaging examination of M. C. Escher's art, and Lincoln's canny observations of the symbolic politics of anomaly suggest a more than merely marginal role for paradoxes and anomalies.[41] Again, an example from the Christian tradition is instructive. The "mystery" of Christ as god incarnate bridges an "unbridgeable" conceptual gap between created and creator through a paradoxical and recursive form of mediation.

Hofstader coined the term "strange loop" to refer to the systematic exploitation of paradox, anomaly, and recursion in the drawings of Escher and in Bach's fugues.[42] Briefly stated, when continuous systems are pushed to their limits, they generate paradoxes. When those paradoxes are aggressively pursued as the organizing principle behind a cosmology, the result is often a recursive or strange-loop cosmology.[43] Just as paradox joins two dissonant figures of speech or meaning in a construct that transcends normal language, so too, a recursive cosmology joins two dissonant cosmological visions and insists that they are somehow compatible or one. The result is a sophisticated cosmology that transcends the limits of normal "rational" cosmology. At the limits of one system we are referred to another, yet this new system is oddly a part of the old, and *vice versa*. Through the use of recursion propounders of cosmologies can assert discontinuity as well as continuity, and in doing so they constitute transcendence simultaneously with a totalistic cosmos. Reality can be dual (or even

40. The mutual creation of Indian gods is discussed by Wendy Donniger O'Flaherty in *Dreams, Illusion, and Other Realities* (Chicago: University of Chicago Press, 1984), p. 255. Another context for such "mutual creations" is a ritual context in which one recreates primal events and therefore sets up a kind of circular creation.

41. For the account of the dreaming monk, see O'Flaherty, *Dreams*, pp. 207–9.

42. For other examples concerning Gödel's theorem, see Guillen, *Bridges to Infinity*, pp. 118–19.

43. See Hofstader, *Gödel, Escher, Bach*, pp. 67–74. Hofstader also describes a narrow definition of recursivity on pp. 127–52. The example of the two sentences is from p. 21. The notion of recursivity and its relationship to game theory and cosmology has been treated in William Poundstone, *The Recursive Universe: Cosmic Complexity and the Limits of Scientific Knowledge* (Chicago: Contemporary Books, 1985).

multifold) and nondual simultaneously. As in paradox, the meaning is in the perplexing relationship. The very limits of system are used to index the transcendent, and the "mystery" of the sacred can be communicated. This is, to borrow a fitting turn of phrase, a Möbius universe.[44] As we shall see, such recursive strategies have concrete political implications, for they make possible a "politics" of simultaneous differential interpretation.

Such cosmologies are evident in many traditions, though explaining them has always been difficult. Indeed, they have often been overlooked because they defy our attempts to rationalize reality.[45] Yet it is precisely this ability to use the rational to move beyond the rational that makes such cosmologies attractive. They allow a tradition to represent the mystery of the sacred, its simultaneous unity and diversity, its structure and substance, its continuity and discontinuity. Such cosmological schemes are difficult to apprehend and describe. M. C. Escher's drawing "Print Gallery" conveys a more limited though no less recursive world.[46] In this work a man is viewing a painting which twists on itself to become the world in which the same man is standing.

Complex transrational recursive cosmology is, I argue, a common feature of Buddhism, a feature exploited intellectually in the Mahāyāna and practically in the Buddhist tantras. Understanding this continuous yet self-transcendent cosmology and its political implications is a necessary first step in understanding the creation of the *Scripture for Humane Kings*.

The eighth-century monk Kūkai (the reputed designer of the Humane Kings mandala at Tōji), who introduced Esoteric Buddhism to Japan, indicated the centrality of paradox to any understanding of the Buddhist tantras: "The Dharma is beyond speech, but without speech it cannot be revealed. Suchness transcends forms, but without depending on forms it cannot be realized. . . . Since the Esoteric Buddhist teachings are so profound as to defy expression in writing, they are revealed through the medium of painting to those who are yet to be enlightened."[47] The paintings Kūkai speaks of are the two mandalas which graphically depict the cosmology of the Chinese Esoteric Buddhism and Japanese Shingon.[48] Arrayed on the eastern and western walls of the ritual arena, the mandalas and the worlds they describe are recursively related.[49] Eso-

44. See O'Flaherty, *Dreams*, pp. 240–41.

45. The notion of "the Kingdom" in the New Testament is one possible example. See Norman Perrin, *The New Testament: An Introduction* (New York: Harcourt Brace Jovanovich, 1974), pp. 288–91.

46. A reproduction of this work is in Hofstader, *Gödel, Escher, Bach*, p. 714.

47. Yoshido S. Hakeda, *Kūkai: Major Works* (New York: Columbia University Press, 1972), p. 145.

48. The central figure of this cosmology is Mahāvairocana, the great "sun" Buddha. H. P. L'Orange's term "cosmocrat" is perhaps the most appropriate description of him. For L'Orange's notion of the cosmocrat, see "Expressions of Cosmic Kingship in the Ancient World," in *Sacral Kingship*, pp. 481–92.

49. For a more detailed account both of the mandalas and of their recursive relationship, see Charles D. Orzech, "Cosmology in Action: Recursive Cosmology, Soteriology, and Authority in *Chen-yen* Buddhism with Special Reference to the Monk Pu-k'ung" (Ph.D. diss., University of Chicago,

teric practice carried out in the space embraced by the twin mandala involved the ritual realization of the paradoxical identity and nonidentity of saṃsāra and nirvana and of the Two Truths. The Esoteric schools of Buddhism in China, Korea, and Japan were constituted in and through the ritual realization of this paradox, a realization which was simultaneously transcendent and political. This realization is nowhere more apparent than in the second recension of the *Scripture for Humane Kings*. This scripture was central both to Kūkai's Shingon Buddhism and to Pu-k'ung's Chinese Esoteric Buddhism, just as the first version was central to the creation of a new Chinese Buddhism in fifth-century North China. In both versions of the text political authority serves to index soteriological progress. In both sovereign power is recursively linked to the "edge of reality"—to a "transcendent" nirvana—and in both this formulation is conditioned by historical circumstances. As in the example of the Ming Dynasty ritual controversy, my typology will allow us more easily to understand how polity, cosmology, and soteriology constitute the complex religious systems of national protection Buddhism. To come to grips with national protection Buddhism and to understand the role of the *Scripture for Humane Kings* in its creation we must first examine the basic schemata of Buddhist cosmology and their religious and political import.

1986), and Fabio Rambelli's recent interpretations of the notion of recursion in Shingon Buddhism, "Re-inscribing *Maṇḍala*: Semiotic Operations on a Word and Its Object," in *Studies in Central and East Asian Religions* (Copenhagen and Århus: Seminar for Buddhist Studies, 1991), 4:1–24.

2

World, Path, and Authority in Buddhism

> There is no difference at all
> between this world and nirvana;
> between nirvana and this world
> there is no difference at all.
> The limit of nirvana
> is the limit of this world.
> —Nāgārjuna, *Mūlamadhyamakakārikās*, 25:19

The Place of Nirvana

The place of nirvana and the authority of one who has entered nirvana are issues that have plagued and fascinated Buddhists from the very beginning of the tradition. The utter transcendence of nirvana is a common Buddhist theme. Thus, in the *Khuddakanikāya*, the Buddha proclaims,

> Monks, there is that sphere wherein is neither earth nor water, fire nor air: it is not the infinity of space, nor the infinity of perception; it is not nothingness, nor is it neither idea nor nonidea. . . . Monks, there is an unborn, unbecome, unmade, unconditioned. Monks, if there were not an unborn, unbecome, unmade, unconditioned, then we could not here know any escape from the born, become, made, conditioned.[1]

1. Beyer, *Buddhist Experience*, p. 199, translating "Udāṇa" from *Khuddakanikāya*. Note that "earth nor water, fire nor air" refers to the lowest manifestations of the world system, while "it is not the in-

But it is also undeniable that "cosmological" assumptions undergird Buddhist notions of the path to salvation and the relationship of that path to the exercise of legitimate authority.[2] Indeed, the "sphere wherein is neither earth nor water . . . neither idea nor nonidea" is a description of the bottom and pinnacle of a well-known Buddhist cosmology. Eliade called the problem of the "cosmology" of nirvana "the paradox of the unconditioned." The paradox is often articulated as an inquiry into the "mode of being of the 'nirvanaized one,'" and the question is whether a Buddha enters total extinction or some other form of existence. This question is one of "Fourteen Difficult Questions" (*caturdaśāvyākṛtavastūni*), which include cosmological probings on the eternality or perishability of the world. Concerns over the locus and state of enlightened persons both before and after death, or over the nature and fate of the cosmos were part of a common background of cosmological inquiry that early Buddhism shared with emerging Hindu and Jain traditions. In one account the Buddha refuses to say whether "the saint exists" or "does not exist" after death, and through an analogy he demonstrates to his questioner that either assertion "does not fit the case."[3] Nāgārjuna put it more succinctly:

> After his final cessation
> the Blessed One isn't is
> (isn't isn't) isn't is and isn't
> isn't isn't is and isn't.[4]

The question only leads to a conundrum; reality is paradoxical.

While some Buddhist traditions thus label cosmological inquiry irrelevant to or even detrimental to the pursuit of enlightenment, others speak of the

finity of space" refers to the four supreme trances of the formless realm, which are the "summit" of the universe as well as the most advanced states to be achieved in the practices of "calming" (Pāli, *sammatha*, Chinese *chih*).

2. Buddhist traditions have generated a prodigious array of world systems under a variety of labels. Thus we find constant reference to *saṃsāra* or the cycle of birth and rebirth, to various *dhātu* or *loka* as in the terms *trisāhasramahāsāhasralokadhātu*, and to various *kṣetra* or "fields," as in *Buddhakṣetra*. Perhaps the closest term to our cosmology is *lokaprajñapti* or "world-teachings." Abhidharma texts differentiate between the "receptacle world" (Sanskrit *bhājanaloka*) and the "world of beings" (*sattvaloka*). None of these is a precise equivalent for our term "cosmology," but cosmology and cosmography have a long pedigree in discussions of Buddhist world-systems, so I will continue the usage. For an overview, see Louis de La Vallée Poussin, "Cosmogony and Cosmology (Buddhist)," in James Hastings, ed., *Encyclopedia of Religion and Ethics*, 13 vols. (Edinburgh: T & T Clark, 1908–27), 2:129–38.

3. The story is found in Warren, *Buddhism in Translations*, pp. 123–28, translating *Majjhimanikāya Sutta* 72.

4. Beyer, *Buddhist Experience*, p. 214, with minor modifications. Beyer's citation is to Nāgārjuna, *Mādhyamaka-śāstra*, or *Mūlamādyamakakārikās* 25:17–18. For an alternate translation, see Streng, *Emptiness*, p. 214.

Buddha's sovereignty over the world, and they expend great effort cataloging that world. A well-known passage from the *Majjhimanikāya* is emblematic of this theme of sovereignty:

> As soon as he is born, the *bodhisattva* takes seven steps, facing the North, and utters the lion's "roar," exclaiming, "I am the highest in the world, I am the best in the world, I am the eldest in the world; this is my last birth; there will not be another life for me henceforth."[5]

Remarking on this passage, Eliade underscored the Buddha's abolishing or transcending of the self, of space and time.[6] We should note that the Buddha's proclamation is based on early Indian presuppositions about the yogic path, a path described as a progressive mastery of the self, of space, and of time, in a gradual climb to the summit of the world. In other words, the paradox of the "nirvanaized one" is a statement both about his mastery of the world and his simultaneous transcendence of that world.

Anticosmological strands in early Buddhism are well documented, yet many discussions of nirvana, especially in the Mahāyāna and the tantras, reverberate with a deep concern for the world. So too, scholars have noted that "the seemingly acosmological nature of nirvāṇa in early Mahāyāna presupposed a cosmology," and the words of Nāgārjuna cited at the head of this chapter are a confirmation—at least for some Buddhists—of nirvana's engagement with the world.[7] One of the most striking passages in the *Scripture for Humane Kings* describes a cosmic hierarchy stretching from petty kings up to the lord of the entire universe. This pinnacle of existence somehow both is and is not the state of nirvana.

> If a ***bodhisattva*** abides in absolutely inexpressible [numbers of] Buddha-states he becomes the great quiescent heavenly king of the fourth trance, lord of the triple world, and cultivating absolutely inexpressible Teachings attains the ***samādhi*** which exhausts reality and [he] is the same as a Buddha in deeds and station. Having exhausted the

5. *Majjhimanikāya* 3, 123, quoted in Mircea Eliade, *A History of Religious Ideas*, trans. Williard R. Trask, vol. 2, *From Gautama Buddha to the Triumph of Christianity* (Chicago: University of Chicago Press, 1982), p. 73.

6. Eliade, *History of Religious Ideas*, 2:73, 105.

7. Faure, *Rhetoric of Immediacy*, p. 70, has borrowed this argument from Paul Mus, who first noted that cosmological development in the early Mahāyāna was taking place on an intermediate level between this world and nirvana. This intermediate level corresponded to the relics of the Buddha (*sarīra*, *sarīradhātu*). For Mus's argument, see *Barabudur*, 1:60–84. It is interesting to speculate that the growing importance of relics, both to lay and monk, could have been an impetus to cosmological speculation.

sources of the triple world [he nevertheless] teaches and transforms all beings just as in a Buddha-realm. (T 245 8.827a27–b1)

In this passage and in others like it, cosmology and authority, the path and the goal, are functions of each other. The bodhisattva has "exhausted the sources of the triple world," yet continues to "teach" and "transform" beings "just as in a Buddha-realm." Far from being an elimination of the worldly, for many Buddhists nirvana is implied by the very structure of the world. Many Buddhist scriptures expressed this paradoxical "cosmology" of nirvana in the idiom and iconography of Indian kingship, and clearly the *Scripture for Humane Kings* is no exception.[8] The framework of the scripture consists of systematic correlations between actual rulership, levels of mastery of the Buddhist Teaching, and advancement both in salvific means and in cosmic location. The fundamental premise of the *Scripture for Humane Kings* is that the world, the path, and authority are functions of one another and that nirvana and the world are paradoxically related.

Like every religion, Buddhism is a discourse about the world, and sovereignty is a convenient idiom for representing religious authority. An often overlooked dimension of Buddhism is the insistence—sometimes quite literal—that achievement on the path is inextricably bound up with authority, that the Buddha is not only "world renouncer," but also has been and is "world conqueror."[9] With few exceptions modern scholars have interpreted such language allegorically. These reductive allegorizations dismember Buddhism by lopping off Buddhist notions of polity. Buddhist teachings must be understood

8. The two best discussions of the use of kingship imagery in Buddhism are Paul Mus, "Le Bouddha paré: Son origine Indienne," *Bulletin de l'École française d'Extrême Orient* 28 (1926): 153–280, and Snellgrove's "Notion of Divine Kingship," pp. 204–18. Balakrishna G. Gokale's "Early Buddhist Kingship," *Journal of Asian Studies*, 26.1 (1966): 15–22, also provides a useful sketch of early attitudes and historical realities. Frank E. Reynolds and Mani B. Reynolds' translation of *Three Worlds According to King Ruang: A Thai Buddhist Cosmology* (Berkeley: Institute of Buddhist Studies, 1982) is an extensive discourse on the relations among authority, cosmology, and salvation. Buddhist ritual abounds with imagery borrowed from royal pomp and circumstance. For instance, Buddhas and bodhisattvas receive consecration or *abhiṣeka*, a rite with ancient connections to Indian kingship. For consecration and Indian kingship more broadly, see Johannes C. Heesterman, *The Ancient Indian Royal Consecration* (The Hague: Mouton, 1957); Louis Dumont, "The Conception of Kingship in Ancient India," *Contributions to Indian Sociology* 6 (1962): 48–77; Jan Gonda, *Ancient Indian Kingship from the Religious Point of View* (Leiden: E. J. Brill, 1966); Heesterman, *The Inner Conflict of Tradition: Essays in Indian Ritual, Kingship, and Society* (Chicago: University of Chicago Press, 1985). Also Ronald Inden, "Lordship and Caste in Hindu Discourse," in Audrey Cantlie and Richard Burghart, eds., *Indian Religion* (London: Curzon Press; New York: St. Martin's Press, 1985); and John F. Richards, ed., *Kingship and Authority in South Asia*, South Asia Publications Series 3 (Madison: University of Wisconsin Press, 1978).

9. Tambiah, *World Conqueror and World Renouncer*.

not merely as championing a metaphoric sovereignty, but as advancing a comprehensive vision of the cosmos, of authority, and of a path in which achievement is both "worldly" and "transcendent." To reimagine this Buddhism, to grasp the message of the *Scripture for Humane Kings* and other scriptures that likewise speak of sovereignty, we must carefully attend to positive Buddhist recognitions of the world so that the biases of our own world do not blind us to their shapes. But we must also take care that we do not merely replicate one or another Buddhist world, thereby abandoning interpretation entirely. Using the typology of cosmologies outlined in Chapter 1, I examine here the basic strands or themes of Buddhist cosmology and their deployment in complex recursive cosmologies in the Mahāyāna. The imagery of Indian kingship played a central role in these complex cosmologies. Neither mere allegory nor a pandering to the exigencies of survival in the world, sovereign imagery became the vehicle for a Buddhism claiming at once world conquest and world transcendence. This "royal" Buddhism was conceptualized in the Mahāyāna and put into practice in the tantras.

The World in Buddhism

In an important recent book Randy Kloetzli reexamines the world conqueror and world renouncer strands of Buddhist cosmological imagery and proposes an expansion of this two-strand typology. A review of Kloetzli's insights and difficulties is a convenient framework for thinking through the major strands of Buddhist cosmological imagery and for formulating a taxonomy that is both flexible and analytically useful.[10] Kloetzli characterizes one of the cosmological currents in Buddhism by its use of images of time and motion and the other by its use of space and light.[11] Building on this distinction, Kloetzli argues for a new four-fold typology of Buddhist cosmology composed of two main types and two subtypes. He calls the main types the "*sāhasra*" (thousands) cosmology and the "*asaṅkhyeya*" (innumerable) cosmology, in accordance with the mathematical imagery found in each. Each main type has two variants or subtypes, the *cakravāla* and the Pure Land.[12]

10. I have reviewed Kloetzli's work in more detail in my dissertation and in a review, "Answering Difficult Questions," which appeared in *History of Religions* 24.3 (1985): 282–84.

11. Randy Kloetzli, *Buddhist Cosmology: From Single World System to Pure Land: Science and Theology in the Images of Motion and Light* (Delhi: Motilal Banarsidass, 1983), p. ix.

12. This is the first work to take a fresh look at Buddhist cosmology since Louis de La Vallée Poussin and Willibald Kirfel scouted the topic now three-quarters of a century ago. For La Vallée Poussin's classic essay, see "Cosmogony and Cosmology (Buddhist)," 2:129–38. Also see Willibald Kirfel, *Kosmo-*

Though Kloetzli focuses on *sāhasra* and *asaṅkhyeya* images, he begins with an extended discussion of the *cakravāla*. The *cakravāla* is presumed by all Buddhist cosmological traditions, and it is the essential building block or basic element of descriptive Buddhist cosmology.[13] The *cakravāla* cosmology and references to it as the "triple world" (*tribhūmika, tridhātuka, triloka*) are found throughout the Pāli scriptures and in Mahāyāna and Vajrayāna texts. The *cakravāla* cosmology presents a world of moral/physical divisions comprising the familiar Indian Mt. Meru cosmology. The world is divided into the *kāmadhātu*, or the lower realms of coarse sensual desires, and the upper *rūpadhātu*, or realm of form. The top station of Mt. Meru in the *kāmadhātu* is the heaven of Lord Indra (*trāyastriṃśa*), while the top of the *rūpadhātu*, and thus of the cosmos, is the heaven of Maheśvara or Śiva, the *akaniṣṭha*.[14] Certain sentient forces exist outside of the realm of form in the "formless" realm or *ārūpya*.

The *cakravāla* takes its name from its configuration. The cosmos is composed of seven concentric golden mountain ranges (*cakra*) with Mt. Meru (or Sumeru) at the center and the outer *cakravāla* wall of iron at the perimeter. The intervening spaces between the mountain ranges are filled with seas and land masses (*dvīpa* or "islands") located at the cardinal points in the oceans around the seventh mountain range. The entire disk is said to rest on a circle of water supported upon wind, which in turn rests on space (*ākāśa*).

If one were to climb the central mountain (as one may through reincarnation or through the advanced practice of enstatic trance or *samathā*), one would ascend through the various levels of the cosmos, first passing through the *kāmadhātu*, which includes an assortment of hells, the realms of the ghosts (*pretas*), animals, humans, *asuras*, and the *kāmadevas* (including the Tuṣita heaven and the heaven of Indra). Leaving the *kāmadhātu*, one ascends to the *rūpadhātu* or *brahmaloka* crowned by the *akaniṣṭha* heaven at the summit of the universe. The *rūpadhātu* encompasses the four *dhyāna* heavens or heavens which can be accessed in advanced trance (the fourth of these is described in the passage

---

graphie de Inder (Bonn: K. Schroeder, 1920). Moving far beyond the confines of South Asia, Kloetzli argues persuasively that Buddhist cosmological imagery can be understood as a part of scientific and mathematical speculation across the ancient world. See, for example, his use of Archimedes' "The Sand Reckoner" to determine the underlying meaning of the phrase "the sands of the *Gaṅgā*, in *Buddhist Cosmology*, pp. 113–31.

13. I am obviously indebted to Kloetzli for the descriptive material in the next few pages. His discussion of the *cakravāla* cosmology may be found in *Buddhist Cosmology*, pp. 23–50. A synopsis of these systems can be found in La Vallée Poussin's "Cosmogony and Cosmology (Buddhist)."

14. For the development of Śiva as lord of the *akaniṣṭha* heaven in esoteric Buddhism, see Iyanaga Nobumi, "Récits de la soumission de Maheśvara par Trailokyavijaya d'après les sources Chinoises et Japonaises," in Michel Strickmann, ed., *Tantric and Taoist Studies in Honor of R. A. Stein, Mélanges Chinoises et Bouddhiques* 22 (1985): 633–745.

from the *Scripture for Humane Kings* quoted earlier). Thus the *cakravāla* maps a sort of pilgrim's progress, wherein the lower realms and the realm of the starry sky and its correlate teachings must be successively mastered to gain access to the *brahmaloka* and the most refined summit of consciousness.[15]

While the *cakravāla* is the basis of Buddhist cosmology, it is frequently met in two expanded forms: the *sāhasra* or "thousands" form and the *asaṅkhyeya* or "innumerable" form. The *sāhasra* represents a mathematical expansion of the *cakravāla*-cosmology and is found throughout Buddhist literature, in the *Pāli* scriptures (for example in the *Aṅguttaranikāya*), in the *Jātakas*, in the works of Buddhaghoṣa, Vasubandhu, the *Prajñāpāramitās* and elsewhere. Frequently described as the *trisāhasra mahāsāhasralokadhātu* (often translated as the "three-thousand great-thousand world system"), the *sāhasra* is characterized by the division of the *brahmaloka* or *rūpadhātu* into horizontally arranged multiples of thousands of *cakravāla* worlds, all of which are dominated by a single Buddha just as in the common *cakravāla*.[16]

The image of other Buddha-worlds like our own but independent of it is associated with the appearance of *asaṅkhyeya* and Pure Land imagery. Found in the *Prajñāpāramitās*, the *Lotus Sūtra* and the *Vimalakīrtinirdeśa*, *asaṅkhyeya* designates a cosmology composed literally of "innumerable" *cakravāla* worlds, each with its own Buddha. Under certain circumstances these "Buddha-lands of the ten directions" (*daśadigbuddha*) become visible. Kloetzli considers the Pure Land to be a subtype of *asaṅkhyeya* cosmos.[17]

Although Kloetzli's taxonomy provides an excellent vehicle for examining the meaning of mathematical imagery in Buddhist traditions, it has limited value for our exploration of the religious and political import of Buddhist cosmology. The basis of this inadequacy is the fact that the *cakravāla* is an element, implicit or explicit, in all Buddhist world descriptions, and its meaning depends on the context in which it is embedded. Without careful attention to the context of a cosmological image, its meaning cannot be determined, and conflicting or contradictory interpretations result.[18]

15. Kloetzli, *Buddhist Cosmology*, pp. 47–50. The upper levels of the path constituted by the four "formless" trances can be found in Buddhaghoṣa's *Viśuddhimagga*, chapters 10 and 23. For a translation see Beyer, *Buddhist Experience*, pp. 206–11. Edward Conze has a convenient table of these states in *Large Sūtra on Perfect Wisdom*, pp. 670–71.

16. Kloetzli, *Buddhist Cosmology*, pp. 51–82.

17. Ibid., pp. 91–111, describes the *asaṁkhyeya* cosmology. Kloetzli's comments about the Pure Lands are found on pp. 136–37.

18. Although the *cakravāla* is often associated with the Nikāya tradition, Kloetzli relies on later sources, notably Vasubandhu's *summa* of the Abhidharma tradition, the *Abhidharmakośa* and Nāgārjuna's massive commentary on the *Pañcaviṁśatisāhasrika-Prajñāpāramitā*, the *Mahāprajñāpāramitāśāstra* to formulate a full and clear picture of it. Vasubandhu's great *summa* of the Sarvāstivādin Abhidharm-

For instance, Kloetzli characterizes the *cakaravāla*-cosmos as a solid gradient of *substance* from the coarse *kāmadhātu* through ever subtler matter of the *rūpadhātu* and describes a continuous graded path to salvation, a salvation accomplished over time through *personal* striving, self transformation, and achievement.[19] "The basic drama, then, is the passage of the Buddhist monk absorbed in trance . . . to the world of Brahma, there to journey through the various meditation realms and finally to move beyond the cosmos into nirvāṇa."[20] The path depicted here is a continuous ascent to the summit of the world and thence out of the world into nirvana. Yet as Kloetzli notes, Vasubandhu's *Abhidharmakośa,* which is his primary source of information on the *cakravāla,* also presents the entire world system as a series of relative *positional* measurements. There, each level of the cosmos corresponds to a certain type of body, a certain life span, and various physical measurements such as body size, length of day, and so on.[21] Kloetzli then argues that "it will become increasingly evident that this aspect of the Buddhist cosmos is a statement that all measurement is ultimately empty." In the terms of my typology this *cakravāla* is *structural* and *positional* in nature.[22]

It is quite clear that the first discussion of the *cakravāla* is couched in what I have called *personal* imagery, whereas the second discussion is couched in *positional* imagery. But where is the emphasis in each of these descriptions to be placed? If, as in the first case, the emphasis is on the progressive ascent up the cosmic mountain, then the scheme is *continuous*. But if the emphasis is placed on the total break between this world and nirvana, then the scheme is *discontinuous*. Similarly, if in the second case, the emphasis is placed on the replication of structure throughout all the Buddha-worlds, then the imagery of emptiness is markedly *continuous*. If the emphasis is placed on the gaps between these visionary worlds and on their usual invisibility, then the scheme is *discontinuous*. How are we to determine the *significance*—political, religious, or other-

---

ist persuasion was written before his conversion to the Vijñānavādin (Yogācāra) school at the hands of his brother Asaṅga. See Louis de la Vallée Poussin, trans. and annot., *L'Abhidharmakośa de Vasubandhu,* 3 vols. (Paris: Paul Geunther, 1923–25). A translation of the *Pañcavimśati* is available in Conze, *Large Sūtra on Perfect Wisdom*. Also see Étienne Lamotte, trans. and annot., *Traité de la grande vertu de la sagesse de Nāgārjuna (Mahāprajñāpāramitā-śāstra)*, 3 vols. (Louvain: Bureaux du Muséon, 1944–70).

19. Kloetzli, *Buddhist Cosmology*, pp. 49–50.

20. Ibid., p. 50.

21. As the passage at the head of this chapter indicates, the *Scripture for Humane Kings* presumes such correlations. When we examine the system globally, we find that beings in the hells have nearly infinitesimal life spans, though they spend long eons in the hells by being reborn in them instantaneously. Conversely, beings in the heavens have immensely long life spans. Kloetzli has an excellent series of charts depicting these relationships in *Buddhist Cosmology*, pp. 32–39.

22. Ibid., p. 44.

wise—of cosmological imagery? Turning to descriptions of the *cakravāla* embedded in the larger cosmological compendia of the *Abhidharmakośa* and the *Mahāprajñāpāramitāśāstra* results in yet another methodological quandary. First, both of these texts advance markedly *positional* concerns. The *Abhidharmakośa* of the Sarvāstivādins is concerned with *dharma* analysis and classification while the *Mahāprajñāpāramitāśāstra* is a refutation of that analysis on the basis of the structure and relativity of universal emptiness. Second, the *Abhidharmakośa* presumes the ultimate *discontinuity* between the samsaric world and the nirvanic world. The *Mahāprajñāpāramitāśāstra*, meanwhile, presumes certain *continuities* in the cosmos.[23]

My point is that without considering the context in which the *cakravāla* (or any of its derivatives) appears, it is impossible to determine whether a *cakravāla* represents a continuous ascending path toward the summit of the cosmos, a radical discontinuity between this world and nirvana, or a skillful deployment of both continuous and discontinuous notions. Where the ultimate soteriological goal is emphasized, the aim is not merely to "master" the cosmos but to transcend it utterly. The significant gap or *discontinuity* implied in this use of the *cakravāla* must be recognized. The pilgrim's progress and the process of the path end abruptly. Thus many of the texts of Nikāya Buddhism contend that when a Buddha or an arhat dies, he is totally extinct in this cosmos.[24] Yet where a graded series of meditative exercises (*samathā*) is emphasized, the sequential continuity of the cosmos is foregrounded, and with it the mastery of the cosmos. It is therefore of vital importance to recognize the contexts of a cosmology as determining factors in its interpretation.

Aside from the meaning of mathematical imagery in Buddhist cosmological speculation, Kloetzli's real contribution is his highlighting of the roles of imagery of time and motion and space and light in Buddhist cosmology. As I will demonstrate, the sophistication of and the compelling nature of the Buddhist tradition lie in its use of these images not merely one at a time, but in multiple configurations that articulate relationships between the world, the path, and authority in specific historical contexts.

23. Including the notion that Buddhas and bodhisattvas *never* enter nirvana as a totally "other" state. See Kloetzli's discussion of this notion in *Buddhist Cosmology*, on pp. 110–11.

24. Throughout this study I have followed John Strong's lead in using "Nikāya Buddhism" (Buddhism of the schools) to indicate Buddhist traditions usually labeled Hīnayāna. While it raises problems of its own, this label was occasionally used in the tradition and avoids the misleading and pejorative designation promoted by the Mahāyāna. See John S. Strong, *The Experience of Buddhism: Sources and Interpretations* (Belmont, Calif.: Wadsworth, 1995), p. 86. Richard S. Cohen has recently warned of the pitfalls of taking too seriously the Mahāyāna/Hīnayāna taxonomy in "Discontented Categories: Hīnayāna and Mahāyāna in Indian Buddhist History," *Journal of the American Academy of Religion* 63.1 (1995): 1–25.

A Taxonomy of Buddhist Cosmologies

When we use the typology I advanced in Chapter 1 to examine Buddhist cosmologies, we find that some use the causal, temporal, and *personal* idiom of inborn substances and their interaction, while others emphasize the structural, a-temporal, or *positional* visionary apprehension of reality in trance. I call these the *rupic* cosmology and the *dharmic* cosmology.[25]

I have chosen the terms *rupic* and *dharmic* for two reasons. Each term indicates a coherent cosmological thread in the language of Buddhism, yet each is free of any single historical context. The terms emerge in the early distinction between the Buddha's physical body, or *rūpakāya*, and his "body" of teachings, his *dharmakāya*. The first represents the conditioned world, a body subject to time and karmic causality, and therefore changeable and perishable. The second represents the unconditioned world, the world of the Teaching, imperishable, timeless, unchanging. *Rupic* cosmology is personal and is correlated with the practices of calming (*samathā*) and the mastery of the universe of time and of motion, while *dharmic* cosmology is positional and correlated with insight (*vippasanā*), with transcendence of the universe, and with visionary experience.

The *rupic* cosmos is the "commonplace" world of persons, substances, time, motion, and the operation of the laws of karma and *pratītyasamutpāda* (co-dependent arising.)[26] Contrasting with the *rupic* cosmology, the *dharmic* cosmology represents the universe of the enlightened, the visionary apprehension

25. A similar distinction has been used by John Strong in his analysis of *avadāna* stories. Basing his work on that of Paul Mus, Strong distinguishes *rupalogical* from *dharmalogical* results flowing from a given meritorious act. See John Strong, "The Transforming Gift: An Analysis of Devotional Acts of Offering in Buddhist Avadāna Literature," *History of Religions* 18 (February 1979): 222–27, and his *Legend of King Aśoka*, pp. 108–9.

26. This *rupic* cosmology might also be called the *rupic-nirmanic* cosmology, a term suggested to me by Frank Reynolds. Reynolds has used the terms "rupic" and "dharmic" in his "Multiple Cosmologies and Ethics." The term *rūpa* is important primarily though not exclusively in the early Buddhist tradition. *Rūpa* is the form or substance of the world, and in many Nikāya Buddhist traditions this cosmology is not salvific, though it is the medium through which the Buddhist teaching manifests. However, John Clifford Holt has persuasively argued that certain aspects of this cosmos can indeed be salvific. See his *Buddha in the Crown: Avalokiteśvara in the Buddhist Traditions of Sri Lanka* (New York: Oxford University Press, 1991), esp. with respect to Natha Deviyo. The Buddha's physical body, his *rūpakāya* is thus distinguished from his *dharmakāya* or his "Body of Teaching." The notion of *nirmāṇas*, of personal transformations or extensions of the Buddha as salvific forces in the world of *saṃsāra*, is not unknown in Nikāya Buddhism and is a pervasive theme in the Mahāyāna and in Esoteric Buddhism. *Nirmāṇas* are transformations of the Buddha's own substance and are explicitly salvific. On the topic of *rūpa*, see Stcherbatsky, *Central Conception*, pp. 11–15. Also Maryla Falk, *Nama-rūpa and Dharma-rūpa: Origins and Aspects of an Ancient Indian Conception* (Calcutta: University of Calcutta, 1943).

of the structure of reality, both as inexpressible and as the Dharma, the "firmly structured" reality of the Buddhist Teaching.

The terms *rupa* and *dharma* are found together in many Buddhist traditions, and their relationship is crucial to an understanding of Buddhist cosmology. While the terms evoke broad cosmological themes, they avoid the pitfalls of tying a typology to one particular Buddhist cosmological description and its historical circumstances. Consequently, any given cosmological description may, and usually does, entail both *rupic* and *dharmic* elements. The significance and configuration of these elements, whether they are viewed in terms of fundamental *continuity* or *discontinuity*, depend upon context and historical circumstances. Generally speaking, Mahāyāna cosmologies are dominated by themes of continuity while Nikāya Buddhist cosmologies are discontinuous, but this is not always the case, and as we shall see, the exceptions are of particular interest.[27] Indeed, the fifth-century "Mahāyāna" *Scripture for Humane Kings* is structured around the relationship between continuous and discontinuous *rupic* cosmologies.

The two major cosmological idioms, one emphasizing the instantaneous, positional Buddha's-eye view of the world, the other emphasizing the gradual development and transformation of the person, reflect a tension that runs through Buddhist traditions.

Rupic Cosmologies: Transformation and Substance

Focused on a single Buddha, *rupic* cosmologies are closely linked to the imagery of substance, time, and progressive motion toward purity. In terms of the distinction drawn in Chapter 1 between personal and positional cosmologies, *rupic* cosmologies are markedly personal. Thus the *Jātaka*s extol the disciplined development of virtue throughout the Buddha's past lives. *Rupic* cosmologies in the Mahāyāna focus on the gradual, organic maturation and transformation of the bodhisattva in progress through the ten stages along a personal path of achievement, and when the goal is reached the bodhisattva is anointed as sovereign of the triple world in the palace of the *akaniṣṭha* heaven.[28] Personal transformation is identical with the bodhisattva's exercise of "skillful means"

27. This is, of course, a generalization and refers to emphases or tendencies. Things are more complex when we look, for instance, at the notion of *icchāntika* in the Mahāyāna, or at any number of Nikāya Buddhist texts. Moreover, John Holt's recent work on Avalokiteśvara in Sri Lanka indicates that the *pratītyasamutpāda* cosmos can indeed have a salvific function in Nikāya Buddhism.

28. For a detailed discussion of the bodhisattva path, see Har Dayal, *The Bodhisattva Doctrine in Buddhist Sanskrit Literature* (London: Routledge & Kegan Paul, 1932; reprint, Delhi: Motilal Banarsidass, 1970), and more recently on the path and its relationship to the Two Truths, Huntington and Wangchen, *Emptiness of Emptiness*. Part two of this book is a translation of Candrakīrti's *Entry into the Middle Way* (*Madhyamakāvatāra*).

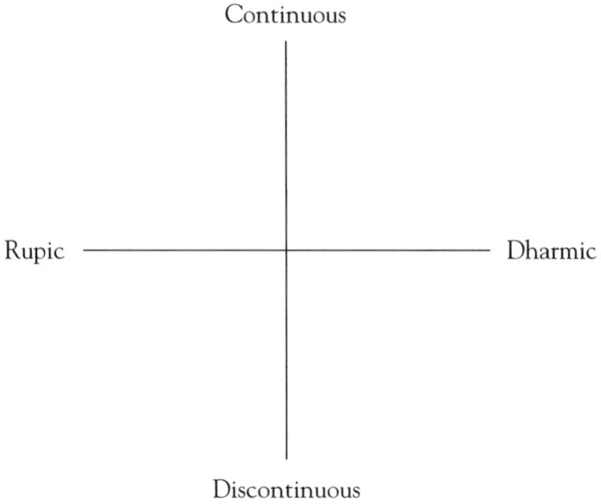

Fig. 2. Buddhist cosmological choices

(*upāya*), his extension of himself in *nirmāṇas* or "transformed" guises for the purpose of saving sentient beings. The bodhisattva path, outlined in its classic form in the *Daśabhūmikā sūtra* and trod over three "incalculable" eons, culminates in the summit of personal perfection, complete self-transformation, the transformation of others, and the mastery of the forces of *pratītyasamutpāda* and the karmic universe.[29]

This process is the dominant concern in texts such as the *Bodhisattva bhūmi*, the *Laṅkāvatāra Sūtra*, the *Awakening of Faith in the Mahāyāna*, The *Lion's Roar of Queen Śrīmālā*, and the *Ratnagotravibhāga*, with their language of seed-nature or lineage (Chinese, *chung-hsing*, Sanskrit *gotra*) and "fruit."[30] According to these texts, beings have the seed of Buddha-nature (*Fo chung-hsing*), which must be cultivated gradually and brought to maturity. This gradual maturation is accomplished through the elimination of "adventitious" defilements and is a prominent element in Yogācāra teachings and in the *Tathāgatagarbha* tradition.[31]

29. See Daisetz Teitaro Suzuki, *Studies in the Laṅkāvatāra Sūtra* (London: Routledge & Kegan Paul, 1930; reprint, Boulder: Prajna Press, 1981), pp. 202–36, for an excellent discussion of the bodhisattva.

30. Suzuki, *Studies in the Laṅkāvatāra Sūtra*, esp. 175–79, 254–63. Yoshito S. Hakeda, trans. and comm., *The Awakening of Faith* (New York: Columbia University Press, 1967). Alex Wayman and Hideko Wayman, trans. and intro., *The Lion's Roar of Queen Śrīmālā* (New York: Columbia University Press, 1974). For a full translation and study of the *Ratnagotravibhāga*, see Takasaki Jikido, *A Study on the Ratnagotravibhāga (Uttaratantra): Being a Treatise on the Tathāgatagarbha Theory of Mahāyāna Buddhism* (Rome: Istituto Italiano per il Medio ed Estremo Oriente, 1966). Still the classic study of *Tathāgatagarbha* is David Seyfort Ruegg, *La théorie du Tathāgatagarbha et du Gotra: Études sur la sotériologie et la gnoséology du bouddhisme* (Paris: École Française d'Extrême-Orient, 1969).

31. The line between Yogācāra and *Tathāgatagarbha* is often blurred, though proponents of these tendencies have sometimes been rivals, and some of their tenets are diametrically opposed. See Rob-

The *rupic* cosmology focuses on a single Buddha. Even in the enormously extended *sāhasra* form the cosmos is a single "Buddha-field" (*Buddha-kṣetra*). The various salvific manifestations of the Buddha are all personal transformations or extensions of him—his *nirmāṇas*—manifest through his transformative power of *adhiṣṭhāna*.[32] The *Awakening of Faith* says, "[He who has fully uncovered the original enlightenment] is capable of creating all manner of excellent conditions because his wisdom is pure. The manifestation of his numberless excellent qualities is incessant; accommodating himself to the capacity of other men he responds spontaneously, reveals himself in manifold ways, and benefits them."[33]

In texts of the *Tathāgatagarbha* and Yogācāra traditions, the final goal, the place of nirvana, is assimilated to the conditioned, transformative cosmos in two ways. The first is through reference to the *dharmic* vision of the paradoxical identity of *saṃsāra* and *nirvana*. The second is through pivotal intermediaries. Thus the *saṃbhogakāya* or "body of bliss" attained by the bodhisattva as a reward for the fulfillment of vows acts as a kind of bridge or interface between enlightenment and unenlightened beings. Similarly, *Tathāgatagarbha* is itself both the matrix or womb out of which enlightenment is born (the conditioned world) *and* the embryo of enlightenment itself. Although the cosmology of these texts is preeminently personal, motifs that form the other major strand of Buddhist cosmological traditions—the *dharmic* cosmology—are always present.

The *Dharmic* Cosmology: Vision and Structure

The *dharmic* cosmology is a cosmology of light which makes possible a vision of the structure of reality. It is the cosmology of the Buddha in nirvana; it represents the ultimate vision of the cosmos as perceived by the enlightened. *Dharmic* cosmologies are markedly positional. This is particularly apparent in the Abhidharma texts of Nikāya Buddhism, which seek to classify all the dis-

ert M. Gimello, "Chih-yen (602–668) and the Foundations of Hua-yen Buddhism" (Ph.D. diss., Columbia University, 1976), pp. 265–67, 272–73. Some texts such as the *Ratnagotravibhāga* are clearly *Tathāgatagarbha*, treating topics of *garbha*, *gotra*, and so on. Many more such as the *Nirvana Scripture*, the *Laṅkāvatāra Scripture*, or the *Awakening of Faith* treat these topics as well as favorite Yogācāra topics. Further, fifth- and sixth-century Chinese tended to blend these teachings. For a brief summary of Yogācāra and its relationship to *Tathāgatagarbha*, see Paul J. Griffiths, Noriaki Hakamaya, John P. Keenan, and Paul L. Swanson, *The Realm of Awakening: Chapter Ten of Asaṅga's Mahāyānasaṅgraha* (New York and Oxford: Oxford University Press, 1989), pp. 3–45. For a study of these texts in Chinese *situ*, see Diana Y. Paul, *Philosophy of Mind in Sixth-Century China: Paramārtha's Evolution of Consciousness* (Stanford: Stanford University Press, 1984), and again, Gimello, "Chih-yen," esp. pp. 277–81.

32. Sometimes translated as "grace" or as "empowerment," *adhiṣṭhāna* is a direct cognate of *superstitio* the "overstanding" power or aid of divinity.

33. Hakeda, *Awakening of Faith*, pp. 41–42.

crete "elements" (*dharmas*) of the world, and in Mahāyāna scriptures such as the *Lotus Sūtra* and the *Pañcavimśatisāhaśrika-prajñāpāramitā*, both of which open with a stunning series of visions revealed by the Buddha from his trance, the "king of concentrations" (*samādhirāja*):

> the Lord on that occasion put out his tongue. With it he covered the great trichiliocosm and many hundreds of thousands of *niyutas* of *kotis* of rays issued from it. From each one of these rays there arose lotuses . . . and on those lotuses there were, seated and standing, Buddha-frames demonstrating [the] dharma. . . . They went in all ten directions to countless world systems in each direction, and demonstrated dharma to beings.[34]

In contrast to *rupic* cosmologies, *dharmic* cosmologies in the Mahāyāna are not limited to a single Buddha-field. Indeed, we are told that "world systems as numerous as the sands of the Ganges were illuminated by His [the Tathāgata's] splendour (*raśmirddhibala*)." The emphasis is on the visionary experience of the numberless Buddhas of the ten directions of the universe (*daśadigbuddha*).[35]

This cosmological theme found in the *Avataṃsaka*, the *Vimalakīrtinirdeśa*, the *Lotus*, and other texts is accompanied by a shift away from the *rupic* cosmology's primary concern with the process of salvation and the removal of defilements through long arduous discipline. Instead these texts extol the instantaneous vision of the structure of the cosmos. The rhetoric of time, substance, and transformation is eclipsed by a rhetoric of space, vision, and structure. Subitism, not gradualism, is the leitmotif of these texts.[36] Positional motifs dominate these scriptures. Thus visions of the countless Buddhas and *Buddhakṣetras* of the ten directions produced by the light of the Buddha's smile in the *Pañcavimśati* are reminiscent of tableaus found in the great cave-temples of Ellora or Yün-kang and are the equivalent of the vision of a mandala given to initiates in various branches of Esoteric Buddhism.[37] The position of every

34. See Conze, *Large Sūtra on Perfect Wisdom*, pp. 38–44. The quotation is from page 39. For the image in the *Lotus Sūtra*, see Hurvitz, *Lotus Blossom of the Fine Dharma*, pp. 286–87.

35. Conze, *Large Sūtra on Perfect Wisdom*, p. 39. For Kloetzli's discussion of it, see *Buddhist Cosmology*, pp. 94–98, and for the limitless world systems, pp. 113–31. The *Mahāprajñāpāramitāśāstra* also discusses this passage on pp. 431–528. For a discussion of the *raśmirddhibala* and the *daśadigbuddha*, see Kloetzli, *Buddhist Cosmology*, pp. 103–11.

36. For a many-faceted examination of subitism and gradualism in Buddhist thought, see Peter N. Gregory, ed., *Sudden and Gradual: Approaches to Enlightenment in Chinese Thought* (Honolulu: University of Hawaii Press, 1987).

37. For Ellora, see Geri H. Malandra, *Unfolding a Maṇḍala: The Buddhist Cave Temples at Ellora* (Albany: State University of New York Press, 1993). James O. Caswell has provided a penetrating analysis of the caves at Yün-kang in *Written and Unwritten: Buddhist Caves at Yüngang* (Vancouver: University of British Columbia, 1988).

element is immediately visually apparent, and each element fulfills a structural role in a galactic fashion; each element is a replication of the structure of the single cosmos.

The basis of this revelation is said to be the absolute emptiness (*śūnyatā*) and therefore the interpenetration of all *dharmas* or constituent parts of the *dharmadhātu* (cosmos). This notion of emptiness dissolves the personal cosmology of the path, a point made clear in the Buddha's response to Śāriputra's query about how the bodhisattva should "course in Transcendent Wisdom":

> The Bodhisattva, the great being, coursing in transcendent wisdom, truly a Bodhisattva, does not review a Bodhisattva, nor the word "Bodhisattva," nor the course of a Bodhisattva. . . . And why? Because the Bodhisattva, the great being, is actually empty of the own-being of a Bodhisattva and because transcendent wisdom is by its own-being empty.[38]

The point of this passage is that realization of the total interdependence of all things, including the path, nirvana, bodhisattvahood, and so on, and their complete lack of personal and individual self-existence makes possible the vision of the Buddhas of the ten directions. Indeed, the Buddhas of the ten directions are nothing other than the structure of emptiness itself. The process of the personal *rupic* cosmos here is reduced to an instantaneous vision of infinite numbers of cosmological structures in space. All reality is luminous and empty, interpenetrating as in the various jewels of Indra's net or in Śuddhodana's vision of Maitreya's tower in the *Gandhavyūha sūtra*.[39] The supreme vision of the *Pañcavimśatisāhasrika-prajñāpāramitā* is the vision of innumerable (*asaṅkhyeya*) worlds and Buddhas. The "Buddha's eye-view," the *dharmic* perspective, is the dominant idiom. The world it depicts is timeless, impersonal, structural, and positional.[40]

38. Conze, *Large Sūtra on Perfect Wisdom*, p. 57. Conze's translation uses the term "perfect wisdom." "Own-being" is a translation of Sanskrit *svabhāva*, a word indicating a self-existent substance or entity.

39. For a discussion of the *Gaṇḍhavyūha sūtra* (which has been incorporated into the massive *Avataṁsaka Sūtra*), see D. T. Suzuki, *On Indian Mahāyāna Buddhism*, ed. Edward Conze (New York: Harper & Row, 1968), pp. 147–226; Francis Cook, *Hua-yen Buddhism: The Jewel Net of Indra* (University Park: Pennsylvania State University Press, 1977). On the Gaṇḍhavyūha Sūtra and Barabudur, see Jan Fontein, *The Pilgrimage of Śudhana: A Study of the Gaṇḍhavyūha Illustrations in China, Japan, and Java* (The Hague: Mouton, 1967). For the notion of the interpenetrating universe and its relationship to the bodhisattva stages, see Luis O. Gomez, "The Bodhisattva as Wonder Worker," in *Prajñāpāramitā and Related Systems: Studies in Honor of Edward Conze*, ed. Lewis Lancaster, Berkeley Buddhist Studies Series no. 1 (Berkeley: Institute of Buddhist Studies, 1977), pp. 221–61.

40. Similar observations may be made of the "monistic" and "dualistic" traditions of advaita and visisthadvaita in Hinduism. As will become apparent, the issue is not merely one of cosmological speculation. Such issues have soteriological and political implications.

Few Buddhist works, however, use *rupic* or *dharmic* imagery exclusively. Indeed, the compelling nature of much of Buddhist cosmology lies precisely in its sophisticated use of both types of cosmological imagery to play "the edge." Thus one might argue (as Kloetzli does) that the immense spaces present in *asaṁkhyeya* cosmologies constitute a profound discontinuity, a startling contrast to the continuity of matter in other Buddhist cosmologies. This would seem to reflect the growing place of emptiness in the Mahāyāna tradition. But as I have noted, an interpretation of a cosmology depends on whether it is situated in a discontinuous or a continuous context. The vision of the Buddhas of the ten directions—their emptiness notwithstanding—is often contextualized as fundamentally *continuous*, all lands are simultaneously accessible in the soteriological vision. There is a hidden continuity of structure to the universe, a structure that is absolutely and instantaneously everywhere. The apparent epistemological discontinuity of the cosmos—why it is that we don't *always* see as the Buddha sees—dissolves in the recursive relationship between *saṃsāra* and nirvana. Discontinuity, personal development, time, and even space may, in such cases, be interpreted as continuous, instantaneous, interpenetrating, and positional. The first stage of the path contains within it the last stage of the path. The personal *rupic* cosmology is paradoxically the positional *dharmic* cosmos, yet they are paradoxically different.

This hidden continuity, asserted in the face of apparent discontinuity, is used effectively to inscribe more complex and recursive cosmological notions. Perhaps the most widely known expression of this tension is the famous Two Truths doctrine expounded in Nāgārjuna's *Fundamentals of the Middle Way* (*Madhyāmakakārikā*).[41]

Nāgārjuna states that there are two kinds of truth, two kinds of reality: that which is conditioned, governed by the everyday operation of the laws of *pratītyasamutpāda* and karma, and that which is absolute and unconditioned, the reality of nirvana, of the awakened ones. Then, he states that these two realities are nondual. In the terms of my discussion in Chapter 1, *saṃsāra* and nirvana are recursively related; their relationship is constituted across the "edge of reality."

The Two Truths did not appear with Nāgārjuna and the Mahāyāna, and this is especially obvious if we regard the Two Truths as a statement reflecting cosmological, rather than linguistic, analytic, or pragmatic concerns.[42] Nāgār-

41. For an analysis of the Two Truths, see T.R.V. Murti, *The Central Philosophy of Buddhism* (London: Allen & Unwin, 1955), pp. 228–55, and Streng, *Emptiness*, esp. pp. 39–40, 144–46.

42. I am not suggesting that Nāgārjuna's work does not serve as an "antidote" (*tui-hsiang*) to certain kinds of mental constructs. It does. Whether he intended it to do so or whether he was engaging in sophisticated cosmological thinking is beside the point. If we simply go along with traditional interpretations of his work, we abdicate our responsibilities as interpreters. For one of the best examinations of Madhyāmika, see Huntington and Wangchen, *Emptiness of Emptiness*.

juna's presentation, like that ascribed to the Buddha in refusing to discuss the existence of the arhat after death, is a reformulation and soteriological reinterpretation of two cosmologies, which, as far as we can ascertain, have coexisted in Buddhism from the time it emerges into the light of history. These cosmologies are the very basis of Buddhist accounts of the world, of authority, and of the path to salvation.[43] Thus, one can view Buddhism as a religion that creatively brings together two contradictory worldviews: the *rupic* world of karmic causality and the *dharmic* and highly structural world of the Buddha in nirvana.[44] The world of karma both is and is not the world of *mokṣa*. Buddhist worlds are constructed in and across the chasm separating these two cosmologies. Reality is indicated not by one view or the other but by the "edge" or relationship between the two views, a relationship whose particular emphases and import depend on historical context.

Thus we can see that there are two distinct strands of Buddhist cosmology, each of which may be interpreted in a continuous *or* in a discontinuous fashion. These are the personal *rupic* cosmology and the positional *dharmic* cosmology. In its purest form the *rupic* cosmos emphasizes the world of time, process, and the gradual personal transformation of the impure to the pure. Its aim is the mastery of the universe. The *dharmic* cosmology emphasizes the instantaneous visionary apprehension of the structure of reality. Its aim is the utter transcendence of the cosmos. In texts where the *dharmic* cosmology is dominant, the personal, temporal, and process-oriented dimensions of the *rupic* cosmology are encompassed by their status as reflections of fundamental emptiness and of one another. The structural identity between *saṃsāra* and nirvana is emphasized. The number of Buddhas is infinite, filling the ten directions of the universe. But each is "empty," and they are positional replications of one another. In those texts where the *rupic* cosmology is the dominant concern, this vision of ultimate reality is relegated to a secondary position, and the transformative link between *saṃsāra* and nirvana is highlighted, usually in terms of a mediating link such as the *saṃbhogakāya*, the *tathāgatagarbha*, or

43. Frank Reynolds has pointed to precursors of the Two Truths doctrine in Theravada Buddhism, noting that a creative tension exists between what he calls the *pratītyasamutpāda* cosmogony and the "Buddha" cosmogony, and that these categories have ethical echoes throughout the tradition. See Reynolds, "Multiple Cosmogonies and Ethics," pp. 203–24. Reynolds actually discusses four cosmologies, two aligned with the *saṃsāric* world and *pratītyasamutpāda* and two aligned with the pursuit of the *Dhamma*.

44. This is a common interpretation of Buddhism, perhaps best represented by Melford Spiro's *Buddhism and Society: A Great Tradition and Its Burmese Vicissitudes* (New York: Harper & Row, 1970). Spiro argues that Buddhism is split between a "kammatic," lay-oriented path and a "nibbanic," monastically oriented path. Unfortunately, Spiro ties the "kammatic" orientation too closely to the laity and the "nibbanic" orientation too closely to monks. Buddhism is not unique in this wedding of two cosmologies. Much of the Indian religious heritage stems from the creative interaction of Vedic householder traditions with a variety of renunciant traditions.

even the *cakravartin* ("wheel-ruler" or sovereign). Buddhist worldviews almost always combine both *rupic* and *dharmic* elements in a complex and finely nuanced mix. The religious and political significance of this mix depends on context.

Siddhi and Salvation

The relationship between two main types of cosmology in the Buddhist tradition has been interpreted in many ways over the centuries. Sometimes the emphasis seems to fall on the causal cosmology, on the world of the path; at other times the emphasis is clearly on the goal, to the seeming omission of how to get there. These relationships are mirrored in Buddhist notions of soteriology (salvation) or "accomplishment" (*siddhi*) and in Buddhist notions of sovereignty.

The origins of the *rupic* and *dharmic* strands of Buddhist cosmology might well be found in a historical accident that brought together two distinct modes of soteriological endeavor. Exercises involving enstatic states ("calming," Pāli *samathā*) are thought to have been part of pan-Indian Upanishadic heritage. These are the states leading to progressive mastery of the "stuff" (both mental and physical) of the cosmos. In contrast, insight into the truths proclaimed by the Buddha ("seeing," Pāli *vippasanā*) lead to the eradication of ignorance and release from the cycle of rebirth. Both kinds of achievement are commonly styled sovereignty or mastery, and both figure prominently in my discussion of Buddhist notions of authority.[45]

Siddhi (Chinese *hsi-ti*, *ch'eng-chiu*) is the general term for soteriological accomplishment as well as for the attainment of "lesser" ends.[46] It can refer to the attainment of enlightenment or all-knowledge (*samyaksaṃbuddha*), the manifestation of supernormal powers concomitant with advance on the path, as

45. The relationship between these types of mastery stirred considerable debate in early Buddhist traditions over whether wisdom alone or mastery of various "enstatic" states alone can lead to nirvana. Thus some argued for the notion of *cetovimutti* (liberation of the mind), some for *paññāvimutti* (liberation by means of wisdom), and yet others for *ubhatobhāgavimutti* (liberation in both ways). Paul J. Griffiths, *On Being Mindless: Buddhist Meditation and the Mind-Body Problem* (La Salle, Ill.: Open Court, 1986), has traced these arguments succinctly. See the extended note 47 on pp. 153–54. Nathan Katz also examines the issue at greater length in *Buddhist Images of Human Perfection* (Delhi: Motilal Barnasidass, 1982), especially pp. 96–106.

46. For a brief treatment of the role of the *siddhis* in Buddhism and their pre-Buddhist background, see Donald K. Swearer, "Control and Freedom: The Structure of Buddhist Meditation in the Pāli Suttas," *Philosophy East and West* 23 (December 1973): 443–52, and Eliade, *Yoga*, pp. 85–100; 177–85; 383–84.

well as to selfish ends. Three classifications of *siddhi* are widely used and can help us sort out the relationship between *siddhi* and cosmology.

The first classification of *siddhi* is found in the "Sampasadaniya sutta" of the *Dīghanikāya*. This classification distinguishes two types, those *siddhis* which are "noble" and those which are "ignoble," the latter conducing to further involvement with the world, the former to the transcendence of it.[47] Although the distinction between noble and ignoble *siddhi* is superficially similar to that drawn in Esoteric texts between *lokottara* (supramundane) and *laukika* (mundane) *siddhi* (which I discuss in Chapters 5 and 6), it is based on a radically discontinuous cosmology.[48] Ignoble attainments are not salvific; they do not lead to transcendence of the world but to further entanglement in it.

The most frequently drawn distinction—and that which results in the most quoted formulation—is between the *abhijñā* ("superknowledges") and the *siddhis* (Pāli, *ṛddhi*, "supernormal powers"). The lists of *abhijñas* and of *siddhis* appear to have been formalized quite early in Buddhist history and are taken up in Nikāya Buddhist and Mahāyāna texts alike. The account reproduced in Buddhagosạ's *Visśudhimagga* is representative.[49] The "superknowledges" (*abhijñās*) are:

1. The heavenly ear [*divya-crotra*]. "With the heavenly ear, perfectly pure and surpassing that of men, he [the Buddha or adept] hears sounds, celestial as well as human, far as well as near."
2. The knowledge of others' thoughts [*para-citta-jñāna*]. "With his own mind he encompasses the minds of other beings."
3. The recollection of former lives [*purva-nivās-ānusmṛti-jñāna*]. "He recalls his manifold former lives . . . 'There I was, that was my name, that was my family, that was my caste. . . . It is thus that he recalls his manifold previous lives, with all their modes, in all their details."
4. The knowledge of the decease and rebirth of beings, or the heavenly eye [*divya-cakṣus*]. "With the heavenly eye . . . he sees beings as they are about to die or find a new rebirth . . . and he sees that whatever happens to them happens in accordance with their deeds."

From the same source we find a typical list of *siddhi* (*ṛddhi*): "Being one, he becomes many; having become multiple, he becomes one; he enjoys the ex-

47. Swearer, "Control and Freedom," p. 449.

48. The *Dīghanikāya* example is based on a discontinuity between this world and nirvana, whereas that commonly found in Esoteric traditions is based on continuity between this world and nirvana. John Holt discusses a similar taxonomy in Śri Lanka in *Buddha in the Crown*, pp. 19–26.

49. The *Visśudhimagga* ("Path of Purity") is very much a Nikāya Buddhist text. The translation used here is that of Edward Conze, *Buddhist Scriptures* (Harmondsworth, England: Penguin Books, 1959), pp. 130–33.

perience of becoming visible or invisible; he goes unimpeded through a wall, a rampart, or a mountain; he travels cross-legged in the sky, like a winged bird; he dives up and down the earth as if it were water; he touches and feels with his hands the sun and the moon, which are so potent and powerful; he can reach as far as the *Brahmaloka* with his body."[50]

A third classification is that presented by Asaṅga (the Mahāyāna theologian of the second century C.E.), in his *Bodhisattva-bhūmi*. Asaṅga distinguishes two types of *siddhi*, *pariṇāmiki* (*pien shen-tsu*), commonly translated as "powers of transformation," and *nairmāṇiki* (*hua shen-tsu*), "powers of creation."[51] Asaṅga lists sixteen different types of *pariṇāmiki* powers: a bodhisattva can shake buildings, realms, or even infinite numbers of worlds; he can emit simultaneous streams of flame and cold water from his limbs; he can illumine buildings, worlds, and so on; he can show all the worlds and Buddha-fields to other creatures; he can transmute the four elements into one another; he can pass through walls, and so on; he can reduce and increase the size and volume of things; he can make things and forms enter his body; he can assume the external appearance and speech of different kinds of congregations; he can make himself visible and invisible; he can control and dominate all creatures; he can control and surpass the *siddhis* of others (excepting Buddhas and bodhisattvas who are his peers or betters); he can confer intelligence and understanding on others; he can confer mindfulness on others; he can comfort creatures so that they may pay attention to preaching without distress; he can emit rays that allay the torments of the various hells. Asaṅga lists two types of *nairmāṇiki* powers: the bodhisattva can create transformation bodies (*kāya-nirmāṇam*), and a bodhisattva can create and project a voice to preach the *Dharma*.[52]

The common translation of the terms *pariṇāmiki* and *nairmāṇiki* as "power of transformation" and "power of creation" obscures an important distinction between the two powers.[53] Indeed, if we examine the list, the majority of the first sixteen "transformative" powers involve some abrogation of common notions of space or involve powers of light that defy normal spatial boundaries and

50. Ibid., pp. 122–30, with minor modification. The quotation on the *ṛddhis* is from Dayal, *Bodhisattva Doctrine*, p. 113. For the classic sources see Griffiths, *On Being Mindless*, p. 195.

51. Dayal, *Bodhisattva Doctrine*, p. 113, and Gomez, "Bodhisattva as Wonder-worker," p. 230. The Chinese translation is *P'u-sa ti c'hin ching* (T 1581 30.888–959). *Siddhi* (*shen-tsu*) is discussed at 30.896c6–897b26.

52. Dayal, *Bodhisattva Doctrine*, pp. 113–15. Actually, several subtypes are discussed here. See T1581 30.897b26–c15 and continuing discussion through 899.

53. See *A Sanskrit-English Dictionary*, comp. Monier Monier-Williams (Oxford: Clarendon Press, 1898), p. 556, col. 2, where *nairmāṇiki* is given as "measure," "reach," "extent," "transform," "pith or best of anything." *Pariṇāmiki* is given as "subject to development or evolution," *nairmāṇiki* seems to have etymological connections with the idea of essence, and both seem to mean transform. The Chinese terms *pien shen-tsu* (*pariṇāmiki*) and *hua shen-tsu* (*nairmāṇiki*) both mean to change or transform.

limitations. *Pariṇāmiki* powers involve the negation or transcendence of bodily limitations, and particularly of human bondage to spatial, material, and temporal circumstances. This transcendence is usually accomplished through luminous visions. The *nairmāṇiki* or "creative" powers, on the other hand, are concerned with the multiplication or emanation of bodies or forms that are transformations or extensions of the originator himself. *Nairmāṇiki* powers involve the personal substantive extension or *transformation* of the bodhisattva. Thus I advocate rendering *pariṇāmiki* as "powers of vision, illusion" or "light" and *nairmāṇiki* as "powers of transmutation."

Though there are some exceptions in Asaṅga's list, the distinction provides us with a guideline for a new analysis of the superknowledges and the supernormal powers which places them within a comprehensive cosmological framework. It also provides a rationale for understanding the other *abhijñas* and classifications of *siddhi*. If we consider, for instance, Buddhagoṣa's list of *abhijñas* and his comments on them, it becomes clear that these may be classified as *pariṇāmiki* because of their structural and light-related nature. For example, the "heavenly eye" is so termed "because it spreads a brilliant supernatural light . . . it has a great power of penetration and can discern objects that are hidden behind walls or other obstructions."[54] Thus the *pariṇāmiki* type of powers is based in the perceptions available to Buddha or those same perceptions that they induce in others in order to produce the thought of enlightenment. These powers reveal some part of ultimate reality as it is, as a timeless structure, or hint of its interconnectedness, a vision of the whole which is positional. The *nairmāṇiki* type of power is used by Buddhas and bodhisattvas to project themselves into the temporal and substance-based process of transformation in order to aid beings.

Thus one can see that *nairmāṇiki siddhi* are associated with the *rupic* strand of cosmological thinking, with the notion of transmutation and mastery of the world of substance, with progress through time along the soteriological path, and with the enstatic practices labeled *samathā* (calming). *Pariṇāmiki siddhi* is connected with the *dharmic* strand of cosmological thinking, with a vision of the universe in its absolute and timeless structure, with the practice of *vipassanā* (wisdom or insight).

It is tempting, at this juncture, to leave the correlation as it is, a simple equivalence between the powers of vision and the *dharmic* cosmology and the powers of transmutation and the *rupic* cosmology.[55] But one further issue must be

54. Conze, *Buddhist Scriptures*, p. 133.

55. For a similar analysis from the standpoint of the canonicity of the *Jātaka* literature, see Arnold Aronoff, "Contrasting Modes of Textual Classification: The Jātaka Commentary and Its Relationship to the Pali Canon" (Ph.D. diss., University of Chicago, 1982).

addressed which my approach helps to make clear. This concerns light-related experiences.

Not all the photic displays in Buddhist traditions can be classified as powers of vision and related to the positional *dharmic* cosmology. Take, for example, the following excerpts from the *Śrīmālādevi sūtra*, a text in the *Tathāgatagarbha* tradition:

> At that very instant, the Lord approached in the space [in front], and she saw the inconceivable body of the Buddha seated there, emitting pure light rays . . . [Queen Śrīmālā says:] May the Lord now protect me and quicken the seed of enlightenment.

And again:

> Lord, the embrace of the Illustrious Doctrine will perfect all the innumerable Buddha natures . . . at the time of new differentiation of the worlds there came a great cloud which poured down innumerable colors and poured down innumerable jewels. In the same way, this embrace of the Illustrious Doctrine pours down countless maturations of merit and pours down countless knowledge jewels.[56]

This interpretation of photic experience in the *Tathāgatagarbha* tradition is strikingly different from that encountered in transcendent wisdom texts. In the *Tathāgatagarbha* tradition and in *rupic* cosmologies as a whole, light is seminal, it impregnates and causes development of seeds rather than illuminating a visionary structure, as in the *Prajñāpāramitās*.[57] The interpretation of photic experiences in the *Śrīmālādevi sūtra* and other such texts is determined by their context in the *rupic* cosmology.

To sum up my argument, thus far I have shown that the Buddhist tradition contains two distinct cosmological schemes, one personal, the other positional. I have called the personal strand of Buddhist cosmology the *rupic* cosmology, and the positional tendencies, *dharmic* cosmology. Each of these strands may be interpreted in a *continuous* or in a *discontinuous* manner depending on the context. Buddhist notions of soteriology, as represented in *siddhi* also are of

56. Wayman and Wayman, *Lion's Roar*, pp. 60–61, 69–70.

57. The notion that light is seminal in nature and that it is manifested in the crystallized form is found elsewhere in the history of religion and must be distinguished from the light of vision. See Mircea Eliade, "Spirit, Light, and Seed," *History of Religions* 11 (August 1971): 1–30, and his "Experiences of the Mystic Light," in *The Two and the One*, esp. pp. 24–26, "The Light Solidified." Gerardo Reichel-Dolmatoff reports a similar seminal and crystalline light in his *Amazonian Cosmos: The Sexual and Religious Symbolism of the Tukano Indians* (Chicago: University of Chicago Press, 1971), esp. pp. 48–52. One might mention, in passing, similar notions in Christianity, such as the *Logos-spermatikos*.

two varieties. The first, powers of transmutation or evolution, are closely aligned with the *rupic* cosmology and with the mastery of the world. The second, the powers of vision, are associated with the *dharmic* cosmology and with transcendence of the world.

In spite of the fact that some Buddhist traditions espouse a negative attitude toward cosmology, most are based on a mixture of two cosmologies and sophisticated notions of the relationships between them. Each cosmological type is mirrored in notions of *siddhi* that give a characteristic flavor to individual Buddhist traditions. The *rupic* cosmos and the *dharmic* cosmos, continuity and discontinuity, are often inextricably and paradoxically identified. These two cosmologies and the relationship between them are also reflected in the "body politic," in the images of Buddhas, bodhisattvas, and *cakravartins*.

Cosmology, Authority, and the Politics of the Buddhist Body

From the earliest times the body of the Buddha (and by extension all simulacra of the Buddha, including stūpas, texts, images, and monks and nuns and their robes) has been the object of veneration and a powerful semiotic index.[58] The *Scripture for Humane Kings* promotes an elaborate ritual display of Buddhist images and Buddhist monks as the antidote to the End of the Teaching (*fa-mo* rather than the usual *mo-fa*).[59] In fifth-century North China this display of Buddhist bodies (monks, statues, texts, and so on) promoted by flamboyant royal patronage functioned as a sign that the temporal decay of Buddhism had been halted and that the clock had been turned back to the period of the Correct Teaching (*cheng-fa*). This constituted a visible reversal of an earlier attempt to eradicate all images of Buddhist authority from the Chinese body politic. The Buddhist body became the canvas for conflicting notions of cosmology, soteriology, and polity. At one extreme the body was described as "crumbling, diseased, wounded," and at the other "like a priceless jewel of lapis lazuli."[60] The potency of the Buddhist body and its ambivalent associations with kingship date to the earliest historical records of Buddhism. While

58. Bernard Faure has explored the semiotics of monastic robes in "Quand l'habit fait le moine: The Symbolism of the *Kaṣāya* in Chan/Zen Buddhism," *Cahiers d'extrême-asie* 8 (1995): 335–67.

59. Or perhaps, the "End-Teaching," the last of three periods during which the Buddhist Teaching has fallen into decline.

60. The first quotation is from P. Lal, trans., *The Dhammapāda* (New York: Farrar, Straus & Giroux, 1967), p. 89. The second is from the vows of Bhaiṣajyaguru, the "Healing Buddha," translated by John S. Strong in *The Experience of Buddhism*, p. 191.

some texts regard kings and kingship with particular disdain, others assert that both the Buddha and the *cakravartin* possess the thirty-two major and eighty minor signs of authority.[61]

Three main theories of the body of the Buddha emerged; that of the triple body of the Buddha, that of the double body of the Buddha, and that of the *cakravartin*. Although the *cakravartin* is usually treated separately from the body of the Buddha, its proper orbit is in relationship to the imagery and ideology of the body of the Buddha. I will take up the double and triple body theories first and then turn to the *cakravartin*.

The development of theories concerning the Buddha's body is widely acknowledged to have its roots in an early distinction between the Buddha's physical body, *rūpakāya*, and his "body" of teachings, his *dharmakāya*, the first representing the conditioned world, a body subject to karmic causality and therefore changeable and perishable, the second representing the unconditioned or transcendent state, the world of the Teaching, imperishable, timeless, unchanging. Thus the two bodies correlate roughly with the two cosmologies I have delineated above (*rupic* and *dharmic*), and with the two types of *siddhi* (*nairmāṇiki* and *pariṇāmiki*). This early dual-body theory was further refined into the *nirmāṇakāya/dharmakāya* theory found in the Mādhyamika-leaning *Prajñāpāramitās* on the one hand and, into the more developmental scheme of *nirmāṇakāya/saṃbhogakāya/dharmakāya* found in texts associated with the Yogācāra and *Tathāgatagarbha* traditions.[62] The significance of the Buddha's body further depends on whether the universe is seen as fundamentally *continuous* or fundamentally *discontinuous*.

In continuous *rupic* cosmologies in the Mahāyāna we can observe a single Buddha and his bodies, which are extensions of himself produced through his powers of transmutation, while in continuous *dharmic* cosmologies all of the numberless Buddhas are equally "transformations," are equally empty, and are made visible through the powers of light.

61. The thirty-two major and eighty minor marks of a Buddha are found in a number of texts, including in *Mahāvyutpatti* 17. For a list, see Leon Hurvitz, *Chih-I (538–597): An Introduction to the Life and Ideas of a Chinese Buddhist Monk, Mélanges chinois et bouddhiques* 12 (1960–1962): appendixes K and L, 353–60.

62. The literature on the Buddha-bodies has been steadily growing. An excellent place to start is Suzuki, *Studies in the Laṅkāvatāra Sūtra* pp. 308–38. Also see Mus, "Le Bouddha paré." For other work on the Buddha-Bodies, see Nagao Gadjin, "On the Theory of the Buddha-Body," *The Eastern Buddhist* 6 (May 1973): 25–53; reprinted in L. S. Kawamura, ed. and trans., *Mādhyamika and Yogācāra: A Study of Mahāyāna Philosophies* (Albany: State University of New York Press, 1991), pp. 103–22. For an interesting perspective from the Theravāda tradition, see Frank Reynolds, "The Several Bodies of the Buddha: Reflections on a Neglected Aspect of the Theravāda Tradition," *History of Religions* 16 (May 1977): 374–89. The *Bukkyo daijiten* has a compact overview at 4452b–4454a. "Busshin," in *Hōbōgirin*, 2: 174b–185a, is perhaps the best succinct treatment of the topic.

Transcendent Wisdom scriptures expressly align the two-body theory with the Two Truths.[63] The key to this body theory lies in its emphasis on the emptiness of all *rupic* forms, which is the basis for their mutual visibility and activity. All time and all space are illumined and immediately apprehended just as a single image is reflected endlessly in the fabled net of Indra.[64] Thus in the famous passage quoted from the *Pañcavimśati-sāhasrikā-prajñāpāramitā*, the light rays issuing from the Buddha's outstretched tongue result in the visibility of "Buddha-frames demonstrating dharma. . . . They went in all ten directions to countless world systems."[65] In the *Avataṃsaka sūtra* (*Hua-yen*) we are told that "it would take eternity to count all the Buddha's universes. In each dust-mote of these worlds are countless worlds and Buddhas."[66] All of these worlds are visible and freely interpenetrate because of their emptiness.[67] Over and over again we are told that the Buddha "knows," "observes," "sees." "A Bodhisattva who dwells in this supreme *samādhi*, sees infinite lands, beholds infinite Buddhas, delivers infinite sentient beings . . . demonstrates infinite miracles . . . [etc.]"[68] The *nirmāṇakāya* is the *dharmakāya* and *vice versa*. The point is clearly the vision of the structure and emptiness of the cosmos, a vision which is underscored by the infinities of universes and "transformations." Authority in this type of system is one based on structural repetition. The Buddha is "cosmocrat" by virtue of his pervasive structural reality.

The three-body theory developed in Yogācāra and *Tathāgatagarbha* texts is founded on the notion of the substance and transmutation of the Buddha's own person. The *Ratnagotravibhāga*, which amounts to a lengthy recapitulation of this point, says,

> Tathāgatahood consists in the manifestation of the three bodies of a Buddha. The element of the Tathāgata is therefore the cause of their attainment. . . . As it is said: "In each being there exists in embryonic form the element of the Tathāgata, but people do not look through to that."[69]

63. An example is in Conze, *Large Sūtra on Perfect Wisdom*, pp. 254–55.

64. For the net image, see Cook, *Hua-yen Buddhism*, p. 4.

65. Conze, *Large Sūtra on Perfect Wisdom*, p. 39.

66. Garma C. C. Chang, *The Buddhist Teaching of Totality: The Philosophy of Hwa Yen Buddhism* (University Park: Pennsylvania State University Press, 1974), pp. 4–5.

67. Ibid., pp. 60–63.

68. Ibid., p. 7.

69. This passage is from the *Ratnagotravibhāga*, trans. and edited by Edward Conze in collaboration with I. B. Horner, David Snellgrove, and Arthur Waley, eds., *Buddhist Texts Through the Ages* (New York: Harper Torchbooks, 1964), 216–17. Takasaki's rendering of the passage is in *A Study of the Ratnagotravibhāga*, pp. 290–91. Conze's "element" and Takasaki's "essence" both render the Sanskrit *dhātu*. For an extended discussion of the three bodies, see Takasaki, pp. 326–31. John Keenan has raised the possibility that the *saṃbhogakāya* developed in Pure Land circles before developing in Yogācāra. Such

In the case of the three bodies it is precisely the salvific mediation between the world and enlightenment which is emphasized; their emptiness is secondary. The emphasis on the transformative and teaching function of the bodhisattva is closely aligned with the three-body scheme and particularly with the *saṃbhogakāya*, which, in turn, is connected with the idea of *adhiṣṭhana*.[70] The term *adhiṣṭhāna* has its roots in the Pāli scriptures where *adhitthana iddhi* is the power of the Buddha's self-multiplication. It is found throughout the Mahāyāna and has a range of meanings. These include decision, resolution, self-determination, to stand on or insist on, basis, to oversee, a residence or abode, and a benediction.[71] Its basic meaning seems to be to take a stand or position, in its metaphorical and literal senses, as well as to provide a basis for, as in benediction. This "basis" is the foundation for transcendent wisdom's existence in the world. It indicates, to borrow a convenient phrase, "a place on which to stand," as well as the stand taken.

Through his power of *adhiṣṭhāna* the Buddha creates "Tathāgata-frames" (Buddha universes, *tathāgatavigraha*) and, of course, Tathāgatas. One's place in the cosmos, one's body, and one's stage on the path are inextricably linked.[72] In the case of a Buddha or an advanced bodhisattva the force of his *adhiṣṭhāna* and his vow, not his *karma*, creates the *nirmāṇa* body and the place on which it stands.[73] He has mastered the *pratītyasamutpāda* world and now uses this mastery to generate salvific transmutations of himself for the benefit of sentient beings. Here the importance of the third element or the intermediary body, the *saṃbhogakāya* must be noted.

Saṃbhogakāya literally means a "body attained as a reward," in this case as a reward for having perfected certain bodhisattva practices. Kiyota sums it up nicely, "*Saṃbhogakāya* is the instrument through which the historical man realizes *dharmakāya*, it is symbolic of the perfection of bodhisattva practices, and it is the instrument through which the Dharma penetrates the world of sentient beings."[74] In other words, the body which apprehends enlightenment

---

development would be an example of a "bridge" term, in this case a body for a place which is itself "betwixt and between" nirvana and this world. See Keenan, "Pure Land Systematics in India: The *Buddhabhūmi Sūtra* and the Trikāya Doctrine," *Pacific World*, n.s., 3 (Fall 1987): 29–35.

70. On *adhiṣṭhāna*, see Suzuki, *Studies in the Laṅkāvatāra Sūtra*, pp. 202–5, 356, and *Bukkyō daijiten*, 436b–437a.

71. On *vikkubana*, see *The Pāli Text Society's Pali-English Dictionary*, ed. T. W. Rhys-Davids and William Stede (London: Pāli Text Society, 1921–25; reprint, New Delhi: Oriental Books, 1975), p. 613b, and for *adhittani*, p. 28b. For *adhiṣṭhāna*, see *Sanskrit-English Dictionary*, p. 22b.

72. Kloetzli, *Buddhist Cosmology*, pp. 65, 109.

73. For an analysis of the relationship between a vow and one's body, see John Strong, "Making Merit in the Aśokāvadāna: A Study of Buddhist Acts of Offering in the Post Parinirvana Age" (Ph.D. diss., University of Chicago, 1977), and his article "The Transforming Gift."

74. Minoru Kiyota, *Shingon Buddhism* (Tokyo and Los Angeles: Buddhist Books International, 1978), p. 58. The Sino-Japanese designations of this body's two-fold function are *tzu-shou yung-shen* (the body

also points the other way, it is the sovereign lord of the cosmos, and it exercises sovereignty in the practice of the salvation of beings. But it is those very acts which produce enlightenment. The *Laṅkāvatāra sūtra* explains this as the "twofold sustaining power (*adhiṣṭhāna*) of all the Buddhas."[75] The *saṃbhogakāya*, then, is a kind of third term that I mentioned above; it indicates a bridge across the "edge" of reality, it is a place where the unconditioned meets the conditioned; where the *dharmic* world meets the *rupic* world.

In Yogācāra and *Tathāgatagarbha* traditions, in such texts as the *Awakening of Faith*, we can observe a link between the *saṃbhogakāya* and the transmutation or evolution of defiled mind into pure *bodhi*.[76] This transmutation takes place in the *ālaya* or "storehouse consciousness," which is equated with the middle of the Yogācāra Three Truths.[77]

Although the focus of the *rupic* cosmology as manifested in the three-body theory of the Mahāyāna is on transmutation, one must recognize the recursivity of this transmutation which enables a differential interpretation. Thus in the *Laṅkāvatāra sūtra* the ultimately real and the imaginary are linked by the relative reality symbolized as the *ālaya* consciousness. So too the Buddha's *dharmakāya* and the forms in the world, the *nirmāṇakāya*, are linked by the *adhiṣṭhāna* of the *saṃbhogakāya*. The relationship between *saṃsāra* and nirvana is central to the Mahāyāna version of the *rupic* cosmology, but in these texts it is cast in terms of pivotal intermediaries, the *ālaya*, the *tathāgatagarbha*, the *saṃbhogakāya*, or the second of the Three Truths. It is the transformation between purity and defilement.

One of the most striking and yet common features of the *saṃbhogakāya* is its representation in full royal regalia. Although we can understand the theories of the Buddha-bodies in relationship to Buddhist cosmology, a full appreciation of their import emerges only when we consider Buddhist images of kingship. The tendency to use the idioms and trappings of kingship to discuss Buddhas and bodhisattvas is present in all branches of Buddhism in virtually all periods, and it takes a more "concrete" form in discussions of "Buddhist" kingship. Though a full discussion of the topic would take us far afield, it is vital that we understand the logic of this association and the primary forms in which it manifests.

---

used to effect one's own enlightenment) and *ta-shou yung-shen* (the body used to effect the enlightenment of others).

75. Daisetz Teitaro Suzuki, trans., *The Laṅkāvatāra Sūtra* (London: Routledge & Kegan Paul, 1932; reprint, Boulder: Prajna Press, 1978), pp. 87–89.

76. Though in some *Tathāgatagarbha* thought a sort of absolute duality between defilements and pure mind sets up an interesting *discontinuous rupic* world.

77. Kiyota, *Shingon Buddhism*, p. 59. For a detailed treatment of the relationship between the bodies, the *ālaya*, and the Three Truths, see Griffiths et al., *Realm of Awakening*, especially pp. 9–12, 23ff., 57ff., 63ff.

The linkage—both positive and negative—between rulers and Buddhas emerges following Aśoka's rule, which provided a fertile store of images relating the "king of kings" or "wheel-ruler" (*cakravartin*).[78] Later Buddhist thinkers propose a systematic ranking of *cakravartins* associated symbolically with the metals gold, silver, copper, and iron, with the number of continents that each rules, and with the mode of conquest applied.[79] This imagery was taken up in the Mahāyāna and so permeates the tradition that the figure of the bodhisattva is virtually unthinkable without it.[80]

The most often quoted early instance of the equation between Buddhas and kings occurs in the *Mahāparinibbāna-sutta:*

> 'And as they treat the remains of a king of kings, so, Ānanda, should they treat the remains of the Tathāgata. At the four cross roads a dāgaba should be erected to the Tathāgata. And whosoever shall there place garlands or perfumes or paint, or make salutation there, or become in its presence calm in heart—that shall long be to them for a profit and a joy.'[81]

It is obvious that the equivalence in death between the Tathāgata and the king of kings is meant to redound to the benefit of the Tathāgata. But just what is being gained through this equivalence? To answer this question we can examine two depictions of the "righteous ruler" (*Dharmarāja*) which appear in early Buddhist dialogues. The "Aggañña-suttanta" of the *Dīghanikāya* tells the story of King Mahāsammata, the "great elect," who after the end of the paradisial golden age is elected king in an effort to bring order out of anarchy.[82] As payment for his services he receives an allotment of rice. In this case kingship is the first step back to order after the fall, but it is also an indication of that very fallen state. In contrast, the "Cakkavatti-sīhanānda-suttanta," also

78. For Aśoka in history and in legend and for the notion of the *cakravartin*, see Strong, *Legend of King Aśoka*, esp. pp. 44–55.

79. This imagery is central to the *Scripture for Humane Kings*. For the most systematic presentation of the typology, see Vasubandhu's *Abhidharmakośa*, 3:197.

80. See especially Mus, "Le Bouddha paré," pp. 153–278.

81. T. W. Rhys-Davids, trans., *The Mahā-parinibbāna Suttanta*, in *Buddhist Suttas* (New York: Dover, 1969), p. 93. In this quotation and hereafter I have silently changed diacritic marks to conform with modern usage. Gregory Schopen provides a detailed linguistic analysis of this passage, in which he argues for distinguishing between injunctions meant for monks and those enjoined upon the laity in "Monks and the Relic Cult in the *Mahāparinibbānasutta:* An Old Misunderstanding in Regard to Monastic Buddhism," in Koichi Shinohara and Gregory Schopen, eds., *From Benares to Beijing: Essays on Buddhism and Chinese Religions* (Oakville, Ontario: Mosaic Press, 1991), pp. 189–92.

82. For this story, see T. W. Rhys-Davids, trans., *Dialogues of the Buddha*, 3 vols., Sacred Books of the Buddhists, nos. 2–4 (London: Pāli Text Society, 1899–1921), 3:79–94.

in *Dīghanikāya*, associates the *cakravartin* Dalḥanemi with the golden age.[83] It is only with his passing that the decline commences. These passages are emblematic of two distinct Buddhist attitudes toward kingship and the world at large. On the one hand, kingship represents the discontinuity between the temporal world and the *Dharma*. On the other hand, kingship is the embodiment of the *Dharma*, and wise rule can stave off or even reverse the decline of the teaching. This second perspective is often treated as an allegorical afterthought and as an attempt by Buddhists to borrow the charisma of kingship or by kings to legitimate their claims vis-à-vis the samgha. I think something much subtler and more important is going on.

With respect to my inquiry, one strand of Buddhism emphasizes the discontinuity between the world and nirvana. It distinguishes sharply between the supernormal powers that lead to entanglement with the world and the insight that leads to transcendence of the world, and it sees kingship and enlightenment as antithetical. Buddhist schools dominated by a positional or *dharmic* cosmological stance that is also discontinuous (these are usually but not always Nikāya Buddhist) emphasize insight and wisdom, the *abhijñās* (superknowledges) rather than the supernormal powers. The doctrine is obsessively classified and structured, as in the *Abhidharmakośa*, and even personal concerns, such as the various transformative powers, are placed in a structural grid (if not rejected outright).[84] This approach is exemplified in the Abhidharma. The *rūpakāya* of the Buddha is regarded as a perishable thing, totally distinct from the eternal truth, the Dharma, or Teaching. It has no salvific power. The *cakravartin* is sharply distinguished from the Buddha, and as in the case of "Mahāsammata," he may be regarded as a sign of the fallen state of the world, a sign that we have entered the period of the "end of the Teaching." The pursuit of enlightenment and kingship rest on fundamentally antithetical assumptions concerning the structure of reality.[85]

In Buddhist schools dominated by the personal *rupic* strand of cosmology that is also discontinuous (again, usually but not always Nikāya Buddhist), we find a different picture. Buddhas and kings are of different "lineages." The emphasis is on the path to purity effected through the discipline, to be "born" into the family of the Buddha. Yet in the *Jātakas* and elsewhere the Buddha's

83. Rhys-Davids, *Dialogues*, 3:59–76. Also see Tambiah, *World Conqueror and World Renouncer*, pp. 42–47.

84. For Sarvāstivādin doctrines, see André Bareau, *Les sectes bouddhiques du petit véhicule* (Saigon: École Française d'Extrême-Orient, 1955), esp. pp. 131–37, 259–61.

85. A *cakravartin* has perfected meritorious action while a *pratyeka-Buddha* has perfected meditation, thus forming a dyad representing the *rupic* world and the *dharmic* world. Only a full Buddha has perfected both. See the *Abhidharmakośa*, 3:56–57. Strong, *Legend of King Aśoka*, has a compact summary of materials regarding the *cakravartin* on pages 44–49.

rūpakāya begins to take on salvific significance, and its special substance continues to be present in the temporal world in the form of relics. It is no accident that these same tales emphasize the meritorious activities of Śākyamuni performed in his past lives, culminating in his last birth as Prince Vessantara.[86] Nor is it accidental that traditions emerged which place Śākyamuni as heir to the throne and that extol his miraculous deeds and those of his disciples, both during life and through relics after death.[87] In these tales the *rūpakāya* is important because it is the vehicle of Teaching. The continued presence of the Buddha either in the relics or in assertions of the *arhat*'s ability to live until the *pralaya* or end of the eon emphasize the importance of continued personal presence of the Buddha and an attempt to circumvent or forestall the stark discontinuity between the Buddha and the world after he has passed into *parinirvāṇa*. Indeed, the abhidharmist Vasubandhu balked at the notion of the complete extinction of the Buddha in *parinirvāṇa*, for if the Buddha is extinct, to whom do we go for refuge?[88]

The other strand of Buddhism emphasizes the continuity between the world and nirvana. Supernormal attainments are valued as indicators of advancement on the path and kingship is seen as a manifestation of the *Dharma*. By this move Buddhism claims the world for nirvana and nirvana for the world. Cosmologically speaking, kingship is deployed in a continuous and totalistic fashion to assert that nirvana undergirds the structure of the world and manifests in sovereignty. At the same time sovereignty becomes more than total power. It comes to point beyond totality to the infinite. The positive appreciation of the *cakravartin* Dalḥanemi, the royal bodhisattva, and so on all point down this road; and at the end of this road is the *saṃbhogakāya*, "which is established in the great kingship of the *Dharma*."[89]

Thus, in Buddhism kingship can have four distinct roles. In *rupic* worlds emphasizing *discontinuity*, Buddhas and *cakravartins* represent different "lineages" (Sanskrit *gotra*). In *dharmic* worlds focusing on *discontinuity*, Buddhas and *cakra-*

86. For the *Vessantara Jātaka*, see Strong, *Experience of Buddhism*, pp. 23–26. The "spin" on Vessantara is that he is the king who gives everything away.

87. E. B. Cowell, ed., *The Jātaka: or Stories of the Buddha's Former Births*, 6 vols. and index (London: Pāli Text Society, 1895–1913; reprinted in 3 vols., London: Luzac, 1969), for the Jātakas. I would probably put the *Mahāparinibbāna Suttanta* in this category as well as the *Mahāvastu*. See Rhys-Davids, *Mahāparinibbāna Suttanta*, and J. J. Jones, trans., *Mahāvastu*, 3 vols. (London: Luzac, 1949). The text is a production of the Lokottaravādin branch of the Mahāsāṃghikas, the same tradition that is connected with the *Tathāgatagarbha* in the latter text by the same school, *The Lion's Roar*. For the origins of the Mahāsāṃghikas, see Janice J. Nattier and Charles S. Prebish, "Mahāsāṃghikā Origins: The Beginnings of Buddhist Sectarianism," *History of Religions* 16 (February 1977): 237–72.

88. By avoiding a simplistic bifurcation of Buddhism into "Hīnayāna" and "Mahāyāna" and instead concentrating on the various cosmological strands in Buddhist tranditions we see that even the most systematic Buddhist theology is multiple.

89. From the *Trikāyastava*, quoted in Strong, *Experience of Buddhism*, p. 154.

vartins are representative of markedly different and even opposing structures. In a *rupic* tradition emphasizing *continuity* Buddhas and *cakravartins* are part of the same family and occupy the same continuum, the *cakravartins* having equal merit to but less insight than the Buddhas. In a *dharmic* tradition emphasizing *continuity* Buddhas and *cakravartins* are structural replications or images of one another. Buddhist cosmological themes and their implications can be summarized as follows:

Continuous

Rupic cosmology	*Dharmic* cosmology
Nairmāṇiki siddhi	*Pariṇāmiki siddhi*
Three bodies	Two bodies
Cakravartin will become Buddha	*Cakravartin* is Buddha

Discontinuous

Rupic Cosmology	*Dharmic* Cosmology
Adhitthana iddi	*Abhijñās*
Rūpakāya (relics important)	*Dharmakāya* (teachings important)
Cakravartin of different lineage	*Cakravartin* of opposing structure

Rather than viewing theories of the Buddha's body as purely "theological" and notions of kingship in Buddhism as mere "politics," we can view the various Buddha-body theories and theories of Buddhist kingship as functions of cosmology and as embedded in the relationship between *saṃsāra* and nirvana. Buddhist bodies (monastic or royal), then, are indices of salvific authority, and their display and veneration encode attitudes toward and negotiation of Buddhist worldviews. Buddhist cosmology is complex and very often joins continuous and discontinuous, *rupic* and *dharmic*, themes in sophisticated ways. The fifth-century *Scripture for Humane Kings* is a case in point, and as we shall see it recursively joins continuous and discontinuous *rupic* cosmologies to craft a comprehensive Buddhist response to local concerns in fifth-century North China.

PART TWO

The Transcendent Wisdom Scripture for Humane Kings and the Creation of National Protection Buddhism

3

The Genealogy of Humane Kings

> Texts are worldly, to some degree they are events, and, even when they appear to deny it, they are nevertheless part of the social world, human life, and the course of historical moments in which they are located and interpreted.
>
> —Edward Said

The Place of the Humane Kings

The *Prajñāpāramitā Scripture for Humane Kings Who Wish to Protect Their States* (*Jen-wang hu-kuo po-jo-po-lo-mi ching*) claims to be a "Transcendent Wisdom" (*Prajñāpāramitā*) scripture specifically bequeathed by the Buddha to "humane kings" (*jen-wang*). As with any "new" revelation, its acceptance depended on the suspension of certain kinds of evaluation. The text itself begins this process of suspension, boldly proclaiming that "the ***Mahāprajñāpāramitā*** expounded by the Seven Buddhas (of the past) and the ***Prajñāpāramitā*** that I now expound are identical and without the slightest difference" (T 245 8.829c2–4). Yet the very existence of such a proclamation simultaneously asserts and undermines its claims to authority. Though new revelations attempt to become "timeless by suppressing their temporality," such suppression always falls short of its goal, and all texts bear the signs of the world in which they were created.[1] But what was the world in which this text was created?

The *Scripture for Humane Kings* configures Buddhist notions of the world, the path, and authority in ways that indicate both its Buddhist and its Chinese parentage. Though well within the norms of the Buddhist tradition, the *Scripture for Humane Kings* deploys *dharmic* and *rupic* strands of cosmology in a complex recursive formation, reinterpreting the bodhisattva path in response to circumstances in fifth-century North China. Rather than being simply a reiteration of Buddhist ideas, the scripture represents a complex process of adaptation which resulted in a new "Chinese" form of Buddhism. This chapter and the next examine the typological and contextual dimensions of the emergence and use of the scripture in fifth- and sixth-century North China. Chapters 5 and 6 examine the recreation of the scripture as an integral part of the emerging Esoteric Buddhist tradition of the eighth-century Chinese court. We may safely conclude that the texts we have were the product, not merely of a single author, but of a cumulative religious and political process over several centuries.

On a cursory reading one is tempted to regard the *Scripture for Humane Kings* as a bald attempt to curry favor with rulers, an attempt to make Buddhism useful and attractive to people concerned with the very real and often intractable problems of war, famine, and disease. Careful study of the scripture soon disabuses us of this facile opinion. Chinese rulers, Confucian scholars, Buddhist catalogers, lay devotees, and even Taoists found this scripture both compelling and troubling. Although it presents familiar Buddhist topics such as the bodhisattva path, its deployment of these topics led to suspicions of a non-Indian origin. The bodhisattva path presented in the fifth-century *Scripture for Humane Kings* is decidedly idiosyncratic, and its terminology is unlike that of widely available Mahāyāna scriptures. Its chapter "The Two Truths" presents not two, but three truths. Its predictions of the timing and causes of the End of the Teaching (*fa-mo* in the idiom of the scripture) are likewise unique. Furthermore, the scripture is structured by a three-fold typology of "seed-natures" or "lineages" (Chinese *chung-hsing*, Sanskrit *gotra*), which has no exact canonical counterpart and which looks very odd in a "Transcendent Wisdom" scripture. Finally, the scripture turns all the bodhisattva stages and perfections into an exercise in one perfection, that of forbearance (*jen*, Sanskrit *kṣānti*).

In the course of this chapter and the next I will introduce the *Scripture for Humane Kings*, examine its notions of cosmology and authority, and explore

1. Barbara Herrnstein Smith, "Contingencies of Value," in Robert Von Hallberg, ed., *Canons* (Chicago: University of Chicago Press, 1984), p. 32. For the "techniques" employed to accomplish this suppression and the efforts to ferret out forgery, see Anthony Grafton, *Forgers and Critics: Creativity and Duplicity in Western Scholarship* (Princeton: Princeton University Press, 1990).

its "imagery of succession, of paternity, of hierarchy."[2] The first steps in this process describe the text and its contexts, following its traces through Chinese history. Then I explore the major components of the scripture, focusing on the path it outlines. The path outlined in the scripture inscribes an intricate hermeneutic seam in which continuous and discontinuous *rupic* notions of the world and authority are joined to *dharmic* notions.

An Outline of the *Scripture for Humane Kings*

Although the *Scripture for Humane Kings* is now little known and seldom read, it was one of the most important Buddhist texts in East Asia and the charter for Buddhist cults of national protection (*hu-kuo*).[3] The *Scripture for Humane Kings* circulates in two versions; the first, which dates from the fifth century, has traditionally been regarded as a translation from Sanskrit into Chinese by Kumārajīva (Chiu-mo-lo-shih), while the second version was produced under imperial auspices in the eighth century by the monk Pu-k'ung chin-kang (Amoghavajra), the great proponent of Esoteric Buddhism.[4]

2. Edward Said, *Beginnings: Intention and Method* (New York: Basic Books, 1975), p. 162.

3. For an overview of Buddhism and state protection, see Jacques May, "Chingo kokka," *Hōbōgirin*, 4:322–27, and Robert Duquenne, "Daigensui," in *Hōbōgirin*, vol. 6, esp. pp. 621ff.

4. The version attributed to Kumārajīva (T 245) and that of Pu-k'ung (Amoghavajra, T 246) are available in Takakusu Junjirō and Watanabe Kaigyoku, eds., *Taishō shinshū daizōkyō*, 85 vols. (Tokyo: Taishō issaikyō kankō-kai, 1924–32). For an introduction to and description of the text, see M. W. DeVisser, *Ancient Buddhism in Japan: Sūtras and Ceremonies in Use in the Seventh and Eighth Centuries A.D. and Their History in Later Times*, 2 vols. (Leiden: E. J. Brill, 1935), 1:116–42. DeVisser's study includes a summary translation of approximately one fourth of the text. Very little work has been done on the scripture since DeVisser's pioneering study. Tamura Enchō has a brief overview of the text's history up to 660 in "Early Buddhism in Japan," *Studies in History*, Fukuoka: Bulletin of the Faculty of Literature, Kyushu University, 13 (1971): 75–79. A partial English translation that covers *exactly* the same portions translated by DeVisser (albeit with updated translations of technical terminology) may be found in Edward Conze, trans., *The Short Prajñāpāramitā Texts* (London: Luzac, 1973), pp. 165–83. This update was done by Lewis Lancaster. About two-thirds of my translation (see Part III herein) has appeared privately on compact disc as part of the Ninnōkyō USA Project in 1995, carried out by Shingon Buddhist International Institute, with the permission of Penn State Press. Mochizuki discusses the texts in *Bukkyō daijiten*, 4105c–4107a. More recently, Satō Tetsui, Yoritomi Motohiro, and Makita Tairyō have gone over the same ground. Satō Tetsui's *Zoku tendai daishi no kenkyū* (Kyoto: Hyakkaen, 1981), pp. 72–112, discusses the *Scripture for Humane Kings* as well as other related Chinese scriptures. His arguments are summarized in Paul L. Swanson's *Foundations of T'ien-t'ai Philosophy: The Flowering of the Two Truths Theory in Chinese Buddhism* (Berkeley: Asian Humanities Press, 1989), pp. 45–48. Yoritomi's argument is in *Chūgoku mikkyō no kenkyū* (Tokyo: Daitō shuppansha, 1979), pp. 160–74. Makita Tairyō's summary of the issue is in his *Gikyō kenkyū* (Kyoto: Kyōto daigaku jinbun kagaku kenkyūjo, 1976), esp. pp. 44–47. One of the best studies of the scripture is by Rhi Khiyong, "*Inwang Panya-kyŏng* kwa hoguk pulgyo," which appeared in *Han'guk Pulgyo yŏn'gu* (Seoul: Han'guk Pulgyo

The basic plan of both versions of the *Scripture for Humane Kings* is identical, and a considerable portion of the eighth-century version is either a paraphrase of or identical in wording to the fifth-century version of the text. Although many differences between the two versions are minor, the eighth-century recension makes major departures from its predecessor. In the eighth-century recension Pu-k'ung substituted Esoteric *vidyārājas* (Chinese *ming-wang*, Lords of Illumination) drawn from the *Sarvatathāgatatattvasaṃgraha* for the fifth-century "Great-howl bodhisattvas," and he appended a long *dhāraṇī* to the text in a fashion common in Esoteric reworkings of previously "translated" scriptures.[5] Pu-k'ung also eliminated the earmarks of Six Dynasties Buddhism, purging the text of references to "Prince Moonlight" (Yüeh-kuang wang), the Three Truths, and its unusual timing of the prediction of apocalyptic decline.[6] He also eliminated Taoist vocabulary and brought the scripture's terminology of the stages of the path in line with that commonly used in Chinese translations of Transcendent Wisdom scriptures.

According to Buddhist hermeneutical schemes presented in the commentaries, the *Scripture for Humane Kings* teaches "inner" and "outer" forms of protection (*nei wai hu*). An explicit analogy is drawn between kings and bodhisattvas, between the techniques used by kings and *cakravartins* to "nurture" and "protect" their states (*hu-kuo*) and those used by bodhisattvas to "nurture" and "protect" the Buddha-fruit (*hu-fo-kuo*).[7] The seventh-century T'ien-t'ai

Yŏn'guwŏn, 1982), pp. 163–93. Osabe Kazuo's work is the most reliable and recent work on the Esoteric use of this text. See his *Tōdai mikkyōshi zakkō* (Kobe: Kōbe shōka daigaku gakujutsu kenkyūkai, 1971), pp. 90–92, and his *Tō Sō mikkyōshi ronko* (Kyoto, 1982). Also see the brief discussion in Yamazaki Hiroshi, *Zui tō bukkyōshi no kenkyū* (Kyoto: Hōzōkan, 1967), pp. 244–45, and my own discussion in Chapter 5.

5. On the production of the text, see *Chiu t'ang shu*, by Liu Hsü et al., 945 A.D. (Peking: Chung-hua shu-chü, 1971), "Tai-tsung huang-ti chüan," vol. 9, no. 11, p. 10. The correspondence between Pu-k'ung and the emperor on this matter is collected in Yüan-chao's *Tai-tsung-ch'ao ssu-k'ung ta-pien-cheng kuang-chih san-tsang ho-shang piao-chih-chi*, T 2120 52.831b19–c20 and 832a25–b12 (hereafter *Collected Documents*) and is discussed at length in Chapter 5. On the *vidyārājas*, see Jean Przyluski, "Les Vidyārāja: Contribution à l'histoire de la magie dans les sectes mahāyanistes," *Bulletin de l'École Française d'Extrême-Orient* 23 (1923) [Hanoi, 1924]: 301–18.

6. For a full discussion of "Prince Moonlight" (Yüeh-kuang wang) in Six Dynasties times, see Erik Zürcher, "Prince Moonlight: Messianism and Eschatology in Early Medieval Chinese Buddhism," *T'oung Pao* 68 (1982): 1–59; also *Bukkyō daijiten*, 758a–759b and 4199b–4200b, on the relationship between Prince Moonlight and King Prasenajit, the main interlocutor of the text.

7. The earliest commentary on the scripture, *Jen-wang po-jo ching shu* (T 1707 33.314b–359a), is by the famous *Mādhyamika* proponent Chi-tsang. Although it purports to be Kuan-ting's record of T'ien-t'ai founder Chih-i's commentary on the scripture, Satō Tetsui dates the *Jen-wang hu-kuo po-jo ching shu* (T 1705 33.253b–286a) between 664 and 734 in the early T'ang dynasty. See Satō Tetsui, *Tendai daishi no kenkyū*, pp. 548–54. I will refer to this commentary as the T'ang T'ien-tai commentary. Produced by Pu-k'ung's close disciple Liang-pi, who was instrumental in the production of the new translation of the *Scripture for Humane Kings*, the *Jen-wang hu-kuo po-jo-po-lo-mi-to ching shu* (T 1709 33.429a–523b) is the standard commentary on the Esoteric version of the scripture. Three ritual commentaries

Commentary on the Scripture for Humane Kings outlines the text as follows: "The major portion of the text is divided into four: the earlier three chapters explicate inner protection, while the chapter on 'Protecting the State' explicates outer protection. The chapter on 'Offering Flowers' explicates the rewards of kindness and worship, and the chapter on 'Receiving and Keeping' explicates the scripture's overall import."[8]

Traditional analyses like this one underscore the dual agenda of this text, which pursues both the highest vision of transcendent emptiness and more "mundane" political and personal protection. Averting disasters and achieving the vision of the "edge of reality" (*bhūtakoṭi*) are linked through kings and the bodhisattva path.

Like most Mahāyāna scriptures, the *Scripture for Humane Kings* begins with a prologue describing the locale of its revelation and the various beings assembled to hear the Buddha preach. King Prasenajit and the kings of fifteen other "great states" contemporary with the Buddha figure prominently in the assembly.[9] The Assembly is outlined as follows:

1. *Bhikṣus* (monks), all of whom have attained the state of *arhat*.
2. Great *ṛṣi pratyekabuddhas*[10]
3. Bodhisattva-*mahāsattvas*
4. Worthies adhering to the five (lay) precepts (*wu-chieh hsien*)
5. Women of pure faith adhering to the five precepts who are *arhats*

are attributed to Pu-k'ung and were probably produced under his supervision. These are the *Jen-wang hu-kuo po-jo-po-lo-mi-to ching t'o-lo-ni nien-sung i-kuei* (T 994 19.514a–519b), *Jen-wang pan-jo nien-sung fa* (T 995 19.520a–522a), and *Jen-wang po-jo t'o-lo-ni shih* (T 996 19.522a–524b). DeVisser gives a synopsis of these commentaries in *Ancient Buddhism in Japan*, 1:158–75, and I deal with them in Chapter 6. *Fo-shuo jen-wang hu-kuo p'an-jo-po-lo-mi ching shu* (T 1706 33.286b–313c) is by Shan-yüeh of the Sung dynasty. A modern Mandarin commentary on the fifth-century scripture, *Jen-wang hu-kuo ching chiang-i*, was published by Yüan-ying (Taipei: Wen-shu ch'u-pan-she, 1989). For a brief overview of the commentaries, see Kunikazu Kimura, "Differences in the Doctrines of the Various Commentaries of the *Ninnōkyō*," *Indogaku bukkyōgaku kenkyū* 29 (March 1981): 120–21.

8. The quotation is from T 1705 265a12–14. I read *hsiang-miao* not in its usual sense of "appearance" or "countenance" but as "import."

9. King Prasenajit figures prominently in early Buddhist materials and in Chinese translation of those materials. He is the preeminent ruler among the Buddha's contemporaries. For a synopsis of legends relating to Prasenajit, see *Bukkyō daijiten*, 4199b and 4371a.

10. These are beings who gain enlightenment through their own analysis of the twelve-fold chain of causation (*nidāna*) and who, from the Mahāyāna point of view, enter a premature state of cessation and thereby do not teach others or even complete the path themselves. It is interesting that the eighth-century recension omits these and that the adjective applied here (*ṛṣi*, *ta-hsien*) is a common Taoist designation for "immortals" who inhabit remote mountain fastnesses. On the *pratyekabuddha*, see Ria Kloppenborg, *The Paccekabuddha: A Buddhist Ascetic* (Leiden: E. J. Brill, 1974), and the brief but helpful discussion in Peter N. Gregory, *Tsung-mi and the Sinification of Buddhism* (Princeton: Princeton University Press, 1991), pp. 100–101.

6. Those in the seven "worthy" stages (*chi-hsien chu*)
7. Nine *brahmadevas*
8. Various gods and "sons of heaven" (*t'ien-tzu*) of the desire realm
9. The kings of the sixteen great states and their entourages
10. Beings of the five destinies
11. Other beings from all directions
12. Transformations from the Pure Lands of the ten directions
13. Transformation Buddhas along with their eight-fold assemblies (T 245 8.825a7–b9)

The assembly inscribes three hierarchies. Those in numbers 1 through 3 are listed in ascending order according to the fruit of their practice (from the point of view of the Mahāyāna, of course): *arhat*, *pratyekabudda*, bodhisattva-*mahāsattva*. Numbers 4 through 11 are listed in descending order according to their practice, from the highest (laymen adhering to the five precepts) through various "kings" (heavenly and earthly), through "other beings." Numbers 12 and 13 are Buddha assemblies from other *cakravāla*s than our own. None of this is particularly startling (if we leave aside what in South Asian circles would raise eyebrows—women *arhats*). But it is notable that in this assembly the kings of this world occupy the second from the lowest rung of the cosmic hierarchy, just above "beings of the five destinies" and "other beings."

Low and even questionable status notwithstanding, we are informed that "this scripture is entrusted to all the kings of states and not to monks and nuns" (whom the scripture characterizes as corrupt) (8.832b22–24). Thus, these "kings" may be viewed either as the lowest rung of the path or as the indispensable foundation of the path. These very kings constitute both the first stages of the path and the last bastion of order in the degenerate age of the End of the Teaching.[11] As we shall see, the kings occupy an ambivalent position in the scripture and the ordering of this initial assembly is echoed in the path detailed in the scripture.

As if in response to signs of the imminent End of the Teaching, the second chapter of the *Scripture for Humane Kings* begins with the king's unspoken query asking how rulers may protect their states in these latter days of the Teaching. The Buddha gives voice to the question in the minds of his audience, proclaiming that he will first discuss how bodhisattvas protect and nourish the practices of the ten stages; only then will he turn to protection of the state (8.825b13–15). Much of this chapter revolves around how one properly "con-

11. Ironically, many Chinese during the Six Dynasties period regarded the presence of celibate clergy as indicative of another sort of decline. The growing numbers of monks and nuns—once viewed as no more than a foreign curiosity—came to be regarded as a dangerous "cancer" at the heart of Chinese society. I will take up this issue in Chapter 4.

templates" (*kuan*) reality, a reality which escapes all opposites and which culminates in the perception of the "edge of reality."

Chapter 3 describes the path in fifty-two stages, beginning with exercises propaedeutic to the path itself and progressing to complete Buddhahood.[12] Of particular interest is the use of terminology closely associated with the *Ti-lun* (Yogācāra) and the "Womb of the Thus-come One" (*Tathāgatagarbha*) schools and the explicit analogy drawn between kings and bodhisattvas.[13] The *Scripture for Humane Kings* constructs a typology of "seed-natures" or "lineages" inspired by Yogācāra and *Tathāgatagarbha* works. This typology signals a relationship between the *Scripture for Humane Kings* and other fifth-century Chinese compilations, such as the *Scripture of the Original Acts That Serve as Necklaces for Bodhisattvas* (*P'u-sa ying-lo pen-yeh ching*, T 1485), the *Scripture of Brahma's Net* (*Fan-wang ching*, T 1484), the *Vajrasamādhi Scripture* (*Chin-kang san-mei ching*, T 273), as well as the no-longer-extant Taoist work, the *Scripture on the Original Forms*.[14] Like the *Scripture for Humane Kings*, the *Scripture of the Original Acts* divides the path into lineages and correlates various "wheel-rulers" (*cakravartin*) with the bodhisattva stages.[15]

Chapter 4 presents a discussion of the Two Truths, a topic hotly debated by fourth- and fifth-century Chinese intellectuals. As I have mentioned, the fifth-century version of the text is the *locus classicus* of the "Three Truths," a doctrine which became the cornerstone of the T'ien-t'ai school and which had great significance for the Chinese assimilation of Buddhism in later T'ien-t'ai and Hua-yen schools.[16]

In chapter 5 the Buddha finally addresses the question of how "humane-kings" (*jen-wang*) protect and cultivate their states, and chapter 6 consists of a brief series of "wonders" or "miracles" characteristic of many Mahāyāna scriptures. (I will examine these in Chapter 4 herein.)

12. A compact and classic treatment of his path is in Dayal, *Bodhisattva Doctrine*, esp. pp. 278–91.

13. The term *ju-lia-tsang* (Sanskrit *Tathāgatagarbha*) is not used in the scripture, though *fo-tsang* (Sanskrit *Buddhagarbha*) is used.

14. The *Scripture of the Original Acts that Serve as Necklaces for Bodhisattvas* seems to have been directly influenced by the *Scripture for Humane Kings*. Both scriptures have a forty-two-stage path modeled on that of the *Avataṃsaka* coupled with the ten stages of firm belief as a propaedeutic. For a discussion, see Steven Bokenkamp, "Stages of Transcendence: The *Bhūmi* Concept in Taoist Scripture," in Buswell, *Chinese Buddhist Apocrypha*, esp. pp. 124–25.

15. T 1485, 24.1011c and 1012c; 1016a. Indeed, its description of rulers uses the same classification: "Advanced stage are iron wheel-rulers, intermediate are scattered like grain, introductory are kings among men" (1017a19–33). Overall the style of the scripture is remarkably like that of the *Scripture for Humane Kings*. For an analysis of the influences on the *Scripture for Humane Kings*, see Satō, *Tendai daishi*, esp. pp. 686–707.

16. On discussions of the Two and Three Truths in Six Dynasties Buddhism and the rise of T'ien-t'ai theory, see Swanson, *Foundations of T'ien-T'ai Philosophy*. On Chinese assimilation of Buddhist ideas at the end of the Six Dynasties period, see Gimello, *Chih-yen (602–668) and the Foundations of Hua-Yen Buddhism*, and for later development of these trends, see Gregory, *Tsung-mi*.

Chapter 7 presents the path once more, and adds to it both predictions of troubling events that will portend the End of the Teaching as well as rituals to forestall such events. The eighth and final chapter reiterates the dire prophecies of the end times and details the deeds of rulers which lead to such calamities, once again admonishing all concerning their obligations to uphold and protect the Teaching. The chapter titles in the two versions are shown as follows:

Chapter Number	Fifth-Century Version	Eighth-Century Version
1	Prologue	Prologue
2	Contemplating Emptiness	Contemplating Thus-Come Ones
3	Bodhisattva's Teaching and Transformation	Bodhisattva Practices
4	The Two Truths	The Two Truths
5	Protecting the State	Protecting the State
6	Offering Flowers	The Inconceivable
7	Receiving and Keeping	Receiving and Keeping
8	The Charge	The Charge

All in all, the *Scripture for Humane Kings* comes across to a reader today as a blend of Transcendent Wisdom, Yogācāra, and *Tathāgatagarbha* traditions combining the *dharmic* and *rupic* strands of Buddhism tailored to Chinese "imperial" audiences and interests. Yet the cut of the tailoring and its contextual significance are anything but obvious. To begin to understand its underlying structure and significance we must first begin to fix its contexts, contexts which can be traced in the earliest notices taken of it.

The Early History of the *Scripture for Humane Kings*

Early references to the scripture as well as suspicions of its Chinese provenance are found in Buddhist catalogs and historical sources. Pre-T'ang dynastic histories contain only two references to "humane kings." Both are from the *[Liu]-Sung History* (*Sung-shu*) compiled by Shen Yüeh at the beginning of the sixth century, and these simply refer to "the humane king's rule."[17] Until the sixth

17. *Hsin-chiao pen sung-shu*, vol. 7.3.28.2.1.7, p. 1793, and 7.3.55.2.42, p. 2349. I am indebted to the East Asian Library of the University of Washington for access to their Database of the Twenty-Five Chinese Dynastic Histories.

century the phrase "humane king" was almost totally absent from official Chinese discourse.[18]

Seng-yu's *Ch'u san-tsang chi-chi*, of 515, which contains the earliest extant catalog mention of the scripture, lists the text under the category "translator's [name] lost": "*Jen-wang hu-kuo po-jo-po-lo-mi ching* one chüan."[19] Later, in an introduction to a commentary on the Transcendent Wisdom Scriptures (*Prajñāpāramitā*), Emperor Wu of the Liang dynasty is quoted as remarking: "Now, as for the *Jen-wang po-jo* . . . it is regarded as a suspect scripture, therefore I will leave it aside and not discuss it."[20]

The next catalog mention occurs in 594 in Fa-ching's *Chung-ching mu-lu*, which notes that an earlier listing attributes the work to Dharmarakṣa (Chu Fa-hu) but the heading of the same text attributes the translation to Kumārajīva.[21] Fa-ching goes on to comment: "Now if we consider this scripture, from start to finish, its meaning and style are unlike translations by these two worthies, therefore it has been entered into the list of suspect [scriptures]" (where it is the second member of the list). At the end of his list of twenty-one suspect scriptures Fa-ching adds: "In many cases, the colophons to the titles [giving the translator's name, etc.] vary among the various catalogues. The style and doctrine [of these texts] are also ambiguous in nature. It has yet to be established whether they are genuine or spurious. The matter requires further examination."[22] This entry takes on added significance as Fa-ching's catalog was compiled in an effort to legitimize Buddhism in the Sui.[23] The illicit reputation of the *Scripture for Humane Kings* must have been too well known to give it an authoritative lineage.

Yet a mere three years later, in 597, just that move was made. Fei Ch'ang-fang provided the much-needed authoritative lineage of translators for the *Scripture for Humane Kings* in his *Li-tai san-pao chi*, listing three translations of the text by the great savants Dharmarakṣa, Kumārajīva, and Paramārtha (Chen-ti).[24] Fei's effort was mounted in the face of a revival of interest in Taoism, and

18. See my comments on the classical corpus in Chapter 4.

19. *Ch'u san-tsang chi-chi*, T 2145 55.29c19. Kyoko Tokuno has provided succinct evaluations of the major Chinese Buddhist catalogues in "The Evaluation of Indigenous Scriptures in Chinese Buddhist Bibliographic Catalogues," in Buswell, *Chinese Buddhist Apocrypha*, pp. 31–74.

20. *Ch'u san-tsang chi-chi*, T 2145 55.54b. Emperor Wu of the Liang Dynasty was one of the most famous patrons of early Chinese Buddhism. See Kenneth Chen, *Buddhism in China: A Historical Survey* (Princeton: Princeton University Press, 1964), 124–28.

21. *Chung-ching mu-lu*, T 2146 55.126b–c.

22. Quoting Kyoko Tokuno's translation of the passage in "The Evaluation of Indigenous Scriptures," p. 41. See *Ch'u san-tsang chi-chi*, T 2145 55.126c.

23. On the catalog see Robert E. Buswell Jr., *The Formation of Ch'an Ideology in China and Korea: The Vajrasamādhi-sūtra, A Buddhist Apocryphon* (Princeton: Princeton University Press, 1989), pp. 34–35. For another discussion, see Hayashiya Tomojirō, *Kyōroku kenkyū* (Tokyo: Iwanami Shoten, 1941), pp. 77–79.

24. *Li-tai san-pao chi*, T 2034 49.62c, 64c, 78a, 79a, 99a and 101c. See Tokuno, "Evaluation of Indigenous Scriptures," pp. 43–47, for an assessment of Fei Ch'ang-fang's work.

in the context of inter-religious rivalry Fei "deliberately distorted many textual references, falsely attributing to famous translators Buddhist texts that were then circulating as anonymous in order to give them more credibility."[25]

For the next fifteen years the text disappeared from view, a period corresponding roughly from the fall of the Sui (618) through the reign of the T'ang founder Kao-tsu (Li Yüan, reigned 618–26).[26] This absence is probably due to the close relationship between the *Scripture for Humane Kings*, the nascent T'ien-t'ai school of Buddhism, and the rulers of the now-deposed Sui dynasty.

Later sources, such as the *Chronicle of Buddhas and Patriarchs* (*Fo-tsu t'ung-chi*, compiled late tenth century by Chih-p'an), show little reticence in accepting the *Scripture for Humane Kings* as canonical. Thus, the *Chronicle* records that a "humane kings maigre feast" took place in 559 under the auspices of Emperor Wu (r. 557–60) of the Ch'en dynasty (557–87).[27] Other references also point to the Ch'en dynasty. According to the *Chronicle of Buddhas and Patriarchs*, in 586 the Emperor Hsiao (r. 583–87) installed the T'ien-t'ai founder Chih-i at the Kuang-wu monastery and commanded him to lecture on the *Scripture for Humane Kings*. The emperor is reported to have performed a three-fold prostration during this event, and Chih-i was assailed by objections from five prominent monks.[28] The text also figures in the biography of Chih-i enshrined in the *Chronicle of Buddhas and Patriarchs*. There the *Scripture for Humane Kings* is cited as the source of Chih-i's doctrine of Three Truths; the *Scripture of the Original Acts That Serve as Necklaces for Bodhisattvas* (*P'u-sa ying-lo pen-yeh ching*, T 1485) is cited as the source of his Three Contemplations; and the *Nirvana Scripture* is cited as the source of his doctrine of Three Knowledges.[29] Less than a century later the *Scripture for Humane Kings* had found its way through Korea and on to Japan.[30]

25. Buswell, *Formation of Ch'an Ideology*, p. 35. Hayashiya's discussion of Fei's catalog is in Hayashiya, *Kyōroku kenkyū*, pp. 82–85.

26. For T'ang reign dates I am following Paul Kroll, "Basic Data on Reign Dates and Local Government," *T'ang Studies*, no. 5 (1987): 95–104.

27. *Fo-tsu t'ung-chi*, T 2035 49.352b. For Chih-p'an and his work, see Jan Yün-hua, ed. and trans., *A Chronicle of Buddhism in China, 581–960 A.D.* (Santiniketan: Visva-Bharati Research Publications, 1966).

28. *Fo-tsu t'ung-chi*, T2035 49.247c, 182c.

29. Ibid., 186b. The influential Pure Land master Hui-yüan (532–92) used the scheme of the Five Forbearances found in the *Scripture for Humane Kings* to structure the three highest insights in his analysis of the path. See Kenneth Tanaka, *The Dawn of Pure Land Buddhist Doctrine: Ching-ying Hui-yüan's Commentary on the Visualization Sūtra* (Albany: State University of New York Press, 1990), pp. 87–88.

30. The *Samguk yusa* (T 2039, vol. 49), compiled by Iryŏn (1206–89) in 1285, contains references to "Humane Kings" performances. See, for instance, 974a9, 999b17. For other references to the scripture in Korea and to its use in Esoteric circles, see Henrik H. Sørensen, "Esoteric Buddhism in Korea," in his edited volume *The Esoteric Buddhist Tradition*, SBS Mongraphs no. 2 (Copenhagen and Århus: Seminar for Buddhist Studies, 1994), 73–96. Also on Korea, see Tamura Enchō, *Studies in History*,

The next record of the *Humane Kings* is in the first month of 630, when the second T'ang emperor T'ai-tsung (Li Shih-min, r. 626–49) commanded all the monks of the capitol to set aside the twenty-seventh day of each month for the recitation of the *Scripture for Humane Kings* in order to secure blessings for the state and its officials.[31] Twice more the *Chronicle of Buddhas and Patriarchs* cites T'ai-tsung as encouraging the use of the scripture and for the setting up of "high seats" in accord with the provisions in the text. The latest such reference is in 639.

The use of the scripture in the mid-T'ang is closely tied to Esoteric Buddhism and is documented in the *Chronicle of Buddhas and Patriarchs* and—at last—corroborated in contemporary sources. In 742 Hsüan-tsung (Li Lung-chi, r. 712–56) commanded the Esoteric master Pu-k'ung to lecture on the *Scripture for Humane Kings*.[32] More extensive use of the *Scripture for Humane Kings* came some twenty years later in the aftermath of the great rebellion of An Lu-shan. The year 765 was not a good one for the emperor Tai-tsung (Li Yü, r. 762–79). The Tibetan invasion of the Chinese heartland was only the latest in a long series of uprisings and disasters which threatened the T'ang dynasty's precarious hold on power in the years following the rebellion.[33] An avowedly Buddhist emperor, Tai-tsung invoked the protection and aid of the Buddha in convoking a "humane kings" assembly according to the *Scripture for Humane Kings*. Thus, in 765 he agreed to Pu-k'ung's request both to perform the rites and to produce a new translation of the scripture.[34] Tai-tsung provided a preface for the new recension and allowed the scripture to be recorded in the official catalog, thus putting the empire's imprimatur on it and settling the issue of the scripture's authority as genuine revelation.[35] The scripture occupies the lion's share of space in the last T'ang catalog of scriptures, a catalog produced by Pu-k'ung's disciple Yüan-chao in 786.[36] Tai-tsung

---

pp. 79–82. For the use of scripture in Japan, see DeVisser, *Ancient Buddhism in Japan*, 1:175. The first notice of the use of the scripture in Japan was in 660. See DeVisser, 1:116.

31. *Fo-tsu t'ung-chi*, T2035 49.363b–c.

32. Ibid., 365b–c, 456a, 374b.

33. The classic study of the rebellion is by Edwin G. Pulleyblank, *The Background of the Rebellion of An Lu-shan* (London: Oxford University Press, 1955). Also see the treatment by Denis Twitchett, "Hsüan-tsung (reign 712–56)," in Denis Twitchett, ed., *The Cambridge History of China*, vol. 3, part 1 (Cambridge: Cambridge University Press, 1979), pp. 443–63.

34. For the correspondence between Pu-k'ung and the emperor on this matter, see T 2120 52.831b–832b and my discussion in Chapter 6.

35. The preface is in T 246 8.834a14–b25.

36. Yüan-chao produced the *Ta-t'ang chen-yüan hsü-k'ai-yüan shih-chiao lu* in 786 (hereafter *Supplement* T 2156, vol. 55) and 800 the *Chen-yüan hsin-ting shih-chiao mu-lu* (hereafter *New Recension* T 2157, vol. 55). He is also responsible for the *Collected Documents*, a collection of correspondence between the Esoteric master Pu-k'ung and the emperors Hsüan-tsung, Su-tsung, and Tai-tsung (T 2120, vol. 52), which I examine in Chapter 6.

was not the last ruler to turn to the *Scripture for Humane Kings*. References abound during the later T'ang and throughout subsequent dynasties.

By the beginning of the sixth century then, we have clear evidence of the existence of a *Scripture for Humane Kings*, though it is not associated with the name of any translator. Though its provenance and status are "dubious," the text appears to have found some currency in the mid- to late-Ch'en dynasty. During the Sui dynasty the scripture is associated with Chih-i and the fledgling T'ien-T'ai school. The *Li-tai san-pao chi* of 597 fixes the text's lineage of translators, and thus its claims to canonicity, with versions attributed successively to Dharmarakṣa, Kumārajīva, and Paramārtha. During the ascendancy of the first T'ang emperor the scripture disappears from view, only to resurface during the reign of T'ai-tsung. In 742 Hsüan-tsung commanded Pu-k'ung to lecture on the text, and his grandson Tai-tsung had Pu-k'ung produce a second "translation." Anonymous circulation of the text in the fifth and sixth centuries gave way to semicanonical and canonical circulation in the seventh century, and finally, in the eighth century to a new, fully canonical "translation" under imperial auspices.

Thus we can be assured that the *Scripture for Humane Kings* was composed in Chinese of South and East Asian parts. The arguments for an East Asian origin have been ably summarized by Satō Tetsui and others.[37] Though it was written in Chinese, the prosimetric style of the scripture imitates Chinese translations of South Asian Buddhist scriptures. The language is largely monosyllabic, and much of the prose is in four- or five-word phrases with some parallelism between phrases. Buddhist technical vocabulary is rendered in a variety of ways. A relatively small number of terms (boldfaced and italicized in my translations) use Chinese to transliterate Sanskrit vocabulary. These words would have had a distinctly foreign ring to Chinese ears and would serve to bolster the authentic "flavor" of the text. But most terms represent standard renderings of Buddhist technical vocabulary in a style current in the fifth century. The *chi* (Sanskrit *gāthā*) in the fifth-century text are in both seven- and five-footed forms dominated by parallelism.[38]

The *Scripture for Humane Kings* thus has a curious, though by no means unique history. Several pressing questions face us. What can the path outlined in the *Scripture for Humane Kings* tell us about issues of authority in fifth-century

37. A summary of the arguments is in Appendix B.

38. There are also some clear links between a *gāthā* (*chi*) that appears in chapter 5 (8.830b) and one that appears in K'ang Seng-hui's 261 translation of the *Liu-tu chi ching* (T 152 3.22c–23a, Sanskrit, *Sadpāramitāsaṅgraha sūtra*, a collection of *avadāna*) and in the *Scripture of the Wise and the Foolish* (T 202 4.426b–c, *Hsien-yü ching*), which was translated in 445. For an analysis of the language of the scripture and its relationship to these and other texts, see Satō, *Tendai daishi*, pp. 688–94, and my comments in Chapter 5.

North China? What does the unique path outlined in the scripture have to do with the specific circumstances that produced the text? What were the discursive restraints that impelled the Buddhist establishment to canonize the *Scripture for Humane Kings*, giving it a complete pedigree of translation, and what prompted its "retranslation" in the mid-T'ang?

To address the first of these questions in another way, just what was it about the *Scripture for Humane Kings* that prompted Emperor Wu to "leave it aside" when it was a text that might serve to bolster his own claims of sovereignty? The answer in its simplest form is that the path outlined in the *Scripture for Humane Kings* appeared to violate certain key taxonomic boundaries, both within the genre of Transcendent Wisdom literature and within Chinese Buddhism as it had been formulated up to that time. The anomalies in the path outlined in the *Scripture for Humane Kings* reflect a Chinese reworking of the relationships among the world, the path, and Buddhist notions of authority. Paradoxically, these anomalies served in the long run to position the *Scripture for Humane Kings* as an authoritative Chinese Buddhist scripture.

The Problematic Nature of the *Scripture for Humane Kings*

As the charter for Buddhist state cults throughout East Asia, the *Scripture for Humane Kings* has been the object of numerous commentaries, and its efficacy for avoiding illness, bringing rain, and preventing fires was celebrated in a *pien-wen* and in miracle tales.[39] Such broad application is enjoined in the text itself, which was to be employed if any of the following "seven difficulties" (*ch'i-nan*) arose:[40]

> [If] the sun and moon lose their appointed courses or a red sun or a black sun comes out, or two, three, four, or five suns simultaneously shine or

39. The *pien-wen* (*Wei jen-wang po-jo ching chiang-ching pien-wen*) was found among texts exhumed in Tun-huang, Pelliot 3808, dated to the Latter T'ang Dynasty in 933–34 in the reign of Ming-tsung. There are relatively few copies of the *Scripture for Humane Kings* among the Tun-huang finds, and most are fragmentary. These include Stein numbers 124, 3472, 4528, and 7242; Peking numbers 3481–3; and Pelliot number 3971, as well as the *pien-wen*. All but Pelliot 3971 appear to be from the fifth-century recension of the text. Pelliot 3971 is a fragment of a pronouncing guide, apparently for the great *dhāraṇī*. Japanese miracle tales concerning the efficacy of expounding the text may be found in D. E. Mills, *A Collection of Tales from Uji: A Study and Translation of Uji Shūi Monogatari* (Cambridge: Cambridge University Press, 1970), pp. 238 and 425–26.

40. A fully annotated translation of this passage is found in Appendix A.

the sun is eclipsed and does not shine, or halos surround the sun, one, two, three, four or five halos appear. At times of such wonders [you should] recite this scripture. These constitute the first difficulty.

[If] the twenty-eight mansions lose their courses, or Venus, the Yama star, the Wheel star, the Demon star, Mars, Mercury, the Wind star, the Blade star, the Southern Dipper, the Northern Dipper, the great stars of the Five Wardens, all of the stars of state rulers, the stars of the three dukes, and of the one hundred officers, and all such stars each are transformed, [you should] recite and expound this scripture. These constitute the second difficulty.

[If] great fires burn the state and the myriad people are incinerated, [if] demon fires, dragon fires, deva fires, mountain spirit fires, human fires, forest fires, rebel fires, or other such wonders [occur, you should] recite and expound this scripture. These constitute the third difficulty.

[If] great floods inundate the people and the seasons are reversed: in winter it rains and in summer it snows. In winter there is lightning and thunder resounds, and in the sixth month the rain freezes and there is frost and hail. There are red rains, black rains, and green rains and it rains dirt and rock and stones. Rivers flow in reverse, sweeping along stones and floating mountains. At times of such wonders [you should] recite and expound this scripture. These constitute the fourth difficulty.

[If] great winds blow killing the myriad people, and the mountains, rivers, and forests of the state are extinguished all at once. [If] there are unseasonable typhoons, black winds, red winds, green winds, heavenly winds, earthly winds and fire winds, [then] at times of such wonders [you should] recite and expound this scripture. These constitute the fifth difficulty.

[If] heaven, earth and the state are scorched by excessive heat, and ponds dry up, the grass and trees wither and die, and the five grains do not ripen and the soil becomes hard and the myriad people perish, [then] at times of such wonders [you should] recite and expound this scripture. These constitute the sixth difficulty.

[If] rebels arise from the four directions to invade the state, or within and without [the borders] rebels arise, [and there are] fire rebels, water rebels, wind rebels, and demon rebels, [and] the people are in chaos and warfare and plunder are on the rise, [then] at times of such wonders [you should] recite and expound this scripture. These constitute the seventh difficulty. (T 245 8.832b26–c22)

A more frightening picture of the future is surely hard to come by, especially when we remember that the temporal, meteorological, cosmological, agricultural, and social order were all the direct responsibility of the Chinese emperor.[41] But this prediction would be all the more frightening were there not some obvious cause for the catastrophes as well as a method to deal with them, which, of course, the scripture provides. Indeed, the first instances of the text's recorded use describe the construction of an altar with one hundred Buddha-images and imperial invitation of one hundred masters of the Teaching as prescribed in the scripture. If sufficient offerings and recitations were performed, then "the calamities would be extinguished."[42]

In keeping with its claims of genuine revelation, the *Scripture for Humane Kings* opens in the same fashion as do other authoritative Buddhist revelations, staking a claim based on an "auditory" witness traced back to the Buddha's disciple Ānanda: "Thus have I heard. Once, when the Buddha was residing on Vulture Peak in the capitol . . ." (T 245 8.825a7).[43]

The time and the signs of an imminent revelation are also specified: "At that time . . . on the eighth day of the first month of the year, Śākyamuni Buddha was poised at the tenth stage and entered the great quiescent-abode ***samādhi*** and his mindfulness caused a great brilliance which illuminated everything in the triple world" (825b9–11).[44] These opening lines are standard fare in Mahāyāna Buddhist scriptures, but the "charge" or commission laid on the audience in the eighth and final chapter is anything but standard: "The Buddha told King ***Prasenajit,*** 'I warn you and the others, that after my ex-

41. There are numerous sources on the role of the sovereign in Chinese calendrical and cosmological thinking. Among the best are Henry Rosemont, ed., *Explorations in Early Chinese Cosmology* (Chico, Calif.: Scholars Press, 1984), and John B. Henderson, *The Development and Decline of Chinese Cosmology* (New York: Columbia University Press, 1984). Hsü Dau-lin's "Crime and Cosmic Order," *Harvard Journal of Asiatic Studies* 30 (1970): 111–25, is especially interesting.

42. Recitation is a common component in the use of Buddhist scriptures. The rituals are described at T 245 8.829c20–830a9 and T 246 8.834c16–835b13.

43. For reflection on the translation of this stock opening phrase, see John Brough, "Thus Have I Heard . . . ," *Bulletin of the School of Oriental and African Studies* 13.2 (1950): 416–26.

44. Both versions of the text indicate this date. It is very typically Chinese to specify a date, and very unlike Transcendent Wisdom texts originating in South Asia. The date corresponds to the *Li-ch'un*, which celebrates the rebirth of spring and the birth of rice and grains. See Juliet Bredon and Igor Mitropanow, *The Moon Year: A Record of Chinese Customs and Festivals* (Shanghai: Kelly & Walsh, 1927), p. 132. The issue of the dating of the Buddha's *parinirvāṇa* was an important one in fifth- and sixth-century China, not only with regard to the timing of the End of the Teaching (which one account dates to 485 C.E.), but also because Buddhist notions of time were almost revolutionary to the Chinese. For a detailed account of these issues, see Hubert Durt, "The Dating of the Historical Buddha (Part I)," in Heinz Bechert, ed., *Symposien zur Buddhismusforschung*, 4, 1 (Göttingen: Vandenhoeck & Ruprecht, 1991), pp. 458–89. The Buddhist encyclopedia *Fa-yüan chu-lin* contains a long discussion of dates of the End of the Teaching at T 2122 53.1005a–1013a. Stephen F. Teiser treats Tao-shih and his *Fa-yüan chu-lin* in "T'ang Buddhist Encyclopedias: An Introduction to *Fa-yüan chu-lin* and *Chu-ching yao-chi*," *T'ang Studies* 3 (1985): 109–28. Liang-pi spends several lines in an explanation of equivalences between Indian and Chinese calendars in his commentary on the *Scripture for Humane Kings*, but does not really throw any light on why this date is mentioned (T 1709 33.448c18–449a2).

tinction in eighty years, eight hundred years and eight thousand years, when there is no Buddha, no Teaching, no Community, no male or female lay devotees, this scripture's three jewels will be entrusted to all the kings of states'" (833b13–14).[45] Although the scripture claims to be about the highest realization of Transcendent Wisdom, it simultaneously claims that kings, not monks, are the recipients and guarantors of this revelation. Although Buddhist discourses about sovereignty and enlightenment are commonly conjoined, the way their union is realized in the *Scripture for Humane Kings* was interpreted alternately as a paradigm for Buddhist notions of authority and as a distortion of those same notions. If this were not enough to call attention to the scripture, then its doctrine of Three Truths insured notoriety. Although the innovation seemed to many a sure sign of forgery, the growing T'ien-t'ai movement in the sixth century used the *Scripture for Humane Kings* as the charter for its theory of Three Truths.

As we have seen, the earliest notices of the *Scripture for Humane Kings* raise doubts about its authenticity. The basis for such doubts and the ways these doubts were assuaged are keys to understanding how the scripture was generated, how it entered the East Asian Buddhist canon, and why it became one of the most important Buddhist texts in China, Korea, and Japan from the fifth through the nineteenth centuries.

Emperor Wu's Doubt: Path and Paternity in the *Scripture for Humane Kings*

The Emperor Wu of the Liang dynasty was clearly uncomfortable with the *Scripture for Humane Kings* as a Transcendent Wisdom scripture, but probably not because the scripture mixed two distinct strands of Buddhist tradition. As I noted in Chapter 2, the blending of *dharmic* and *rupic* worldviews is a hallmark of Buddhism. In keeping with other Transcendent Wisdom scriptures, the *Scripture for Humane Kings* presents both the temporally oriented *rupic* development of the bodhisattva (and the prophecy of the End of the Teaching) and the atemporal *dharmic* vision of the structure of reality in emptiness. So what might have caused the emperor's doubt?

Emperor Wu may have had his doubts occasioned by certain unique details of the scripture such as the Three Truths, the peculiar timing of the End of

45. Both Chi-tsang's commentary (T 1707 33.357c8–26) and the T'ang T'ien-t'ai commentary (T 1705 33.284b9–24) discuss the periodization at some length, linking it to when the Buddha's direct disciples finally died and so forth.

the Teaching, references to the apocalyptic figure of "Prince Moonlight," or the use of Taoist terminology. He may also have balked at the status and role assigned by the scripture to kings.

The *Scripture for Humane Kings* repeatedly proclaims itself a Transcendent Wisdom scripture, and some of the *dharmic* trappings of the genre certainly are present. The predication of the scripture is signaled by a dazzling display of light emitted by the Buddha, a light which first "illuminates all the triple world" and then "all the other Buddha-lands in all directions, lands numerous as the sands of the ***Gaṅgā***" (825b10–13). The discussion of the Two Truths and of emptiness found in chapters 3 and 4 are couched in classic pairs of opposites: "not single, not dual, . . . not existent, not nonexistent," and so on (T 245 8.829b24–26).[46] The series of miraculous events listed in chapter 6 of the text is dominated by the *pariṇāmiki* powers of vision and light, wherein Buddhas and assemblies of the ten directions are illuminated, the sizes of objects are altered, and so on (830c12–831a16).[47]

The *Scripture for Humane Kings* repeatedly asserts its status as Transcendent Wisdom, both within the frame of didactic tales, such as that of "Spotted Foot" in chapter 5 ("they expounded this ***Prajñāpāramitā***'s eight trillion verses") and in outright assertion ("Great king! The ***Mahāprajñāpāramitā*** expounded by the seven Buddhas and the ***Prajñāpāramitā*** that I now expound are identical and without the slightest difference" [829c2–4]).[48] Indeed, from the very outset the *Scripture for Humane Kings* attempts to preempt questions concerning its paternity and its temporality (and therefore its authority), immediately proclaiming its relationship to other Transcendent Wisdom Scriptures:

> At that time all in that great assembly engendered a doubt, each saying to themselves, "The world-honored one, possessing the four fearlessnesses, the eighteen unique characteristics of a Buddha, and the body of the Teaching with its five kinds of vision, has already, in the twenty-ninth year [of his ministry], expounded, on behalf of me and the great assembly, the ***Mahāprajñāpāramitā,*** the Adamanitine ***Prajñāpāramitā,*** the *Celestial Kings' Inquiry Concerning the* ***Prajñāpāramitā*** and the Brilliant Praise ***Prajñāpāramitā,*** so why has the Thus-come One shone forth this great light?" (8.825b19–24)

Though self-promotion is one characteristic of the genre, the prominent inscription of such a challenge should be taken seriously. These must be the Chi-

46. Also see the list of emptinesses at T 245 8.826a13–15.

47. Compare T 246 840c16–841a20 and the translation in Part Three.

48. The seven Buddhas are usually enumerated as Vipaśyin, Śikhin, Viśvabhū, Krakucchanda, Kanakamuni, Kāśyapa, and Śākyamuni. See *Mikkyō daijiten*, 976a–b, and "Bodai," in *Hōbōgirin*, 1:90.

nese translations from which the author of the *Scripture for Humane Kings* took some of his cues concerning the bodhisattva path, the Two Truths, and the doctrine of emptiness. Yet an examination of these translations reveals little in the way of extensive verbatim borrowing.[49] Rather, the author of the *Humane Kings* seems to have used the overall intellectual tenor and description of the Transcendent Wisdom Scriptures and to have relied on their prestige in compiling his new scripture.

All of this striving for legitimacy cannot disguise a gaffe that tips us off to the scripture's Chinese paternity. The compiler of the *Scripture for Humane Kings* cites the *Mahāprajñāpāramitā* and the *Brilliant Praise Prajñāpāramitā* as two distinct *Prajñāpāramitā* scriptures. They are, however, two translations from the same scripture. The *Brilliant Praise*, first translated by Dharmarakṣa in the mid-third century, is a partial version of the *Mahāprajñāpāramitā* (the *Pañcavimśati*). The full *Mahāprajñāpāramitā* was translated by Kumārajīva in the early fifth century.[50]

Notwithstanding this gaffe (which very few of the author's contemporaries could have caught), the *Scripture for Humane Kings* has many of the *dharmic*

49. For example, although the "three falsities" (*san-chia*) and the list of twelve types of emptiness are found in the *Mahāprajñāpāramitā*, the list of emptinesses in the *Scripture for Humane Kings* has more in common with those of the *Nirvana Scripture*. For more details, see Appendix B and Satō, *Tendai daishi*, p. 691.

50. The first is the *Pañcavimśati-sāhaśrika-prajñāpāramitā* (T 223, 403–4) translated by Kumārajīva. See *Bukkyō daijiten*, 4729b–4731a. The second is the *Vajra-cchedika-prajñāpāramitā*, also translated by Kumārajīva sometime between 402 and 414. See *Bukkyō daijiten*, 1347a–1348b. The last scripture cited, the *Brilliant Praise Prajñāpāramitā* (T 222), was translated by Dharmarakṣa (Chu Fa-hu) in 286 and is actually an incomplete version of the *Pañcavimśati*. See *Bukkyō daijiten*, 4730a and 1048b, and Erik Zürcher, *The Buddhist Conquest of China: The Spread and Adaptation of Buddhism in Early Medieval China*, 2 vols., Sinica Leidensia 11 (Leiden: E. J. Brill, 1972), pp. 68–71 and 339–40 n. 182. I have found no references to the "Heavenly Kings" text, either in the *Bukkyō daijiten* or elsewhere. However, there are a number of chapter titles in extant Transcendent Wisdom translations that could possibly be the text in question. These include the "Questions" chapter of the *Brilliant Praise* (T 222 8.210b) in which the four Lokapālas raise questions, or the "Questions on the Abodes" chapter of the *Pañcavimśati*, with its alternate titles in the Sung manuscript "Heavenly Rulers" and in the Yüan and Ming manuscripts as "Heavenly Kings" (T 223 8.273b). All of these are translations, respectively, by Dharmarakṣa (Chu Fa-hu) and Kumārajīva of the same Sanskrit work. Interestingly, another text, the *Pravara-deva-rāja-pariprccheda* (The Transcendent Wisdom Scripture Enunciated to the Victorious Heavenly Kings) (T 231), in a translation attributed to Upaśūnya during the Ch'en (565), has some remarkable similarities to the *Scripture for Humane Kings* in tone, phrasing, and concerns. It actually includes a discussion of "humaneness" and "forbearance" (689a), a generalized prediction of the End of the Teaching with this text as the cure (704b), as well as a protective *dhāraṇī* (713c), and manuscripts from the Sui and T'ang found in the Shōsō-in in Nara have a preface to the *Scripture for Humane Kings* tacked on the end—a preface that quotes the passage above listing the four previously preached Transcendent Wisdom Scriptures (725c22–726a22). For the text and Upaśūnya, see *Bukkyō daijiten*, 2698a–b and 761b. Clearly, someone during the Sui regarded the "Heavenly Kings" text mentioned in the *Scripture for Humane Kings* as the *Pravara-deva-rāja-pariprccheda*.

(and *rupic*) trappings of a "genuine" South Asian Transcendent Wisdom scripture. So whence Emperor Wu's suspicion?

Numerous idiosyncracies in the *Scripture for Humane Kings* might have raised the specter of forgery, not the least of which is the appearance of Taoist terminology:

> Great king, this ***prajñāpāramitā*** is the spiritual basis of the mind-consciousness [*hsin-shih chih shen-pen*] of all Buddhas, ***bodhisattvas*** and of all beings. It is also called the spirit-tally [*shen-fu*], it is also called the ghost-expelling pearl [*p'i-kuei-chu*], it is also called the wish-fulfilling pearl [*ju-i-chu*], it is also called the state-protecting pearl [*hu-kuo-chu*], it is also called the mirror of heaven and earth [*t'ien-ti-ching*], it is also called the spirit king of the dragon jewels [*lung-pao shen-wang*]." (832c23–26)

This passage notwithstanding, the *Scripture for Humane Kings* is remarkably free of Taoist influence. Since the scripture appears to have been written in the 470s, this freedom may well be the result of the Taoist inspired anti-Buddhist persecution of the 450s.[51]

Arguably the most influential of the scripture's idiosyncracies is the enunciation of a doctrine of Three Truths. Embedded in the chapter titled "The Two Truths" we find the following passage:

> If a ***bodhisattva*** sees beings, sees one or sees two, then he does not see one and does not see two. This one and two is the truth of the preeminent meaning [*ti-i-i ti*]. Great king, if there is existence or nonexistence [*jo yu jo wu*], then this is worldly truth. [One can] use three truths to embrace all the constituents: the truth of emptiness, the truth of form, and the truth of mind. I have preached that all constituents do not transcend the Three Truths. Personalist views and the five aggregates are empty and, indeed, all constituents are empty. (829b26–c1)[52]

While some scholars have maintained that this passage and especially

51. I argue the case on dating the scripture later. Satō discusses the passage but really has little to say about it. It is significant that the *Scripture for Humane Kings* is called a "spirit-tally" (*shen-fu*), a phrase which plays upon a long tradition of Taoist palladia. See Anna K. Seidel, "Imperial Treasures and Taoist Sacraments: Taoist Roots in the Apocrypha," in Michel Strickmann, ed., *Tantric and Taoist Studies in Honor of R. A. Stein*, vol. 2, *Mélanges chinoise et bouddhiques* (Brussels) 21 (1983): 291–371.

52. The passage is, of course, the *locus classicus* of the T'ien-t'ai school's teaching of the Three Truths, and the T'ang T'ien-t'ai commentary discusses this at T 1705 33.279c13–21.

Chih-i's elaboration of the Three Truths simply makes explicit certain implicit trends in South Asian Mādhyamika thought, it nonetheless constitutes a very visible doctrinal departure from the norm, though, as we shall see in Chapter 4, it is one in keeping with the emphasis on the *rupic* strains which are so markedly present in the text.[53]

Also striking is the *Scripture for Humane Kings*'s timing of the onset of apocalyptic times. The timing of the onset of the apocalyptic era is calculated in multiples of eight, a scheme unique in Buddhist literature.[54] The only parallel is the prediction of the End of the Teaching found in the *Nirvana Scripture*, which, like that found in the *Scripture for Humane Kings*, is unusual. Indeed, the *Nirvana Scripture* shares more than a few idiosyncrasies with the *Scripture for Humane Kings*.[55] The basic story of the *Nirvana Scripture* is the well-known narrative of the end of the Buddha's life and ministry, his death and its aftermath. As the "last" preaching of the Buddha, the scripture had a wide following among fifth-century Chinese Buddhists.

Evidence for direct borrowing by the *Scripture for Humane Kings* is circumstantial, but several things are striking when we examine the "northern text," which was immensely influential during the period of the compilation of the *Scripture for Humane Kings*. The *Nirvana Scripture*, like the *Scripture for Humane Kings*, speaks of "inner" and "outer" forms of protection: "Good sons! In the Correct Teaching of the Buddha there are two kinds of protection, the

53. Swanson argues convincingly that such trends were incipient in South Asian traditions. See his *Foundations of T'ien-T'ai Philosophy*, esp. pp. 121–23, 155–56.

54. For a detailed study of these apocalyptic predictions, see Jan Nattier, "The *Candragarbha-sūtra* in Central and East Asia: Studies in a Buddhist Prophecy of Decline" (Ph.D. diss., Harvard University, 1988), esp. p. 1–97. Nattier's revised dissertation, *Once Upon a Future Time: Studies in a Buddhist Prophecy of Decline* (Berkeley: Asian Humanities Press, 1991), covers the same ground but adds more context, including some material on the "Aggañña-suttanta" and the "Cakkavati-sihānanda-suttanta." See pp. 7–15 for these works and pp. 27–118 for the types of decline theory and their manifestations in East Asia.

55. The "Nirvana Scripture" in China comes in two basic flavors (a Nikāya Buddhist version and a Mahāyāna version). The *Mahāparinibbānasutta*, no. 16 of the *Dighanikāya* in the Pāli canon, is attributed as a translation of (T 7) by Fa-hsien of the Eastern Chin dynasty. The Mahāyāna version, the *Mahāparinirvāṇasūtra*, was translated twice. The first translation was made by Fa-hsien and Buddhabhadra; the second translation was done by Dharmakṣema in 421 under the Northern Liang dynasty. This translation circulated in South China with alterations made to its chapter divisions by Hui-yen, Hui-kuan, and Hsieh Ling-yün. Dharmakṣema's unmodified version was henceforth known as the "Northern" text, while that of Hui-yen et al., as the "Southern" text. See Ch'en, *Buddhism in China*, pp. 113–20. Fa-hsien's Mahāyāna translation is T 376, vol. 12, the Northern text is T 374, and the Southern text is found in T 375. The Nikāya Buddhist version has been translated by T. W. Rhys-Davids. Although Yamamoto Kōshō has translated the Mahāyāna version of the text in its entirety into English, it is marred by stilted style and a lack of apparatus. See *The Mahāyāna Parinirvana Sūtra*, 3 vols. (Ube, Japan: Karinbunko, 1973–75). Portions of the text are available in English in Samuel Beal, *A Catena of Buddhist Scriptures from the Chinese* (London: Trübner, 1871; reprint, Taipei: Ch'eng Wen, 1970).

first is inner, the second is outer. Inner protection refers to adherence of the prohibitions, while outer protection has to do with clan and relatives."[56]

The *Nirvana Scripture* also uses the same phraseology as the *Scripture for Humane Kings* to discuss the Two Truths, speaking of "worldly truth" (*shih-ti*) and the "truth of the preeminent meaning" (*ti-i i ti*).[57] In some places discussions of forbearance (*jen*) and kingship occur alongside the form of address "kind sir" or "humane sir" (*jen che*), and these discussions, like those of the *Scripture for Humane Kings*, often refer to kings.[58] The term "Lion-howl bodhisattva" (*shih-tzu ho p'u-sa*) occurs both in the text and as a section title, calling to mind the "Great-howl bodhisattvas" (*ta-ho p'u-sa*) of the seventh chapter of the *Scripture for Humane Kings*.[59] So too, King Prasenajit has a major role in the *Nirvana Scripture* (T 374 12.542a ff.).

But it is the *Nirvana Scripture*'s timing of the End of the Teaching which most vividly calls to mind the *Scripture for Humane Kings*. Eschewing the common five-hundred and thousand-year form of the prediction of the End of the Teaching, the *Nirvana Scripture* instead uses a seven-hundred-year period: "The Buddha told Kāśyapa, 'Seven hundred years after my *parinirvāṇa* this Māra Pāpīyas will gradually destroy my Correct Teaching.'"[60] Elsewhere in the same text we find: "Good Sons. After my *parinirvāṇa* the Correct Teaching will not yet be extinguished for yet some eighty years."[61] This phrase coupled with the *Nirvana Scripture*'s willingness to depart from the standard chronology could be the origin of the prediction of the End of the Teaching after "eighty, eight-hundred, and eight-thousand years" which we find in the fifth-century *Scripture for Humane Kings*.[62] It is likely that the *Nirvana Scripture* with its prominent and somewhat eccentric *rupic* themes influenced the composition of the *Scripture for Humane Kings*.

More alarming than its eccentric timetable for the End or its kinship with the *Nirvana Scripture* is the disjunction between the path depicted in authoritative scriptures and that detailed in the *Scripture for Humane Kings*. Indeed, while the *Scripture for Humane Kings* follows the preparatory path involving the efforts of the *śrāvaka* and then the ten bodhisattva "stages," its terminology and its configuration are quite odd, as is the role of kings in turning back the End of the Teaching and establishing the Correct Teaching (*cheng-fa*).

56. This occurs in a discussion of the Buddha's family (T 374 12.559c10–11).

57. As, for example, on 564a17ff.

58. Ibid., 551a–b.

59. See, for example, "Lion-howl bodhisattva" (T 374 12.541b–542b).

60. T 374 12.402c26. The seven-hundred-year prediction is also found in the *A-nan ch'i-meng ching*, T 494 14.785a–b.

61. T 374 12.421c26.

62. Although I have searched for one, I can find no apparent link between this prediction and datable events.

Path in the Fifth-century *Scripture for Humane Kings:*
(T 245 8.826b21–827b1; 827b8–828a8)[63]

I. Forbearance of Self-control (*fu-jen*) or the Womb of Sages (*sheng-t'ai*) is constituted by:
   A. The Ten Grades of Faith (*shih-hsin: shih-shan*) which include three levels: Those in the Inferior and Intermediate levels are the Scattered kings, while those in the Superior level are Iron wheel-rulers of one continent.
   B. The Acquired lineage (*hsi-chung-hsing*, Sanskrit *samudānītagotra*) in which one is a Copper wheel-ruler of two continents.
   C. The Innate lineage (*hsing-chung-hsing*, Sanskrit *prakṛtishthagotra*) in which one cultivates "Dry Knowledge" (*kan-hui*), the Ten Minds, and the Ten Stoppings (*shih-chih*). As a result one becomes a Silver wheel-ruler of three continents.
   D. Lineage of the Way (*tao-chung-hsing*) in which one cultivates the Ten Firm Minds (*shih chien hsin*) and, as a result, becomes a Wheel-turning king of four continents, and initiates the Bodhisattva path.

II. Forbearance of [Firm] Belief (*hsin-jen*) is constituted by:
   A. Stage of Effective Illumination (*shan-chüeh*) 100 Cakravartin/Jambudvīpa
   B. Stage of Abandoning Success; Path-opener (*li-ta*) 1000/King of Trāyastriṃśas heaven
   C. Stage of Brilliant Wisdom (*ming-hui*) 10,000/King Yama

III. Forbearance of Obedience (*hsün-jen*) is constituted by:
   A. Stage of Blazing Wisdom (*yen-hui*) 100,000/King of Tuṣita heaven
   B. Stage of Victorious Wisdom (*sheng-hui*) 10,000,000/King of heaven of Transformative Joy
   C. Teaching Manifests stage (*fa-hsien*) 100,000,000/King of heaven Sovereign over the creations of others.

IV. Forbearance of Birthlessness (*wu-sheng-jen*) is constituted by:
   A. Far-reaching stage (*yüan-ta*) Trillion/King of First Brahma heaven
   B. Equable Discernment stage (*teng-chüeh*) million numberless/King of Second Brahma heaven
   C. Wisdom's Light stage (*hui-kuang*) million *asaṅkyeya* numberless/King of Third Brahma heaven

63. This outline of the path contains abbreviated references to practices the text says characterize each of its levels as well as the number of "Buddha-fields" over which a bodhisattva rules and the level of the cosmos attained. For instance, under the Forbearance of [Firm] Belief we are told that a bodhisattva who attains the stage of "abandoning success" rules over one thousand Budda-fields and is lord of the *Trāyastriṃśas* heaven. Compare the chart of the path in the eighth-century scripture in Appendix C.

V. Forbearance of Quiescent Extinction (*chi-mieh-jen*) is constituted by:
   A. Hard to Top stage (*nan-ting*) Unspeakable/King of Fourth Brahma heaven
   B. Stage of Equanimous Wisdom (*teng-hui*)
   C. Stage of Comprehensive Knowledge (*yüan-chih*)

Each level of the path is correlated with the number of "Teachings" (*fa-men*) employed to save beings and with sovereignty over increasingly exalted realms culminating in the status of "lord of the triple world." While certain other scriptures make such correlations between practice and sovereign recompense, few make it an integral and important element of the path.[64] The *Scripture for Humane Kings*, like the *Bodhisattvabhūmi*, the *Daśabhūmikā*, and the *Avataṃsaka* (translated in 385–433, 297, and 418), takes as a base line a bodhisattva path of ten stages (*ti*, Sanskrit *bhūmi*), and like the *Avataṃsaka* it embeds these stages in an extended path of forty-two stages which encompass the path of the *śrāvaka* as preparation to the career of the bodhisattva.[65] But the names of the stages in the fifth-century *Scripture for Humane Kings* are unique, so much so that Pu-k'ung "rectified" them in his eighth-century recension of the text.[66] Thus it seems clear that the *Scripture for Humane Kings* postdates the *Avataṃsaka* and its ten-stage bodhisattva path but does not use what had become the normative terminology for the bodhisattva stages.[67]

That the bodhisattva path in the *Scripture for Humane Kings* departs from the norm and that the scripture reiterates the path in prose and poetry no less than

64. The *Daśabhūmikā* and the *Mahāyānāvatarā* make direct correlations between advancement on the path and levels of cosmic sovereignty which are the fruit of practice. The *Scripture for Humane Kings* is likely modeled on these and in turn is the model for a similar scheme in the *Scripture of the Original Acts That Serve as Necklaces for Bodhisattvas* (*P'u-sa ying-lo pen-yeh ching*, T 1485). See Iyanaga Nobumi's "Daijizaiten," in *Hōbōgirin*, vol. 6, esp. the chart on pages 742–44. Also see Dayal, *Bodhisattva Doctrine*, pp. 238–91.

65. The *Bodhisattvabhūmi* was translated by Dharmarakṣema sometime between 385 and 433 (T 1581, *P'u-sa ti-chih ching*) and by Gunavarman between 367 and 431 (T 1582, 1583, *P'u-sa shan chieh ching*). The *Daśabhūmika* was translated in 297 by Dharmarakṣa (T 285, *Chien pei i-ch'ieh chih te ching*), by Kumārajīva between 402 and 409 (T 286, *Shih-chu ching*), and again in 418 by Buddhabhadra as chapter 22 of the *Avataṃsaka* (T 278, *Ta-fang kuang fo hua-yen ching*). The path in the *Scripture for Humane Kings* shows the influence of the *Daśabhūmika* translations of Kumārajīva and Buddhabhadra. See Satō, *Tendai daishi*, pp. 691–93.

66. Dharmarakṣa's early version of *Daśabhūmika* (T 285, vol. 10) also has a somewhat eccentric listing of the stages. One should note that the *Scripture for Humane Kings* is not consistent in using designations for the bodhisattva stages. For example, while the seventh chapter describes the tenth stage as "consecration" (*kuan-ting*), the third chapter describes it as "hard to top," or "difficult to surmount" (*nan-ting*). There are several other variants in the text.

67. In fact, as Satō has shown, the latest text quoted by the *Scripture for Humane Kings* is the *Scripture of the Wise and the Foolish* (*Hsien yü ching*), which was translated in 445. See Satō, *Tendai daishi*, p. 692.

four times shows that its generation was, at least in part, an answer to some sort of pressing taxonomic question. Indeed, the path presented in the *Scripture for Humane Kings* is at once a cosmology and a hierarchical prescription concerning authority. It is, however, an anomolous and somewhat peculiar hierarchy.

Certainly the *Scripture for Humane Kings* contains both *rupic* and *dharmic* cosmological motifs. But how these motifs are related in the path is more to the point. The *Scripture for Humane Kings* is not at all a typical Transcendent Wisdom scripture. Rather, the *rupic* concerns of the path and the prophecy of the End of the Teaching have been packaged in a *dharmic* Transcendent Wisdom container. Moreover, there are *two* distinct *rupic* cosmologies in this scripture, one of which is continuous, the other discontinuous.

That *rupic* motifs dominate the scripture is nowhere more apparent than in the scheme of lineages (Chinese *chung-hsing*, Sanskrit *gotra*) derived from the Yogācāra and *Tathāgatagarbha* traditions and their uncomfortable fit with the framework of the path of the five forbearances.[68] The initial stages of the path (corresponding to the first "forbearance of self-control," Chinese *fu-jen*) are comprised of those practicing the "ten virtuous acts" (*shih-shan*) toward the Buddha, the Teaching, and the Community. These "bodhisattvas arouse the great mind [of enlightenment]. Having long been separated in the sea of suffering of the triple world, the intermediate and the inferior of these are petty kings, while the superior ones are iron wheel-rulers of one continent" (827b14–15).[69] Beings who have trod this path are then reborn possessing acquired lineage and become "copper wheel-rulers of two continents." Those who have advanced to the innate lineage are "silver wheel-rulers of three continents," while those of the lineage of the Way become full *cakravartins* of all four continents (827b16–17).

68. The scheme of two "seed-natures," that which is "acquired" (*hsi-chung-hsing*, Sanskrit *samudānīta gotra*) and that which is "innate" (*hsing-chung-hsing*, Sanskrit *prakṛitistha gotra*), is found in *Bodhisattvabhūmi* (T 1581, 30.888a–889b), as well as in later works such as Hsüan-tsang's translation of the *Yogācārabhūmi* (*Yü-chieh shih-ti lun*, T 1579 30.478b–480b). Rendering *chung-hsing* as "seed-nature" is awkward, so I have opted for rendering it as "lineage." The term certainly calls to mind "lineage," but Chinese usually use the word *tsu* when referring to ascent and descent. Ruegg has a helpful discussion in *La théorie du Tathāgatagarbha et du Gotra*, esp. pp. 86–94, 185–88. Also relevant are the Waymans' *Lion's Roar of Queen Śrīmālā;* Jikidō Takasaki's study and translation of the *Ratnagotravibhāga*, *A Study on the Ratnagotravibhāga;* S. K. Hookham's *The Buddha Within: Tathāgatagarbha Doctrine According to the Shentong Interpretation of the Ratnagotravibhāga* (Albany: State University of New York Press, 1991); and Sallie B. King, *Buddha Nature* (Albany: State University of New York Press, 1991). Early Chinese thinkers were heavily influenced by synthetic works such as the *Nirvana Scripture* and the *Laṅkāvatāra* and they tended to mix Yogācāra and *Tathāgatagarbha* thought. For a brief overview, see Paul, *Philosophy of Mind in Sixth-Century China*, esp. pp. 46–48 and 132–33.

69. These "petty kings" "scattered like rice" may indeed be a reference to the figure of Mahāsammatha, the "great elect" who brings order out of chaos in "Aggañña suttanta" of the *Dīghanikāya*.

The "acquired lineage" (*hsi-chung-hsing*) and the "innate lineage" (*hsing-chung-hsing*) are Chinese translations of the Sanskrit terms *samudānīta gotra* and *prakṛitishtha gotra*. According to the *Bodhisattvabhūmi*, innate lineages "are termed innate because they are attained through the nature of things as regards the developing continuities [of sentient beings] from beginningless time. Lineages attained by practice are so called because they are attained through a series of cultivating good roots from the start" (T 1579 30.478c).[70] Yogācāra and *Tathāgatagarbha* texts like the *Bodhisattvabhūmi*, *Ratnagotravibhāga*, and the *Śrimālādevi sūtra* employ these distinctions.

In India the language of "lineage" implies some innate and substantive distinction among beings. It appears to have been adopted by Buddhists as a strategy for endowing low-caste Hindu converts with a lineage parallel to that asserted by the three higher castes.[71] Early Mahāyāna usage of "lineage" is designed to emphasize the discontinuity between the two "Hīnayāna" vehicles of the *Śrāvakayāna* ("the vehicle of the Auditors") and the *Pratyekabuddhayāna* ("the vehicle of the solitary Buddha") and that of the bodhisattvas of the Mahāyāna ("the great vehicle"). Thus, in texts such as the *Mahāvyutpatti* and the *Bodhisattvabhūmi* individuals are typed according to their lineage. Those with *śrāvaka* lineage will become *śrāvaka*, and so forth.[72] This use of the language of lineage is clearly *rupic*, personal, and discontinuous. However, Mahāyāna texts that emphasize the ultimate single vehicle (Sanskrit *ekayāna*) use the language of lineage to explain various levels on a single, continuous path.

In the *Scripture for Humane Kings* the acquired lineage and the innate lineage are coupled to the term "lineage of the Way." Indeed, the "lineage of the Way" (*Tao-chung-hsing*) has no equivalent in South Asian scriptures. It is, however, found in the *Scripture of the Original Acts That Serve as Necklaces for Bodhisattvas* (*P'u-sa ying-lo pen-yeh ching*, T 1485), a Chinese scripture modeled in part on the *Scripture for Humane Kings*, which has a five-lineage system.[73] "Lineage" is also—and most obviously—a key concern in Chinese culture. As we shall see, Buddhism was perceived by many Chinese as destructive to the family, the state, and to cosmic order itself. Thus, while this system of lineage carries with it a strong flavor of discontinuity between types or lineages of beings, and while questions of lineage raise disturbing issues for many Chinese, the entire system is subsumed into another system: that of the five forbearances.

70. Quoted in Paul J. Griffiths et al., *The Realm of Awakening*, p. 88 n. 37. I have not tried to improve on the translation. Simply put, innate *gotra* is the result of deeds in previous existences. Acquired *gotra* is the result of good deeds practiced in the present life.

71. See Dayal, *Bodhisattva Doctrine*, pp. 51–52.

72. Ibid., pp. 52–53 and 75–76, on the different "work" (*caryā*) of each *gotra*.

73. T 1485 24.101b25–26.

By far the most glaring anomaly in the path outlined in the *Scripture for Humane Kings* is its transformation of the six perfections into variations on the perfection of forbearance (*jen*, Sanskrit *kṣānti*):

> The Buddha said, "Great King, the five forbearances are the ***bodhisattva*** teachings: forbearance of self-control, [in] superior, intermediate, and inferior [levels], forbearance of [firm] belief, [in] superior, intermediate, and inferior [levels], forbearance of obedience, [in] superior, intermediate, and inferior [levels], forbearance of the birthlessness [of constituents in] superior, intermediate, and inferior [levels], and forbearance of quiescent extinction, [in] superior and inferior [levels]. These are what are called the cultivation of the ***Prajñāpāramitā*** by all Buddhas and ***bodhisattva***s. (8.826b21–c28)[74]

While wisdom is often given the status of first among equals in its pairing with skillfull means (*upāya*) or compassion (*karuṇā*) in Transcendent Wisdom scriptures, the *Scripture for Humane Kings* presents the entire path under the rubric of "five forbearances" (*wu-jen*), which are ultimately subdivided to yield "fourteen forbearances" (*shih-ssu jen*). No other Transcendent Wisdom text and, for that matter, no other Mahāyāna text, does this.

This collapsing of the path into a single virtue is not fully compatible with the division of the first forbearance into the practice of the ten virtues and the three lineages. Indeed, the scripture is ambiguous here. The following extended passage underscores the intimate link between the five forbearances and the three lineages:

> Good sons, initially arousing the signs of trust, beings [numerous as] the sands of the ***Gaṅgā*** cultivate the forbearance of self-control, and before the three jewels they produce the ten minds characteristic of the acquired lineage. [The ten minds are now listed, as in T 246.] Having accomplished this ***bodhisattva***s are able, within a limited scope, to transform beings [and they have] transcended the two vehicles and all the good stages. All Buddhas and ***bodhisattva***s have cultivated the ten minds which are the womb of the sages.
>
> Next [they] arouse the dry wisdom[75] of the innate lineage [already] possessed of the ten minds. That is, the four-fold mental stopping,[76]

74. Dayal, *Bodhisattva Doctrine*, covers *kṣānti-pāramitā* on pp. 209–16.

75. "Dry wisdom" (*kan-hui*, Pāli *paññāvimutti*, *sukha-vipassanā*) tends to indicate one who has attained certain meditative insight but who has not attained the five penetrations (Pāli, *abhiññā*). For a discussion of the term, see Katz, *Buddhist Images of Human Perfection*, pp. 81, 78–83, and Chi-tsang, T 1707 33.329a27–b12.

76. *Ssu-i-chih*.

> [viz. that the] body, feelings, mind, and constituents are impure, painful, impermanent, and selfless. The three-fold mental stopping,[77] that is the three eras: forbearance concerning past causes, forbearance concerning present causes and fruits, and forbearance concerning future fruit. These ***bodhisattvas***, moreover, are able to transform all beings and they are already able to transcend the view of self and of beings and other such thoughts, and even heterodox and inverted thoughts are unable to ruin them.
>
> Next there are the ten stages of the lineage of the Way. These contemplate form, intellect, mind, feelings, and actions and attain the forbearance of discipline, the forbearance of view, the forbearance of fixed [concentration], the forbearance of wisdom, and the forbearance of liberation. [They] contemplate the causes and fruits of the triple world [and attain] the forbearance of emptiness, the forbearance of wishlessness, the forbearance of signlessness, and contemplate the two truths and the voidness of reality. [Knowing that] all constituents are impermanent, is called the forbearance of impermanence. [Knowing that] all constituents are empty [they] attain the forbearance of birthlessness. These ***bodhisattvas*** of the ten firm minds are wheel-turning kings and, moreover, [they] are able to transform the four [continents of the] world and produce the good roots of all beings. (8.826b25–c10)

The *Scripture for Humane Kings* argues for the salvation of all beings and underscores the kinship of all lineages by saying that "all Buddhas and ***bodhisattvas*** nurture the ten minds which are the womb of the sages," and that:

> [those in] the intermediate and inferior grades of good [faith] are kings scattered like grain,[78]
> and those in the superior grade of the ten good faiths are iron wheel-rulers.
> Those of the acquired lineage are copper wheel-rulers of two continents,
> and the silver wheel-rulers of three continents are of the innate lineage.
> Those of the lineage of the Way, firm in merit, are *cakravartins* whose seven treasures illuminate the four continents.
> These thirteen [*sic*] persons are in the womb of the sages which is the forbearance of self-control. (T 245 8.827b15–18)

The use of the lineage scheme in the *Scripture for Humane Kings* establishes a

77. *San-i-chih*.

78. One wonders if the "kings scattered like grain" (*su-san wang*) are an oblique reference to Mahāsammata from the *Dīghanikāya*. The word "grain" (*su*) has the extended meaning "tithe" and calls to mind the tithe of rice given to the king to maintain order in the time of the End of the Teaching.

taxonomic discontinuity among the lineages, and between the lineages and those practicing the ten virtues on the one hand, and those on the bodhisattva path on the other. Thus, petty kings have not yet firmly established a lineage and "like a feather blown hither and thither" they can backslide (831b7–8).

The order of the assembly described at the opening of the scripture reflects these discontinuities, first listing in *ascending* order those on the path who have *already* acquired a lineage (*bhikṣu/arhats*); those of the innate lineage (*pratyeka-buddhas*); and those of the lineage of the Way (*bodhisattva-mahāsattvas*), comprising the three vehicles and the three lineages. The list then proceeds in *descending* order to list "worthies adhering to the five (lay) precepts" (*wu-chieh hsien*), women of pure faith adhering to the five precepts who are *arhats*, those in the seven "worthy" stages (*chi-hsien chu*), the nine *brahmadevas*, the various gods and "sons of heaven" (*t'ien-tzu*) of the desire realm, the kings of the sixteen great states and their entourages, and all the other beings of the five destinies. These beings are still striving to acquire a lineage. The kings of the sixteen states (to whom the scripture is entrusted) are next to last in the secondary of the two lists. Finally the scripture lists the "transformations of the Pure Lands" and the "Buddhas and their retinues" from these lands, all of whom are, of course, of the lineage of the Way.

For the moment I would like to call attention to the "lowly" kings who practice pious acts. These pious acts which support the Saṃgha and its teaching mission are described as the "womb of the sages." In other words, such acts are the beginning of the path for all beings and represent a sort of continuity with later stages of the path. Yet such kings *have not yet surely established a lineage* and can backslide. The ambivalent position of these kings is underscored by the five forbearances, which constitute the overall framework of the path. Once again there is a fundamental *kinship* not only between petty rulers and the great *cakravartins* but also between all rulers and the advanced bodhisattvas. All are practicing "forbearance." The correlate of this position is that the ten bodhisattva stages proper are proclaimed kings:

> If a **bodhisattva** abides in one hundred Buddha-states[79] he becomes the king of the four [continents] of ***Jambudvīpa,***[80] and cultivating one-

79. Where the eighth-century text reads Buddha-*kṣetra*, the fifth-century text specifies a Buddha-state (*fo-kuo*). A Buddha-*kṣetra* is a Buddha-land, that is, the cosmological locale which is the karmic "reward" for the bodhisattva's great deeds. The classic treatment of Buddha-*kṣetra* is Teresina Rowel, "The Background and Early Use of the Buddha-Kṣetra Concept," *Eastern Buddhist* 6 (1933): 191–246, 379–431; and 7 (1936): 131–45.

80. In traditional Buddhist cosmology Jambudvīpa is the continent where "India" is located. For this and the following cosmological locales, see Kloetzli, *Buddhist Cosmology*, esp. the charts on pp. 32–39. Chi-tsang makes it quite clear that a king's land is a transformation and recompense for his meritorious deeds. See Chi-tsang, T 1707 33.334a4–16 and 335a7–8.

> hundred Teachings [he uses] the mind of equanimity of the two truths to transform all beings.
>
> If a ***bodhisattva*** dwells in one thousand Buddha-states he becomes the god-king of the ***Trāyastriṃśās***,[81] and cultivating one thousand Teachings, [he uses] the ten good paths to transform all beings. (8.827a9–13)[82]

And so on up to the state of complete Buddhahood. By terming all on the path, from petty kings through Buddhas as "kings" (*wang*), the *Scripture for Humane Kings* erases with one hand the distinction between bodhisattvas (we can for all practical purposes read "monks" here) and kings. Bodhisattvas are indeed kings, and all rule "lands" of sizes proportional to their stage of practice and lineage. The result is that kingship ceases to function as what Bruce Lincoln has termed a "taxonomizer."[83] Instead, the taxonomizers are related to advancement on the path characterized by the ten faiths and the lineages.

Thus kings may be understood as bodhisattvas and vice versa, while at the same time, they may be sharply distinguished from and subordinated to "bodhisattvas," since they have not yet firmly acquired a lineage. In the first instance the hierarchy is based on *rupic* continuity. In the second it is based on *rupic* discontinuity. The scripture thus facilitates simultaneous differential interpretation. The long-term success of the *Scripture for Humane Kings*, I would argue, hinged on this quality. P. Steven Sangren has argued that such ambiguity is fundamental to Chinese social relationships: "In the politics of Chinese social relations, this contextual shifting is expedient precisely because it provides a means for both parties in a relationship to understand the nature of their relationship differently."[84] As we shall see in Chapter 4, this understanding is based on practice.

This taxonomic sleight of hand whereby kings may be understood both as outsiders who have not firmly established their Buddhist "credentials" and as "bodhisattvas" on the path of the five forbearances is instantiated by the homophonic play on the word *jen*. The *Scripture for Humane Kings* draws a *parallel* between kings who nurture or protect (*hu*) their states and bodhisattvas who nurture and protect (*hu*) the Buddha-fruit.[85] Thus both kings and bodhisatt-

81. The heaven located atop Mt. Meru, its lord is Śakra or Indra.

82. The ten good paths or acts are not killing, stealing, committing adultery, lying, uttering harsh words or words that cause enmity, not gossiping, being greedy, angry, or entertaining wrong views. Compare the translation of the eighth-century text.

83. Lincoln, *Discourse and the Construction of Society*, pp. 131–41.

84. P. Steven Sangren's *History and Magical Power in a Chinese Community* (Stanford: Stanford University Press, 1987), p. 185, amounts to an extended meditation on this quality of Chinese social relations.

85. The words we pronounce *hu* in modern Mandarin were homophones in Ancient Chinese. For more on this, see the discussion in Chapter 4.

vas nourish and protect their offspring. This "nourishing" analogy, which is developed by commentators in the hermeneutical scheme of inner and outer "nourishing" or "protection," is coupled with the statement that the preparatory stages of the path constituted by the Ten Faiths are trod by common kings and are the "womb of the sages," thus implying that kings are the maternal "womb" in which the seed of the Buddha-fruit is nurtured. Kings are then likened to mothers, bodhisattvas to embryos, and Buddhas are thereby given birth. Kings, then, are *Tathāgatagarbha*. This identity further enables interesting hermeneutical possibilities; *Tathāgatagarbha* texts interpret the *Tathāgatagarbha* both as the container of the embryo of Buddhahood *and* as the embryo itself. Thus the role of kings is to be protectors and guardians—or mothers—of the Saṃgha. At the same time the practices characteristic of kingship—particularly the protection of the Teaching—lead to the acquisition of Buddhist lineage (*hsi-chung-hsing*) and realization of one's innate Buddhahood (*hsing-chung-hsing*) and thus to full deployment of the Way (the practices and progress of the bodhisattva, *tao-chung-hsing*).[86] The scheme of the five forbearances sets out a *continuous* progress from king through Buddha, and through it effectively erases the taxonomic line between bodhisattvas and kings. But the lineage scheme clearly indicates that petty kings as yet have not firmly acquired a lineage. Here a stark *discontinuity* exists and acquisition of a lineage is possible only through a regimen of flamboyant giving (Sanskrit *dāna*). But at the same time the protection analogy sets up a *parallel* development of inner and outer nourishing in which certain acts are seeds which bear fruit, and these acts, seeds, and fruit are congruent but *not continuous*, invoking the other interpretation of *Tathāgatagarbha* as container but *not* the embryo contained. These relationships are schematized as follows:

Discontinuous Interpretation

Kings: bodhisattva/monks :: no *gotra* : *gotra*
outer : inner
womb : embryo
humaneness : forbearance
dāna (giving) : *prajñā* (wisdom)

Continuous Interpretation

Kings *are* bodhisattva/monks :: all are born from forbearance/womb of the sages
outer *is* inner
womb *is* embryo
humaneness *is* forbearance
dāna (giving) *is* *prajñā* (wisdom)

86. Such hermeneutical coupling is, of course, found in the familiar "two wheels of the Dharma" scheme and is prominent in the *Aśokāvadāna* and ultimately rests on the ambiguous relationships between *kṣatriya* and Brahmin castes.

In typical Buddhist fashion this double *rupic* world of kings/bodhisattvas, the temporal decay of the teaching and the notion of lineage, is packaged in the *dharmic* proclamation of emptiness and the Two Truths, forming a nicely recursive package. To realize the emptiness of all *dharmas*, to approach the edge of reality, is also to proclaim and progress upon the path of kings/bodhisattvas. Advancement on the path of kings/bodhisattvas evident in proper practice turns back the End of the Teaching, and establishes the Correct Teaching in the vision of true emptiness and the edge of reality. Forbearance is simultaneously path and goal. Thus the scripture plays on simultaneous continuities and discontinuities in the path to open up the possibility of simultaneous yet different interpretations of kings and bodhisattvas. With this gap the *Scripture for Humane Kings* has created an opportunity to weld together two quite hostile worldviews and polities in a recursive manner. As we shall see, the conjunction of these interlocking schemes at the foundation of the *Scripture for Humane Kings* makes possible a differential understanding of the relationships between monks and the government while it simultaneously supports the thesis that all alike are kings. Both may claim precedence though a differential deployment of the hermeneutical schemes in the text. The conjunction or disjunction of the categories of king and bodhisattva in the text is symptomatic of a deeper taxonomic issue, an issue of 'lineage' or *hsing*, and whether one could be both "Buddhist" and "Chinese." This taxonomic issue is at once *the* issue of the fifth and sixth centuries and the very heart of the *Scripture for Humane Kings*.

4

The End of the Teaching and the Creation of Chinese Buddhism

> After the five turbulent eras ***bhikṣu, bhikṣuṇī,*** the four classes of disciples, the heavenly dragons and all of the eight-fold spirit-kings, the kings of states, the great officers, the heirs apparent and princes will be haughty [and hold themselves in] great esteem and extinguish and smash my Teaching. . . . You should know at that time that it will not be long before the Correct Teaching is about to be extinguished.
>
> —*Scripture for Humane Kings* (T 245 833b17–25)

Language and Authority in the *Scripture for Humane Kings*

The seam at the heart of the *Scripture for Humane Kings* brings together *dharmic* imagery with continuous *and* discontinuous *rupic* imagery. It uses the language of Transcendent Wisdom and lineage to join rulers and bodhisattvas in a fraternity of the path of forbearance while simultaneously invoking an interpretation of kings as nurturing of but subservient to the saṃgha. Kings and bodhisattvas both are and are not alike, and both are linked to the *dharmic* imagery of the edge of reality. This complex recursive strategy is epitomized by the terms "humane/forbearing," and these terms are linked to the circumstances of the scripture's composition. In this chapter I trace the relationship between forbearance (Chinese *jen*[a], Sanskrit *kṣānti*) and the Confucian virtue of humaneness (*jen*[b]).[1] The conjunction of these terms leads us beyond the text of the *Scripture for Humane Kings* to its context in the assimilation debates in fifth-century north China. Finally, I show how the *Scripture for Humane Kings* played a significant role in the rise of the first truly Chinese school of Buddhism, Chih-i's T'ien-t'ai.

As I have shown, the *Scripture for Humane Kings* is unique in its eccentric elevation of the perfection of forbearance (*jen po-lo-mi*, Sanskrit *kṣānti pāramitā*) as *the* key perfection of the path and in its taxonomy of lineages. These eccentricities point beyond the confines of the text and its theological models to the circumstances of its composition. The very language of the text's title leads directly to a crucial social and ideological issue.

In contrast to normative Transcendent Wisdom scriptures the *Scripture for Humane Kings* subsumes the entire bodhisattva path under a scheme of five forbearances, which are subdivided into fourteen forbearances. The title of the scripture does not use the term forbearance (*jen*[a]), however, but rather the homophonous word "humane" (*jen*[b]). The ambiguous relationship between kings and bodhisattvas has already been noted, but this ambiguity is made more cogent by the pun on words that to this day remains homophonous in Mandarin—*jen*—and which were both pronounced *ńźi̯ĕn* in Six Dynasties and T'ang times.[2] While the content of the scripture describes forbearing kings and

1. The word *jen* should not be translated as "benevolent." For an insightful discussion of the etymology and translation of the term, see Peter Alexis Boodberg, "The Semasiology of Some Primary Confucian Concepts," in *Selected Works of Peter A. Boodberg*, comp. Alvin P. Cohen (Berkeley and Los Angeles: University of California Press, 1979), pp. 36–38. Also see Victor Mair's comments in *Tao Te Ching*, p. 107. Tu Wei-ming has an excellent discussion of the term in two articles, "The Creative Tension Between Jen and Li" and "Li as a Process of Humanization," in *Humanity and Self-Cultivation: Essays in Confucian Thought* (Berkeley: Asian Humanities Press, 1979), pp. 5–16 and 17–34. It is notable that while many Chinese Buddhist scriptures draw heavily on Taoist terminology, the *Scripture for Humane Kings*, with only minor exceptions, focuses on the language of virtuous kingship which had long been associated with (though not the sole property of) Confucian state ideology.

2. Bernard Karlgren and others have reconstructed the pronunciations of archaic and ancient Chinese in part by an examination of ancient rhyming dictionaries. The T'ang Dynasty pronunciation of the term has been reconstructed as ˛ńźi̯ĕn and ʻńźi̯ĕn for *jen* and *jen*. Bernhard Karlgren's *Analytic Dictionary of Chinese and Sino-Japanese* (Paris: Librairie Orientaliste Paul Geunther, 1923; reprint, New York: Dover, 1974), p. 271. Also see his *Grammatica Serica Recensa* (Stockholm: Museum of Far Eastern Antiquities, 1964 reprint of the Bulletin of the Museum of Far Eastern Antiquities, no. 29, 1957), no. 388 **nien*, p. 110, and no. 456 *nien*, p. 125. The *Pronouncing Dictionary of Chinese Characters in Archaic and Ancient Chinese, Mandarin, and Cantonese* (Hong Kong: Chinese University of Hong Kong Press, 1979), gives the same reading based on Karlgren's work. We can be assured that the words were homophones because of this linguistic work and because commentaries obviously presume this. Several other words indicate a possible use of rhyme, assonance, and consonance to heighten the effect. These include the words *hua* (Chou: **xua*), *Fo* (Chou: **biuət*), *kuo* (Chou: **kua*), *kuo* (*kuək*), and *hu* (Chou: **yo*). Thus, to *yo kuək* and to *yo kua* have a good chance of having been deliberately alike in sound, though we may never know for certain. For the most recent work on T'ang pronunciation the reader should consult Edwin G. Pulleyblank, *Lexicon of Reconstructed Pronunciation in Early Middle*

bodhisattvas and seldom uses the term "humane," its title evokes humane kings, and in this linguistic fortuity lies much of the power and brilliance of the work.[3] Fully to appreciate this pun we need to explore the connotations of the phrase humane kings (*jen-wang*) in fifth-century China.

The particular locution "humane kings" (*jen-wang*) is almost entirely absent from classical Chinese literature before the sixth century, and all evidence points to the *Scripture for Humane Kings* as its source. While the first appearance of the phrase "humane king" in the official histories is in the sixth century (*Liu-*) *Sung shu*, the individual terms "humane" and "forbearing" are ubiquitous. *Daikanwa jiten* contains a full eight pages of definitions for "humane" and two pages for "forbearing."[4] Of works in the classical canon *Shih-chi* (the *Book of Poetry*) uses the word *jen* the least, amounting to two occurrences of each term. There, "humane" first occurs in the "Shu yu t'ien":

> To the hunt Shu has gone, / And people there are none
> Remaining in the street. / Perhaps a few you'll find;
> But none like Shu *so kind*, / So graceful, will you meet.[5]

Jen occurs only once more, again with the same sense of "kindness."[6] *Jen* or "forbearing" is also found in the "Hsiao pien," where it has the sense of "callous," and in "Sang jou," where it means "hard-hearted" or "indifferent."[7] Only later does the term take on the more positive meaning of forbearing.

Once we look past the early material of the *Shih-chi* to works more pointedly didactic in intent, we find the term "humane" among the most important in the classical Chinese moral vocabulary. In the *Analects*, in *Mencius*, and so forth it becomes the much-sought *summum bonum*, or as Legge often translates it, "perfect virtue." The *Analects* portray humaneness as the central teaching of Confucius:

Chinese, Late Middle Chinese, and Early Mandarin (Vancouver: University of British Columbia Press, 1991), *nin*, p. 265, and *Middle Chinese: A Study in Historical Phonology* (Vancouver: University of British Columbia Press, 1984), and his remarks on Karlgren's work and work based on it in his review article, "The Reconstruction of Han Dynasty Chinese," *Journal of the American Oriental Society*, 105.2 (1985): 303–8. I also treat evidence from relevant commentaries below.

3. The term "forbearing" is ubiquitous in the scripture. Aside from titles, the term "humane" appears only three times in the body of the scripture; twice at the end of chapter 4 (T 245 8.829c16, 22) and once in chapter 5 (T 245 8.830b19).

4. *Daikanwa jiten*, 1.577c–584d and 4.955a–957a.

5. Translation by James Legge, *The Book of Poetry: Chinese Text with English Translation*, (China: The Commercial Press, n.d.), p. 89. The phrase is *mei ch'ieh jen*, roughly "kindly and fair"; the emphasis is mine.

6. Ibid., p. 113 ("Lu ling"), in the same phrase "kindly and fair" *mei ch'ieh jen*.

7. Ibid., pp. 255–57, 391–93.

> The Master said, "I have not seen a person who loved virtue [*jen*], or one who hated what was not virtuous. He who loved virtue would esteem nothing above it. He who hated what is not virtuous, would practise virtue in such a way that he would not allow anything that is not virtuous to approach his person."[8]

Indeed, in the *Analects* humaneness subsumes all the other virtues, just as in the *Scripture for Humane Kings* forbearance subsumes all the other bodhisattva virtues.[9] Hall and Ames, in their recent probing of the ethical and religious meanings of the *Analects*, choose to render *jen* as "authoritative person." They point out that prior to its prominent use in the *Analects*, *jen* is unimportant.[10] Citing Peter Boodberg's work on the term, they argue for a dynamic, socially lived definition of *jen* that denotes the "qualitative transformation of the person and achievement of authoritative humanity."[11] The *Mencius* so abounds with discussions of humaneness, kingship, and forbearance that one can hardly read the *Scripture for Humane Kings* without thinking of it. We read, for instance, that "he who, using virtue, practices humaneness is the sovereign of the kingdom," that "the humane man [*jen*[b] *jen*[c]] has no enemy under heaven," that "all men have some things which they cannot bear [*jen*[a]];—extend that feeling to what they can bear, and humaneness will be the result."[12] In another passage humaneness, forbearance, and man come together in praise of the earliest kings: "When they exerted to the utmost the thoughts of their hearts, they called in to their aid a government that could not endure [*jen*[a]] to witness the sufferings of men [*jen*[c]]:—and their humaneness [*jen*[b]] overspread the kingdom."[13]

While humaneness became the all-encompassing characteristic of the "authoritative" and integrated person for the Confucian tradition, it was not without detractors. The *Tao-te ching* pointedly says, "Abolish humaneness and abandon righteousness, the people will once again be filial and kind."[14] Certainly, after the fall of the Han and during the centuries prior to the compo-

8. James Legge, *Confucius* (1893; reprint, New York: Dover, 1971), p. 167, bk. 4, chap. 6.

9. Munro notes that it occurs in 58 of the 499 chapters of the *Analects*, and that "human-heartedness" comes to encompass all the individual virtues. Munro, *Concept of Man in Early China*, pp. 28–29.

10. David L. Hall and Roger T. Ames, *Thinking Through Confucius* (Albany: State University of New York Press, 1987), pp. 111–13. The authors critique modern psychologizing of the term by Ch'an and others as well as its objectivization by Fingarette.

11. Ibid., p. 114.

12. Legge, p. 196 (translating *Mencius*, bk. 2, pt. 1, chap. 3.1; p. 479 (translating bk. 6, pt. 2, chap. 3.3); and p. 493 (translating bk. 7, pt. 2, chap. 31.1). Here and below I have substituted "humaneness" where Legge uses "benevolence," and I have supplied the Chinese in brackets.

13. Legge, *Mencius*, p. 290, translating bk. 4, pt. 1, chap. 1.5.

14. "Kind" (*tz'u*) in this case does not render "forbearing" (*jen*). See Mair's translation of the *Tao Te Ching* 63 (19), p. 81.

sition of the *Scripture for Humane Kings* Confucian virtues had a dedicated following, or at least there was a cadre of officials who found the incantation of these terms legitimating. But we must not lose sight of the fact that the terms were heavily freighted and of questionable utility.

The word "forbearing" (*jen*[a]), as we have seen in the *Shih-chi*, is sometimes meant in the sense opposite of caring, or compassionate.[15] Yet it also commonly occurs as "patient," or "enduring," as in the *Kuan-tzu*.[16] It is in this latter sense that it translates the Sanskrit term *kṣānti*, "patient endurance" or "forbearance," in Buddhist *Jātaka* tales. Indeed, an early translation renders "Śākyamuni" as "[he who is] able to forbear" (*neng-jen*). Hsi Ch'ao (336–77) writes in his "Convert's Vademecum" (*Feng fa-yao*):

> It is said in the *Ch'a-mo-chieh ching*: "Of all the (virtues) practiced by the bodhisattva, that of forbearance . . . is the greatest. If he is scolded and abused he will be silent and not answer; if he is beaten and punched, he will undergo it without joining issue. If he meets with anger and hatred, he will face (his opponents) with tenderness; if he is slandered, he will not think about the evil (of their words)." It is also said in the *Fa-chü ching*: "The forbearing heart is like earth; the practice of forbearance is like a threshold." This is because (the earth and the threshold) hold the dust and receive (all) impurities, and always (patiently) bear being trodden upon.[17]

But such assertions of identity between Buddhist and Confucian values were not to be found in authoritative *Buddha vaccana* until the advent of the *Scripture for Humane Kings* a full century after Hsi Ch'ao.

The genius of the *Scripture for Humane Kings* lay, in part, in the use of homophony to encode the ambiguous relationship between kings and monks, and between Confucian and Buddhist virtues. Paradoxically, Buddhism and Confucianism have the same goal; forbearing Buddhists and humane kings are identically "authoritative persons." The linguistic resonance between humaneness and forbearance was further enhanced by a similar turn of phrase linking bodhisattvas who protect the Buddha-fruit (*hu Fo-kuo*) with kings who protect their states (*hu-kuo*), both of whom "transform" (*hua*) the people. This linguistic strategy calls to mind the recursive relationship between the temporal and the timeless, between the End of the Teaching and the Correct Teaching.

15. Thus, in the *Kuo yü* it is defined as the opposite of righteousness (*I*) and of compassionate (*tzu*). See *Daikanwa jiten*, 4.955a.

16. *Daikanwa jiten*, 4.955a.

17. Quoted in Zürcher, *Buddhist Conquest of China*, 1:170, with minor modifications.

The role of such deliberate linguistic coincidences—"puns"—has attracted relatively little attention from scholars of religion. Work that has been done has largely been carried on in psychology and anthropology. Freud wrote extensively on "wit," jokes and puns as displacements of and disguised manifestations of conflicts that have been repressed into the unconscious mind. This unconscious "ambivalence" acts subversively through the structure of conscious expression.[18] Building on Freud's work, the anthropologist Mary Douglas examined joking rituals and puns, and she contends that such matters are funny precisely because there is a hidden, antihierarchical meaning or a reverse hierarchy concealed in a normally accepted structure or turn of phrase. Juxtaposition and context reveal this hidden subversion.[19]

In the case of a pun, language is used simultaneously to reveal and to conceal. A word functions in its normal role while undermining that role with an alternative interpretation. The alternative interpretation refers to and is dependent on the "normal" meaning for its existence and vice versa. There are "inner" and "outer" meanings, neither of which can exist without the other and which refer to one another in a recursive manner. Once raised to consciousness, the simultaneous duality and singularity of meaning is inescapable. Or, in the words of the *Scripture for Humane Kings*, "If a **bodhisattva** sees beings, sees one [truth] or sees two [truths] this certainly is not seeing one and not seeing two. This 'one' and 'two' is the Preeminent Truth" (829b26–27). Like the paradox of *saṃsāra* and nirvana and the paradox of the Two Truths, humane/forbearing is, in a peculiarly Buddhist way, a joke. Simultaneous and differential interpretations are generated from the same "text." In the *Scripture for Humane Kings*, the Transcendent Wisdom of forbearing bodhisattvas and the humaneness of the sage-kings of Confucian antiquity are joined in an ambivalent embrace.

The import of this linguistic convergence was not lost on Buddhist commentators. Liang-pi, a contemporary of Pu-k'ung who aided in producing the eighth-century recension of the text, writes in his *Commentary on the Scripture for Humane Kings*:

> The word humane [*jen*[b]] is equivalent to the word person [*jen*[c]]. This is because the correct understanding of "person" is "one who is anxious [about relations]." Therefore he thinks of relations. According to the

18. Sigmund Freud, "Wit and Its Relations to the Unconscious," in *The Basic Writings of Sigmund Freud,* trans. and ed. A. A. Brill (New York: Modern Library, 1938), pp. 633–803, but esp. 636–37, 649ff., and 655ff.

19. Mary Douglas, "The Social Control of Cognition: Some Factors in Joke Perception," *Man*, n.s., 3.3 (1968): 361–76. The subversion can be overt, as Bruce Lincoln has pointed out in his study of political slogans in *Discourse and the Construction of Society*, pp. 17–26.

> "Ta-chuan" of the *Shu-ching*, Shun did not seek prominence, yet was lofty, he did not go [abroad in the world], yet he was [cognizant of what was] distant, He was reverent toward heaven and heaven was humane. The *Li chi* [*Book of Rites*] says: Mutual filiality above and below is referred to as humaneness. (T 1709 33.434c22)

Clearly, for Liang-pi the scripture's title intends an identification with the traditional Confucian sage-king, whose virtue is centered in relations in society and the virtuous transformation of that society. As I have shown, a key assertion of the *Scripture for Humane Kings* is that bodhisattvas are kings, and they cultivate qualities that protect and nurture their eventual achievement of Buddhahood, qualities which are founded on the succor and transformation of all sentient beings. Conversely, kings tread the bodhisattva path.

In the Buddhist context the pun on humaneness/forbearance is enhanced by its allusion to one of the most famous of *Jātaka* tales—one widely known in China—"The Preacher of Forbearance" (*Kṣāntivadijātaka*).[20] In this tale, the king of Kāśī brutally tortures the Buddha in his previous incarnation as an ascetic practitioner of the *kṣānti-pāramitā* (*jen-p o-lo-mi*). The ascetic, hacked into a bloody mass by the king's henchmen, proves his inner mastery of forbearance, refusing to become angry at this injustice. The king, however, has demonstrated his complete lack of mastery over others or over himself.

The *Scripture for Humane Kings* bridges the Buddhist and Confucian contexts in a series of strikingly "personal" linguistic parallels. Both "humane kings" and "kings of forbearance" "transform" (*hua*) the people. Both "cultivate," "nurture," or "protect" (*hu*) their "states" (*kuo, ti*, Sanskrit *bhūmi*). Various commentaries on the *Scripture for Humane Kings* take this linguistic bridge as a starting point in elucidating a deep structural continuity between true Confucian kingship or "outer protection" (*wai-hu*) and the pursuit of enlightenment of "inner protection" (*nei-hu*). According to an early T'ang commentary (attributed falsely to the T'ien-t'ai master Chih-i):

> Because the humane king is he who explicates the Teaching and disseminates virtue here below he is called "humane." Because he has transformed himself he is called "king." The humane king's ability is to protect [*hu*]. What is protected is the state. This is possible because the humane king uses the Teaching to order the state. Now if we con-

20. For this tale see H. T. Francis and E. B. Cowell, eds., *The Jātaka* (London: Luzac, 1969), 3:26–29. For a study of this *Jātaka*, see Graeme MacQueen, "The Conflict Between External and Internal Mastery: An Analysis of the *Khāntivadi Jātaka*," *History of Religion* 20 (February 1981): 242–52. For the tale in China, see E. Chavannes, trans., *Cinq cents contes et apologues extraits du Tripiṭaka chinois* (Paris: Adrien-Maisonneuve, 1962), 4:113–14.

sider the *Prajñā-[pāramitā]*, its ability is to protect. The humane king is he who is protected. Because he uses the *Prajñā-[pāramitā]* the humane king is tranquil and hidden. Thus, if he uses his ability to propagate the Teaching, the king is able to protect [the state], and it is the *Prajñā-[pāramitā]* which is the [method of] protection. Moreover, one who is humane is forbearing [*jen-che jen yeh*]. Hearing of good he is not overjoyed, hearing of bad he is not angry. Because he is able to hold to forbearance in good and bad, therefore he is called forbearing. (T 1705 33.253b28–253c4)

For this unknown T'ien-t'ai commentator of the seventh century the protection and transformation of the "underheaven" (*t'ien-hsia*) is of a piece with the cultivation of forbearance and the transformation of oneself through the teachings of Transcendent Wisdom. Sage-king and bodhisattva cultivate identical qualities and behave in the same way in pursuit of the same goals. Pushing on from personal to the more positional implications of this identity, the commentator underlines the text's emphasis on the identity of the Two Truths and their basis in emptiness (*śūnyatā*):

The origin of this [identity] is in Śākyamuni's Teaching, where he perceived the *dharmas* of all births. Knowing birth one can really see all the *dharmas* of extinction. If [all alike are] extinguished, then [all] are empty. Because of this emptiness the six worlds and so on and the state are immutable and do not change. If the triple world is entirely bound together then the king is tranquil and hidden. This is what the two vehicles have attained and named humane king. (T 1705 33.253c4–9)[21]

Shan-yüeh, a commentator of the Sung dynasty (960–1280), explicates the equivalence differently:

Moreover, the Buddha explains how two words have the same meaning and how homophonous words can be regarded as different. . . . First, as to the four words, "humane kings protect states," this is the important point which gave rise to the scripture. "Humane king" refers to emperors and kings, both ancient and modern who possess Tao. In modern terminology humane is the dissemination of virtue, while the total

21. The notion of the king being "hidden and tranquil" certainly has Taoist overtones and calls to mind the idea of inner sagehood and outer kingdom developed in Kuo-hsiang's treatment of Chuang-tzu. "Seeing the *dharmas* of all births" refers to the "forbearance of the birthlessness" or unoriginated nature of all things (*wu-sheng-jen*, Sanskrit *anutpattikadharmakṣānti*).

> transformation of oneself constitutes kingship. This is especially apparent in the humane king's application of virtue. (T 1706 33.286c6–17)

In this interpretation one who is enlightened ("possesses Tao") has as an inner goal self-transformation, which constitutes true kingship and which necessarily manifests itself in the exterior dissemination of virtue, or humaneness. This notion follows precisely the implications of the *Kṣāntivadijātaka*. The commentators thus make it clear that the pun is more than a mere coincidence of language and that a hidden continuity lies beneath the apparently different goals of kingship and enlightenment. The outer common meaning of the "humane king" involves the transformation of the state, while the inner meaning is the cultivation of Buddhahood and the transformation of oneself. Yet both result in the transformation of all sentient beings through forbearance/humaneness.[22]

What seems initially a facile pun based on the sounds of the words "humane" and "forbearing," is in fact coupled to the recursive relationship signified by the ambiguous terminology of kingship and the path to produce a sophisticated conceptual doubling designed to evoke the deepest structures of both the Buddhist and the Confucian traditions. The humane king has the virtue of forbearance, the sovereign is the saint, and both seek to attain and protect the "state." Both bear the signs of authority. They are different yet the same. Enabled by this *double entendre* rulers could and would use the scripture to bolster their sovereign claims (Liang emperor Wu's doubts notwithstanding). Monks could point to the scripture as evidence of the deep continuity between Buddhism and Confucianism, between monks and emperors, and of the superiority of the former over the latter. But what circumstances could have led to such an assertion of identity in the face of well-established notions to the contrary?

The Problem of Assimilation in Fifth-Century North China

Though the *Scripture for Humane Kings* presents kings and bodhisattvas as cousins, the prophecy of government persecution of the saṃgha which will hasten the End of the Teaching points to darker realities. Prophetic revelations such as these often cloak the immediate past and the present as a vision of the future. In this encoding of political realities we have an opportunity to

22. Recall that the *Nirvana Scripture* regards outer transformation as pertaining to the family and clan, while inner transformation pertains to oneself.

observe the social and historical dynamics that produce such revelations.[23] Indeed, the prophecy of the End of the Teaching in the *Scripture for Humane Kings* marks the creation of a new vision of the Chinese Buddhist state and the emergence of a new taxonomy, in which being both Buddhist and Chinese was not a contradiction.

While the *Scripture for Humane Kings* owes much to the Transcendent Wisdom Scriptures, the *Avataṃsaka*, and the *Nirvana Scripture*, their presence and circulation in the middle of the Six Dynasties period is a necessary but not a sufficient cause of its production. It might even be said that the wide circulation of these Buddhist texts with their elaborate ordering of beings on the path was both a contributing cause of and an answer to a profound sense of disorder.

For many in fifth-century China, a visible sign of chaos was the growing presence and prominence of foreigners and their foreign religion taking root on Chinese soil. What had earlier been a mere curiosity was now perceived as a threat. By the fifth century monks and monasteries were everywhere, yet even their champions saw them as foreign. In 402 the great defender of the Buddhist clergy Hui-yüan wrote to Huan Hsüan, the ruler of North China:

> Even if the Way is not realized its Ritual must always be preserved. If the Ritual is preserved the *dharma* can be propagated, and if the *dharma* can be propagated the Way may be sought. . . . Moreover, the *kaṣāya* is not a garment (fit to be worn) at an imperial audience; the *pātra* is not a vessel [fit to be used] in the palace. Soldiers and civilians [must] have a different appearance; foreigners and the Chinese must not mix [*jung hua pu tsa*]. If [the monastic rules of] people who shave their heads and mutilate their bodies become mingled with the Rites of China [*Hsia chih li*], this is a sign of the mutual interference of different species [*tse shih lei-hsiang she chih hsiang*], something which makes me feel uneasy.[24]

Hui-yüan's defense of the faith, his championing of the rights of clergy to be free from the necessity to venerate family and empire, was argued on the premise that Buddhist and Chinese were exclusive taxonomic species that "must not mix." Between this statement, which was dominant both among Chinese

23. My thinking on this issue has been stimulated by Lawrence E. Sullivan's comments in "The End of Myth: Reflections on the Terminal Character of Beginnings," a public lecture delivered at the University of North Carolina at Chapel Hill, October 30, 1993.

24. Zürcher, *Buddhist Conquest of China*, 1:259, quoting *Hung ming chi* (T 2102 52.84a23–27), compiled by Seng-yu between 515 and 518. The structure of this passage is apparently modeled on the *Ta-hsüeh*. For a translation see Wing-tsit Chan, *A Sourcebook in Chinese Philosophy* (Princeton: Princeton University Press, 1969), pp. 86–87.

and "foreigners" in North China into the early sixth century, and the pronouncements of the *Scripture for Humane Kings* and later of its commentaries in the seventh century, there is a world of difference.[25] In the seventh-century T'ien-t'ai commentary quoted above the homophonous terms *jen* are taken as a sign of a deep harmony between Buddhist and Confucian goals.

But during the four-hundred chaotic years between the fall of the Han after 185 and the rise of the Sui in 618 there was a common belief in the profound distinction or discontinuity between Chinese (*hsia, hua*) and other peoples (*jung, fan*).[26] Nevertheless, the assertion of equivalence between Confucian models of ideal behavior and Buddhist ones was not an invention of the *Scripture for Humane Kings*. Sun Ch'o, for instance, had argued in the fourth century that "[the Duke of] Chou and Confucius are identical with the Buddha; the Buddha is identical with [the Duke of] Chou and Confucius!"[27] Chih Tun's fourth-century introduction to his "Eulogy on an Image of the Buddha Śākyamuni" begins thus: "The way to establish others (in virtue) consists of humaneness (*jen*) and righteousness (*i*); thus the foundation of humaneness and righteousness is that what is meant by the Way and its virtue."[28]

But prior to the sixth century the position staked out by Sun Ch'o and Chih Tun was that of a small minority. The taxonomy was clear, Buddhist and Chinese were mutually exclusive categories, both intellectually and on the ground. Moreover, monks and kings were as compatible as oil and water. This widely held perception of incompatibility cuts across the social and political climate of the Northern Wei (Pei Wei, 424–533), the climate which nurtured the *Scripture for Humane Kings*.

Scholars often speak of the Northern Wei as the precursor of the great unified empire of the Sui and T'ang periods, and they have good reason to do so. Legal systems, city planning, religious festivities, and social structures that emerged during the Northern Wei held sway for hundreds of years and influ-

25. The number of Buddhist foundations in the Northern Wei dynasty remains quite meager until well into the 480s, no doubt a testimony to the persecution of the 440s and 450s and the liberalization of the 480s, of which the *Scripture for Humane Kings* was a part. For figures on monastic foundations, see Jacques Gernet, *Buddhism in Chinese Society: An Economic History from the Fifth to the Tenth Centuries*, trans. Franciscus Verellen (New York: Columbia University Press, 1995), p. 6.

26. The issue of Chinese ethnocentricity, in both ancient and modern times, is the subject of many studies. For the period in question see Zürcher, *Buddhist Conquest of China*, 1:264–80. For an overview, see Wang Gungwu, "Early Ming Relations with Southeast Asia: A Background Essay," in John King Fairbank, ed., *The Chinese World Order: Traditional China's Foreign Relations* (Cambridge: Harvard University Press, 1968), esp. pp. 42–45.

27. The argument is put forward in *Yü tao lun*, which is preserved in *Hung ming chi* (T 2102 54.17a7, the whole context is from 16b–17c). This argument includes issues of humaneness and the role of the Buddha as the cosmic ruler.

28. Quoted with modification from Zürcher, *Buddhist Conquest of China*, 1:177. The allusion is to *Lun-yü* (*Analects*) 4.28.2.

enced the development of societies, morals, and cities as far away as Korea and Japan.

An outline history of the T'o-pa rulers of the Northern Wei is really quite straightforward. Originally the ruling tribe in the Tai state (338–76), the T'o-pa were conquered and dispersed by Fu Chien only to rise again after the fall of the Latter Ch'in (384–417).[29] In a series of wars the T'o-pa unified north China by bringing down the Hsia and the Western Ch'in in 431, and the Northern Liang in 439. In the meantime, campaigns against South China brought it a large part of Honan in 431, including the old capital of Loyang. This, and the growing centrality of Chinese bureaucrats and great families in the empire, set the stage for the move of the capital to Loyang in the last decade of the fifth century, bolstering T'o-pa claims to be the rightful rulers of all of China.[30] Uprisings by non-sinified tribes led to the fragmentation fo the T'o-pa empire into the Northern Ch'i (550–76) and Northern Chou (557–79). It was a former T'o-pa vassal—the future Sui emperor Wen—who went on to unify all of China for the first time in four hundred years.

But this simple outline tells us little about the context of the *Scripture for Humane Kings*. More to the point were changes taking place in the society in the north. As Wolfram Eberhard puts it: "Thus in the years between 440 and 490 there were great changes not only in the economic but in the social sphere. The Toba declined in number and influence. Many of them married into rich families of the Chinese gentry and regarded themselves as no longer belonging to the Toba. In the course of time the court was completely sinified."[31] Indeed, the early preoccupation of the Northern Wei government with a nine-tiered ranking of families was an early symptom of the assimilation problem, and what at the beginning of the century was very much a Central Asian society was by

29. For a synopsis of early T'o-pa history, see Peter A. Boodberg, "The Language of the T'o-pa Wei," *Harvard Journal of Asiatic Studies* 1 (1936): 167–85, and Wang Chung-lo, *Wei chin nan-pei ch'ao sui ch'u t'ang shih* (Shanghai: Jen-min ch'u-pan she, 1979), esp. pp. 364–408. For Fu Chien, see Michael C. Rogers, *The Chronicle of Fu Chien: A Case of Exemplar History* (Berkeley and Los Angeles: University of California Press, 1968), esp. pp. 22–32.

30. On sinification and the move to Lo-yang, see Wang Chung-lo, *Wei Chin nan-pei ch'ao sui ch'u t'ang shih*, pp. 391–404.

31. Wolfram Eberhard, *A History of China*, 4th. ed. (Berkeley and Los Angeles: University of California Press, 1977), pp. 145–46. A chronicle of this transition is available in Leon Hurvitz, trans., *Wei Shou: Treatise on Buddhism and Taoism: An English Translation of the Original Chinese Text of "Wei-shu" CXIV and the Japanese Annotations of Tsukamoto Zenryū* (Kyoto: Jimbungaku kenkyū jo, 1955). Kenneth Ch'en's *Buddhism in China: A Historical Survey* (Princeton: Princeton University Press, 1964) also contains a convenient synopsis on pages 145–83. Wang Chung-lo analyzes the assimilation debate as a three-party affair; those "conservatives" who resisted assimilation to Chinese ways, "middle of the roaders" who opted for a mix of T'o-pa and Chinese customs, and the "party of change" who sought to abandon T'o-pa ways for those of the Chinese. See Wang Chung-lo, *Wei chin nan-pei ch'ao*, pp. 395–401.

the end fully sinified. Emperor Hsiao-wen (r. 471–500) pushed a series of measures before and after the move to Lo-yang, including a revision of government offices to bring the Wei into line with Chinese practice, the banning of traditional T'o-pa dress and language at the court, and the abandonment of the T'o-pa surname in favor of the Chinese surname Yüan. The transfer of the seat of government to Lo-yang in 494 was the most visible of the sinifying measures, and the decision to abandon the traditional P'ing-ch'eng site for imperial mausoleums marked a clean ritual break with T'o-pa roots.[32] In actuality, the government program of sinification only confirmed the reality of the absorption of the T'o-pa into Chinese culture. According to the "Bibliographic Treatise" of the *History of the Sui* (*Sui shu*): "When the Later Wei first took control of the Central Plains, all of the commands for the disposition of their armies were given in 'barbarian' language [*i-yü*]. Later, when they had become tainted by Chinese customs (*jan Hua-su*) many of them could no longer understand their own tongue. So they began to teach it to each other, calling it their 'national language' [*kuo-yü*]."[33] It was precisely in this context of intense social and cultural flux with its preoccupation with ranking and ethnic purity that the categories "Buddhist/Western" (*hsi*, *fan*) and "Chinese" (*hsia*, *hua*, *han*) were being sorted out. This is also the context for the ranking schemes found in the *Scripture for Humane Kings* and the *P'u-sa ying-lo pen-yeh ching*.

Scholars have made the reasonable supposition that initially Buddhism, a religion of "foreigners," made common cause with the T'o-pa aristocracy, and that as sinification progressed rulers became more disposed toward "Confucian" ways and trappings. Indeed, the complex relationship between Confucian and Buddhist notions of sovereignty and between the timeless vision of the Two Truths and the temporal decay of the End of the Teaching found in the *Scripture for Humane Kings* seems to call to mind the persecution of Buddhism in the context of sinification. Suffice it to say that Buddhism, with its foreign associations, did not sit well with certain members of the aristocracy, who wished to be seen as "Chinese." As we have already seen, to be Buddhist was by definition to be *not* Chinese. Seen in this light, the persecution of Buddhism initiated in 446 was an attempt to assert a purified definition of Chineseness. To be Chinese one had to expunge Buddhism from one's discourse as well as from one's life and politics.

32. Wang Chung-lo, *Wei chin nan-pei ch'ao*, esp. pp. 398–401.

33. From Chang Wu-chi's "Ching-chi chih," in *Sui-shu*, 4.32.947, quoted by Victor H. Mair, "Buddhism and the Rise of the Written Vernacular in East Asia: The Making of National Languages," *Journal of Asian Studies* 53.3 (1994): 727. According to Mair, Tabgatch language, under the influence of Buddhism, may have been partially responsible for the idea of and the eventual rise of written vernacular Chinese.

Banning the Buddhist Body: The Persecution of 445

The persecution of Buddhism under the Emperor T'ai-wu (reigned 424–52) was preceded by a buildup of anti-Buddhist sentiment among key Confucian and Taoist officials who may be viewed as the radical vanguard of the forces of sinification. Playing on a variety of anti-Buddhist sentiments ranging from moral repugnance toward the monastic life, to charges that monks were idle parasites, to imperial dismay at a seemingly unending string of "Buddhist bandit" uprisings, the Celestial Master K'ou Ch'ien-chih (fl. 425–48) and the influential minister Tsui Hao (381–450) pursuaded Emperor T'ai-wu by 444 of the damaging influences of Buddhism on the body politic, and he promulgated the following edict:

> Those *śramaṇa* persons borrow the vain falsehoods of the Western barbarians and recklessly create disaster and calamity. Theirs is not the way to make uniform the effects of government or to spread earnest virtue through the world. From princes and dukes on down, if there be persons who are privately supporting *śramaṇas*, they shall all send them to the officials; they may not conceal them. The limit is the fifteenth day of the second month of this year. Anyone who exceeds the limit without surrendering the *śramaṇas* shall himself die. If anyone harbors them, the whole family shall be executed.[34]

The proximate cause of emperor's attempts to eradicate Buddhism was the alleged discovery on monastic grounds of arms, wine-making apparatus, and "rooms for debauchery" during the rebellion of K'ai Wu (445). Following on the heels of the alleged discovery, an edict was issued ordering that the *śramaṇas* of Ch'ang-an be killed and that Buddha-images be burnt and broken.[35] Kung-tsung, the crown prince regent, offered memorials countering this policy, saying that "the sins were not the sins of the portraits and statues." He was

34. Hurvitz, *Wei Shou*, pp. 65–66. Richard B. Mather has rendered a good account of K'ou's Taoism in "K'ou Ch'ien-chih and the Taoist Theocracy at the Northern Wei Court, 425–451," in Anna Seidel and Holmes Welch, eds., *Facets of Taoism: Essays in Chinese Religion* (New Haven: Yale University Press, 1979), pp. 103–22. On anticlericism in the period, see Zürcher, *Buddhist Conquest of China*, 1:254–85. Millennial uprisings led by "Buddhist bandits" occurred throughout the Northern Wei rule with major uprisings in 402, 473, 481, 490, and so on. For an account, see Gernet, *Buddhism in Chinese Society*, pp. 286–89, and Tsukamoto Zenryū, *Shina bukkyōshi kenkyū, hokugi-hen* (Tokyo: Kōbundō, 1942), esp. 246–90.

35. Recounted in Hurvitz, *Wei Shou*, pp. 64–66. Economic considerations may also have contributed to this persecution as they did in other such episodes. See Gernet, *Buddhism in Chinese Society*, pp. 20–21.

not heeded.[36] The reasons for the prohibition were cogently presented by the emperor in an edict that reads in part:

> Formerly, a reckless Sovereign of the Latter Han believed in and was led astray by evil and deceit. On the false pretext that he had dreamt of them, he served the malignant demons of the barbarians and thereby disturbed Heaven's order. From of old the Nine Provinces had never had such a thing in their midst. Its exaggerated grandiloquence is not based on human nature. In later ages, among ignorant lords and sovereigns gone astray, there was not one who was not dazzled by it. Therefore government and education have not been observed, propriety and righteousness have greatly decayed. The way of the demons prospered and looked upon the law of kings as it were nought. Since then each age has passed through disorder and calamity. Heaven's punishment has been quick to come, and the people have perished utterly. . . . We will completely shake off the barbarian gods and annihilate their vestiges. . . . If from now on there be any who dare serve the barbarian gods or make images, statues, or figures in clay or bronze, they shall be executed with their whole households. . . . When there are extraordinary men, only then can there be extraordinary acts. Were it not for Us, who could do away with this age-old counterfeit? Let the officials proclaim to the generals of garrisons and the governors that all Buddhist reliquaries, images, and barbarian scriptures are to be completely destroyed and burnt, and that the *śramaṇas*, without distinction of youth or age, are all to be buried alive.[37]

What is clear from these edicts and from the persistence of monastic leaders who, like T'an-yao, secretly continued to wear their robes, is that the visible presence of Buddhism, its robes, relics, images, and so on came to be viewed as the signs of disputed authority and cultural struggle in the Northern Wei.[38] Buddhism was portrayed by some as a foreign "demon" religion incommensurate with and destructive of "true" Chinese polity. The body politic was to be cleansed by the eradication of all bodily signs of Buddhist authority. The persecution of Buddhism that began in 444 was the first comprehensive attempt (but certainly not the last) to enforce a deeply felt distinction between Buddhists and Chinese.

The prohibition was gradually relaxed, especially after the death of Tsui Hao, the counselor responsible for much of the anti-Buddhist propaganda, in 450.

36. Hurvitz, *Wei Shou*, p. 66.
37. Ibid., pp. 66–67, promulgated 446 C.E.
38. Ibid., p. 69.

As Leon Hurvitz recounts it: "Households of earnest believers were able secretly to hold their services. The extreme among the *śramaṇas* still secretly wore religious habits and repeated their incantations. Only they could not openly practice the religion in the capital."[39] With the death of Tsui Hao and soon thereafter of the emperor, a more moderate approach to Buddhism's relation to the state was pursued. The architect of this policy was T'an-yao, appointed "Saṃgha Superintendent" by the Emperor Wen-ch'eng (r. 452–56).

The appointment of a Saṃgha superintendent signals a shift to a more accommodating approach to the Buddhist/Chinese question, but we would be wrong to see the shift as a complete reversal of imperial policy toward Buddhism. As Saṃgha superintendent, T'an-yao was the monk charged with oversight of monastic affairs in the mid-fifth century, and he was the architect of a new government Buddhism. Indeed, official policy was designed to transform Buddhism into an arm of the state, and T'an-yao became the head of a bureaucracy staffed by lay officials or nominal "monks."[40] The new *śramaṇa* superintendent was not an independent head of the Saṃgha. Rather, he was appointed by the emperor and tonsured by the emperor's hand.[41] The religious rationale for this government Buddhism was supplied by the first *śramaṇa* superintendent Fa-kuo, who justified government service of monks by direct identification of the emperor as the Buddha. In contrast to Hui-yüan's rigorous defense of clerical independence, Fa-kuo said that "T'ai-tsu is enlightened and loves the Way. He is in his very person the Thus-Having-Come-One. *Śramaṇas* must and should pay him all homage. . . . He who propagates the teaching of the Buddha is the lord of men. I am not doing obeisance to the Emperor, I am merely worshipping the Buddha."[42]

If T'an-yao lived to see the *Scripture for Humane Kings*, it must have made him angry. T'an-yao, like many other monks, had suffered through Emperor T'ai-wu's persecution, only to be elevated to a position in which he could repair the damage done and, hand in hand with the new emperor, build a new state religion. His activity can be seen as an attempt to put forward a new tax-

39. Ibid.

40. "Below" the *śramaṇa* superintendent T'an-yao were the *tu-wei-na* or "*wei-na* general" and the *wei-na*, which Tsukamoto points out were not equivalent of the South Asian monastic *karmadāna* or "overseer" but rather were "officials not of an autonomous clergy but of a secular government concerned with the regulation of ecclesiastical affairs." See Hurvitz, *Wei Shou*, p. 76 n. 4, and 83. If one of Emperor T'ai-wu's aims was to control Buddhism, that aim was also pursued by his successors. Indeed, as Anna K. Seidel has noted, imperial Taoist worship also continued. See Seidel, "Imperial Treasures and Taoist Sacraments," pp. 352–58.

41. When the proclamation "restoring" Buddhism was promulgated, the emperor personally tonsured the new *śramaṇa* superintendent Shih-hsien and four others. See Hurvitz, *Wei Shou*, pp. 71, 78, and 78 n. 1.

42. Ch'en, *Buddhism in China*, p. 146, and Hurvitz, *Wei Shou*, p. 53.

onomy, which articulated a Buddhist-Confucian rapproachment in the wake of the disastrous persecution. Tan-yao may even have known who compiled the *Scripture for Humane Kings*, though we, at this remove in time, can only make more or less educated guesses. Was it someone in the monastic circles of the capital who opposed the institution of "Saṃgha Superintendent" (a distinct possibility given its dictum: "If any of my disciples, ***bhikṣu*** and ***bhikṣuṇī*** establish registration and serve as officials they are not my disciples"). Was it a refugee monk from the conquered Northern Liang dynasty to the northwest? Many were the monks who would object to the monastic census, government control of ordination, and continued proscriptions on the making of images. There were not a few who felt the employ of soldiers and criminals in "Saṃgha" and "Buddha households" for monastic works projects was a flagrant violation of rules of the discipline.[43]

The controversial nature of the *Scripture for Humane Kings* is evident when we consider the range of possible relationships between Buddhism and the Chinese state. The position espoused by Fa-kuo and his successor, T'an-yao, was one in which the emperor was expressly identified as the Tathāgata or as a bodhisattva and which promoted state control of monastic affairs. We will take this as position one, where *identification* (of the emperor with the Buddha) is coupled with *dependence* (of monastic institutions on state institutions). Logically opposite to this identification and dependence would be the *rejection* of any identification of the ruler with the Buddha as well as an assertion of monastic *independence* from state institutions. Such a position was espoused by Hui-yüan in response to Huan Hsüan's attempts to rein in the Southern clergy.[44]

Between these two positions are two other logical positions. One could *reject* all identity between the ruler and Buddhist paradigms while calling for the *control* or suppression of Buddhist institutions, as did certain traditionalists and advocates of "sinification," some of whom were responsible for the great persecution. Finally, one might expressly *identify* the ruler as a *cakravartin* or even as a bodhisattva while calling for the *independence* of clerical institutions and the subservience of the state to the clergy. This is the position taken in the *Scripture for Humane Kings*, a position which was a direct challenge to that promoted by the Samgha superintendents and the Northern Wei government. In the *Scripture for Humane Kings* we read the traces of one strand of opposition to the dependence of the samgha on the state and one of the two emerging taxonomies in which one could speak of being both Buddhist and Chinese.

43. Though in fact there is considerable support in South Asian sources for such practices.

44. Zürcher, *Buddhist Conquest of China*, 1:154–59, 204–53. David Farquhar discusses later movements to identify emperors with bodhisattvas in "Emperor as Bodhisattva in the Governance of the Ch'ing Empire," *Harvard Journal of Asiatic Studies* 38.1 (1978): 5–34.

Ritual Politics and the Creation of the *Scripture for Humane Kings*

For much of the third and fourth centuries Buddhism had had two appeals. On the one hand it provided a new source of ideas and religious philosophy for the intelligentsia. On the other hand Buddhism touted its apotropaic value: it promulgated and was seen as offering superior powers of healing, prognostication, and protection. From the perspective of rulers, however, it must have seemed a bit thin on protection. Certainly there were rulers like Emperor Wu of the Liang dynasty who sought the salvific ends of Buddhism at least as much as its "worldly" benefits, but for most, praying monks appeared to offer little obstruction to a warlord and a sizable army. The salvific philosophy of the Transcendent Wisdom Scriptures seemed of little practical or immediate use. Little wonder then, that scriptures such as the *Scripture of the Golden Light* (*Chin-kuang ming ching*, Sanskrit *Survaṇaprabhāsa*) that promised military aid, albeit of a "spiritual" kind, were favorites of rulers.[45]

From very early on the *Scripture for Humane Kings* was paired with the *Scripture of the Golden Light*, and both were used under the Ch'en dynasty in the Emperor-Bodhisattva cult.[46] The *Scripture of the Golden Light* has often been translated, from Sanskrit into Chinese, Khotanese, Tibetan, and so forth. The first Chinese version is by Dharmakṣema in the earth fifth century, and versions followed by Paramārtha and I-ching.[47] The *Scripture of the Golden Light*, like the *Scripture for Humane Kings*, promises that "for those who hear this sutra . . . misfortunes are forever extinguished."[48] Like the *Scripture for Humane Kings*, it also concerns itself centrally with kings, kingship, and in this case with the four guardian kings (*lokapāla*) who form the main object of the teaching. In the "Chapter on the Four Great Kings" the guardians vow that they

45. The *Scripture of the Golden Light* is found in three Chinese versions. The *Chin-kuang-ming ching* (T 663, vol. 16) was translated by T'an Wu-ch'an under the Northern Liang dynasty. The *Ho-pu chin-kuang-ming ching* (T 664) was the effort of Dharmarakṣa and Pao-kuei and dates from the Sui dynasty. During the early T'ang dynasty I-ching rendered it as *Chin-kuang-ming tsui-sheng wang ching* (T 665). For an overview of Buddhist scriptures used in state protection cults in East Asia, see Jacques May, "Chingokokka," in *Hōbōgirin*, 5:322a–327a.

46. Mark Lewis, "The Suppression of the Three Stages Sect: Apocrypha as a Political Issue," in Buswell, ed., *Chinese Buddhist Apocrypha*, pp. 209–10. For a translation of the *Survaṇaprabhāsa*, see R. E. Emmerick, trans., *The Sūtra of the Golden Light: Being a Translation of the Survaṇabhāsottamasūtra*, Sacred Books of the Buddhists, vol. 27 (London: Luzac, 1970).

47. For a brief overview of its history of translation, see Emmerick, *Sūtra of the Golden Light*, introduction, p. x.

48. Ibid., 2.

> with the twenty-eight great generals of the *Yakṣas*, and with numerous hundreds of thousands of *Yakṣas* will continually watch over, guard and protect the whole of *Jambudvīpa* with our divine eye. . . . When, dear Lord, a king of men should hear this excellent *Survaṇabhāsa*, king of Sūtras, and having heard it, should give protection, should give salvation, assistance, defence from all their enemies to those monks who hold the chief Sūtras, we, dear lord, the four great kings, will give protection, will give salvation, assistance, defence, peace, welfare to that king of men and to the beings in all regions.[49]

Where the *Scripture of the Golden Light* promises that the great *Lokapālas* will come to the aid of devoted rulers, the *Scripture for Humane Kings* promises that "Great Howl Bodhisattvas" (*ta-li ho p'u-sa*) and their military retinues will come to the aid of rulers in need. According to the scripture, a ruler who ritually demonstrates the Correct Teaching will be aided by the five "Great Howl Bodhisattvas," who will come to protect the state, the person, or whatever is endangered:

> Great king, if in future eras there are all the kings who receive and hold the three jewels I will send the five great-power **bodhisattva**s to protect their states. First Chin-kang-ho[50] ***bodhisattva,*** his hand grasping a thousand jewel-emblem discus will go to protect that state. Second Lung-wang-ho[51] ***bodhisattva,*** his hand grasping a golden wheel lamp, will go to protect that state. Third Wu-wei-shih-li-ho[52] ***bodhisattva,*** his hand grasping a chin-kang-cudgel, will go to protect that state. Fourth Lei-tien-ho[53] ***bodhisattva,*** his hand grasping a thousand-jeweled lasso, will go to protect that state. Fifth Wu-liang-li-ho[54] ***bodhisattva,*** his hand grasping a fifty-blade discus, will go to protect that state. [These] five great masters with five thousand great spirit kings will go to your state and greatly promote blessings and benefit. It is fitting that you establish [their] images and worship them. (833a9–17)

But the *Scripture for Humane Kings* goes further, for it directly links the teach-

49. Ibid., 24. Similar statements arise throughout the work, as well as punitive warnings in case of royal neglect of the *saṃgha*. In such cases there are bandit uprisings, and so on. See p. 38. For the Chinese text of the passage, see T 663 16.341a4–18.

50. Vajra-howl.

51. Dragon-king howl.

52. The fearless ten-power howl.

53. Thunder-and-lightening howl.

54. Limitless-power howl.

ing and cultivation of the path as well as the public recitation and veneration of the scripture with the protection of the state.

As I have shown, this "Teaching" erases the distinction between monks and kings, replacing it with a hierarchy of bodhisattva-kings beginning at the lowest levels of visible "worldly" rulers. These rulers practice "outer protection," the visible manifestation of which is the support of the Saṃgha and, more specifically, the ostentatious ritual veneration of the text of the *Scripture for Humane Kings* and the monks who propound it:

> The Buddha said, "Great king, you should make nine colored banners nine *chang* long, nine colored flowers two *chang* high, one thousand branched lamps five *chang* high, nine jade screens and nine jade wrappers.[55] Also make a jeweled table on which to place the scripture. When the king travels [*hsing shih*] always keep this scripture one hundred paces in front of him, always with the light of one thousand [lamps]. This will ordain that—within a radius of one thousand *li*—the seven difficulties will not arise and crimes and transgressions will not be produced. When the king is not traveling [*chu shih*] make seven jeweled tents and within them make seven high seats upon which to place the scripture rolls, and each day worship, scatter flowers and burn incense [before them] as though you were serving your father and mother or serving the god ***Śakra.*** (832c26–833a4)[56]

Thus, the ruler is physically to demonstrate the proper hierarchical relationships constituting the path by publicly venerating the *Scripture for Humane Kings*. Such display of Buddha images and Buddhist teachers stands in striking contrast to the proscription of precisely such displays during Emperor T'ai-wu's persecution. The *Scripture for Humane Kings* flaunts the display of Buddhist "bodies," making such display the prerequisite of "protection." What had heretofore been separate and unthinkable categories, or to quote Hui-yüan, this "mutual interference of different species" which was at all costs to be avoided, is now the hallmark of proper rule, the sign of "authoritative human-

55. The T'ang dynasty T'ien-t'ai commentary interprets the measurements as follows: "Nine signifies the sufferings of beings . . . two *chang* signifies the two truths, the ten lamps signify the merit of the ten good [acts] . . . five *chang* high [means they] illuminate the five ways [of rebirth]" (T 1705 33.284c21–285a2).

56. Flamboyant royal expenditures were one of the characteristic marks of the growth of Buddhism in Chinese culture. See Gernet, *Buddhism in Chinese Society*, p. 6. It is interesting to note that here the text serves as its own ritual commentary and that there are no independent ritual manuals for the performance of the rite according to the fifth-century version of the text. All manuals found in Chinese and later Japanese collections are keyed to the eighth-century text, which, for grand ritual performance, apparently supplanted the fifth-century version completely.

ity." Moreover, the *Scripture for Humane Kings* makes the very public display of imperial subservience a prerequisite for the establishment of the Correct Teaching, and such displays were intended to counter the official subservience of the Samgha to the state.

This reversal strongly suggests that the great persecution and the state Buddhism established thereafter form the historical backdrop for the composition of the text. Obviously, the *Scripture for Humane Kings* could not have been compiled earlier than scriptures that it borrows directly from, such as the *Avataṃsaka*, which was translated between 418 and 420, the *Nirvana Scripture* of 421, and the *Scripture of the Wise and the Foolish*, which dates from 445.[57] But why not locate the text a century later with the Chou dynasty persecution of Buddhism?

There are numerous reasons for a mid- to late-fifth rather than a mid-sixth century date for the *Scripture for Humane Kings*. As I detailed in Chapter 3, mentions of "humane kings" begin to show up in the Liu-Sung dynastic history and in Seng-yu's catalog entry in the *Ch'u-san-tsang chi-chi* of 515. To place the text later we would have to account for these references.

Other reasons take us back to the prophecy itself. I suggest that a hitherto overlooked indication of the date of the text is found in the prophetic admonition concerning government infringement upon the independence of the Saṃgha. In the description of the dire "last times" in chapter eight we find these statements: "Soldiers and slaves will be made *bhikṣu* and receive preferential treatment . . ." [*ping nu wei pi-ch'iu shou pieh-ch'ing fa*, 833b23],[58] and "If any of my disciples, ***bhikṣu*** and *bhikṣuṇī* establish registration and serve as officials they are not my disciples. This is the law for soldiers and slaves" (833c13–18).

Satō Tetsui and other scholars rightfully point to these passages as indication that the *Scripture for Humane Kings* was written in the aftermath of the great persecution. But closer examination highlights two key elements of the prophecy which bear on the circumstances attendant to the production of the text. These are the statement that "soldiers and slaves will be made *bhikṣu*," and that "they will establish superintendents [*t'ung-kuan*] to regulate the community

57. My attempt to narrow the dating by looking at the creation of and terminology for *saṃgha* comptrollers and registration of monks—first instituted under the Northern Wei with the appointment of Fa-kuo in 398—has proved inconclusive. The *Scripture for Humane Kings* uses a neutral term for "*saṃgha* Comptroller": *t'ung-kuan*, instead of *tao-jen t'ung* (used until the time of Tan-yao) or the later term *Sha-men t'ung*.

58. "Preferential treatment" (*pieh-ch'ing*) indicates direct contact between lay donors and particular monks. Some Vinaya, such as that of the Dharmagupta, allowed such contact while others such as the Sarvāstivāda and the *Brahmajāla* (*Fan-wang ching*, T 1484, vol. 24) prohibited it in favor of contact through a monastic representative. See *Hōbōgirin*, 1:66a–b, s.v. "bessho." Pu-k'ung's eighth-century recension of the text expunges this remark, replacing it with "there is no difference between [such laws and] the laws governing soldiers and slaves and so forth [*yu ping-nu fa teng wu yu i*]" (T 246 8.844b14).

and will set up registration of monks." One possible, but not entirely satisfactory interpretation fo the phrase "soldiers and slaves will be made *bhikṣu*" is that this refers to a "secular" bureaucracy that controlled the Saṃgha. Another interpretation is that it refers to a key element of T'an-yao's new government Buddhism. One of T'an-yao's efforts at promoting the spread of Buddhism was his establishment of Saṃgha (*seng-shih-hu*) and Buddha (*fo-t'u-hu*) households.[59] Following the Wei subjection of an era in the Shantung region, much of the local Chinese population was relocated to the area around Ta-t'ung and reduced to slavery.[60] T'an-yao sought both to help these people and to promote Buddhism by organizing the refugees into Saṃgha households to cultivate grain, a part of which was paid in to a local Saṃgha storehouse to be redistributed during times of famine. Buddha households were constituted using slaves and criminals to do monastic work ("sprinkling and sweeping"), and some of these even took monastic vows. Indeed, slaves were often donated to the Saṃgha as a form of meritorious action, and these slaves helped the monasteries open up new, often marginal uplands. The Saṃgha was also able to grow its own slaves, and when the children of slaves reached the correct age they were ordained, thus preventing their transfer back to the government or to private individuals. The practice apparently began in the mid-fifth century and had become such a problem that by 517 the court attempted to ban such ordination.[61] These new organizations began functioning between 470 and 476 and probably laid the foundation for the tremendous expansion of monastic foundations in the 480s.[62] Monastic registration took place in 477. These circumstances closely match the prophetic denunciations of the *Scripture for Humane Kings*. Thus it is most likely that the *Scripture for Humane Kings* was

59. Tsukamoto Zenryū has a study of these organizations, "Hokugi no sōgiko butsotoko," in *Shina bukkyōshi kenkyū, hokugi-hen*, pp. 165–213. The portion of this work concerning T'an-yao has been translated into English by Galen E. Sargent, "Tan-yao and His Times," *Monumenta Serica* 16 (1957): 363–96. Wei Shou's comments on the households are in Hurvitz, *Wei Shou*, pp. 72–73.

60. It was a common T'o-pa practice to use captives as slaves, and slaves were an important part of the Northern Wei economy. Slaves were classified as "government" and "private," and were counted in alloting land to be opened up for cultivation. See Wang Chung-lo, *Wei chin nan-pei ch'ao*, esp. 370–76, and Wang Yi-t'ung, "Slaves and Other Comparable Social Groups During the Northern Dynasties (386–618)," *Harvard Journal of Asiatic Studies* 16 (1953): 301–44.

61. Jacques Gernet points out the precedents in Vinaya for the institution of monastic slaves in *Buddhism in Chinese Society*, pp. 100–103. These South Asian precedents notwithstanding, T'an-yao's use of slaves is also perfectly in keeping with T'o-pa use of slaves and could be seen as a continuation of government policy which perhaps conveniently dovetailed with Vinaya precedents. For the order attempting to ban ordination of the children of slaves, see Hurvitz, *Wei Shou*, p. 90.

62. The exact dating of the establishment of these institutions is in dispute. Some sources designate the earlier date of 470, others 476–77. Tsukamoto argues convincingly for the latter date. See his discussion in *Shina bukkyōshi kenkyū, hokugi-hen*, pp. 171ff. and 182–191.

written sometime soon after 477 by a monastic opponent of T'an-yao.[63] The end of which it speaks is a present reality; the beginning it would make is in the future.

Thus the *Scripture for Humane Kings* presents us with a confluence of several interests, ideologies, and concerns. The scripture is a direct descendent of the Transcendent Wisdom Scriptures, the *Avataṃsaka*, and the *Nirvana Scripture*, all of which were rendered into Chinese by the third decade of the fifth century. But the concerns that brought forth and shaped the scripture and its cohorts (such as the *Scripture of the Original Acts* and the *Scripture of Brahma's Net*) were dominated by tensions in the polity of North China in the mid-fifth century. As we have seen, these tensions—especially tensions concerning the assimilation of T'o-pa peoples to Chinese society—bear a direct relationship to the assimilation of Confucian to Buddhist polity as presented in the *Scripture for Humane Kings*. If the persecution of Buddhism under the Northern Wei marks the forceful advocacy of a separation of Buddhists from Chinese, the *Scripture for Humane Kings* marks a just as forceful advocacy of the essential identity of Buddhists and Chinese and of Buddhist and Confucian polity. But the premise of this identity is the rejection not of state support of Buddhism, but of the state control of Buddhism promoted in the aftermath of the great persecution. The prophecy of the End of the Teaching in the *Scripture for Humane Kings* is a call for the establishment of a new Buddhism in North China and an attack on the state Buddhism instituted in the 470s. The flamboyant prestations enjoined by the scripture simultaneously constitute the sign of "authoritative humanity" and the sign of the Correct Teaching, a Correct Teaching displayed in the ritual submission of the emperor to the Saṃgha.

The Politics of the Three Truths

The political context of the *Scripture for Humane Kings* helps us make sense of its use of Buddhist cosmology and also helps us understand some of the scripture's idiosyncracies. What made the *Scripture for Humane Kings* an especially powerful work was its harnessing of Buddhist notions of the world, authority, and the path to the apocalyptic prediction of the End of the Teaching and to the concerns of a fifth-century Chinese audience. While the apocalyptic motif is found in other Mahāyāna scriptures, in the *Scripture for Humane Kings*

63. Tsukamoto, in a passing remark, situates the *Scripture for Humane Kings* in this milieu. Ibid., p. 210.

the *rupic* notion of the End of the Teaching is fully integrated both with the bodhisattva path and with the duties of kings. Moreover, the scripture encourages simultaneous but different interpretations of the relationship between the Saṃgha and the state and between monks and kings.

As we have already seen, the prediction of the "end-time" probably reflects the recent persecution of Buddhism between 445 and 450 in North China, the "restoration" that followed it, and a call to establish a new beginning, and to restructure the relationship between the clergy and the government. One issue, however, remains. Why does the scripture proclaim a doctrine of Three Truths?

One possible interpretation of the appearance of Three Truths in the *Scripture for Humane Kings* is that they were not meant to conflict with the doctrine of Two Truths but rather were merely supplemental explanation of an abstruse point of Buddhist doctrine. While such a proposition could conceivably have been the case at some stage of the composition of the text, it is obviously *not* the case in the text as we have it. The *Scripture for Humane Kings* proudly proclaims the Three Truths in verses (Sanskrit *gāthās*) throughout the text.

From the perspective of Buddhist doctrine the Three Truths was arguably the most important contribution of the *Scripture for Humane Kings* to the development of indigenous systems of Chinese Buddhism. Chih-i, the founder of the T'ien-t'ai school, repeatedly cited the *Scripture for Humane Kings* along with the *Scripture of the Original Acts* as the basis for his construction of the Three Truths as "empty," "provisional," and "middle."[64] Paul Swanson has examined the philosophical roots and the import of Chih-i's formulation and concluded that though such a position was hinted at in South Asian Buddhist works, its development in China was one of the characteristics of the assimilation of Buddhism to East Asia. References to the Three Truths are strewn throughout the *Scripture for Humane Kings*, but the key passage reads as follows:

> If a ***bodhisattva*** sees beings, sees one or sees two, then he does not see one and does not see two. This one and two is the truth of the preeminent meaning [*ti-i-i ti*]. Great king, if there is existence or nonexistence [*jo yu jo wu*], then this is worldly truth. [One can] use three truths to embrace all the constituents: the truth of emptiness [*k'ung-ti*], the truth of form [*se-ti*], and the truth of mind [*hsin-ti*]. I have preached that all constituents do not transcend the three truths. Personalist views and

64. For a brief discussion of the Three Truths in Chih-i's work, see Neal Donner and Daniel B. Stevenson, *The Great Calming and Contemplation: A Study and Annotated Translation of the First Chapter of Chih-i's Mo-ho chih-kuan* (Honolulu: University of Hawaii Press, 1993), pp. 9–13. For a more extensive discussion and an appraisal of the *Scripture for Humane Kings*, see Swanson, *Foundations of T'ien-t'ai Philosophy*, esp. pp. 38–56.

the five aggregates are empty and indeed, all constituents are empty. (829b26–c1)[65]

The first sentence of this passage is no different from many other such pronouncements in Transcendent Wisdom or Mādhyamaka literature. So too, given the strong *Tathāgatagarbha* and Yogācāra elements in this text, the notion of three truths consisting of "emptiness," "form," and "mind"—the first two corresponding to *paramārthasatya* and *saṁvṛitisatya* and the third corresponding to the notion that all we know of the world is mental representation—is not remarkable. On the other hand, to propose Three Truths in the context of a chapter titled the "Two Truths" does seem a bit cheeky.

I propose one possible answer to this puzzle. If we keep in mind my exploration of the links between cosmology, notions of authority, and notions of salvation, what might we surmise from a system that so boldly proposes Three Truths? The key soteriological problem in a *dharmic* scheme that asserts the fundamental continuity of the cosmos is the problem of the place of nirvana and the apparent discontinuity between this world and nirvana. The assertion of the identity of samsara and nirvana and the doctrine of the Two Truths is an answer to the fundamental conundrum of *dharmic* cosmologies. Likewise, the issue in a *rupic* scheme that asserts the fundamental continuity of the cosmos is the place of ignorance and defilement, or how it happens that we are ignorant of our true and inherent nature. Putting it in global rather than in individual terms, how is it that the Teaching declines? The Three Truths would seem to answer this conundrum through a pivotal "truth" that can mediate enlightenment and ignorance, the eternal Teaching and its temporal demise. Thus, while the *dharmic* Two Truths formulation logically raises soteriological conundrums, the *rupic* Three Truths scheme erases those conundrums by proposing the inherent qualities of enlightenment in all beings—a useful doctrine in the face of difficult issues of ethnic assimilation.

But a more concrete possibility also presents itself. In a rigorous Two Truths formulation, the End of the Teaching is ever linked to the Correct Teaching

65. The passage is, of course, the *locus classicus* of the T'ien-t'ai school's teaching of the three truths and the T'ang dynasty commentary attributed to Chih-i (T 1705) has a discussion of this at 279c13–21. Chi-tsang's comments are as follows: "The master Tripiṭaka said, 'The basic nature of all constituents is the truth of emptiness. Common people take outward form and regard it as reality, and this is called the truth of form. People in the three vehicles who are cultivating the way are without mental outflows, and this is called the truth of mind.' If we discuss birth and death, and nirvana, each has three truths. The three truths of birth and death: gods, humans, and the four great elements are the truth of form. The eight cognitions are the truth of mind, and transcending birth and death without nirvana is the truth of emptiness. The three truths of nirvana: the real form of gods and humans is the truth of form. The two minds of reality are called the truth of mind, and being without birth and death's four inverted views is called the truth of emptiness" (T 1707 33.343a2–8).

through a recursive identity. Paradoxically, the golden age and the last age, the eternal *Dharma* and temporality are identical yet different, and this identity is realized through insight. Pu-k'ung's eighth-century recension of the *Scripture for Humane Kings* foregrounds the Two Truths aspect of the text by eliminating all references to Three Truths. But the sheer number of references to the Three Truths in the fifth-century *Scripture for Humane Kings* indicates that they were somehow an important part of the message. Close examination of the Three Truths and Chi-tsang's initial comments on them is instructive: "The basic nature of all constituents is the truth of emptiness [*k'ung-ti*]. Common people take external forms and regard them as reality, and this is called the truth of form [*se-ti*]. People in the three vehicles who are cultivating the Way are without mental outflows, and this is called the truth of mind [*hsin-ti*]" (T 1707 33.343a2–8).[66] It is notable that "cultivation of the Way" is the basis for realizing that "forms" are in fact "empty." This realization is achieved through practice, which, of course, constitutes the visible signs of authority. The proper display of the signs of authority—robes, images, rituals—are indications that the Correct Teaching has been actualized and that the End of the Teaching has been averted. In other words, the truth of mind is manifest in ritual display and worship of the Buddhist body.

From this perspective the doctrine of the Three Truths is in complete harmony with the *rupic* agenda of the scripture, and it may not be too far-fetched to argue that the three-fold assembly described at the opening of the scripture—clerics (bodhisattvas striving on the path), laity (kings and pious laypeople), and the Buddhas of the ten directions—represents the Three Truths: the truth of mind, the truth of form, and the truth of emptiness, as well as the three-fold polity of Chinese Buddhists, Confucians, and (non-Chinese) Buddhists.[67] Just as the words "forbearing" and "humane" are joined in the sound *ńẓi̯ěn*, the Two Truths of emptiness and form are somehow joined in the third Truth of the Preeminent Meaning. Here we can observe the complex adaptive system we call Buddhism in the process of evolution. The seam joining *dharmic* and *rupic*, continuous and discontinuous worlds, the past and the future, good

66. The passage continues, "If we discuss birth and death, and nirvana, each has three truths. The three truths of birth and death: gods, humans, and the four great elements are the truth of form. The eight cognitions are the truth of mind, and transcending birth and death without nirvana is the truth of emptiness. The three truths of nirvana: the real form of gods and humans is the truth of form. The two minds of reality are called the truth of mind, and being without birth and death's four inverted views is called the truth of emptiness" (T 1707 33.343a2–8).

67. Note that this taxonomy is not fully commensurate with the lineage taxonomy outlined in the path and the order of the assembly given in the prologue of the scripture. Here we can see one of the "seams" of the text where two quite different sets of analogies jostle one another. Compare with my analysis in Chapter 3.

rulers and bad, Confucians and Buddhists, inscribes in theological terms a new vision of polity. It is a vision that conceives a truly *Chinese* Buddhism.

Lineage and Canon: The Making of Chinese Buddhism

The model of a Chinese Buddhist polity set forth in the *Scripture for Humane Kings* was, however, under an increasingly severe handicap. As Buddhism became a permanent part of the Chinese religious landscape, the importance of authoritative lineages tracing texts and teachings back to the holy lands of South Asia also grew. In cases where a text circulated anonymously and gained importance in Chinese Buddhism, a lineage of translators became a necessity. In Chinese Buddhism of the fifth and sixth centuries the "translator" functioned to characterize and shape the discourse surrounding the text.

As I have shown, the *Scripture for Humane Kings*, in enunciating the identity of "forbearance" and "humaneness" and the identity of Buddhist and Confucian ideologies grew in stature and importance. It is no surprise, then, that by the end of the sixth century there was a marked shift in the discourse surrounding the *Scripture for Humane Kings*, a shift that involved both the creation of a genealogy of authoritative translations and the imprimatur of imperial authority. Both the choice of translators and the timing of the construction of this textual lineage are significant. Both are related to the rise of the T'ien-t'ai movement.

The facts of the creation of this lineage are quite clear. As in Seng-yu's *Ch'u-san-tsang chi-chi* of 515, Fa-ching's *Chung-ching mu-lu* of 594 regards the *Scripture for Humane Kings* as "suspicious" and casts doubt on attributions of it to Dharmarakṣa or Kumārajīva. This long-held position of Buddhist catalogers was summarily reversed when, in 597, Fei Ch'ang-fang legitimated the text by providing an authoritative lineage of translators for it in his *Li-tai san-pao chi*. There he lists three translations of the text, attributing them successively to Dharmarakṣa, Kumārajīva, and Paramārtha.[68] Fei's reversal of long-held suspicions concerning this and many other dubious scriptures was a part of efforts to enhance the standing of Buddhism vis-à-vis Taoism during the Sui. But Fei's particular construction of an illustrious ancestry for the *Scripture for Humane Kings* involved more than a simple affirmation of its canonicity.

In the context of sixth-century China, Dharmarakṣa, Kumārajīva, and Paramārtha were indeed names to conjure with. Dharmarakṣa was the greatest translator and propagator of Buddhism prior to Kumārajīva, with the conser-

68. *Li-tai san-pao chi*, T 2034 62c, 64c, 78a, 79a, 99a and 101c.

vative *Tsung-li chung-ching mu-lu* of Tao-an listing 154 works under his name.[69] Originally born in Tun-huang around 230 of Indian and Scythian parents, he entered the order early in life, had wide acquaintance with Confucian works, and traveled extensively. He was noted as the translator of the *Kuan-tsan ching* (a partial version of the *Scripture on Transcendent Wisdom in 25,000 Verses*), the first complete version of the *Lotus of the True Teaching* (T 263, *Saddharma-puṇḍarīka*), the *Vimalakīrtinirdeśa*, the *Sūraṅgamasamādhisūtra*, and the *Sukhavatīvyūha*. His work was widely seen as building the foundation of Buddhism in north China and setting the stage for Tao-an and Kumārajīva in the centuries that followed.

Kumārajīva was born in Kucha in 350 and studied the Sarvāstivāda in Kashmir before his conversion to the Mahāyāna.[70] His accomplishments as a scholar and wizard are said by some to have led Fu Chien's commander Lu Kuang to conquer Kucha in 384, taking Kumārajīva captive as an adviser. After the conquest in 401 of Lu Kuang's Later Liang state, Kumārajīva was shipped to Ch'ang-an where he served as a court adviser. In the following years until his death in 413 he translated and corresponded widely, providing for the first time fully accurate translations of Mahāyāna and especially Mādhyamika doctrines into Chinese. In the period between 402 and his death, Kumārajīva translated the *Amitābhasūtra*, the *Scripture on Transcendent Wisdom in 25,000 Verses*, the Mādhyamika texts *The Treatise on the Middle* and the *Treatise on the Twelve Gates*, as well as *The Treatise on the Great Transcendent Wisdom* (Mahāprajñāpāramitā śāstra, this latter is thought by some to be his own work commenting on Nāgārjuna). During the same period he also retranslated the *Lotus of the True Teaching* and the *Vimalakīrtinirdeśa*. In his last years he produced translations of the *Scripture on the Ten Stages* and the *Treatise on the Completion of Truth*.

Paramārtha (Chen-ti, "Ultimate Truth") was born in India and arrived in Canton in 546 and had an audience with the Emperor Wu of the Liang dynasty in 548 where he would have stayed but for the rebellion which brought down the Liang.[71] During his wanderings in this time of upheaval he nonetheless produced translations of the *Scripture of the Golden Light* (*Survaṇapra-*

69. For his biography, see *Kao-seng chuan* (T 2059 50.326c2–327a12). A good summary of Dharmarakṣa's life and work may be found in Zürcher, *Buddhist Conquest of China*, 1:65–70, and also in T'ang Yung-t'ung, *Han wei liang chin nan-pei ch'ao fo-chiao shih*, 2 vols. (Peking: Chung-hua shu-chü, 1983), 1:110–16.

70. For his biography see *Kao-seng chuan* (T 2059 50.330a10–333a12). Brief summaries of his life and works are found in Zürcher, *Buddhist Conquest of China*, 1:226–27, and Ch'en, *Buddhism in China*, 81–83. For a more detailed treatment, see T'ang Yung-t'ung, *Han wei*, 1:196–229.

71. His biography is in *Hsü kao-seng chüan* (T 2060 50.429c6–431a6). A brief biography is found in Ch'en, *Buddhism in China*, 134–35. Diana Paul, *Philosophy of Mind in Sixth-Century China*, treats Paramārtha's life in the context of the Ti-lun school in China.

bhāsa) in 552 and the *Diamond-cutter* (*Vajracchedikā*) in 562. In the years following 562 he translated a series of Yogācāra works by Asaṅga and Vasubandhu, including the *Viṁśatikā*, and the *Mahāyānasaṃgraha*. He spent the last years of his life in the environs of Canton.[72]

The earliest and most persistent attribution of the *Scripture for Humane Kings* is to Dharmarakṣa and Kumārajīva, and later attributions are to Paramārtha. By the time of the Sui, only the "Kumārajīva version" was extant; that is, the Kumārajīva attribution was the most important one. Both Dharmarakṣa and Kumārajīva were translators of the *Lotus of the True Teaching* and of major Transcendent Wisdom, Mādhyamika, and bodhisattva path texts. By contrast, Paramārtha is associated with the Yogācāra (Chinese *Ti-lun*) movement, whose impact in China peaked during the late fifth and early sixth centuries. Thus, attributions to Dharmarakṣa, Kumārajīva, and Paramārtha borrow not only the prestige of the two greatest translators before the sixth century, but they also place the *Scripture for Humane Kings* in an impeccable lineage of texts related to the Transcendent Wisdom teachings and the *Lotus* while simultaneously invoking Yogācāra and *Tathāgatagarbha* traditions. Style aside, it is an eminent and suitable lineage for the *Scripture for Humane Kings*.

By the time the attributions of translators were fixed by Fei Ch'ang-fang's *Li-tai san-pao chi* in 597, the *Scripture for Humane Kings* was of signal importance to the fledgling T'ien-t'ai school, a school in the process of establishing its religious and political hegemony. The *Scripture for Humane Kings* provided the scriptural basis for a key T'ien-t'ai doctrine of the Three Truths, and it provided ideological justification for the school's relationship with the Sui rulers. Thus the choice of translators was not merely a case of finding prestigious names to help its circulation; it was a case of what kind of prestige was needed. Further, canonizing this text by providing it with "translators" underscored at once both its genuineness as a product of the holy land and its centrality in the creation of a new discourse in which one could claim to be a Chinese Buddhist. Ironically, the limits of the new taxonomy are asserted in this act of canonization: Chinese can be at once Chinese and Buddhist, but "scripture" is not a product of China—it is Indian. Commentary is acceptable as a Chinese mode of Buddhist literature; "scriptures" produced by Chinese are, however, "forgeries."[73] Chinese concerns created the *Scripture for Hu-*

72. See Paul, *Philosophy of Mind in Sixth-Century China*, pp. 31–37. T'ang Yung-t'ung's treatment is in *Han Wei*, 2:615–25.

73. Jacques Derrida once remarked on a similar blind spot in Lévi-Strauss's analysis of the "savage mind": "It could perhaps be said that the whole of philosophical conceptualization, which is systematic with the nature/culture opposition, is designed to leave in the domain of the unthinkable the very thing that makes this conceptualization possible: the origin of the prohibition of incest." Jacques Derrida, in "Structure, Sign, and Play in the Discourse of the Human Sciences," in Hazard Adams and Leroy Searle, eds., *Critical Theory Since 1965* (Tallahassee: Florida State University Press, 1986), p. 87.

mane Kings. At the same time, the cultural economy of a newly emerging Chinese Buddhism necessitated the erasure of its paternity and the creation of a South Asian genealogy.

T'ien-t'ai's Canon and the *Scripture for Humane Kings*

It is hard to imagine that the doctrine of the Three Truths was the sole motivating factor in the canonization of the *Scripture for Humane Kings*. Other issues were likely more pressing, particularly the political ones. Fei Chang-fang's catalog stands at the confluence of some key events in Chinese Buddhism, and it is intimately linked to the rise of the T'ien-t'ai school. The T'ien-t'ai school of Buddhism is perhaps the most famous of the Chinese Buddhist schools and the first well-organized and fully sinified interpretation of Buddha-*vaccana* in China. The school's name is derived from the mountain retreat of its "founder," Chih-i, whose name is virtually inseparable from that of the school.

Along with major texts such as the *Mahāprajñāpāramitā*, and the *Lotus Sutra*, Chih-i regularly quotes the *Scripture for Humane Kings* and the *Scripture of the Original Acts That Serve as Necklaces for Bodhisattvas*. Arguments in his major works, such as the *Great Calming and Contemplation* (*Mo-ho chih-kuan* T 1911), the *Meaning of the Four-fold Teaching* (*Ssu chiao i* T 1929), the *Profound Meaning of the Lotus of the Teaching* (*Fa-hua hsüan-i* T 1716), the *Profound Commentary on the Vimalakīrṭi Scripture*, (*Wei-mo ching hsüan-shu* T 1777), and the *Meaning of the Triple Contemplation* (*San kuan i*), are strewn with quotations from the *Scripture for Humane Kings*, illustrating the nature of the path, the Adamantine *Samādhi* (*chin-kang-ting san-mei*), the Three Truths, and so on.[74] He clearly relied upon it as authoritative.

The facts of Chih-i's life are well enough known that a brief summary will suffice here. Though descended of northerners who fled south in 317, Chih-i's first real immersion in "northern" Buddhism began when he journeyed to Mt. Ta-hsien in the late 550s to study discipline under the direction of Hui-

74. References to the *Scripture for Humane Kings* are found in *Mo-ho chih-kuan* 3 (T 1911 46.21b), 5 (46.53a), and 6 (46.72b, 84c); the *Ssu chiao i* 8 (T 1929 46.751b–752c), 11 (762c–763c), 12 (765a, 766c). These citations are frequently found in conjunction with citations from the *Scripture of the Original Acts That Serve as Necklaces of the Bodhisattvas* and the *Nirvana Scripture*, and the one at *Ssu chiao i*, 46.738, is an involved discussion of forbearance. Citations involving the three truths include *Fa-hua hsüan-i* (T 1716 33.704c); *Wei-mo ching hsüan shu* (T 1777 38.525b and 534c); *Ssu chiao i* (T 1929 46.727c); and *San kuan i* in *Wan-tzu hsu-tsang ching* (Hong Kong reprint of *Dai-nihon zokuzōkyō*), 98.76a. References also may be found in works attributed to Chih-i such as *Ssu nien-ch'u* 3 (T 1918 46.567b, 568a, 571c, 577b). For a recent study and translation of the first chapter of the *Great Calming and Contemplation*, see Donner and Stevenson, *The Great Calming and Contemplation*.

k'uang. There he is said to have concentrated on the *Lotus*, the *Wu-liang i ching*, and the *P'u-hsien kuan ching*.[75] He left by 560 and proceeded north to Mt. Ta-su on the border between the Ch'en (557–89) and the Northern Ch'i (550–89), where he studied contemplative discipline, the Lotus, and *Prajñāpāramitā* under the direction of Hui-ssu.

Seven years later Chih-i returned to the Ch'en capital at Chin-ling with a band of followers where he preached to prominent members of the court.[76] Chih-i was in the Ch'en capital at the Wa-kuan ssu until he made his first trip to Mt. T'ien-t'ai in 575, just after the initiation of Emperor Wu's persecution of Buddhism in the Northern Chou dynasty. The proscription in the north was reminiscent of a proscription under the Wei more than a century earlier. It was coupled with a memorial to the throne by a "renegade" Buddhist Wei Yüan-sung arguing for the dismantling of Buddhist and Taoist ecclesiastical structures and their replacement by a "Buddha world" *within* the framework of the Chou state.[77]

Whether Chih-i thought the proscription in the north was a herald of things to come in the south is now impossible to say. In any event, Chih-i remained on T'ien-t'ai for ten years until, in 585, he was coaxed to return to the capital by the Ch'en emperor. Shortly after his return to Chin-ling the emperor instructed Chih-i to move from the Ling-yao ssu to the Kuang-tse ssu, a monastery occupied by Emperor Wu of the Liang dynasty before he ascended the throne. Soon thereafter Chih-i was instructed to preach on the *Scripture for Humane Kings*.[78] In Hurvitz's words: "The religious meeting at the Kuang-tse-ssu was apparently a very great event, attended by the Emperor himself and by many important laymen and clerics, including the monkish officials Hui-heng and Hui-k'uang. If the *pieh-chüan* is to be taken at face value, these two monks bombarded Chih-i with objections, all of which he demolished with ease."[79] Chih-i's exposition of the *Scripture for Humane Kings* was in all prob-

75. *Hsu kao-seng chüan*, T 2060 50.564b9–11.

76. Hurvitz, *Chih-I*, pp. 109–10. Chih-i's correspondence from this time, preserved in *Kuo-ch'ing po lu* (T 1934), includes his reference to "the Humane King's capacious Way" (49.799b23), and the reply (799c24) calls Chi-i the "forbearing master" (*jen-shih*). Discussions of kingship are also preserved at 817b25–28, c23–24, and 823b19–21.

77. Hurvitz, *Chih-I*, pp. 119–20. It is interesting to note that this amounts to a variation of a scheme proposed under the Northern Wei and is reminiscent of Fa-kuo's identification of the emperor with the Buddha.

78. Hurvitz, *Chih-I*, p. 133.

79. Ibid., 134–35. *Hsü kao-tseng chuan* (T 2060 50.565c9–12, 27–566a3) also records the event. The biography of Chih-i in the *Fo-tsu t'ung-chi* records other details, including the name of the Hall (T'ai-chi t'ien), that the event took place in the fourth month of 586, and that one hundred seats were set up (in accordance with the prescription of the *Scripture for Humane Kings*. 182c). On 247c we are also told that Chih-i lectured on both the *Ta chih-tu lun* and the *Scripture for Humane Kings*, and that in 587 at the Kuang-yu monastery a similar series of lectures was held which the emperor personally attended and at which he made three prostrations in honor of the text. Duplicate references are found

ability part of the ritual exposition that the scripture recommends in times of trouble. Chih-i continued to preach at the capital for another three years until he fled the city before the advancing Sui army in 589.

The new Sui ruler (Emperor Wen, r. 589–605), a devout Buddhist and a shrewd politician, realized that the major disruption of patronage and of civil and clerical institutions in the south would take some effort to mend. As a result, the Sui set on a policy of currying the favor of famous southern clerics, and particularly of Chih-i. Thus, in 589 and 590 Chih-i was drawn into a correspondence with scions of the Sui and with Emperor Wen himself. Of great interest to our exploration is that protection of the state quickly comes to the forefront of the correspondence and remains one of its major themes. The most important correspondence was between Chih-i and Yang Kuang, the future Emperor Yang. This correspondence was to continue after Chih-i's death with other members of the T'ien-t'ai school, and notably with Kuan-ting, Chih-i's disciple and recorder.

In the political climate of the first unification of China in four hundred years it is no surprise that the protection of the state forms a constant theme in this correspondence. Nor is it surprising to see occasional references to the *Scripture for Humane Kings*. Setting the tone for these exchanges is Emperor Wen's edict concerning public and private religious works:

> The ideal of the Thus-come One's teaching is uniformity and the thoughtful care of the bodhisattvas is fundamentally without distinctions. Therefore they are capable of saving all species, of bringing salvation to living creatures. Our position being that of a sovereign among men, we have continuously glorified the Three Treasures. We have ever spoken of the ultimate principle and have disseminated and clarified the Mahāyāna. All the teachings are open and clear; in their substance there is no distinction between "we" and "they." How much less in religious works should there be distinction between public and private.[80]

Yet this profession of nondiscrimination was not always the reality. Writing in 592 to Yang Kuang, Chih-i forwarded complaints voiced by southern clerics that rather than repairing monasteries the government was tearing them down or plundering them for other projects. In a carefully worded protest Chih-i in-

---

at 353b and 456a. It is a pity that the influential *Jen-wang po-jo ching shu* (T 1705) is not actually the work of Chih-i, for from it we seek clues to trace the founder's attitudes concerning the *Scripture for Humane Kings*. As it stands, the commentary is a reflection of the centrality of the *Scripture for Humane Kings* in the canon of the early T'ang T'ien-t'ai school.

80. Hurvitz, *Chih-I*, p. 143 n. 1, is quoting Arthur Wright's translation, of a passage in *Li-tai san-pao chi* (T 2034 49.108a–b), with minor modifications.

voked the image of the sovereign as protector of the Teaching, beginning, "Your Highness has always been a true defender of the Faith, a veritable bodhisattva of mercy."[81]

As we have seen, Chih-i's two major works, the *Profound Meaning of the Lotus of the Teaching* and the *Great Calming and Contemplation*, produced in Chiang-ling in 593 and 594, are strewn with references to the *Scripture for Humane Kings*. Shortly thereafter in 595, during a brief stay at Chiang-tu, we find the first overt reference to the *Scripture for Humane Kings* in Chih-i's correspondance with Prince Kuang. Apparently Chih-i had given his partially completed commentary on the *Vimalakīrtinirdeśa* to the prince, who then wrote to request the rest of the work. Chih-i's reply opens by flattering the prince, "The Humane King's encompassing Way embraces beings who are his trust, and shelters the bodhisattvas of the ten stages, responding to beings as a great family."[82] But Chih-i's use of notions for which the *Scripture for Humane Kings* forms a background are nowhere clearer than in a long missive written to Yang Kuang three days before his death. In part it reads,

> Happily I encountered an illustrious age, and thus was a pillar in a bridge to the Sun of Buddhahood. I beg to place my reliance in Imperial glory, also to enjoy the strength of the multitude and, in order to encourage those who have the [karmic] nexus, to repair these three places: first, in order to raise up and glorify the Law of the Buddha of the three ages; next to protect the land of the Great Sui [*wei yung-hu ta sui kuo-t'u*]; last, for the sake of all the multitudinous beings of the Sphere of the Law.[83]

In his last surviving letter, to be delivered to Yang Kuang after his death, Chih-i writes:

> I deficient in the Way, early encountered a superior [karmic] nexus. When I first raised up my heart [to bodhi], upwardly I hoped for the forbearance of the truth of the birthlessness of constituents [*wu-sheng jen*], downwardly I sought purity of the six senses. . . . Universal action and universal learning, these are the conduct of the bodhisattva. *When the Tathāgata becomes extinct, the Teaching is entrusted to the sovereign of the realm*. . . . After my life is over, if I have any spiritual power, I vow to protect the territories of Your Highness. If the effect of my vow spreads

81. Hurvitz, *Chih-I*, pp. 147–48.
82. *Kuo-ch'ing po-lu*, T 1934 46.807b23. See Hurvitz, *Chih-I*, pp. 156–58 on the sequence of events.
83. Hurvitz, *Chih-I*, p. 165.

abroad, with it I will respond to Your Highness' kindness, in keeping with my own original wish.[84]

The correspondence and patronage of Yang Kuang survived the death of Chih-i. Letters continued between members of the school and the new monarch of the realm, Emperor Yang, and these often touch on the protection of the state. The *Kuo-ch'ing po lu* itself, compiled by Kuan-ting, commences with an elaborate invocation of protection.[85] Indeed, shortly before his ill-fated Korean expedition of 611 Emperor Yang summoned Kuan-ting, Chih-i's disciple and recorder, who it should be noted, was by now the author of two commentaries on the *Scripture for Humane Kings*.[86]

Though we cannot pin down with certainty that the *Scripture for Humane Kings* was *the* model for the relationship between Chih-i, Kuan-ting, and Yang Kuang, their correspondence indicates its profound influence. Curiously, the year Chih-i retired from the capital to T'ien-t'ai (594–95) was also the year of the publication of the *Chung-ching mu-lu*, which still questioned the authority of the *Scripture for Humane Kings*. The year Chih-i died (597) saw the publication of Fei Chang-fang's *Li-tai san-pao chi* and the effective canonization of the *Scripture for Humane Kings* through its attribution of a lineage of translators. This "nexus" of circumstances along with Chih-i's use of the Three Truths underscores that the fates of the new T'ien-t'ai school, the Sui sovereign, and the *Scripture for Humane Kings* were intimately intertwined.

On entering China Buddhism was already a complex adaptive system that had developed in response to the needs of South and Central Asian communities. It brought with it a sophisticated repertoire of multiple cosmologies and notions of authority. This repertoire served it well in China, and in the *Scripture for Humane Kings* we can discern how the application of continuous and discontinuous strands of Buddhist cosmology enabled different interpretations of the relationship between imperial and monastic authority. The *rupic* themes of lineage, of the apocalyptic time of the End of the Teaching, and the long path of the bodhisattva are recursively linked to the *dharmic* theme of the timeless Correct Teaching and nirvana through the ritual practice of "true" kingship. Thus, the cosmology of the scripture is no mere ornamental flourish, nor is the scripture a crude attempt to curry royal favor. Rather, it is a sophisticated application of Buddhist notions of cosmology and

84. Hurvitz's translation, with minor emendations and emphasis added, *Chih-I*, pp. 166–69. The original is *Kuo-ch'ing po-lu*, T 1934 46.809c–810c. "When the Tathagata becomes extinct . . ." at 810a16–23 is an allusion to the fifth-century recension of the *Scripture for Humane Kings*, T 245 8.832b21–25.

85. *Kuo-ch'ing po-lu*, T 1934 46.794a23–796b.

86. Hurvitz, *Chih-I*, p. 180. These are unfortunately no longer extant.

authority to create a new Buddhism for new historical circumstances. This process of adapting Buddhist notions of authority to Chinese needs was expressed in a distinctly Chinese manner. With the scheme of the five forbearances and the pun on the word *jen* the *Scripture for Humane Kings* skillfully played "the edge" in a way that is both Buddhist and Chinese. Transcendent Wisdom indeed shaped and was shaped by the politics of fifth-century North China.

It is very likely that these circumstances gave birth to the lineage of translators Fei Chang-fang attributes to the *Scripture for Humane Kings*. The canonization of the *Scripture for Humane Kings* is of a piece with the birth of the first truly Chinese school of Buddhism, and this is a fitting home for the first Chinese scripture to proclaim the identity of Buddhist and Confucian ideologies. With the birth of the T'ien-t'ai school, we see the birth of a Buddhism which was something of a cross between that of T'an-yao and that advocated in the *Scripture for Humane Kings*. But the story does not end here. The fifth-century version of the *Scripture for Humane Kings* was superseded some 150 years later by a new "translation" produced under imperial auspices by the Esoteric master Pu-k'ung, and it is to the esoteric *Scripture for Humane Kings* that we may now turn.

5

Esoteric Turns

> Humane kings treasure this scripture and its meaning is noble and it protects the state. In translations of previous eras its principles have not yet been [fully] transmitted. (*Fo-tsu t'ung chi,* 377c–378a)
>
> —Emperor Tai-tsung

New World and New Scripture: The Esoteric School and the Mid-T'ang Court

In marked contrast to the mystery surrounding the origin of the first version of the *Scripture for Humane Kings*, the second version was produced on imperial order by the monk Pu-k'ung (Pu-k'ung chin-kang, Sanskrit Amoghavajra) with the aid of his disciples Liang-pi, Fei-hsi, Yüan-chao, and others in 765–66, and we have an imperial preface for the text as well. The only "mystery" surrounding this second version of the text is how anyone could retranslate a text for which there was certainly no South Asian "original." While the canonization of the first version of the *Scripture for Humane Kings* is intimately connected with the T'ien-t'ai school, the second version of the text is closely tied to the rise to prominence of Esoteric Buddhism (*Mi-chiao*, tantra, or Vajrayāna) in the mid-T'ang dynasty.[1]

1. The relationship between "Esoteric" "tantric" and Vajrayāna Buddhism has been made unnecessarily complex by sloppy use of terminology. Tantras or "warp" books proliferated in India across reli-

As I have shown, the fifth-century author of the *Scripture for Humane Kings* tailored the *rupic* and *dharmic* fabric of Buddhist cosmology to specific historical circumstances, creating a distinctively Chinese image of Buddhist state polity. The success of the scripture lay in its promotion of a Saṃgha-state partnership in which monks and rulers could understand their relationship both in similar and in different terms. This relationship was expressed in the path of the five forbearances and instantiated in the word *jen* (forbearing/humane). In the eighth century the monk Pu-k'ung modified the scripture to fit the needs of his new Esoteric Buddhist ideology and the historical circumstances of his imperial patrons. Pu-k'ung's Esoteric Buddhism taught the practical realization of the Two Truths, the simultaneous achievement of mundane and supermundane goals in the recursive cosmos of ritual performance. In keeping with this new emphasis Pu-k'ung eliminated all references to the Three Truths. As I will demonstrate, Pu-k'ung's new recension of the *Scripture for Humane Kings* reflected the demands of Esoteric ideology and those of political expediency. The linguistic emblem of these demands is the great *dhāraṇī* Pu-k'ung inserted in the seventh chapter of the scripture. By examining Pu-k'ung's new version of the scripture we can trace some of the adaptations of the complex system now recognizable as Chinese Buddhism.

The historical, political, and doctrinal matrices of Chinese Esoteric Buddhism and the material and intellectual circumstances that gave rise to the new recension of the *Scripture for Humane Kings* are the focus of this chapter. The starting point for this examination is the "esoterization" of Chinese religion that began in the mid-T'ang.[2]

---

gious and sectarian boundaries by promoting techniques for realization. Some scholars have as "tantric" any technique in which the adept visualizes him or herself in the body of the divinity. Vajrayāna Buddhism properly speaking is the systematic blending of tantric practices with Buddhist Mahāyāna theology which took place in North India from the eighth century onward. Esoteric Buddhism (*Mi-chiao*) is usually identified as the system of tantric practice and Mahāyāna theology which took form in China under the leadership of Pu-k'ung, and it encompasses traditions that draw their lineages from him and other T'ang dynasty teachers. *Chen-yen* (Japanese *Shingon*, Sanskrit *Mantra*) is also used to designate this movement. I think this designation is a projection of Japanese sectarian notions on Chinese Esoteric Buddhism. I prefer to reserve the term *Chen-yen* as a translation of *mantra* in all but a few cases. Chinese Esoteric Buddhism is further blended with Vajrayāna teachings in the late ninth century through the efforts of the last wave of Indian Buddhist missionaries and translators, and then in the twelfth century and after by teachings imported by the Mongols. Giuseppe Tucci's "The Religious Ideas of the Vajrayāna" arguably remains the best overall introduction to Indo-Tibetan Vajrayāna. Virginia Vacca's translation of it is found in his *Tibetan Painted Scrolls* (Rome: Libreria Dello Stato, 1949), 1:209–49.

2. Yoshioka Yoshitoyo has characterized post-T'ang Buddhism as consisting of Ch'an, Pure Land, and tantra, or Esoteric Buddhism. I think it is safe to say, even more generally, that post-T'ang religion consisted of a process that organized the religious world around a few key genera, while in and between those genera we find a growing elaboration, variation, and adaptation of specific rites. One such process might be characterized as the spread and fusion of esoteric rites into popular religious settings and the concomitant elaboration of new forms of religious and social organization. See *Dōkyō to bukkyō*, vol. 1 (Tokyo: Nihon gakujutsu shinkōkai, 1959), p. 369.

Between the third century and the beginning of the eighth century, South and Central Asian Buddhist texts, focused on ritual and studded with *mantras* and *dhāraṇīs*, began first to trickle and then to pour into China.[3] This piecemeal transmission continued until Śubhakarasimha (Shan-wu-wei), arrived in Ch'ang-an in 716. Shortly thereafter (721) Vajrabodhi (Chin-kang-chih) and his disciple Pu-k'ung arrived in the T'ang capital to propagate and articulate comprehensive systems of Buddhist Esoterism (tantra). Perhaps the last significant test in the piecemeal transmission was the *Scripture of the Amoghapāśa Dhāraṇī, The Sovereign Lord of Spells*, translated by Ratnacinta (d. 721).[4] *The Scripture of the Amoghapāsá Dhāraṇī* is actually a small compendium of

3. Chou I-liang's "Tantrism in China," *HJAS* 8 (March 1945): 241–332, remains the best source on Chinese Esoteric Buddhism in English. His treatment of early "tantric" material in China is on pages 241–48. Material on Japanese Shingon, by comparison, abounds. Hakeda's *Kūkai: Major Works* gives access to the writings of Pu-k'ung's spiritual grandson, and works by Minoru Kiyota and Taikō Yamasaki give some access to Japanese Esoteric thought and practice, but see reviews by James H. Sanford, *Monumenta Nipponica* 44.3 (Autumn 1989): 383–85, and my "Reality Words," *History of Religions* 30.2 (November 1990): 213–15. The works of Tajima Ryūjun, *Étude sur le Mahāvairocana-Sūtra (Dainichikyō)* (Paris: Adrien Maisonneuvre, 1936) and *Les deux grandes maṇḍalas et la doctrine de L'ésoterism Shingon* (Paris: Presses Universitaires de France, 1959), are coming from within the Shingon tradition but are more comprehensive, though hard to get. In Japanese the classic work on Esoteric Buddhism remains Ōmura Segai's *Mikkyō-hattatsu-shi*, 5 vols. (1918; reprint, Tokyo: Kokusho Kankōkai, 1972), though some of his more radical conclusions have been shown to be unfounded. More recently, the works of Matsunaga Yūkei, especially *Mikkyō no reikishi* (Kyoto: Heiryaku-ji shoten, 1969) and *Mikkyōkyōtenseiritsu shiron* (Kyoto: Hōzōkan, 1980), bring to bear considerable new scholarship on the many-faceted East Asian Esoteric tradition. Though much of Japanse scholarship has been driven by both Japanocentric and Shingon agendas, Osabe Kazuo has explored the Chinese developments of the Esoteric School. His *Tōdai mikkyōshi zakkō* focuses on Pu-k'ung and his school, while his *Tō Sō mikkyōshi ronko* treats various "miscellaneous" developments, including the increasing importance of *Susiddhi* and rites for ghosts and so on. Finally, for tantrism in East Asia and the relative paucity of sexual symbolism, see Rolf Stein. "Quelques problèms du tantrisme chinoise," *Annuaire du Collège de France* (1974): 499–508, and "Nouveaux problèms du tantrisme Sino-Japanais," ibid. (1975): 481–88. For further bibliography in French Chinese and Japanese, see my "Seeing Chen-yen Buddhism."

4. My translation of portions of the scripture appeared in Victor Mair, ed., *The Columbia Anthology of Traditional Chinese Literature* (New York: Columbia University Press, 1994), pp. 116–20. The original Chinese version is T 1097, vol. 20. A polished version based on this text by the Brahman Li Wu is T 1096. Ratnacinta was reputedly descended from a line of Kasmiri kings and entered the Buddhist order as a boy. He excelled at chanting and meditation and developed a reputation as a strict follower of the Vinaya (rules of the discipline). He came to Loyang in 693 and was lodged in a succession of monasteries translating scripture until he moved to the T'ien-chu ("India") monastery at Lung-men in 707. From that time until his death at the age of over one hundred years in 721, he lived a simple life in quarters constructed entirely in Indian fashion. During this period he did not work on translation, though other Indians living with him made grammatical improvements on his translations, notably on the *Amoghapāsā Dhāraṇī*. For an overall study of Ratnacinta, see Antonino Forte, "The Activities in China of the Tantric Master Manicintana (Pao-ssu-wei: ?–721 A.D.) from Kashmir and His Northern Indian Collaborators," *East and West*, n.s., 34, nos. 1–3 (September 1984): 301–45. Forte argues that the scripture was not widely circulated but gives no evidence for this argument. Since a polished version was prepared, it seems that circulation of the text was intended. Apparently Ratnacinta and Śubhakarasiṃha were acquainted. See Chou, "Tantrism in China," p. 267.

rituals designed to serve a variety of religious needs ranging from curing illness to prolonging life to worshiping Amoghapāśa in a quest for enlightenment. Amoghapāśa, "the Unfailing Lasso," is a manifestation of Avalokiteśvara, whose devices—including the lasso or lifeline—save those in danger. Texts such as this, which may be expanded and contracted or modified as need and local concern dictate, were common as Esoteric Buddhism spread across India, Central Asia, and into China.

Although "tantric" Buddhist teachings had been slowly sifting into China since the third century, the Esoteric teachings which developed in Central Asia and India from the third through the seventh centuries remained eclipsed in China until the arrival of the Indian missionary Śubhakarasiṃha in 716.[5] The arrival of this *ācārya* ("teacher") initiated the growth of systematic understandings and applications of tantric techniques that coalesced to become the various lineages of Chinese Esoteric Buddhism.

Since the time of T'an-yao highly educated monks propagating the teachings quickly became servants of the state. The great *ācāryas* of the eighth century were not free to do as they pleased. On arrival at the court they were placed under house arrest as "guests" in government monasteries where they could be watched and interrogated. Once accepted they were put to work in the service of the state with teams of translators, rendering texts and performing rituals to augment state policy, to ensure seasonable rain, to repel invasion and put down uprisings, and to help promote the well-being of the imperial family and its ancestors. Thus, their teachings were shaped both by their particular religious ideologies and by imperial needs. Chinese Esoteric Buddhism in the eighth century was driven by political utility. As Osabe has argued, the organization of Pu-k'ung's teachings was based on the *Sarvatathāgatatattvasaṃgraha* (*STTS*).[6] But its articulation was determined in large part by state policy. For

5. The definition of and earliest dates of Buddhist tantrism are still debated. Some scholars, such as Alex Wayman, argue for an early date of the Buddhist tantras; possibly as early as the fourth century. His argument is in "The Early Literary History of the Buddhist Tantras, Especially the *Guhyasamāja Tantra*," in *The Buddhist Tantras: Light on Indo-Tibetan Esoterism* (New York: Samuel Weiser, 1973), pp. 12–23. Matsunaga Yūkei, *Mikkyō no rekishi*, and Kenneth Eastman have been cautious about such early dating of the tantras. See Eastman, "The Eighteen Tantras of the Vajraśekhara/Māyājāla" (paper presented to the 26th International Conference of Orientalists in Japan, Tokyo, 1981), pp. 4ff., who argues that while evidence from Tun-huang and elsewhere indicates Pu-k'ung did have the *STTS* (contra Ōmura, *Mikkyō-hattasu-shi*, pp. 476–90), there is little evidence for systematic Buddhist Esoterism before the seventh century. A brief resume of the paper appeared in *Transactions of the International Conference of Orientalists in Japan* 26 (1981): 96–96. John R. Newman's "The Outer Wheel of Time: Vajrayāna Buddhist Cosmology in the Kālacakra Tantra: (Ph.D. diss., University of Wisconsin, 1987) pp. 43–69, provides an overview of the dating problems of Esoteric Buddhism. Finally, Todd Gibson has recently pointed out the importance of Central Asia in the creation of Buddhist tantra in "Inner Asian Contributions to the Vajrayāna," *Indo-Iranian Journal* 38 (1995): 1–21.

6. Osabe, *Tōdai mikkyōshi zakkō*, p. 164.

this reason eighth-century Esoteric Buddhism was constituted as a loose complex of rituals for specific purposes devoted to specific divinities.[7]

When he arrived in Ch'ang-an, Śubhakarasiṃha was met with considerable suspicion by the T'ang emperor Hsüan-tsung.[8] The emperor was as interested in Taoism and the occult as he was suspicious of persons of reputedly vast power and insight. He impounded forthwith Śubhakarasiṃha's Sanskrit texts (and we can presume he placed him under careful surveillance). Apparently convinced that Śubhakarasiṃha's knowledge would be of more use than harm, the emperor returned the texts, and the *ācārya* was ensconced in an imperial monastery and put to work translating the teachings he had brought with him.[9] It was Śubhakarasiṃha who translated what became one of the two chief texts of East Asian Esoteric Buddhism, the *Mahāvairocana Scripture* (MVS).[10] The emperor's trusted servant, the Ch'an monk I-hsing, became Śubhakarasiṃha's disciple, and thus esoteric knowledge and techniques were applied to everything from the calendar to the making of rain.[11]

Four years later in 720, Vajrabodhi arrived after a circuitous journey, which had begun at the great north Indian monastic university Nālandā and taken him to the flourishing Vajrayāna center of Śrī Vijaya (present day Sumatra).[12]

7. This practical context has tended to be overlooked in studies of East Asian Esoteric Buddhism in favor of explanations of the overall "system." Ironically, the importance and result of this practical context is recognized in medieval Japanese manuals, which detail rites for specific circumstances and divinities (Chinese *pieh-ts un*, Japanese *besson*).

8. Hsüan-tsung (Li Lung-chi, 685–762) became heir apparent in 710 and reigned from 712 to 756.

9. For most of his life Śubhakarasiṃha lived and worked at the Hsi-ming monastery in Ch'ang-an. For the Hsi-ming monastery, see Anonino Forte, "Daji," in *Hōbōgirin*, 6: 700–701. See Chou, *Tantrism in China*, p. 264. Śubhakarasiṃha's biography is translated in Chou, pp. 251–72. The original of Chou's biography of Śubhakarasiṃha is *Sung kao-seng chüan*, T 2061 50.714b1–716a17. Other sources are Li Hua's *Shan-wu-wei-hsing-chüan*, T 2055 50.290a, and the same disciple's *Shan-wu-wei san-tsang ho-shang-pei-ming*, T 2055 50.290a–291c. On the sources used by Tsan-ning, the compiler of the *Sung kao-seng chüan*, see Chou, pp. 248–51.

10. For the MVS, see Tajima, *Étude sur le Mahāvairocana-Sūtra*, and Iyanaga Nobumi's excellent "Liste des abréviations (Bibliographie commentée)," which appears in "Récits," pp. 643–55. Yamamoto Chikyo has recently published a full translation of the text, making it available for the first time in English. The translation, however, lacks critical apparatus and is cast in a stilted, sometimes incomprehensible English. Notwithstanding, it is a useful and welcome contribution by one of Japan's foremost scholars of Shingon Buddhism. See *Mahāvairocana Sūtra* (Delhi: International Academy of Indian Culture and Aditya Prakashan, 1990.

11. I-hsing's biography is in *Sung kao-seng chüan*, T 2061 50.732c7–733c24. Osabe Kazuo gives a detailed treatment of this influential Esoteric/Ch'an monk in *Ichigyōzenji no kenkyū* (Kobe: Kōbe shōka daigaku gakujutsu kenkyūkai, 1963). Ch'an readily adopted esoteric techniques, as is apparent in evidence both from central China and from Tun-huang. For these, see Tanaka Ryōsho, "Tōdai ni okeru zen to mikkyō to no kōshō," *Nipponbunkkyōgakkai nempō* 40 (1975): 109–24, and Kenneth W. Eastman, "Mahāyoga Texts at Tun-huang," *Bulletin of the Institute of Cultural Studies Ryukoku University* 22 (1983): esp. 53–58.

12. Vajrabodhi's biography is found in Chou, "Tantrism in China," pp. 272–84. The original text is *Sung kao-seng chüan*, T 2061 50.711b6–712a22. There are also two biographies in Yüan-chao's *Chen-*

There is little direct evidence that Vajrabodhi and Śubhakarasiṃha were companions, but it is hard to imagine their not knowing each other and sharing texts during the years the two were active in the T'ang court. Vajrabodhi, like his predecessor, served the emperor in a variety of ways, but he was especially prized for wielding supranormal powers.[13] He is responsible for the first Chinese translation of the *STTS*, and on his death in 745 a stupa was built for him outside the eastern capital at Lo-yang.[14]

We do not know for sure when Pu-k'ung, Vajrabodhi's chief disciple, linked up with his master, but our earliest records place Pu-k'ung at Vajrabodhi's side.[15] Pu-k'ung succeeded his master as a mature man of Central Asian roots, but unlike his master he had spent all but his earliest years in the T'ang capital. Ensconced in the Ta Hsing-shan monastery (originally established by the Emperor Wen of the Sui dynasty), Pu-k'ung became the first fully initiated *ācārya* who was comfortable both in East Asian and South Central Asian languages

---

yüan hsin-ting shih-chiao mu-lu, T 2157, vol. 55, the first by Vajrabodhi's lay disciple Lu Hsiang (875b1–876b27), and the second, shorter notice by K'un-lun-weng (876b29–877a21). For the Kingdom of Śrī Vijaya, see D. A. Nilakanta Shastri, "Śrī Vijaya," *Bulletin de l'École Française d'Extrême-Orient* 40 (1940); 239–313.

13. For Vajrabodhi's exploits, see Chou, *Tantrism in China*, esp. 276–84.

14. Pu-k'ung requested this stūpa for his master. See T 2120 52.836a18–b15; also see Vajrabodhi's biography in Chou, *Tantrism in China*, p. 283. Vajrabodhi's "translation" (T 866 18.239b–253c) is a truncated rendition of the *STTS* comprising only the first part of the longer, four-part scripture, which we know from Sanskrit, Tibetan, and the later Chinese translation of Dānapāla (Chinese *Shih-hu*, T 882). Pu-k'ung's translation is similarly truncated, with a focus on the establishment of the mandala and its chief divinities. Neither translated the subsequent material on Trilokyavijaya or on the various "secret" *siddhis*. For a comparison of the contents of the Tibetan, Sanskrit, and full Chinese versions, see Chandra and Snellgrove, *Sarva-Tathāgata-Tattva-Saṅgraha*, pp. 8–10. The *Taishō* references given in the table on page 8 are in error. Eastman details the cycle of texts and their availability in "Eighteen Tantras."

15. Pu-k'ung's biography is translated by Chou, *Tantrism in China*, pp. 284–307. The original is *Sung kao-seng chüan*, T 2061 50.712a24–714a20. Pu-k'ung's disciple Chao Ch'ien compiled *Ta-pien-cheng kuang-chih pu-k'ung san-tsang hsing-chuan*, T 2056 50.292b–294c. Several eulogies and a stele biography by his disciple Fei-hsi, as well as Pu-k'ung's collected correspondence with three emperors and his autobiographical last will, are in Yüan-chao's *Collected Documents*, T 2120 52.826c–860c, which I examine in Chapter 6. On Pu-k'ung's origins, see Chou, p. 285 n. 1, and appendix M, pp. 321–22. There are conflicting reports concerning Pu-k'ung's birthplace. Some sources point to Sri Lanka, others to Central Asia, Although Yüan-chao says that Pu-k'ung linked up with Vajrabodhi in Śrī Vijaya, there is much evidence to the contrary. Both Chou and, more recently Todd Gibson, have argued that Pu-k'ung was from Sogdiana. See Gibson, "Inner Asian Contributions to the Vajrayāna," pp. 10–11. It is also doubtful that Pu-k'ung accompanied Vajrabodhi all the way from Śrī Vijaya, since Pu-k'ung says that Vajrabodhi told him of the discovery of the esoteric scriptures in an iron stūpa in Central India and the loss of the larger version of the *STTS* in a typhoon. The tale is related in *Chin-kang ting ching ta yü-ch'ieh pi-mi hsin ti fa-men* (Instructions from the Teaching of the Secret Heart of Mahā Yoga of the Scripture of the Diamond Summit), T 1798 39.808a19–b28, and is translated by me in Donald S. Lopez, ed., *Buddhism in Practice* (Princeton University Press, 1995), pp. 314–17. For the kingdom of Śrī Vijaya, see Shastri, "Śrī Vijaya," pp. 239–313.

and cultures.[16] In Pu-k'ung's work we see the systematic adaptation of the Esoteric teachings to Chinese circumstances and concerns.

Soon after his master's death Pu-k'ung received permission to travel to India to seek the latest version of the text that was to become the charter of his teachings, the *STTS*.[17] The mission aimed at garnering the full teachings of the text which was "tossed overboard" years earlier during Vajrabodhi's voyage to China. Pu-k'ung returned in 746 with texts, teachings and gifts from India and from King Śilamega of Sri Lanka.[18] These were presented to the emperor, and not long afterward Pu-k'ung was summoned to the palace to set up an altar for the emperor's consecration (*kuan-ting*, Sanskrit *abhiṣeka*) as a disciple in the Esoteric school.[19] Until the An Lu-shan rebellion in 756 Pu-k'ung remained at court in the emperor's service performing various kinds of ceremonies and translating and commenting on esoteric texts. He was honored with the purple robe and the rank of third degree.[20]

Although Pu-k'ung gained more prominence than his predecessors and found a following among the elite of the day, the Esoteric teachings remained in the shadow of Hsüan-tsung's Taoist interests, though it is clear that the emperor used both ideologies to bolster his personal and dynastic aims.[21] But with the rebellion of 756 and the ensuing chaos of the next eight years, all of this changed.

Hsüan-tsung and the court fled south in the night before the advancing rebel armies, in an episode that is among the best known Chinese history and litera-

16. Thus I refer to Pu-k'ung by his Chinese name while I refer to Śubhakarasiṃha and Vajrabodhi by their Sanskrit names. Pu-k'ung's monastic headquarters was located in Ch'ang-an and was one of the largest official temples in the realm. See Chou, *Tantrism in China*, p. 294. For Pu-k'ung's origins, see note 15.

17. For the *STTS*, see David L. Snellgrove's introduction to Lokesh Chandra and D. L. Snellgrove, *Sarva-Tathāgatha-Tattva-Sangraha*, Śata-piṭaka Series, vol. 269 (New Delhi: Mrs Sharada Rani, 1981), pp. 5–67. Iyanaga Nobumi summarizes the evidence for all three *ācāryas* having the *STTS* in "Recits," pp. 656–57.

18. See Chou, *Tantrism in China*, pp. 288–93, for an account of the pilgrimage. It is of interest that Pu-k'ung's pilgrimage coincides with the expulsion of *hu* barbarians precipitated by continuing tension between the *hu* and the Chinese empire. For this, see Gibson, "Inner Asian Contributions," pp. 17–18 and note 87.

19. In this and most other cases the *abhiṣeka* referred to the preliminary initiation into Esoteric Buddhism. See Chou, *Tantrism in China*, p. 293, *MVS*, T 848 18.33a–b; and Vajrabodhi's extensive treatment in *STTS*, T 866 18.248c–252c, and the treatment in *Mikkyō daijiten*, 409c–410c and *Bukkyō daijiten*, 811c–813c. An English account is available in Yamasaki, *Shingon*, pp. 175–81.

20. See Chou, "Tantrism in China," pp. 293, 296, 300, on Pu-k'ung's honors and ranks.

21. For Taoist legitimation of the emperor, see Charles David Benn, "Taoism as Ideology in the Reign of the Emperor Hsüan-Tung (712–755)" (Ph.D. diss., University of Michigan, 1977). For an in-depth study of a Taoist ordination early in the eighth century, see Benn, *The Cavern Mystery Transmission: A Taoist Ordination Rite of A.D. 711* (Honolulu: Univeristy of Hawaii Press, 1991).

ture.[22] The heir apparent, Su-tsung (Li Heng, r. 756–62) regrouped to the north at Ling-wu, while Pu-k'ung was trapped in the capital, now held by the rebels. Soon after receiving word of the emperor's abdication Pu-k'ung began secretly communicating vital information to Su-tsung and performing rites invoking the *vidyārāja* Acala in an effort to defeat the rebels.[23] During this period loyalist generals patronized Pu-k'ung, and some, such as the famous Ko Shu-han, received both counsel and *abhiṣeka*.[24]

After the loyalist forces had recaptured the two capitals, Pu-k'ung wrote memorials of congratulations and was invited to the palace (758–59). He soon reestablished an altar for *abhiṣeka*, "the primary gate to the Mahāyāna," and those for *homa* used for "averting disasters, increase, subjugation, and joy," and he consecrated Su-tsung as *cakravartin* possessing the "seven treasures."[25] In the following few years, until Su-tsung's death in 762, Pu-k'ung became a close and powerful confidant of the imperial family; and years later the Lady Chang, Su-tsung's empress, wrote a funeral eulogy for Pu-k'ung.[26]

By the time T'ang Emperor Tai-tsung (Li Yü, r. 762–79) came to the throne in May 762, the empire he inherited was largely a thing of the past. The rebellion of An Lu-shan, which had brought an ignominious end to the long and peaceful reign of his grandfather, had left its marks on what was now little more than the corpse of a great empire. His own father, Su-tsung, had indeed retaken the capital, but his power to rule was reduced to a fraction of that of Hsuan-tsung. Rival warlords with independent armies flouted requests for payment of tax revenue. In any case, taxes were nearly impossible to collect from a population decimated by war and attendant famine; many now were refugees, and tax rolls were useless. The sale of monastic ordination certificates to finance the suppression of the rebels had further reduced the taxable population.[27]

22. For the famous story, see Howard Levy, *Harem Favorites of an Illustrious Celestial* (T'ai-chung: Chung-t'ai 1958), pp. 132–33.

23. The episode is mentioned in Chou, "Tantrism in China," pp. 294–95, and in T 2120 52.827c24–828a24, where Pu-k'ung tells of his "*adhiṣṭhāna* rites" on behalf of Su-tsung, though no mention is made of Acala. However, Fei-hsi's stele biography preserved in the *Collected Documents* (T 2120 52.849a1–5) specifically states that it was Acala who was invoked. The import of this will becomes apparent when we examine the Esoteric rites connected with the *Scripture for Humane Kings*. Iwazaki Hideo treats the events in "Fukusanzo to shuso tenno," *Mikkyō gakku kenkyū* 18 (1987): 112–29 (and on Fudō/Acala, pp. 114–15), as does Yamazaki Hiroshi, in *Zui tō bukkoyōshi no kenkyū*, 242–45.

24. Iwazaki Hideo, "Pu-k'ung and Ko Shu-han," *Journal of Indian and Buddhist Studies* (*Indogaku bukkyōgaku kenkyū*) 34 (March 1986): 514–17. For a list of Pu-k'ung's disciples in court, see note 31.

25. PCC, T 2120 52.829b25–28. These are four of the standard five *homa* or immolation rites in the Esoteric school. I discuss them in Chapter 6, and Chou, "Tantrism in China," p. 295, outlines them briefly.

26. Her eulogy is in *Collected Documents*, T 2120 52.847b25–c13.

27. On the sale of monk certificates in the aftermath of the rebellion, see Gernet, *Buddhism in Chinese Society*, pp. 52–56.

What little the lords of the northeast and southwest had they kept for themselves. Tai-tsung's situation looked ominously like that of the rulers of the Latter Han, or even like that of the ancient Chou kings who stood as powerless figureheads, pushed this way and that by the whims of jockeying warlords.[28]

In this precarious environment Tai-tsung exploited every source of power, every possible bolster for his legitimacy. Among the court fixtures who had stood by his grandfather and father was the monk Pu-k'ung who had slowly been shaping the teachings of Esoteric Buddhism, now comprised of two lineage transmissions (his own and that of Śubhakarasiṃha), into a comprehensive vision of rulership and attainment.

While Taoist ideology had dominated the reign of Hsüan-tsung, now the situation was reversed. Fresh ideas were needed, and Tai-tsung reached out to Pu-k'ung and the Esoteric Buddhist teachings for aid. Esoteric ideology promoted the role of the *cakravartin* and his cosmocratic powers of transformation, and these notions comported well with traditional ideas of the transformative virtue (*te*) of the Confucian sage-king.[29] It was during this period that the newly coalescing system of teachings became known as Esoteric Buddhism (*Mi-chiao*).

Esoteric Buddhism now found itself in the role of legitimating the Confucian world order. It was under Tai-tsung's reign that many of *Mi-chiao*'s distinctive rituals came into being. Pu-k'ung became a regular in the palace and early in the reign gained privileged free access to the inner palace, where he established an "inner chapel for *homa* and *abhiṣeka*.[30] He became Tai-tsung's *abhiṣeka* mas-

28. For appraisals of Tai-tsung, see Denis Twitchett, ed., *The Cambridge History of China*, 14 vols. projected, vol. 3, *Sui and T'ang China, 589–906*, part 1 (Cambridge: Cambridge University Press, 1979), pp. 483–97, 571–80.

29. There is considerable argument over the meaning of the word *te*, which is commonly translated as "virtue," and which I translate as "transformative virtue." Granet and others, using examples from anthropology, noted the *mana*-like quality of virtue. Proper action caused, as if by a magical vital force, an appropriate response. Donald J. Munro has put forward some powerful arguments against the *mana* thesis based on careful textual and etymological work. He notes that *te* means to "look up to" or to "emulate" and that the force of the word is based on the emulation of exemplary models. See Munro, *Concept of Man*, pp. 99–116, 124–28, and his appendix, "The Origin of the Concept of *Te*," pp. 185–97. Victor Mair has argued for translating the word as "integrity" (at least in the context of the *Tao te Ching*. See pages 133–35 of his translation of this work). I usually explain *te* to my students as similar to harmonics on a guitar. If a certain note on one string is struck, a note on another string vibrates in harmony with it. Whether one agrees with the "mana" interpretation or not, the underlying notion is based on the ability of virtue to transform everything around it. It is a highly personal and continuous notion. The *Analects* are full of examples. Perhaps the classic example is the case of the sage-emperor Yü's exercise of virtue over arms against the Miao aborigines cited in James Legge and Clae Waltham, "The Counsels of the Great Yü," in *Shu Ching: Book of History, A Modernized Edition of the Translations of James Legge* (London: George Allen & Unwin, 1972), pp. 24–25.

30. *Collected Documents*, T 2120 52.840a19. This is revealed in a missive requesting that seventy-one translations be added to the imperial catalog of Buddhist texts. First on this list was the *Sarvatathā-*

ter and *guru* as well as the tutor of several other high court figures, including the chief ministers Wang Chun, Yüan Tsai, and Tu Hung-chien.[31] Men such as the powerful eunuch and military commander Yü Ch'ao-en competed to build Pu-k'ung chapels. Pu-k'ung reared one of Tai-tsung's daughters and nursed her in her illness.[32] He was soon appointed to a post in the Directorate of State Ceremonial (the office charged with oversight of monks and nuns as well as foreign guests), and he was accorded a series of high ranks and honors including the title "Master of the State" (*kuo-shih*), finally becoming, shortly before his death, duke of Su, with a fiefdom of three thousand households.[33]

---

gatatattvasaṃghraha. See 839a. This "inner chapel" (*nei tao-ch'ang*) appears to have been the "longevity hall" (*ch'ang-sheng tien*) of the Ta-ming palace. For its history, see Chou, "Tantrism in China," appendix C, pp. 310–11. The biography of Wang Chin in the *Chiu T'ang shu*, 118.3417 (hereafter *CTS*), discusses the chapel. Jacques Gernet has translated the relevent passage in *Buddhism in Chinese Society*, pp. 292–93.

31. A partial list of Pu-k'ung's patrons and disciples includes the emperors Hsüan-tsung, Su-tsung, and Tai-tsung; members of the Imperial Family Tu-ku Kuei-fei (queen), Prince of Han (son of previous queen), and Princess Hua-yang (queen's daughter, Pu-k'ung's adopted daughter); the government officials Liu Chu-lin (gov. gen. of Ling-nan-tao; Chou, *Tantrism in China*, 288–89 n. 22), Ko-shu Han (mil. gov. gen., Chou, pp. 294 n. 46, *CTS* 104.10a–14b), Li Yüan-tsung (comm. of religious affairs, Li Fu-kuo Chou, 295, *CTS* 184.7a–9b), Wang Chin (prime minister, Chou, 296 n. 61, *CTS* 118.10), Li Hsien-ch'eng (eunuch), Liu Hsien-ho (eunuch), Yen Ying (censor general), Yü Ch'ao-en (eunuch, comm. imper. army), and Yüan Tsai (prime minister, Chou, 330, appendix S, *CTS* 118.1a–6b); the monks Fei-hsi, Vajrabodhi, Han-kuang (T 2061 50.879c), Hui pien, Li-yen (Kuchean monk), Ch'ien-chen (Chou, 298 n. 67, T 2061 50.736b–737a), Hui-lang (Chou, 301 n. 85), Yüan-chiao, Hui-chao, Hui-kuo, Chüeh-ch'ao, Liang-pen, Tzu-lin, Li-yen, and Hui-lin; the lay disciples Chao Ch'ien (lit. council to emp. Chou, 300 n. 79); the taoist Lo Kung-yüan; and Hsü Hao (calligrapher). See Ōmura Seigai, *Mikkyō hattatsu-shi*, 3: 701–26; Chou, *Tantrism in China*, pp. 288–89, 293–97, Appendix S, pp. 329–30; and Benn, "Taoism as Ideology," pp. 297–300, passim.

32. Pu-k'ung adopted the princes of Hua-yang as his daughter, and cared for her until her death. Chou, *Tantrism in China*, p. 299; for a series of memorials concerning her, see *Collected Documents*, T 2120 52.843a16–b6, 843c14–844a4, 844a5–15. The princess's name is indicative of the Taoist proclivities of her father. Hua Yang is the name of the grotto-heaven purportedly secreted beneath Mao-shan, the home of Shang-ch'ing Taoism. On the Hua Yang grotto, see Edward H. Schafer, *Mao Shan in T'ang Times* (Society for the Study of Chinese Religions, Monograph 1, 1980), pp. 1–5. On the Mao Shan tradition more generally, see Michel Strickmann, "On the Alchemy of T'ao-hung-ching," in Holmes Welch and Anna Seidel, eds., *Facets of Taoism* (New Haven: Yale University Press, 1975), pp. 123–92, and "The Mao-shan Revelations, Taoism and the Aristocracy," *T'oung Pao* 63 (1977): 1–64.

33. For the Directorate of State Ceremonial, see Chou, "Tantrism in China," p. 296 and appendix P, pp. 325–26. For Pu-k'ung's awards and honors, see Chou, p. 300 and n. 82; also *Collected Documents*, T 2120 52.845c23–846b2, for the imperial edict enfeoffing Pu-k'ung. Pu-k'ung had already been awarded a nominal office of the first rank, third class (*kai-fu i-t'ang san ssu*). This new award was a substantive office (*Su-kuo-kung*). For the system of offices and ranks, see Ts'en Chung-mien, "The T'ang System of Bureaucratic Titles and Grades," trans. P. A. Herbert, *Tang Studies* 5 (1985): 27–28. The title *kuo-shih* originally had close connections with Taoist messianic movements. See Anna K. Seidel, "The Image of the Perfect Ruler in Early Taoist Messianism: Lao-tzu and Li Hung," *History of Religions* 9 (November 1969, February 1970): 227 n. 35 and 234.

Pu-k'ung oversaw a series of building projects, both in the capital and in the provinces. The most important of these was the rebuilding of the five monasteries on Mt. Wu T'ai and the conversion of one of them, the *Chin-ko ssu* ("Golden Pavilion") into the mountain headquarters of the Esoteric school, replete with altars for *abhiṣeka* and *homa*.[34] Among his other duties, Pu-k'ung was often called upon to control the weather and to nullify the effects of comets and unfavorable asterisms, and he promulgated a cult of the emperor as *cakravartin*.[35] He regularly prayed for the prolongation of the emperor's life and performed rites for the protection of the state and for the salvation of the imperial ancestors, tasks he passed on to his disciples as their primary responsibilities when he died in 774.[36] On his death, the emperor grieved at the loss of his friend and canceled court for three days. A sumptuous state funeral was held and eulogies and biographies were written by high court officials.[37] During his activity in China, Pu-k'ung had translated more texts from Sanskrit to Chinese than any other individual except the seventh-century monk Hsüan-tsang.[38]

Pu-k'ung had become the most powerful Buddhist cleric in the history of China and developed a new paradigm of religious polity for Esoteric Buddhism. A prominent element of this new polity was his new recension of the *Scripture for Humane Kings*. Between the mid-eighth and the mid-ninth centuries Esoteric Buddhism had been developed into a coherent system of thought and

34. For a survey of all of the relevant documents on this project, see Raoul Birnbaum, *Studies on the Mysteries of Mañjuśrī: A Group of East Asian Maṇḍalas and Their Traditional Symbolism* (Society for the Study of Chinese Religions, Monograph no. 2, 1983), pp. 7–38. Shortly after Pu-k'ung's death, his disciple Hui-shao requested to go to Wu-t'ai to perform *homa* rites for the protection of the state, and this was permitted by Tai-tsung (*Collected Documents*, T 2120 52.839b1–17).

35. For Pu-k'ung's efficacy in weather and comet control, see Chou, *Tantrism in China*, pp. 298–99. Various groups, both in and opposed to the government, attempted to identify the emperor or one or another charismatic monk with Maitreya, some other Bodhisattva, or as a *cakravartin* modeled on the popular legends of the Emperor Aśoka. For a summary of these trends, see Farquhar, "Emperor as Bodhisattva," pp. 5–34, and esp. 11–24. For a masterful study of the use of titles such as "Golden Wheel Ruler" or *cakravartin* during the Reign of the T'ang Empress Wu, see Antonino Forte, *Political Propaganda and Ideology in China at the End of the Seventh Century* (Naples: Istituto Universitario Orientale, 1976), esp. pp. 125–70, where the author includes an overview of the Buddhist legends in China, the concept of the *cakravartin*, and the predictions that the Empress Wu was also the coming Bodhisattva Maitreya. On the popularity of the Aśoka legends in China, see Jean Przyluski, *The Legend of the Emperor Aśoka in Indian and Chinese Texts*, trans. Dilip Kumar Biswas (Calcutta: Firma K. L. Mukhopadhyay, 1967), and Strong, *Legend of King Aśoka*.

36. *Collected Documents*, T2120 52.844b8–13.

37. Chou, "Tantrism in China," pp. 301–2. For eulogies honoring Pu-k'ung, see T 2061 52.847a2–852a.

38. For this dimension of Pu-k'ung's work and its context in the learning of Sanskrit in China, see R. H. Van Gulik, *Siddham: An Essay on the History of Sanskrit Studies in China and Japan* (Nagpur: International Academy of Indian Culture, 1956).

practice adapted to Chinese circumstances. This Chinese Esoteric Buddhism flourished until the twelfth century before being absorbed into Vajrayāna Buddhism under the Yüan Dynasty or dispersed as ritual techniques into other Buddhist institutions and into Taoist practice and folk belief.

Although some Esoteric teachings and texts had already spread throughout East Asia, the disciples of Śubhakarasiṃha, Vajrabodhi, and Pu-k'ung were the key links in the spread of a more comprehensive Esoteric Buddhism throughout East Asia. The teachings were exported to Korea by Hyŏnch'o (Chinese Hsüan-chao), Yirim (Chinese I-lin), and Pulga Saui (Chinese Pu-k'e-ssu-i), who were disciples of Śubhakarasiṃha; by Hyech'o (Chinese Hui-ch'ao) who was a disciple both of Vajrabodhi and of Pu-k'ung, and by Hyeil (Chinese Hui-i) and Ojin (Chinese Wu-chen) who were disciples of Pu-k'ung's disciple Hui-kuo.[39] At the beginning of the ninth century Japanese pilgrims such as Saichō (767–822), the founder of esoteric *Tendai*, and Kūkai (774–835), founder of *Shingon*, came to the T'ang to study under the disciples of the great *ācāryas*.[40] In the tenth through twelfth centuries Indian missionaries carried the latest Vajrayāna teachings from the great monastic centers of Nālandā and Vikramaśila to Tibet and Central Asia where they became the foundation of Tibetan Buddhism. But the crucial shaping of this comprehensive form of East Asian Esoteric Buddhism was carried out by Pu-k'ung in the context of the mid-T'ang court. The new recension of the *Scripture for Humane Kings* was a key element in Pu-k'ung's nascent esoteric religious ideology, an ideology expressed as the union of twin goals of mundane and supermundane benefit.

39. Henrik H. Sørensen's excellent "Esoteric Buddhism in Korea" is, to my knowledge, the only overall treatment of the topic in a Western language. It appears in Henrik H. Sørensen, ed., *The Esoteric Buddhist Tradition*, SBS Monographs no. 2 (Copenhagen and Arhus: The Seminar for Buddhist Studies, 1994), pp. 73–96. For these monks, see pp. 81–85. Hyech'o is the only one of these on whom we have considerable resources. See Jan Yün-hua, "Hui-ch'ao and His Works: a Reassessment," *The Indo-Asian Culture* (New Delhi) 12, no. 3 (January 1964): 177–90, and Yang Han-sung, Jan Yün-hua, Iida Shotaro, and Laurence W. Preston, trans. and eds., *The Hye-Ch'o Diary: Memoir of the Pilgrimage to the Five Regions of India*, Religions of Asia Series 2 (Seoul: UNESCO Collection of Representative Works, 1984), pp. 14–20, for a brief biographical sketch. For more, see Sørensen, "A Bibliographical Survey of Buddhist Ritual Texts from Korea," *Cahiers d'Extrême-Asie* 6 (1991–92): 159–200.

40. Esoteric texts and teachings had already reached both Korea and Japan prior to the eighth century and the garnering of more complete Esoteric teachings were the motivation for Korean and Japanese pilgrimages to China. Saichō studied with Shun-hsiao, who was apparently in Śubhakrasiṃha's lineage, and Kūkai studied with Hui-kuo, a direct disciple of Pu-k'ung. For Saichō, the vexed relationship with the two strands of T'ang Esoterism, and the relationship between Tendai and esoteric teachings, see Paul Groner, *Saichō: The Establishment of the Japanese Tendai School* (Berkeley: Berkeley Buddhist Studies Series, 1984), esp. pp. 38–64, and on the central role of Tendai Esoterism, Stanley Weinstein, "The Beginnings of Esoteric Buddhism in Japan: The Neglected Tendai Tradition," *Journal of Asian Studies* 34.1 (1974): 177–91. The best English introduction to Kūkai remains Yoshito Hakeda, *Kūkai: Major Works*, but see my article "Seeing *Chen-yen* Buddhism," for an appraisal of traditional biases in Shingon accounts of Kūkai's transmission.

The Esoteric Teachings

The Esoteric Buddhism of Pu-k'ung and his disciples draws together lineage teachings focused upon two major texts, the *Mahāvairocana Sūtra* (*MVS*) and the *Sarvatathāgatatattvasaṃgraha* (*STTS*), and on certain secondary texts such as the *Scripture for Humane Kings*. Both major texts begin with a description of the cosmic "sun" Buddha Mahāvairocana and his palace at the summit of the form realm in the Akaniṣṭha heaven. The palace, which is the very cosmos itself, is Mahāvairocana's "grace" (*adhiṣṭhāna*), a grace which is simultaneously the ultimate nature of reality or emptiness (*śūnyatā*) and the transformative process of the cosmos itself.[41] Extending and expanding the idiom of sovereignty found in the Mahāyāna, these texts proclaim themselves the "Great Teaching Kings of the Mahāyāna" and delineate a practice that aims at once for world transcendence and world conquest.

Like many Mahāyāna scriptures each of these texts contains two types of cosmology. One is the *rupic* cosmology of progress and process, exemplified by the bodhisattva path, by the imagery of seeds and fruit, families (*kula*), and the language of substance and time. The other is the *dharmic* cosmology *of* vision and light emphasizing the structure and instantaneousness of emptiness.[42] As I have argued, these two cosmologies provide much of the dynamic tension and

41. For Mahāvairocana, see Charles D. Orzech, "Mahāvairocana," in Mircea Eliade, ed., *Encyclopedia of Religion* (New York: Macmillan, 1987), 9:126a–128b. The *MVS* (T 848, vol. 18) is found both in Chinese and in Tibetan translations. Tajima Ryūjun's *Étude sur le Mahāvairocana-Sūtra* provides extensive bibliography and covers the Tibetan translations, pp. 141–48. More recent bibliography may be found in Shuchi-in Daigaku Mikkyō gakki, ed., *Mikkyō-kankei-bunken-mokuroku* (Kyoto: Dōshisha shuppan, 1986), section IV.2.b.

For the title of the *STTS* in its various reconstructions and various translations, see Kiyota, *Shingon Buddhism*, pp. 22–24, and Tajima Ryūjun, *Les deux grandes maṇḍalas*, pp. 21–22. The Tibetan version dates from the beginning of the eleventh century by Rin-chen bzang-po and Śraddhākaravarma (Tohoku no. 479). For the Sanskrit version, see K. Horiuchi, ed., *Tattvasaṃgraha-Sūtra* (Kōyasan: Kōyasan University Press, 1968–70). For an overview of the *STTS*, see David L. Snellgrove's introduction to Chandra and Snellgrove, *Sarva-Tathāgatha-Tattva-Saṅgraha*, pp. 5–67, and Iyanaga, "Récits," pp. 656–57. Abridged versions of the first of this scripture's sections were made by Vajrabodhi (T 866, vol. 18), Pu-k'ung (T 865, vol. 18), and by Prajñā (744–810, T 868, vol. 18). On Prajñā and his patronage under Te-tsung's reign, see Chapter 6 and Yoritomi Motohiro, *Chūgoku mikkyō no kenkyū*, pp. 1–107. A full translation which matches the Tibetan was produced by Dānapāla (Shih-hu, fl. 982–1017) is T 882, vol. 18. Pu-k'ung's outline of the complete scripture is in *Rites of the Eighteen Assemblies* (*Shih-pa-hui chih-kuei*, T 869 18.284c–287c). Also see Eastman, "Eighteen Tantras," pp. 1–4, and the bibliography in *Mikkyō-kankei-bunken-mokuroku* IV.2c. Iyanaga summarizes the evidence for all three *ācāryas* having the *STTS* in "Recits," pp. 706–7 n. 143.

42. For a discussion of the two texts, see Orzech, "Cosmology in Action," chap. 3. Traditional scholarship has repeatedly tried to pigeonhole each of these texts as predominantly Yogācāra or Mādhyamika. These efforts might serve some heuristic purpose, but as is the case with any text which is self-consciously synthetic, they blend many strands of the Buddhist tradition.

creativity of Buddhism, as well as its adaptability. In Esoteric Buddhist teachings, the world of process stands in the same relationship to the world of vision as *saṃsāra* stands to nirvana in the Two Truths. Unlike the Mahāyāna, here successful practice involves the immediate ritual realization of the Two Truths or, in the words of Śubhakarasiṃha and I-hsing, "The three unimaginable periods of time (*triasaṅkhyeyakalpa*) are nothing other than the accomplishment of enlightenment (*bodhi*); if in the course of a single life one frees oneself from erroneous attachments, why discuss a period of time?" (*Ta-jih ching shu* 1796 39.600c19).[43]

Esoteric Buddhism teaches the *ritual* realization of the identity of nirvana and *saṃsāra*, of emptiness and the world of images, of the Buddha and of every person. The practitioner seeks to realize the complete interchangeability of signs through a process of iconic simulation and manipulation, through an *imitatio dei* called the "three mysteries" (*san-mi*). These "mysteries" are the mysteries of body, speech, and mind. In Esoteric ritual the practitioner's body becomes Mahāvairocana's body (or the body of some other Buddha or bodhisattva), its posture and trappings based on iconography. The practitioner's speech becomes Mahāvairocana's speech or mantra (*chen-yen*). Finally, the practitioner's mind becomes Mahāvairocana's mind in the process of meditation and visualization. In the performance of ritual the *ācārya* both conquers and transcends the world.

As in other forms of tantric Buddhism, Esoteric Buddhism is concerned with the construction of a ritual reality, a universe which emerges in the *sādhana* experience.[44] Pu-k'ung's Esoteric Buddhism is based on Central and South Asian tantric teachings and focuses on *chen-yen* (Sanskrit mantra) or "reality words." *Chen* designates the real, apprehended through words, meditation, and image: reality to be grasped through images, a reality which is none other than the emptiness and simulation of all reality.[45] While Mahāvairocana's "grace" is present in all simulacra or images, it is ritual art, first as an exterior mandala or icon, and then as the mandala realized in the heart and body of the practi-

43. The great *Commentary on the Mahāvairocana Scripture* (T 1796, vol. 39) was written by I-hsing on the basis of oral commentary by Śubhakrasiṃha and should be regarded as a product of both men. Wilhelm Kuno Müller's "Shingon-Mysticism: Śubhakrasiṃha and I-hsing's Commentary to the Mahāvairocana-Sūtra, Chapter One, An Annotated Translation" (Ph.D. diss., University of California, Los Angeles, 1976), provides an entrée into the commentary as well as extensive bibliography. A rearrangement of the *Commentary* by Chih-yen and Wen-ku is the preferred version in the Japanese Taimitsu tradition. Ōmura Seigai provides a summary of the contents of the *Commentary* in *Mikkyō hattasu shi*, 3:370–414.

44. On the *sādhana* and its importance, see Agehananda Bharati, *The Tantric Tradition* (New York: Rider, 1965), pp. 13–17, 228–78, and Sanjukta Gupta, "Tantric Sādhana: Pūja," in Sanjukta Gupta, Dirk Jan Hoens, and Teun Goudriaan, eds., *Hindu Tantrism* (Leiden: E. J. Brill, 1979).

45. *Chen-yen* and Shingon are sometimes translated as "true-word," which unfortunately does not convey the sense of mantra as sound which somehow taps to the root of reality, nor does it convey the host of Chinese associations connected with Taoist "realized-persons" (*chen-jen*, often translated as "immortals").

tioner, and as ritual action itself which becomes the most instructive of simulacra.[46] As I will demonstrate, Pu-k'ung "esoterized" the *Scripture for Humane Kings* so that it points beyond itself to instantiation in ritual action.

Unlike later Shingon Buddhism or even certain strands of late T'ang Esoteric Buddhism, Pu-k'ung's teachings did not place equal emphasis on the *MVS* and the *STTS*. The most significant ideological factor in his Buddhism was the *STTS*, which provided the architectonic "grammar" for structuring, restructuring, and integrating a wide variety of practical and religious goals. The central role of the *STTS* as the ideological touchstone and grammar of Pu-k'ung's Esoteric teachings is enshrined in his story of the origin of the "yoga" teachings in an "Iron Stūpa" in central India. The legend of the Iron Stūpa recounts the origins of Pu-k'ung's Esoteric Buddhism and the "reappearance" of its key text and rites contained in the *STTS*. The story was related by Pu-k'ung based on the oral teaching of his master Vajrabodhi and is found in *Instructions on the Gate to the Teaching of the Secret Heart of Mahā-yoga of the Scripture of the Diamond-Tip* (T 1789 39.808a19–b28, *Chin-kang-ting ching ta yü-chia pi-mi hsin ti fa-men i-kuei*).[47]

Pu-k'ung's story begins with a typical "outlining" discourse that both situates the reader and sets the stage for the genealogy of the text and its transmission to China. The tale begins with a great worthy (*ta-te*, Sanskrit *bhadanta*) during the time of the End of the Teaching, who through the use of Mahāvairocana's mantra had gained a vision of Mahāvairocana and of a teaching that has traditionally been identified with the "Essential Rites for Vairocana" (T 849 and *chüan* seven of the *MVS*, T848). Using these techniques he then opened the iron stūpa (that is, he entered the mandala). Once inside the stūpa his education consisted of a course in the *STTS*, and we are informed that the text of

46. The amount of scholarship on mandalas is staggering and rivals work on Esoteric Buddhism as a whole. For an introduction, see Tajima, *Les deux grandes maṇḍalas*. Perhaps the classic work is Toganoo Shōun, *Mandara no Kenkyū* (Kōyasan: Kōyasan daigaku, 1927; reprinted in *Toganoo zenshū*, vol. 4, Kyoto, 1959). Lokesh Chandra, *The Esoteric Iconography of Japanese Maṇḍalas*, Śatapitaka Series no. 92 (New Delhi: International Academy of Indian Culture, 1971), includes a summary of major Japanese scholarly work on the mandalas. There is considerable disagreement as to the origins of the seventh *mandala*. The *Vajradhātu Mandala*'s nine-fold arrangement poses special problems. It is described by Tajima, *Les deux grandes maṇḍalas*, pp. 162–97, by Toganoo Shōun, *Mandara no kenkyū*, pp. 204–62, and by Kiyota, *Shingon Buddhism*, pp. 93–104. Note the contrasting arrangements of Tibetan *Vajradhātu Mandalas* in David L. Snellgrove, *Buddhist Himalaya: Travels and Studies in Quest of the Origins and Nature of Tibetan Religion* (New York: Philosophical Library; Oxford: Bruno Cassirer, 1957), pp. 227–42, and by Giuseppe Tucci in "Gyantse ed I suoi Monasteri, Part I: Descrizione Generale dei Tempi," in vol. 4 of his *Indo-Tibetica* (Rome: Accademia d'Italia, 1941). Much of the classic Japanese scholarship on the mandalas has been sketched out in Englsh in Adrian Snodgrass, The *Matrix and Diamond World Maṇḍalas in Shingon Bddhism*, 2 vols. (New Delhi: Aditya, 1988), and in Ulrich Mammitzsch, *Evolution of the Garbhadhātu Maṇḍala* (New Delhi: Aditya, 1991). Both works stick to doctrinaire Shingon interpretations.

47. See note 15.

the *STTS* available in China is but a superficial outline of the truly comprehensive scripture contained in the iron *stūpa*. A longer "outline" than that now extant was supposed to have been brought with Vajrabodhi from India, but this text, which is described as "broad and long like a bed, and four or five feet thick," was tossed overboard during a typhoon. We are left with the obvious conclusion that the complete and Correct Teaching is still available through initiation.[48]

Time and again Pu-k'ung frames his life and mission in terms of the Five Wisdoms in the *STTS*, and its five-fold mandalic structure became the template for new rituals for his imperial and aristocratic patrons. Pu-k'ung states this plainly to his successors and to the Emperor Tai-tsung in 771, requesting that the texts he had labored to translate over a thirty-year period be entered into the official imperial catalog: "Among the teachings I have translated, the Yoga of the Tip of the Vajra (the *STTS*) is the path for quickly becoming a Buddha. As for the remaining sections of the mantra teachings, these I present to help the state avoid disasters, to keep the stars on their regular courses, and to insure that the wind and rain are timely" (T 2120 52.840b1–2). Reading these comments from the perspective of later Japanese Shingon tradition with its dual emphasis on the *STTS* and the *MVS* we might mistakenly assume that Pu-k'ung relied on the teachings of the *STTS* for enlightenment and on the *MVS* for "worldly" goals. An examination of T'ang ritual texts from Pu-k'ung's lineage shows instead that the *STTS* and its central teachings not only provided the quick path to enlightenment, they also provided the basic structure or "template" for the key rituals of Pu-k'ung's state-protection Buddhism. What is more, only the most advanced students were granted full initiation to this teaching and Pu-k'ung took care to single them out: "Many are the disciples who have entered the altar to receive the *Dharma*. Eight of them have been nurtured and established in the [Yoga of the] Five Sections [the *STTS*], and two of these have died, leaving six persons [so trained]. These are: Han-kuang of the Chin-k'o [monastery], Hui-chao of Silla, Hui-kuo of the Ch'ing-lung [monastery], Hui-lang of the Ch'iung-fu [monastery], and Yüan-chao and Chueh-chao of the Pao-shou [monastery]" (T 2120 844a28–b2).[49] The *MVS* is clearly *secondary* in Pu-k'ung's tradition.[50]

48. Pu-k'ung's *Indications of the Rites of the Eighteen Assemblies* (*Shih-pa hui chih-kuei*, T 869 18.284c–287c) outlines this more comprehensive text. It is notable that the fifteenth assembly consists of the *Guhyasamāja yoga* (*Pi-mi chi-hui yu-chieh*, T 869 18.827a28–b7). For more on this, see Eastman, "Eighteen Tantras," pp. 42–60.

49. The Yüan-chao mentioned here is not the Yüan-chao who compiled the *Collected Documents*.

50. Iyanaga summarizes the evidence for all three *ācāyas* having the *STTS* in "Recits," pp. 706–7 n. 143. Although acknowledging that elements of both the *MVS* lineage and the *STTS* lineage come together in Pu-k'ung, Osabe makes it abundantly clear that the *STTS* provides the underlying structure of Pu-k'ung's Esoteric Buddhism and that this Buddhism is a "state-protection Buddhism." See *Tōdai mikkyōshi zakkō*, esp. pp. 164, 165–80 and 89–105. Pu-k'ung's pronounced leanings toward the

The Structure of Esoteric Ritual

Before we can examine Pu-k'ung's ritual manuals and how mandalas connected with the *Scripture for Humane Kings* were produced from them, a brief overview of Esoteric ritual and the templates from the *STTS* is in order. The purpose of ritual (*sādhana*) is *siddhi* (Chinese *ch'eng-chiu*, sometimes transliterated as *hsi-ti*), a term which literally means the attainment of a goal. In Esoteric Buddhism the basis of *siddhi* is often defined as the realization of the identity of the practitioner's body (*mudrā*), speech (*mantra*), and mind (*samādhi*) with those of the "basic divinity" (Chinese *pen-ts'un*, Japanese *honzon*). Some treatments of Esoteric Buddhism tend to overintellectualize the tradition by focusing on the mental component. Esoteric ritual involves all three components, mental, sonic, and somatic. When *siddhi* is considered from the perspective of ultimate enlightenment, *anuttarasaṁyaksambodhi*, then one refers to it simply as *siddhi*, or more specifically as *lokottara siddhi* (*ch'u-shih ch'eng-chiu*, or *ch'eng-chiu hsi-ti*). It is in this state that the vision of the "emptiness" and interchangeability of all images is realized. Cosmologically speaking, this *siddhi* is *dharmic*. Soteriologically speaking, it is *pariṇāmiki*. When this attainment is channeled toward action in the conditioned universe through images, mandalas, and mantras, it is referred to as mundane *siddhi* (*laukika siddhi*, *shih-chien ch'eng-chiu*) and is manifested through application of supernormal powers used to aid in the salvation of beings. Cosmologically speaking, mundane *siddhi* is *rupic*. Soteriologically speaking, it is *nairmāṇiki*. Though the purpose of any given ritual might be predominantly *dharmic* or *rupic*, all rites assume both goals.

This "dual" structure is often described in terms of "inner" and "outer" dimensions of performance. Rituals are articulated in terms of the inner versus the outer cosmos, the human body and the divine body, the samsaric cosmos and the nirvanic cosmos. These relationships are established and manipulated mentally, sonically, and physically through the use of visualization, mantra, *homa*, *abhiṣeka*, and *nyāsa*.[51] Such correspondences are repeatedly articulated

---

STTS are evident in his correspondence, as I will demonstrate below. Elsewhere, such as in the *Tou-pu t'o-lo-ni mu* (T 903 898c–900a), attributed to Pu-k'ung but probably the work of a disciple, both traditions are mentioned, and yet other disciples, such as his biographer Chiao Ch'ien, make pointed reference to Pu-k'ung's teachings as comprised by the *STTS and* "the method of setting up the *mandala* according to the *Mahākarunagarbhamaṇḍala* of the MVS" (see T 2056 292c5ff. and 283a6–9). Some Japanese scholars, such as Ono Gemmyo, have argued on the basis of *mandala* iconography that Pu-k'ung is the author of the pure "dual *mandala*" tradition. See, for instance, Chandra, *Esoteric Iconography*, p. 37. It seems clear that Pu-k'ung used the teachings of the MVS but not in a "double" sense as in Japan. The double mandala tradition probably arose in the generation after P-k'ung, and it never came to be the all-encompassing ideological emblem that it did in Japan.

51. On *nyāsa* (the localization of divine powers in the body), see Bharati, *Tantric Tradition*, pp. 273–74; Eliade, *Yoga*, pp. 210–11; and the *Mahāvairocana Sūtra*, T 848 18.22a–22b, 38–38c.

in the Esoteric texts and commentaries. For instance, in discussing *homa* (immolation), one text in the *STTS* cycle says that the outer *homa* is the fire altar, the sapwood, and so on, while in the "adamantine inner *homa* . . . total enlightenment is the flame and my own mouth is the hearth."[52] Although *siddhi* is thus of "two types," each attainment implies and requires the other.[53]

The ultimate soteriological element of Esoteric ritual is "identification," or the generation of the adept in the body of the divinity for the purpose of insight into emptiness. Nevertheless, most rites, such as those of the *Scripture for Humane Kings*, focus on the *effect* of such identification in the world. Thus, most rituals are apotropaic, and the adept, acting as the divinity, secures various sorts of blessings for a community. The apotropaic dimension of Esoteric ritual has not escaped scholarly attention. Stephan Beyer's *Cult of Tārā* demonstrates this dual goal in Tibetan rites to Tārā and the articles of William Stablein demonstrate the process in Newar healing rituals.[54] Indeed, the two kinds of *siddhi* may be considered the ritual realization of the Two Truths, a realization in which the adept simultaneously becomes "world renouncer" and "world conqueror."

The cultivation of *siddhi* is the aim of the Esoteric teaching, and Esoteric rituals, whether of the Indian, Tibetan, Chinese or Japanese variety, exhibit a highly regular structure based on the metaphor—harking back to the Vedas—of inviting a guest for dinner. "At the most fundamental and overt level, both Vedic and Tantric rituals are banquets in honor of the gods."[55] This is so in Vedic ritual (much else is, of course, going on), in *pūjā* ("offering"), which characterizes popular Hindu worship, and in the various rites of the tantras. Indeed, if we examine the sixteen traditional *upacāras* or "attendances" of house-

52. From the *Chin-kang-feng-lo-ko i-ch'ieh yu-ch'ieh yu-ch'i ching*, attributed to Vajrabodhi, T 867 18.266a12–21. Examples abound throughout the tradition.

53. The root texts of the tradition discuss not only the attainment of enlightenment but also the attainment and use of supernormal powers. Rites used to obtain these *siddhi* comprise a large part of the latter portions of the *STTS*. So too, texts aimed at immediate "worldly" goals almost always point out the soteriological and transcendent insight gained in such practices. I detail these dimensions below and in the next chapter.

54. Stephan Beyer, *The Cult of Tārā: Magic and Ritual in Tibet* (Berkeley and Los Angeles: University of California Press, 1973), esp. pp. 254–58. See William Stablein, "A Descriptive Analysis of the Content of Nepalese Buddhist *Pūjas* as a Medical-Cultural System with Reference to Tibetan Parallels," in A. Bharati, ed., *In the Realm of the Extra-Human: Ideas and Actions* (The Hague: Mouton, 1976), pp. 165–73, and his "Tantric Medicine and Ritual Blessings," *The Tibetan Journal* 1 (1976): 55–69. For the Buddhist theory of disease and its relationship to practice, see Paul Demieville, "Byō," in *Hōbōgirin*, vol. 3, esp. pp. 249–63.

55. Wade T. Wheelock, "The Mantra in Vedic and Tantric Ritual," in Harvey P. Alper, ed., *Mantra* (Albany: State University of New York Press, 1989), p. 111. For an introduction to and brief bibliography on the vast topic of Vedic ritual, see Jan C. Heesterman, "Vedism and Brahmanism," in *Encyclopedia of Religion*, 15:217b–242a. For the metaphor of the "guest" in Vedic ritual, see J. C. Heesterman, *The Broken World of Sacrifice: An Essay in Ancient Indian Ritual* (Chicago: University of Chicago Press, 1993), esp. pp. 36–39, 188–89.

hold and temple *pūjā*, we find remarkable correspondence with *homa* and other esoteric rites.[56] Not surprisingly, one mainstream tradition in Japanese Shingon (*Chūinryū* of Koyasan) divides most rituals into five modules based on the guest metaphor: purification, construction, encounter, identification, and dissociation.[57]

However the stages of ritual are divided, what occurs is the construction of a world—of a mandala—in which the adept and the Buddhas, bodhisattvas, or guardian divinities can meet. This fundamental mandalic structure is a simulacrum of the cosmos with Mahāvairocana enthroned in the palace at the summit of the realm of form (the *akaniṣṭha* heaven). The ritual construction of the mandala is the construction of the universe. The process of construction culminates in the consecration (*abhiṣeka*) of the adept.[58] Realizing the complete identity of his body, speech, and mind with that of Mahāvairocana, the fully initiated adept is consecrated Lord of the Triple World. This "lordship" involves both world transcendence (*lokkotara siddhi*, Chinese *ch'u shih-chieh ch'eng-chiu*) and world conquest (*laukika siddhi*, Chinese *shih-chieh ch'eng-chiu*). This element of "world conquest" was taken quite seriously in East Asia and royal patrons endowed grand temples with permanent mandalas/altars for *abhiṣeka* and *homa*. Indeed, the Esoteric focus on various "simulacra" made the religion an ideal vehicle for ostentatious displays of wealth which characterized the mid-T'ang elite.

The Esoteric ritual system of Vajrabodhi, Pu-k'ung, and their disciples at first seems labyrinthian. One is confronted with hosts of divinities, Buddhas, and bodhisattvas, with seemingly endless ritual texts and ritual variations. In fact the system is quite straightforward, even when we take into account the tendency to ritual accretion and elaboration over time. As in Taoist rituals scrutinized by Kristofer Schipper, and in alchemical texts studied by John Read, we find here an architectonic ritual paradigm or template out of which specific rituals are constructed to meet specific needs. These rituals are themselves composed by stringing together a series of "rites" in a sort of boilerplate fashion.[59]

56. For a convenient overview of *pūja* and relevant bibliography, see Nancy E. Auer Falk. "Pūja," in *Encyclopedia of Religion*, 12:83a–85a. The list of the sixteen *upacāras*, "invocation," "offering a seat," "greeting," "water," and so on, is on page 84a.

57. For this analysis, see Richard K. Payne, "Feeding the Gods: The Shingon Fire Ritual" (Ph.D. diss., Graduate Theological Union, University of California, Berkeley, 1985), pp. 219ff. Payne's thesis has been published as *The Tantric Ritual of Japan: Feeding the Gods: The Shingon Fire Ritual* (New Delhi: Aditya, 1991).

58. The process begins on T 866 18.237c and runs through 239b.

59. Kristofer Schipper, *The Taoist Body*, trans. Karen C. Duval (Berkeley and Los Angeles: University of California Press, 1993). For Schipper's discussion of rituals and rites, see pp. 75–80. According to John Read, "Alchemical ideas were limited in number, so that alchemical artists and writers were forced to seek novelty by means of slight alterations in their modes of expressing familiar tenets. Their emblematic drawings, like their expressions, often give rise to a feeling that they have been constructed

Ritual elaboration typically takes place through the embedding or nesting—sometimes recursively—of independent modules or rites into larger ritual structures, a process which usually involves some modification of the original ritual's concern.[60]

At the highest level, the architectonic paradigms—the "cosmological" outlines or templates—are laid down in the root texts of the tradition, whether the *STTS* or the *MVS*.[61] Each scripture details a distinctive mandala structure.[62] Thus, when we examine the *STTS*, we find a systematic procedure for constructing a mandala/altar based on the relationships of its constituent divinities. These relationships govern the construction of the mandala/altar and the progress of the ritual, from the establishment of boundaries, through the visualization of its central divinity, to the visualization of its subsidiary divinities or their *bīja* or *samaya*. The scripture gives the name and mantra of each divinity, his or her *mudrā*, and an iconographic description for the purpose of visualization.[63] In the case of the MVS the mandala unfolds as a lotus to reveal

from "standard parts." *Prelude to Chemistry: An Outline of Alchemy: Its Literature and Relationships* (Kila, Mont.: Kessinger, 1992), p. 238.

60. Fritz Staal has made similar arguments concerning Vedic ritual. See his "Ritual Syntax," in M. Nagatomi et al., eds., *Sanskrit and Indian Studies* (Dordrecht: D. Reidel, 1980), pp. 119–42.

61. In addition to these two scriptures, the *Susiddhikara* (T 893) was seen in certain late T'ang Esoteric lineages as a third, integrating principle uniting the *MVS* and the *STTS*. For these developments, see R. Misaki, "On the Thought of Susiddhi in the Esoteric Buddhism of the Late T'ang Dynasty," in *Studies of Esoteric Buddhism and Tantrism in Commemoration of the 1,150th Anniversary of the Founding of Koyasan* (Kōyasan: Kōyasan University Press, 1965), pp. 255–81, and Kazuo Osabe, "On the Two Schools of Garbhodbhava Esoteric Buddhism in the Latter Period of the T'ang Dynasty and the Method of the Three *Siddhis*," in the same collection, pp. 237–54. Osabe goes into greater depth in *Tōdai mikkyōshi zakkō*, pp. 209–52.

62. In the case of the *STTS* we find a five-fold structure composed of four Buddhas arranged at the cardinal directions surrounding Mahāvairocana. In turn, each of these Buddhas is the center of a similar cardinal and recursive arrangement. The divinities are seated on lotus thrones which rest on a lunar disk. In the *MVS* Mahāvairocana is surrounded at the cardinal and interstitial directions by Buddhas and bodhisattvas, but these stand alone and are not, as in the *STTS*, the center of further cardinal deployments. Each Buddha or bodhisattva is seated on a lunar disk which rests on a lotus (the reverse of the *STTS*).There are many treatments of the two main mandalas. The *Vajradhātu maṇḍala* is described by Tajima, *Les deux grandes maṇḍalas*, pp. 162–97, by Toganoo Shōun, *Mandara no kenkyū*, pp. 204–62, and by Kiyota, *Shingon Buddhism*, pp. 93–104. Note the contrasting arrangements of Tibetan *Vajradhātu Maṇḍalas* in Snellgrove, *Buddhist Himalaya*, pp. 227–42, and by Giuseppe Tucci in "Gyantse ed I suoi Monasteri, Part I." A convenient introduction to the *Garbhadhātu mandala* is found in Tajima, *Les deux grandes maṇḍalas*, pp. 55–141, and Toganoo, *Mandara no kenkyū*, pp. 63–188. The recent publication of works by Mammitzsch, *Evolution of the Garbhadhātu Maṇḍala*, and Adrian Snodgrass, *Matrix and Diamond World Maṇḍalas in Shingon Buddhism*, makes some of the classic work of Shingon exegetes available in English, though without advancing the analysis of the tradition. For further bibliography, see notes 41 and 46.

63. For example, the key "template" text for the teachings of the *STTS* in the mid- to late-T'ang was Vajrabodhi's *Scripture Outlining the Meditations and Chants in the Yoga of the Vajra Summit* (*Chin-kang-ting yü-ch'ieh chung lüeh-ch'u nien-sung ching*, T 866 18.223b–253c. The text is a truncated version of a much longer Sanskrit text. This translation renders only the first part of the full text and

a pyramid-like hierarchy of Mahāvairocana surrounded by the Buddhas of the cardinal directions and the interstitial bodhisattvas arranged on the eight petals of a lotus throne. In the most common graphical arrangements (the so-called *Genzu* mandala in Shingon) eleven other halls emanate from the petals representing the activities of the bodhisattvas. The *MVS* also classifies all of its divinities into three categories: Buddha, Vajra, and Padma.

In the *STTS* Mahāvairocana, seated in the *karma* assembly, is surrounded by four Buddhas representing four aspects of his wisdom. Unlike the pyramid-like hierarchy of the *MVS* each of these Buddhas is the center of another five-fold configuration that recursively replicates the larger pattern. Altogether, the scripture describes the five Buddhas, sixteen *prajñā* bodhisattvas, and sixteen *samādhi* bodhisattvas. These latter are divided into female *pūjā* and male *prajñā* bodhisattvas. Thus thirty-seven divinities comprise this mandala. The *STTS* classifies its divinities into Buddha, Vajra, Padma, Ratna, and Karma, in accord with the type of wisdom and mandala described in the text. While the *MVS* includes the Vajra-beings, they play a much more prominent role in the *STTS*.

Ritual "application" for specific purposes starts with the fundamental template, which governs the deployment of the mandala/altar itself, the names and iconography of the divinities in it, and their mantras and *mudrās*. Each ritual manual (Sanskrit *kalpa*, "ordinance," Chinese *i-kuei*, or *fa*, "method") is structured by the template in the form of the chief divinity for the ritual. Thus, in the esoteric ritual for Humane Kings, the *Prajñāpāramitā* bodhisattva of the *STTS* is the central divinity. Much of the rest of a given ritual, its subsidiary divinities and sequences of rites, is drawn from the *STTS*. Indeed, the construction of the mandala/altar is largely a matter of using boilerplate sequences appropriate to the *STTS*. These sequences include the purification of the adept and the site, and the construction of the mandala/altar, the expulsion of hindrances or evil influences, the invitation of the three "departments" (in this case Buddhas, bodhisattvas, and Vajra-beings) of the *STTS*, offerings (water, thrones, incense, lamps, and so on), meditation on the chief divinity, and exit rites (usually the reverse of preparatory sequences). All are structured according to the template of the *STTS* using sequences recognizable in a variety of ritual texts by their identical procedures, mantras, *mudrās*, and divine names.[64] This modular approach makes the system learnable, infinitely expandable, and easily adapted to whatever needs a new context might require.

---

focuses on the establishment of the great mandala and instructions for the initiation of disciples. The actual construction of the mandala begins at 227a. Each of the five central divinities is named and their mantras, *mudrās*, and iconography are detailed. Shih-hu (Dānapāla) provided the first full Chinese translation of the *STTS* (T 882) at the end of the tenth century.

64. One example of such "boilerplate" is based on the *Shih-pa kuei-yin*, which Shingon exegetes consider to be Kūkai's account of his master Hui-kuo's teaching. The text is T 900 18.781c–783c. It sets out a standard sequence of worship keyed to a series of *mudrā*. This sequence does in fact reflect

The teachings of Vajrabodhi, Pu-k'ung, and his disciples are permeated with images of sovereignty; with kings, *cakravartins*, and royal bodhisattvas. One key expression of this imagery is the division of all manifestations, functions, and attributes divinities into "wheel bodies" (*lun shen*, Sanskrit *cakrakāya*).[65]

> According to the Sanskrit text of the Yoga of the Summit of the Vajra [the *STTS*] in the possession of Tripiṭaka (Pu-k'ung) . . . the five bodhisattvas[66] manifest bodies differentiated in accord with two kinds of wheel. In the first—the Wheel of the [Correct] Teaching—***bodhisattvas*** manifest their bodies of truth [*chen-shih shen*] because this is the body received as recompense for the practice of vows. In the second—the Wheel which brings about the Teaching—[they] display their bodies of wrath [*wei-nu shen*] because it is the body which, arising from Great Compassion, manifests as anger.[67]

Thus each of the five Buddhas of the *STTS* have three forms: Buddha, bodhisattva, and wrathful *vidyarāja*.[68] Buddhahood—the state of enlightenment itself—is represented as the "Wheel body of the Self-nature" (*tzu-hsing lun shen*,

---

sequencing found in T'ang dynasty manuals. For an outline of the sequence and the mudras, see *Mikkyō daijiten*, 2:888a–889b. For the T'ang manuals and their sequencing, see the tables of correspondence in Hatta Yukio's *Shingon jiten* (Tokyo: Hirakawa shuppansha, 1985), pp. 255 and 264–67. Hatta's dictionary is one of the most important works for the study of East Asian Esoteric Buddhism to be produced in recent decades. For a review, see Ian Astley-Kristensen, "Two Sino-Japanese DhāraṇīDictionaries," *Temenos* 23 (1987): 131–34. My Appendix D, "Boilerplate sequences in Pu-k'ung's Teachings," compares these sequences in key T'ang dynasty and Japanese texts.

65. Kiyota translates *lun shen* as "Wheel-body" (*Shingon Buddhism*, pp. 103–4). Unfortunately this is both meaningless and clumsy in English, and it misses the metaphorical, mythical, and cosmological connotations of the term (discus, realm/*cakravala*, ruler/*cakravartin*, and so on). I suggest *lun shen* abbreviates the phrase *chuan-lun shen*, "wheel-turning body or "body which turns the wheel of . . ." Thus, *Cheng-fa-lun shen* should be read as "body [which turns] the Wheel of the Correct Teaching," and *Chao-ling-lun shen* as the "body [which turns] the Wheel which Commands [or "brings about"] the Teaching." For the sake of fluid English I call these the "Body of the Correct Teaching" and the "Body of Command," respectively. See Ian Astley-Kristensen's analysis of the term in *The Rishukyō: The Sino-Japanese Tantric Prajñāpāramitā in 150 Verses (Amoghavajra's Version)*, Buddhica Britannica Series Continua III (Tring, U. K.: The Institute of Buddhist Studies, 1991), pp. 136 and 207.

66. "Bodhisattvas" (*p'u-sa*) here refers to the Buddhas Mahāvairocana, Ratnasaṁbhava, etc., in their compassionate activities.

67. Liang-pi is probably quoting—with some elaboration—his own comments in *Instructions for the Rites, Chants, and Meditations of the Prajñāpāramitā-dhāraṇī Scripture for Humane Kings Who Wish to Protect Their States* (T 994, 19.514a-519b, *Jen-wang hu-kuo po-jo-po-lo-mi-tuo ching t'ou-lo-ni nien-sung i-kuei*, hereafter *Instructions*), 514a24–28. I will treat this commentary in Chapter 6. The "wheel-bodies" are also covered briefly in *Bukkyō daijiten*, 1857c–1858a, 1315b, and 623a.

68. These three are similar to the "families" of the *MVS*, and it is tempting to see these wheel bodies as indicative of the influence of the *MVS*. Perhaps their inspiration is in the *MVS*, but as the quotation indicates, in Pu-k'ung's manuals they are clearly framed in terms of the *STTS*.

Sanskrit *svabhāvacakrakāya*). Apotropaic rites focusing on the beneficent teaching activities of bodhisattvas appear to invoke the "Body [which turns] the Wheel of Correct Teaching" (*cheng-fa lun shen*, Sanskrit *sadharmacakrakāya*). These beings have the term *vajra* (*chin-kang*) prefixed to their names. The chastizing and wrathful manifestations who are transformations of the Buddhas and bodhisattvas are designated the "Body [which turns] the Wheel of Command" (*chiao-ling lun shen*, Sanskrit *Ādeśanācakrakāya*). The term *vidyarāja* (*ming-wang*) is suffixed to their names, and they are activated in rites of subjugation and in situations where beings forcefully resist the teaching.[69] Liang-pi identifies the Correct Teaching body of each of the five Buddhas. For instance, the Correct Teaching form of Mahāvairocana of the *STTS* is Vajrapāramitā (the chief divinity of the Humane Kings ritual), and this form represents the body of Mahāvairocana, who having just achieved the state of total enlightenment, sets in motion the wheel of the Teaching "to transform and guide beings" to the other shore (T 1709 33.516b12–16). In apotropaic ritual one or two "wheels" (the Correct Teaching form and the Wrathful form) may be activated. Although there are no extant graphic representations of these wheels from eighth-century China, the Wheel bodies and their associations were given physical expression in Kūkai's *Ninnōkyō mandara*, which still survives in the lecture hall of Tōji.[70]

The Esoteric teachings of Vajrabodhi and Pu-k'ung constitute a complex system based on South and Central Asian principles and adapted to the circumstances of the T'ang court. This "quick path" (of Esoteric ritual) uses both the imagery of the bodhisattva path, of seed and family, and the visual imagery of emptiness experience of ritual. Not surprisingly, an examination of Esoteric ritual based on these texts often reveals marked recursiveness. The practitioner generates, worships, and identifies with a Buddha, a bodhisattva, or even a divinity such as Maheśvara. This attainment is at once *dharmic* and *rupic*, for in ritual performance, path and goal are one. One's own achievement of enlightenment is simultaneously salvific ritual action on behalf of others. In some rituals one preaches to and initiates other beings (in the communities, in the hells, and so on), who then are visualized as saving and initiating others—in a process that wraps around on itself in just the sort of "strange loop" I discussed

69. It is tempting to identify the Wheel body of the Self-nature with the *Dharmakāya*, the Body of the Correct Teaching with the *Samboghakāya*, and the Body of Command with the *nirmāṇakāya*. From this perspective the Body of Command proceeds from the Body of the Correct Teaching in a fashion reminiscent of medieval Christian arguments about the Son and the Holy Spirit. Some Shingon exegetes do exactly this. See, for instance, the entry in *Mikkyō daijiten*, 2:844a–b, "sanrinzin," T'ang Esoteric teachings do not specify whether the Body of the Correct Teaching is a *samboghakāya* or a *nirmāṇakāya*. Indeed, in terms of ritual practice, both the Body of the Correct Teaching and the Body of Command are forms of the Buddha's compassion (compassion and wrath aroused by compassion).

70. See *Mikkyō daijiten*, 4:1764c–1767a.

Virūpākṣa (Śiva)				Bahuśrauta
	Yamāntaka Vajrayakṣa	Amoghasiddhi Akṣobhya	Vajradaṁṣṭra Vajrasattva	
Śakra	Acala	Mahāvairocana	Vajrapāramitā	Brahmadeva
	Kuṇḍalivajra Trailokyavijaya	Amitābha Ratnasaṁbhava	Vajratīkṣna Vajraratna	
Virūḍhaka				Dhṛtarāṣṭra
	COMMAND	SELF-NATURE	CORRECT TEACHING	

Fig. 3. The Wheel Bodies and the Tōji Lecture Hall

in Chapters 1 and 2.[71] Thus the savior becomes the object of salvation in the process of ritual. The adept and those he seeks to exorcise/initiate become ritual clones of one another. All are suffering, all are saviors, in a ritual experience where *saṃsāra* and nirvana collapse. This dual structure forms the underpinning of Esoteric Buddhism and most of its texts in China.

The attainment of *siddhi* is the ritual actualization of Esoteric soteriology in a "recursive" cosmos. The realization of the basic divinity (*pen-tsun*) of the rite is the realization of one's own enlightenment and the simultaneous purification of one's world. As I will demonstrate in Chapter 6, the ritual expulsion and subduing of demons and epidemics is identical with the process of the elimination of *kleśas* in the *homa* rite, a rite which results in the attainment of enlightenment both by the demons and by the exorcist.

As a result of this dual emphasis, both Esoteric and Vajrayāna practices have been excoriated as materialistic. But evaluations of these systems as materialistic fundamentally misunderstand the nature of the Esoteric Buddhism in China and its role in the development of Buddhism from the mid-T'ang onward.[72] It is this "refusal to distinguish between the everyday world and the experience of nirvana" that forms the context for Esoteric practice and for the new vision of polity which emerged with the Esoteric school in the mid- to late-T'ang dynasty. This refusal, coupled with a system designed to be shaped by whatever tradition it is resident in is the fundamental context for the new recension of the *Scripture for Humane Kings*.

71. Staal discusses recursive nesting, wherein a ritual composed of the same sequence of rites as the main ritual is nested into that main ritual. See "Ritual Syntax," pp. 132–35. I discuss recursion in Esoteric rites for the salvation of beings in the other realms of existence in "Seeing *Chen-yen* Buddhism, pp. 101–9, in "Esoteric Buddhism and the *Shishi* in China," in Henrik H. Sørensen, ed., *The Esoteric Buddhist Tradition*, (SBS Monographs no. 2 (1994): 51–72, and more briefly in "Saving the Burning-Mouth Hungry Ghost," in Donald S. Lopez Jr., ed., *Religions of China in Practice* (Princeton: Princeton University Press, 1996), pp. 278–83.

72. Many scholars of Buddhism regard the pursuit of enlightenment as somehow necessarily detached from the various "applications" of ritual to everyday life. Such interpretations do violence to the basic principles of Esoteric Buddhism and betray a modern, Western bias against anything in religion that seems remotely magical, worldly, or political. David Snellgrove is among the few who have questioned this notion. In his *Indo-Tibetan Buddhism: Indian Buddhists and Their Tibetan Successors*, 2 vols. (Boston: Shambala, 1987), Snellgrove has argued that "central to tantric practice is the refusal to distinguish between the everyday world (*saṃsāra*) and the experience of nirvana" (1:160). In fact, Snellgrove defines the Vajrayāna as essentially concerned with both enlightenment and practical ends, "such as gaining prosperity, offspring, a particular woman, good harvests or rainfall, overcoming adverse influences such as various kinds of disease-causing evil spirits, curing the effects of poison, etc. It is sometimes suggested that while the tantras, later classified as inferior, cater for the more mundane requirements, the superior ones are concerned with more truly religious objectives. In fact all tantras are interested in precisely the same objectives, whether supramundane or mundane" (1:235–36, and see 238 on *siddhis*). I have detailed the biases of traditional scholarship on Esoteric Buddhism in "Seeing *Chen-yen* Buddhism," pp. 87–97.

The Rebirth of a Chinese Buddhist Scripture

The second recension of the *Scripture for Humane Kings* (765–66) was prepared by Pu-k'ung at the request of the T'ang Emperor Tai-tsung and was a key text in the propagation of the Esoteric school in eighth- and ninth-century China and later in Korea and Japan.[73] In the tenth month of 765 Tai-tsung, ruling precariously over a now very decentralized empire and under the threat of an immanent Tibetan invasion to the North and West, ordered Pu-k'ung to produce a new version of the *Scripture for Humane Kings*. According to the *Chronicles of the Buddhas and the Patriarchs* Tai-tsung asked Pu-k'ung

> to set up one hundred high seats and to preach upon the *Scripture [for Humane Kings.]* The emperor descended for worship. As soon as it was done the bandits were pacified. An imperial edict said: "Humane kings treasure this scripture and its meaning is noble and it protects the state. In translations of previous eras its principles have not yet been [fully] transmitted." Thereupon, by imperial order Pu-k'ung Tripiṭaka *śramaṇa*, Fei-hsi, Liang-pi, and the rest were ordered to retranslate [it] in the Southern Peach Garden of the Ta-ming palace. The emperor personally read [the two translations] side by side and saw that although the two scriptures, new and old, matched in terms of principle, the new version was more comprehensive. [He] thereupon composed a preface for it. (*Fo-tsu t'ung chi*, T2035 377c–378a).[74]

73. The *sūtra* and the attendant rites have been used in suppressing rebellions, in sectarian warfare, and in repelling Mongol and American invasions of the Japanese islands. For Korea, see Sørensen, "Esoteric Buddhism in Korea," and for Japan see DeVisser, *Ancient Buddhism in Japan*, 1:121, 182–83.

74. The *Chiu t'ang shu* (*Old T'ang History*) notes that the rite was expressly ordered by Pu-k'ung's patron, the Emperor Tai-tsung, and it was carried out at the Hsi-ming and Tse-sheng monasteries in the capital both for the repulsion of enemies and for the promotion of rain. *Chiu t'ang shu*, by Liu Hsü et al., 945 (Peking: Chung-hua Shu-chü, 1971), Tai-tsung huang-ti chuan IX, no. 11, p. 10. The correspondence between Pu-k'ung and the emperor on this matter is found in Yüan-chao's *Collected Documents*, T 2120 52.831b19–c20 and 832a25–b12. *Fo-tsu t'ung chi*'s details obviously derive from these sources and the preface to T 994 and 995. All versions of the edict to translate the *Scripture for Humane Kings* also note that the same team retranslated the *Scripture of the Esoteric Teaching of the Mahāyāna* (*Ta-ch'eng mi-yen ching*, T 681, vol. 16), which had originally been translated by Divakara. The new recension is T 682. The *Scripture of the Esoteric Teaching* is composed primarily of *gāthās*, and while it does include many of the same themes—humaneness, a hierarchy of kings (736c), and relationships between humaneness and "Buddha lineage" (737c)—it appears to bear no more relationship to the *Scripture for Humane Kings* than that it too was a retranslation of an earlier scripture. In *Chūgoku mikkyō no kenkyū*, pp. 175–81, Yoritomi Motohiro attempts to link the *Scripture for Humane Kings* with ritual manuals for the protection of the state devoted to Vaiśravana. It is likely that someone in Pu-k'ung's circle authored the manual in question (T 1249 21.227c–230a).

Indeed, the joint forces of P'u-ku Huai-en, a military commander of Uigur origin, and the Tibetans had penetrated deep into Chinese territory when P'u-ku Huai-en died suddenly. The death was attributed to Pu-k'ung's ritual, a ritual that his disciple Fei-hsi notes was dedicated to the *vidyārāja* Acala.[75] In 767 Pu-k'ung requested an imperial edict to provide for the ordination of monks for the performance of the rite that was to be used repeatedly as a centerpiece of Pu-k'ung's state cult. Thirty-seven monks (the number of the central deities of the *Vajradhātu maṇḍala*) were ordained by imperial edict to chant the scripture and perform the rites on Mt. Wu-t'ai, to "establish the state as a field of merit."[76]

As we have seen, the previous success and popularity of the text rested in large part on its solution to the issue of the "Chineseness" of Buddhism, an issue it resolved by clever use of linguistic similarity to underscore soteriological links between bodhisattvas who protect the Buddha-fruit and kings who protect their states. In this new vision of the cosmos, kings and monks alike were sovereigns treading the same path. Just as surely, kings ranked as the lowliest on the path and could only show their progress through flamboyant prestations to the Saṃgha. Pu-k'ung reconfigured the text to emphasize the recursive cosmology of the Two Truths, a reconfiguration in keeping with the dual attainment of enlightenment and protection in Esoteric ritual.

The *Scripture for Humane Kings* once again served as a vehicle linking Chinese and Buddhist notions of authority and salvation, but it could not do this without modification. The scripture had to become an expression not only of the deep harmony between the goals of bodhisattvas and Chinese emperors, but also of Esoteric cosmology, polity, and salvific action in the context of the T'ang court. Pu-k'ung's new "translation" thus involved changes at several levels of the text: in terms of its surface appearance, in terms of its internal ideological consistency, and in terms of Esoteric practice.[77]

The *Scripture for Humane Kings* was written in a prosimetric form common to many Six Dynasties Buddhist scriptures. Thus the surface appearance of the text inherited by Pu-k'ung and Liang-pi was decidedly archaic, both in its style and in its vocabulary. Nearly three centuries had passed since its composition and, much like the King James Bible in the twentieth century, its language was anything but current (though it is, in places, more varied and more elegant than the eighth-century recension). Pu-k'ung retained much of this style and thus both versions of the scripture emulate the four-word phrasing and par-

75. For the circumstances of 765, see C. A. Peterson, "Court and Province in Mid- and Late-T'ang," in *The Cambridge History of China*, vol. 3, pt. 1, esp. pp. 490–91. For Fei-hsi's comment, see *Collected Documents*, T 2120 52.849a1–5.

76. *Collected Documents*, T 2120 52.835b17–c9.

77. Yoritomi, *Chūgoku mikkyō no kenkyū*, has a nice synopsis of the changes between the old and new versions at pp. 172–74.

allelism typical of the "church" language popularized by Kumārajīva's translations. Yet the earlier version tends to be terse, and the latter version often verbose.[78] In terms of prosody, the earlier scripture contains three verse segments, the first and the longest in chapter 3 is a summary of the path in seven-word lines marked by strong parallelism and no rhyme.[79] The second, which appears in the fourth chapter, is made up of strongly parallel five-character lines. The final *gāthā* of the earlier text appears in chapter 5 and is in fact quoted from the *Scripture of the Wise and Foolish.*[80] As this was supposed to be a retranslation, Pu-k'ung followed the form and style of these verses very closely, making minor changes in phrasing and occasional additions as warranted by his own theological agenda. He did, however, add a long *gāthā* in five-character lines as well as a *dhāraṇī* to chapter 7. Pu-k'ung was also forced to make some changes in "technical" vocabulary. The specialized vocabularies of Chinese Buddhism had undergone considerable evolution, and some of these vocabularies were already archaic when the scripture was first composed. Astronomical terms, for instance, had been regularized with the growing presence in China of Indian astrology.[81] Thus, in the passage describing the "seven difficulties" (*ch'i-nan*) in the fifth-century text we find,

> [If] the twenty-eight mansions lose their courses, or Venus, the Yama star, the Wheel star, the Demon star, Mars, Mercury, the Wind star, the Blade star, the Southern Dipper, the Northern Dipper, the great stars of the Five Wardens, all of the stars of state rulers, the stars of the three dukes, and of the one hundred officers, and all such stars each are transformed, [you should] recite and expound this scripture. These constitute the second difficulty.[82]

It is notable that even Chi-tsang has to gloss the terms that already appear archaic. Pu-k'ung's version reads:

78. Compare T 245 8.832a3–9 and T 246 8.842a7–11, which treats the fifth bodhisattva stage. For work on the language of early Buddhist scriptures, see Mair, "Buddhism and the Rise of the Written Vernacular"; Erik Zürcher, "A New Look at the Earliest Chinese Buddhist Texts," in Koichi Shinohara and Gregory Schopen, eds., *From Benares to Beijing: Essays on Buddhism and Chinese Religion in Honor of Professor Jan Yün-hua* (Oakville, Ontario: Mosaic Press, 1991), pp. 277–304, and Zürcher's "Late Han Vernacular Elements in the Earliest Buddhist Translations," *Journal of the Chinese Language Teachers' Association*, 12.3 (1977): 177–203.

79. Although there is no rhyme scheme, there is certainly much assonance.

80. Hsien-yü ching, T 202 4.426b–c. See my comments in Chapter 3, notes 39 and 67, and later here in Chapter 5.

81. Compare T 245 8.832c1–22 and T 246 8.843a18–b5. For Indian astrology in China, see Raoul Birnbaum, "Introduction to the Study of T'ang Buddhist Astrology," *Bulletin: Society for the Study of Chinese Religions* 8 (Fall 1980): 5–19, and Edward Schafer, *Pacing the Void: T'ang Cults of the Stars* (Berkeley and Los Angeles: University of California Press, 1977), esp. pp. 1–20 and his bibliography.

82. A fully annotated version of this passage is in Appendix A.

The second is when the stars and asterisms lose their courses, or when comets or Jupiter, Mars, Venus, Mercury, Saturn, and so on each are transformed or appear in the daytime.

Gone are the lunar mansions, the "blade star," the stars of the dukes, and so on.

In part, Pu-k'ung's renovation of the language and style of the text involved eliminating the remaining earmarks of Chinese composition, of silencing any overtly Chinese voices, whether or not the redactors were aware of them as such. For instance, the story of King P'u-ming, which appears in chapter 5 of the fifth-century text includes a *gāthā* which begins:

In the fires of the ***kalpa*'s** end *ch'ien* and *k'un*[83] are thoroughly incinerated, ***Sumeru*** and its great oceans are all reduced to ashes.
The fortune of the heavenly dragons[84] is exhausted and in their midst[85] all is withered and dead. The two virtues[86] have even perished, how can the state endure?
Birth, old age, sickness and death wheel around without interruption, affairs crowd in [on us][87] and we wish to flee, grief and pity do us harm.
Desire is deep and calamities are heavy, and our ulcers and illnesses are without external [cause].[88]
The triple world is all suffering, what can the state rely upon?
(T 245 8.830b5–10)

This story and the *gāthā* are in fact lifted from two earlier translations, the *Scripture of the Wise and the Foolish* (T 202 426b, *Hsien-yü ching*, Sanskrit *Dama-muka nidāna sūtra*, first translated by Hui-chüeh and others in the third century) and the *Assembled Scriptures [Concerning] the Six Pāramitās* (T 152 3.22c29–23a4, *Liu-tu chi ching*, translated by K'ang Seng-hui, also in the third century).[89]

83. *Ch'ien* and *k'un* are heaven and earth, respectively, in the idiom of the first two hexagrams of the *I-ching*.

84. "Heavenly dragons" (*t'ien-lung*) can refer simultaneously to emperors and to dragons.

85. It is possible to construe this as "in the middle" or even "in the middle [country]."

86. The "two virtues" (*liang-i*) refers to the two primordial dimensions of *yin* and *yang* in the language of the *I-ching* or *Scripture of Changes*. Chi-tsang discusses theses without so much as batting an eyelash.

87. My reading of this line is tentative.

88. Following Chi-tsang's reading of the passage, T 1707 33.346a2–3.

89. The *Hsien yü ching* has been translated into English from the Tibetan version by Stanley Frye, as *The Sūtra of the Wise and the Foolish* (Dharamsala: Library of Tibetan Works and Archives, 1981). See *Bukkyō daijiten*, 934b–935a. For the *Liu-tu chi ching*, see *Bukkyō daijiten*, 5072a–b. Zürcher, *Buddhist Conquest of China*, discusses K'ang Seng-hui (mid-third century) and the *Liu tu chi ching* briefly at 1:51–55. Interestingly, both of these early translations mention humaneness (*jen*) in this tale, and K'ang Seng-hui's goes to some length in discussing the "teaching of virtue and humaneness" appropriate to kings (*wang che wei te jen fa*, T 152 3.23c1ff.). Neither version of the *Scripture for Humane Kings* dwells on this.

The extensive interpolation of unmistakably Chinese terms such as the designations of the first two hexagrams of the *Scripture of Changes* (*I-ching*) *ch'ien* and *k'un* in these early translations, simply raised too many questions about texts containing them. Pu-k'ung's rendition is considerably different:

The fires of the ***kalpa*** rage, the great-thousand [worlds] are all destroyed,
 Sumeru and its great oceans are obliterated without a trace.
Brahma and ***Śakra,*** all of the gods and dragons, and all sentient beings are
 exterminated as well, how much more so this body.[90]
Birth, old-age, sickness, and death, grief and pity, suffering and vexation,
 hatred and affection, harass us and we desire to escape.
Love and desire bind and incite us, and we inflict ulcers and illnesses on
 ourselves; the triple world is without peace, what joy has the state?
(T 246 8.840b15–20)

Similarly, Pu-k'ung eliminated all references to the popular Six Dynasties messianic figure of "Prince Moonlight" (*Yüeh-kuang wang*), even when it meant substituting new material in its place.[91] Gone too is the Taoist flavored passage on the scripture as the "spirit-tally."[92]

Pu-k'ung also smoothed over a gaffe in the fifth-century text where the author unwittingly cites two different translations of a single Transcendent Wisdom text. The fifth-century version reads:

> The great enlightened world-honored one has already, during the twenty-ninth year [of his ministry], on behalf of me and the others of the great assembly preached the ***Mahāprajñāpāramitā,*** the *Adamantine-**prajñāpāramitā,*** the *Celestial King's Inquiry-**prajñāpāramitā,*** and the *Brilliant Praise* ***prajñāpāramitā.*** Why has he [now] done this?" (T 245 825b20–26)

Pu-k'ung's version corrects the list to eliminate the error:

> The great enlightened world-honored one has previously expounded for us the ***Mahāprajñāpāramitā*** and the Adamantine-***prajñāpāmitā,*** the Celestial Kings Inquiry on the ***Prajñāpāramitā,*** the Larger ***Prajñā-***

90. Liang-pi says that Brahma here indicates the lords of the four trance-heavens, while Śakra is lord of the "heaven of the thirty-three" or *Trāyastrimśās*. In the fifth-century text this stanza ends, "the two virtues (yin and yang) have even perished, how can the state endure?"

91. For the passages on Prince Moonlight, see Appendix A.

92. T 245 8.832c23–26, cited and translated in Chapter 3, p. 85 and Appendix A, p. 285.

> ***pāramitā*** and so forth,[93] and countless innumerable ***Prajñāpāramitās***. Why then, has the Thus-come One today emitted this great light?"

The eighth-century recension of the *Scripture for Humane Kings* also dispenses with the odd eight-based prediction of the End of the Teaching in favor of the normative five- and ten-based prediction. Pu-k'ung's text scraps the eccentric terminology of the ten bodhisattva stages used in the fifth-century text, replacing it with the familiar ten stages that had by the T'ang achieved normative status.

Although Pu-k'ung sought to eliminate overtly Chinese traits in the *Scripture for Humane Kings*, we would be mistaken to assume that the text had been purged of local Chinese concerns. Rather, the concerns have changed, and their integration into the body of the text has been made to appear seamless. For instance, as a government official in a Buddhism that was for all intents and purposes an arm of the government, Pu-k'ung could not retain the proclamation that "If any of my disciples, ***bhikṣu*** and ***bhikṣuṇī,*** establish registration and serve as officials they are not my disciples." The questions of assimilation and clerical independence so important in the fifth century had receded from active concern. State Buddhism was an institution with a long and honorable Chinese pedigree. Not surprisingly the line was dropped from the new recension of the text.

Beyond the reconstruction of the surface of the text, Pu-k'ung's eighth-century recension sought to eliminate ideological anachronisms and elements inconsistent with Esoteric doctrine. To this end Pu-k'ung expunged all mention of the Three Truths, which not only marked the text as anomalous and "T'ien-t'ai" (which, to an *ācārya* of South Asian orientation, probably amounted to the same thing), but which also contradicted key elements of Pu-k'ung's esoteric teachings, especially its promotion of the Two Truths and the strong recursion between *dharmic* and *rupic* cosmologies. The continuous and discontinuous *rupic* structure of the path found in the fifth-century scripture was left largely untouched, for as we shall see, Pu-k'ung made frequent use of the double meaning of humane/forbearing kings. But the elimination of the Three Truths had the effect of bringing the *dharmic* dimensions of the scripture *as* a Transcendent Wisdom Scripture to the fore.

Pu-k'ung was not content, however, merely to regularize terminology and to eliminate dissonant voices. In a number of cases significant additions were made to the text, additions which enhance its Transcendent Wisdom flavor.

93. The first is the 25,000-line *Praja ñāpāramitā*: the second is the well-known *Diamond Sūtra*. Liang-pi notes that the *Diamond Sūtra* is the ninth "assembly" of the *Mahā-prajñāpāramitā*, the Celestial Kings Inquiry is the sixth assembly, and the Larger is the second assembly (T 1709 33.450a3–10). For more on this see Chapter 3, pp. 83–84.

Thus, while a large portion of the text is nearly identical with its fifth-century predecessor, in other places whole sections were added.[94] Chapter 2 of the fifth-century text is titled "Contemplating Emptiness." Pu-k'ung's chapter 2, "Contemplating the Thus-come One," retains virtually all of the early version and inserts the following passage at the end of the chapter:

> At that time the World-honored One said to King ***Prasenajit,*** "By what signs do you contemplate the Thus-come One?" King ***Prasenajit*** answered, "I contemplate his body's real signs; [I] contemplate the Buddha thus: Without boundaries in front, behind, and in the middle; not residing in the three times and not transcending the three times; not residing in the five aggregates, not transcending the five aggregates; not abiding in the four great elements and not transcending the four great elements; not abiding in the six abodes of sensation and not transcending the six abodes of sensation; not residing in the three realms and not transcending the three realms; residing in no direction, transcending no direction; [neither] illumination [nor] ignorance and so on. Not one, not different; not this, not that; not pure, not foul; not existent nor nonexistent; without signs of self or signs of another; without name, without signs; without strength, without weakness; without demonstration, without exposition; not magnanimous, not stingy; not prohibited, not transgressed; not forbearing, not hateful; not forward, not remiss; not fixed, not in disarray; not wise, not stupid; not coming, not going; not entering, not leaving; not a field of blessings, not a field of misfortune; without sign, without the lack of sign; not gathering, not dispersing; not great, not small; not seen, not heard; not perceived, not known. The mind, activities and senses are extinguished and the path of speech is cut off. It is identical with the edge of reality, and equal to the [real] nature of things. I use these signs to contemplate the Thus-come One." (T 246 8.836a22–b5)

Although these additions are not as striking as the addition of the great *dhāraṇī*, they are part of an overall strategy to enhance the Transcendent Wisdom dimensions of the text while pointing beyond the text to a new ritual context. Pu-k'ung also replaced the "great howl bodhisattvas" of the fifth-century scripture with esoteric *vidyārājas*, and he made the text's application dependent on the proper use of the *dhāraṇī* he added to the seventh chapter:[95]

94. Chapter 7 is another instance. Pu-k'ung's text adds a substantial *gāthā* at T 246 8.842c11–843a5.

95. On the *vidyārājas*, see Przyluski, "Les Vidyārāja," pp. 301–18; the entry in *Bukkyō daijiten*, 4779a–c; and Robert Duquenne, "Daitoku myōō," *Hōbōgirin*, 6:652–70.

> Namo ratna-trayāya, nama ārya-vairocanāya tathāgatāyarhate saṃyaksambuddhāya, nama ārya-samanta-bhadrāya bodhisattvāya mahāsattvāya mahākārunikāya, tad yathā: jñāna-pradīpe akṣaya-kośe pratibhānavati sarva-buddhāvalokite yoga-pariniṣpanne gambhīra-duravagāhe try-adhva-pariniṣpanne bodhi-citta-saṃjānāni [844a] sarvābhiṣekābhiṣikte dharma-sāgara-sambhūti amogha-śravaṇe mahā-samanta-bhadra-bhūmi-niryāte vyākaraṇa-pariprāptāni sarva-siddha-namaskṛte sarva-bodhi-sattva-saṃjānāni bhagavati-buddhamāte araṇe akarane araṇakaraṇe mahā-prajñā-pāramite svāhā! (T 246 8.843c20–844a9)[96]

According to the text this *dhāraṇī*

> is the speedy gate[97] originally cultivated and practiced by all the Buddhas. Should a person manage to hear this single writ, all his crimes and obstructions will be completely eliminated. How much more benefit will it produce if it is recited and practiced! By using the august power of the Teaching, one may cause states to be eternally without the host of difficulties." (843c16–18)

The practice of the *dhāraṇī* will invoke the Buddha's aid, and he will

> command the ***bodhisattva-mahāsattva*s** of the five directions to assemble and go to protect any state wherever and whenever in the future the kings of states establish the Correct Teaching and protect the three jewels. (T 26 843b24–26)

The *vidyārājas* and the *dhāraṇī* are the most obvious marks of a new Esoteric ritual context for the *Scripture for Humane Kings*. These changes are signs of a new conception of the relationship between the emperor and the *ācārya*, a relationship actualized beyond the confines of the text in a new ritual context in which the Esoteric master was both "world renouncer" and "world conqueror."

96. I have rendered the *dhāraṇī* in Sanskrit since it does not appear in the fifth-century text and since this *dhāraṇī* was likely composed by Pu-k'ung. Hatta Yukio has reconstructed the *dhāraṇī*. See *Shingon jiten*, p. 246.4. For mantras and *dhāraṇī*s more generally, see Alper, *Mantra*.

97. Liang-pi's commentary indicates that "speedy" *su-chih* modifies "gate" (T1709 33.516c18–19).

6

Lords of Light

The *Scripture for Humane Kings* in Esoteric Practice and Esoteric Polity

> I possess ***dhāraṇī*** which can [afford] wonderous protection. It is the quick teaching originally practiced by all the Buddhas. If a person manages to hear this single writ, then all his crimes and obstructions will be completely eliminated. How much more benefit will it produce if it is recited and practiced! By using the august power of the Teaching, one may cause states to be eternally without the host of difficulties. (T 846 8.843c16–20)
>
> —Pu-k'ung's recension of the *Scripture for Humane Kings*

Esoteric Hermeneutics: A Confluence of Meanings

The reworking of the *Scripture for Humane Kings* and the new *dhāraṇī* added to its seventh chapter flow directly from the premise that the Esoteric teaching is the best method for the pursuit both of enlightenment and of "worldly" goals. As we have seen, the notion of the intimate relationship between supramundane and mundane *siddhi*, between inner and outer *homa* ("immolation"), and between enlightenment and compassionate action on behalf of others is found in the root texts of the tradition and is the basis for apotropaic ritual. This pursuit of a "dual goal" is implicit as well in Esoteric cosmology, and it is the key for understanding the importance of the recasting of the *Scripture for Humane Kings*. Now that we have examined how the matrix of Esoteric teachings and historical circumstances shaped Pu-k'ung's recension of the *Scripture of Humane Kings*, we can turn both to the larger context of Esoteric Buddhism and to its application in ritual and polity. In this chapter I will first explore how Pu-k'ung used indigenous Chinese religious symbolism to articulate Esoteric ideology. Then I will explore how—in Pu-k'ung's words—"The Correct Teaching patterns the state" (*Cheng-fa li kuo*) in rituals based on the *Scripture for Humane Kings*. In turn, I will explore how these rituals were central to the emergence of a comprehensive vision of Chinese Buddhist State polity in the major documents of the Esoteric school. This vision of polity constitutes yet another transformation of the Buddhist themes of mastery and transcendence of the world.

Pu-k'ung's Esoteric Buddhism was articulated in terms of the interdependence of the achievement of enlightenment and the defense of the state.[1] This Esoteric Buddhism was not a static tradition imported from South Asia and Central Asia and isolated from its Chinese environment. As I have noted, the *dharmic* and *rupic* strands of Buddhist cosmology and their expression in the modular structure of Esoteric Buddhist ritual constituted a system readily adaptable to new contexts and new needs. During three decades of activity in the T'ang court, Pu-k'ung moved beyond his teacher Vajrabodhi to develop rituals for his imperial patrons, often drawing on previous Buddhist teachings such as the *Scripture for Humane Kings* and on indigenous religious ideologies.

It was fortuitous for the Esoteric masters that they arrived at the court in the early to mid-T'ang. It has often been said that until the reunification of North and South under the Sui, there had been two disparate emphases in Chinese Buddhism. Buddhism in the South was dominated by intellectuals. It was literate and aimed at the acquisition of insight. Buddhism in the North, under the non-Han rulers, emphasized the pragmatic benefits of healing, prognostication, and in general, the supranormal powers of monks such as Fo T'u-teng.[2] However much such divisions are a function of our sources, it seems apparent that the Sui and T'ang ruling families united the two cultures and provided precisely the right climate for Esoteric Buddhism, which likewise aggressively united the pursuit of enlightenment and transformative activity in the world. This was a useful alliance, particularly under Emperor Tai-tsung, when all the legitimation that the emperor could muster was barely enough to keep the empire together.

In this endeavor, the Esoteric *ācāryas* applied hermeneutic techniques reminiscent of techniques of "matching meanings" (*ko-i*), which had long since been abandoned by translators.[3] Established as a method of translating Bud-

1. Osabe, *Tōdai mikkyōshi zakkō*, pp. 90–91.

2. The historical and geographical division of emphasis in early Chinese Buddhism oddly parallels the two sorts of *siddhi*. For the split between Northern and Southern Buddhism, see Ch'en, *Buddhism in China*, pp. 121–212. For the wonderworker Fo T'u-teng, see Arthur Wright, "Fo-T'u-Teng: A Biography," *Harvard Journal of Asiatic Studies* 11 (1948): 321–71.

3. On *Ko-i*, see Ch'en, *Buddhism in China*, pp. 68–69; Zürcher, *Buddhist Conquest of China*, 1:184; T'ang Yung-t'ung, "On Ko-yi, the Earliest Method by Which Indian Buddhism and Chinese Thought Were Synthesized," in W. R. Inge et al., eds., *Radhakrishnana: Comparative Studies in Philosophy* (Lon-

dhist technical vocabularies in the early Six Dynasties, *ko-i* brought together indigenous Chinese terms and notions in the service of communicating South Asian Buddhist ideas. Though *ko-i* effectively ended as a rigid means of translating with the advent of Kumārajīva in the early fifth century, the *hermeneutic reality* of using Chinese culture to communicate Buddhist notions did not abate; rather, it became more sophisticated.[4] The Esoteric *ācāryas*, especially the sinified Pu-k'ung and his immediate Chinese disciples, raised this technique to an art.

Foremost among the indigenous traditions Pu-k'ung made use of were mythology, speculation, and ritual practice surrounding the figure of the sage-king. This tradition was the foundation of Chinese imperial ideology and was also central in Taoism.[5] One of its many expressions during the mid-T'ang was the cult of T'ai-i and speculation centered on cosmological diagrams associated with the *Lo-shu* and the *Ho-t'u*.[6]

During the Han (206–20 B.C.E.) and Six Dynasties (220–589) numerological, prognosticatory, and cosmological speculation coalesced to form the structural principles for a wide-ranging cosmological system based on the five activities (or "five elements," *wu hsing*) and their disposition in nine "palaces" (*chiu kung*). In these speculations the universe was envisioned as a square of three by three or nine "palaces," the central palace representing the emperor,

---

don: Allen & Unwin, 1951), pp. 276–86; and Fung Yu-lan, *A History of Chinese Philosophy*, 2 vols., trans. Derk Bodde (Princeton: Princeton University Press, 1953), 2:241–42.

4. The task of interpretation in the context of "sinification" is perceptively treated in Robert M. Gimello, "Random Reflections on the 'Sinification' of Buddhism," *Bulletin of the Society for the Study of Chinese Religions*, no. 5 (Spring 1978): 52–89, and Peter N. Gregory, *Tsung-mi and the Sinification of Buddhism* (Princeton: Princeton University Press, 1991), esp. his comments on "doctrinal classification" (*p'an-chiao*), pp. 93–114.

5. For Taoism and imperial ideology, see Benn, "Taoism as Ideology," esp. pp. 14–55, and Seidel, "The Image of the Perfect Ruler in Early Taoist Messianism," pp. 216–47, and "Imperial Treasures and Taoist Sacraments."

6. The best recent work relating to the *T'ai-i* cult is Marc Kalinowski's "la transmission du dispositif des neuf palais sous les six-dynasties," in Michel Strickmann, ed., *Tantric and Taoist Studies*, vol. 3, *Mélanges chinoises et bouddhiques* (Brussels) 22 (1985): 773–811. Kalinowski criticizes the use of the terms *lo-shu* and *ho-t'u* as equivalents for a magic square of nine as a neo-Confucian anachronism. Seidel has explored the early use of the *ho-t'u* and *lo-shu* in the apocrypha in "Imperial Treasures and Taoist Sacraments," pp. 297–308. Other treatments include Fung Yu-lan, *History of Chinese Philosophy*, vol. 2, chap. 2, "Tung Chung-shu and the New Text School," and chap. 3, "Prognostication Texts, Apocrypha, and Numerology During the Han Dynasty." Also, Marcel Granet, *La pensée chinoise* (Paris: Éditions Albin Michel, 1934; reprint, 1968), pp. 127–279. Briefer and more engaging are the articles by Schuyler Cammann, "The Magic Square of Three in Old Chinese Philosophy and Religion," *History of Religions* 1 (August 1961): 37–80; "Islamic and Indian Magic Squares," parts 1 and 2, in *History of Religions* 8 (February 1969): 181–209 and 271–99. Also, "Old Chinese Magic Squares," in *Sinologica* 7 (1962): 14–53. For the Ho-t'u, see Michael Saso, "What Is the Ho-T'u?" *History of Religions* 17 (February–May 1978): 399–416. Henderson treats the diagrams in his *Development and Decline of Chinese Cosmology* (New York: Columbia University Press, 1984), pp. 59–87.

the outer palaces representing the provinces of the empire. The lord of the central palace is T'ai-i, the "Great Monad" or "unity." Through numerological speculation and the use of homology one could divine the orderly processes and transformations of the natural world, the alternation of *yin* and *yang*, and the cyclic transformations of the five "activities" and the five seasons.

By the time of the Emperor Wu of the Han dynasty (r. 140–87 B.C.E.), T'ai-i had been homologized to the sovereign in the palace of the pole star who ruled the eight other sectors of the heavens.[7] In later centuries the earthly emperor was equated with this heavenly ruler. It was thought that the emperor, as the ruler of the nine courts, should circulate from one court to another in imitation of the transformative process of the universe. By adhering to the proper ritual activity, the color of garments, and so on, the emperor could bring himself into harmony with the transformations of the cosmic order, and in turn this virtuous behavior could influence these transformative processes for the good of the empire. This notion found expression in discussions of a *Ming-t'ang* or "Bright Hall," a cosmic palace modeled on the T'ai-i numerology, in which the emperor "circulated," performing rituals according to the season. Few were the emperors who actually built a *Ming-t'ang*, though the notion of such a cosmic palace was entertained in most reigns.[8]

Nonetheless, speculation led to the actual construction of such edifices down through Chinese history, and a cult of T'ai-i was active during the time of Emperor Hsüan-tsung and Pu-k'ung when nine thrones were set up and the various stellar lords were "circulated" each year.[9] Moreover, certain Taoist initiation rites made extensive use of this nonary configuration.

7. For this palace and its divinity, see Schafer, *Pacing the Void*, pp. 45–53.

8. There are several sources on the *ming-t'ang*. The dated but classic volume is by W. E. Soothill, *The Hall of Light: A Study of Early Chinese Kingship*, ed. Lady Hosie and G. F. Hudson (London: Lutterworth Press, 1951). Wechsler's *Offerings of Jade and Silk*, pp. 195–211, focuses on the T'ang Dynasty. Comments on the *ming-t'ang* may also be found in Granet, *La pensée chinoise*, pp. 90–99, 175–84, 210–29. Henri Maspero has a piece on the structure, "Le Ming-Tang et la crise religieuse chinoise avant les Han," *Mélanges chinois et bouddhiques* (Brussels) 9 (1951): 1–17. John S. Major includes the *ming-t'ang* in his "Five Phases, Magic Squares, and Schematic Cosmology," which appears in Henry Rosemont, ed., *Explorations in Early Chinese Cosmology* (Chico, Calif.: Scholars Press, 1984), pp. 133–66. Also see Paul Wheatley, *The Pivot of the Four Quarters: A Preliminary Enquiry into the Origins and Character of the Ancient Chinese City* (Chicago: Aldine, 1971), pp. 470–71, n. 129. Antonino Forte has reexamined the history of the *ming-t'ang* in his recent *Mingtang and Buddhist Utopias in the History of the Astronomical Clock: The Tower, Statue, and Armillary Sphere Constructed by Empress Wu* (Paris: École Française d'Extrême-Orient, 1988). A detailed account may also be found in the great Ch'ing Dynasty encyclopedia, the *Ku-chin t'u-shu chi-ch'eng* (Taipei: Wen-hsing shu-tien, 1964), in the "Explanation of the T'ai-i Spirit," *p'eng* 490:16–20.

9. Kalinowski, "La transmission," p. 780, points out that this is the only documented pre-Sung dynasty confluence of the nonerian T'ai-i cult and imperial ritual independent of *ming-t'ang* ideology. See esp. his note 31. Also see Cammann, "Magic Square of Three," pp. 37–78; the description in the "Explanation of the *T'ai-i* Spirit," *peng* 490, pp. 16–20; the account in the *Chiu t'ang shu*, pp. 929–39; and

It is hard to imagine that such an important ideological and ritual complex dealing with Chinese cosmic sovereignty would have been ignored by Buddhists. Indeed, I would suggest it was not. One of the most striking features of Japanese Shingon Buddhism is its dual mandala configuration. The *Garbhakośadhātu* mandala is drawn from the *MVS*, whereas the *Vajradhātu* mandala is based on the *Sarvatathāgatatattvasaṃgraha.*[10] The text of the *STTS* presents a series of four sets of six mandalas in a fashion typical of Vajrayāna ritual texts. The mandalas are integrated vertically in the text through the "template" or paradigm presented as the *mahāmaṇḍala* in the first part of the text. But sometime during the last half of the eighth century what was to become the standard *Vajradhātu* mandala emerged in China. This arrangement is based on the *mahāmaṇḍala* described in the translations of Vajrabodhi (T 866) and Pu-k'ung (T 865). The *mahāmaṇḍala* constitutes a central court surrounded by eight other courts. The first six courts beginning with the central court are drawn from the first segment of the *STTS*, the seventh is drawn from the second segment, while the two last courts are drawn from later sections of the text.[11] Although certain nonary arrangements are found in Vajrayāna texts or systems of India, Tibet, or Central Asia, a nine-fold *Vajradhātu* mandala is decidedly anomalous.[12] I think it quite likely that this arrangement was an adaptation of Esoteric ritual inspired by the T'ai-i cult and its ideological underpinnings.

Another intriguing example of Pu-k'ung's "matching of meanings" is found in the meditation on the structure of emptiness and its transformations as practiced in the technique called "The Five Permutations of the *bīja* A" (*A-tzu wu-lun*). This technique involves the sequential visualization of the Sanskrit "seed-syllable," the *bīja* A, the primordial symbol of emptiness and enlightenment through five permutations as *a*, *ā*, *aṃ*, *aḥ*, and *āḥ* (or *āṃḥ*). Each letter is associated with a direction, a Buddha and an element. Śubhākarasiṃha propounded a set of interpretations for the technique in which the initial *a* represents the first move toward enlightenment produced by the commencement

the "Altars of the Nine Courts," in the *T'ang hui-yao* (The Essentials of the T'ang), compiled by Wang P'u (922–82) in 100 *chüan* (Kiangsu shu-chü, 1884), *chüan* 10b:17–23. The last is a full description.

10. The literature in Japanese on the relationship between the *Genzu* mandalas used in Shingon and mandalas found in a variety of T'ang sources is massive, and the English literature on the topic is growing rapidly. For a convenient summary, see Yamamoto Chikyō, *Introduction to the Maṇḍala* (Kyoto, 1980), pp. 64–82.

11. For the first segment, see The *Vajradhātu Maṇḍala* is described by Tajima, *Les deux grandes maṇḍalas*, pp. 162–97; by Toganoo, *Mandara no kenkyū*, pp. 204–62; and by Kiyota, *Shingon Buddhism*, pp. 93–104. Note the contrasting arrangements of Tibetan *Vajradhātu Maṇḍalas* in Snellgrove, *Buddhist Himalaya*, pp. 227–42, and by Tucci in "Gyantse ed I suoi Monasteri, Part I."

12. Any arrangement of center and cardinal points with the four interstitial points will generate a nine-fold structure. Also, certain ways of drawing the *Gharbadhātu* mandala involve a nine-fold and an eighty-one-fold division of the sacred space. But the stacking of nine variants of the *mahā*-mandala as found in the Japanese *Vajradhātu* mandala is unique.

of practice. It is equated with the Buddha Akṣobhya, the center, and the element earth. The final *āmḥ* represents the attainment of enlightenment, Mahāvairocana, and space or *ākāśa*.[13]

Pu-k'ung instituted a new set of associations with this key meditative technique. He adds the Chinese set of transformative "activities" (*wu-hsing*) and the seasons to the traditional Indian set of elements, and he begins with Mahāvairocana and the element earth at the center, ending with Amoghasiddhi and water. Pu-k'ung's system portrays a cycle or a loop like the system of Chinese activities it is modeled on. Enlightenment and transformation through skillful means are forever in a cycle, forever transformations of one another. Now Mahāvairocana is associated with the center, the color yellow, the earth, and the square, rather than with the traditional blue or white, *ākāśa* and roundness. The attribution is significant when we consider that the traditional Chinese archetype of the sovereign at the center of the *Lo-shu* is the Yellow Emperor at the center of the square earth![14]

Pu-k'ung was an astute practitioner of the art of interpretation, an art essential in the construction of a Chinese Esoteric Buddhism. The dual emphasis of Esoteric ritual and ideology and its insistence on the recursive relationship between *dharmic* and *rupic* strands of Buddhism was to serve as a framework for the adaptation of a variety of indigenous Chinese and Buddhist practices, ideas, and texts. Like the creator of the *Scripture for Humane Kings* three hundred years earlier, Pu-k'ung's interpretive skill helped to realize a Chinese Esoteric Buddhist practice and polity, and this skill is manifest in his rites for the protection of the state.

Esoteric Religion on Imperial Altars: Pu-k'ung's Rituals for Humane Kings

Although the *Scripture for Humane Kings* is entrusted to "the kings of states and not to ***bhikṣu***s and ***bhikṣuṇī***s, ***upāsaka***s and ***upāsikā***s . . . because nothing but the august strength of kings is able to establish it,"[15] Pu-k'ung's ritual commentaries make it clear that the *ācārya* is the primary actor and the true

13. See *Hōbōgirin*, fasc. 1, pp. 1a–6a. Also, Tajima, *Étude sur le Mahāvairocana-Sūtra*, pp. 15–16, *Les deux grandes maṇḍalas*, pp. 73–75, and in English, Taikō Yamasaki, *Shingon: Japanese Esoteric Buddhism* (Boston and London: Shambhala), pp. 195–215.

14. For the assertion of this symbolic complex in the early T'ang Dynasty immediately preceding the years of Pu-k'ung's activity, see Wechsler, *Offerings of Jade and Silk*, p. 113.

15. T 246 8.843a11–12.

sovereign. Like the role of the emperor as flamboyant patron of the Saṃgha in the fifth-century text, the role of the emperor in the updated version of the scripture is one of support and veneration, but more specifically, support and veneration of the Esoteric school and its ritual program. Although the recitation and ritual veneration of text and monks prescribed in the fifth-century scripture are retained in the new recension, they are marginalized by the new *dhāraṇī* and the rites that actualize its power.

A common thread running through all of Pu-k'ung's writings was the interdependence of the achievement of enlightenment and the protection of the state. The two goals were recursive, just as nirvana and *saṃsāra* are two and yet are not two. Ostensibly, *all* Esoteric rituals served to further both goals, but some rituals were tailored to one purpose or the other. An examination of T'ang ritual texts from Pu-k'ung's lineage shows instead that the *STTS* and its central teachings not only provided the quick path to enlightenment, they also provided the basic structure or "template" for the key rituals of Pu-k'ung's state-protection Buddhism.

When we examine ritual manuals produced by Pu-k'ung and his successors, we find that ritual aid for the state fell into two broad categories. Some rituals were for the express welfare of the imperial family, both living and dead, while others were designed to protect and maintain the state and the cosmic order more generally.[16] Whether it involved an Esoteric revamping of earlier

16. The most prominent of these are the "distribution" rites (*shih-shih*). Since their appearance in the late T'ang, the *shih-shih* have formed the ritual core of the Ghost Festival and of rites for the recently dead. The relative silence over just what ritual experts are saying and doing has much to do with indigenous as well as modern scholarly prejudices against esoteric traditions in general and Chinese esoteric ritual, both Taoist and Buddhist, in particular. I have examined these prejudices in my article "Seeing *Chen-yen* Buddhism." Both Pu-k'ung and Śikṣānanda translated manuals for rituals used to alleviate the suffering of beings in the lower realms, rituals which found immediate application in rites for the dead and in the yearly Ghost Festival. These texts serve both as guides to practice and as accounts of the origin of the rites. They include The *Conditions and Causes Which Gave Rise to the Teaching to Ānanda Concerning the Essentials of the Yoga [Tradition] on Distribution of Food to Burning Mouths* (T 1318 and 1319), the *Dhāraṇī Sūtra for Saving the Burning-Mouth Hungry Ghost* (T 1313 and 1314), and the ritual text *Distributions of Food and Water to Hungry Ghosts* (T 1315). This last text presents a ritual, centered on the use of mantra, for magically multiplying offerings of food and water to alleviate the suffering of the countless beings in the lower realms. The new techniques of offering are given authoritative charter through an account of the ritual's origins, an account which is associated with these rites into this century. The earlier rites connected with the Chinese *Yü-lan-p'en Scripture* have been treated by Stephen F. Teiser, *The Ghost Festival in Medieval China* (Princeton: Princeton University Press, 1988). Teiser has also explored the emergence of the Chinese vision of the underworld in his study and translation, *The Scripture on the Ten Kings and the Making of Purgatory in Medieval Chinese Buddhism* (Honolulu: University of Hawaii Press, 1994). For an exploration of the *shih-shih* rites, see Orzech, "Esoteric Buddhism and the *Shishi* in China." I have translated the story of the origin of the *shih-shih* rites in appendix 2 of that publication, and have also done an updated translation titled "Saving the Burning-Mouth Hungry Ghost."

Buddhist texts and rituals or the production of new rituals, Pu-k'ung and his successors consistently followed the template set out in the *STTS*.[17]

Three ritual commentaries on Pu-k'ung's new recension of the *Scripture for Humane Kings* are attributed to Pu-k'ung (though likely the joint product of Pu-k'ung and his close disciples).[18] The most important of these commentaries is *Instructions for the Rites, Chants, and Meditations of the* ***Prajñāpāramitā Dhāraṇī*** *Scripture for Humane Kings Who Wish to Protect Their States* (T 994, 19.514a–519b, *Jen-wang hu-kuo po-jo-po-lo-mi-tuo ching t'o-lo-ni nien-sung i-kuei*, or *Instructions*).[19] *Instructions* outlines the establishment of the mandala/altar, the order of the rites in the ritual, and gives instructions on the contemplation of the great *dhāraṇī*.[20] The *Method for Chanting the Humane Kings* ***Prajñā*** *[pāramitā]* (T 995, *Jen-wang po-jo nien-sung fa*, or *Method*) also outlines the ritual and focuses on its mantra sequences. The *Translation of the Humane Kings* ***Prajñā***-*[pāramitā] Dhāraṇī* (T 996, *Jen-wang po-jo t'o-lo-ni shih*, or *Translation*) is an exegesis of the key *bīja* or seed syllables of the major *dhāraṇī* of the text.

The *Instructions*, the *Method*, the *Translation*, and Liang-pi's great commentary on the *Scripture for Humane Kings* include only partial accounts of specific rites such as the inner visualizations of the adept. Like rainmaking rituals and other such performances there is no exhaustive ritual commentary dating from later Chinese use of the text. Nevertheless, when we examine these ritual manuals with knowledge of the template drawn from the *STTS* and of the specific boilerplate sequences found in other late-T'ang manuals in Pu-k'ung's lineage, we can "flesh out" the full performance. The "cohort" of the Humane Kings manual includes the *Kuan-tzu-tsai p'u-sa ju-i-lun nien-sung i-kuei* (T 1085), the *Wu-liang-shou ju-lai kuan-hsing kung-yang i-kuei* (T 930), and the *Chin-kang-ting lien-hua-pu hsin nien-sung i-kuei* (T 873). Our knowledge of these ritual performances is further corroborated both by T'ang sources contemporary with Pu-k'ung and by ritual manuals preserved in the medieval Japanese Shingon and Tendai collections.[21] These are intimately linked to state protection. The *Zuzō-*

17. Again, we have the various "Ghost Festival" texts already cited as well as the rainmaking scriptures (T 989–990), rites for the worship of Amitabha (T 930), and so on.

18. Osabe sees these ritual commentaries as indicative of Pu-k'ung's transformation of Vajrabodhi's Esoteric Buddhism into an Esoteric Buddhism of state-protection designed to serve Chinese needs. Indeed, Liang-pi (T 1709 33.516b–ff.) details the rites in his commentary and the continuity is striking. See Osabe, *Tōdai mikkyōshi zakkō*, pp. 89–95.

19. Though it is attributed to Pu-k'ung, the opening passages and the preface indicate that it was the product of the master and his disciple Liang-pi. The preface was composed by Hui-ling of Pu-k'ung's Hsing-shan monastery. For the comments in the preface, see T 994 19.514a6–7.

20. For these ritual commentaries, see Osabe, *Tōdai mikkyōshi zakkō*, and DeVisser, *Ancient Buddhism* 1:158–76. Toganoo, *Mandara no kenkyū*, pp. 370–71, treats these briefly.

21. For instance, *Collected Documents* (T 2120) is replete with references to *homa* and *abhiṣeka* performed at the Esoteric altars of the inner palace (*nei tao-ch'ang*); at Pu-k'ung's home monastery, the Hsing-shan ssu; and at the Golden Pavilion (Chin-k'o ssu) on Mt. Wu-t'ai. For the *homa* rite, see

shō, the *Kakuzenshō*, the *Asabashō*, the *Besson-zakki*, and the *Byakuhōkushō* all preserve medieval Japanese versions of mandalas and altar layouts for the *Scripture for Humane Kings*. Although these manuals must be used with caution, they clearly reflect the overall structure and sequencing of rites known from T'ang dynasty sources.[22] Finally, Jokei's ninth-century *Kaguraoka shidai*, which preserves Shingon ritual sequences connected with the *Vajradhātu* (*STTS*), demonstrates a remarkable continuity with eighth-century T'ang rituals in Pu-k'ung's lineage. Almost certainly Pu-k'ung's rituals were not as punctilious as those found in modern-day Shingon or in medieval *Taimitsu* and *Tomitsu* manuals, but the template and the sequencing or ritual modules are nearly identical.

Any ritual and the mandala and altar layouts for its performance will follow the "grammar" or "template" of the *STTS*—the five-fold mandala structure and the Wheel body taxonomy—but will vary in "vocabulary," details, divinities, and so forth depending on its purpose. The specific configuration of the mandala/altar—the "vocabulary," if you will—depended upon the purpose at hand. These variations are explained in *Instructions*, which is divided into five unequal parts. Part 1, "The Five Bodhisattvas Manifesting Their Awesome Virtue," discusses the relationship of the key divinities and their Wheel Bodies to the *STTS*. Part 2, "Rites for Constructing the Mandala," sets out the procedures to be followed in establishing the mandala/altar. Part 3 details the rites for "Entering the Ritual Arena" (actually the order or sequence of rites comprising the ritual program). Part 4 presents a "Translation of the Phrases of the *Dhāraṇī* and the Method for Its Contemplation." Part 5 sets out the "Visualization of the *Dhāraṇī* According to the Wheel of Characters."[23]

The purpose of part 1 is to situate the divinities of the ritual within their proper orbits of association with the *STTS*. Beginning in the east with Vajrapāṇi and proceeding to the south (Vajraratna), west (Vajratīksna), north (Vaj-

---

Michel Strickmann, "*Homa* in East Asia," in Fritz Staal, ed., *Agni*, 2 vols. (Berkeley and Los Angeles: University of California Press, 1982), 2:418–55, and Payne, *Tantric Ritual of Japan*.

22. See Appendix D, "Boilerplate Sequences in Pu-k'ung's Teachings." The following Japanese manuals all contain material on the rites for Humane Kings. The *Zuzōshō* (Taishō supplement, vol. 3) was compiled by Ejo in 1139; the *Bessonzakki* (Taishō supplement, vol. 3) was compiled by Shinkaku (1117–80); the *Kakuzenshō* (Taishō supplement, vol. 4) was the work of Kakuzen (1143–1218), and in the same volume is the *Kakuzen hitsu Ninnōkyōhō*. The *Asabashō* (Taishō supp., vol. 9) was compiled by the Tendai monk Shōchō (1205–82); and the *Byakuhōkushō* (Taishō supp., vol. 6) was compiled by Ryōzen (1258–1341). These commentaries purport to contain materials of the oral traditions passed on from Chinese to Japanese initiates. While it is obvious this later material must be used judiciously, the conservative nature of the tradition, the clear continuity with T'ang ritual manuals (immediately obvious in examining Hatta Yukio's tables in *Shingonjiten*, pp. 255–67), and the example of the ghost rites (for which we have later Chinese ritual commentaries) means that we can use this material with some confidence.

23. Part 2 of *Instructions* details strikingly Indian procedures for setting up the ritual arena, and with it we enter the ritual process proper, including the purification of the ground with cow dung and cow urine. *Hōbōgirin*, 3:279–80, "Chakuji," has a discussion of these procedures.

rarakṣa), and center (Vajrapāramitā), *Instructions* first quotes the initial description of each divinity from Pu-k'ung's translation of the *Scripture for Humane Kings*. It then identifies each with its "Wheel body" forms derived from the five chief divinities of the *STTS*. For example, Vajrapāṇi is identified with Samantabhadra (P'u-hsien p'u-sa) as the Body of the Correct Teaching who eliminates subtle defilements (*kleśa*), while his Body of Command is Trilokyavijayavajra (*Chiang san-shih chin-kang*), who subdues the *māras* and Maheśvara.[24] This list thus describes three possible mandala/altar deployments with Vajrapāramitā/Mahāvairocana/Acalavajra seated at the center. Depending on the need at hand (teaching and purification of subtle defilements, enlightenment, or the pacification of calamities, the subjugation of enemies, and so on) the *ācārya* employs Vajrapāramitā or Acalavajra as the central divinity.[25] The associations outlined in part one of *Instructions* are presented in table 1.

Table 1. The Divinities in the Esoteric ritual

	Body of Correct Teaching	STTS	Function	Body of Command	Function
East	Vajrapāṇi	Samantabhadra	eliminates kleśa	Trilokyavijaya	subdues Māra/ Maheśvara
South	Vajraratna	Ākāśagarbha	fulfills desires	Kuṇḍalivajra	subdues asuras
West	Vajratīksna	Mañjuśrī	severs obstacles	Yamāntaka	subdues evil dragons
North	Vajrarakṣa	Vajradamṣṭra[26]	eliminates sins	Vajrayakṣa	subdues rakṣasas and yakṣas
Center	Vajrapāramitā	Mahāvairocana	subdues demons	Acalavajra	subdues māras

24. In the *Sarvatathāgatatattvasaṃgraha* Vajrapāṇi, the "great rakṣa" subdues Maheśvara. For a fascinating analysis of this conversion of a Hindu divinity into a Buddhist protector, see Iyanaga, "Recits."

25. Mahāvairocana is likely not to be the central divinity of the ritual, since other rituals have total enlightenment as their primary goal, though the *dharmic* experience of visionary light is a central part of the visualization of Prajñāpāramitā bodhisattva. See the original at T 994 517b20ff. I will discuss the use of Vajrapāramitā and Acalavajra further.

26. *Mikkyō daijiten*, 2:676a–677b identifies this figure as "Vajra tooth" from Amoghasiddhi's court in the first mandala from the *STTS*. He is equated with Vajrayakṣa in the Vajradhātu mandala. Vajradamṣṭra is the name given the beneficent form of this bodhisattva in the *Garbha* mandala, where he is placed in Vajrapāṇi's court. His vow is to devour the causes of suffering. See Snodgrass, *Matrix and Diamond World Maṇḍalas*, 1:332. Osabe, *Tōdai mikkyōshi zakkō*, pp. 92–93, opines that the ritual program of the Humane Kings predates the dichotomy of the Garbhadhātu and Vajradhātu mandalas and methods. While I agree with the spirit of Osabe's remark, putting the issue in terms of the Shingon dual mandala system is still anachronistic.

Part 2 of *Instructions* stipulates requirements for siting and constructing a mandala/altar as well as procedures for painting the divinities and arranging objects on the altar. The sequence of the rites strung together to form the ritual is invariant, though particular rites may be nested into other rites in accordance with the goal of the performance. First, the *ācārya* decides which sort of mandala/altar to construct. Although most rituals involve the visualization of the mandala in the body, an external prepainted mandala or a three-dimensional altar may or may not be available. Moreover, both interior and exterior mandalas may consist of full images in either two or three dimensions, *bīja* (the fundamental sonic expressions of divinities), or *samaya* (the "pledge," in this case a symbolic representation of the meditative state of divinities).[27] Part 2 also stipulates proper times and colors of vestments, as well as the seating position of the *ācārya* appropriate to the divinity evoked and the purpose of the ritual.[28] For example, in the case of the rites outlined in *Instructions* the central divinity will commonly be Prajñāpāramitā bodhisattva or Acalavajra.[29] The former is the Body of the Correct Teaching of Mahāvairocana. The latter is Mahāvairocana's wrathful Body of Command. If the rite is being performed for pacification of calamities (*śāntika*), the *ācārya* is dressed in white, faces north—the direction of Vajrarakṣa/Vajrayakṣa—and visualizes the focal divinity, the offerings, and so on, as white in color and he chants calmly and silently. If for increase (*pauṣṭika*) he wears yellow and faces Vajrapāṇi/Trailokyavijaya—yellow in color—in the east. He chants calmly and under his breath. If the rite is for subjugation (*abhicāraka*) he wears black and faces Vajraratna/Kuṇḍali—visualized as black in color—in the south. He inwardly arouses great compassion and outwardly assumes an awesome, angry demeanor and shouts out the chants. If for attraction (*vaśīkarana*) the *ācārya* wears red and faces Vajratīksna/Yamāntaka—visualized as red in color—in the west. He chants in a joyous and fierce voice. These four types of rites are *homa* (immolation), and we know from other sources that the shapes of *homa* altars also vary in accordance with the purpose of the ritual.[30] For pacification

27. The four main types of mandalas are the *Mahā-maṇḍala*, which is the mandala constructed with painted images of the deities; the *Samaya-maṇḍala* consisting of the symbolic forms of the deities; the *Dharma-maṇḍala*, which uses the *bīja* or "seed-syllables" of the deities; and the *karma-maṇḍala*, which represents the forms of the deities in unpainted images.

28. See *Instructions*, T 994 19.515c–516a18, for the colors, times, and directions. For types of *homa*, see Snodgrass, *Matrix and Diamond World Maṇḍalas*, 1:82–96. For a full discussion of contemporary *homa* (which closely matches medieval Japanese manuals), see Payne, *Tantric Ritual of Japan*.

29. Although *Instructions* details the iconography of Prajñāpāramitā bodhisattva, contemporary evidence and evidence from Japanese manuals show that Acala is often favored.

30. On the shapes of *homa* altars, the first systematic appearance of rites of "pacification," "subjugation," and "increase," see Bodhiruci's *I-tzu-ting lun-wang ching* ("The Scripture of the Cakravartin of the Single-character Uṣṇīṣa," T 951 19.261c–263b) and Strickmann's comments in "*Homa* in East Asia," pp. 434–47.

the altar is circular. For increase the altar is square. For subjugation the altar is triangular, while for attraction the altar is in the form of a lotus. Thus depending upon the purpose of the ritual, one generates a mandala that is simultaneously stereotypical and tailored to specific circumstances.

Although no graphic mandalas can with certainty be dated to the T'ang, a variety of mandalas are preserved in medieval Japanese manuals. Figure 4 reproduces a Humane Kings mandala from the *Asabashō*.[31]

The basic sequence of rites that compose the ritual is outlined in section 3 of *Instructions* and begins with the preparation of the *ācārya*.[32] These rites involve the purification of body, speech, and mind, the performance of the "pledges" (*samaya*) of the three "departments" of Buddha, bodhisattva, and vajra beings, and the protection of the *ācārya* by donning "armor." The next sequence of rites involves visualizing, securing, and embellishing the ritual space. Only then can the deities be welcomed to the ritual arena, where they are offered water, jeweled thrones, incense, and so on. Having assembled and worshiped the divinities, the *ācārya* moves to the visualization and identification with the chief divinity of the ritual and the contemplation of the syllables of the great *dhāraṇī*. Finally, having accomplished the purpose of the ritual, the *ācārya* performs a series of exit rites that reverse the entry rites. Among these are a final set of offerings, the transfer of merit to all beings, the dissolving of the ritual space, and departure. *Homa*, when it is performed, focuses on Acala and is nested into the series of offerings after the divinities have "taken their seats," and before the identification sequence. Some T'ang manuals carefully detail some sequences while abbreviating others.[33] Throughout the performance the text (in the Pu-k'ung recension) resides on the altar, and a group of monks chant it as specified in the *Scripture for Humane Kings* itself. The ritual as it appears in section 3 is translated in the following pages. I have supplied the sequence divsions numbered I–IV.[34]

31. The mandala reproduced in Figure 4 is from *Asabashō*, Taishō Supplement, vol. 9, illustration 19.

32. The same order is outlined in *Method*, T 995 19.520a–521c.

33. For instance, *Instructions* gives the barest indication of the exit rites (T 994 19.515c), while *Method* specifies each step (T 995 19.521c).

34. I have labeled and numbered I–IV the specific rites, which consist largely of "boilerplate." I have found it convenient to use a somewhat different terminology and division of the sequence from that used by the Chūinryū of Kōyasan. *Instructions* is representative of T'ang Esoteric manuals in Pu-k'ung's lineage. It is structured around the *mudrā* and mantra sequences and includes ritual instructions concerning what to do, how to make the *mudrās*, and other "stage" directions (in normal typeface), liturgy to be recited by the *ācārya* (in quotation marks) and the mantras to be chanted (boldface). Bold italics represent transliterated Sanskrit terms appearing in the Chinese. Pictures of the mudrās can be found in Hatta's *Shingon jiten* under their corresponding mantras and at the front of volume 1 of *Mikkyō daijiten*. The spareness of *Instructions* contrasts with the elaborate ritual laid out in the *Byakuhōkushō* (Taishō supplement, vol. 6, pp. 198c–217c), though one should note that exactly the same sequence of ritual modules is present there.

Fig. 4. A Humane Kings Mandala from *Asabashō*

[I. Preparation of the *Ācārya* and the Arena]
If the practitioner seeks relief from calamities [*śāntika*]:

First: You must bathe and put on freshly cleaned clothes. If you are a householder, receive the lay precepts. Caring naught for your own life [you] should arouse the fervent mind of the Great Vehicle seeking *siddhi*. Toward numberless beings arouse the compassionate vows of the mind of salvation. In this manner you will be able to swiftly achieve *siddhi*. On entering the ritual arena do a full prostration in veneration to all the Triple Jewel throughout the *Dharmadhātu*. Kneeling on the right knee, repent all transgressions of the triple karma (body, speech, mind), request that the Buddhas of ten directions turn the wheel of the Correct Teaching, and beseech all Tathāgatas to long abide in the world.

[The practitioner then says,] "All the merit that I, (insert name), cultivate shall be dedicated to the achievement of unsurpassed enlightenment. I vow that, together with all beings of the *Dharmadhātu*, the ***siddhi*** we seek shall quickly attain fulfillment."

Next: Assume the cross-legged position. In case there are deficiencies that have not been cleansed, take the hands and rub [them with] incense and, arousing the fervent mind, make the purification *mudrā*. With care and humility clasp the hands like an unopened lotus blossom. Chant the mantra:

Om svabhāva-śuddhāh sarva-dharmāh sarvabhāva-śuddho 'ham[35]

Chant this mantra three times. While you chant it, move the mind to magnanimity and [reflect]: "All *dharmas* are originally pure, therefore my body is also completely pure." Then with eyes closed visualize all the multitudes of ritual arenas, the assemblies of Buddhas and bodhisattvas that everywhere fill the void. Hold every sort of supernal incense and with triple karma resolute and sincere, face them to pay your respects.

One: Make the *mudrā* of the Buddha department ***samaya.*** Place your two hands before your heart, making a fist with the fingers crossed and inside, while the thumbs are upright. Chant the mantra:

Oṃ jina-jik svāhā[36]

Silently chant this mantra three times and release the [*mudrā*] above your head. Because of making this *mudrā* and chanting this Buddha department ***samaya*** mantra, all of the Buddhas of the *Dharmadhātu* of the ten directions will assemble like a cloud and totally fill the void. [They] empower the practitioner [who will thus] be freed from all obstacles, and your vow cultivating the purification of the triple karma will be swiftly accomplished.

Two: Make the *mudrā* of the Bodhisattva department ***samaya.*** As before [clasp] your hands before your heart and make a fist [this time] with the left thumb inside. Chant the mantra:

Oṃ aloki svāhā[37]

Just as before chant it three times and release [the *mudrā*] above your head. Because of making this *mudrā* and chanting this Bodhisattva department ***samaya*** mantra Kuan-yin and all the other bodhisattvas of the *Dharmadhātu* of

35. *Shingon jiten*, no. 1808.
36. Ibid., no. 242, the heart mantra of the "Buddha-department."
37. Ibid., no. 64, the heart mantra of the "Bodhisattva-department."

the ten directions will assemble like a cloud and totally fill the void. [They] empower the practitioner [whose] triple karma [thus] becomes pure and without any affliction. This is called bodhisattvas carrying out the vow of great compassion and it will cause one who seeks it to attain complete fulfillment.

Three: Make the *mudrā* of the Vajra department ***samaya*** as in the previous *mudrā* [but] extend the left thumb while enclosing the right thumb in the palm. Chant the mantra:

Oṃ vajra-dhṛk svāhā[38]

As before chant it three times and release [the *mudrā*] above your head. Because of making this *mudrā* and chanting this Vajra department ***samaya*** mantra, all of the Vajra [beings] of the *Dharmadhātu* of the ten directions will manifest their wrathful bodies and assemble like a cloud and fill the void. [They] empower the practitioner [whose] triple karma becomes firm as a diamond. This is called the sages carrying out the Buddha's awesome spirit. Using the strength of their vows [they] are able to protect the state and cause it to be without calamities, and even this insignificant body will be without troubles.

Four: (516c) Make the *mudrā* of protecting the body. Again use the *mudrās* and chant the mantras of the three departments and empower the five places—that is the two shoulders, heart, throat, top of head—and release [the *mudrā*] above your head. Forthwith you will be protected by stout Vajra armor. Because of this empowerment the entire body of the practitioner glows with an awesome radiance. All the *māras* who would obstruct and harass [you] do not dare to look [at you] and they quickly flee.

Five: (516c–517a) Make the exorcism *mudrā* and then the *mudrā* of the Vajra quarter jewel-realm. Use the previous Vajra department *mudrā* and chanting the mantra circle the altar turning to the left. Make three circuits. Forthwith you will be able to exorcise all the powerful *māras* and, as a consequence of the goodness of all Buddhas and bodhisattvas, all those who are hidden will be exposed and they will flee far from [the Buddha's] world. Make three circuits to the right, as you like, big or small. This will complete the Vajra quarter jewel-realm. All the Buddhas and bodhisattvas will not disobey you. How much more is it true for those who would harass you, and you will be able to obtain their expedient devices. Release the [*mudrā*] above your head.

[II: Summoning and Feting the Divinities]

Six: Make the *mudrā* of inviting the sages to descend to the altar. Use the previous *mudrās* of the three departments and chant their mantras. [This time]

38. Ibid., no. 1090, the heart mantra of the "Vajra-department."

move your thumbs toward your body summoning them three times. Immediately the air before you will fill up with the sages of the three departments, each going to his proper place without obstructing another. They wait silently.

Seven: *Mudrā* offering *agra*-perfumed water. As above using two hands respectfully offer the ***maṇi***-bejeweled vessel filled with perfumed water. Hold it at eyebrow level and chant the mantra:

Om vajrodaka ṭha hum[39]

Just as above chant it three times while moving your heart to magnanimity. Next bathe all the sages and release [the *mudrā*] above your head. Because of this ***agra*** water, during each and every stage—from the stage of victorious understanding and practicing of the Teaching to the stage of the *Dharma*-cloud—all the Buddhas and bodhisattvas of the *Dharmadhātu* of the ten directions will protect you and you will obtain all their *abhiṣekas*.

Eight: *Mudrā* presenting jeweled thrones. As above, with care and humility, clasp your hands with thumbs and little fingers matching and slightly bent. The remaining six fingers are spread and a little bent, like a lotus blossom just opening. Chant the mantra:

Oṃ kamala svāhā[40]

By making this *mudrā* and chanting this mantra, you cause the jeweled thrones which are presented to be received and used by the sages as though they were real, and this causes the practitioner to reach the state of fruition[41] and to attain the Vajra-firm jeweled-throne.

Nine: Make the *mudrā* of universal offering (517a–b). As above, clasp your two hands. The five fingers are interlaced with the right pressing on the left. Place it above your heart and chant the mantra:

Namaḥ sarvathā kham udgate sphara hīmaṃ gagana-khaṃ svāhā[42]

By your making this *mudrā* and chanting this mantra—moving the mind to magnanimity—it rains all [types] of offering vessels in all of the ritual arenas of all ocean-like assemblies of Buddhas and bodhisattvas all about the *Dharmadhātu*. On the first recitation numberless vessels are filled with incense paste, which is daubed on all the sages. On the second recitation every sort of flower garland adorns [the sages]. On the third recitation all sorts of incense is burned

39. Ibid., no. 1498.

40. Ibid., no. 123.

41. The "state of fruition" or attainment indicates the completion or outcome or attainment of the goal of practice.

42. *Shingon jiten*, no. 1711.

as offering. On the fourth recitation it rains superb divine food and drink, which is properly arranged in the jeweled vessels and offered everywhere. On the fifth recitation it rains all sorts of bejeweled lamps, which are offered before all the Buddhas and bodhisattvas. Because of the strength of the empowerment [conferred by] chanting this mantra, in all the ocean-like assemblies the offerings of incense and so on all are completely real and are used by the sages and, as for the practitioner, you are certain to obtain recompense.

[III: Contemplation of the Chief Divinity of the Ritual]

Ten: Make the fundamental *mudrā* of ***Prajñāpāramitā.*** Place your hands back to back with the index and little fingers enclosed in the palms with the thumbs pressing on the index fingers. Place [the *mudrā*] above your heart and chant the *dhāraṇī* from the scripture seven times.[43] Because of making this *mudrā* and chanting this *dhāraṇī* the practitioner immediately transforms his own body into ***Prajñāpāramitā bodhisattva*** and he becomes the mother of all Buddhas. The image of the bodhisattva is seated cross-legged on a white lotus. His body is golden colored, and he has many precious necklaces adorning his body. On his head is a jeweled crown with two (pieces of) white silk hanging down the sides. In the left hand is the Sanskrit text of the ***Prajñā***[*-pāramitā*]. His right hand is held before his breast making the *Dharmacakramudrā;* thumbs pressing on the "head" of the fourth finger. Now, meditate on the bodhisattva from head to toe. All the pores of his body emit a multicolored radiance, which fills the *Dharmadhātu*. Each ray transforms into countless Buddhas, who fill up the void, and on behalf of the assembled beings in all these worlds they expound the profound teaching of the ***Prajñāpāramitā,*** which causes the ***samādhi*** of the abode of enlightened comprehension. After you the practitioner complete this contemplation, release the *mudrā* above your head. Grasp the prayer beads and clasp hands together and with a resolute heart chant this mantra:

Om Vairocanamā (la) svāhā[44]

Chant this three times and empower the rosary by touching it to your head.[45] Then bring it before your heart. With the left hand receiving the bead and the right hand moving the bead, focus on union and abide in the Buddha-mother ***samādhi.*** Contemplate it without interruption, and chant [the mantra either] 108 or 21 times. When you have finished, touch the rosary to your head and put it back in its place. Make the ***samādhi*** *mudrā*. Lay your hands across each other just below the navel with the right pressing on the left. [Sit] with upright

43. Section 4 of *Instructions* gives a word-by-word explication of the *dhāraṇī* (T 994 19.518a–519a). Section 5 gives instructions for interior visualization of the *dhāraṇī* in "wheels" of words.

44. *Shingon jiten*, no. 1541.

45. Literally, "by wearing it on your head."

posture, closed eyes, and head slightly inclined, and concentrate on your heart. Visualize a bright round mirror which [expands] from one *hasta* in breadth gradually [to fill] the entire *Dharmadhātu*. Set out the characters in line revolving to the right, and contemplate them in sequence. Their effulgent radiance shines everywhere. Proceed from the outside toward the inside until reaching the character *ti*. Then go from the inside toward the outside. Gradually contemplate all the characters. When you have been around once start over again. When you reach the third repetition your mind will be quiescent and concentrated, and you will clearly comprehend the meaning of that which you contemplate: "No production, no extinction, all is the same throughout the *Dharmadhātu*. Not moving, not quiescent, meditation and wisdom are the twin conveyance. Forever beyond all signs, this is the contemplation of ***Prajñāpāramitā samādhi***." Make the Prajñāpāramitā *mudrā* and chant the ***dhāraṇī*** seven times and release [the *mudrā*] above your head.

[IV. Exit Sequence]

Next: Make the *mudrā* of universal offering. As previously, move your mind [to magnanimity] and follow the sequence of offerings. Before the sages dedicate the merit produced to the fulfillment of all vows on behalf of the state and the family, and for the benefit of others. Thereafter transfer [the merit] to beings so they may turn to the Pure Land, turn to the edge of reality, [and] turn to seeking unsurpassed **bodhi** and vow that all beings will swiftly arrive at the other shore.

Next: Make the previous *[Vajra]-dhātu mudrā* and chant the previous mantra three times circling to the left, which will complete the dissolution of the [*Vajra*] realm.

Next: As previously, make the *mudrās* of the three departments and chant the previously (used) mantras three times, all the while moving your thumbs toward the outside. This will complete the departure, and the sages will each return to their original land. The practitioner should make a prostration and leave.

Not only are the exit rites highly abbreviated but the *homa* rite is conspicuously absent (though it is alluded to in section two). This vagueness has little to do with "secrecy." Rather, it is simply a matter of convenience. To outline the full sequence of rites in every manual is neither necessary nor practical. An *ācārya* already knows the basic template and the sequencing of rites which are strung together to compose the appropriate ritual performance.

I would like now to examine the iconography of the Humane Kings ritual, especially as it pertains to the chief divinity in section three of *Instructions*, Prajñāpāramitā bodhisattva. Let us recall that Pu-k'ung's translation of the *Scrip-*

ture for Humane Kings, *Instructions*, and Liang-pi's commentary on the *Scripture for Humane Kings* identify Prajñāpāramitā bodhisattva as Mahāvairocana's Body of the Correct Teaching, his form just after he had reached enlightenment and set the "Wheel of the Teaching" into motion.[46] In *Instructions* she holds a text in one hand while giving the *Dharmacakra mudrā* with the other. Both *Instructions* and Liang-pi's commentary identify Mahāvairocana's Body of Command as Acalavajra, and Liang-pi provides even more detail on the iconography of the wrathful forms than on the beneficent forms. In Liang-pi's commentary Prajñāpāramitā bodhisattva does not make the *dharmacakra mudrā* but instead grasps the "vajra discus" (*chin-kang lun*), which represents Mahāvairocana's teaching.[47]

Next to Avalokiteśvara, Acala is perhaps the most frequently encountered Buddhist divinity in East Asia. This fierce *vidyārāja* is the chastising form of Mahāvairocana and is usually portrayed seated in full lotus posture on a rocky crag, with a dreadlock hanging down his left side. His face is a fierce grimace, with one or two fangs protruding. Wreathed in flames and smoke, he holds a noose in his left hand and a sword in his right hand, symbolic of his subjugation of demons (*māras*) and cutting off of evil defilements. Throughout East Asian and Tibetan Esoteric Buddhism he is intimately linked with Agni, the Vedic god of fire, and with the *homa* rite (Japanese *goma*).[48]

According to Fei-hsi's *Hsing-chuang*, it was Acalavajra that Pu-k'ung invoked to come to the aid of Su-tsung when he was regrouping his forces at Ling-wu, and evidence from Japanese manuals indicates that the wrathful forms led by Acalavajra are commonly used in the Humane Kings ritual. Why then do these texts give both wrathful and beneficent forms while section 3 of *Instructions* focuses only on the beneficent forms? When are the wrathful Lords of Light (*vidyārāja*) led by Acala employed?

An examination of Japanese ritual manuals indicates some ambiguity, at times identifying *both* Prajñāpāramitā bodhisattva and Acala as chief divinities of the ritual. *Zuzōshō*, in its brief account first cites Prajñāpāramitā bodhisattva as chief, then Acala, but it does not attempt to clarify the issue.[49] *Byakuhōkushō* indicates that Acala is the "esoteric" form of Prajñāpāramitā-

46. T 1709 33.516b11–20.

47. See Liang-pi, T 1709 33.515c–516b. The "discus" is described on 516b15 and the description of Acala is on 516b17–21. *Byakuhōkushō*, 200b, also provides a description. For a complete description of a *śāntika* or "pacification" *homa* to Acala in contemporary Shingon practice, see Payne, *Tantric Ritual of Japan*, pp. 95–142. The modern rite agrees remarkably well with that laid out in *Byakuhōkushō*.

48. For a comparison of the types of *homa* throughout Asian Buddhist systems, see Strickmann, "*Homa* in East Asia" and Payne, *Tantric Ritual of Japan*, esp. pp. 60–63. Acala's iconography is the subject of *Nippon no bijutsu* 3, no. 238 (March, 1987), *Fudō myōō zō*. Images connected with the Humane Kings rites are plates 4 (p. 4) and 37–43 (pp. 29–32).

49. T supp. 3.2a.

bodhisattva.[50] It cites a variety of precedents in various oral traditions, finally arguing that while Prajñāpāramitā bodhisattva is the basic divinity of the ritual (*pen-tsun*, Japanese *honzon*), the aim of protection makes it clear that Acala and the other wrathful forms are used in most circumstances.[51]

When we examine the iconography of Acala in the Humane Kings performances as found in Japanese manuals, we find that Acala's noose has been replaced with an eight-spoked vajra wheel. *Byakuhōkushō* says that the wheel is substituted for Acala's usual noose because of the iconography of Acala's alter ego, Prajñāpāramitā bodhisattva.[52] This may refer to the "spoked wheels" discussed in section 5 of *Instructions*. Evidence from the T'ang and from Japanese manuals points to the centrality of Acala *vidyārāja* and the other wrathful forms in Pu-k'ung's rituals for Humane Kings, and it seems as though Acala's unusual iconography comes to embody both the Body of the Correct Teaching and the Body of Command, an arrangement which calls to mind the unique tripartite mandala of the Tōji Lecture Hall.[53] This ambiguity is likely a direct result of Pu-k'ung's emphasis on the twin goals of enlightenment and protection. Like *saṃsāra* and nirvana they are paradoxically one and yet two. Acalavajra turns the "wheel of command" to eliminate the obstructions to the Teaching while Prajñāpāramitā bodhisattva turns the wheel of the Correct Teaching. Which form employed depends upon the need, but the two forms are inextricably related.

Once again an examination of Japanese manuals sheds some light on *how* the actual procedure involving beneficent and wrathful forms takes place. It is not possible to say for certain that Pu-k'ung's rituals followed these procedures, but given the conservative nature of the tradition something like what follows must have been the case. It is also hard to say just how elaborate Pu-k'ung's ritual performances were, but given his royal patrons and permanent facilities in the palace, performances after the An Lu-shan rebellion were likely grand events. We get some idea of what these performances may have looked like when we examine medieval Japanese manuals such as the *Bessonzakki*, the *Kakuzenshō*, or the *Byakuhōkushō*. These manuals specify the need for two or more altars; that of the chief divinity and the *homa* altar to its left (see figure 5).[54]

50. *Byakuhōkushō* has a discussion concerning why Prajñāpāramitā bodhisattva cannot be the chief divinity of the rite and why the Esoteric dimension of the rite uses Acala. See T supp. 6.200a–203c.

51. *Byakuhōkushō*, T supp. 6.202c1–5, 21–24, 26, and 28.

52. Ibid., 203b–c, for the iconography.

53. See Figure 3.

54. Sometimes there were two more altars for the various saints and for the twelve devas. See, for instance, the *Kakuzenshō*, T supp. 3.313a, or *Bessonzakki*, T supp. 3.144a–b. The diagram in Figure 6 is from *Byakuhōkushō*, T supp. 6.211b.

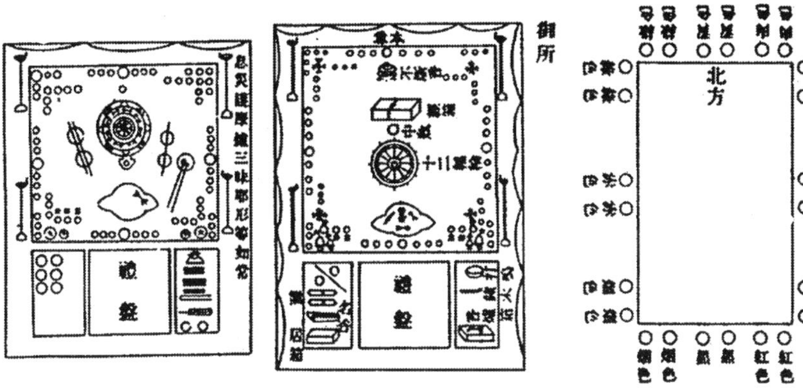

Fig. 5. Altars from *Byakuhōkushō*.

The ritual for Humane Kings as detailed in *Byakuhōkushō* follows the outlines found in *Instructions* and *Method*, filling in gaps, and providing supplementary details according to a variety of oral transmissions. In accord with other Japanese traditions Acala and the other four *vidyārājas* are usually the focus of the ritual, though Prajñāpāramitā bodhisattva is also invoked (T 6.213c16–214c3). Compared to the bare-bones sketch in *Instructions* the rite in *Byakuhōkushō* is a grand event. While the leading *ācārya* is performing the rite at the main altar, a company of monks chants the scripture without interruption, now loudly, now silently, depending on the time and purpose.

Just after the *ācārya* at the main altar has made the offering of thrones and has sounded the bell that signals the opening of the identification rite, the *homa* master commences his rite at yet another altar (215b29–c9). As stipulated in *Instructions* he visualizes himself as Prajñāpāramitā bodhisattva, crowned with five Buddhas, with golden skin, seated on a white lotus-throne, his left hand holding the text of the *Prajñāpāramitā*, his right hand forming the *Dharmacakra-mudrā* (215c10–18). He then commences the standard *homa* sequence, empowering the hearth, utensils, and so on and visualizing within himself Mahāvairocana's seed-syllable *vaṃ*, which transforms into a *stūpa* (Mahāvairocana's *samaya*) and then into Mahāvairocana himself (215c20–216a7).[55] Making a series of offerings, he then visualizes the seed-syllable *hrīḥ* in his heart transforming into a twelve-spoked vajra-wheel, and the wheel then transforming into Acala (216a8–10). Shortly thereafter he visualizes the seed syllables of the five *vidyārāja* of the rite, and each syllable changes into the *samaya* or symbol of each *vidyārāja*, thus constituting the full mandala of the rite (216a21–25). A series of standard *homa* offerings follows: incense, oil, sapwood,

55. The *ācārya* visualizes his mouth, the hearth, and Mahāvairocana's mouth as identical.

and so on.[56] At the close of the rite a *gāthā* is offered that expressly identifies the incineration of interior evil with the elimination of calamities (216c8–28). Both the rite at the main altar and that at the *homa* altar end with the standard series of exit rites sketched out in *Instructions*, *Method*, and in other T'ang manuals. Aside from reversing the entry rites, taking off the "armor," and deconstructing the ritual space, these rites dedicate the merit gained to insure that all beings will benefit and gain suitable rebirths. This and the merit gained by listening to the scripture will result in their eventual rebirth in better realms or stations of life.[57]

Although Pu-k'ung's rituals were probably not as grand as the elaborate tripartite ritual in the *Byakuhōkushō,* we can nonetheless discern the basic elements behind *Instructions*. First, the chanting of the scripture and the offerings to the monks performing the service date back to the fifth-century text, and these have been retained. Second, the worship and identification with Prajñāpāramitā bodhisattva and the chanting of the great *dhāraṇī* from Pu-k'ung's text is performed at the main altar/mandala. Third, a *homa* invoking Acala and through him the other four *vidyārāja* is performed at a subsidiary homa altar, the shape of which would be determined by the purpose of the ritual. A key part of establishing the Correct Teaching is the removal of obstacles of both an internal and an external nature. Once again we see a simultaneous play of "inner" and "outer" meaning, recalling the "inner" forbearance of the bodhisattva and the "outer" protection of the Humane King. Here, the outer *homa* is the fire altar and the consumption of the ghee, the sapwood, and so on represent the elimination of calamities, enemies, or epidemics. However, in the inner *homa* of the *ācārya*'s meditation it is the *kleśas* or defilements which are destroyed. "Total enlightenment is the flame and my own mouth is the hearth" (T 867 18.266a12–21).

In Chapter 5 I argued that in the Esoteric Buddhist tradition the notion of the Two Truths and the realization of the identity of *saṃsāra* and *nirvana* is actualized in the practice of ritual. Esoteric ritual has a dual yet not dual goal, for one attains both mundane ends (*laukika siddhi*) as well as the supramundane end of enlightenment—the Buddha-fruit (*lokkotara siddhi*). The two strands of Buddhist cosmology, the *rupic* and the *dharmic* are joined in the physical, sonic, and mental experience of ritual. The structure of ritual itself is based on recursive principles. Rites such as the *homa* are recursively nested into the main ritual. Moreover, the attainment of the goal, the repulsion of

56. The *śāntika homa* for Acala detailed by Payne, *Tantric Ritual of Japan*, pp. 95–142, almost exactly matches this material from *Byakuhōkushō*.

57. We must not forget that the scripture promises great merit to those who even hear one word of it (T 246 8.836a). From the overall perspective, what we have is a ritual realization of the dual function of *Dharma* and *Daṇḍa*, of "world renunciation" and world conquest. For *Dharma* and *Daṇḍa* see Tambiah, *World Conqueror and World Renouncer*, pp. 23–53.

the invaders, is of a piece with their conversion and with the purification and enlightenment of the *ācārya* himself. The *homa* rite itself has a double meaning, an inner as well as an outer performance; it is a ritual "pun" based on the Two Truths, and it results in a ritual sovereignty that entails both the conquest and the transcendence of the world.

Pu-k'ung's ritual system as extrapolated from the *STTS* was framed as a comprehensive vision of salvation and polity. At once the servant of the imperial court and a cosmic sovereign, Pu-k'ung skillfully applied the recursive vision of the cosmos to the role of the *ācārya*. As we shall see from his correspondence, Pu-k'ung regarded himself as a servant to the Confucian sage-king. Yet he also considered himself the counterpart to the *cakravartin*, and in his ritual roles, he often functioned not only as Prajñāpāramitā bodhisattva, the Teacher, but also as Acalavajra, the protector. Thus while serving the transformative ends of the sage-king, Pu-k'ung was in some sense the manipulator of and even the origin of those transformations. He was at once a transformation and the source of transformation. From one perspective every one of Pu-k'ung's Esoteric rites was the practical realization of the Two Truths. In ritual, the *ācārya* is the Lord of Light (*vidyārāja*), the chastising world conqueror and the enlightened world renouncer. Yet the *ācārya*'s role in the Chinese court was to be the religious adviser of the *cakravartin*/sage-king. As in the fifth-century *Scripture for Humane Kings*, the roles of the monk and the emperor were subject to simultaneous and yet differing interpretations. Thus the unusual importance of the scripture for the construction of Esoteric polity in the second half of the eighth century and beyond.

A New Buddhist-State Polity: Pu-k'ung, Yüan-chao, and the *Collected Documents*

The first version of the *Scripture for Humane Kings* offered a new model of the relationship between Buddhism and the Confucian state, a model which played on the identity and difference between Confucian humaneness and Buddhist forbearance. So too the new recension of the text was central to Pu-k'ung's vision of a kind of dual polity that played on the identity and difference between the goals of the *ācārya* and the Son of Heaven. The emerging Chinese Esoteric Buddhism is intimately related to Pu-k'ung's political role in the mid- and late-T'ang court, and it is in this role that the *Scripture for Humane Kings* looms large. Indeed, the protection of the state, the nurturing of the imperial house, and the rewriting of the *Scripture for Humane Kings* are of a single piece with Pu-k'ung's emerging Esoteric doctrine and practice.

In this regard we are particularly fortunate in having not only voluminous scriptures and commentaries from Pu-k'ung's hand and from his disciples, along with several contemporary biographical accounts and notices, but also, unique for the T'ang period, an extensive collection of personal and public correspondence, much of it with the T'ang emperors. We also have two "catalogs" from the end of the eighth century compiled by the same man who compiled Pu-k'ung's correspondence. Through this historical and autobiographical material we can examine Pu-kung's notions of Esoteric polity, and we can trace the outlines of the Esoteric school and the place of the *Scripture for Humane Kings* in it through the second half of the eighth century.

The bulk of this correspondence was collected by Pu-k'ung's disciple Yüan-chao in *Collected Documents* (T 2120). The correspondence is comprised of letters between Pu-k'ung, Su-tsung, and Tai-tsung as well as assorted other communications connected with the Esoteric school, including Pu-k'ung's testamentary epistle. These documents provide us an inside view of Pu-k'ung's understanding of his own position and goals.[58]

Collected Documents is supplemented by two further works by Yüan-chao. The *Ta t'ang chen-yüan hsü kai-yüan shih-chiao lu* (Supplement to the Catalog of Buddhist Teachings of the K'ai-yüan Period Compiled During the Chen-yüan Period of the Great T'ang Dynasty, T 2156 55, hereafter *Supplement*), and the more expansive *Chen-yüan hsin-ting shih-chiao mu-lu* (New Recension of the Catalog of the Buddhist Teaching Compiled in the Chen-yüan Period, T 2157, vol. 55, hereafter *New Recension*) present us with a picture of one branch of the Esoteric School after the death of Pu-k'ung in 774 up until the year 800 when the latter catalog was compiled.[59] These are invaluable sources for the lineage teachings of Pu-k'ung just prior to Kūkai's arrival, and the *Scripture for Humane Kings* figures prominently in them. I will first examine Pu-

58. T 2120 52.826c–860c. Raffaello Orlando, "A Study of Chinese Documents Concerning the Life of the Tantric Buddhist Patriarch Amoghavajra (A.D. 705–774)" (Ph.D. diss., Princeton University Press, 1981), has translations of about one-quarter of the documents in this collection and lists the contents of others. His work attempts little in the way of interpretation and studiously avoids any exploration of Esoteric Buddhism. Orlando stresses from the beginning that "this dissertation is an examination of Amoghavajra's public life" as revealed in this collection (Abstract, p. 1). Thus, while Orlando's study complements Chou's study of the biographies of the *ācāryas*, it avoids dealing with the driving force of Pu-k'ung's public life: Esoteric ritual and ideology. Also, since Orlando is not a specialist in Esoteric Buddhism, some of his translations obscure important doctrinal or ritual matters. Thus I have in some cases used Orlando's translations and in other cases I have either modified his translations or translated pieces he ignored. Osabe Kazuo has translated the entire text into Japanese in *Kokuyaku Issaikyō* (Tokyo: Daitō shuppansha, 1930–), "Gokyōbu," 98:476–604.

59. Jacques Gernet cites ca. 778 as the date of this collection but gives no rationale, and Orlando merely places it at the end of the eighth century. The last piece in the collection is dated 4 December 781, which appears to rule out 778. For this and other reasons I give below, I believe the text must be dated to the mid- to late-780s. Gernet's comment appears in *Buddhism in Chinese Society*, p. 338 n. 65. For the manuscripts on which the Taisho edition is based, see Orlando, "Study," p. 42.

k'ung's notions of Esoteric polity as evident in the *Collected Documents*. Then I will examine notions of Esoteric polity after the death of Pu-k'ung as demonstrated by all three collections. As we shall see, the *Scripture for Humane Kings* plays a prominent role in Pu-k'ung's lineage teachings in the last quarter of the eighth century, and through these teachings in the formation of Esoteric Buddhism throughout Asia.

Pu-k'ung's Construction of Esoteric Polity in the *Collected Documents*

The documents presented by Yüan-chao in the *Collected Documents* had a didactic purpose. That purpose was to articulate an Esoteric state polity modeled on the relationship between Pu-k'ung and the Emperors Su-tsung and Tai-tsung. I will examine the overall structure and intent of the collection below. For the moment my aim is to present Pu-k'ung's understanding of Esoteric polity as found in his correspondence.

To this end I have analyzed the contents of the *Collected Documents* according to recurring themes:

1. Documents couched strictly in Buddhist idiom or on strictly Buddhist topics make up 11 of the 66 pieces, and 5 of these are from imperial hands (16 percent).
2. Documents couched strictly in Confucian or Taoist idioms constitute only 6 items (1 percent).
3. Documents in which analogies are drawn between Buddhist and Confucian or Taoist ideas, 19 items (29 percent).
4. Documents that present Pu-k'ung as bodhisattva or "master" constitute 10 items (15 percent), of which 7 are from imperial authors.
5. Documents that speak of the emperor as *Cakravartin*, *Dharmarāja*, "Golden-Wheel Ruler," or of the imperial claim to the *Dharmacakra* constitute 9 items (14 percent), all but one from Pu-k'ung.
6. There are 18 documents (27 percent) in which ritual activity is performed "on behalf of the State" or "for the protection of the State," 14 of which are by Pu-k'ung.
7. Fourteen documents, all by Pu-k'ung, speak of rites to lengthen the emperor's life (21 percent). These were usually presented on imperial birthdays.
8. Thirty-two, all by Pu-k'ung, documents speak of the powers of the sage king and his virtuous "transformation" of the realm (48 percent).[60]

60. There is some overlap in certain of the documents. Thus the total of 140 percent.

It is apparent that a high proportion of the documents deal with rituals for the emperor and the protection of the state. What is interesting is that Pu-k'ung took two distinct tacks in these memorials. On the one hand, he presented himself in the guise of the ever-loyal Confucian minister, using the idiom of an officer serving the virtuous sage-king, whose transformative virtue is equated with the transformative influence of the *cakravartin*. On the other hand, Pu-k'ung used the idiom of the bodhisattva and imperial *abhiṣeka*-master, who in ritual could assume the role either of the world renouncer or of the world conqueror.

In certain memorials the roles are skillfully combined—the perspective constantly shifting. Pu-k'ung was a shrewd politician, as is evident in his continued high status in a court notorious for its intrigues. But this skill was based on his understanding of the principle strands of Buddhist tradition as they were embodied in the *STTS* and on his understanding of the culture of the Chinese court. We must also remember that the ability to shift the lines between insider and outsider and to do so in ways that allow both parties to understand the same relationship differently is a primary desideratum of Chinese religious and political life.

Under certain circumstances Pu-k'ung unambiguously played the part of a servant of the state. His rhetoric in the following memorial congratulating Su-tsung on his choice of the Lady Chang as his empress could just as well have been written by a non-Buddhist.

> As for the empress, I have heard that of Heaven and Earth it is she who gives birth to the myriad creatures. Now! The alternation first of yang then of yin is regarded as the [workings of] the Tao. [You] use spirit [virtuous example] to transform the masses and she nurtures the people. Of old [the empress] was regarded as the reason for the flourishing of the august sage-king [*sheng-wang*]. Yea, the virtue of the empress is displayed and her yielding nature sets a pattern [for the people]. . . . On high you have matched the luminous mandate. Here below you harmonize yourself with the virtue of earth. You are in accord with the heart of the people, and you are concerned over the world's mother. These two virtues have already set auspicious [forces in motion]. In the whole kingdom who does not offer praise and congratulations? Moreover [because] I serve the Tao I have long been showered by your favor. I joyously express my regards. (T 2120 52.828c13–23)

In like manner there are a few memorials that stick strictly to Buddhist language, though half of these are by an emperor writing to Pu-k'ung.[61]

61. See, for instance, the imperial reply in *Collected Documents*, T 2120 52.828a19–24.

But the overwhelming bulk of memorials by Pu-k'ung skillfully blend imagery of the Chinese sage-king with that of Esoteric Buddhism. These memorials reflect Pu-k'ung's direct involvement in key areas of imperial perogative, the well-being of the imperial ancestors, of the imperial family itself, and the guarantee of the proper order and processes in the heavens and the atmosphere, processes indicative of the transformative virtue of the Confucian sage-king.[62] Here Pu-k'ung used the Esoteric notions of the universe as the varied transformations of Mahāvairocana's *adhiṣṭhāna* as the basis of his weather and astronomical control.[63] Take, for example, the following memorial in which Pu-k'ung expresses his thanks to the emperor for the rain that he (Pu-k'ung) had been called upon to bring:

> The *sramana* Pu-k'ung says: An imperial servant arrived bearing [your] sage instructions, ordering me to pray for rain for the K'ang-yang area, and that the rain should come before seven days had past. I heard the command and obeyed, for it is the Lord who commands and the officer who follows, and I am your humble servant. The emperor sees with the eyes of all and hears with the ears of all. Heaven is high yet heeds the lowly, the grief of the farmers. This may be called the emperor's brilliance. Now, when the edict was promulgated I forthwith went to the *bodhimaṇḍa* and concentrated my resources and united my mind. In order for me to accomplish the will of heaven I must rely on the fine and subtle teachings which have been bequeathed by all the Buddhas. One must arrive at sincerity and then one can respond to the spirits. . . . Dancing for joy, I send up this memorial of congratulations.

The imperial reply follows:

> You have wonderous practice, complete understanding and great compassion! You are profoundly concerned about the state and your humane [*jen*] concern permeates the living beings. At the pure altar you prayed for sweet dew, exerting yourself day and night. . . . In no time at all it rained, thus the green sprouts have revived and the harvest will be timely. I have seen your expansive virtue and it both shames and encourages me. (841a2–18)

The timeliness of the rains was one of the central responsibilities of the Confu-

62. I treat Pu-k'ung's rites for the succor of imperial ancestors in "Seeing *Chen-yen* Buddhism," and in "A History of the *Shi-shi* in China."

63. There are several notices of Vajrabodhi, Pu-k'ung, and their disciples being called upon to promote good weather or to transform the baleful influences of comets and unusual asterisms. Pu-k'ung's biography contains several stories of his rites for making rain and his ability to prevent the disastrous consequences of comets. See Chou, "Tantrism in China," pp. 277 and 302–3, for example.

cian sage-king and they were indicative of his continued right to rule. Pu-k'ung specifically portrays himself as the humble servant of the Confucian sage-king, but this service consists of using Buddhist methods to bring about rain.

Pu-k'ung's self-understanding and its foundation in Esoteric notions concerning cosmology and authority was indispensible to his maintenance of this dual role. In a memorial to Su-tsung, dated 17 March 758, Pu-k'ung expressed his appreciation of a gift of incense in a way that simultaneously evokes his roles as Confucian servant and as an *ācārya* who put in motion the "Wheel of Command" to protect the empire:

> The *śramaṇa* Pu-k'ung says: Your majesty gave me rare incense; through your messenger you bestow upon me great favor. I am speechless with delight. . . . I have dedicated my life to the Buddhist cause. . . . I have prayed with the strength of the all-embracing [bodhisattva] vow that I would encounter the triumphant appearance of a *cakravartin*. . . . [During the early part of the rebellion] your majesty's noble plans were carried out by you alone, yet the Teaching mysteriously contributed [toward victory]; the gang of bandits was fragmented and destroyed and the imperial portents have returned to their normative state. . . . In the tenth month you cleansed the palace by setting up an assembly to drive out evil influences, when you rectified your rule by granting official titles, you went up to the *bodhimaṇḍa* for *abhiṣeka*. . . . Already you have showered me with gifts. When can I ever repay you? It is proper that I reverently bathe the statues at the appointed times and that I perform the *homa* rites at the half moon in order that the thirty-seven divinities [of the *Vajradhātu* mandala] may protect your earth, my brilliant king [*ming-wang, vidyārāja*] and that the sixteen protectors[64] might guard your majestic spirit, so that you may live as long as the southern mountain, eternally, without limit. (827c24–828a24)[65]

In this memorial we meet with several themes that are standard in the collection: thanks for patronage, alternating Buddhist and Confucian readings of sovereign authority and the role of the emperor, and mention of "prayers" and rituals for the protection of the state and the emperor himself.

Closer examination of the memorial reveals Pu-k'ung's political and rhetorical skills. In the first line Pu-k'ung proclaims himself a grateful servant, appearing to locate himself in the Confucian hierarchy, far below the Son of Heaven.

64. It is not clear whether this refers to the sixteen "bodhisattvas" of the cardinal layout of the *mahāmaṇḍala* of the *STTS*, to the sixteen deva protectors of the law, or to sixteen Vajra divinities which appear among the twenty deva in the *Vajradhātu maṇḍala*. For the first two of these possibilities, see *Mikkyō daijiten*, 2:899b–900c. For the last, see *Bukkyō daijiten*, 2416a–2417b.

65. I have followed Orlando's translation, in "Study," pp. 45–49, with minor modifications.

Yet suddenly he shifts, proclaiming his dedication and bodhisattva vows and his hopes of encountering a *cakravartin*. From this perspective Pu-k'ung would seem to possess the higher authority. But just as suddenly the scene is shifted back to the Confucian perspective, emphasizing the emperor's power in the rebellion, and then just as suddenly it shifts back again with an oblique reference to Pu-k'ung's invocation of Acala while in the occupied capital, proclaiming that "the Teaching mysteriously contributed toward victory." The outcome shifts us back again; the "imperial portents have returned to their normal state" and these portents are, of course, indicative of the transformative virtue of the sage-king. But this is no sooner proclaimed than we are then told of Pu-k'ung's performance of exorcistic rites and an *abhiṣeka*, which refers to the *cakravartin abhiṣeka* Pu-k'ung bestowed on Su-tsung. Predictably, the next sentence takes us back into the servant mode, with Pu-k'ung protesting his indebtedness to the emperor. But how he then will repay the emperor is to "perform the *homa* rites," and so on, in other words ritually to take charge of the protection of the state and the person of the emperor.

All of this shifting back and forth leaves us seriously in doubt as to which man is in charge in what ways, but it also gives each man room to maneuver, to play a double role as need arises before two audiences: Buddhist and "Confucian." Pu-k'ung pops back and forth from servant to sovereign to servant in this and in a number of other memorials. Just when he seems to be proclaiming a classical Two Wheels situation where the *ācārya* is the otherworldly counterpart to the *cakravartin* (or where the emperor is supported by the sage/savior of Taoist lore), he shifts into his role as "turner" of the Wheel of Command. Similarly, the emperor's role by implication moves back and forth between that of the ultimate source of transformative virtue and that of a subordinate performer.

Perhaps no single passage better exemplifies Pu-k'ung's consummate blending of Esoteric Buddhist and Chinese idioms than this, from a letter congratulating Tai-tsung on ascending the throne: "Your majesty has inherited the Heavenly [Mandate] and ascended the throne. Sage government will be renewed. The Correct Teaching patterns the state and is in proper correspondence with the noumena [*cheng-fa li-kuo, yü ling he-ch'i*]" (T 2120 52.829c17–830a11).

This was Pu-k'ung's first official letter to Tai-tsung after he ascended the throne, and it was accompanied by a statue of Marīci and the text of the *Dhāraṇī of the Great Buddha's Uṣṇīṣa*.[66] The occasion was Tai-tsung's birthday (this

66. Probably T 944a 19.100a–102c, *Ta fo-ting ju-lai fang-kuang hsi-tan-tuo po-tan-lo t'o-lo-ni*. T 944b 19.102c–105b contains the reconstructed siddham text. It is one of a cycle of texts that harness the power of Śākyamuni as lord of the various transformations of nature and astral phenomena. For more on this cycle of texts, see "Bucchō," in *Hōbōgirin*, 2:148–50, and Hubert Durt, "Daibucchō," in

was the first of many birthday greetings), and it is notable that Pu-k'ung ties together the Correct Teaching, which according to the *Scripture for Humane Kings* comes about as the result of proper Buddhist rule, and that this is "in proper correspondence with the noumena," a phrase evoking a hoary tradition of Taoist and Confucian notions of "tallies" between rule of the world and the Heavenly order of things.[67] Reading this correspondence vividly highlights our sense of Pu-k'ung's skillful interweaving of Esoteric Buddhism and Chinese ideology.

Yüan-chao and Esoteric Polity 775–800 C.E.

The *Scripture for Humane Kings* was crucial in this deft negotiation of Buddhist and Chinese worlds. Indeed, the scripture was more than simply another "application" of Esoteric notions. Rather, it played a key role in the articulation of a comprehensive vision of polity in Pu-k'ung's lineage. Yüan-chao's *Collected Documents* and his two catalogs provide us details of Pu-k'ung's lineage teachings from just after the *ācārya*'s death in 774 until just before the arrival of Kūkai from Japan in 802. The *Scripture for Humane Kings* and the documents that discuss it are the "manifesto" of East Asian Esoteric Buddhism. These documents present a paradigmatic portrait of the ideal religious polity as realized in joint rule by emperor and *ācārya.*

Yüan-chao was one of the most prominent monks in the last half of the eighth century.[68] He became an acolyte at the age of ten to the great *vinaya* (discipline, Chinese *lü*) expert Ching-yün of the Hsi-ming monastery. As he matured he became something of a polymath, mastering not only *vinaya* but also the *Vimalakirṭi scripture*, the *Vijñaptimātrata*, the *Nirvana scripture*, and Hua-yen teachings. He also studied ritual as well as the teachings of Confucius and Mo-tzu. He served as "recorder" (*pi-shou*) in a number of translation projects, including the one at An-kuo monastery, which involved comparison of old and new *vinaya* commentaries.[69]

Although Chih-p'an's biography of Yüan-chao is found in the *Vinaya* master's section of the *Lives of Eminent Monks Compiled During the Sung Dynasty*,

---

Hōbōgirin, 6:596–98. Also related are T 937 and 950. For Marīci, see Benyotosh Bhattacharyya, *An Introduction to Buddhist Esoterism* (Varanasi: Chowkhamba Sanskrit Series Office, 1964), chap. 13.

67. The passage evokes the notion of *ling-pao* with its plethora of connotations. For an overview, see Max Kaltenmark, "Ling-Pao: note sur un terme du taoisme religieux," *Mélanges publies par l'Institut des Hautes Études Chinoises* (Brussels) 2 (1960): 559–88.

68. Yüan-chao of the Hsi-ming Monastery was a scholar of Vinaya and a disciple of Pu-k'ung (who was himself a specialist in the Sarvāstivādin Vinaya). His biography is in *Sung kao-seng chüan*, T 2061 50.804b17–805c20. Also see *Bukkyō daijiten*, 303c–304a, and *Mikkyō diajiten*, 161c–162a.

69. For his biography, see *Sung kao-seng chüan*, T 2061 55.804b17–805c21.

Yüan-chao's close connection to the Esoteric school is evident in all of his works. Indeed, the Esoteric and *vinaya* schools had a strong affinity for each other, and Yüan-chao was typical in this regard.

Yüan-chao's *Collected Documents* is odd in several ways. The 133 pieces contained in it at first seem a hodgepodge. The first 101 pieces follow chronological sequence. The last 32 do not, and these include material that could have been interspersed among the previous pieces. *Collected Documents* was written during Te-tsung's reign (Li Kua, r. 779–805), yet any mention of him or of the *ācāryas* active at that time is conspicuously absent. A careful examination of the contents of the *Collected Documents* reveals a method behind these oddities.

The *Collected Documents* is broken up into six *chüan*, the first beginning in the reign of Su-tsung, with the recapture of the T'ang capitals during the An Lu-shan rebellion.[70] The first *chüan* chronicles Su-tsung's establishment of Pu-k'ung as the protector of the state. Many of the pieces in the first *chüan* are concerned with Pu-k'ung's establishment of an *abhiṣeka* altar for the protection of the state. The end of the first *chüan* moves into the reign of Tai-tsung with the letter cited above accompanied by the text on the Buddha's *uṣṇīṣa* and by a statue of the divinity Marīci.

Just at this point Yüan-chao has placed the exchange concerning the retranslation of the *Scripture for Humane Kings*, including a letter of thanks from Pu-k'ung for the emperor's new preface for the scripture.[71] Two imperial edicts conclude the section, the first conferring the nominal rank of *k'ai-fu* and the title *ta-hung-chiao san-tsang* on Pu-k'ung's late teacher Vajrabodhi, the second conferring the rank *t'e-chin* and the title *ta-kuang-chih Pu-k'ung san-tsang* on Pu-k'ung.[72]

The document thus begins with Pu-k'ung's involvement in the denouement of the An Lu-shan rebellion and establishes a parallel between the emperor as head of state and the Buddha (and, by implication, the *ācārya*). The first section of *Collected Documents* presents us with a major disaster that is rectified by close cooperation between the emperor and the *ācārya* and by new forms of ritual action and honors by the emperor. It then goes on to portray the institutionalization of the Correct Teaching in this dual sovereignty under the new emperor Tai-tsung.

The second *chüan* portrays the growing and continued effectiveness of the relationship between the *ācārya* and the Son of Heaven. It begins with a re-

70. Yüan-chao's biography in the *Sung kao-seng chüan* mentions a *Pu-k'ung san-tsang pei piao-chi* in seven *chüan*. While this must be *Collected Documents* (T 2120), the fact that Tsan-ning mentions a seven-*chüan* version raises questions of the odd organization of the six-*chüan* version. Yüan-chao tells us in his preface to *Collected Documents* that the text is in six *chüan*. See *Sung kao-seng chüan* by Tsan-ning, T 2061 50.805b11.

71. Items 16, 17, and 18, in Orlando's numeration (T 2120 52.831b19–832a25).

72. T 2120 52.832b13–c17 and 832c18–833a26.

quest by Pu-k'ung for funds to renovate the monasteries on Mt. Wu-t'ai and to establish an Esoteric center there devoted to Mañjuśrī for the protection of the state. Under these conditions, the rebellions that do occur are quickly put down. Indeed, in the exchange of letters concerning the rebellious disobedience of the regional military commander Chou Chih-kuang, who was killed on imperial orders, Pu-k'ung remarks that "one can see that the power of the sage-king [*sheng-wang*] in this event achieved success without fighting, and the compassion of the humane king [*jen-wang*] ultimately saved lives" (52.834c6–7). Moreover, in the exchange concerning the renovation of the five monasteries on Mt. Wu-t'ai Pu-k'ung says that their purpose is the constant recitation of the *Scripture for Humane Kings* and the *Scripture of the Esoteric Teaching of the Mahāyāna* (835c3–5).[73] Mañjuśrī was thereafter established as the official patron of the empire, and Pu-k'ung was ordered to establish temples to Mañjuśrī and Samantabhadra in the T'ang ancestral seat of T'ai-yüan. The exchange concerning T'ai-yüan expressly orders "the chanting of the *Scripture for Humane Kings* by the monks of the combined temples on behalf of the seven imperial forbears from Kao-tsu through Su-tsung" (838a17–8). Pu-k'ung takes on the role of "Master of the State" (*kuo-shih*) and teaches the multitudes.

Chüan 3 is the beginning of the end. Commencing with a list of scriptures he has translated on behalf of the state (including the *Scripture for Humane Kings* and its commentaries and ritual manuals), Pu-k'ung sums up his life's work of translating texts for the dual purpose of enlightenment and the protection of the state, requesting the emperor grant the texts official recognition by entering them in the imperial catalog. Mañjuśrī cloisters are set up in all official monasteries, and Pu-k'ung is instrumental in insuring seasonable rain. The princess Ch'iung Hua is given into Pu-k'ung's care: she dies, and Pu-k'ung makes arrangements for the funeral.[74] The section ends with Pu-k'ung's testament, which apparently cements the relationship between the emperor and the Esoteric school after Pu-k'ung's death.

The fourth section of *Collected Documents* begins with a request for monks to recite *sūtras* at Pu-k'ung's quarters and at the new Mañjuśrī temple on behalf of the state (845b27–c22). Pu-k'ung falls ill and is granted great rank and honors by the emperor. He writes a final farewell letter to the emperor and dies in 774. The rest of section 4 is composed of eulogies and commemorative pieces written by members of the court, including the chief minister Yüan Tsai.[75] Fei

73. The *Ta-ch'eng mi-yen ching* (T 681, vol. 16) was retranslated along with the *Scripture for Humane Kings*. See Chapter 5, note 65.

74. This is the princess Hua-yang referred to in Chapter 5, note 32.

75. Pu-k'ung's patrons and disciples included a number of future chief ministers as well as the current chief minister, Yüan Tsai. For Yüan Tsai, see Twitchett, *Cambridge History of China*, vol. 3, pt. 1, *Sui and T'ang China*, 589–906, pp. 496–97, 576–78. Also see Chapter 5, note 31.

Hsi's stele biography extols Pu-k'ung's aid to Su-tsung during the An Lu-shan rebellion, noting that Pu-k'ung performed rites invoking the aid of the *vidyā-rāja* Acala (*pu-tung*) to repulse the usurpers (849a15). Posthumous honors are bestowed upon Pu-k'ung by the emperor. The *chüan* ends with a memorial by Hui-lang, Pu-k'ung's successor as master of *abhiṣeka*, thanking the emperor for the posthumous honors.

The fifth and sixth sections of the *Collected Documents* are quite odd. Most of the documents in the fifth section portray Hui-lang as stepping into Pu-k'ung's relationship with Tai-tsung, with predictable success. Rain is timely, rebellions are put down, and all is well.

The most apparent oddity in *chüan* 5 is the break in the chronological sequence that prevails up to document 101. From this point on, the themes remain the same—the close cooperation of the Esoteric school with the emperor for the protection and well-being of the state. But most of the documents of *chüan* 5 that are out of chronological order are by persons other than Pu-k'ung or Hui-lang. Many of these documents are written by Pu-k'ung's other fully initiated disciples: Chüeh-chao, Hui-kuo, and Hui-sheng.

This is also the pattern of the sixth and final section of *Collected Documents*. Here we find documents about rebellion, rain, and, prominently, the Wui-t'ai complex. The next to last memorial is a letter of thanks to the emperor for appointing Hui-lang as abbot of Pu-k'ung's Hsing-shan monastery (a post Pu-k'ung never held). The final document is a stele biography by Yen Ying, which was set up in Pu-k'ung's cloister (near his new *stūpa?*). Dated 781, it is the only item in the collection dated after Tai-tsung's death. It presents Hui-lang as the seventh patriarch and extols the relationship between Pu-k'ung and Tai-tsung.

Thus the dominant structure of this collection is the portrayal of a joint Esoteric Buddhist polity comprised of the *ācārya* and the Son of Heaven. Through the careful arrangement of a wealth of documents, Yüan-chao shows again and again that this is the ideal polity for the empire, and that the *Scripture for Humane Kings* is the emblem of that polity. *Collected Documents* is a hagiographic version of Esoteric polity, of the ideal of simultaneous protection of the state and pursuit of enlightenment.

But other issues are less obvious. Was this the only aim of *Collected Documents*? Is there a reason for its beginning when it does? What of its odd arrangement in the fifth and sixth sections? Who was the intended audience? Why are there no documents from Te-tsung's reign?

Our first clue to the answers to these questions lies in the last document of the collection. Yen Ying's stele biography is the only work dated from the reign of Te-tsung. No communication between the Esoteric school and the emperor is recorded after Tai-tsung's death in 779. The 781 date of Yen Ying's stele establishes a terminus a quo for the collection. Yüan-chao died in 800, and we know that he was commissioned to edit a number of collections including *Collected Documents* after 781.[76] *Collected Documents* was thus written sometime during the last twenty years of the century, during the reign of Te-tsung. Te-tsung came to the throne as an energetic forty-year-old bent on wresting some of the control of the empire back from provincial warlords. He did not share his father's regard for the Esoteric masters, and indeed, he put an end to Esoteric rites in the palace and cut back patronage to the school.[77]

With this in mind, let us look at the major players in the *Collected Documents* again. Two emperors are covered, Su-tsung and Tai-tsung, and two *ācāryas*, Pu-k'ung and Hui-lang. Pu-k'ung is paired first with Su-tsung and then with Tai-tsung. When Pu-k'ung dies, the pair is made up of Tai-tsung and Hui-lang. But when Tai-tsung dies, Hui-lang is stranded; the seventh patriarch has no willing partner to insure the ideal polity. The structure is incomplete; Te-tsung is noticeably absent.

A second clue is in the beginning of *Collected Documents*. The opening of the collection and its themes of dual sovereignty not only comport with the dual purpose of Esoteric ideology as established by Pu-k'ung, they also present a forceful argument for continued patronage of the school in a time of imperial distress. During the years 782–85 Te-tsung was beset by a series of rebellions brought on by his stubborn pursuit of renewed imperial control over the nominally loyal warlords, who had entrenched themselves after the An Lu-shan rebellion. What began in 782 as moderate success for imperial forces soon turned into a nightmarish repeat of the events thirty-seven years earlier during the An Lu-shan rebellion. In 783–84 Te-tsung was forced to flee his capital and to retreat, first to Feng-t'ien, and then toward Szechuan. Not until 785 did he reenter the capital.[78] The parallel with the events of the An Lu-shan rebellion must have been on everyone's mind.

In this context it is obvious why *Collected Documents* begins with a memorial by Pu-k'ung to Su-tsung congratulating him on retaking the western capital and underscoring Pu-k'ung's ritual activity on behalf of the emperor. The context also helps us to understand the following three pieces concerning the retaking of the capitals, pieces which include thanks from the emperor for Pu-k'ung's help, the repeated theme of the protection of the state and the routing

76. Among these were works on the transmission of the Dharma at the An-kuo monastery and a collection of documents relating to I-hsing and the vinaya. The list is on T 2061 55.805b, and I discuss them below.

77. For Te-tsung's reign, see Twitchett, *Cambridge History of China*, pp. 492ff.

78. For the An Lu-shan rebellion, see Twitchett, *Cambridge History of China*, pp. 453–63. For Te-tsung's predicament, see esp. pp. 503–10. For another view of the series of rebellions under Te-tsung, see Denis Twitchett, "Lu Chih (754–805): Imperial Advisor and Court Official," in Denis Twitchett and Arthur Wright, eds., *Confucian Personalities* (Stanford: Stanford University Press, 1962).

of rebel forces, and the documents concerning the new recension of the *Scripture for Humane Kings*. Yüan-chao was drawing a parallel between past and present and implying that what worked for Su-tsung and then so many times for Tai-tsung would work now, if Te-tsung would only try it. Indeed, the portrayal of the idyllic rule of Tai-tsung and Pu-k'ung and the paradigm of dual sovereignty put forward in the *Collected Documents* could have been meant ironically. The ideal polity had been broken and the consequences were clear. Because of the fit between the structure of *Collected Documents* and the circumstances of Te-tsung's early reign I think it is reasonable to date *Collected Documents* to the years 783–85 or shortly thereafter.

In a peculiar way the *Collected Documents* reads like a pseudo-official chronicle of the reign of Tai-tsung from the Esoteric point of view. Like official histories, *Collected Documents* was meant to be a work of edification and to present an exemplary model for behavior to its contemporary readers. *Collected Documents* used the mirror of the past to castigate the present. Thus in his preface Yüan-chao notes the number of works in the collection and says, "Now they are divided into six *chüan*, so that they may be handed down in the future. Those who study them well will know their intent" (T 2120, 826c27–28). The intent was to propagate an ideal model of the relationship between Esoteric masters and the emperor. It was the current emperor, above all, who was the intended audience, and he was being admonished for letting the ideal situation of his predecessor slip away. Thus, in *Collected Documents* the structure or paradigm of dual sovereignty achieves expression in a form that is characteristically Chinese: the didactic history. Perhaps Yüan-chao's aim was accomplished, for Te-tsung soon thereafter reversed his anti-Buddhist position and lavishly patronized the monk Prajñā, a new arrival propagating Esoteric Buddhism in what was to become the last major translation project of the T'ang dynasty.[79]

Yüan-chao, The Esoteric School, and the Legacy of the *Scripture for Humane Kings*

Yüan-chao's two "catalogs," the *Supplement* (T 2156, vol. 55) and the *New Recension* (T 2157, vol. 55), are dated 796 and 800. The later work is indeed a massive catalog of Buddhist scriptures, though one which highlights scriptures of the Esoteric school. But the *Supplement* is no comprehensive catalog

79. For Te-tsung's reversal and the monk Prajñā, see Stanley Weinstein, *Buddhism Under the T'ang* (Cambridge: Cambridge University Press, 1987), pp. 86–99, and for a detailed examination of Prajñā and his work, see Yoritomi Motohiro, *Chūgoku mikkyō no kenkyū*, pp. 1–109.

at all. Instead it is propaganda for the Esoteric school and preeminently for the *Scripture for Humane Kings*.

The large number of Esoteric scriptures in Yüan-chao's catalogs reflects both the fact that these were the scriptures that were "hot" in India and Central Asia in the eighth century and the dominance of Pu-k'ung's Esoteric teachings. While Yüan-chao's *New Recension* includes much from outside of the Esoteric orbit, his *Supplement* is dominated by three concerns: the new recension of the *Scripture for Humane Kings;* the commentary on the *Liu-ch'u ching* (another important text in the *STTS* orbit) and the role of the monk Prajñā in its propagation; and the great *vinaya* commentary produced at the An-kuo monastery.[80] Yüan-chao was involved in these projects as "recorder" and 75 percent of the *Supplement* consists of narrative accounts of these projects.

The *Supplement* is broken into three *chüan* with translations of scriptures in the first, commentaries in the second, and catalogs, memorial stele, and other documents comprising the third *chüan*. Yüan-chao chose to treat both the *Scripture for Humane Kings* and the *Liu-ch'u ching* in the first *and* second *chüan*, since both new "translations" and new commentaries were involved. Much of the material in *Collected Documents* is duplicated in the *Supplement*, not in the context of the history of the Esoteric school but rather as coherent narratives about the *Scripture for Humane Kings* and the other works.

While much of the material in the collection has been reassembled from *Collected Documents* and other sources, occasional new details do appear. There are mentions of 100-seat Humane Kings convocations as well as a narrative of the grand convocation outside the south gate of the city in 765.[81]

The first long narrative to appear in the *Supplement* is the narrative of the history of the transmission of the *Scripture for Humane Kings* and the circumstances of the production of its new recension, of Pu-k'ung's ritual commentaries on the scripture, and of Liang-pi's great commentary (749c–753a with short breaks; 758a–758c; 761c). When we add the prominent role of the *Scripture for Humane Kings* in the *Chen-yüan shih-chiao lu* to its place in *Collected Documents*, it is evident that the *Scripture for Humane Kings* was one of the most visible signs of the Esoteric school in the second half of the eighth century. These documents provided the exempla for a "national protection" Esoteric Buddhism that was exported to Korea and Japan, where it once again underwent complex

80. The *Liu-ch'u ching* (Japanese *Rishukyō*) is a short *Prajñāpāramitā* with decidedly tantric coloring. Pu-k'ung translated the text (T 243 8.784a–786b), and Ian Astley-Kristensen has produced an excellent study and translation of the scripture, *The Rishukyō*.

81. Yüan-chao mentions 100-seat Humane Kings convocations at T 2156 55.751c9–18, including an imperial reply, and another at 55.761c24. The great convocation outside the south gate of the city in 765 is one connected to P'u-ku Huai-en and the Tibetan invasion and the new recension of the *Scripture for Humane Kings*. The account appears at 55.752b27–753b8.

evolution. The *Scripture for Humane Kings* was no mere window dressing for Pu-k'ung's lineage; it was at the heart of the Esoteric vision of Buddhist polity. The original lineaments of this polity emerged in the intersection between the *rupic* and *dharmic* strands of Buddhist cosmology, authority, and salvation and the very local problems of fifth-century north China. Pu-k'ung's recension of the scripture reflects a new deployment of these strands of Buddhist tradition tailored to concerns of the eighth-century T'ang court. Repackaged for decidedly changed circumstances in Yüan-chao's *Collected Documents*, this vision of Esoteric polity moved beyond China to Korea and Japan.[82]

The Hermeneutic Seam: Cross-Cultural Paradigms and Local Meaning

Religion is a complex, open-ended, adaptive system in which local constructions of meaning are applied to other local, but quite new contexts. Pu-k'ung's congratulatory statement to Tai-tsung on the successful assassination of Chou Chih-kuang—"one can see that the power of the sage-king . . . achieved success without fighting, and the compassion of the humane king ultimately saved lives"—is a case in point and epitomizes the emergence and recasting of the *Scripture for Humane Kings*.

As I have demonstrated, Buddhist meaning is generated in the deployment and redeployment of notions about the world, the path, and authority in new contexts in response to new needs. The two major strands of Buddhist cosmology (*dharmic* and *rupic*) thus provide the paradigms or the "grammar" of Buddhism, but outside of scholarly analysis this grammar is inseparable from the complex and evolving language of Buddhism in various historical contexts and in various texts. The negotiation that is part of a living, complex, and changing tradition can often be glimpsed in the disjunctions or seams where divergent meanings are stitched together to respond to the necessities of life. By being attentive to these seams and to the underlying paradigms of a religious tradition we can deepen our understanding of religion in changing social and cultural contexts. By attending to how cosmology, the path, and authority are functions of one another, we can see more clearly how meaning is produced in the application of one local system to another locale. Thus in Chapters 1 and 2 I set out to delineate the basic "grammar" that is a part of the construction of meaning in Buddhist worlds.

But knowing that the basic strands of Buddhism involve *dharmic* and *rupic*

82. *Collected Documents* was among the key texts taken to Japan by Kūkai.

notions about cosmology, soteriology, and authority, that these might be viewed as discontinuous, continuous, or recursive, and that Buddhism often "plays the edge" between world conquest and world transcendence is only helpful when applied in an analysis of a particular historical situation. In analyzing the fifth-century *Scripture for Humane Kings* I have shown that recursively related continuous and discontinuous *rupic* notions were the real heart of the scripture. The words "forbearing" and "humane" are local interpretations of Buddhism's *rupic* and *dharmic* themes with regard to the problem of a Chinese Buddhism. It may well be that the Three Truths is another expression of the same problem. The issue of the Chineseness of Buddhism was the historical "locale" for a politics of transcendence and thus for the appearance of the scripture.

What made sense in the fifth and sixth centuries did not, however, suffice in the eighth century. The development of Esoteric Buddhism in the T'ang court demanded a vision of Buddhism and Confucianism as part of a universal polity for the empire, and this government context coupled with Esoteric emphasis on practice as the realization of the Two Truths led to Pu-k'ung's recasting of the *Scripture for Humane Kings*. Indeed, as I noted at the beginning of this book, Esoteric Buddhism plays out the political ramifications implicit in the relationship between world transcendence and world conquest. Thus, in the new recension of the text the "edge of reality" was instantiated in ritual that explicitly claimed both the goals of enlightenment and specific "mundane" benefits. At least in the Chinese situation, an important factor in the authoritativeness and longevity of a revelation is its ability to simultaneously admit of multiple interpretations. The fifth-century *Scripture for Humane Kings* was designed to do this, and Pu-k'ung's recension fine-tuned and updated the design. In the hands of Pu-k'ung and Yüan-chao, the *Scripture for Humane Kings* became a key element of an Esoteric polity that was ideally constituted as a dual sovereignty of the Son of Heaven and the *ācārya*. The scripture's longevity, both as a charter of East Asian national protection Buddhism and as an object of popular veneration, testifies to its importance as one of the great products of Chinese Buddhism.

PART THREE

The Transcendent Wisdom Scripture for Humane Kings Who Wish to Protect Their States (T 246)

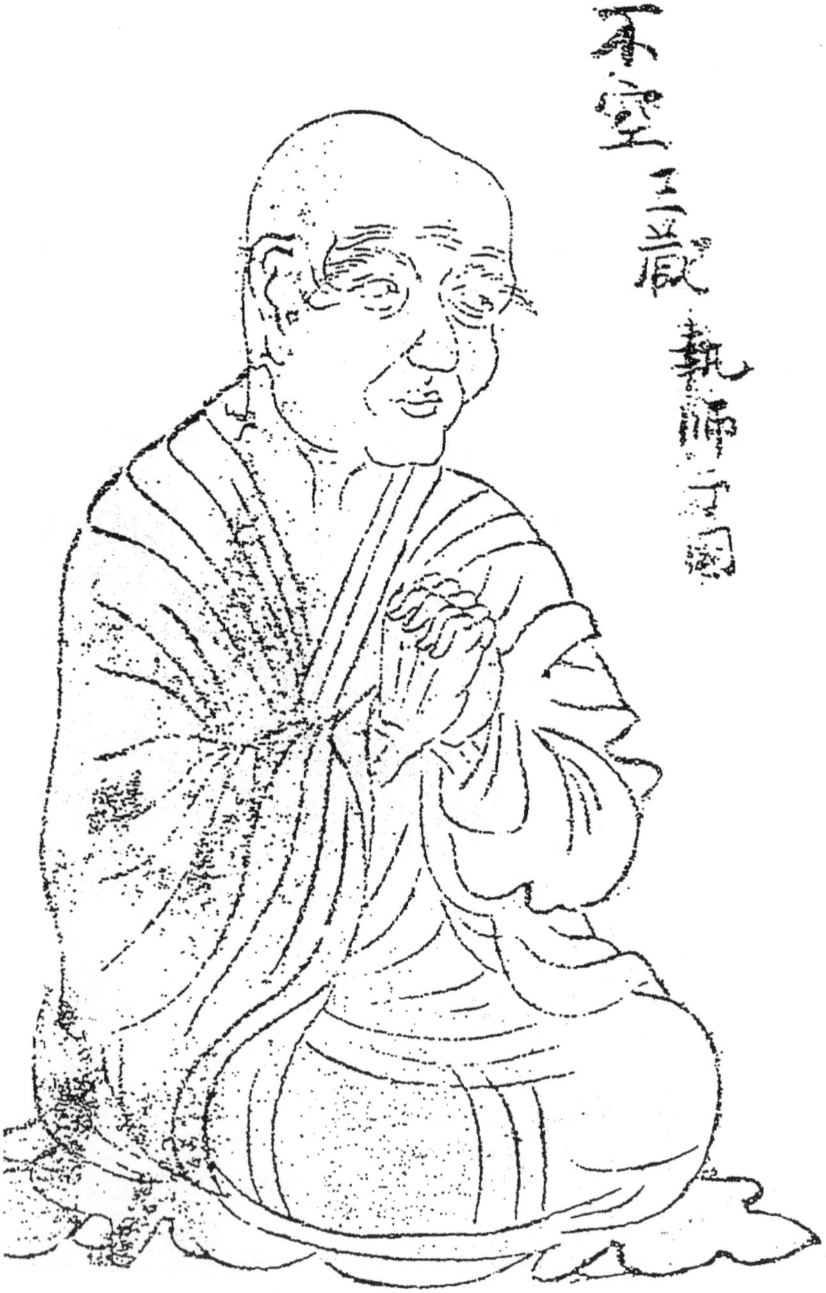
不空三藏
執師子國

1

Prologue

[834c] Thus I have heard. Once the Buddha was residing on Vulture Peak in the Capital[1] together with a great assembly of ***bhikṣu***s, eighteen-hundred in all, every one an ***arhat***.[2] All of their outflows had already been exhausted and

1. The Capital (*She-ch'eng*), literally "city of the king's palace," represents the Sanskrit Rajāgṛha.

2. The fifth-century version of the text lists the total number of the gathered assemblies as "eight trillion." The text begins, as do most Buddhist scriptures, with the characterization of the assemblies present to hear the Buddha preach. While the introduction of the eighth-century version follows or paraphrases the fifth-century version using updated language, there are also a few points at which the texts are substantially different. Each text lists the participants (and their religious accomplishments). The assemblies are as follows:

Fifth-century version (T 245 8.824a–b)	Eighth-century version (T 246 8.834c–835a)
Bhikṣus	Bhikṣus
	Bhikṣunīs
Great *ṛṣi pratyekabuddhas*	
Bodhisattva-Mahāsattvas	Bodhisattva-Mahāsattvas
Worthies Adhering to Prohibitions	Upāsakas and Upāsikās

they would not again be subject to the defilements.[3] Their minds were well freed, their wisdom was well freed. They had already accomplished the nine and ten forms of wisdom.[4] [They had achieved] the three false and real contemplations and the three emptiness-gate contemplations.[5] Those whose [efforts] are [based on] merit and those whose [efforts] are not [based on] merit were totally accomplished.[6]

Women of Pure Faith: Arhats	
Those of Seven Worthy Stages	Those of Seven Worthy Stages
Nine Brahmadevas, etc.	Sixteen Kings
Various Devas / Sons of Heaven	Devas of Desire Realm, Asuras, etc.
Sixteen Kings	
Other Beings of the Five Gati	
Various other beings	
Transformed Pure Lands	Transformed Pure Lands
Transformation Buddhas	Transformation Buddhas

It is immediately apparent that the eighth-century version of the text gives a more abbreviated listing of gods and leaves out the great *ṛṣi pratyekabuddhas* as well as the beings of the five *gati*. The fifth-century version lists women of pure faith who adhere to the prohibitions—all arhats, while the eighth-century version simply calls them bhikṣunī. In either case the attribution of arhat status to women is unusual but not unheard of. The entire introductory chapter of the text is strongly reminiscent of the introductory chapter of the *Lotus Sūtra*. See Hurvitz's translation of *The Scripture of the Lotus Blossom of the Fine Dharma*, pp. 1–21.

3. *Lou* "leakages" or "outflows" corresponds to the Sanskrit *āsrava*. This comment is missing in the fifth-century version of the text.

4. Both texts and commentary read *i pan*, "already managed" or "accomplished," rather than *i pien* "completely eloquent." The Nine and Ten Forms of Wisdom and all other numerical categories are found in the numerical glossary. This sentence and the next two discuss the achievements of these saints in categories based on a division of the path into the achievements of the Auditors (*śrāvakas*) and those of the Bodhisattvas. For a discussion of these stages, see Hurvitz, *Chih-I*, especially pp. 347–49.

5. According to Liang-pi's *Commentary on the Scripture for Humane Kings*, the three false and real contemplations (*san chia-shih kuan*) concern the emptiness of constituents, feelings, and names. The three emptiness-gate contemplations (*san k'ung-men kuan*) concern the recognition that all is empty, signless, and wishless (T 1709 33.440c21–23).

6. This sentence refers to the two-fold division of the "saintly stage" of the path of the Auditors into "those who have more to study" (*yu-hsüeh*), comprised of two sorts of people: those who intellectually cognize the way (*chien-tao*), those who actively cultivate the way (*hsiu-tao*), and those who have nothing more to learn (*wu-hsüeh-tao*). See Hurvitz, *Chih-I*, p. 348. According to Liang-pi, "those whose [efforts] are [based on] merit" (*yu-wei kung-te*) comprise the lower level of those who have nothing more to learn while "those whose [efforts] are not [based on] merit" (*wu-wei kung-te*) are accomplished by effort of discriminating the true from the false, and these comprise the upper level of those who have nothing more to learn (T 1709 33.441b1–15). The fifth-century text follows here: "Those whose [efforts] are [based on] merit and those whose [efforts] are not [based on] merit, who no [longer] studied the ten knowledges, who no [longer] studied the eight knowledges, who had studied the six knowledges, the three roots and the sixteen mental activities, the contemplation that dharmas are false and voidness is real, the contemplation that sensory perception is false and voidness is real, the contemplation that names are false and voidness is real, the Three Contemplative Gates of Emptiness, the Four Truths, the Twelve Causes (*nidāna*): their limitless merit was all accomplished." The eighth-century version places this list below.

Moreover, there were eight hundred ***bhikṣunī,*** every one an ***arhat.***[7] There were also limitless and innumerable ***bodhisattva-mahāsattva***s whose wisdom of reality was impartial, who had forever cut off delusive obstructions, and whose skill-in-means and adroitness had given rise to great acts and vows.[8] Using the four all-embracing virtues, they enrich the lives of sentient beings. Their four immeasurable minds universally shelter all, and they have attained the triple mirror knowledge[9] and the five supranormal powers. They cultivate and practice the boundless [thirty-seven] divisions of **bodhi**-[illumination], and having applied themselves to the magical arts, they surpass all the worlds. They have profoundly penetrated codependent origination, emptiness, signlessness, and wishlessness. Coming and going from the trance of extinction, their manifestations are difficult to fathom. They destroy and subdue ***Māra*** the evil one [with the] twin illumination of the two truths. Their eye of the Teaching is all-seeing and knows the roots of all beings. With the four-fold unobstructed powers of comprehension they expound fearlessness. The wonderous knowledge of the ten directions and the thunderous sounds of the Teaching bring them near to the peerless adamantine-***samādhi.***[10] Such qualities as these were complete [in them].

Moreover, there was an immeasurable assembly of ***upāsaka***s and ***upāsikā***s[11] all of whom had perceived the noble truths. There were also countless beings who had cultivated the seven [stages of] worthy conduct, the states of mindfulness, the abandonments, the supranormal powers, the eight victorious stages [of meditation], and the ten modes of universal contemplation.[12] The sixteen lessons quickened [their] insight [into] the truth.[13]

7. The fifth-century text omits specific reference to *bhikṣunī*.

8. *Bodhisattva-mahāsattva*, a "bodhisatttva-great being." The first half of the sentence refers to how bodhisattvas benefit themselves, the second half to how they benefit others.

9. The triple mirror-[like] knowledge (*san ming-chien-ta*) includes insight into the conditions of one's previous lives, insight into the conditions of other beings' lives, and insight into the causes and conditions of the present life that will lead finally to Nirvana. The use of the word "mirror-like" (*chien*) seems a Chinese imposition. Liang-pi, T 1709 33.442b28–443a3, has an extensive discussion of this knowledge.

10. This is the *chin-kang san-mei* or *vajra-samādhi*, which appears extensively in the *Mahāparinirvāṇa Scripture* (a major influence on the *Scripture for Humane Kings*) and later in the *Scripture of the Adamantine Samādhi*. It came to stand for supreme enlightenment, inclusive of all previous "stages" and is intimately connected with the notions of innate, and "sudden" enlightenment. It is often characterized as the total quiescence or immobility of body and mind. See Buswell, *Formation of Ch'an Ideology*, especially pp. 26–27 and 104–15.

11. Male and female lay devotees.

12. The seven stages of worthy conduct (*ch'i hsien hsing*) are a preparatory path, and it is followed by the seven stages of sage conduct (*ch'i sheng hsing*). The four states of mindfulness, the four right efforts, and the four elements of supranormal powers, along with the five moral faculties, constitute the first seventeen steps of the thirty-seven *Bodhipākṣika dharmas*. Liang-pi has an extensive discussion of these. For a list, see Hurvits, *Chih-I*, p. 344.

13. The sixteen lessons (*shih-liu hsin-hsing*, sometimes the *shih-liu ti-kuan* or the *shih-liu hsing-hsiang*)

The kings of the sixteen great states and King ***Prasenajit*** were also present, each with upwards of ten million retainers.[14] There were, moreover, the kings of the six heavens of desire, ***Śakra devanam-indra*** and the rest, with their retinues of countless gods, all the great ***brahma***-kings of the four pure heavens of form together with their retainers and countless gods; and all the transformations of countless beings of the various destinies.[15] The ***Asura***s and their retainers were also present in like numbers.

[835a] There were also the transformed manifestations of pure lands of the ten directions and the manifestations of one billion lion thrones, and on [each of these] were Buddhas broadcasting the essentials of the Teaching. In front of each seat a flower appeared; these one billion flowers were massed together like a jeweled canopy.[16] On each of these flowers there were, moreover, countless transformation Buddhas and countless ***bodhisattva***s. The four-fold and eight-segmented assemblies were all immeasurable.[17] Each of the Buddhas in their midst expounded the ***Prajñāpāramitā,*** and this scene was replicated in all of the Buddha lands of the ten directions, lands as numerous as the sands of the ***Gaṅgā.***[18] And all those who had come to the great assembly made obeisance to the feet of the Buddha, withdrew to one side, and sat down.

At that time, on the eighth day of the first month of the year,[19] the World-

---

refers to consideration of the four noble truths from each of four perspectives connected with the stage of recognizing the Way (*chien-tao*) mentioned above. Liang-pi enumerates these at T 1709 33.446b2–15. "Insight into the truth" (*ti-hsien-kuan*) is comprised of three distinct stages: viz., "discriminative insight" (*chien hsien-kuan*), "insight into causality" (*yüan hsien-kuan*), and "insight into circumstances" (*shih hsien-kuan*). See note 9. This sentence is so condensed that my rendering of it is quite tentative.

14. The states are traditionally listed as Vaiśālī, Kosala, Śrāvastī, Magadha, Kapilavastu, Kuśinagara, Kauśāmbī, Pañcāla, Paṭaliputra, Mathurā, Uṣa, Puṅyavardhana, Devāvatāra, Kāśī, and Campā. They are enumerated in chapter 8 of the sutra.

15. My translation of *t'ien-tzu* as "gods" would certainly have the ring of Chinese imperial authority to the Chinese reader, where it commonly means "the Son of Heaven" or "Emperor." Liang-pi has an extensive excursus on Buddhist cosmology as defined by the assemblies here (T 1709 33.446b–448b). For an English accounting of Buddhist cosmology, see Kloetzli, *Buddhist Cosmology*.

16. For the symbolism of the jeweled canopy or *gandhakuṭī*, see John Strong, "Gandhakuṭī: The Perfumed Chamber of the Buddha," *History of Religions* 16 (1977): 390–406.

17. The four-fold assembly is constituted by human beings: monks and nuns, female and male lay devotees. The eight-segmented assembly is constituted by nonhumans: gods, nāgas, yakṣas, gandharvas, asuras, garudas, kiṃnaras, and mahoragas. See *Bukkyō daijiten*, 2.1800a and 5.4223c–4224a.

18. The transcription of *prajñāparamitā* here is *po-jo-po-lo-mi-to*, which was apparently introduced by Hsüan-tsang in the seventh century. The earlier text uses the more common spelling, which is without the final "*to*." For the image of the "sands of the Ganges," see Kloetzli, *Buddhist Cosmology*, pp. 113–24.

19. It is very typically Chinese to specify a date, and while Indians routinely insert chronograms in their colophons, it is unusual in Perfect Wisdom literature. Both versions of the text indicate this date. Compare T 245 8.825b10. The date corresponds to the *Li-ch'un*, which celebrates the rebirth of spring and the birth of rice and grains. See Bredon and Mitropanow, *Moon Year*, p. 132. Liang-pi spends several lines in an explanation of equivalences between Indian and Chinese calendars, but does not really throw any light on why this date is mentioned (T 1709 33.448c18–449a2).

honored One entered the wonderous ***samādhi*** of great quiescence and calm[20] and all of the pores of his body emitted a brilliant light that illuminated the Buddha-lands of all the ten directions, lands numerous as the sands of the ***Gaṅgā.*** Then the countless gods of the desire realm rained down masses of marvelous flowers. All the gods of the form realm also rained down heavenly flowers. The various colors alternated in a most lovely manner. Then [the beings of] the formless realm rained down incense and flowers. The incense was like ***Sumeru*** and the flowers like cartwheels. Flowers descended in clouds time and again on the great assembly, and the entire Buddha-realm quaked and shook in six ways.[21]

At that moment all in the great assembly reflected thus: "The great enlightened World-honored One has previously expounded for us the ***Mahāprajñāpāramitā*** and the Adamantine-***prajñāpāramitā,*** the Celestial Kings Inquiry on the ***Prajñāpāramitā,*** the Larger ***Prajñāpāramitā*** and so forth,[22] and countless innumerable ***Prajñāpāramitā***s. Why then, has the Thus-come One[23] now emitted this great light?"

Then King ***Prasenajit*** of ***Śrāvastī*** thought to himself, "The Buddha's present manifestation is an extraordinary sign. Assuredly this is the rain of the Teaching and it will bring universal blessings and joy." So [he] asked Jewel-Cover, Stainless [Fame], and all the rest of the ***upāsaka***s and ***Śāriputra, Subhūti*** and all the rest of the great auditors, and ***Maitreya,*** Lion-roarer, and all the rest of the ***bodhisattva-mahāsattva***s: "What does this demonstration of the Thus-Come One portend?"[24] Then, in all the [various] great assemblies there were none able to answer. ***Prasenajit*** and the others, relying on the Buddha's spiritual power, extensively produced music.[25] All the gods of the desire

20. The "wonderous *samādhi* of great quiescence and calm" (*ta chi-ching miao san-ma-ti*) is glossed by Liang-pi as "the supreme trance" (*sheng-ting*).

21. A stock phrase portending a great event. There are several sets of six shakings. One set is derived from the *Mahāprajñāpāramitā* when the east rises while the west sinks, and so on.

22. The first is the 25,000-line *Prajñāpāramitā,* the second is the well-known *Diamond Sūtra*. Liang-pi notes that the *Diamond Sūtra* is the ninth "assembly" of the *Mahāprajñāpāramitā*, the Celestial Kings Inquiry is the sixth assembly, and the Larger Prajñāpāramitā is the second assembly (T 1709 33.450a3–10). The fifth-century text lists the first three and the Brilliant Praise *prajñāpāramitā* (*kuang-tsan*) and specifies that the Buddha had already preached these "in the twenty-ninth year" (825b21–25). The T'ien-t'ai commentary attributed to Chih-i discusses the significance of the year in the context of the Buddha's ministry (T 1705 33.264b16–20). Pu-k'ung's change amends what by the eighth century was an obvious gaffe; that the *Mahāprajñāpāramitā* and the *Kuang-tsan* are two translations of the same scripture. For more on this, see Chapter 3.

23. "Thus-come One" renders *ju-lai*, Sanskrit *tathāgata*.

24. Jewel-Cover is Ratnachattra, Stainless Fame is Vimalakīrti, Lion-Roarer is the Sanskrit Siṃhanāda. This latter is often an attribute of the Buddha, but here it has been personalized as a separate being. He is a major figure in the Mahāyāna version of the *Mahāparinirvāṇa sūtra*. See Liang-pi, T 1709 33.450b2–3.

25. "Relying on the Buddha's spiritual power" (*ch'eng fo shen-li*) is a stock phrase. The passage seems peculiar and is meant to indicate that the assemblies began singing spontaneously.

and form realms played an offering of music and the sound of innumerable divas permeated the three thousand great thousand universe.[26]

At that moment the World-honored One again sent forth innumerable ***asaṅkhyeya*** beams of light, and their brilliance was variegated. In each beam of light a jeweled lotus appeared, each with a thousand petals, all of golden color. And on [every flower] there was a transformation Buddha proclaiming the essentials of the Teaching.[27] This Buddha-light illuminated Buddha-lands of the ten directions, [countless as the] sands of the ***Gaṅgā.*** These wonders did have a cause.

The Buddha-lands of [the ten] directions [included:] On the east the ***bodhisattva-mahāsattva*** P'u-kuang;[28] in the southeast the ***bodhisattva-mahāsattva*** Lien-hua shou;[29] in the south the ***bodhisattva-mahāsattva*** Li-yu;[30] in the southwest the ***bodhisattva-mahāsattva*** Kuang-ming;[31] in the west the ***bodhisattva-mahāsattva*** Hsing-hui;[32] in the northwest the ***bodhisattva-mahāsattva*** Pao-sheng;[33] in the north the ***bodhisattva-mahāsattva*** Sheng-shou;[34] in the northeast the ***bodhisattva-mahāsattva*** Li-ch'en;[35] at the zenith the ***bodhisattva-mahāsattva*** Hsi-shou;[36] and at the nadir the ***bodhisattva-mahāsattva*** Lien-hua sheng.[37] Each of them with countless hundreds of thousands of ***bodhisattva-mahāsattvas*** all had come hither bearing various sorts of incense, scattering various flowers, and making countless musical offerings to the Thus-come One. They did obeisance at the Buddha's feet, silently withdrew and were seated, and they folded their hands in homage and single-mindedly contemplated the Buddha.[38]

26. I have chosen diva, a female opera singer (not to be confused with *devas*) to render *chi-yüeh* (Sanskrit *gandharvas*), as the etymology of diva indicates a divine musical performer. The three-thousand great thousand world is a common description of the universe in T'ien-t'ai teachings. For a full discussion, see Kloetzli, *Buddhist Cosmology*, pp. 52–64.

27. These "Transformation Buddhas" (*hua-fo*) are *nirmāṇas*, apparitional bodies produced by the Buddha.

28. "Universal Light," Sanskrit *Samantaprabha*.

29. "Lotus-hand," Sanskrit *Padmapāṇi*.

30. "Abandoning-sorrow," Sanskrit *Vigatāśoka*, this latter construction according to DeVisser, *Ancient Buddhism in Japan*, 1:127.

31. "Shining-light," Sanskrit *Raśmiprabhāsa*.

32. "Conduct of wisdom," which DeVisser and Rahder tentatively reconstruct as "He who is disposed to good conduct," Sanskrit *Caritramati*.

33. "Precious-conqueror," which DeVisser reconstructs as *Ratnajaya*. Another possibility is *Ratnaketu*.

34. "Receiver of Victory," Sanskrit *Jayapratigraha*.

35. "Abandoning the dusty [world]," Sanskrit *Vigatarajas*.

36. "Receiver of joy," Sanskrit *Nandapratigraha*.

37. "Lotus conqueror," Sanskrit *Padmajina*.

38. "Single-mindedly contemplated the Buddha" is the lead in to the next chapter, "Contemplating the Thus-come One."

2

Contemplating the Thus-come One

[835b] At that time the World-honored One arose from ***samādhi,*** and seated on the lion throne he addressed the great assembly, "I know that the sixteen [great kings] and the kings of all the other states have been thinking, 'The World-honored One's great compassion bestows universal boon and blessing. How may I and all the other kings protect[1] our states?' Good sons! On behalf of all the ***bodhisattva-mahāsattva***s I will first speak of the protection of the Buddha-fruit and of nurturing the practices of the ten stages.[2] You and the others should listen carefully. Listen carefully, and ponder it well."

Then, when the great assembly and King ***Prasenajit*** and the others heard what the Buddha said, all offered words of praise, "Excellent, excellent!" Then

1. Here and in the following paragraphs *hu* is translated as both "protect" and "nurture" so as to make a more fluid English translation. The word has both connotations.

2. The "ten stages" (*shih-ti,* Sanskrit *daśabhūmi*) are the ten stages traversed by *bodhisattvas* in the quest for enlightenment. These are detailed in the next chapter.

they scattered countless exquisite jeweled flowers which transformed in midair into a jeweled canopy and, moreover, in that great assembly there was no one it did not cover.

At that moment King ***Prasenajit*** rose from his seat and paid obeisance to the Buddha's feet. Clasping his hands and kneeling, he asked the Buddha, "World-honored One, how do the ***bodhisattva-mahāsattva***s protect the Buddha-fruit, how do they nurture the practices of the ten stages?"

The Buddha replied to King ***Prasenajit,*** "With regard to the protection of the Buddha-fruit, all the ***bodhisattva-mahāsattva***s abide thus: Teaching and transforming all [beings, whether] born from eggs, from the womb, generated from dampness, or from metamorphosis, they do not contemplate the signs[3] of form, nor do they regard form as feeling, thinking, volition, or consciousness. So too inverted views of the self, of permanency, bliss, personality, and purity,[4] of the four [*bodhisattva*] virtues, the six perfections,[5] the Two Truths, the Four Truths, the power of fearlessness, and so on, and all of the practices. It is so even for ***bodhisattva***s and Thus-come Ones.[6] They contemplate neither signs nor thusness. How can this be? This is because the nature of all constituents is simply reality itself.[7] It neither comes nor goes; it is neither born nor extinguished. Identical with the edge of reality,[8] the nature of constituents is nondual, is undifferentiated, and is like the void. The signs of the aggregates, the sense media, and the elements are without 'me' and 'mine.'[9] This is how ***bodhisattva-mahāsattva***s practice the ***Prajñāpāramitā.***"

King ***Prasenajit*** said to the Buddha, "World-honored One, if ***bodhisattva***s and beings are not different in nature, [835c] then what signs do ***bodhisattva***s use to transform beings?" The Buddha said, "Great king, the nature of constituents, of form, feeling, thinking, volition, and consciousness; of permanency, bliss, personality, and purity, is neither in form, nor in the formless.[10] Moreover,

3. "Signs" or characteristics (*hsiang*) translates the Sanskrit term *lakṣaṇa*.

4. Permanency, bliss, personality, and purity are the four *viparyaya* (*ssu-tao*) or inverted beliefs refuted by the Buddhist teachings of impermanence, suffering, the lack of self, and impurity. An alternate list refers to the notion that Nirvana is not a state of permanence, and so on. See *Bukkyō daijiten*, 2.1962a. These four qualities, however, also serve as descriptions of the *Tathāgatagarbha*.

5. Literally, the "six ferries," these are the six bodhisattva "perfections" (*pāramitā*).

6. This passage seems unnecessarily convoluted in the eighth-century version of the text. The meaning of the passage is readily evident from the fifth-century version.

7. Literally, the "true reality" (*chen-shih*), here standing for "true thusness" (*chen-ju*). "Constituents" (*fa*, Sanskrit *dharma*) are the basic constituents making up reality. For this theory, see Stcherbatsky, *Central Conception of Buddhism*.

8. "The edge of reality" (*chen-chi*, Sanskrit *bhūtakoṭi*) is ultimate reality, or ultimate truth.

9. The earlier version of the text clearly indicates that what is completely lacking is signs of me and mine (T 245 8.825c24–25). In the eighth-century text, "signs" (*hsiang*) is at the head of the phrase. I have followed Liang-pi's parsing of the text for my translation (T 1709 33.454a3).

10. "The nature of constituents" translates *fa-hsing* (Sanskrit *dharmatā*), the Dharma-nature or fundamental nature of all constituents.

form, feeling, thinking, volition, and consciousness; permanency, bliss, personality, and purity are neither pure nor impure. How can this be? This is because all the constituents by nature are completely empty. It is because of worldly truth, because of the three false views, [that] the constituents of all sentient beings' aggregates, sense media, and elements create blessings and misfortune, immobility and activity, and so forth. [Therefore,] cause and fruit all exist.[11] [Therefore] all the practices cultivated by the worthies and sages[12] of the three vehicles, right up to the attainment of the Buddha-fruit, all are said to exist. The sixty-two views are likewise said to exist. Great king, if one is attached to names and signs and to discriminating all the constituents of reality and the activities and fruits of the six destinies, the four kinds of births, and the three vehicles, then [one] does not see the real nature of all constituents."

King ***Prasenajit*** said to the Buddha, "The true nature of all constituents is pure and impartial. Neither existent nor nonexistent, how can knowledge of it be elucidated?"[13] The Buddha said, "Great king, in knowing and elucidating the real nature there is neither existence nor nonexistence. Why is this? This is because the nature of constituents is empty. It is the same [with] form, feeling, thinking, volition, and consciousness, the twelve sense media, the eighteen elements, the self,[14] the six elements, the twelve-fold [chain of] causation, the Two Truths, and the Four Truths. All are completely empty. So too are all constituents [like this], even birth, even extinction, even existence, and even emptiness; every moment is also like this.[15] Why is this so? In every instant of thought there are ninety moments, and in one moment there are nine hundred productions and extinctions. This is because all existent things are made of constituents and [the constituents] are entirely empty. [One] uses the profound ***Prajñāpāramitā*** to see that all constituents are entirely empty—empty inside, empty outside, empty inside and outside; empty of emptiness, great emptiness, supreme emptiness! Existence is empty. Nonexistence is empty[16]—beginningless emptiness. Endless emptiness. Dispersion is empty, the basic nature is

11. Following Liang-pi's explanation at T 1709 33.454c15–455a2.

12. "Worthies" (*hsien*) and "sages" (*sheng*) indicate the two lowest rungs of the path. See Hurvitz, *Chih-I*, pp. 346–48 and chapter 3 of the sutra.

13. The terms "existent" (*yu*) and "nonexistent" (*wu*) were key terms in the fifth-century debates surrounding the *prajñāpāramitā* and the Mādhyamika teachings. For a discussion, see Swanson, *Foundations of T'ien-T'ai Philosophy*.

14. The "self" (*shih-fu*) usually translated the Sanskrit *puruṣa*, or "person," which is often a synonym for *atman*, but with a sense of the "spirit" or "essential" humanity. The word is missing in the earlier version of the text.

15. A "moment" (*ch'a-na*, Sanskrit *kṣaṇa*) is generally thought of as the shortest measure of time.

16. Literally "not-acting" (*wu-wei*) is empty, here using the vocabulary of classical Taoism. The fifth-century version reads: "Existence is empty, nonexistence is empty, beginnings are empty, the nature is empty, the preeminent truth (*ti-i-ti*) is empty, the ***Prajñāpāramitā*** is empty . . . " (T 245 8.826a14–15).

empty, individuality is empty, all constituents are empty.[17] The ***Prajñāpāramitā*** is empty. Causality is empty, and the Buddha-fruit is empty. The emptiness of emptiness is therefore empty. [Yet] because all existence is composed of constituents, aggregations of constituents therefore exist. Sensory aggregates therefore exist. Name aggregates therefore exist. Causal aggregates therefore exist. Fruition aggregates therefore exist.[18] The six destinies therefore exist. The ten stages therefore exist. The Buddha-fruit therefore exists. Everything is completely existent.

Good sons! If a ***bodhisattva*** abides in the signs of constituents, the signs of self, or the signs of persons, or has a view of beings, and on their behalf abides in the world, then [that person] is not a ***bodhisattva.*** Why is this? This is because all constituents are completely empty. If, in regard to all constituents, [the *bodhisattva*] has attained the unmoving state, then there is no birth, no extinction, no signs, no absence of signs, nor should he give rise to [such] views. Why is this? [This is because] all constituents are entirely thusness.[19] All Buddhas, the complete Teaching, and the entire Community are likewise thusness. [When] the very first instant of sagely wisdom manifests before [one], the complete eighty-four thousand stanza ***Prajñāpāramitā***[20] calls it the stage of Joy.[21] [When it is] a conveyance which exhausts obstacles and liberates, it calls it a vehicle. When signs of mutability are extinguished, it calls it the adamantine concentration. [836a] When substance[22] and signs are viewed impartially it calls it all-knowledge.[23]

Great king, the words and phrases[24] of this ***Prajñāpāramitā*** are the same as those preached in concert by hundreds of Buddhas, by thousands of Buddhas, and by all of the hundreds of thousands of ten thousands of hundreds of thousands of Buddhas. If there is a person in the three thousand great thousand worlds—worlds numerous as the sands of the ***Gaṅgā***—who, replete with the seven treasures, uses them as offerings which cause all sentient beings in the

17. "Individuality" (*tzu-hsiang*, Sanskrit *svalakṣaṇa*) indicates the signs or marks of individual self-existence independent of other entities.

18. The word "aggregate" (*chi*) indicates a collection of *dharmas*.

19. "Thusness" (*ju*) indicates the ultimate reality of things.

20. The fifth-century version cites the *Brilliant Praise Prajñāpāramitā* (*Kuang-tsan po-jo-po-lo-mi*).

21. *Huan-hsi ti, Pramuditā bhūmi,* the first of the bodhisattva stages. I am following Liang-pi's interpretation and parsing of this line (T 1709 33.456b29–c7).

22. Emending "propriety" (*li*) with "substance" (*t'i*) in accordance with Liang-pi (T 1709 33.459a18).

23. This last comment is missing from the fifth-century version. "All knowledge" (*i-ch'ieh chih-chih*) is the omniscient state of Buddhahood, the last stage of the path.

24. "Words" (*wen-tzu*) is a common translation of the Sanskrit *vyañjana*, a distinguishing mark or sign, while the Chinese indicates the written characters, and thus my translation. "Sentences" (*chang-chü*) often renders the Sanskrit word *pada*, most exactly, "feet" or "propositions." As Liang-pi indicates, the true text is not that written with ink (T 1709 33.459a27–b8).

great-thousand worlds to attain the fruit of ***arhat***-ship,[25] this does not compare with a person who gives rise to one thought of pure faith in this scripture. How much more so if one is able to receive and hold to it, to read and recite and expound one sentence of it? Why is this? The nature of the text is transcendent[26] and is without the signs of textuality. [The text] is neither the Teaching nor other than the Teaching.[27] Therefore ***prajñā*** is empty; therefore the ***bodhisattva*** is also empty. And why is this? In the ten stages, each and every stage has an "initial production," an "abiding production," and a "final production." These thirty productions are entirely empty. Moreover, all-knowledge is also entirely empty.

Great king! If a **bodhisattva** perceives a realm, perceives knowledge, perceives a doctrine, or perceives sensation, this is not the perception of a sage, but the perception of a dunce. The fruit and recompense of sentient beings in the three worlds is void and false. In the realm of desire, discrimination creates all karma. In the realm of form, the four trances of purity and calm create karma. In the formless realm, the four trances of emptiness give rise to karma. The karmic fruit in the [three realms of] existence is entirely empty. The fundamental ignorance of the triple world is likewise empty. The station of sagehood and all the sages are without outflows or birth and extinction.[28] In the triple world the remaining habits of ignorance—the recompense of change—are also entirely empty. The **bodhisattva** of the [stage of] equal enlightenment[29] and the attainment of the adamantine concentration[30] as well as the cause and the fruit of the [final] two deaths are empty too; so too is the state of all-knowledge.[31] [With] the Buddha's unsurpassed enlightenment[32] the seeds of knowledge reach maturity.[33] Discrimination [of true from false] and nondiscrimination [which results in nirvana][34] are extinguished in the truly pure

25. The fifth-century version specifies "the four fruits of the seven worthies" (T 245 8.826a26–27).

26. *Wen-tzu-hsing li*, following Liang-pi's commentary, the "real nature of the text abandons all signs of self nature," therefore my rendering "transcendent." See T 1709 33.459c21–23.

27. I have rendered the double negative in this phrase (*fei fa, fei fei fa*) as neither . . . nor.

28. "The station of sagehood" (*sheng-wei*) refers generally to the Buddhist life.

29. *Teng-chüeh*, or *samyaksaṃbodhi*, is the fifty-first and next to the last stage on the path.

30. *Chin-kang ting* (alternately *chin-kang san-mei*) or *Vajrasamādhi*, the ultimate trance or absorption attained in the last stage of the bodhisattva.

31. Following Liang-pi (T 1709 33.461b25–29), "the cause and fruit of the final two deaths" indicates that even at these most advanced stages not all of the seeds of karma have been eliminated. But, as the text points out, even these are entirely empty.

32. "Unsurpassed enlightenment" (*Wu-shang chüeh*) is the Sanskrit *anuttarasamyaksaṃbodhi*.

33. Literally, "they are complete."

34. I am reading *mieh*, "extinguish," as the verb in this sentence. "Discrimination" (*tse*, *pravicaya*) and "nondiscrimination" (*fei-tse*, *tse-mieh*, *pratisaṃkhyānirodha*) are, respectively, the second member of the second component of the "seven components of perception" (*ch'i-chüeh-chih*, *sapta bodhyangi*)

realm of the Teaching. [True] nature [and knowledge of its] signs,[35] equanimity and response to needs, are also empty.[36]

Good sons! If a person cultivates and practices the ***Prajñāpāramitā,*** discourses on it and listens to it, [that person] may be compared to a deaf-mute magician.[37] The character [of principles and things][38] is the same as the nature of constituents; it is likewise vacuous and empty. All constituents are entirely thusness.[39] Great king, the ***bodhisattva-mahāsattvas***' protection of the Buddha-fruit is accomplished like this!"

At that time the World-honored One asked King ***Prasenajit,*** "By what signs do you contemplate the Thus-come One?" King ***Prasenajit*** answered, "I contemplate his body's real signs; [I] contemplate the Buddha thus: Without boundaries in front, behind, and in the middle; not residing in the three times and not transcending the three times; not residing in the five aggregates, not transcending the five aggregates; not abiding in the four great elements and not transcending the four great elements; not abiding in the six abodes of sensation and transcending the six abodes of sensation; not residing in the three realms and not transcending the three realms; residing in no direction, transcending no direction; [neither] illumination [nor] ignorance and so on. Not one, not different; not this, not that; not pure, not foul; not existent or nonexistent; without signs of self or signs of another; without name, without signs; without strength, without weakness; without demonstration, without exposition; not magnanimous, not stingy; not prohibited, not transgressed; not forbearing, [836b] not hateful; not forward, not remiss; not fixed, not in disarray; not wise, not stupid; not coming, not going; not entering, not leaving; not a field of blessings, not a field of misfortune; without sign, without the lack of sign; not gathering, not dispersing; not great, not small; not seen, not heard; not perceived, not known. The mind, activities and senses are extinguished and the path of speech is cut off. It is identical with the edge of reality, and equal to the [real] nature of things. I use these signs to contemplate the Thus-come One."

---

and the extinction which results from distinguishing false from true. The point here is that both of these are transcended. See Hurvitz, *Chih-I*, p. 345.

35. Following Liang-pi's reading at T 1709 33.461c11–13.

36. There are two pairs here: the fundamental nature of things, their *hsing*, and knowledge of the signs of things, their *hsiang* (*lakṣana*), and then the state of equanimous repose of enlightenment or *p'ing-teng*, and response to the needs of beings or *ying-yung*.

37. This passage is not found in the fifth-century text. Its import is that all this talking and listening is, basically, empty.

38. Liang-pi points out that the first *fa* in this phrase means the "principles and things" (*li-shih chih fa*) that constitute reality (T 1709 33.461c24–25).

39. The fundamental reality of things (*i-ch'ieh fa chieh ju yeh*).

The Buddha said, "Good sons! If you do as you have said, [you will gain] the strength and fearlessness of the Buddhas and Thus-come Ones, and your merit will be like the sands of the ***Gaṅgā***. Only the Unique Teaching is like this.[40] One who cultivates the ***Prajñāpāramitā*** ought to contemplate in this manner. If he contemplates otherwise it is a heterodox contemplation." And when this doctrine was spoken countless numbers of the great assembly attained the clarity of the eye of the Teaching.[41]

40. The "unique Buddhist teaching" (*pu-kung fa*) is equivalent to the Sanskrit *āveṇika-buddha-dharma*.

41. The state at which the outflows have ceased.

3

The Bodhisattva Path

At that time King ***Prasenajit*** said to the Buddha: "World-honored One, [concerning] ***bodhisattva-mahāsattva***s who nurture the practices of the ten stages; how should they cultivate the path? How do they transform beings? Further, by what signs do they abide in and plumb [reality?]"

The Buddha said, "Great king, all ***bodhisattva-mahāsattva***s rely upon the teaching of the five forbearances in order to cultivate the path. These are called the forbearance of self-control, the forbearance of [firm] belief, the forbearance of obedience, and the forbearance of the birthlessness [of all constituents], each of which is divided into superior, intermediate, and inferior stages. The [final forbearance], the forbearance of quiescent extinction, also has superior and inferior stages. This is what is called ***bodhisattva***s cultivating the ***Prajñāpāramitā.***

Good sons! First, in the stage of the forbearance of self-control,[1] they give

1. The forbearance of self-control (*fu-jen*) indicates the development of patience with the disciplines that lead to insight into the causes of suffering and thus the eradication of defilements.

rise to the acquired lineage by cultivating the practices of the ten abodes.[2] At the beginning they arouse the mental signs: the mass of existent beings—as numerous as the sands of the ***Gaṅgā***—and they see the Buddha, the Teaching, and the Community. They arouse the ten [grades of] faith and these are called: the trusting mind, the mind of remembrance, the mind of zealous progress, the mind of wisdom, the mind of fixed concentration, the mind of nonretrogression, the mind of discipline, the mind of will, the mind of protecting the Teaching, and the mind of transference.[3] Applying these ten minds can, to a limited extent,[4] transform all beings. They surpass the two vehicles and all the good stages.[5] This is how ***bodhisattva***s begin to nurture the mind, and because of this these [ten kinds of mind] are referred to as the "womb of the sages."

Next, ***bodhisattva***s [of] the innate lineage cultivate ten kinds of ***pāramitā,*** which give rise to the ten antidotes.[6] This refers to contemplating that the constituents of the body, the feelings, and the mind are impure, cause endless suffering, and are selfless. Controlling passion, anger, and delusion—the three roots of misfortune—they arouse magnanimity, compassion, and wisdom—the three roots of good fortune. They investigate the three periods: past causes of forbearance, present causes and effects of forbearance, and future effects of forbearance. ***Bodhisattva***s at this station extensively benefit beings, and transcend thoughts of the self, others, beings, and so on, and heterodox and inverted views can no longer harm them.

2. The "acquired lineage" or the "lineage resulting from previous practice" (*hsi-chung-hsing*, Sanskrit *samudānīta-gotra*) is the inherited nature that is the direct result of one's past good actions. See *Bukkyō daijiten*, 2469b, and the discussion in Chapters 3 and 4 of the study. Both the commentaries of Liang-pi (T 1709 33.464a19–b1) and the T'ien-t'ai commentary attributed to Chih-i (T 1705 33.269b18–21) take great pains to distinguish the "lineage" scheme in this scripture from that of the five (or six) lineages that appear in the *P'u-sa ying-lo pen-yeh ching* (T 1485 24.1012b25–c5). Neither the elements of practice nor the interpretation of the terms matches up. The ten abodes (*shih-chu*) are the propaedeutic to the path and are listed by Hurvitz, *Chih-I*, pp. 363–64.

3. The fifth-century text orders the list differently (T 245 8.26b), as do later T'ien-t'ai lists. See Hurvitz, *Chih-I*, p. 363.

4. Liang-pi explains "to a limited extent" (*shao-fen*) by reference to the *Hua-yen ching*. What they will accomplish in a later stage through the "ten virtues" (*shih-shan*, equivalent to the *shih-hsin* or ten grades of Bodhisattva faith) is termed "extensive" (*kuang-ta*) transformation; this, in contrast, is "limited" (T 1709 33.465c12–14).

5. Liang-pi glosses the two vehicles as "those who have more to learn" (*yu-hsüeh che*) and "those who have no more to learn" (*wu-hsüeh che*). See note 6 to chapter 1 of the sūtra. The "good stages" (*shan-ti*) are the first nine of a ten-stage scheme that appears in the *Mahāprajñāpāramitā*. The bodhisattva path commences with stage 9, and the previous eight are the "good stages" (T 1709 33.465c15–22).

6. The innate lineage (*hsing-chung-hsing*, Sanskrit *prakritịstha-gotra*) indicates the stage at which one comes to recognize the true nature of oneself and the world. See *Bukkyō daijiten*, 2469b. For Liang-pi's discussion, see T 1709 33.466a2–12. The ten antidotes, or means of responding to and controlling defilements (*shih-tui-chi*, Sanskrit *pratipakṣa*) are designed to combat *kleśa* or the "defilements." *Bukkyō diajiten*, 3320c–3321a.

Next ***bodhisattva***s of the lineage of the Way cultivate the ten transferences and give rise to the ten kinds of forbearing mind.[7] That is, the contemplation [836c] of the five aggregates: form, feeling, thinking, volition, and consciousness; and the attainment of the forbearance of the discipline, the forbearance of fixed meditation, the forbearance of wisdom, the forbearance of liberation, and the forbearance of views of liberation.[8] Contemplating cause and effect in the triple world, they attain the forbearance of emptiness, the forbearance of signlessness, and the forbearance of wishlessness.[9] Contemplating the two truths, falseness and truth, and that all constituents are impermanent, they attain the forbearance of impermanence. [When they realize] that all constituents are empty, they attain the forbearance of birthlessness. ***Bodhisattva***s of this station are wheel-turning kings who are able extensively to transform and benefit all beings.[10]

Next are ***bodhisattva***s forbearing of [firm] belief.[11] This refers to the stage of joy,[12] the immaculate stage,[13] and the luminous stage,[14] [wherein bodhisattvas] are able to sever the three obstructions of bondage to defilements of form.[15] They practice the four all-embracing ***bodhisattva*** virtues: giving, loving speech, beneficent action, and mutual aid. They cultivate the four immeasurable minds:[16] the immeasurable mind of pity, the immeasurable mind of compassion, the immeasurable mind of joy, and the immeasurable mind of complete impartiality [toward beings]. Using the four comprehensive vows, they sever all bondage, constantly transform beings, cultivate Buddha wisdom, and at-

7. The "lineage of the Way" (*tao-chung-hsing*) indicates the stage at which the bodhisattva initiates acts characteristic of the path in the Mahāyāna, acts of supererogation or "transference" (*hui-hsiang*) whence the merit gained is redirected toward the salvation of all other beings. Liang-pi notes that this is the commencement of the "sagely path" (*sheng-tao*), and that the seeds of one's acts are imbued with the Way (T 1709 33.446c20–23). Hurvitz, *Chih-I*, pp. 364–65, lists the ten transferences as " the ten degrees of diversion."

8. This last forbearance implies that bodhisattvas at this level learn not to entertain misleading views of liberation (*chieh-t'o chih chien*).

9. Both versions of the text read *hsiang*, "thought," here instead of *hsiang*, "sign." Liang-pi, however, reads "sign," and the context among two of the other three "gates to liberation" argues for amending the text (T 1709 33.467a17).

10. They are thus *cakravartin*. Again these "extensively transform" beings (*kuang-hua*), while those in earlier stages transform beings to a "limited extent" (*shao-fen hua*).

11. The "forbearance of [firm] belief" (*hsin-jen*) refers to the stage in which the bodhisattva patiently and steadfastly accepts the Teaching.

12. What follows is the standard enumeration of the ten bodhisattva stages. *Huan-hsi*, Sanskrit *pramuditā*, is roughly "pleasurable." The names of the ten stages in the fifth-century text are different and unique. See Appendix A for these.

13. *Li-kou*, Sanskrit *vimala*, is "stainless." Hence my translation "immaculate."

14. *Fa-kuang* is a common translation of Sanskrit *prabhākari*, or "luminous."

15. Liang-pi notes that these are anger, lust, and delusion, which are conquered in stages 1, 2, and 3, respectively (T 1709 33.467b19–21).

16. I amend the text here in accordance with the Sung, Yüan, and Ming editions.

tain unsurpassed enlightenment.[17] They abide in the three gates of liberation: the gate of emptiness, the gate of signlessness, and the gate of wishlessness, and this is root of all the activities of the ***bodhisattva-mahāsattva*s** from the first stage of the arousal of [enlightened] mind to the attainment of all-knowledge. [Thus they] bring benefits and blessing, peace and tranquility, to all beings.

Next are ***bodhisattva*s** forbearing of obedience.[18] This refers to the stage of radiant wisdom,[19] the invincible stage,[20] and the stage disposed toward enlightenment.[21] They are able to sever the three obstructions of bondage to defilements of mind.[22] They are able physically to travel to the myriad Buddha-lands of the ten directions, and to manifest unspeakable spiritual penetrations that transform, benefit, and bless beings.[23]

Next are ***bodhisattva*s** forbearing of the birthlessness [of all constituents].[24] This refers to far-reaching stage,[25] the immovable stage,[26] and the stage of effective intelligence.[27] They are able to sever the three obstructions of the material and mental habits,[28] and they are able to manifest unspeakable numbers of bodies, according to the appropriate class or type, in order to enrich all beings.

17. "Unsurpassed enlightenment" (*wu-shang chüeh*) is a common translation of the Sanskrit *anuttarasamyaksaṃbodhi*.

18. The "forbearance of obedience" (*hsün-jen*) indicates the state where one comes to accept and follow the long path toward enlightenment.

19. *Yen-hui* commonly renders the Sanskrit *aricișmatī*.

20. *Nan-sheng*, rendering the Sanskrit *sudurjayā*, "unconquerable."

21. *Hsien-ch'ien* renders Sanskrit *abhimukhī*, which has been variously translated as "directly facing" or "face to face." The underlying meaning is that one comes face to face with the realization that one will attain enlightenment.

22. Liang-pi notes that these are lopsided views, attachment to the notion of Hinayāna nirvana, and the aggregated causes and karma of the triple world. They occur, respectively, in the fourth, fifth, and sixth stages (T 1709 33.468a17–20).

23. According to Liang-pi, the fourth-stage bodhisattvas can travel to a *koṭī* (either 100,000 or 1,000,000) of Buddha-lands, the fifth-stage to one hundred *koṭī*, the sixth to one thousand *koṭī* (T 1709 33.468b6–8).

24. The "forbearance of the birthlessness [of all constituents]" (*wu-sheng-jen*, *anutpattikadharmakṣānti*) refers to the forbearance or willingness to accept the birthlessness or fundamentally unproduced nature of all constituents (*fa*, *dharmas*) of reality. The bodhisattva enters this forbearance at the seventh stage and it becomes the focus of his enlightenment, replacing the four truths. For more, see Suzuki, *Studies in the Laṅkāvatāra Sūtra*, pp. 125–27, 226–28, and Edward Conze, *Buddhist Thought in India*, pp. 221–22.

25. *Yüan-hsing* renders Sanskrit *dūraṃgamā*, sometimes translated as "far advanced." See, for example, Huntington and Wangchen, *The Emptiness of Emptiness*, p. 185.

26. *Pu-tung* renders Sanskrit *acalā*. Hypostatized, the stage becomes the Acalā *vidyārāja*, a popular divinity, especially in East Asian Esoteric Buddhism.

27. *Shan-hui*, Sanskrit *sādhumatī*. I am using R.A.F. Thurman's translation of the term from his *Holy Teaching of Vimalakīrti: A Mahayana Scripture* (University Park: Pennsylvania State University Press, 1976).

28. In the seventh stage they eliminate all the subtle forms of karmic fruit; in the eighth stage they cut off all effort (*kung-yung*); and in the ninth stage they eliminate unhindered obstructions (*wu-ai*). See Liang-pi, T 1709 33.468b22–24.

Next is the forbearance of quiescent extinction;[29] Buddhas and ***bodhisattvas*** alike rely on this forbearance. [Those] abiding in the rank of the inferior forbearance of the adamantine concentration are called ***bodhisattvas***: those in the superior forbearance are called all-knowing.[30] Contemplating the supreme truth, they have severed the signs of ignorance. This is [called] equal enlightenment.[31] The state of nonduality in which signs and signlessness are equivalent refers to the eleventh stage of all-knowledge. [Here] there is neither being nor nonbeing. Profoundly quiescent, neither coming nor going, [the saint] constantly abides in the unchanging. This is the same as the nature of constituents, the edge of reality, and so on.[32] Their causeless great compassion continually transforms beings; and riding the vehicle of all-knowledge, they come to transform the triple world.

Good Sons! [As for] all the defilements of all types of beings, [this] karma is differentiated and ripens to fruition [according to] the twenty-two roots, and it does not transcend the triple world. [As for] all the instruction of the Buddhas, the response-bodies and the body of the Teaching, are no exception to this.[33] If someone says that there is yet another world and other beings, then this is the heterodox doctrine proclaimed in the *Scripture of Great Existence*.[34]

29. *Chi-mieh jen*, Sanskrit *vyupasama-kṣānti*. For the term "quiescent extinction" as a synonym for nirvana, see *Bukkyō daijiten*, 2158a.

30. Here the text has skipped over the tenth stage, *fa-yün*, *Dharmamegha*, or Cloud of the Teaching. It is mentioned in proper sequence in the summary *gāthā* below. As Buswell has noted in his *Formation of Ch'an Ideology in China and Korea*, p. 107, the fifth-century text is more explicit about the link between the Vajrasamādhi and the state of all-knowledge: "Buddhas and ***bodhisattvas*** alike use this forbearance to enter the adamantine ***samādhi***" (T 245 8.826c21–22).

31. This entails the ability to view all things impartially. The Chinese is *p'ing-teng chüeh*. See *Hōbōgirin*, 3:275.

32. The "edge of reality" (*chen-tse*, *bhūtakoṭi*) is identical with the fundamental dharma-nature (*fa-hsing*). I am using Robert Buswell's rendering of the term *bhūtakoṭi*.

33. The "response bodies" (*ying-hua shen*, Sanskrit *nirmāṇakāya*) are the bodies created deliberately by Buddhas and bodhisattvas so that they may come to the aid of beings. In some cases the "response" bodies (*ying-shen*) are the bodies used to aid humans, while "transformation" bodies (*hua-shen*) are used to aid other sorts of beings. The "body of the Teaching" (*fa-shen*) is the *dharmakāya*, the ultimate reality. Both the fifth- and eighth-century recensions are identical in identifying *nirmāṇakāya* and *dharmakāya*, but do not mention the third body or "recompense" or "enjoyment" (*pao-shen*, *saṃbhogakāya*) gained by advanced bodhisattvas. It is also possible to construe the passage as "all the response bodies created by the Body of the Teaching." Compare T 245 8.826c29–827a1. I have tried to retain the parallelism of the passage at the expense of smooth English phrasing.

34. The fifth-century version of this passage is far more elegant: "The defilements of all the beings do not transcend the womb of the triple world; all beings' recompense [ripens according to] the twenty-two roots and does not transcend the triple world; all Buddhas—their response bodies and the body of the Teaching—also do not transcend the triple world. Outside of the triple world there are no beings. What would the Buddha have to transform? Therefore I say, outside the womb of the triple world there is not a single living being. This doctrine [of a place transcending the triple world] is preached in the heterodox *Scripture of Great Existence*. It has not been preached by the seven Buddhas" (T 245 8.826c–827a). The *Scripture of Great Existence* (*Mahābhāva-sūtra?*) is not attested in the Chi-tsang's

Great King! I have always preached to all beings that only one who completely severs [837a] the ignorance of the triple world is called a Buddha, and that when the self-nature is pure, it is called the nature of original enlightenment,[35] and this wisdom is none other than the complete wisdom of all the Buddhas.[36] Hence, what constitutes the basis of beings is the very basis of the practice of all the Buddhas and ***bodhisattvas***. And the very basis of the practice of ***bodhisattvas*** is the fourteen forbearances contained in the teaching of the five forbearances."

The Buddha said: "Great king! Previously you asked, 'How do the ***bodhisattvas*** transform living beings?' ***Bodhisattva-mahāsattvas*** transform them like this. [All things] from the beginning of the first stage up till the very last stage, from the abode of self-centered practice to the abode of Buddha practice, are due to all-knowing.[37]

If a ***bodhisattva-mahāsattva*** abides in one hundred Buddha-***kṣetra***,[38] he becomes a wheel-turning king of ***Jambudvīpa***.[39] He cultivates one-hundred glorious Teachings and uses the ***dāna pāramitā*** to abide in equanimity and to transform all the beings of the four quarters of the world.[40]

---

commentary. Liang-pi's commentary glosses the *Scripture of Great Existence* as a Vaiśeṣika work (T 1709 33.469c12–14). Most references in the index of the Taisho canon appear to derive from the fifth-century version of the *Scripture for Humane Kings*. However, a commentary by Chi-tsang on the *Śata-śāstra* of Āryadeva quotes the title of the *Ta-yu ching* and certainly refers to Vaiśeṣika doctrines (T 1827 42.281a3). The commentary attributed to Chih-i contrasts the position of the *Ta-yu ching* with that of the "two vehicles" (of Śrāvakas and Pratyekabuddhas), who maintain that no beings exist outside the triple world. Both are mistaken (T 1705 33.272a1–5). My thanks to Iyanaga Nobumi (personal communication) for information on the *Ta-yu ching*.

35. Nature of original enlightenment, *pen-chüeh-hsing*.

36. *I-ch'ieh chih-chih* is clumsy to render into English. It indicates the special form of "all-knowledge" (*i-ch'ieh-chih*) distinctive to Buddhas alone, and not characteristic of the auditors (*śrāvaka*) or the self-enlightened (*pratyekabuddha*).

37. "All-knowing" here is *i-ch'ieh chih-chien*.

38. A Buddha-*kṣetra* is a Buddha-field or Buddha-land, that is, the cosmological locale which is the karmic "reward" for the bodhisattva's great deeds. The classic treatment of Buddha-*kṣetra* is Teresina Rowel's "The Background and Early Use of the Buddha-Kṣetra Concept."

39. A *chuan-lun-wang* or *cakravartin*. In traditional Buddhist cosmology, Jambudvīpa is the continent where "India" is located. For this and the following cosmological locales, see Kloetzli, *Buddhist Cosmology*, esp. the charts on pp. 32–39. Chi-tsang makes it quite clear that a king's land is a transformation and recompense for his meritorious deeds. See T 1707 33.334a4–16 and 335a7–8.

40. The fifth-century text does not contain the word "glorious" (*ming*), the presence of which makes rendering the passage something of a problem (T 245 8.827a10–11). It literally says, "[He] cultivates one hundred teachings' glorious gates [*hsiu pai-fa ming-men*]." As previously indicated, "Teaching-gates" (*fa-men*) is best rendered simply as "Teachings," unless the passage makes the "gate" metaphor explicit. The four quarters of the world is literally the "four underheavens" (*ssu-t'ien-hsia*), and in the fifth-century version is Jambhu-(dvīpa)'s four heaven's kings. This probably means he is king of the four (under) heavens, that is, the four continents, and not that he is lord of the four heavens or that he becomes a guardian king of one of the four directions (*Lokapāla*).

If a ***bodhisattva-mahāsattva*** dwells in one thousand Buddha-***kṣetra,*** he becomes the king of the ***Trayastriṃśa***s heaven.[41] He cultivates one thousand glorious Teachings and he discourses on the ten good paths, transforming all living beings.[42]

If a ***bodhisattva-mahāsattva*** dwells in ten thousand Buddha-***kṣetra,*** he becomes king ***Yama.*** He cultivates ten-thousand glorious Teachings, and relying upon the four trance states, he transforms all living beings.[43]

If a ***bodhisattva-mahāsattva*** dwells in one hundred thousand Buddha-***kṣetra,*** he becomes the king of the ***Tuṣita*** heaven.[44] He cultivates one hundred thousand glorious Teachings and uses the seven divisions of ***bodhi***-illumination to transform all living beings.

If a ***bodhisattva-mahāsattva*** dwells in ten million Buddha-***kṣetra,*** he becomes the king of the heaven of transformative joy.[45] He cultivates ten million glorious Teachings and uses the Two Truths and the Four Truths to transform all living beings.

If a ***bodhisattva-mahāsattva*** dwells in one hundred million Buddha-***kṣetra,*** he becomes the king of the heaven sovereign over the creations of others.[46] He cultivates one hundred million glorious Teachings and his knowledge of the twelve causes transforms all living beings.[47]

If a ***bodhisattva-mahāsattva*** dwells in one billion Buddha-***kṣetra,*** he becomes king of the ***Brahma*** [heaven] of the first trance.[48] He cultivates one billion glorious Teachings and through the wisdom of skillful means and artifice transforms all living beings.

If a ***bodhisattva-mahāsattva*** dwells in one trillion numberless Buddha-***kṣetra,*** he becomes king of the ***Brahma*** [heaven] of the second trance. He cultivates one trillion numberless glorious Teachings and his double illumi-

41. The heaven located atop Mt. Meru, its lord is Śakra or Indra.

42. The ten good paths or acts are not killing, stealing, committing adultery, lying, uttering harsh words, or words which cause enmity, not gossiping, being greedy, angry, or entertaining wrong views.

43. Yama has long been viewed as the lord of the dead in Indoeuropean mythology. In this scheme he occupies the heaven just above the summit of Meru in the realm of desire. The four trance states (*shih ch'an-ting*) lead to the four "trance-heavens" enumerated below.

44. Next on the ascent of the cosmos, the *Tuṣita* heaven is the locale of Maitreya's pure land where he, like Śākyamuni before him, awaits his last birth.

45. *Lo-t'ien*, Sanskrit *Nirmāṇarati*, is the fifth and next to the last heaven in the realm of desire. Its inhabitants enjoy magical creations of their own making.

46. *Tzu-tsai-t'ien*, Sanskrit *Paranirmitavaśavartin*, is the highest heaven in the realm of desire. Its lord, Maheśvara, is the basis for all the transformations of the realm of desire, and he derives pleasure from these transformations.

47. The "twelve causes" (*shih-erh yin-yüan*, Sanskrit *nidāna*) are the twelve links in the chain of co-dependent origination or *pratītyasamutpāda*.

48. Equivalent to the first level of the realm of form and the first of four "trances" (*ch'an*, Sanskrit *dhyāna*) mastered by the Buddha on the night of his enlightenment.

nation,[49] impartiality, spiritual penetrations, and wisdom resulting from his vow transforms all living beings.

If a ***bodhisattva-mahāsattva*** dwells in hundreds of trillions of ***asaṅkhyeya*** Buddha-***kṣetra,*** he becomes a king of the ***Brahma*** [heaven] of the third trance. He cultivates one hundred trillion numberless glorious Teachings and using the four-fold unobstructed wisdom[50] transforms all living beings.

If a ***bodhisattva-mahāsattva*** dwells in absolutely unspeakable numbers of Buddha-***kṣetra,*** he becomes the great king of the ***Brahma*** [heaven] of the fourth trance, lord of the triple world. He cultivates absolutely unspeakable numbers of glorious Teachings and having attained the ***samādhi*** which exhausts phenomenal reality he is identical with a Buddha who has exhausted the springs[51] of the triple world and, just as in a Buddha Land, everywhere brings [837b] benefit to beings.

This is [what is meant by] ***bodhisattva-mahāsattva***s manifesting all the bodies of kings in order to transform [beings] and to provide instruction in [worldly] affairs. So it is also with the Thus-come Ones of the ten directions. They realize unsurpassed enlightenment and constantly, throughout the universe, benefit and bless beings."[52]

At that time all in the great assembly immediately rose from their seats and offered unspeakable numbers of flowers and burned unspeakable [sticks of] incense, they made offerings to, worshiped, and praised the Thus-come One. Just then King ***Prasenajit*** came before the Buddha and using a ***gāthā*** [sang this] praise:

World-honored One! guiding master of adamantine body, mind coursing in quiescent extinction, turning the wheel of Teaching,
Your eight-fold perfect speech expounds the Teaching [on behalf of others].[53] Thence, millions of beings attain the Way.
Thence gods and people all cultivate renunciation and are able to practice all of the **bodhisattva** Way.

49. "Double illumination" or "twin elucidation" (*shuang-chao*) is the ability to elucidate and comprehend the Two Truths, and it was met with in chapter 1 of the sūtra in the description of the assemblies present to hear the scripture.

50. The four-fold unobstructed wisdom (*ssu-wu-ai chih*, Sanskrit *pratisaṃvid*) was also an attribute of the *bodhisattvas* in the first chapter of the scripture. For its definition, see the "Glossary of Numerical Terms."

51. Reading "springs" (*yüan*) for "source" (*yüan*) as in the Sung, Yüan, and Ming editions.

52. "Unsurpassed enlightenment" is *anuttarasamyaksaṃbodhi*. The "universe" (*fa-chieh*) is the *dharmadhātu*.

53. A Buddha's speech is said to have these eight characteristics: never hectoring, never misleading or confused, fearless, never haughty, perfect in meaning and in flavor, free from harshness, and suited to the context.

The fourteen ***bodhisattva***s are able truly to comprehend the merit of the wonderful gate of the teaching of the five forbearances.

The three worthies and the ten sages[54] are in the midst of the practice of forbearance, yet it is only the Buddha who is able to exhaust origination.

The ocean of the Buddha, Teaching, and Community, [is the] womb of the three jewels with limitless merit gathered in it.[55]

Bodhisattvas in the ten [grades of] good [faith] arouse the great mind; [after] long being separated in the ocean of the wheel of suffering of the triple world.

The intermediate and inferior ranks of good [faith] are kings, scattered like grain, while the superior among the ten [grades of] good [faith] are iron-wheel kings.[56]

[Those who have] acquired lineage are copper-wheel kings of two continents, silver-wheel kings of three continents are of the stage of innate lineage.

Firm in [faith] and merit [those of] the lineage of the Way are wheel-turning kings; their seven treasures and golden wheel [rules] four continents.

The thirty persons in the womb of the sages of the forbearance of self-control [master] the ten abodes, the ten practices, and the ten transferences.[57]

All the Buddhas of the three times have studied in them, and there is no one who is not born of this forbearance of self-control.

The basis of all ***bodhisattva*** practice is therefore arousing the mind of faith, and this is difficult [to accomplish].

But if [one] attains the mind of faith, one will not retrogress and will enter the birthless Way of the first stage.

Transforming and benefiting oneself and others in complete equanimity is called the initial arousing of the mind of the ***bodhisattva.***

The ***bodhisattva*** of the joyous stage is a wheel-turning king, [who] initially illuminates the Two Truths and the principle of equanimity.[58]

In accord with circumstances they transform beings roaming the one hundred states, and their acts of ***dāna*** purify and benefit the flock of beings.

Entering the reality of ***prajña*** is called "abiding," and abiding produces meritorious acts and is called a "stage."

54. The three worthies (*san-hsien*) and the ten sages (*shih-sheng*) refer to the early segments of the path as outlined above.

55. My rendering of this stanza follows Liang-pi's explanation (T 1709 33.472a23–472b5).

56. *Cakravartins* possessing the iron wheel rule only a single domain.

57. The fifth-century text lists the ten [grades of] faith (*shih-hsin*), the ten [grades of] stopping (*shih-chih*), and the ten [grades of] firm mind (*shih-chien-hsin*).

58. The fifth-century text reads, "The bodhisattva of good perception is king of the four worlds (reading *t'ien* here as *t'ien-hsia* as in the body of the text) who simultaneously illuminates the Way of the Two Truths and equanimity."

In the first abode [one] concentrates on the host of merit and [abides] immovable in the supreme meaning.[59]
The ***bodhisattva*** of the immaculate [stage] is king of the ***Trāyastriṃśā***s and manifests forms in the six realms in thousands of states and lands.
His discipline is complete; his purity is entirely perfect. Forever transcending error and impervious to all transgression or loss
[He abides in] the signless, causeless real nature without substance, without birth, and without dualistic views.[60]
The ***bodhisattva*** of the luminous stage is King ***Yama,*** whose response forms go to all the tens of thousands of Buddha-***kṣetra.***
[837c] Well able to [achieve] unimpeded ***samādhi,*** hidden and manifest [he] is sovereign of all the three insights.[61]
The joyous, immaculate, and luminous are able to extinguish material bonds of all defilements.
Comprehensively contemplating all of the karma of body and speech, their illumination of the purity of the nature of constituents is complete.
Bodhisattvas of radiant wisdom vigorously progress through hundreds of thousands of ***kṣetra*** as kings of ***Tuṣita.***[62]
[Their] knowledge of reality, of quiescent extinction, and of skillful means [and their] penetration of the truth of birthlessness illumines emptiness and existence.
Bodhisattvas of the invincible [stage] have attained equanimity [and rule] ten million states as god-kings of transformative joy.[63]
Contemplating the truth of the emptiness of emptiness and the lack of the two signs,[64] they send their forms everywhere throughout the six destinies.
Bodhisattvas of the [stage] disposed toward enlightenment are sovereign kings.[65] They perceive the causes of birth and that signs are nondual.
And the light of their knowledge of supreme truth is able to fill [the

59. The fifth-century text reads, "[abides] immovable in the preeminent truth" (*ti-i i,* T 245 8.827b26).

60. Here the fifth-century version reads: "[He abides in] the causeless, signless, third truth, without death, without birth, and without the two views" [*wu-yüan wu-hsiang ti san ti, wu ssu wu sheng wu erh-chao,* T 245 8.827b28].

61. The eighth-century text departs entirely from the fifth-century text for these two lines. "The brilliant wisdom of emptiness illumines King Yama whose response forms guide the flock of beings in ten thousand states. Forbearing of mind they are in the midst of the nondual, triple truth, and leaving existence and entering nonexistence they transform beings" (T 245 827b29–c1).

62. "Vigorously progress" (*ching-chin*), literally pure progress, represents *vīrya,* one of the six *pāramitā* or bodhisattva perfections.

63. Here, as previously, the fifth-century text reads, "The victorious wisdom of the self-penetrating clarity of the three truths . . ." (T 245 8.827c6).

64. The signs of self and other.

65. Kings of the *Paranirmitavaśvartin,* the highest heaven in the realm of desire, as explained above.

universe], and they proceed to transform beings throughout one hundred million lands.[66]

[Those in] the stages radiant wisdom, invincible, and disposed toward enlightenment are able to cut off the three obstructions and all delusion.

Their empty wisdom is quiescent in causeless contemplation, [and] turning round[67] they reflect that the mind is empty, an immeasurable realm.

***Bodhisattva*s** of the far-reaching [stage], kings of the first trance, abide in the signless and birthless forbearance.

Their skillful means and excellent artifice are [applied with] complete equanimity [as they] constantly transform the flock of beings in one billion lands.

Entering the stage of immovability from which the teaching flows, forever without life allotments[68] [they] transcend all existence.

Constantly contemplating the supreme truth and shedding light on non-duality, [they have passed] twenty-one lives coursing in emptiness and quiescence.

In accordance with the love of the Teaching, the great scholar of the far-reaching [stage] alone is able to cut off habits of ignorance.

***Bodhisattva*s** of the immovable stage are kings of the second trance. They attain transformation bodies [which are] self-sustaining.[69]

And they are able throughout a trillion ***kṣetra*** to transform beings in accordance with their forms and types.

Having comprehensive knowledge of limitless ***kalpa*s** of the three epochs, they are immovable in the [truth] of the supreme meaning.

Bodhisattva*s** of [the stage of] effective intelligence are kings of the third trance. They are able to manifest [themselves] simultaneously in thousands [of worlds, worlds numerous as the sands of the] ***Gaṅgā.

Always coursing in actionless and empty tranquility, in a single instant they comprehend Buddhist teachings[70] [numerous as] the sands of the ***Gaṅgā.***

Bodhisattva*s** of the teaching-cloud [stage] are kings of the fourth trance, transforming flocks of beings in hundreds of thousands of numberless [worlds, worlds numerous as the sands of the] ***Gaṅgā.

Beginning with entry to the complete understanding of the adamantine

66. The fifth-century text reads, "The light of the great wisdom of the Three Truths [of the stage] disposed toward enlightenment . . . " (T 245 827c9).

67. They are contemplating their own mind (*huan-chao*), a turning around to contemplate one's own mind.

68. "Without life allotments" (*wu fen-tuan*), in other words, they are no longer at the mercy of past acts that govern their incarnations.

69. In other words, they can produce *nirmāṇas* that exist on their own to save beings.

70. "Buddhist teachings" (*fo-tsang*) may also be rendered as the Buddhist treasury or even as womb of the Buddhas.

[concentration], they have already traversed the eternity of twenty-nine births.
In the inferior stage of the contemplation of forbearance of quiescent extinction, [they have but] one [more] turn to [the stage] of sublime enlightenment,[71] [which is] equal to the unequaled.
The stages immovable, effective intelligence, and teaching-cloud eliminate the remnants of previously existing habits of ignorance.[72]
The signs of habits of ignorance [are erased] and their consciousness is completely revolutionized.[73] The principles of the Two Truths are completely [realized], and there is nothing which has not been exhausted.
Correctly enlightened and signless in the universal realm of the Teaching, thirty lives are exhausted and enlightenment is complete.
Calmly illuminated and actionless [in] real liberation, the response manifestations of their great compassion are without equal.
Profoundly unmoved and always in peaceful seclusion, their light is everywhere [yet] nothing is illuminated.
[838a] Having received the fruit of the abodes of the three worthies and the ten sages, it is only a Buddha who dwells in a pure land.
All beings temporarily abide, [yet when they] ascend to the adamantine source, they are perpetually immovable.
The merit of the Thus-come One's triple karma[74] is limitless, and consequently all beings equally experience his compassion.
The king of the Teaching, the unsurpassed, a tree among men, universally shelters all beings [and brings them] immeasurable light.
His speech constantly expounds the Teaching, with its plenitude of meaning, while his mind [abides in] the causeless illumination of quiescent extinction.
A Lion among men for the sake of expounding the profound doctrine so rare,
Innumerable lands all quake and the great assembly is overjoyed.
The World-honored One has well expounded the fourteen kings [of forbearance] and therefore I now honor him.

At that time, the great assembly—as vast as trillions of sands of the ***Gaṅgā***—heard what the Buddha, the World-honored One, and King ***Prasenajit*** had said concerning the limitless merit of the fourteen forbearances. They attained

71. "Sublime enlightenment" renders *miao-chüeh.*

72. The "remnants of ignorant habits" (*wu-ming hsi*) are the traces or seeds of former acts that remain in the "storehouse consciousness" (*ālayavijñāna*) and which impel one, even in the absence of continued defilements, to a new rebirth.

73. *Vijñāna-parāvṛtti.*

74. There are several groups of three karmic inheritances, the one meant here is likely body, speech, and mind.

the benefit of the great Teaching, and on hearing the Teaching, they were awakened and attained the forbearance of birthlessness and entered the state of uprightness.[75]

At that time the world-honored one proclaimed to the great assembly, "Ten thousand ***kalpa***s ago in the Teaching-realm of the King Dragon-brilliance this king ***Prasenajit*** was a ***bodhisattva*** of the fourth stage and I was a ***bodhisattva*** of the eighth stage. Now, before me, he has produced this great lion's roar. Thus, thus, thus as he said, he has attained the real meaning, the imponderable meaning! These matters are only known among Buddhas.

"Good sons! These fourteen forbearances, all of the Buddha's Teaching-bodies,[76] all of the ***bodhisattva*** practices, are imponderable! Immeasurable! Why is this? This is because all Buddhas are born in the ***Prajñāpāramitā,*** transformed in the ***Prajñāpāramitā,*** and are extinguished in the ***Prajñāpāramitā.*** [Yet] in reality all the Buddha's births are no birth, their transformation no transformation, and their extinction no extinction. Preeminent and non-dual, of neither signs nor signlessness, neither self nor others, neither coming nor going—this is because they are like the void.

"Good sons! The nature of all sentient beings is without birth and extinction. This is because all aggregations of constituents are illusory transformations and possess the signs of the [five] aggregates, the sense media, and the elements. [They] are without conjunction or dispersal. Constituents are the same as the nature of reality[77] because they are quiescent and empty. The self-nature of all sentient beings is pure, and all of their acts are without bondage or liberation. They produce neither cause nor fruit, nor lack of cause or lack of fruit. All the suffering they undergo, which are known as defilements—the sign of self or of others—is all because of emptiness.[78] The universe is empty,[79] empty without sign, without doing, not in accord with inverted views, not in accord with illusion, without the signs of the six destinies, without the signs of the four [types] of birth, without the signs of sages, and without the signs of the three jewels. This is because of emptiness.[80]

"Good sons! Deepest ***prajñā*** is without knowing, without viewpoint, is not [838b] action, not causality, not abandoning and not receiving.[81] [It is] cor-

75. The "state of uprightness" (*cheng-wei*) is glossed by Liang-pi as the first *bhūmi* or bodhisattva stage (T 1709 33.475b17–18).

76. "All of the Buddha's teaching bodies" indicates not only the *dharmakāya*, but also the *nirmāṇa-kāya* and *saṃbhogakāya*. See Liang-pi, T 1709 33.475c14.

77. "Nature of reality" translates *fa-hsing*.

78. The rendering of this line is tentative.

79. The *Dharmadhātu* (*fa-ching-chieh*) is empty.

80. In other words, from the ultimate point of view, from the point of view of the supreme truth (which is not a point of view, I might add), all is emptiness.

81. The line recalls the famous essay of Kumārajīva's disciple Seng-chao (374–414), "Prajñā is not Knowledge" (*Po-jo wu chih lun*). For a full treatment of Seng-chao, see Walter Liebenthal, *Chao Lun:*

rectly abiding in contemplation without signs of illumination. Therefore, one who practices this path is like emptiness. [Because] the signs of constituents are thusness, whether there is something [one wants to] attain or nothing [one wants to] attain, all are unattainable. Thus ***prajñā*** is not identical with the five aggregates, nor is it something apart from the five aggregates; it is not identical with beings, nor is it something apart from beings; it is not identical with the world, nor is it something apart from the world; it is not identical with the practice of liberation, nor is it abandoning the practice of liberation.[82] Thus all signs are imponderable. Therefore, none of the practices cultivated by the ***bodhisattva-mahāsattva***s reach a conclusion, but are in the practice [itself]. The knowledge of all the buddhas is like a phantasm—[they] attain the signs of nonabiding in the midst of transformation. Therefore, the fourteen forbearances are unfathomable.

"Good sons! This treasury of merit I have just expounded is of great benefit to all living beings. Compared to it even the preaching of the ***bodhisattva***s of the ten stages—as innumerable as the sands of the ***Gaṅgā***—which would result in trillions of merits, would be just like a single wave in the sea. Yet all the Buddhas of the triple world are able to know this reality, and all in the worthy and sage [stages] whole-[heartedly] extol it. For this reason I have now outlined a small portion of its merit.

"Good sons! These fourteen forbearances have been practiced and cultivated by all ***bodhisattva***s, in all the worlds of the ten directions past and present. They have been revealed by all the Buddhas, and all the Buddhas and ***bodhisattva-mahāsattva***s of the future will do likewise. If a Buddha or ***bodhisattva*** attains all-knowledge but does not do it from this 'gate,' then he is not at the abode [of all-knowledge]. Why is this? This is because the paths of all Buddhas and ***bodhisattva***s are the same.

"Good sons! Should a person be able to give rise to one thought of pure faith on hearing of abiding forbearance, active forbearance, transferring forbearance,[83] joyous forbearance, immaculate forbearance, luminous forbearance, radiant wisdom forbearance, invincible forbearance, disposed toward enlightenment forbearance, far-reaching forbearance, immovable forbearance, effectively intelligent forbearance, teaching-cloud forbearance, and sublime enlightenment forbearance, then this person will transcend all suffering and difficulties—for hundreds of ***kalpa***s, thousands of ***kalpa***s, or unimaginable numbers of ***kalpa***s, ***kalpa***s equal to the sands of the ***Gaṅgā.*** He will not be

---

The Treatises of Seng-chao, 2d revised edition (Hong Kong: Hong Kong University Press, 1968). Also Richard Robinson, *Early Mādhyamika in India and China* (Madison: University of Wisconsin Press, 1967), pp. 123–55 and 212–21.

82. Liang-pi glosses "the practice of liberation" (*hsing-chieh*) as "contemplative knowledge" (*kuan-chao-chih*).

83. In other words, the ten abodes, the ten acts, and the ten transferences of the preparatory path.

born in the evil paths, and not long thereafter will attain ***anuttarasamyaksaṃbodhi.***"

At that moment one million identically named space-store ***bodhisattvamahāsattvas***,[84] together with the limitless and innumerable great assemblies who had come [with them], jumped for joy that they were to inherit the Buddha's awesome spirit. Buddhas of the ten directions, as numberless as the sands of the ***Gaṅgā*** appeared everywhere, each in a ritual arena, expounding the fourteen forbearances, just as our World-honored One had, without any differences, and each and every one joyously, in like [manner], proclaimed the cultivation of this ***Prajñāpāramitā.***

Then the World-honored One said to King ***Prasenajit,*** "You previously asked, 'What signs do you use to abide in contemplation?' ***Bodhisattvamahāsattvas*** contemplate in this manner: taking up illusory transformation bodies, they recognize illusory transformation and correctly abide in equanimity without distinction between other and self. It is thus that one contemplates transformation and [838c] benefits living beings. Thus, all living beings long ago and in distant ***kalpas***, from the first ***kṣaṇa*** of consciousness were differentiated from trees and rocks. In birth after birth they become impure or pure, and each individual is the basis for inumerable pure and impure consciousnesses. From that initial ***kṣaṇa*** there are inexpressible ***kalpas*** to the final adamantine ***kṣaṇa,*** and there are absolutely inexpressible [states of] consciousness [there between]. At birth, all sentient beings possess the two constituents of form and mind. Form designates the form aggregate, while mind designates the other four aggregates. All of these by nature cohere and obscure reversion to reality.

"Great king! This single constituent of form gives birth to innumerable forms. When the eye perceives it, it is form. When the ear hears it, it is sound. When the nose encounters it, it is fragrance. When the tongue perceives it, it is taste. When the body feels it, it is sensation. When firm and supporting it is called earth. When moist and wet it is called water. When warm it is called fire. When light and moving it is called wind. It gives birth to the abodes of the five cognitions and gives name to the five primary colors.[85] Thus it develops and evolves from a single form and a single mind to produce inexpressible and innumerable forms and minds. All because they are illusory.

"Good sons! The perceptions of sentient beings are dependent upon the worldly convention. Whether 'existent' or 'nonexistent' the productions of sentient beings are vain thoughts like memories and the production of karma and the receiving of the fruit [of these acts] is called worldly truth. All of the beings of the triple world and the six paths—the ***Brahmans***, the ***Kṣatriyas***,

84. *Ākāśagarbha.*

85. The "five cognitions" are *wu shih-ch'u* or *parijñānas.*

and the ***Vaiśyas*** have the view of self, of the form constituent and the mind constituent, which is like something seen in a dream.

"Good sons! All names are completely established upon falsehood. Before the Buddha appeared, the illusory teachings of worldly truth were without names and without meanings, and even without the signs for substance. [They were] without the name for the triple world, and without names for good and evil recompense in the six destinies. It is because of this that all of the Buddhas manifest themselves on behalf of sentient beings, to preach innumerable names in the triple world, in the six paths, both those pure and those impure. Thus, all are like the sounds of breath. All constituents and signs are momentary; they do not abide. From one ***kṣaṇa*** to the next they are neither the same nor different. Quickly arising and just as quickly extinguished, they are not cut off, nor are they continuous. This is because all existence is made of constituents [and these] are like flames. All the constituents' signs—that is [what we] call the realm of form, the realm of sight, and the realm of sight-perception, all the way to the realm of the Teaching, the realm of consciousness and the realm of intellect—are like lightning flashes. Signs are not fixed, existence and nonexistence are not different, like a second moon.[86] All constituents are causally constructed, and the constituents of the aggregates, the sense media and the elements, are like waves on water. All constituents are causally constructed, and all sentient beings, all causes and fruits of the same time, all causes and fruits of different times, and the good and bad of the three eras are like clouds in the air.

"Good sons! ***Bodhisattva-mahāsattvas*** abide in non-discrimination, in lacking any sign of 'this' or 'that,' 'self' or 'other.' They continually practice transformation and benefit without the signs of transformation and benefit. Therefore, you should know that the defilement and attachment of the ignorant obstructed consciousness is void; the signs [constitute] bondage. The illuminating vision and knowledge of the ***bodhisattva*** is like [that of] an illusionist, lacking any substantial sign, like a conjured blossom.[87] This is how ***bodhisattva-mahāsattvas*** abide in the benefit of themselves and others and thus contemplate reality."

When this teaching had been expounded, limitless numbers of men and gods in the great assembly attained the forbearance of self-control, the [triple] emptiness and the forbearance of the birthlessness [of constituents].[88] [Whether in] the first stage, the second stage, or [even] on up to the tenth stage, countless ***bodhisattvas*** acceded to "once-returning."

86. My rendering of this line is tentative. The import seems to be that everything is at base empty of self nature, without support, like a second moon seen by someone because of an eye disease, or in a delusion, a dream, a hallucination, or a reflection.

87. Literally, like a flower [appearing in mid-] air.

88. Following Liang-pi's reading of the passage (T 1709 33.482b15–16). The "triple emptiness" refers either to the empty, the signless, the wishless, or to the emptiness of self, constituents, and all things.

4

The Two Truths

[839a] At that time, King ***Prasenajit*** said to the Buddha, "World-honored One, is the worldly truth contained in the supreme truth or not?[1] If you say it does not exist [within it], then wisdom should not be [called] dual. If you say it does exist [within it], then wisdom ought not be [called] single.[2] What of this matter

1. Much of this brief discourse on the Two Truths is either identical with or a close paraphrase of the fifth-century text. There are, however, a few important divergences. The fifth-century text concludes with a short paragraph on the name of the text (T 245 8.829c16–21). Pu-k'ung has removed this paragraph and placed it at the conclusion of the entire text (T 246 8.844c19–25). Pu-k'ung has also added a concluding couplet to the *gāthā*, and he regularly substitutes "supreme truth" (*sheng-i ti*) for "truth of the preeminent meaning" (*ti-i i-ti*), though one such reference remains. Pu-k'ung also eliminated all references to the Three Truths.

2. "If [you] say it does not exist (*wu*) . . . If [you] say it exists (*yu*) . . ." I have rendered the terms of the question as "existence" and "nonexistence," since these are the key terms of the Chinese philosophical debate on the issue. Liang-pi's commentary notes that if one speaks and hears, then the truth is not single, if one does not speak and hear, then the truth is not dual. "Not two, not one, then this is the truth of the preeminent meaning [*ti-i i ti*]." He then goes on to quote the earlier "translation"

of the meaning of singularity or duality?" The Buddha said, "Great king, in the past, during the teaching of the Buddha King Dragon-brilliance you had already asked the meaning [of this].[3] Now, I will not explain and you will not listen. Not explaining and not listening, these then are called 'single meaning' or 'dual meaning.'[4] Now, truly listen and I will explain it to you." Then the World-honored One pronounced these stanzas:

The signless supreme truth is not made of the substance of self and other.
The causal [world], like illusory existences, is also not made of self and other.
The nature of constituents at base is without nature, and the supreme truth is likewise empty.
All existent [things are comprised of] illusory constituents; the three falsities collect [to produce] false existences.[5]
Isn't isn't, truth is really nonexistent, [It is] quiescent and extinguished, the supreme emptiness.[6]
All constituents [have] conditioned existence, the meaning of existence and nonexistence is thus.
The basic self of existence and nonexistence is two-fold, like the two horns of cattle.
The enlightened see that they are nondual, the Two Truths are never identical.[7]
The wise see that they are nondual; [if one] seeks duality it cannot be obtained.
[One may not] refer to Two Truths as single, [for] single [truth] cannot be obtained either.[8]

---

and notes that this is the source of its "Three Truths" doctrine (T 1709 33.483a18–29). The T'ang dynasty commentary attributed to Chih-i discusses the Three Truths at length (T 1705 279c13–21).

3. The fifth-century text says, "Great king! You have already asked the meaning of one and two [before] the seven Buddhas of the past" (T 245 8.829a6–7).

4. There is a play on the word "not" here, which above has indicated "nonexistence." The Buddha is chiding Prasenajit, and saying "not explaining" (*wu shuo*), "not listening" (*wu t'ing*).

5. In this and the previous stanza we see explanation first of the supreme position, then of the worldly position. My translation of the second stanza follows Liang-pi's explanation that the "three haves" (*san-yu*) in the stanza are not the same. The first refers to all existent things (*ti*), the second to the illusory existence of the *skandhas*, the third to their unreality (*pu-shih*). The "three falsities" (*san-chia, prajñapti*) refers to the dependent nature of all existence: of all constituents of existence, of all sensation, and of all names (T 1709 33.843b24–c3).

6. "Isn't isn't, truth is really nonexistent" renders *wu wu ti shih wu*.

7. "Never identical" renders *ch'ang pu chi*, literally "always not come up to."

8. Liang-pi points out that to seek the signs of oneness or twoness is to seek signs and miss the truth (T 1709 33.483c12–19).

With respect to understanding, one constantly proceeds from one,
with respect to truth, one constantly proceeds from two.[9]
Comprehending this one and two, one truly enters the supreme truth.
Worldly truth arises from illusion and transformation, just like conjured flowers,[10]
Like reflections or like hair-wheels.[11] Causality thus is illusory existence.
[From] illusion and transformation one perceives [only] illusion and transformation, the stupid call illusion truth,
Illusory teachers see illusory teachings, but truth and illusion alike are completely nonexistent.[12]
If one comprehends constituents thus, then of course one understands the meaning of one and two.
With regard to all constituents everywhere, one should contemplate thus.

"Great king! ***Bodhisattva-mahāsattva*s** dwell in the supreme truth transforming all living beings. Buddhas and sentient beings are one, and not two. Why is this? [This is because] these two—sentient beings and ***bodhi***—are [both] completely empty.

[839b] "By the emptiness of sentient beings one attains true ***bodhi***-emptiness and by the emptiness of ***bodhi*** one attains the true emptiness of sentient beings. By [realizing] that all constituents are empty [one realizes that] emptiness is therefore empty. Why is this? [This is because] ***prajñā*** is signless and the Two Truths are entirely empty. That is, from ignorance all the way to [the state of] all-knowledge there are no signs of self or signs of another. In the truth of the preeminent meaning one sees that there is nothing to be seen.[13] If one prac-

9. The first indicates the enlightened point of view, the second the worldly point of view.

10. Liang-pi identifies "worldly truth" (*shih-ti*) as existence and nonexistence (*yu, wu*), which give rise to illusion and transformation (T 1709 33.484a5–7).

11. "Hair-wheels" (*mao-lun*) are explained by Liang-pi as what is seen when there is something foreign in one's eye (T 1709 33.484a9–11). Buswell, *Formation of Ch'an Ideology in China and Korea*, renders the term "gossamer," while Suzuki (*Laṅkāvatāra Sūtra*) renders it "hair-net." A modern opthamologist would call them "floaters." The fifth-century text reads, "like reflections or like a third hand." The T'ang commentary attributed to Chih-i is of no help with this metaphor, as it gives the general purport of the chapter without analyzing it line by line. Chi-tsang's commentary just says that the line means that worldly truth depends on empty names and is without reality (T 1707 33.340b23–25). Wŏng-ch'ŭk's commentary treats this in a straightforward manner, noting that third hands simply do not occur. A note in the commentary says that one version of the text has "three heads" (*san shou*), but that this is a mistake (T 1708 33.404a21–23).

12. The final two stanzas below do not appear in the fifth-century text. It has, instead, the following: "[This] is called the contemplation of all the Buddhas, and the contemplation of the bodhisattvas is also thus" (T 245 8.829a26).

13. Oddly, here the text uses the expression "truth of the preeminent meaning" (*ti-i i ti*), which was the centerpiece of the fifth-century text and which has otherwise been expunged from the eighth-century recension.

tices then there is no grasping. [Likewise] if one does not practice then there is no grasping. Whether practicing or not practicing, still there is no grasping, for all constituents are devoid of grasping. A ***bodhisattva*** who has not yet become a Buddha takes ***bodhi*** and makes it defilement. Yet when a ***bodhisattva*** becomes a Buddha he takes defilement and makes it ***bodhi.*** Why is this? This is because the truth of the supreme meaning is nondual. This is because all Buddhas, Thus-come Ones, and all constituents are entirely thusness."

King ***Prasenajit*** said to the Buddha, "How is it that of all the Buddhas and ***bodhisattva***s of the ten directions none abandon the written word and [yet they] practice reality?"

The Buddha replied, "Great king! As for the written word, this refers to the scriptures, metrical compositions, prophecies, chants, addresses, stories arising from causality, parables, narratives, birth stories, expanded scriptures, miraculous tales, and dogmatics.[14] Everything which has been expounded, the sounds, the style of language, the words, the phrases, are all thus, without a doubt, signs of reality; but if one is attached to the signs of the written word, then certainly these are not reality either.[15]

"Great king! One who cultivates the signs of reality is similar to [one who] practices literary cultivation. The signs of reality are the very mother of all Buddha-wisdom as well as the mother of the basic wisdom of all sentient beings. This then is what is called the substance of all-knowledge. All Buddhas—those who have not yet achieved Buddhahood and those who have—regard it as the mother of wisdom. All Buddhas who have already attained Buddhahood regard it as all-knowledge. [Those who] have not yet attained [it] regard it as [basic] nature; [those who] have already attained it regard it as [all-] knowledge.

The ***prajñā*** of the three vehicles is neither produced nor extinguished; its self-nature always abides. All sentient beings regard this as awakening to [one's basic] nature.[16] If ***bodhisattva***s neither fetter themselves to the written word nor abandon the written word—being without signs of the written word is not to be without the written word—in this way they are able to cultivate [themselves] without perceiving signs of cultivation. Such a one certainly may be said to cultivate the written word and [yet] is able to attain the real nature of

14. This is the standard taxonomy of Buddhist scriptures, or the "twelve varieties of Buddhist preachment" (*shih-erh pu ching, dvādacakadharmapravacana*). Hurvitz enumerates and briefly discusses these in *Chih-I*, pp. 337–38.

15. The point is not to become attached to the text or to the teaching in a literal fashion. These are merely signs pointing to true reality. Chi-tsang (33.341c1–5) discusses this and, in the words of the T'ang commentary attributed to Chih-i, "The Buddha has made it clear that the vulgar truth exists as text but the real truth does not exist as text" (T 1705 33.256a10–11).

16. The term used here is *chüeh-hsing*.

prajñā. This is the ***Prajñāpāramitā.*** Great king! ***Bodhisattva-mahāsattvas***' protection of the Buddha-fruit, their nurturing of the practices of the ten stages, and protection and transformation of living beings is carried out like this."

King ***Prasenajit*** said to the Buddha, "The nature of reality is one and the types and classes of sentient beings, their origins and actions, are unlimited. Is the Teaching single or unlimited [in number?]"

The Buddha said, "Great king! The Teaching is not single, nor is it unlimited. How is this so? This is because all sentient beings have form-constituents and mind-constituents, the signs of the five aggregates and the views of self and other, as well as all sorts of unfathomable roots and actions. When the Teaching is viewed according to roots, it is unlimited. [But] the nature of all these constituents is not found in signs nor in the lack of signs, and it is not unlimited. If ***bodhisattvas*** go along with all other sentient beings and regard [the Teaching] as single or as multiple, this is certainly not seeing [839c] the meaning of one and two.[17] [When] one understands that one and two are "not one" and "not two," this is the supreme truth. Clinging to one and two as existent or as nonexistent is the worldly or vulgar truth. Therefore, the Teaching is neither one nor two.

"Great king! The ***Prajñāpāramitā*** expounded by all the Buddhas and the ***Prajñāpāramitā*** that I have now expounded are identical and without any difference. If you and the others of the great assembly receive, hold, read, and recite it, and expound and practice it, then this constitutes receiving and holding the teaching of all the Buddhas.

"Great king! The merit of this ***Prajñāpāramitā*** is immeasurable. If all the Buddhas—indescribable as the sands of the ***Gaṅgā***—each and every one a Buddha, were to teach and transform indescribable and unlimited numbers of sentient beings, and each and every one of these beings all became Buddhas,

17. Here the eighth-century text departs from the fifth-century text, which reads: "If a ***bodhisattva*** sees beings, sees one or sees two, then [he] does not see one and does not see two. This one and two is the truth of the preeminent meaning [*ti-i-i ti*]. Great king, if there is existence or nonexistence [*jo yu jo wu*] then this is worldly truth. [One can] use Three Truths to take up all constituents: the truth of emptiness, the truth of form, and the truth of mind. I have preached that no constituent transcends the three truths. Personalist views and the five aggregates are empty and, indeed, all constituents are empty" (T 245 8.829b26–c1). Chi-tsang comments: "The master Tripitaka said, 'The basic nature of all constituents is the truth of emptiness. Common people take outward form and regard it as reality, and this is called the truth of form. People in the three vehicles who are cultivating the way are without mental outflows, and this is called the truth of mind.' If we discuss birth and death, and nirvana, each has three truths. The three truths of birth and death: gods, humans, and the four great elements are the truth of form. The eight cognitions are the truth of mind, and transcending birth and death without nirvana is the truth of emptiness. The three truths of nirvana: the real form of gods and humans is the truth of form. The two minds of reality are called the truth of mind, and being without birth and death's four inverted views is called the truth of emptiness" (T 1707 33.343a2–8). The passage is, of course, the *locus classicus* of the T'ien-t'ai schools teaching of the Three Truths.

and all of these Buddhas and so forth furthermore taught and transformed unlimited and indescribable numbers of beings, and these also all became Buddhas, then the ***Prajñāpāramitā*** expounded by all these Buddhas, the indescribable, unlimited numbers of ***nayutas*** of hundreds of thousands of verses would be inexhaustible. [Moreover,] if you were to choose a single verse from all of these verses and then divide that verse into one thousand parts and then choose one part therefrom and expounded the merit of that part, the merit of that word[18] would still be inexhaustible. How much more so [is this the case with] the merit of these limitless words? If through this scripture a person arouses a single thought of pure faith, [then] this person will transcend one hundred ***kalpa***s, one thousand ***kalpa***s, a billion ***kalpa***s of births and deaths in suffering and difficulty. How much more so [if one] copies it, receives, reads and recites it, and on behalf of others expounds its merit? [Then this person] is no different from all of the Buddhas of the ten directions. [You] should know that all the Buddhas protect and recollect this person and it will not be long before [such a person] will attain ***anuttarasamyaksaṃbodhi***."[19]

When this teaching had been expounded a million persons attained the forbearance of the three emptinesses.[20] Billions of persons attained the forbearance of great emptiness, and unlimited numbers of ***bodhisattva***s attained and abided in the tenth stage.[21]

18. "Word" translates *chu* "statement" or "proposition" as representing the Sanskrit *pada*.

19. "Complete enlightenment."

20. There are several sets of "three emptinesses" (*san-k'ung*). They include "emptiness," "signlessness," "wishlessness"; and emptiness of the self, of constituents, and of all phenomena, and so on. Liang-pi specifies that the meaning here is of the emptiness of the three falsities perceived in the stage of the three worthies, that is, the emptiness of things, sensations, and names (T 1709 33.487b28).

21. Liang-pi indicates that "great emptiness" is the forbearance that sets one out on the Bodhisattva path (T 1709 33.487b29–c1).

5

Protecting the State

[840a] At that time the World-honored One told King ***Prasenajit,*** the others, and all of the other kings of great states, "Listen carefully, Listen carefully, and on your behalf I will expound the method for protecting the state.[1] [Now], in all states, when [things are] on the brink of chaos and there are all [sorts of] disasters, difficulties, or bandits come to wreak havoc, you and the others and all kings should receive and hold, read and recite this ***Prajñāpāramitā.*** Sumptuously adorn a ritual arena and set up one hundred Buddha images, one hun-

1. I have omitted the header to the second fascicle, which simply repeats the title and translators cited at the beginning of the text. "Protecting the state" renders *hu-kuo* and parallels "protecting" or "nurturing" the "Buddha-fruit" (*hu fo-kuo*) and the "practices of the ten stages" (*hu shih-ti hsing*). Protecting the state is regarded by many commentators as "outer protection" (*wai-hu*), while the nurturing of the ten stages is "inner protection" (*nei-hu*). See, for example, the T'ien-t'ai commentary attributed to Chih-i (T 1705 255a19–22) and especially its interpretation of "inner" and "outer" lands (280a4–11). For more on this and on the parallels and puns involved, see the analysis in Chapter 4 of the study.

dred ***bodhisattva*** images, and one hundred seats for Buddhist masters, and invite one hundred masters of the Teaching to expound this scripture. Before all of the seats light all kinds of lamps, and burn all kinds of incense, scatter various flowers and make vast and abundant offerings of clothing and utensils, drink and food, broth and medicines, places of shelter and repose, and all of the usual affairs of offering.[2] Twice each day [the Buddhist masters should] lecture on and read this scripture. If the king, the great officers, ***bhikṣu***s, ***bhikṣunī***s, ***upāsaka***s, and ***upāsikā***s hear, receive, read, and recite it and practice it according to the [prescribed] method, the disorders and difficulties will forthwith be eradicated.

"Great king! In all states there are countless specters and spirits, each of whom has countless minions. If they hear this scripture, they will protect your state. If a state is on the verge of chaos, the specters and spirits form the vanguard of chaos. Because of the chaos of the specters and spirits the myriad people become chaotic. In due course bandits arise and the one hundred surnames perish.[3] The king, the heir apparent, the princes, and the one hundred officers involve one another in scandals.[4]

Transformations and wonders appear in the heavens and on earth. The sun, the moon, and the swarms of stars lose their proper times and regulation. There are holocausts, great floods, great winds, and the like. Everyone should receive, hold, expound and read this ***Prajñāpāramitā*** [when] these difficulties arise. Should [people] receive, hold, read, and recite this scripture, everything they seek, official position, abundant wealth, sons and daughters, wisdom and understanding, intercourse according to their wishes, or recompense in the human and celestial realms, will be attained and satisfied.[5] Illness and difficulty will straightaway be eradicated. Bonds and fetters, cangues, and locks that bind [people's] bodies will be loosed. All transgressions will be completely wiped out, even [if people have] broken the four most serious prohibitions and have committed the five heinous crimes, and even [if they] have violated all the prohibitions and have [committed] transgressions without number.

[840b] "Great king! Long ago ***Śakra-devanamindra*** became the King Born of the Crown [of the Head]; In his desire to eradicate the lord Śakra he led four

2. More detailed ritual prescriptions appear in Chapter 7 of the scripture, in the fifth-century version of Chapter 7 (Appendix A) and, of course, in the esoteric ritual manuals treated in Chapter 6 of the study.

3. The "one hundred surnames" is a stock Chinese expression for "the people."

4. Literally, there are mutual [accusations] of right and wrong (*hu-hsiang shih-fei*).

5. "Intercourse according to their wishes" seems to indicate, at least in Liang-pi's reading, financial and social intercourse (*wang-lai*) and not intercourse of a more private nature (T 1709 33.489b22–23). Here and in certain other instances the text inserts a redundant "all" (*chieh*) in imitation of the translationese of early Chinese Buddhist texts. In these cases the "all" is simply a Sanskrit plural marker.

armies up to the celestial palace.[6] At that time the celestial king immediately used all the Buddha-teachings of the past, and arranged one hundred lofty seats and invited one hundred masters of the Teaching to expound and read this ***Prajñāpāramitā*** scripture. The King Born from the Crown withdrew forthwith, and the heavenly host was at peace.

Great king! Formerly, the king of T'ien-lo had an heir apparent named Spotted-foot.[7] When [Spotted-foot] ascended to the station of king, a heterodox master named Shan-shih bestowed consecration on him.[8] Shan-shih then commanded Spotted-foot to collect the heads of one thousand kings in order to sacrifice them at the altar of ***Mahākāla,*** the great black god.[9] Since Spotted-foot had acceded to the kingship, he had already captured nine-hundred ninety-nine kings, and was merely one king short. [So Spotted-foot] traveled north ten thousand *li* to capture a king named P'u-ming.[10] This king P'u-ming told Spotted-foot, "I wish to listen to one day's ceremonies, to worship the three jewels, and to feed the ***śramaṇas***." Spotted-foot listened and then permitted this. This king [P'u-ming] then relied upon the teaching which had been expounded by all the Buddhas of the past, set up one hundred lofty seats, and invited one hundred masters of the Teaching. In the course of that day's two [ritual] occasions they expounded the ***Prajñāpāramitā***'s eight trillion verses. At that time, from the midst of the assembly, the preeminent master of the Teaching recited these verses on behalf of King P'u-ming:

The fires of the ***kalpa*** rage, the great-thousand [worlds] are all destroyed,
Sumeru and its great oceans are obliterated without a trace.

6. The "King born of the Crown" (*ting-sheng-wang*, so called because he was born of a sack which erupted from his father's head) was a *cakravartin* ruling all four continents, and he attempted to storm the *Trayastriṃśās*, the next "level" of the cosmos, and dethrone its ruler Indra (Śakra). This king was reputedly a past incarnation of Śākyamuni, and the story turns up in various early collections including the *Scripture of the Wise and the Foolish* (*Hsien-yü ching*). The T'ang dynasty T'ien-t'ai commentary discusses it (T 1705 33.280b23–c14), and an English translation of the complete tale is available in Frye, *Sūtra of the Wise and the Foolish*, pp. 223–27. Wang Wen-yin discusses the language of the tale in *Fo-chiao fan-i chih yen-chiu* (Taipei: T'ien hua ch'u-pan shih-yeh kung-ssu, 1985), pp. 375–77.

7. The story appears in the *Laṅkāvatāra Sūtra* (Suzuki translation, chap. 8, pp. 216–17), where we are told that Spotted-foot (*Pan-tsu*, Sanskrit Kalmāṣapāda) and his siblings came by their peculiar markings because their father mated with a lioness. They are used in the *Laṅkāvatāra* as warning concerning the evil consequences of meat-eating. The T'ang T'ien-t'ai commentary (T 1705) tells the story twice (at 33.257c1–258a6 and 280c14–281b12) and goes into considerable detail. Not only was Spotted-foot carnivorous, he is said to have eaten children (280c24–28).

8. Shan-shih means "good-gift."

9. The fifth-century text merely says "family gods" (*chia-shen*). The negative mention of Mahākāla in this eighth-century text indicates that such a cult had spread, perhaps to Central Asia and southwest China.

10. His name means "Universal Brilliance."

Brahma and **Śakra,** all of the gods and dragons, and all sentient beings, are exterminated as well, how much more so this body.[11]
Birth, old-age, sickness, and death, grief and pity, suffering and vexation, hatred and affection, harass us and we desire to escape.
Love and desire bind and incite us, and we inflict ulcers and illnesses on ourselves; the triple world is without peace, what joy has the state?
Existence and action are not real, they arise from causality. Flourishing and decline succeed one another in a flash; one moment there is something, and suddenly there is nothing.[12]
All worlds, or realms, or births, in accordance with karma are causally manifested, like shadows and echoes, and are entirely empty.[13]
Perception floats [up] due to karma and arises by riding on the four elements. Ignorance is bound by passion, born through a succession of selves.[14]
Perception, following karma, moves [from one birth to another], the body lacks a master; [one] should know that the state too is an illusory transformation.[15]

When the master of the Teaching finished the verses, King P'u-ming, having heard the teaching, was enlightened and experienced the emptiness-***samādhi,*** and all of the king's retinue attained the Teaching-eye of emptiness.[16] Thereupon this king was sent to the state of T'ien-lo, and in the assembly of all of the kings spoke these words: 'The humane [kings][17] have arrived at the time of their fate. All of us should chant and hold the ***gāthā*** of the ***Prajñāpāramitā*** pronounced by former Buddhas.' [840c] All of the kings heard this and all were enlightened, attained the emptiness-***samādhi,*** and each and every one chanted

11. Liang-pi says that Brahma here indicates the lords of the four trance-heavens, while Śakra is lord of the "heaven of the thirty-three or *Trayastriṃśās*. In the fifth-century text this stanza ends, "The two virtues [yin and yang] have even perished, how can the state endure?" I have translated the entire fifth-century *gāthā* in Appendix A.

12. The fifth-century text reads: "Existence is based on nonexistence, and causality gives rise to all, what flourishes must decline, what is real must be empty" [*yu pen tzu wu, sheng-che pi shuai, shih-che pi hsü,* T 245 8.830b10–11].

13. The fifth-century text adds, "The state is also [empty] like this" (T 245 8.830b13).

14. This is a particularly difficult line to render and my translation is tentative.

15. "Perception, following karma moves [from one birth to another]" follows Liang-pi's explanation of the line (T 1709 33.491b2–23).

16. The "emptiness *samādhi* is the trance in which one recognizes that the self and the aggregates comprising the person are unreal and insubstantial. It is usually regarded as one of the "three *samādhis*." This is not specified in the fifth-century text, which only mentions the Teaching-eye of emptiness (T 245 8.830b17). Nonetheless, the T'ang dynasty T'ien-t'ai commentary does discuss the three *samādhis* (T 1705 281b20–23). The Teaching-eye of emptiness involves the ability to penetrate appearances and see them for what they are—empty.

17. This is one of the few places in the body of the scripture where "humane" (*jen*[b]) is used, rather than "forbearing" (*jen*[a]).

and held it. Then King Spotted-foot asked all the kings: 'What teaching are you now chanting?' At that time P'u-ming immediately used the above verses as a reply to King Spotted-foot, [and when] the king heard this teaching [he] too realized the emptiness-concentration. He jumped for joy and proclaimed to all the kings, 'I have erred on behalf of a heterodox and perverse master. The fault is not yours. Each [of you may] return to your states and you should invite masters of the Teaching to expound this ***Prajñāpāramitā***.' Then King Spotted-foot bestowed the state upon his brother, left the householder life in order to follow the Way, and attained the forbearance of the birthlessness of [all] constituents.

"Great king! In the past there were, moreover, five thousand kings of states who continuously chanted this scripture [and who gained] protective recompense in this life. [Now] you and the others, the sixteen, and all kings of great states should similarly cultivate the method of protecting the state [and should] receive and hold, read, recite, and expound this scripture. If, in coming ages, all the kings of states, and others, should desire to protect the state or to protect themselves, then they should likewise receive and hold, read, recite, and expound this scripture."

When this teaching was enunciated, countless persons and groups of persons attained conversion to [the state of] nonretrogression.[18] ***Asura***s and others attained birth in the heavens, and all the unlimited and countless gods of the desire and form [realms] attained the forbearance of the birthlessness [of all constituents].

18. "Conversion to the state of nonretrogression" renders *pu-t'ui-chuan*, Sanskrit *avaivartika*.

6

The Inconceivable

[840c] At that time, [when] the kings of the sixteen states and all in the great assembly heard the Buddha expound the profound meaning of this ***Prajñāpāramitā,*** they jumped for joy and scattered trillions of jeweled lotus flowers, which in midair became a jeweled flower-throne.[1] All the Buddhas of the ten directions and their immeasurable great assemblies gathered and sat on this throne and expounded the ***Prajñāpāramitā.***[2] Everyone in this great assembly took up tens of thousands of golden lotus flowers and scattered them over Śākyamuni Buddha. [The blossoms] then coalesced into a flower parasol that

1. Chi-tsang notes in his commentary that "this chapter abundantly illustrates [the effects of] reverential offerings and the cultivation of offerings" (T 1707 33.346c26–27).

2. It is unclear from the phrasing whether a single throne or many thrones were formed. The fifth-century text, however, is quite clear that this is a single throne which all the Buddhas and assemblies sit on together, and thus I have followed the sense of the fifth-century version in making the throne singular. Compare T 245 8.830c16ff.

sheltered everyone in the great assembly.[3] Again they scattered eighty-four thousand ***Puṇḍarīka***[4] blossoms, and in midair these became a dais of white clouds. On this dais was the Buddha Kuang-ming[5] together with all the Buddhas of the ten directions and their limitless great assemblies [before whom they] expounded the ***Prajñāpāramitā.*** Every [member] of the great assembly held a ***mandāra***[6] flower [and they] scattered them before Śākyamuni Buddha and all the great assemblies. [They] also scattered ***mañjūṣaka***[7] flowers, which transformed in midair to become an adamantine palace. In the palace the Buddha-king Shih-tzu fen-hsün[8] discoursed on the supreme ***Prajñāpāramitā*** together with all of the Buddhas and great ***bodhisattva***s of the ten directions. Again they scattered innumerable divine and exquisite flowers and, in midair these transformed into [841a] a bejeweled cloud-canopy that completely covered all the three thousand great thousand worlds. And beneath this cloud-canopy flowers as numerous as the sands of the ***Gaṅgā*** rained down from midair.

When King ***Prasenajit*** and all in the great assembly had seen these events, they sighed [at the] miraculous occurrence.[9] [Prasenajit] clasped his hands before the Buddha and said, "Would that all the Buddhas of the past, present, and future should always preach this ***Prajñāpāramitā;*** would that all living beings should always see and hear it just as we have, today, without any difference."

The Buddha said, "Great king! It shall be as you have said! This ***Prajñāpāramitā*** is the mother of all of the Buddhas and the mother of all of the ***bodhisattva***s. It is the birthplace of every distinctive [form of] merit and spiritual penetration. When all of the Buddhas expound it together its efficacy is multiplied. For this reason you and the others always should receive and keep it."

Then, on behalf of all the great assemblies, the World-honored One displayed inconceivable spiritual penetrations and transformations. One flower entered countless flowers and countless flowers entered one flower. One Buddha-land entered countless Buddha-lands and countless Buddha-lands entered one Buddha-land. One ***guṇakṣetra***[10] entered countless ***guṇakṣetra***s and

3. The T'ang dynasty T'ien-t'ai commentary has a schematic passage listing the various wonderous events that take place in this chapter. It is of particular note because it reads very much like a visualization manual. See T 1705 33.281c7–22.

4. Lotus flowers.

5. His name, *kuang-ming*, means "Brilliant Light."

6. "Coral-tree" flowers, a white flower said to grow in the heaven of Indra.

7. A red flower.

8. The "lion roused to anger."

9. Following Liang-pi, literally a "rare occurrence" (*wei hui-yu*, Sanskrit *abhūtadharma*, T 1709 33.493b12–14). It is also the name of one of the twelve kinds of scriptures or "Buddhist preachments" mentioned above and designates accounts of miracles performed by the Buddha or other deities.

10. A *guṇakṣetra* is literally a land or field of qualities (*guṇa*). Here it likely designates a realm the size of a dust mote. This passage is one of the very few where the eighth-century text departs from the fifth-century text.

countless ***guṇakṣetra***s entered one ***guṇakṣetra.*** Countless great oceans entered into one of the [Buddha's] hair follicles. Countless [Mt.] ***Sumeru***s entered a mustard seed. One Buddha-body entered countless bodies of living beings and countless bodies of living beings entered one Buddha-body. The large appeared small and the small large. The pure appeared defiled, the defiled pure. These Buddha-bodies were inconceivable, the bodies of sentient beings were inconceivable, and the very world was inconceivable.

And when the Buddha had displayed these spiritual transformations, ten thousand women converted their female bodies [into those of men] and attained the spiritual penetration ***samādhi.*** Countless gods and humans attained the forbearance of the birthlessness of constituents; countless ***asura***s and others converted to the ***bodhisattva*** path, and ***bodhisattva***s numerous as the sands of the ***Gaṅgā*** in [their] present bodies became Buddhas.[11]

11. The fifth-century text is slightly different in tone and certain details: "When the Buddha had displayed these ***ṛddhi-pāda,*** all the devas of the ten directions attained the Buddha-transformation ***samādhi.*** Bodhisattvas [numerous as] ten [times] the sands of the ***Gaṅgā*** manifested their bodies becoming Buddhas; the eight classes of kings, [numerous as] three [times] the sands of the ***Gaṅgā*** converted to the bodhisattva path; ten thousand women attained the spiritual penetration ***samādhi*** in their present bodies. Good sons, this ***Prajñāpāramitā*** is of benefit to the triple world. It has been expounded in the past, it has now been expounded in the present, and it shall be expounded in the future. Listen carefully, listen carefully! Ponder it well and put it into practice" (T 245 831a11–16).

7

Receiving and Keeping This Scripture

[841a] When King ***Prasenajit***[1] witnessed the Buddha's spiritual transformations—the Universally-shining Thus-come one[2] manifest on one thousand flower daises, and on one thousand flower petals one thousand transformation-body Buddhas, and amidst these thousand flower petals countless Buddhas preaching the ***Prajñāpāramitā***[3]—[he] addressed the Buddha, "World-honored One! Such an unfathomable ***Prajñāpāramitā*** cannot be comprehended and cannot be known. How can all the good sons understand and apprehend this scripture and expound it on behalf of others?"

The Buddha said, "Great king! Listen carefully now! From the initial practice of forbearance to the adamantine concentration, [bodhisattva-mahāsattvas]

1. The fifth-century text reads "Prince Moonlight" (*Yüeh-kuang wang*).
2. The "World-honored Universally-shining one" (*pien-chao ju-lai*) is a common title for Mahāvairocana, the "Great Sun Buddha" of the Esoteric tradition. See Orzech, "Mahāvairocana."
3. The fifth-century text attributes all these wonders to Śākyamuni.

cultivate the thirteen gates of contemplation according to the Teaching, and all [those] who have become masters of the Teaching rely upon and are established [by these]. You and the others of the great [841b] assembly should treat [such masters] as Buddhas and make offerings to them, and should respectfully offer them hundreds, thousands, ten thousands, or millions of heavenly and wonderful incense and flowers.

Good sons![4] Those masters of the Teaching [who are] ***bodhisattvas*** [at the stage of] acquired lineage, whether ***bhikṣu***s, ***bhikṣunī***s, ***upāsaka***s or ***upāsikā***s, cultivate the practices of the ten abodes. Seeing Buddha, Teaching, and Community, they arouse the ***bodhi***-mind. They have compassion and sympathy and bring benefit and blessing to all living beings. They contemplate their own bodies and all the roots in the six realms and see that all is impermanent, is suffering, is empty, and is selfless.[5] Understanding karmic acts, birth and death, and ***nirvana,*** they are able to benefit themselves and others with abundance, peace, and joy. Whether they hear praise of the Buddhas or disparagement of the Buddhas, their minds are concentrated and immovable.[6] Whether they hear that there is a Buddha or that there is no Buddha, their minds remain concentrated and they do not retreat. The three [kinds of] karma do not cause them loss and they promote the six points of harmonious reverence.[7] Through their skill in means and adroitness they discipline beings. They diligently study the ten wisdoms and their spiritual penetrations transform and benefit [beings]. Those in the inferior rank cultivate the eighty-four thousand [verse] ***Prajñāpāramitā.***

Good sons! Before [the stage of] acquired forbearance,[8] through a thousand

4. The wording of this section and the next are quite different in the fifth-century text, although the same topics are covered. See the appendix on variants. In his commentary Chi-tsang spends considerable time unpacking the various stages of the path and comparing the terminology here with that of the *P'u-sa ying-lo pen-yeh ching*. See T 1707 33.349c, 350a, and so on. The T'ang T'ien-t'ai commentary also engages in this comparison and in trying to work out equivalences between the unusual terminology of the fifth-century *mārga* presented here and that of other texts. See, for example, T 1705 33.272c, 275b19–22.

5. My reading of "six realms" (*liu-chieh*) follows Liang-pi, who emphasizes that they are places, that is, the six destinies (*liu-ch'ü*, T 1709 33.496a13–19). He also points out that the "old scripture" omits this and instead elaborates the "four roots."

6. This calls to mind the story of "Never Disparaging" (*Sadāparibhūta*), the bodhisattva who never belittled others but always praised them saying they would all one day become Buddhas. The story is found in the *Lotus Sūtra*. See Hurvitz, *The Scripture of the Lotus Blossom of the Fine Dharma*, pp. 279–85.

7. Liang-pi indicates that the three kinds of karma (*san-yeh*) refer to actions of body, speech, and mind, a reading one would expect in an Esoteric context such as this (T 1709 33.496b18–25). He also notes that the "old scripture" runs the three kinds of karma and the six points of harmonious reverence together. The six points of harmonious reverence have to do with monastic concord. See the numerical glossary.

8. In the phrase "before [the stage of] acquired forbearance" (*hsi-jen yi-ch'ien*), acquired forbearance (*hsi-jen*) refers to the stage of acquired lineage (*hsi-chung-hsing*).

kalpa*s** they practice the ten good [acts], advancing and backsliding, light as a feather that follows the wind east or west. Once they arrive at the state of forbearance and enter the company of those correctly fixed [on truth], then they will not commit the five rebellious acts and will not slander the Correct Teaching.[9] This is because they know that the signs of the self and of constituents[10] are entirely empty, and they dwell in the state of liberation[11] for one ***asaṅkhyeyakalpa. Cultivating this forbearance [they are] able to give rise to the victorious actions.[12]

Next are ***bodhisattva*s** [of the stage of] the innate lineage, who abide in nondiscrimination and cultivate the ten wise contemplations.[13] Therefore they renounce wealth and life.[14] Therefore they adhere to the pure commandments. Therefore they are humble. Therefore they benefit themselves and others. Therefore they are not confused by birth and death. Therefore they have a profound perception of signlessness. Therefore they apprehend existence as though it were a phantasm. Therefore they do not seek after recompense. Therefore they attain unobstructed understanding. Therefore at every moment they manifest the Buddha's spiritual powers. Therefore they have the antidotes for the four inverted [beliefs], the three unfortunate roots, the delusions of the triple world and its ten inverted [views]. Views of self are every moment [recognized as] void and false, and they understand that names are false, perceptions are false, and that things are false[15] and are all unattainable. [They comprehend] that the self and others are signless and they abide in the contemplation of reality.[16] [Those of this] intermediate rank cultivate and practice the eighty-four thousand ***Prajñāpāramitā*** and in two ***asaṅkhyeyakalpa*s**

9. "Correct Teaching" here and below is *cheng-fa*, Sanskrit *saddharma*.

10. Liang-pi says the phrase "signs of self" indicates recognition that the aggregates or *skandhas* are empty, while the phrase "[signs of the] constituents" indicates the recognition that all dharmas are empty (T 1709 33.497a15–17).

11. Liang-pi points out that "this is the station of the forbearance of self-control and it has two names. Because they hope for the fruit of *bodhi* it is called 'provisions' [*tzu-liang*, Sanskrit *śambhara*], because they hope for the fruit of nirvana it is called 'liberation.' Because this refers to the 'liberation' portion it is called the 'station of liberation'" (T 1709 33.497b1–3).

12. Liang-pi indicates these are the "ten degrees of action" (*shih-hsing*) that constitute the basis of the next stage, the stage of the innate lineage (*hsing-chung-hsing*). See T 1709 33.497b9–10 and for the "ten degrees," Hurvitz, *Chih-I*, p. 364.

13. According to Liang-pi, the "ten wise contemplations" (*shih hui kuan*) are none other than the "ten degrees of action" (T 1709 33.497c24–25).

14. Liang-pi says that renunciation here (*she*) means "giving" (*shih*), because they have a mind of renunciation they excel at giving (*dāna*), and the wealth here is not only material, but the wealth of the Teaching. They are further not attached to their bodies (T 1709 33.498a3–6). This paragraph in the fifth-century version speaks of eliminating the ten inverted views (T 245 8.831b16).

15. The "three false" things (*san-chia*, *prajñapti*).

16. "Reality" here is *chen-ju*, Sanskrit *tattva*.

they perform all of the victorious acts and attain the state of the forbearance of firm [belief].

Next are the ***bodhisattva*s** of the lineage of the Way, who abide in the forbearance of firm [belief]. Contemplating the nature of all constituents they attain [the realization that all is] without birth and extinction. Their four immeasurable minds smash all darkness. Constantly visualizing all the Buddhas, they vastly and abundantly worship them. Constantly studying all the Buddhas, they abide in the mind of transference.[17] The good roots they cultivate all proceed to[18] the edge of reality,[19] and while in ***samādhi*** they are able to perform extensively Buddhist affairs.[20] Manifesting every sort of body, they practice the four kinds of concerted action. Dwelling in nondiscrimination, they transform and benefit beings. Their wisdom is completely enlightened and they have profoundly investigated [reality]. All [of their] actions and vows have universally been cultivated and practiced, and as masters of the Teaching they are able to transform and manage living beings. Good at contemplating the five aggregates, the triple world, the two truths, and the signlessness of self and other, they attain the nature of reality. Although they continually cultivate the supreme [841c] truth they nevertheless undergo birth in the triple world. Why is this? This is because the fruit of their karma is not yet completely exhausted, and because of this they are born according to the Way among men and gods. The superior [among these] cultivate and practice the eighty-four thousand ***Prajñāpāramitā*.** [During] three ***asaṅkhyeyakalpa*s** they cultivate the dual benefit and their practice greatly flourishes.[21] They attain excellence at moderating and subduing [the passions] and at all the ***samādhi*s**, and abiding in victorious contemplation, [they] cultivate the practices of departing [the world]. Because of this they are able to realize the state of equanimous sagacity.

Next are the ***bodhisattva-mahāsattva*s** of the joyous stage, who transcend the stage of dullness, are born in the family of the Thus-come One,[22] and abide in the forbearance of equanimity. Commencing with knowledge of signlessness, they illuminate the supreme truth and [they maintain] equanimity of the single sign [that is, of the signless] whether there are signs or not. Because they have cut off all ignorance and have extinguished the desires of the triple world

17. "Transference" is *hui-hsiang hsin*.

18. I read *ju* in the fourth tone.

19. "Edge of reality" *shih-chi*, Sanskrit *bhūtakoṭi*.

20. In other words, though absorbed in *samādhi* they simultaneously act on behalf of all beings.

21. I amend "lack" (*wu*) with "broadly" (*kuang*), following Liang-pi's commentary (T 1709 33.500a25–27). "Dual benefit" refers to their benefiting of themselves and others.

22. *Ju-lai chia* indicates they will achieve complete Buddhahood. Like the fifth-century text this comment is part of the argument about the different *gotra*. See my analysis in Chapters 3 and 4 of the study.

they will avoid countless deaths and births in the future. Making great compassion the head, they give rise to all the great vows; through the wisdom of skillful means, every moment they cultivate and practice countless victorious activities. Because they [adhere] neither to realization nor to nonrealization, they are completely learned; because they neither abide nor do not abide, they are inclined toward all-knowledge; because they practice in the realm of birth and death, they are unmoved by the ***māra***s; because they have departed from me and mine, there is nothing they fear; because they lack the signs of self and other, they constantly transform beings; because of the force of their sovereign vows, they are born in all the pure lands.

Good sons! This initial enlightened wisdom is not suchness, is not knowledge, is not existent, is not nonexistent, it is devoid of the signs of duality. The marvelous function of skillful means is not overturned and does not abide, it is not in motion and not quiescent. The sovereignty of the two-fold benefit is like water and wave, which are not the same yet not different.[23] The knowledge that gives rise to all the ***pāramitā***s is neither the same nor yet different.

Through four ***asaṅkhyeyakalpa***s they fulfill the cultivation and practice of ten million activities and vows. ***Bodhisattva***s of this stage are free of the fruits of karma in the triple world and do not create it anew, but because of the strength of their wisdom they have taken up vows to be reborn. At every moment they constantly practice ***dāna pāramitā,*** and their giving, loving words, beneficial acts, and work together with others is vastly purifying,[24] and they are well able to abide peacefully while benefiting beings.

Next are the ***bodhisattva-mahāsattva***s of the immaculate stage. [With] the four immeasurable minds of supreme quiescent extinction they have cut off anger and the rest of the habits. They have cultivated all the practices, that is to say, they have renounced all injury and theft, they are without depraved thoughts, and they have attained truthful speech, harmonious speech, gentle and persuasive speech, regulated and disciplined speech. They always practice a giving attitude, always arouse a compassionate attitude, and abide in an attitude of correct truth. Quiescent and calm, sincere and good, they have renounced obstacles involving the breaking of prohibitions, and they practice contemplation of great compassion without interruption. During five ***asaṅkhyeyakalpa***s they fulfill the pure commandments of the ***pāramitā.*** Their resolve is fierce, and they have forever abandoned all defilements.

Next are the ***bodhisattva-mahāsattva***s of the luminous stage, who dwell in

23. Liang-pi explains that "the two-fold benefit is sovereign" refers to the benefit the bodhisattva gains for himself in terms of wisdom, and the benefit to others through his skillful means. Therefore, it is the sovereignty of two-fold benefit (T 1709 33.502a21–23).

24. These are the four all-embracing virtues (*ssu-she fa*).

nondiscrimination and who have eradicated ignorance. Through the forbearance of signlessness they have attained the triple illumination,[25] and they completely understand that in the three eras[26] there is no coming and no going. [842a] Relying upon the four calm states, the four formless concentrations, and nondiscriminatory knowledge, they sequentially follow [the path]. They completely fulfill the supreme concentrations and attain the five supernormal powers. They manifest bodies large and small, hidden and evident, that are able to exist on their own. Their heavenly eye is pure and completely sees all realms; their heavenly ear is pure and completely hears all sounds. Using the knowledge of the minds of others, they know the minds of sentient beings. [Through their experience of] former abodes they are able to discern countless distinctions.[27] In [the course of] six ***asaṅkhyeyakalpa***s they practice all the ***pāramitā***s of forbearance and attain total control [over the defilements],[28] and they benefit and comfort [beings].

Next are the ***bodhisattva-mahāsattva***s of radiant wisdom, who cultivate the practice of the forbearance of obedience. Because there is nothing they lay hold of,[29] they are forever spared births in trifling bodies or with biased views. They have practiced to completion the limitless ***bodhi*** methods[30]—the states of mindfulness, the abandonments, the supranormal powers, the moral faculties, the moral powers, the components of perception, and the path.[31] For the sake of the desire for accomplishment they are strong, and nothing can frighten them from the distinctive Buddhist Teaching. In [the course of] seven ***asaṅkhyeyakalpa***s they practice innumerable ***pāramitā***s of vigor, have long abandoned indolence, and universally benefit beings.

Next are the ***bodhisattva-mahāsattva***s of the invincible stage, who use the four fearlessnesses and follow thusness.[32] Pure and equanimous they are without signs of bias and have cut off the delight in seeking the ***nirvana*** of the little

25. The "triple illumination" consists of knowledge of former births of oneself and others, knowledge of the future conditions of rebirth of oneself and others, and knowledge concerning the exhausting of present defilements that will lead to nirvana (T 1709 33.504a5–7).

26. That is, past, present, and future.

27. "Distinctions" here or "discriminations" would be Sanskrit *pariccheda*.

28. "Total control" (*ta tsung-chih*) can in some contexts mean "dhāraṇī," but here it does not.

29. *She-shou* is literally "gather and receive." Liang-pi explains that the ***bodhisattva-mahāsattva***s realize thusness and there is nothing to attach to in it (T 1709 33.504c18–20).

30. Generally the *p'u-t'i fen-fa*, the thirty-seven *bodhipāṣika dharmas*, but here the seven "divisions," which are then enumerated (as Liang-pi, T 1709 33.505a8–12 notes, quoting the *Discourse on the Ten Stages* or *Shih-ti lun*).

31. These are the four states of mindfulness, the four abandonments, the four supranormal powers, the five moral faculties,the five moral powers, the seven components of perception, and the eight-fold path.

32. "Thusness" here renders *chen-ju*.

vehicle. They have collected all merit and they have completely contemplated all truths: the noble truth of suffering, the truths of the origin, extinction, and path [to extinguish suffering], the worldly and the supreme—they contemplate limitless truths.[33] So that [they may] benefit beings they practice all the arts: literature, medicine, eulogies, drama, crafts, spells, heterodox ways, strange discourses, and divination of fortunate and unfortunate events, all without [committing] a single error. However, toward sentient beings they do not commit acts of injury or harrassment. Rather, in order to benefit [sentient beings] they manifest all [of the above arts], gradually causing them to abide in unsurpassed ***bodhi***. In all of the stages they know the exits from the path and the obstructions on the path.[34] During [the course] of eight ***asaṅkhyeyakalpa***s they constantly cultivate ***samādhi*** and give rise to all of the practices.

Next are the ***bodhisattva-mahāsattva***s of the stage disposed toward enlightenment.[35] These attain the superior [grade] of the forbearance of obedience, and abiding in the three gates of liberation they are able to exhaust the triple world's collection of causes and collection of karma and the coarser manifestations, practices, and signs.[36] On the level of great compassion they contemplate all of birth and death: ignorance, obscuring acts which collect in consciousness as seeds, name and form, the six abodes of sensation, contact, perception, desire, grasping, existence, birth, old age, and death,and so on.[37] All have their cause in attachment to the self and are the karmic fruit of ignorance. Because of nonduality they are neither existent nor nonexistent, [they have neither] a single sign nor are they signless.[38] During nine ***asaṅkhyeyakalpa***s they practice hundreds of ten thousands of empty, signless, wishless ***samādhi***s, and they attain all the limitless illumination of all the ***prajñāpāramitā***s.

Next are the ***bodhisattva-mahāsattva***s of the stage of far-reaching activity. They cultivate the forbearance of the birthlessness [of constituents] and real-

33. The first four are, of course, the Four Noble Truths, the last two are the Two Truths.

34. My phrasing follows Liang-pi, T 1709 33.505c21–23. Compare the fifth century text at T 245 8.832a5–7.

35. Again, I am following Robert Buswell's rendering of the term *hsien-ch'ien* or *abhimukhī*. See Buswell, *Formation of Ch'an Ideology in China and Korea*, p. 26.

36. Liang-pi notes that "collection of causes" (*chi-yin*) refers to inborn seeds of defilement and cognition, while the "collection of karma" (*chi-yeh*) refers to the seeds of fortune and misfortune (T 1709 33.506a16–17). The Chinese word *chi* or "collection" is a poor translation for the presumed Sanskrit term *samudāya*, which means "original," "origination," or "arising together." Thus, Liang-pi's "inborn" (*chu-sheng*).

37. These are, of course, the twelve *nidāna* of the chain of codependent origination.

38. Liang-pi explains that these correspond to the three gates of liberation, the empty (not existent or nonexistent), the signless (having a single sign or without signs), and the wishless (because of nonduality) (T 1709 33.506c1–12).

ize that constituents are without distinctions,[39] and have cut off all the fruits of karma and the subtle manifestations, practices, and signs. Abiding in the trance of extinction, [they nonetheless] give rise to triumphant acts; and [842b] although constantly in quiescent extinction they extensively transform beings. They demonstrate and enter the path of the auditors while pursuing Buddha-wisdom, they likewise demonstrate heterodox ways and appear as King ***Māra*** and follow worldly [ways] even though they have left the world. During ten ***asaṅkhyeyakalpa***s they practice hundreds of ten-thousands of ***samādhi***s, they adroitly [apply] skillful means to broadcast the treasury of the Teaching[40] [and] all their adornments are complete.[41]

Next are the ***bodhisattva-mahāsattva***s of the immovable stage, who abide in the forbearance of the birthlessness [of constituents].[42] Their essential [grasp of reality] cannot be augmented or diminished[43] and they have cut off all [extraordinary] action.[44] Their minds and mental conditions are calm and quenched, and they are without the signs of body or mind, as if void and empty. For these ***bodhisattva***s neither the Buddha-mind, the ***bodhi***-mind, nor the ***nirvāṇa***-mind arise.[45] Because of their original vow [they possess] all of the Buddha's empowerments,[46] and are able, in a single instant of thought, to give rise to wise acts.[47] [With their] double illumination and equanimity they use the ten powerful wisdoms, and everywhere in unspeakable great thousands of worlds all beings, according to [their type], are universally benefited.[48] During one thousand ***asaṅkhyeyakalpa***s they fulfill hundreds of ten-thousands of great vows. [Their] minds and mental conditions [are constant whether] entering the various destinies or all-knowledge.[49]

39. *Fa wu-pieh* indicates they realize the thusness of constituents. Liang-pi, T 1709 33.506c27–28.

40. Literally, the "Dharma-womb" (*fa-tsang*).

41. "Adornments" (*chuang-yen*) are the various virtues and perfections.

42. This is the intermediate stage of the forbearance of birthlessness.

43. Following Liang-pi's reading of the passage (T 1709 33.507c3–6).

44. Again, following Liang-pi's explanation, in earlier *bhūmis* the bodhisattva must apply vigorous effort, but by the eighth stage all has become "natural" (T 1709 33.507c6–21).

45. In other words, the notion of attaining Buddhahood, and so on, does not even occur at this stage, for the ***bodhisattva-mahāsattva***s are free even of such subtle forms of attachment and striving.

46. "All of the Buddha's empowerments" (*chia-chih*, Sanskrit *adhiṣṭhāna*). Empowerments is sometimes rendered "grace" or "graces," and it indicates both the empowerment to practice and the power to benefit beings. The Sanskrit term *adhiṣṭhāna* is an etymological cousin to the Catholic term *superstitio*, to "over-stand," or to empower by grace. For a more detailed discussion, see *Bukkyō daijiten*, 436b, and Suzuki, *Studies in the Laṅkāvatāra Sūtra*, pp. 202–5.

47. Liang-pi notes that these are acts (*yeh*, karma) that benefit beings (*li-sheng yeh*) (T 1709 33.508b15–16).

48. The bodhisattvas of this stage manifest themselves in forms suitable to the type of being they wish to aid, therefore "according to [their type]."

49. This line is particularly difficult to render and I have tried to follow the sense discussed by Liang-pi (T 1709 33.508c5–8) and that displayed in the fifth-century text (T 245 8.832a26–27).

Next are the ***bodhisattva-mahāsattva***s of the stage of effective intelligence,[50] who abide in the superior stage of the forbearance of the birthlessness [of constituents]. [They have] extinguished the signs of mind and mental conditions and have realized the wisdom which is sovereign and have cut off all obstructions. They use the great spiritual penetrations and cultivate the power of fearlessness, and they excel at being able to guard and protect the Teaching-treasury of all the Buddhas. [They have] attained the unobstructed understanding of the [fundamental nature of] constituents and their [various] meanings,[51] and they discourse upon and expound the Correct Teaching without interruption or exhaustion. In the space of a single ***kṣaṇa*** they are able to enter inexpressible numbers of worlds. In accord with all the questions and difficulties of beings [they utter] the single sound of their comprehension of the ***Śakya*** and universally bring about joy. During ten thousand ***asaṅkhyeyakalpa***s they are able to manifest all the Buddha's spiritual penetrations and powers—as many as hundreds of ten thousands of sands of the ***Gaṅgā***—and the inexhaustable store of the Teaching [brings] benefit, increase, and complete fulfillment.

Next are the ***bodhisattva-mahāsattva***s [of the stage of] the Teaching-cloud, with limitless wisdom, discriminating reflection, and [clear] contemplative perception. From their arousal of the mind of faith though hundreds of ten thousands of ***asaṅkhyeyakalpa***s they have extensively amassed limitless auxiliary disciplines [in order that they might] augment boundless great fortune and wisdom. [They have] realized karmic independence[52] and have cut off hindrances to spiritual penetration. In a moment's thought [they are] able—everywhere in the insignificant and numberless states of the ten directions of hundreds of thousands of ***asaṅkhyeya*** worlds—to know completely all beings' thoughts and activities and roots in the superior, intermediate, and inferior [states, so that they] may discourse on the three vehicles and universally promote the practice of the **[*Prajña*]-*pāramitā*.** Entering the abode of Buddha-action they are strong and without fear and follow the Thus-come One to quiescent extinction where the basis [of consciousness] is reversed.[53]

Good sons! Everything from the initial practice of forbearance to the ada-

50. I am following Buswell, *Formation of Ch'an Ideology in China and Korea*, on the rendering of *shan-hui* as "effectively intelligent" (Sanskrit *sādhumatī*).

51. Liang-pi says that "constituents" here represents the "self-sign" (*tzu-hsiang*, Sanskrit *svalakṣaṇa*) of all things, while their "meanings" represents "all the different signs of constituents" (T 1709 33.509a4–6). In other words, the so-called self-nature of all things is emptiness, while they nonetheless have conventional distinguishing signs or characteristics.

52. Liang-pi explains that "karmic independence" (*yeh-tzu-tsai*) refers to their experience of thusness (T 1709 33.509c12–14).

53. "Where the basis [of consciousness] is reversed" (*chuan-i*, Sanskrit *āśrayapāravṛtti*) refers to relinquishing the defiled seeds remaining in the *ālayavijñāna*, the eighth or "storehouse" consciousness, and thus attaining complete enlightenment.

mantine concentration may be called the conquest of all defilements. The signless forbearance of belief illuminates the supreme truth, extinguishes all defilements, and gives birth to liberating wisdom. Gradually [*bodhisattvas*] subdue and eradicate [defilements], and they use the mind of birth and extinction to attain [what is] beyond birth and extinction. If this mind is extinguished then ignorance is extinguished. None of the knowledge attained before the adamantine concentration may be termed seeing. Only the Buddha's sudden understanding, [842c] the knowledge which is all-knowledge, achieves the name seeing.

Good sons! Adamantine ***samādhi***s manifested before this are in no way comparable to the unequaled [final *samādhi*].[54] It is as if a person ascends a great and lofty platform and thus can see everything—there is nothing this person does not comprehend. Attaining the state of liberation—one signed or signless, without birth and without extinction—is like the edge of reality and so on, it is the same as [the fundamental] nature of constituents. [With a] replete treasury of merit [these beings] abide in the state of the Thus-come [One].

Good sons! In this way all the ***bodhisattva-mahāsattva***s receive and hold, understand and expound [the teaching], and going to all the Buddha-***kṣetra*** of the ten directions, they benefit and pacify living beings and they perceive the signs of reality. They are as I am now, [my] equal without difference.

Good sons! All of the Thus-come [Ones] of the teaching lands of the ten directions have relied on this gate to achieve Buddhahood. Should someone say they have attained Buddhahood in another way, [know] this to be the exposition of **Māra,** not the exposition of the Buddha. Therefore you and the others should likewise know, likewise see, and likewise trust and understand."

At that time, wishing to reiterate the meaning of this proclamation, he pronounced this ***gāthā:***

Self-controlled forbearing ***bodhisattva***s, long nourished in the Buddha Teaching, are firmly established in the thirty minds,[55] and are called nonretrogressing.

First they experience equanimous nature and [they are] born in all the Buddha families, and from the initial attainment of awakening this is termed the joyous stage.

Distancing themselves from impurities, such as wrath, and so on, and all sorts of obstructions, they keep all the prohibitions and are virtuous and pure. This is called the immaculate stage.

54. Liang-pi has an extended note on this, the upshot of which is that previous meditative attainments all pale before the supreme achievement of Buddhahood. See T 1709 33.511a–c.

55. "Thirty minds" refers to the ten sorts of trusting mind (*shih-hsin*), the ten abodes (*shih-chu*), and the ten kinds of supererogation (*shih-hui-hsiang*), discussed above and in Chapter 3 of the study.

Extinguishing obstructions and ignorance and achieving all the concentrations,[56] their illumination is the cause of wisdom's light. This is called the luminous stage.

In the pure ***bodhi*** branches[57] they leave far behind personal and biased views and their wisdom is radiant. This is called the stage of radiant wisdom.

Really understanding all the truths, and the world's every artifice, they bring every sort of benefit to the flock of beings. This is called the invincible stage.

Investigating the teaching of the causes of birth, from ignorance to old age and death, they are able to be profoundly certain. This is called the stage disposed toward enlightenment.

Skilled in means and in ***samādhi*** and manifesting innumerable bodies they excel in responding to the flock of beings. This is called the far-reaching stage.

Abiding in the ocean of signlessness, the empowerment of all the Buddhas masterfully[58] smashes the vehicle of ***Māra.*** This is called the immovable stage.

Attaining the four unobstructed comprehensions, with a single sound [*bodhisattvas*] explain everything, [843a] and those who hear them are overjoyed. This is called the stage of effective intelligence.

Wisdom like a secret cloud, everywhere filling the realm of the Teaching[59] while universally raining down the sweet dew of the Teaching—this is called the stage of the Teaching-cloud.

Complete, [in a] world without outflows,[60] with an always pure, liberated body, quiescent extinction [which is] unthinkable—this is called all-knowledge.

The Buddha told King ***Prasenajit:*** "After my extinction, when the Teaching is about to be extinguished because of the bad karma created by all beings, [this bad karma will] cause every sort of disaster to arise in all the states. All the kings of states and others—the heir apparent, the sons of kings, the empress, and concubines, and all of their retainers, the one hundred officers and the one hundred surnames—should, in order to protect themselves, receive

56. "Concentrations" here is *ch'an-ting*.

57. This does not appear as either one of the seven *bodhyaṅgas* or as one of the thirty-seven *bodhipākṣika dharmas*, thus I take it to refer generally to the seven *bodhyaṅgas* as a group.

58. The term is *tzu-tsai*, which is often translated as self-existent or sovereign, neither of which makes a fluid English translation.

59. The *Dharmadhātu*.

60. Following Liang-pi, T 1709 33.512c25–27.

and keep this ***Prajñāpāramitā,*** [and if they do they will] all attain peace and happiness. I have entrusted this scripture to the kings of states and not to ***bhikṣu***s and ***bhikṣunī***s, ***upāsaka***s and ***upāsikā***s. Why is this? Because nothing but the august strength of kings is able to establish it. Therefore you and the others always should receive and hold, read, recite and expound it.

Great king! The great thousand worlds that I have just transformed [are comprised of] one hundred one hundred hundred thousand ***Sumeru***s and one hundred one hundred hundred thousand suns and moons. Each and every ***Sumeru*** has four continents[61] and this ***Jambhu*** continent [is made up of] sixteen great states, five hundred medium-size states and one hundred thousand small states. If the seven difficulties arise in any of these states, then in order to be rid of the difficulties, all of the kings of these states [should] receive, keep and expound this ***Prajñāpāramitā.*** The seven difficulties will be extinguished forthwith and the states will become peaceful."

King ***Prasenajit*** then asked, "What are these seven difficulties?"[62] The Buddha said, "The first is when the sun and moon lose their appointed courses and the sun's color changes, to white, red, yellow, or black, or when two, three, four, or five suns simultaneously shine; or when the moon's color changes to red or yellow, or when the sun and moon are eclipsed, or circles, one, two, three, four, or five circles appear [around them]. The second is when the stars and asterisms lose their courses, or when comets or [the planets]—Jupiter, Mars, Venus, Mercury, Saturn, and so on—each are transformed or appear during the day. The third is when dragon conflagrations, demon conflagrations, human conflagrations, forest conflagrations, and great conflagrations arise all around and incinerate the myriad things.[63] The fourth is when the seasons are altered and cold and heat are irregular, when in winter there is rain, thunder, and lightning, and when in summer frost, ice, and snow appear. It rains dirt and rock and even boulders,[64] or it hails when it should not and the rains turn red or black, or when rivers overflow, sweeping along stones and floating mountains.

61. The text uses the Chinese term "under-heavens" (*t'ien-hsia*) here.

62. Chi-tsang's discussion of the seven difficulties is also helpful in understanding this list. It is found at T 1707 33.354b22–355c.

63. I have translated *huo* here as "conflagration" in accordance with the sense of Liang-pi's glosses: Dragon fires (*lung-huo*) are thunderous sounds (of rocks? *p'i-li*, see *Daikanwa jiten*, 24530), demon fires (*kuei-huo*) are plagues or epidemics, human fires (*jen-huo*) are when one meets with unfavorable karmic conditions for future rebirths because of wielding supernormal powers for worldly gain, forest fires (literally, "tree fires" [*shu-huo*]), when prolonged drought causes forests to combust (T 1709 33.513c11–14). The fifth-century text has a slightly different list: "demon fires, dragon fires, *deva* fires, mountain-spirit fires, human fires, tree fires, bandit fires" (T 245 8.832c9–10). Obviously, these are not all "fires" in the literal sense of the word. See the complete translation of the fifth-century passage in the appendix.

64. Liang-pi's take on this runs from the straightforward "it rains boulders" to the supranormal "*asura* wars" (T 1709 33.513c23–28). Such phenomena are found during volcanic eruptions.

The fifth is when violent winds arise to obscure the sun and moon, destroy houses, and uproot trees. Stones and boulders fly about. The sixth is when heaven and earth are scorched by excessive heat; ponds dry up, the grass and trees wither and die, and the one hundred grains do not ripen. The seventh is when rebels arise from the four quarters and make raids both inside and outside the borders. Clashes between armies occur and the one hundred surnames perish and die.

[843b] Great king! I will now outline what to do if all these difficulties [arise]—if the sun does not appear during the day and the moon does not appear at night, if in the heavens there are all sorts of calamities, [such as] no clouds, rain, or snow, or if on earth there are all sorts of calamities [such as] landslides and earthquakes or, moreover, if blood flows, demons and spirits manifest themselves, and birds and beasts behave in uncanny ways. [If there are] these sorts of calamities and difficulties without measure and without bounds then, in the case of each and every calamity, all should receive and hold, read, recite, and expound this ***Prajñāpāramitā.***"

As soon as the kings of the sixteen states had heard what the Buddha had said, they were all thoroughly terrified. King ***Prasenajit*** questioned the Buddha, "World-honored One!" Why is it that heaven and earth have these calamities?"

The Buddha said, "Great king, this is because on the ***Jambhu*** continent, in countries and cities great and small, all the people are unfilial to their fathers and mothers and do not revere their teachers and elders. ***Śramaṇa***s and ***Brāhmaṇa***s, kings of states and great officers do not put into practice the Correct Teaching. From these come all evils, [and] difficulties flourish.

"Great king! The ***Prajñāpāramitā*** enables the production of all Buddha-teachings, of all ***bodhisattva*** liberation teachings, of the unsurpassed teachings of all the kings of states, and of the teachings by which all sentient beings are saved. Like a ***maṇi***-gem it possesses a host of virtues and is able to save one from poisonous dragons [and from] all of the evil demons and spirits. [It is able to] satisfy a person's desires.[65] Like the famed wish-fulfilling pearl it is able to respond to the wheel-king's [every wish].[66] It is able to command ***Nanda*** and ***Upananda*** and all the great dragon kings to send down rains and sweet waters to moisten the grasses and trees. It is like a light placed on a high pole in the night illuminating heaven and earth, brilliant as if the sun had come out. This ***Prajñāpāramitā*** is like this! You and all the other kings should make jeweled banners and canopies, burn incense, scatter flowers, and make extensive offerings. Jeweled boxes encasing splendid scriptures should be en-

65. Literally, "a person's mind."
66. Following Liang-pi, T 1709 33.515a22–23.

sconced on jeweled tables. When you wish to travel always have [the scripture] in front of you. Whenever you stop erect seven jeweled tents and assemble jewels [to form a table] upon which to set the scripture. [You] should present every sort of offering, as though serving your father and mother, as though all the gods were serving ***Śakra.***[67]

"Great king! I can see [that in] all the states, all human kings[68] have attained [the status of] emperor or king entirely because in the past they served five hundred Buddhas with reverential offerings. And all those sages who have attained the fruit of the Way have come to be born in this state to produce great blessings and benefit. But if the king's felicity is exhausted in a time when there is no Way, and the sages have abandoned him, then calamities, difficulties, and strife arise.

"Great king! I will command the ***bodhisattva-mahāsatva***s of the five directions to assemble and go to protect any state wherever and whenever in the future the kings of states establish the Correct Teaching and protect the Three-Jewels.

"[From the] East, Chin-kang-shou[69] ***bodhisattva-mahāsattva,*** [his] hand grasping a diamond-cudgel and shedding green light, together with four hundred thousand ***bodhisattva***s will go to protect that state.

"[From the] South, Chin-kang-pao[70] ***bodhisattva-mahāsattva,*** [his] hand grasping a diamond-***maṇi*** and [843c] shedding a sunlight-colored light, together with four hundred thousand ***bodhisattva***s will go to protect that state.

"[From the] West, Chin-kang-li[71] ***bodhisattva-mahāsattva,*** [his] hand grasping a diamond-sword and shedding golden light, together with four hundred thousand ***bodhisattva***s will go to protect that state.

"[From the] North, Chin-kang-***yakṣa***[72] ***bodhisattva-mahāsattva,*** [his] hand grasping a diamond-bell and shedding a ***vaiḍūrya*** light, together with four thousand ***yakṣa***s will go to protect that state.

"[From the] Center, Chin-kang-***pāramitā***[73] ***bodhisattva-mahāsattva,*** grasping a diamond-discus and shedding a five-colored light, together with four thousand ***bodhisattva***s will go to protect that state.

"These five ***bodhisattva-mahāsattva***s, each with their seemingly countless great hoard, will produce great benefit in your states. You should set up their images and make offerings to them."

67. The fifth-century text goes into greater detail concerning the dimensions of various ritual apparatus. See Appendix A.

68. *Jen*[c]*-wang.*

69. Adamantine-hand, Sanskrit Vajrapāṇi.

70. Adamantine-jewel, Sanskrit Vajraratna.

71. Adamantine boon, Sanskrit Vajratikṣṇa.

72. Adamantine-*yakṣa,* Sanskrit Vajrayakṣa.

73. Adamantine-*pāramitā,* Sanskrit Vajrapāramitā.

At that time, Chin-kang-shou ***bodhisattva-mahāsattva*** and the others forthwith rose from their seats, prostrated themselves at the Buddha's feet, stepped to one side and said to the Buddha: "World-honored One. Because of our original vows we have received the Buddha's spiritual power. If in all the states of the worlds of the ten directions, there is a place where this scripture is received and held, read, recited, and expounded, then I and the others go there in an instant, to guard and protect the Correct Teaching or to establish the Correct Teaching. We will ensure that these states are devoid of all the calamities and difficulties. Swords, troops, and epidemics all will be entirely eliminated.

World-honored One! I possess a ***dhāraṇī*** which can [afford one] wondrous protection. It is the speedy gate[74] originally cultivated and practiced by all the Buddhas. Should a person manage to hear this single scripture, all his crimes and obstructions will be completely eliminated. How much more benefit will it produce if it is recited and practiced! By using the august power of the Teaching, one may cause states to be eternally without the host of difficulties." Then, before the Buddha and in unison,[75] they pronounced this ***dhāraṇī:***

> Namo ratna-trayāya, nama ārya-vairocanāya tathāgatāyarhate saṃyak-sambuddhāya, nama ārya-samanta-bhadrāya bodhisattvāya mahāsattvāya mahākaruṇikāya, tad yathā: jñāna-pradīpe akṣaya-kośe pratibhānavati sarva-buddhāvalokite yoga-pariniṣpanne gambhīra-duravagāhe try-adhva-pariniṣpanne bodhi-citta-saṃjānāni [844a] sarvābhiṣekābhiṣikte dharma-sāgara-sambhūti amogha-śravaṇe mahā-samanta-bhadra-bhūmi-niryāte vyākaraṇa-pariprāptāni sarva-siddha-namaskṛte sarva-bodhi-sattva-samjānāni bhagavati-buddhamāte araṇe akarane araṇakaraṇe mahā-prajñā-pāramite svāhā![76]

At that time the World-honored One heard this pronouncement and praised Chin-kang-shou and the other ***bodhisattva***s, saying, "Excellent! Excellent! If there are those who recite and hold this ***dhāraṇī,*** I and all the Buddhas of the ten directions will always be supportive and protective [of them], and all of the evil demons and spirits[77] will venerate them like Buddhas and in not a long time they should attain ***anuttarasaṃyaksambodhi.***

"Great king! I take this scripture and bestow it upon you and the others,

74. Liang-pi's commentary indicates that "speedy" *su-chih* modifies "gate" (T 1709 33.516c18–19).

75. Literally, "with different mouths and the same sound" (*i-k'ou t'ung-yin*).

76. I have rendered the *dhāraṇī* in Sanskrit since it does not appear in the fifth-century text and since this *dhāraṇī* was likely written by Pu-k'ung, who knew Sanskrit. Hatta Yukio has reconstructed the *dhāraṇī*. See *Shingon jiten*, 246.4.

77. Amending the text as suggested in the notes and in Liang-pi's commentary (T 1709 33.519c12).

Vaiśālī, Kośala, Śrāvastī, Magadha, Vārāṇasī, Kapilavastu, Kuśinagara, Kauśāmbī, Pañcāla, Pāṭaliputra, Mathurā, Uṣa, Puṇyavardhāra, Devāvatāra, Kāśī, Campā, and likewise [to all of] the kings of states and so on. All should receive and hold this ***Prajñāpāramitā.***"

At that time when all the great assembly of ***asura***s and others heard what the Buddha said concerning all the calamities and disasters, the hair of their bodies stood on end and they let out a loud cry, saying, "I hope that in the future I will not be born in those states." And at that time the sixteen kings abandoned their kingships and established themselves in the cultivation of the Way of renunciation, possessed of the eight conquering faculties and the ten universal faculties; and they attained the forbearance of self-control, the forbearance of [firm] belief, and the forbearance of the birthlessness of constituents.

At that time all of the gods, humans, and the great assembly of ***asuras,*** and so on scattered ***mandāra*** flowers, ***mañjūṣha*** flowers, ***vārṣika*** flowers and ***sumanā*** flowers as offerings to the Buddha. In accordance with their lineage they attained the three gates of liberation. [They realized that] production is empty, that constituents are empty [and they achieved] the [seven] divisions of ***bodhi*** [illumination].[78] Innumerable and countless ***bodhisattva-mahāsattva***s scattered ***kumunda*** flowers, and ***padma*** flowers as an offering to the Buddha. [As a result] countless ***samādhi***s were displayed before them, and they attained the forbearance of obedience and the forbearance of the birthlessness of constituents. Countless and innumerable ***bodhisattva-mahāsattva***s—as many as the sands of the ***Gaṅgā***—attained [844b] the gate of all ***samādhi***s. They comprehended entirely without obstruction the supreme [truth], the worldly [truth], and equanimity. And always arousing great compassion, [they] greatly benefit living beings in countless millions of hundreds of thousands of ***asaṅkhyeya*** worlds, and in the present life they became Buddhas.

78. The text seems corrupt here.

8

The Charge

[844b] The Buddha told King ***Prasenajit,*** "Now let me caution you and the others. After my extinction the Correct Teaching will be on the point of extinction. After fifty years, after five-hundred years, and after five thousand years there will be no Buddha, Teaching, or Community, and this scripture and the three jewels will be entrusted to all the kings of states to establish and protect.[1] [They should] command all my disciples of the four categories and so on to receive and hold, read, recite, and expound its meaning and principles, and to broadcast its essentials to all beings and cause them to cultivate it in order that they may depart from birth and death.

Great king, after the world [has undergone] the five turbulent eras,[2] all the

1. The eighth-century text departs here from the fifth-century text. Pu-k'ung cites the time periods until the decline in the commonly found multiples of five and ten rather than in multiples of eight as in the fifth-century text. For comparison, see T 245 8.833b13–14 and Appendix A.

2. The "five turbulent eras" (*wu-tu-shih*, Sanskrit *pañcakaṣāyah*) are events that signal the decay of the universe. See *Bukkyō daijiten*, 18a, 1259b–1261a.

kings of states, the heirs apparent, and great officers will turn haughty, [hold themselves in] great esteem, and smash and extinguish my teaching. Openly[3] making laws to control my disciples—the ***bhikṣu*** and ***bhikṣunī***—they will not permit people to leave the family to cultivate and practice the correct Way, and further they will not permit people to make Buddhist ***stūpas*** and images. White-robed [lay people will occupy the] lofty seats [reserved for clergy], while ***bhikṣu***s will stand on the ground. There is no difference between [such laws and] the laws [governing] soldiers, slaves, and so forth.[4] You should know that at that time the extinction of the Teaching will not be long [off].

Great king, all of the causes of the destruction of states are of your own making: [Trusting in] your awesome power you regulate the four-fold assembly and will not permit the cultivation of blessings. All the evil ***bhikṣu***s receive preferential treatment,[5] while ***bhikṣu***s wise and learned in the Teaching single-mindedly befriend one another and hold vegetarian feasts to seek blessings.[6] These heterodox rules are all contrary to my teaching. Thus, the one hundred surnames sicken [and face] limitless sufferings and difficulties. You should know that at that time the state will be destroyed. Great king, at the time of the Teaching's final era,[7] everyone—kings of states, the great officers, and the four classes of disciples—will act contrary to the Teaching and in contravention of Buddhist teaching. They will commit every transgression and, contrary to the Teaching and to the Discipline, bind monks and imprison them. [By this you] will know that the extinction of the Teaching is not long [off].

Great king! After my extinction the four classes of disciples, all the kings of states, the princes, and the one hundred officers and those appointed to hold and protect the Three Jewels will themselves destroy [the Teaching] as worms in a lion's body consume his own flesh.[8] [And these] are not the heterodox [teachers]! Those who ruin my Teaching acquire [the karma of a] great transgression. When the Correct Teaching decays and weakens, the people are

3. *Ming* here means "openly" or "brazenly." I owe this suggestion to Victor Mair.

4. The tone of this chapter in the fifth-century text is much harsher. The version of this passage in the fifth-century text makes it absolutely clear that "soldiers and slaves are made ***bhikṣu***." See T 245 8.833b19–25, the translation of the passage in Appendix A, and Chapters 3 and 4 of the study.

5. *Shou pieh-ch'ing*, literally, "individual invitations." The Dharmagupta Vinaya allows both direct individual donations and donations mediated through the head of the sangha. Other vinayas consider individual invitations a violation of the discipline. See *Bukkyō daijiten*, 4521c, and "Bessho," *Hōbōgirin*, 1:66a–b.

6. The line seems to mean that all the "wise" monks concern themselves with is the cultivation of their own merit.

7. The syntax is "teaching's final era" (*fa-mo shih*), rather than the more common "end teaching" (*mo-fa*).

8. Liang-pi's commentary makes it quite clear that the lion does not eat his own flesh but that worms born of the lion's body eat his flesh, which no other creature will dare to touch (T 1709 33.521c22–26). The image is obviously one of internal corruption.

bereft of proper conduct. Every evil will gradually increase and [the people's] fortunes will be diminished day by day. No longer will there be filial sons, and the six relationships[9] will be discordant. The heavenly dragons will not defend [them], and evil demons and evil dragons[10] will become more injurious day by day. Calamities and monstrosities will intertwine, causing misfortunes to multiply.[11] As is fitting, they will fall into hell or be born as hungry ghosts, and [even] if they should attain human birth, they will be poor and mean, or be victimized by bandits, and all their [good karmic] roots will be insufficient. It is just like a shadow [844c] that follows a form, like an echo that follows a sound, and like a person reading at night, when the fire is extinguished the words [in the book] remain[12]—the fruit of ruining the Teaching is like this![13]

Great king! In generations to come, all the kings of states, the princes, the great officers, together with my disciples, will perversely establish registration [of monks] and institute overseers, and great and small monastic directors,[14] contravening the principle [forbidding] employment [of monks] as lackeys. Then you should know that at that time the Buddhist Teaching has not long [to survive].

Great king! In generations to come all the kings of states and the four classes of disciples should rely on all the Buddhas of the ten directions and [should] constantly practice the Way, establish and disseminate it. And evil monks seeking fame and profit will not rely on my Teaching, and they will go before the kings of states and will themselves utter transgressions and evil, becoming the cause of the destruction of the Teaching. These kings will not distinguish [between the good and evil monks], and trusting and accepting these sayings they will perversely establish regulation [of monastic communities rather than] rely on the Buddhist prohibitions. You should know that at that time the extinction of the Teaching is not long [off].

Great king! In generations to come the kings of states, the great officers, and the four classes of disciples will themselves cause the destruction of the Teaching and the destruction of the state. They themselves will suffer from this, and

9. The "six relationships" are those stipulated in the Confucian teachings between father and son, elder and younger brother, and husband and wife.

10. Liang-pi glosses "evil demons" (*o-kuei*) and "evil dragons" (*o-lung*) as epidemics and natural disasters (T 1709 33.522a9–13).

11. Literally, vertical and horizontal, criss-cross, or, as Liang-pi puts it, "from the four directions there are disasters" (T 1709 33.522a12).

12. A somewhat tortured phrase, but the commentaries are clear that the image is one related to *vāsanā* or the preservation of latent karmic seeds that lead to further rebirth. See Liang-pi, T 1709 33.522a21–27.

13. I emend the text adding a *shih* in accord with the Sung, Yüan, and Ming editions, thus translating the phrase *i fu ju shih* emphatically.

14. *Seng-t'ung.*

it is not the Buddhist Teaching that is to blame. The heavenly dragons will depart, the five turbidities will in turn increase. A full discussion of this would exhaust a ***kalpa*** and would still be unfinished.

As soon as the kings of the sixteen great states heard the exposition [concerning] what was to come and all such warnings, the sound of their pitiful wailing and crying shook the three thousand [worlds]. Heaven and earth were darkened and no light shone. Then, all the kings and the others, each and every one, resolved to receive and keep the Buddha's words and [to forgo] regulation of the four classes [of disciples who] leave home to study the Way. This is in accordance with the Buddha's Teaching.

At that time these assemblies—numberless as the sands of the ***Gaṅgā***—collectively sighed, and said, "It would be fitting that at such a time the world would be empty, a world bereft of Buddhas."

Then King ***Prasenajit*** queried the Buddha: "World-honored One, what should we call this scripture? How am I and the others to receive and keep it?" The Buddha said, "Great king! This scripture is called the ***Prajñāpāramitā*** for Humane Kings Who Wish to Protect Their States. It may also be called the Sweet Dew Teaching Medicine [because] it is like a remedy whose action is able to allay all illness.

"Great king! The merit of this ***Prajñāpāramitā*** is like the void, it cannot be fathomed. If you receive and keep, read, and recite it, the merit obtained will be able to protect Humane Kings and even all beings, like walls, yea, like the walls of a city. Therefore you and the others should receive and keep it."

When the Buddha had finished expounding this scripture, Maitreya, Lion-roarer, and the rest of all the countless ***bodhisattva-mahāsattva***s, ***Śāriputra, Subhūti,*** and the rest, the limitless auditors, and the numberless gods and men of the desire realm, the form realm, and the formless realm, the ***bhikṣu***s and ***bhikṣunī***s, the ***upāsaka***s and ***upāsikā***s, the ***asura***s—all of the great assemblies—heard what the Buddha had said, and all with great joy faithfully accepted and received [it, and put it into] practice.

Appendix A

Major Variants from the Fifth-Century Scripture (T 245)

The eighth-century version of the *Scripture for Humane Kings* I have translated follows closely the fifth-century version in all but a few places. At least half of these texts are identical word for word; for about another 35 or 40 percent, the eighth-century text merely updates or paraphrases the language of the fifth-century version. I have discussed the linguistic details in Chapters 3, 4, and 5 of the study. There are, however, some significant differences between the two recensions. As a product of the esoteric school, the eighth-century version adds a long *dhāraṇī*. It also regularizes the unusual names of the various stages of the path found in the fifth-century text. On the other hand, the eighth-century text leaves out or recasts certain passages that were key to the success of the text in the fifth-century, but which were viewed by Pu-k'ung in the eighth century as aberrant, mistaken, or outmoded.

The Prologue

As noted above in the translation of the prologue of the text there are some differences in the specifics of the various assemblies gathered for the preaching of the *Scripture for Humane Kings*, but most of these are minor. The passage in which Prasenajit and others question the preaching of a new Transcendent Wisdom scripture is, however, important for historical and contextual reasons:

The doubts concerning this scripture are expressed differently.

> The World-honored One, possessing the four fearlessnesses, the eighteen unique characteristics of a Buddha, and the body of the Teaching with its five kinds of vision, has already, in the twenty-ninth year [of his ministry], expounded, on behalf of me and the great assembly, the

> ***Mahāprajñāpāramitā,*** the *Adamantine-**prajñāpāramitā,*** the *Celestial King's Inquiry Concerning the **Prajñāpāramitā*** and the *Brilliant Praise **Prajñāpāramitā,*** so why has the Thus-come One shone forth this great light?"[1] At that time, the lord of ***Śrāvastī,*** King ***Prasenajit,*** who was called "Moonlight," was among the sixteen kings of great states.[2] His meritorious practices [included] the ten stages, the six perfections, the thirty-seven parts [of the Way], and the four objects of unimpeachable purity; and he practiced the ***Mahāyāna.*** (825b20–26)

A different set of bodhisattvas is invoked at the end of the first chapter of the fifth-century version of the text.

> In the Buddha-states [*fo-kuo*] of the other directions [were]: From the South Fa-tsai[3] ***bodhisattva*** together with a great assembly [numbering] five million ***koṭī*** all came hither and entered this great assembly. From the east Pao-chu[4] ***bodhisattva*** together with a great assembly [numbering] nine million ***koṭī*** all came hither and entered this great assembly. From the north Hsu-k'ung-hsing[5] ***bodhisattva*** together with a great assembly [numbering] ten trillion ***koṭī*** all came hither and entered this great assembly. From the west Shan-chu[6] ***bodhisattva*** together with a great assembly [numbering] ten times the sands of the ***Gaṅgā*** came hither and entered this great assembly. (825c2–7)

Chapter 2: Contemplating Emptiness

Aside from its different title and slightly different phrasing there are only a few divergences worth noting. These include the list of "emptinesses" and the use of the idiom "flavor" (*wei*).

1. Chi-tsang's commentary makes it clear that we are talking about the twenty-ninth year, not a period of twenty-nine years (T 1707 33.322a21–23). He considers the text listed here at 314c24–26. The interest in precisely when a text was preached (this supposedly in the thirtieth year) may indicate Chinese interests that emerge as schemes of "dividing the teachings" (*p'an-chiao*) according to when in the career of Śākyamuni they were preached.

2. "Prince Moonlight" (*yüeh-kuang wang*) was an important figure in apocalyptic movements during the Six Dynasties period. According to some legends he was born on the same day as the Buddha and was named "moon" in contrast to the Buddha as "sun." See the T'ang T'ien-t'ai commentary (T 1705 33.264b26–27) and Zürcher's "Prince Moonlight."

3. His name translates as "Dharma-ability."

4. "Jeweled-pillar."

5. "Emptiness nature."

6. "Excellent abode."

> All constituents are empty. Empty inside, empty outside, empty inside and outside, action is empty, nonaction is empty, beginninglessness is empty, the [self-]nature is empty, the [truth of the] supreme meaning is empty, ***prajñāpāramitā*** is empty, the cause is empty, the Buddha-fruit is empty, and the emptiness of emptiness is therefore empty, and therefore, collections of constituents exist. (826a12–15)[7]

> Great king, the renowned flavor of this scripture's sentences [is identical with] the renowned flavor of the sentences preached by hundreds of Buddhas, thousands of Buddhas, tens of hundreds of ten-thousands of Buddhas. (826a24–25)

Chapter 3: *Bodhisattva* Teachings and Transformations

The overall outline of the path found in chapters 3 and 7 of the fifth-century text is very much like that of the eighth-century text. Like the eighth-century text, it has the three lineages[8] combined with the ten abodes and other preparatory levels leading up to the ten stages of the bodhisattva path. However, the names of the bodhisattva stages are unique, and the path is merely sketched out in chapter 3. The path is more systematically presented in chapter 7. Indeed, one wonders why the outline of the path is repeated as it is (four times in the fifth-century text—once each in prose in chapters 3 and 7, once in the *gāthā* in chapter 3, and once in the hierarchy of kings in chapter 3—and five times in the eighth-century version—once each in prose in chapters 3 and 7, once each in the *gāthās* in chapters 3 and 7, and once in the hierarchy of kings in chapter 3). What follows is a long excerpt of the path in the prose of chapter 3 of the fifth-century *Scripture for Humane Kings*.

> The Buddha said, "Great King, the five forbearances are the ***bodhisattva*** teachings: forbearance of self-control [*fu-jen*], [in] superior, intermediate, and inferior [levels], forbearance of [firm] belief [*hsin-jen*], [in] superior, intermediate, and inferior [levels], forbearance of obedi-

7. Chi-tsang glosses all of these terms at T 1707 33.326a22–b16. For example, "The words 'empty inside' mean that within the six *āyatana* there is no spirit of self."

8. The T'ang dynasty T'ien-t'ai commentary examines the differences between the three-lineage scheme of the *Scripture for Humane Kings* and the six-lineage scheme of the *P'u-sa pen-yeh ying-lo ching*. The first three of these six are identical to the three lineages of the *Scripture for Humane Kings*. These are supplemented by the "lineage of the sages" (*sheng chung-hsing*), the "lineage of equal-[minded] enlightenment" (*teng-chüeh hsing*), and the "lineage of excellent-enlightenment" (*miao-chüeh hsing*). Neither these nor the five forbearances of the *Ying-lo* entirely match up. See T 1705 33.269b18–21.

ence [*hsün-jen*], [in] superior, intermediate, and inferior [levels], forbearance of the birthlessness [of constituents in] [*wu-sheng-jen*] superior, intermediate, and inferior [levels], and forbearance of quiescent extinction [*chi-mieh-jen*], [in] superior and inferior [levels]. These are what are called the cultivation of the ***Prajñāpāramitā*** by all Buddhas and ***bodhisattva***s. Good sons, initially arousing the signs of trust, beings [numerous as] the sands of the **Gaṅgā** cultivate the forbearance of self-control, and before the three jewels they produce the ten minds of the acquired lineage.[9] [The ten minds are now listed, as in T 246.] Having accomplished this ***bodhisattva***s are able, within a limited scope, to transform beings [and they have] transcended the two vehicles and all the good stages. All Buddhas and ***bodhisattva***s have cultivated the ten minds, which are the womb of the sages.

"Next [they] arouse the dry wisdom[10] of the innate lineage [already] possessed of the ten minds. That is, the four-fold mental stopping,[11] [viz. that the] body, feelings, mind, and constituents are impure, painful, impermanent, and selfless. The three-fold mental stopping,[12] that is the three eras: forbearance concerning past causes, forbearance concerning present causes and fruits, and forbearance concerning future fruit. These ***bodhisattva***s, moreover, are able to transform all beings, and they are already able to transcend the view of self and of beings and other such thoughts, and even heterodox and inverted thoughts are unable to ruin them.

"Next there are the ten stages of the lineage of the Way. These contemplate form, intellect, mind, feelings, and actions and attain the forbearance of discipline, the forbearance of view, the forbearance of fixed [concentration], the forbearance of wisdom, and the forbearance of liberation. [They] contemplate the causes and fruits of the triple world [and attain] the forbearance of emptiness, the forbearance of wishlessness, the forbearance of signlessness, and contemplate the two truths and the voidness of reality. [Knowing that] all constituents are impermanent is called the forbearance of impermanence. [Knowing that] all constituents are empty [they] attain the forbearance of birthlessness. These ***bodhisattva***s of the ten firm minds are wheel-turning

9. *Hsing-chung-hsing*, Sanskrit *samudānīta gotra*, the "family" or "lineage" which is the result of the practice of good roots. This is not an "inborn" nature, but one resulting from action. See the discussion in Chapters 3 and 4 of the study.

10. "Dry wisdom" (*kan-hui*, Pali *sukha-vipassanā*) tends to indicate one who has attained certain meditative insight but who has not attained the five penetrations (Pāli, *abhiññā*). For a discussion of the term, see Katz, *Buddhist Images of Human Perfection*, pp. 78–83, and Chi-tsang, T 1707 329b5–12.

11. *Ssu-i-chih*.

12. *San-i-chih*.

kings, and moreover, [they] are able to transform the four [continents of the] world and produce the good roots of all beings.

"Moreover, the ***bodhisattvas*** of the forbearance of [firm] belief are referred to as effective illumination],[13] [abandoning] success,[14] and brilliant [wisdom].[15] Those practicing in [these ranks] cut off bondage to the material defilements of the triple world. . . . From the state of effective [enlightenment] to the arrival in ***sarvajña*** these ***bodhisattvas*** use these fifteen minds as the fundamental seeds of all the practices.

"In addition the ***bodhisattvas*** of the forbearance of obedience are those referred to as [blazing] wisdom,[16] victorious [wisdom],[17] and teaching manifests,[18] because they are able to cut off bondage to the mental and other defilements of the triple world. Manifesting a single body in the Buddha states of the ten directions, their limitless and inexpressible spiritual penetrations transform beings.

"In addition the ***bodhisattvas*** of the forbearance of the birthlessness [of constituents] are those referred to as far-[reaching,][19] immovable,[20] and discerning wisdom[21] because they are able to cut off the seeds of the mental and physical and other defilements. They manifest unexpressible spiritual penetrations.

"Next are the ***bodhisattvas*** of the forbearance of quiescent extinction. Buddhas and ***bodhisattvas*** alike use this forbearance to enter the adamantine ***samādhi.*** [Those] in the inferior forbearance are called ***bodhisattva.*** [Those] coursing in the superior forbearance are called ***sarvajña.*** Together they contemplate the truth of the supreme meaning and they have cut off the triple world's mental imprints of ignorance. Having exhausted signs, they are adamantine; having exhausted both signs and the signless, they are ***sarvajña.*** Transcending the worldly truth and the truth of the preeminent meaning, they are at the eleventh stage of ***sarvajña*** awakening. Not existent, not nonexistent, pro-

13. *Shan-[chüeh].*

14. *Li-[ta].*

15. *Ming-[hui].*

16. *Yen-hui*, "blazing wisdom," is the term used for this stage in the *gāthā* later in this chapter and in the seventh chapter, but here the text has *chien*, "seeing."

17. *Sheng-[hui].*

18. *Hsien-fa* is used in the *gāthā* later in the third chapter and in the seventh chapter; here it is *fa-hsien*.

19. *Yüan-[ta].*

20. *Pu-tung* is the same as the eighth stage in the later recension, but in the *gāthā* later in the third chapter and in chapter 7 of the fifth-century version, the stage is listed as "equable discernment," *teng-kuan* or *teng-chüeh*.

21. *Hui-kuang* or "wisdom's light" is the way this stage is listed in the *gāthā* later in chapter 3 and again in chapter 7. Here it appears as "discerning wisdom" (*kuan-hui*).

> foundly pure and calm, forever abiding in the unchanging, they are identical with the edge of reality and the nature of constituents. Their causeless great compassion teaches and transforms all beings, and mounting the vehicle of ***sarvajña,*** they come to transform the triple world." (8.826b21–c28)

> "Great King, I have always said that all beings who cut off the fruit of the defilements of the triple world, [and who do it] completely, are called Buddhas. [When] the self-nature is pure, it is called awaking to ***sarvajña.*** The basic karma of all beings is the basic karma of all Buddhas and ***bodhisattva***s, and it is that which they cultivated in the five forbearances and that [which] the fourteen forbearances bring to completion." [Prasenajit] asked the Buddha, "How does the ***bodhisattva***'s basic karma purify and transform beings?" The Buddha said, "From the first stage up to the last stage, from the place where one practices for oneself to the place of the practice of a Buddha is because of all-knowledge. As for these basic acts, if a ***bodhisattva*** abides in one hundred Buddha-lands. . . . (8.827a4–9)[22]

Chapter Four: The Two Truths

Chapter 4 contains two areas in which it differs from the eighth-century recension of the text. First, it contains an important passage on the Three Truths (rather than the Two Truths—another is found in chapter 7). Second, it contains a passage on the name of the scripture (829c16–21), which appears at the end of chapter 8 (844c19–25) in the eighth-century recension of the text.

The fifth-century scripture specifies *three* truths: vulgar or worldly truth (*su-shih-ti*), "ultimate truth" (*chen-ti*) and "truth of the preeminent meaning" (*ti-i i ti*). This "three truths" formulation becomes the *locus classicus* for the development of Chih-i's T'ien-t'ai doctrine of the Three Truths. Pu-k'ung's recension of the scripture expunges most references to the "truth of the preeminent meaning" and all references to the "Three Truths," and in all instances substitutes "supreme truth" (*sheng-i ti*). Similarly, the "teaching gate" passage in chapter 4 of the fifth-century version reads, "not one, not two, not limitless," while the eighth-century version says, "not one, not limitless."

> If a ***bodhisattva*** sees beings, sees one or sees two, then he does not see one and does not see two. This one and two is the truth of the preemi-

22. Chi-tsang discusses the way that kings transform their lands at T 1707 334a4–16 and 335a7–8.

nent meaning [*ti-i-i ti*]. Great king, if there is existence or non-existence [*jo yu jo wu*] then this is worldly truth. [One can] use three truths to embrace all the constituents: the truth of emptiness, the truth of form, and the truth of mind. I have preached that all constituents do not transcend the three truths. Personalist views and the five aggregates are empty and indeed, all constituents are empty. (829b26–c1)[23]

Chapter 5: Protecting the State

There are two departures of note in this chapter. The first is what appears to be a title for the scripture in the story of King P'u-ming (830b19–20): "Everyone should all chant the ***gāthā*** of the seven Buddhas of the past which appears in the *Humane Kings Inquiry* ***Prajñāpāramitā*** *Scripture*." The eighth-century version reads: "The humane [kings] have arrived at the time of their fate. All of us should chant and hold the ***gāthā*** of the ***Prajñāpāramitā*** pronounced by former Buddhas" (840b28–c1).

The second departure is that the *gāthā* of the fifth-century version contains important differences in wording from that of the eighth-century version. What follows is the fifth-century *gāthā:*

In the fires of the ***kalpa***'s end *ch'ien* and *k'un*[24] are thoroughly incinerated,
Sumeru and its great oceans are all reduced to ashes
The fortune of the heavenly dragons[25] is exhausted and in their midst[26] all is withered and dead.
The two virtues[27] have even perished, how can the state endure?

23. Chi-tsang comments: "The master Tripitaka said, 'The basic nature of all constituents is the truth of emptiness. Common people take outward form and regard it as reality, and this is called the truth of form. People in the three vehicles who are cultivating the way are without mental outflows, and this is called the truth of mind.' If we discuss birth and death, and nirvana, each has three truths. The three truths of birth and death: gods, humans, and the four great elements are the truth of form. The eight cognitions are the truth of mind, and transcending birth and death without nirvana is the truth of emptiness. The three truths of nirvana: the real form of gods and humans is the truth of form. The two minds of reality are called the truth of mind, and being without birth and death's four inverted views is called the truth of emptiness" (T 1707 33.343a2–8). The passage is, of course, the *locus classicus* of the T'ien-t'ai schools teaching of the three truths and the T'ang dynasty commentary attributed to Chih-i has a discussion of this at T 1705 279c13–21.

24. *Ch'ien* and *k'un* are heaven and earth respectively, the first two hexagrams of the *I-ching*. This and the "two virtues" (*erh-yi*) mentioned in the next stanza are further evidence for Chinese composition of the scripture.

25. "Heavenly dragons" (*t'ien-lung*) can refer simultaneously to emperors and to dragons.

26. It is possible to construe this as "in the middle" or even "in the Middle [Kingdom]," i.e., China.

27. The "two virtues" (*liang-i*) refers to the two primordial dimensions of *yin* and *yang* in the language of the *I-ching* or *Scripture of Changes*. Chi-ts'ang discusses these without so much as batting an eyelash.

Birth, old age, sickness, and death wheel around without interruption, affairs crowd in [on us][28] and we wish to flee, grief and pity do us harm.
Desire is deep and calamities are heavy, and our ulcers and illnesses are without external [cause].[29]
All in the triple world involves suffering, what can the state rely upon?
Existence is based on nonexistence and causality gives rise to all. What flourishes must decline and that which is real must be empty.
Beings wiggle about [but] all are like illusions, like echos, completely empty. The state is also like this.
Consciousness and spirit [*chih shen*] are without form [*hsing*], falsehood mounts the four elements[30] and ignorance embraces and nurtures them[31] and makes of them a pleasure vehicle.
Form has no constant ruler and the spirit has no constant home. Form and spirit inevitably depart, surely the existence of the state [is no different]. (830b5–15)

Chapter Six: Scattering Flowers

The eighth- and the fifth-century texts of this chapter are quite similar, though the "lion roused to anger" (*shih-tzu fen-hsün*) has replaced the "Lion howl" (*shih-tzu hou*) of the fifth-century text.

Chapter Seven: Receiving and Keeping [This Scripture]

Chapter 7 of the fifth-century text lacks the long summary *gāthā* of the path found in the eighth-century text. It is also more detailed in its ritual instructions, it has a different set of "protectors," and it includes an interesting passage on the "three truths ***samādhi.***"

The eighth-century recension of the *Scripture for Humane Kings* at this point follows the fifth-century text in repeating the bodhisattva path. This accounting of the path (831a29–832b17) uses the unusual terms for the ten stages we met in chapter 3; however, this presentation is both more systematic and more

28. My reading is tentative.

29. Following Chi-tsang's reading of the passage (T 1707 33.346a2–3).

30. Sung, Ming, and Yüan editions as well as Chi-tsang's commentary all amend the text to read "four snakes" (*ssu-she*), and Chi-tsang glosses this as referring to the four elements. Pu-k'ung's eighth-century recension simply says the four elements (*ssu-ta*).

31. I have amended the text in accordance with Sung, Yüan, and Ming editions.

extended than that of chapter 3 and looks a great deal like the presentations of the path made in the eighth-century version of the text (841b3–842b25). Of note, however, is the complete lack of a summary *gāthā* following the prose description of the path. The *gāthā* that appears in the eighth-century text appears to have been created *de novo* by Pu-k'ung (842c11–843a5).

The description of the "seven difficulties" in the two versions are different. Here is the fifth-century version:

> "Great king! As for the one hundred *koṭī* of *Sumerus* and one hundred *koṭi* of suns and moons, the transformations of which I have just [shown you], each and every *Sumeru* has four continents.[32] This southern *Jambhu* continent [is made up of] sixteen great states, five hundred medium-size states, and one hundred thousand small states, and in these states there are seven [sorts of] difficulties. It is because of these difficulties that all of the kings states should expound and recite the *Prajñāpāramitā*. [When they do so] the seven difficulties forthwith will be extinguished, and the seven felicities straightaway will be produced. The myriad people will be tranquil and the emperor will be joyous."
>
> [King Prasenajit then asked,] "What are these seven difficulties?" [The Buddha said, "If] the sun and moon lose their appointed courses or a red sun or a black sun comes out, or two, three, four, or five suns simultaneously shine or the sun is eclipsed and does not shine, or halos surround the sun, one, two, three, four or five halos appear. At times of such wonders [you should] recite this scripture. These constitute the first difficulty.
>
> "[If] the twenty-eight mansions lose their courses, or Venus,[33] the Yama star,[34] the Wheel star,[35] the Demon star,[36] Mars,[37] Mercury,[38] the

32. The text uses the Chinese term "under-heavens" (*t'ien-hsia*) here.

33. According to Chi-tsang's commentary, if the movements of Venus are regular there is plenty, if it loses its regular movement times will be lean (*Jen-wang-po-jo ching su*, T 1707 33.355a).

34. The text reads *hui-hsing*, which Chi-tsang glosses as "Yama star," (*yen-lo hsing*). He adds that when this star shines, disasters inevitably follow (T 1707 33.355a).

35. According to Chi-tsang, *lun-hsing* is when a brilliant "wheel" appears in the sky; and if the sun, moon, or five planets are in the middle of this wheel, the state will be destroyed. If they move to the right of the wheel, then the state will be at peace. If to the left of the wheel, it is not auspicious (T 1707 33.355a).

36. Chi-tsang notes that the *kuei-hsing* is found in the northeast on the fifteenth day of the ninth month. If it is too close and high (bright?) specters and spirits come to smash the state and spread illness among the people (T 1707 33.355a). Given its position and season, this almost certainly refers to Algol, the eclipsing variable star in Perseus, which varies in brightness. See Schafer, *Pacing the Void*, p. 73.

37. "If Mars is high, rebels arise. If low rebels are subdued" (T 1707 33.355a).

38. Chi-tsang identifies this as the "Damp star" (*shih-hsing*) and as Venus (*T'ai-pai hsing*), though most dictionary definitions give "Mercury" for *shui-hsing*. Its movement through the zoological asterisms (cock, pig, etc.) governs the amount of rainfall (T 1707 33.355a).

Wind star,[39] the Blade star,[40] the Southern Dipper,[41] the Northern Dipper,[42] the great stars of the Five Wardens,[43] all of the stars of state rulers, the stars of the three dukes, and of the one hundred officers, and all such stars each are transformed, [you should] recite and expound this scripture. These constitute the second difficulty.

"[If] great fires burn the state and the myriad people are incinerated, [if] demon fires, dragon fires, deva fires, mountain spirit fires, human fires, forest fires, rebel fires, or other such wonders [occur, you should] recite and expound this scripture. These constitute the third difficulty.[44]

"[If] great floods inundate the people and the seasons are reversed: in winter it rains and in summer it snows. In winter there is lightning and thunder resounds, and in the sixth month the rain freezes and there is frost and hail. There are red rains, black rains, and green rains, and it rains dirt and rock and stones. Rivers flow in reverse, sweeping along stones and floating mountains.[45] At times of such wonders [you should] recite and expound this scripture. These constitute the fourth difficulty.

"[If] great winds blow killing the myriad people, and the mountains, rivers, and forests of the state are extinguished all at once. [If] there are unseasonable typhoons, black winds, red winds, green winds, heavenly winds, earthly winds, and fire winds,[46] [then] at times of such wonders

39. The movement of this star through the zoological asterisms controls the balance of wind and rain. See Chi-tsang, T 1707 33.355a.

40. *Tao-hsing* or "Blade star" is glossed by Chi-tsang as the "Fullness star" (*man-hsing*), and its movement through the zoological asterisms, its "highness" or "lowness," is indicative of warfare, famine, and epidemics (T 1707 33.355b).

41. The Southern Dipper is an asterism comprised of the stars in Sagittarius. See Schafer, *Pacing the Void*, pp. 59–60.

42. An asterism composed of the stars in Ursa Major.

43. Chi-tsang notes that these five correspond to the five elements, wood, water, fire, metal, and earth. Therefore, they refer to the five visible planets.

44. *Huo* might also be translated as "conflagration" in accordance with the sense of Liang-pi's glosses on the similar passage in the eighth-century recension of the text: Dragon fires (*lung-huo*) are thunderous sounds (of rocks? *p'i-li*, see *Daikanwa jiten*, 24530); demon fires (*kuei-huo*) are plagues or epidemics; human fires (*jen-huo*) are when one meets with unfavorable karmic conditions for future rebirths because of wielding supranormal powers for worldly gain; forest fires (literally, "tree fires," *shu-huo*), when prolonged drought causes forests to combust (T 1709 33.513c11–14). Obviously, these are not all "fires" in the literal sense of the word.

45. Chi-tsang ties each color and type of rain to a particular type of supernormal disaster. Thus, red rains signify warfare, black rains signify epidemics, green rains signify famine. Rains of rock and stone signify the anger of immortals and *raksas*, while the reverse flow of rivers signifies rebellions (T 1707 33.355b). Liang-pi's take on this runs from the straightforward "it rains boulders" to the supranormal "*asura* wars" (T 1709 33.513c23–28). Having viewed film taken during the Mt. Pinatubo volcanic eruption in 1991 I am no longer skeptical of it "raining gravel" and even boulders.

46. According to Chi-tsang, black, red, and green winds are so colored by the composition of the sea sand driven before them (T 1707 33.355c).

> [you should] recite and expound this scripture. These constitute the fifth difficulty.
>
> "[If] heaven, earth and the state are scorched by excessive heat, and ponds dry up, the grass and trees wither and die, and the five grains do not ripen and the soil becomes hard and the myriad people perish, [then] at times of such wonders [you should] recite and expound this scripture. These constitute the sixth difficulty.
>
> "[If] rebels arise from the four directions to invade the state, or within and without [the borders] rebels arise, [and there are] fire rebels, water rebels, wind rebels, and demon rebels, [and] the people are in chaos and warfare and plunder are on the rise, [then] at times of such wonders [you should] recite and expound this scripture. These constitute the seventh difficulty." (8.832b26–c22)

The description of the synonyms for the text and of the ritual previous to the *vidyārājas* is both more elaborate and more specific in the fifth-century text:

> "Great king, this ***prajñāpāramitā*** is the spiritual basis of the mind-consciousness [*hsin-shih chih shen-pen*] of all Buddhas, **bodhisattvas** and of all beings. It is also called the spirit-tally [*shen-fu*], it is also called the ghost-expelling pearl [*p'i-kuei-chu*], it is also called the wish-fulfilling pearl [*ju-i-chu*], it is also called the state-protecting pearl [*hu-kuo-chu*], it is also called the mirror of heaven and earth [*t'ien-ti-ching*], it is also called the spirit king of the dragon jewels [*lung-pao shen-wang*]." The Buddha said, "Great king, you should make nine colored banners nine *chang* long, nine colored flowers two *chang* high, one thousand branched lamps five *chang* high, nine jade screens, nine jade wrappers.[47] Also make a jeweled table on which to place the scripture. When the king travels [*hsing shih*] always keep this scripture one hundred paces in front of him, always with the light of one thousand [lamps]. This will ordain that—within a radius of one thousand *li*—the seven difficulties will not arise and crimes and transgressions will not be produced. When the king is not traveling [*chu shih*], make seven jeweled tents and within them make seven high seats upon which to place the scripture rolls, and each day worship, scatter flowers and burn incense [before them] as though you were serving your father and mother, or serving the god **Śakra.** (832c23–833a4).

47. The T'ang dynasty T'ien-t'ai commentary interprets the measurements as follows: "Nine signifies the sufferings of beings. . . . Two *chang* signifies the two truths, the ten lamps signify the merit of the ten good [acts]. . . . Five *chang* high [means they] illuminate the five ways [of rebirth] . . ." (T 1705 33.284c21–285a2).

Compare 843b10–21 and my translation.[48]

The fifth-century text invokes the aid of five "great-howl ***bodhisattva***s" rather than the Esoteric *vidyārājas*, which replace them in the eighth-century text. The passage reads:

> Great king, if in future eras there are all the kings who receive and hold the Three Jewels I will send the five great-power ***bodhisattva***s to protect their states. First, Chin-kang-howl[49] ***bodhisattva,*** his hand grasping a thousand jewel-emblem discus will go to protect that state. Second, Lung-wang-howl[50] ***bodhisattva,*** his hand grasping a golden wheel lamp, will go to protect that state. Third, Wu-wei-shih-li-howl[51] ***bodhisattva,*** his hand grasping a chin-kang-cudgel, will go to protect that state. Fourth, Lei-tien-howl[52] ***bodhisattva,*** his hand grasping a thousand-jeweled lasso, will go to protect that state. Fifth, Wu-liang-li-howl[53] ***bodhisattva,*** his hand grasping a fifty-sword wheel, will go to protect that state. [These] five great masters with five thousand great spirit kings will go to your state and greatly promote blessings and benefit. It is fitting that you establish [their] images and worship them. (833a9–17)

Compare 843b27–c9 and my translation.

The fifth-century text includes a passage listing ten *samādhis*:

> The ***samādhi*** of sublime enlightenment, the ***samādhi*** of complete brilliance, the adamantine ***samādhi,*** the ***samādhi*** of worldly truth, the ***samādhi*** of ultimate truth, the ***samādhi*** of the truth of supreme meaning [*ti i i ti san-mei*]. This three-truths ***samādhi*** [*san-ti san-mei*] is the king of all ***samādhi***s. Moreover, they attained the limitless ***samādhi,*** the seven valuables ***samādhi*** [*chi-ts'ai san-mei*], the twenty-five "existences" ***samādhi,***[54] and the ***samādhi*** of all practices. (833b6–10)

Needless to say the eighth-century scripture omits all of this.

48. Chi-tsang discusses the rite at T 1707 33.356a6–16.

49. His name translates as "Vajra-howl."

50. Dragon-king howl.

51. The fearless ten-power howl.

52. Thunder-howl.

53. Limitless-power howl.

54. Chi-tsang unpacks this list of *samādhis* at T 1707 33.357b10–25, and says that the twenty-five existences *samādhi* indicates the four evil *gathis*, the six heavens of the desire world, the heaven ruled by Lord Brahma, the four trances, the four empty and thoughtless states, and the five pure states. I count twenty-three, but see six heavens of desire in the numerical glossary.

Chapter 8: The Charge

Government Control of the Saṃgha: Some subtle but nonetheless important changes took place in the creation of the eighth-century recension of the *Scripture for Humane Kings*. Two changes found in the final chapter of the text involve the timing and wording of the predictions of the decline of the Buddhist teaching.

The eighth-century text states the periods for the decline of the Teaching as fifty, five hundred, and five thousand years (compare the translation above and 844b6–7). The fifth-century text reads as follows: "The Buddha told King ***Prasenajit,*** 'I warn you and the others, that after my extinction in eighty years, eight hundred years, and eight thousand years, when there is no Buddha, no Teaching, no Community, no male or female lay devotees, this scripture's three jewels will be entrusted to all the kings of states'" (833b13–14).[55]

The conditions causing the fulfillment of the prediction are important for our understanding of the circumstances of the composition of the *Scripture for Humane Kings*. The following passage is particularly important:

> After the five turbulent eras ***bhikṣu, bhikṣuṇī,*** the four classes of disciples, the heavenly dragons and all of the eight-fold spirit-kings, the kings of states, the great officers, the heirs apparent and princes will be haughty [and hold themselves in] great esteem and extinguish and smash my Teaching. Openly making laws to control my disciples—the ***bhikṣu*** and ***bhikṣuṇi***—they will not permit people to leave the family to practice the Way, and further they will not permit the making of Buddhist images or of Buddhist *stūpas*. They will establish superintendents [*t'ung-kuan*] to regulate the community and will set up registration of monks. ***Bhikṣu*** will stand on the ground while white-robed [laymen occupy] high seats. Soldiers and slaves will be made ***bhikṣu*** and receive preferential treatment while knowledgeable ***bhikṣu*** gather single-mindedly to befriend good ***bhikṣu*** and hold vegetarian meetings to seek blessings as in heterodox teachings. All of this is contrary to my Teaching. You should know at that time that it will not be long before the Correct Teaching [*cheng-fa*] is about to be extinguished. (833b17–25)

It is notable that the sentence beginning "They will establish superintendents . . ." is missing from the eighth-century passage and the phrase "soldiers

55. Both Chi-tsang (T 1707 33.357c8–26) and the T'ang T'ien-t'ai commentary (T 1705 284b9–24) discuss the periodization at some length, linking it to when the Buddha's direct disciples finally died and so forth.

and slaves will be made ***bhikṣu*** . . ." [*ping nu wei pi-chiu shou pieh-ch'ing fa*, 833b23] has been modified to read "there is no difference between [such laws and] the laws governing soldiers and slaves and so forth" [*yu ping-nu fa teng wu yu i*, 844b14].

Also missing from the eighth-century recension are the following two passages reemphasizing the opposition to government control: "The monastic community will commit great [acts] contrary to the Teaching, they will commit all [sorts] of transgressions which are contrary to the Teaching and to the Discipline. They bind ***bhikṣu*** according to the laws for prisoners" (833c1–3); and "Great king, in future eras all the kings of states, the heirs apparent, and the four classes of disciples will violate the Buddha's disciples, recording, regulating, and prohibiting them. This is like the laws for commoners and the laws for soldiers and slaves. If any of my disciples, ***bhikṣu*** and ***bhikṣuṇī*** establish registration and serve as officials they are not my disciples. This is the law for soldiers and slaves" (833c13–18).

Miscellaneous Variants Worth Noting

Prince Moonlight: As noted above, Pu-k'ung's recension of the scripture eliminates all references to the apocalyptic complex surrounding "Prince Moonlight" (*Yüeh-kuang wang*, *Yüeh-kuang t'ung-tzu*, *Yüeh-kuang p'u-sa*). Below is a list of these passages.

Prasenajit is identified as "Prince Moonlight" (825b23–25).

In the *gāthā* of chapter 3 Prasenajit refers to himself as Prince Moonlight (828a3).

Immediately following the *gāthā* in chapter 3 Prasenajit is addressed as Prince Moonlight (828a8, 14).

Other noteworthy variations include:

The fifth-century scripture has a few references to the "method of the seven Buddhas"; these are absent from Pu-k'ung's recension.

Sung, Yüan, and Ming editions of the fifth-century text, as well as the modern commentary by Yüan-ying (p. 177), mention the "Ten Kings Scripture" (*shih-wang ching*). This is omitted in the eighth-century version.

Appendix B

The Chinese Provenance of the *Scripture for Humane Kings*

Because of its importance, *The Scripture for Humane Kings* has been discussed in a number of studies. De Visser has a chapter on it in his *Ancient Buddhism in Japan*, and while he lists the dates of its use and discusses the contents of the two versions, he accepts Fei Ch'ang-fang's attribution to Kumārajīva and largely ignores the text's Chinese contexts. The great Japanese buddhologists Mochizuki and Toganoo both discuss the checkered career of this Chinese scripture and, following Fa-ching, conclude it is not to be reckoned among Kumārajīva's works. Mochizuki has a summary of his arguments in *Bukkyō daijiten*, 4105c–4107a. More recently, Satō Tetsui, Yoritomi Motohiro, and Makita Tairyō have gone over the same ground. Satō Tetsui's *Zoku Tendai Daishi no kenkyū*, pp. 72–112, discusses the *Scripture for Humane Kings* as well as other related Chinese scriptures. His arguments are summarized in Paul L. Swanson's *Foundations of T'ien-t'ai Philosophy*, pp. 45–48. Yoritomi's argument is in *Chūgoku mikkyō no kenkyū*, pp. 160–67. Makita Tairyō's summary of the issue is in his *Gikyō kenkyū*, esp. pp. 44–47. What follows summarizes the arguments from these sources and from my own study. The earmarks of Chinese composition include the following:

1. The *Scripture for Humane Kings* is not included in Hsüan-tsang's translation of complete *Prajñāpāramitā* works (Taishō vols. 5–7), and K'uei-chi (632–82) remarks that, according to Hsüan-tsang, "In his travels to the west, he had never heard of the existence of this [*Humane Kings*] scripture."

2. There is no Tibetan version of the text.

3. The *Scripture for Humane Kings* contains some verses virtually identical (T 8 830b5–15) to those found in earlier translations of Jātaka tales found in *Hsien yü ching* and the *Liu tu chi ching* (*Saḍpāramitā-saṁgraha Scripture*). Some of the terminology is unquestionably of Chinese provenance, including terms derived from the *I-ching* and from Taoism.

4. The scripture's list of twelve sorts of emptiness has more in common with the list of eleven sorts of emptiness found in the *Nirvana Scripture* than with the eighteen sorts of emptiness found in the *Pañcaviṃśati prajñāpāramitā*. Indeed, as if in recognition of the anomaly, Pu-k'ung replaced the twelve sorts of emptiness of the earlier text with a list of eighteen sorts of emptiness, which splices the first fourteen emptinesses from *Pañcaviṃśati* with last four of the earlier version of the *Scripture for Humane Kings*.

5. While the fifth-century *Scripture for Humane Kings* is unconventional in the terminology used for the bodhisattva stages, its description of these stages is generally in accord with those laid out in the *Avataṃsaka Sūtra*, which was translated in 428.

6. Details of phrasing in the *Scripture for Humane Kings* can be traced to other translations. For example, the phrase "never committing the five sins nor the six major and twenty-eight minor offenses" is related to a list of offenses found in the *Upāsakā-śīla Sūtra*, which was translated in 426 or 428.

7. Overall, the prophecy found in the *Scripture for Humane Kings* concerning the decline of the Teaching brings to mind some of the circumstances of the persecution of Buddhism that began in 446. As I have shown, the text is a reaction to the post-persecution government Buddhism of T'an-yao.

8. Evidence indicates that the *Scripture for Humane Kings* is closely related to two other Chinese compositions, the *P'u-sa ying lo ching* and *Fan wang ching*, both of which date to the latter half of the fifth century.

9. As I noted above, the *Scripture for Humane Kings* has a close relationship to the *Nirvana Scripture*, both in details of phrasing and in certain subject matter.

10. Attributions of South Asian origins based on Pu-k'ung's imputed use of original Sanskrit texts in his eighth century "re-translation" do not prove there was *a* Sanskrit version of the *Scripture for Humane Kings*. Pu-k'ung would have naturally referred to a number of Sanskrit texts of the Transcendent Wisdom genre in his work on various *parts* of the *Scripture for Humane Kings*. Indeed, the large number of passages identical word for word in both versions strongly suggests that the basis for the eighth-century text was the fifth-century text and not some Sanskrit original.

11. The earlier version of the *Scripture for Humane Kings* includes eschatological material popular during the Six Dynasties. Such material—the seven Buddhas, "Prince Moonlight" (Yüeh-kuang wang), and so on—was expunged from Pu-k'ung's recension.

12. The scripture is the only known Buddhist text that attributes the End of the Teaching to government intervention. Such intervention was an ongoing problem for Six Dynasties Chinese clergy. In a manner far more radical

than that found elsewhere in the Transcendent Wisdom Scriptures, kings are equated with bodhisattvas, and the text is specifically entrusted to kings.

Beyond these arguments the discussion of the Two Truths as three-fold in the early text (but not in the T'ang text) points to a signal Chinese development of the two-truths doctrine, a development that some scholars feel was the result of indigenous Chinese modes of analysis. According to Leon Hurvitz, "the Chinese author of this spurious Sūtra tipped his hand" by using Chinese terms "real truth" (*chen-ti*) and "truth of preeminent meaning" (*ti-i-i ti*) as alternate translations of *paramāthasatya:* "All dharmas are included in the three truths, the 'truth of emptiness,' the 'truth of form,' and the 'truth of mind'" and the "samādhi of the worldly truth, the *samādhi* of the real truth, and the *samādhi* of the truth of supreme meaning. This three truths *samādhi* is the king of *samādhi* among all *samādhi*" (*Chih-I*, pp. 274–75 n. 2).

Appendix C

The Path in Eighth-Century Scripture (T 246 8.836b14–838a8; 841b3–842b26)

The following outline of the path is derived from descriptions in prose and in *gāthā* in Chapters 3 and 7 of the eighth-century scripture (see the translation, pp. 223–34; 256–65), and should be compared with that of the fifth-century scripture in Chapter 3 of the study, pp. 88–89.

I. Forbearance of Self-control (*fu-jen*) is constituted by:
   A. Ten Grades of Bodhisattva Faith (*shih-hsin*, *shih shan*) in two levels: those in inferior and intermediate levels are petty kings. The superior are Iron Wheel-rulers of one continent. Their activities may result in:
   B. Acquired lineage (*hsi-chung-hsing*, Sanskrit *samudānītagotra*) associated with the Ten Abodes of Bodhisattva Wisdom (*shih chu*). These are Copper Wheel-rulers of two continents.
   C. Innate lineage (*hsing-chung-hsing*, Sanskrit *prakṛtishthagotra*) in which one cultivates the Ten Wise Contemplations (*shih hui kuan*, *shih hsing*). These are Silver Wheel-rulers of three continents.
   D. Lineage of the Way (*tao-chung-hsing*) in which one cultivates the Ten Superogatory Activities (*shih hui hsiang*). These are Golden Wheel-rulers of all four continents. This results in:

II. Forbearance of Firm Belief (*hsin-jen*) constituted by:
   A. Joyous Stage (*huan-hsi*) Introductory Level: 100 Buddha-*kṣetra*: Cakravartin/Jambudvīpa
   B. Stainless Stage (*li-kou*) Intermediate Level: 1000: King of Trayastriṃśās Heaven
   C. Luminous Stage (*fa-kuang*) Advanced Level: 10,000: King Yama

III. Forbearance of Obedience (*hsün-jen*) is constituted by:
   A. Stage of Radiant Wisdom (*yen-hui*) Introductory Level: 100,000: King of Tuṣita Heaven
   B. Invincible Stage (*nan-sheng*) Intermediate Level: 10,000,000: King of Heaven of Transformative Joy

- C. Stage Disposed toward enlightenment (*hsien-ch'ien*) Advanced Level: 100,000,000: King of Heaven Sovereign over the creations of others

IV. Forbearance of the Birthless [of Constituents] (*wu-sheng-jen*) is constituted by:

- A. Far-reaching Stage (*yüan-hsing*) Introductory Level: Billion: King of first Brahma Heaven
- B. Immovable Stage (*pu-tung*) Intermediate Level: Trillion: King of second Brahma Heaven
- C. Effectively Intelligent Stage (*shan-hui*) Advanced Level: 100 Trillion: King of third Brahma Heaven

V. Forbearance of Quiescent Extinction (*chi-mieh-jen*)

- A. Teaching-cloud (*Fa-yün*) Introductory Level: Unspeakable: King of Fourth Brahma Heaven
- B. All-knowledge or Excellent Apprehension (*i-ch'ieh chih*) Advanced: Tathāgata

Appendix D

Boilerplate Sequences in Pu-k'ung's Teachings

The modular structure of Esoteric rituals developed by Pu-k'ung and his disciples provided a flexible and easily learned system suited to the dual pursuits of enlightenment and state protection. As Osabe has observed, Pu-k'ung's Esoterism shows the adaptation of tantric Buddhist teachings to the Chinese milieu.[1] In turn, Kūkai and his followers used the same modular structure to adapt the teachings to a variety of Japanese contexts. The lineaments of this structure have recently been laid bare in Hatta Yukio's *Shingon jiten*. Hatta's comprehensive tables and appendixes provide a basis for examination of the underlying ritual structure and the sequencing of individual Esoteric rites in a variety of historical contexts. Hatta's table of rites connected with the *Vajradhātu* (pp. 264–68) are of particular relevance to the procedures concerning the Humane Kings detailed in *Instructions* and *Methods*. In this table Hatta compares the sequencing of rites in eleven manuals connected with the teachings of the *STTS*. He provides a master numbering of all the possible rites that might be nested to produce a specific ritual program. Among the manuals Hatta uses are Japanese manuals of the *Chuinryū* sect of Kōyasan, that attributed to Jōkei (866–900) of the *Kanjūjiryū*, and the *Shih-pa-chih yin* (T 900), supposedly the oral teachings of Pu-k'ung's disciple Hui-kuo as transmitted by Kūkai, and T'ang manuals from the Vajrabodhi/Pu-k'ung lineage.[2] This latter group includes Vajrabodhi's version of the *STTS* (*Chin-kang-ting yu-ch'ieh chung lüeh ch'u nien-sung ching*, T 866) as well as three manuals attributed to Pu-k'ung. These are the *Kuan-tzu-tsai p'u-sa ju-i-lun nien-sung i-kuei* (T 1085, *Ju-i-lun*), the *Wu-liang-shou ju-lai kuan-hsing kung-yang i-kuei* (T 930, *Wu-liang-shou*), and the *Chin-kang-ting lien-hua-pu hsin nien-sung i-kuei* (T 873, *Hsin kuei*).

1. Osabe, *Tōdai mikkyōshi zakkō*, pp. 90–91.

2. Jōkei's *Kaguraoka shidai* represents teachings on the Vajradhātu in the *Kanjūjiryū* tradition. The *Kaguraoka shidai* is the most comprehensive of the manuals surveyed by Hatta. For the manual, see *Mikkyō daijiten*, 230a. For Jōkei's life, see *Mikkyō daijiten*, 1136b–c.

Table 2. Boilerplate Sequence in Pu-k'ung's Teachings

	Hatta	Instructions	Ju-i-lun	Wu-liang-shou	Kagura-oka
Preparation					
1. Worship Triple Jewel	(4)	**		*	*
2. Purify Triple Karma	(9)	*	*	*	*
3. Buddha Department *Samaya*	(10/20)	*	*	*	*
Bodhisattva or Lotus Department *Samaya*	(11/21)	*	*	*	*
Vajra Department *Samaya*	(12/22)	*	*	*	*
4. Armoring the Body	(13)	**	*	*	*
5. Establish Vajra Realm	(35)	**	*	*	*
Welcoming and Feting the Divinities[3]					
6. Offer *Agra* Water	(80)	*	*	*	*
Offer Thrones	(81)	*	*	*	*
Universal Offering	(90)	*	#		*
Homa[4]					
7. *Homa* Sequence				**	
Chief Divinity					
8. Contemplation of Chief Divinity	(95)	*	*	*	*
Exit Sequence					
9. Universal Offering	(106)	**	**	**	*
Dedication of Merit	(108)	**			*
10. Dissolving the Ritual Arena	(109)	**		**	*
Three Departments/Departure	(110, 112)[5]	**	**	**	*
11. Taking Off the Armour	(117–118)		**	**	*
12. Prostration and Exit	(124)	**	**	**	*

Hatta's table clearly demonstrates the direct connection between these manuals and later Shingon manuals. The table also demonstrates Japanese codification of the modular structure and further elaboration on the part of Shingon ritualists. Looking back to the T'ang dynasty context, the table makes it quite obvious that the *Ju-i-lun*, the *Wu-liang-shou*, and the *Hsin kuei* are closely related to the *Instructions* (T 994) and *Method* (T 995). Indeed, Osabe has cogently argued that all of these texts are the product of Pu-k'ung and his heirs.[6]

3. In its full form this sequence of rites includes dispatching a chariot to bring the divinities, welcoming them, and feting them with a variety of offerings including water, garlands of flowers, various kinds of incense, and so on.

4. For a full account of the many subrites, see Payne, *Tantric Ritual of Japan*.

5. This sequence in its full form involves sending off the divinities.

6. Osabe groups these manuals together under the rubric of "the Esoteric Teachings of Pu-k'ung and his milieu." He argues that these texts (and a number of other texts) represent the adaptation of the

In table 2 I compare the sequences of rites in *Instructions* with those in the *Ju-i-lun*, *Wu-liang-shou*, and *Kaguraoka*. In each case the ritual programs involve the same sequences of rites, though some manuals abbreviate, elaborate, or even skip certain details. All use the same mantras or variants of the same mantras.[7] Finally, for our purposes, Hatta's work has one drawback. *Shingon jiten* is a dictionary of mantra, and in the many cases where a sequence of standard rites is briefly referred to *without* mention of the *mudrā* or mantra, Hatta is silent. For instance, Hatta's tables show none of the exit rites for *Ju-i-lun*, or *Wu-liang-shou*. Like these manuals *Instructions* mentions the sequences of rites without specifying the mantra or simply notes, "use the three mantras as before." When we examine the *Wu-liang-shou* and other manuals we find the same kind of abbreviation as in *Instructions*. Indeed, when we take into account indications of rites both when they include mantras and when they merely refer to a rite without actually transcribing a mantra, the high degree of congruence between T'ang rites and Japanese Shingon rites is astounding. In table 2, when a mantra or *mudrā* indicating a correspondence is found in Hatta's table I have marked it with an *. When Hatta is silent but an abbreviated reference to sequences of rites is mentioned in the manuals I have marked them with a **. In one case a mantra is in a text but Hatta skips over it. In this case I have marked it with a #. The boldface headings indicate logical breaks between sequences of rites. My division does not completely correspond to those put forward by various Shingon exegetes. The numbers running down the left side of the table represent discrete sequences of boilerplate rites. I have not included all of the subrites in each. Thus, in the case of the *homa* sequence I have not indicated the establishment of the *homa* altar, the invitation of its deities, the offerings, and so on.

---

tantras to the Chinese scene. Osabe also argues that they represent a joint esoterism of *Vajradhātu* and *Garbhadhātu*, an esoterism influenced by the *Susiddhikara* (Osabe, *Tōdai mikkyōshi zakkō*, pp. 44–48, 89–105). I am in full agreement with Osabe, though I would rather avoid the anachronism of describing Pu-k'ung's teachings as a "conjunction of Vajra and Garbhadhātu teachings."

7. The numbers in parentheses that follow each rite refer to Hatta's sequencing numbers, *Shingon jiten*, pp. 264–68. For the mantra numbers, refer to my treatment of *Instructions* in Chapter 6 of the study and to *Shingon jiten*, pp. 264–68. I have added the sequences from *Instructions* to Hatta's data for comparison.

Glossary of Numerical Terms

Twin or double illumination (*shuang-chao* 雙照). Metaphorically the "light" cast by the perception of the two truths. See Two Truths.

Two-fold or dual benefit (*erh li* 二利). Activities which benefit both oneself and others.

Two signs (*erh hsiang* 二相). Signs of self and other, or subject and object. The enlightened make no such distinctions as "me" and "mine."

Two Truths (*erh ti* 二諦 *satyadvaya*). Relative truth, which is socially, mentally, and linguistically constructed, and absolute truth.

Two vehicles (*erh ch'eng* 二乘). Liang-pi glosses the two vehicles as "those who have more to learn" (*yu-hsüeh che*) and "those who have no more to learn" (*wu-hsüeh che*). See note 6 in the translation of chapter 1 of the sūtra.

Three emptinesses (*san k'ung* 三空). There are several sets of these, for example "emptiness," "signlessness," "wishlessness" and emptiness of the self, of constituents, and of all phenomena.

Three emptiness-gate contemplations (*san k'ung men kuan* 三空門觀). According to Liang-pi, the contemplation of the *vimokṣamukha* or the "gates to liberation": emptiness, signlessness, and wishlessness (T 1709 441a).

Three evil roots or three roots of misfortune (*san chung pu-shan ken* 三種不善根). Passion, anger, and delusion.

Three false contemplations and real contemplations (*san chia-shih kuan* 三假實觀, *prajñapti*). The contemplations on the impermanence and emptiness of constituents (*dharmas*), sensations, and names. See Liang-pi, T 1709 440c.

Three false views (*san chia* 三假 *prajñapti*). To regard things, sensations, or names as ultimately real, when all are, in fact, empty of any permanent reality. See three false contemplations and real contemplations.

Three gates of liberation (*san t'o-men* 三脱門). Emptiness, signlessness, and wishlessness.

Three good roots or three roots of good fortune (*san chung shan-ken* 三種善根). Magnanimity, compassion, and wisdom.

Three [kinds of] acts, triple karma (*san yeh* 三業). There are several lists of these. What is most often meant is both the body, speech, and mind as the producers of karma and the kinds of actions that produce the karma.

Three obstructions (*san chang* 三障). On the gross level these are anger, lust, and delusion. On the mental level these are biased views, attachment to the Hinayana idea of nirvana, and attachment to the coarser manifestations of the aggregated causes and karma of the triple world. On the most subtle level they are the remaining causes of karma, the need for exerting oneself, and other fine obstructions.

Three periods, epochs, or times (*san shih* 三世). Past, present, and future.

Three *samādhis* (*san san mei* [*ti*] 三三昧（地). See three emptinesses and three emptiness-gate contemplations.

Three times (*san chi* 三際). See Three periods.

Three truths (*san ti* 三諦). There are various sets of these. Those in the *Scripture for Humane Kings* are the truths of emptiness, form, and mind (T 245 8.829b26–c1), and worldly truth (*shih ti*), ultimate truth (*chen ti*), and the truth of the preeminent meaning (*ti-i i ti*). These were, in turn, the source for Chih-i's three truths of emptiness (*k'ung*) which is totally "other," yet which is somehow identical with phenomenal existence or provisional truth (*chia*), and the mean or middle (*chung*) reality which transcends the mentally created dichotomy of the empty and the phenomenal.

Three vehicles (*san ch'eng* 三乘). There are numerous lists of three vehicles. Liang-pi indicates that these can refer to the fruit of practice as *śrāvaka*, *pratyekabuddha*, and Buddha, and they may be related to the three lineages outlined in the text (T 1709 455a–b).

Three worthies and the ten sages (*san hsien shih sheng* 三賢十聖). The three worthies are those practicing the ten abodes, the ten practices, and the ten transferences. The ten sages refer to the ten bodhisattva stages (*dasábhūmi*).

Triple illumination or mirror-like knowledge, three insights (*san ming chien* 三明鑑). Insight into the conditions of one's previous lives, insight into the conditions of other beings' lives, and the insight into the causes and conditions of the present life that will lead finally to Nirvana. The use of the word "mirror-like" (*chien*) seems a Chinese imposition. Liang-pi discusses this knowledge extensively at T 1709 33.442b–443a, and 504a.

Triple world, three worlds or three realms (*san chieh* 三界). The world composed of the realm of desire, the realm of form, and the formless realm.

Four categories (*ssu pu* [*ti-tzu*] 四部［弟子］ of disciples) or four-fold assembly. See four-fold eight-segmented assembly. The term may also refer to the four classes of advancement on the path laid out in the *Nikāyas*, i.e. those who have entered the stream, the once-returner, those who never again return, and the *arhat*.

Four comprehensive or vast vows (*ssu hung-yüan* 四弘願). Vows to sever all bondage, to continually transform or save beings, to cultivate Buddha-wisdom, and to attain unsurpassed enlightenment.

Four continents or under-heavens (*ssu t'ien-hsia* 四天下 *dvīpa*). The four continents thought to be at the cardinal directions of the *cakravāla* universe: Purvavideha in the east; Jambudvīpa in the south; Aparacamara in the west; and Uttarakuru in the north.

Four empty thoughtless states (*ssu k'ung wu hsiang* 四空無想). These transic states correspond to the formless realm of the triple world (*ārūpyadhātu*). They are the infinity of space; the infinity of perception; the realm of nothingness; and the realm of neither consciousness nor not-consciousness.

Four evil *gatis* (*ssu o-ch'u* 四惡趣 or *tao* 道)). The four evil destinies, i.e. birth in the hells, as a ghost, an animal, or an *asura*.

Four fearlessnesses (*ssu wu wei* 四無畏). There are two sorts: The first group applies to Buddhas and is the result of omniscience, perfect character, ability to overcome obstacles, and the cessation of suffering. The second sort applies to bodhisattvas and is the result of powers of memory, of moral insight, of rationality, and of the elimination of doubts.

Four formless concentrations (*ssu wu-se-ting* 四無色定). Also called the four trances of emptiness. They are the contemplation of the realm of infinite space, of infinite perception, of nothing at all, and of neither consciousness nor not consciousness. Beyer, the *Buddhist Experience* has a nice translation of these contemplations, pp. 206–9.

Four great elements (*ssu ta* 四大). Earth, water, fire, and air.

Four immeasurables, or immeasurable minds (*ssu wu-liang hsin* 四無量心 *caturi apramanāṇi*). Bodhisattvas who cultivate boundless pity, compassion, joy, and impartiality toward all beings.

Four kinds or types of birth (*ssu sheng* 四生). From eggs, the womb, from dampness, and from metamorphosis.

Four most serious prohibitions (*ssu chung chieh* 四重戒 *pārājikas*). The monastic rules against killing, stealing, sexual misconduct, and lying. Infraction of these rules results in expulsion from the *saṃgha*.

Four noble truths (*ssu ti* 四諦). The truth of suffering, its origin, its cessation, and the path.

Four pure heavens of the form realm (*ssu ssu ching ch'u* 色四靜處). The four heavens at the summit of the realm of form which are accessed through trance, also called the *Brahmalokas*, or heavens of Brahma.

Four reverses or inverted beliefs (*ssu tao* 四倒 *viparyāsa*). Thinking impermanent things are permanent; thinking what has no enduring person or self as having a self; thinking what is impure to be pure; mistaking what leads to misery for what leads to bliss.

Four right efforts (*ssu cheng chin* 四正勤 *catvāri prahāṇāni*). One desires that evil *dharmas* will not arise, that one can abandon those that have already arisen, that good *dharmas* will arise, and that one might augment those that have arisen. See Hurvitz, *Chih-I*, p. 244.

Four states of mindfulness (*ssu nien ch'u* 四念處 *catvāri smṛyupasthānāni*). Recognition that the body is impure, that feelings result in suffering, that the mental states are a series of disconnected moments, and that the constituents of existence (*dharmas*) are co-dependent and transient. These meditations negate the false beliefs in purity, joy, personality (the notion of a self or soul), and permanence. See the four reverses or inverted beliefs.

Four supranormal powers (*ssu ju-i tsu* 四如意足 *catvārā ṛddhipādāḥ*). Four supranormal powers, which are a part of the thirty-seven divisions of *bodhi* illumination. Often listed as supranormal powers of will, of mental exertion, of effort, and of discursive reasoning.

Four transic or calm states (*ssu ch'an-ting* 四禪定). The trances which access the four pure heavens of the form realm.

Four [all-embracing] virtues or kinds of concerted action (*ssu she fa* 四攝法 *catur-saṃgraha-vastu*). The four activities of bodhisattvas which entice beings to come together toward the Teaching: generosity, loving speech, beneficent action, and behavior for mutual aid in a manner consistent with the Teaching.

Four-fold eight-segmented assembly (*ssu chung pa pu* 四衆八部). The four classes of human believers, viz., *bhikṣu*, *bhikṣuṇī*, *upāsakas*, and *upāsikās*, and the eight classes of nonhuman beings, viz., *deva*, *nāga*, *yakṣa*, *gandharva*, *asura*, *mahoraga*, *garuda*, and *kinnara*.

Four-fold unobstructed [powers of] comprehension or wisdom (*ssu wu-ai chih* 四無礙智 or *ssu wu-ai chieh* 四無礙解 *pratisaṁvid*). The dissolution of fear through reliance on the meaning and not the letter of the Teaching; on the Teaching rather than the teacher; on wisdom, not on reasoning; and on authoritative teachings, not on those subject to interpretation.

Five aggregates (*wu wen* 五蘊). The components of a human being. These are form, feeling, thinking, volition, and consciousness. None of these is permanent or eternal.

Five cognitions (*wu shih-ch'u* 五識處 *parijñāna*). Sight, sound, smell, taste, and touch.

Five directions (*wu fang* 五 方). In Chinese cosmology the cardinal directions and the center.

Five forbearances (*wu jen* 五 忍). These are forbearance of self-control, of firm belief, of obedience, of the birthlessness of constituents, and of quiescent extinction. See the description in Chapter 3 of the translation.

Five heinous crimes or rebellious acts (*wu ni tsui* 五 逆 罪). Killing one's father, killing one's mother, killing an Arhat, shedding the blood of a Buddha, or causing a schism in the community.

Five kinds of vision (*wu yen* 五 眼). These are the physical eyes, the divine eye (through which one can see other realms and times), the eye of wisdom or *prajña,* the eye of the teaching, and the Buddha-eye.

Five moral faculties (*wu ken li* 五 根 力 *pañcendriyāṇi, pañca balāni*). The faculties of trust, energy, mindfulness, concentration, and wisdom and the corresponding power associated with each faculty.

Five penetrations. See the five supranormal powers.

Five pure states (*wu ching chu* 五 淨 居). The five highest heavens of the *rūpadhātu* or realm of form, corresponding to the fourth transic state. The topmost of these is the Akaniṣtha heaven, the abode of Śiva, who is lord of the triple-world.

Five supranormal powers or "spiritual penetrations" (*wu shen-t'ung* 五 神 通 *pañcābhijñā*). These are the divine eye, the divine ear, knowing the thoughts of others, knowledge of past and future lives, and knowledge of when one's defilements will cease. Knowledge of magical techniques is sometimes added to make six.

Five turbulent eras or attributes of the turbulent era (*wu tu shih* 五 濁 世 *pañcākaṣāya*). These are usually listed as the five sorts of corruption characteristic of the End of the Teaching: first the *kalpa* decays, and as a result, egoism and excessive passions arise. These cause an increase in suffering and a progressively shortened life span.

Six abodes of sensation or sense media (*liu ch'u* 六 處 *āyatana*). This is the fifth of the twelve causes of codependent origination. Perception involves the conjunction of sense media or 'abodes' (eye, ear, etc.), object, and the mind.

Six destinies or paths (*liu ch'u* 六 趣 *gati*). Types of beings or rebirths: those reborn in the hells, in the heavens as *deva,* as humans, as titans (*asura*), as ghosts (*preta*), and as animals.

Six elements (*liu chieh* 六 界). Earth, water, fire, air, space, and mind.

Six heavens of desire [and the heaven of] Lord Brahma (*fan-wang liu yu t'ien* 梵 王 六 欲 天). These refer to the six heavens in the realm of desire and the heaven ruled by Brahmadeva, the first meditation realm located in the lowest level of the realm of form. See twenty-five existences *samādhi*.

Six perfections or "ferries" (*liu tu* 六度 *pāramitā*). Giving, morality, forbearance, striving, meditation, and wisdom.

Six points of harmonious reverence (*liu ho-ching* 六和敬). Six types of behavior conducive to concord in the community. These are classified in contradistinction with the three karmas. The community worships as a body, its chanting is the expression of unified speech, and its meditation and faith give it unity of mind. The other three points are its unity in observation of the precepts, its unity with regard to doctrine, and its unity as an economic community.

Six relationships (*liu ch'in* 六親). The ideal family relationships between father and son, elder and younger brother, and husband and wife, as stipulated in the Confucian teachings.

Seven components of perception (*ch'i chueh chih* 七覺支 *saptabodhyāngāni*). See the seven divisions of *bodhi* illumination.

Seven difficulties (*ch'i nan* 七難). These are listed in Chapter 7 of the translation. They involve various celestial, meteorological and social disasters.

[Seven] divisions of bodhi-illumination (*ch'i p'u-ti fen fa* 七菩提分法 *sambodhyañga*). These are seven of a list of thirty-seven aids to enlightenment. They are concentration, equanimity, memory of teachings, discrimination between teachings, effort, joy, and ecstasy.

Seven stages of virtue or worthy conduct (*ch'i hsien hsing* 七賢行). The initial seven stages of the path as enumerated in the *Kośa*. They consist of a series of contemplations and are followed by the seven stages of sage conduct.

Seven treasures (*ch'i pao* 七寶). Usually the treasures of a golden-wheel *cakravartin* ruler of all four continents.

Eight victorious stages of meditation or conquering faculties (*pa sheng ch'u* 八勝處). Eight ways in which one gains liberation through specific forms of meditation. Each of the eight is broken into a contrastive pair of subjective and objective. For instance, the first involves subjective desire, which is conquered by meditation on the trifling nature of objects. Liang-pi enumerates these in T 1709 445c–446a, and Robert Thurman gives an excellent account under the term "eight liberations" in *The Holy Teaching of Vimalakīrti: A Mahāyāna Scripture* (University Park: The Pennsylvania State University Press, 1976), p. 153.

Eight-fold path (*pa sheng tao* 八聖道 or *pa cheng tao* 八正道 *aṣṭāngamārga*). These are right views, right discrimination, right speech, right action, right livelihood, right effort, right mindfulness, right concentration.

Nine and ten forms of wisdom (*chiu chih shih chih* 九智十智). A thoroughgoing understanding of the Four Noble Truths based on the common understanding and an enlightened understanding. There is also a separate list of ten forms of wisdom in the Mahāyāna, but given the context, it is the Nikāya Buddhist understanding that applies here. Liang-pi's commentary has an extensive discussion at T 1709 440b–c.

Ten abodes (*shih chu* 十住). As Liang-pi points out, the scripture doesn't specify which of the lists of ten abodes this refers to, but he goes on to cite the list from the *Avataṃsaka:* arousing the mind, controlling the mind, cultivating the activities, acquiring the lineage, skill in means for oneself and others, rectified mind, nonretrogression, scion of the Buddha, prince of the teaching, and consecration as lord of the teaching. See Hurvitz, *Chih-I*, pp. 363–64.

Ten antidotes (*shih tui-chih* 十對治). Means of responding to defilments or *kleśa*. See ten practices and ten inverted views.

Ten directions (*shih fang* 十方). Technically the eight compass points, the zenith, and the nadir. A stock phrase for all directions.

Ten good paths (*shih shan tao* 十善道). These are the same as ten grades of good faith.

Ten grades of (good) faith or ten virtues (*shih hsin* 十信 or *shih shan* 十善). The first ten of the fifty-two stations of the bodhisattva path. They are arousing the mind, trust, remembrance of the Teaching, zealous progress, wisdom, fixed concentration, nonretrogression, discipline, will, protecting or nurturing (*hu*) the Teaching, and transference of merit to others. See Liang-pi, T 1709 465a.

Ten inverted (views) (*shih tien-tao* 十顛倒). According to Liang-pi these are brought under control by the ten antidotes, and these antidotes are in fact the ten wise contemplations or the ten practices. See T 1709 498b–c.

Ten kinds of forbearing mind (*shih jen-hsin* 十忍心). See Chapter 3 of the translation.

Ten kinds of *pāramitā* (*shih po-lo-mi-to* 十波羅蜜多). The six perfections with the addition of four more virtues, viz., skillfull means, vows, strength of purpose, and wisdom.

Ten modes of universal contemplation (*shih pien ch'u* 十徧處 or *shih i-ch'ieh ch'u* 十一切處). Contemplation of the universe from ten different perspectives, viz., earth, water, fire, air, green, yellow, red, white, space, and consciousness.

Ten powers or ten powerful wisdoms (*shih li chih* 十力智 *daśabala*). There are two sets of these, those pertaining to the Buddha and those of bodhisattvas.

The second seems relevant here. These include the power of positive thought, of resolve, of application, of wisdom, of vows, of vehicle, of activities, of nirmanic emanations, of enlightenment, and of teaching.

Ten practices (*shih hsing* 十行). The ten practices follow the ten kinds of faith and the ten abodes in the fifty-two stages of the path. They focus on service to others and include joy at the vision of nirvana, benefiting others, teaching through nonresistance, never deviating from the course, not getting confused, having an impressive appearance to attract others to the teaching, detachment, activities as a savior, being a good model for others, and catching the first glimmer of the truth. See the ten antidotes and the ten inverted views, as well as Hurvitz, *Chih-I*, p. 365.

Ten sorts of trusting mind. See the ten grades of good faith.

Ten stages (*shih ti* 十地 *daśabhūmi*). The ten classic bodhisattva stages. As enumerated in the eighth-century scripture: joyous, stainless, luminous, radiantly wise, invincible, disposed toward enlightenment, far-reaching, immovable, effectively intelligent, Teaching cloud. The *Scripture for Humane Kings* and some other scriptures add all-knowledge (*sarvajñāna*).

Ten transferences or works of supererogation (*shih hui-hsiang* 十回向). Ten ways in which the bodhisattva, refusing to put his own quest first, sees the equality of all things and beings. See Hurvitz *Chih-I*, pp. 364–65, under "The Ten Degrees of Diversion."

Ten universal faculties (*shih i-ch'ieh ch'u* 十一切處). See the ten modes of universal contemplation.

Ten wisdoms (*shih chih* 十智). See the nine and ten forms of wisdom.

Ten wise contemplations (*shih hui-kuan* 十慧觀). See the ten practices.

Twelve classes of scriptures or varieties of Buddhist preaching (*shih-erh pu ching* 十二部經 *dvādaçakadharmapravacana*). These are listed in Chapter 4 of the translation and by Hurvitz, *Chih-I*, pp. 337–38.

Twelve sense media or abodes of sensation (*shih-erh ch'u* 十二處 *āyatana*). Twelve of the eighteen elements involved in perception. Eye and form; ear and sound; nose and smell; tongue and taste; body and touch; mind and phenomena. See the six abodes.

Twelve-fold [chain of] causation [or codependent origination] (*shih-erh in-yüan* 十二因緣 *nidāna*). The twelve codependent causes of suffering and rebirth. They are ignorance, yearning to exist, consciousness, name and form, sense media, contact, feelings, craving, grasping, becoming, birth, and old age and death.

Thirteen gates of the teaching or contemplation (*shih-san kuan-men* 十三觀門). As the scripture indicates, there are fourteen "forbearances" or stages in the path. Excluding the final one there are thirteen.

Fourteen bodhisattvas (*shih-ssu p'u-sa* 十四菩薩 also as fourteen kings [of forbearance] *shih-ssu wang* 十四王). Those who are practicing the fourteen forbearances.

Fourteen forbearances (*shih-ssu jen* 十四忍). The stages of the path taking into account the subdivisions of the five forbearances. See Appendix C, "The Path in the Eighth-Century Scripture."

Sixteen great states and their kings (*shih-liu wang* 十六王). The kings of the sixteen great states contemporary with the Buddha: Vaiśālī, Kośala, Śrāvastī, Magadha, Vārāṇasi, Kapilavastu, Kuśinagara, Kauśāmbī, Pañcāla, Pāṭaliputra, Mathurā, Uṣa, Puṇyavardhara, Devāvatāra, Kāśī, and Campā.

Sixteen lessons (*shih-liu hsin-hsing* 十六心行). The sixteen lessons (sometimes the *shih-liu ti-kuan* or the *shih-liu hsing-hsiang*) refers to consideration of the four noble truths from each of four perspectives connected with the stage of recognizing the Way (*chien-tao*) mentioned above. Liang-pi enumerates these at T1709 33.446b2–15. See Chapter 1, note 13, in the translation.

Eighteen elements or regions (*shih-pa chieh* 十八界 *dhātu*). Taking the same six pairs of abodes or sense media as above and coupling each pair with consciousness yields eighteen abodes or sense media.

Eighteen unique characteristics of a Buddha (*shih-pa pu kung fa* 十八不共法 *āveṇikabuddhadharma*). There are two such sets, one relating to Nikāya Buddhism, the other to the Mahāyāna. According to the Mahāyāna a Buddha is infallible, is not rowdy, does not forget, has unbroken concentration, does not discriminate, is impartial. His will does not falter, nor does his energy flag. His mindfulness is unbroken, he does not abandon concentration, his wisdom never diminishes, and his liberation is unfailing. All his bodily, verbal, and mental acts are imbued with wisdom, and he perceives the past, present, and future without attachment.

Twenty-five existences *samādhi* (*erh-shih-wu yu san mei* 二十五有三昧). The trances which lead to attainment of and transcendence of the twenty-five realms of existence. Fourteen are in the desire realm, seven are in the realm of form, and four are formless. For an enumeration see Hurvitz, *Chih-I*, pp. 339–42.

Thirty minds (*san-shih hsin* 三十心). This refers to the ten grades of faith or trust, the ten abodes, and the ten kinds of transference taken together.

Thirty-seven divisions of bodhi-illumination (*san-shih-ch'i p'u-t'i fen-fa* 三十七菩提分法 *bodhipakṣikadharma*). These aids to enlightenment are the four mindful states, the four right efforts, the four elements of supranormal power, the five moral faculties, the five powers (which correspond to the five moral faculties), the seven "branches" of enlightenment, and the eightfold path. See Hurvitz, *Chih-I*, pp. 344–46.

Sixty-two views (*liu-shih-erh chien* 六十二見). An enumeration of all the wrong views about existence. The right view is selflessness and all the wrong views lean toward either eternalism or nihilism. The *Diganikāya* and the *Brahmajāla sūtra* list these.

Logographs

A-tzu wu-lun	阿字五輪
An-kuo ssu	安國寺
An Lu-shan	安祿山
besson (pieh-tsun)	別尊
Busshin	佛身
ch'a-na	刹那
ch'an	禪
ch'an-ting	禪定
chang	丈
Chang Chiu-ch'eng	張九成
chang-chu	章句
Ch'ang-an	長安
ch'ang-sheng tien	長生殿
chen-chi	真際
chen-jen	真人
chen-ju	真如
chen-shih	真實
chen-shih shen	真實身
Chen-ti	真諦
chen-yen	真言
Ch'en	陳
Cheng-fa	正法
Cheng-fa li kuo	正法理國
Cheng-fa li kuo, yü ling he-ch'i	正法理國與靈和起
cheng-fa-lun shen	正法輪身
cheng-wei	正位
ch'eng-chiu	成就

ch'eng-chiu hsi-ti	成就悉地
ch'eng fo shen-li	成佛身力
chi	偈
chi	集
chi-mieh jen	寂滅忍
Chi-tsang	吉藏
chi-yeh	集業
chi-yin	集因
chi-yüeh	妓樂
ch'i-hsien chu	七賢居
ch'i-nan	七難
ch'i-ts'ai san-mei	七財三昧
chia-ch'ih	加持
chia-shen	家神
Chiang san-shih chin-kang	降三世金鋼
Chiang-tu	江都
chiao-ling-lun shen	教令輪身
chieh	皆
chieh-t'o chih chien	解脱之見
chien hsien-kuan	見現觀
chien-tao	見道
ch'ien	乾
Chih-i	智顗
Chih-p'an	志磐
chih shen	識神
Chih-tun	支遁
Chin-kang-chih	金鋼智
Chin-kang-hou	金鋼吼
Chin-kang-li	金鋼利
Chin-kang-pao	金鋼寶
chin-kang san-mei	金鋼三昧
Chin-kang-shou	金鋼手
chin-kang-ting san-mei	金鋼頂三昧
Chin-ko ssu	金閣寺
Chin-ling	金陵
ching-chin	精進
Ching-yün	景雲
chiu kung	九宮
Chiu-mo-lo-shih	鳩摩羅什

Chu Fa-hu	竺法護
Chu Hsi	朱熹
chu shih	住時
ch'u shih	出世
ch'u-shih ch'eng-chiu	出世成就
chuan	轉
chuan-i	轉依
chuan-lun-wang	轉輪王
chüan	卷
chuang-yen	莊嚴
chüeh-hsing	覺性
Chūinryū	中院流
chung-hsing	種性
Chung-yung chieh	中庸解
erh i	二儀
fa	法
fa-chieh	法界
Fa-ching	法經
fa-ching-chieh	法境界
fa-hsien	法現
fa-hsing	法性
fa-kuang	發光
Fa-kuo	法果
fa-men	法門
fa-mo	法末
fa-mo shih	法末世
fa-shen	法身
fa-tsang	法藏
Fa-yün	法雲
fan	蕃
Fei Ch'ang-fang	費長房
fei fa, fei fei fa	非法非非法
Fei-hsi	飛錫
fei-tse	非擇
Fo chung-hsing	佛種性
fo-kuo	佛國
fo-t'u-hu	佛圖户
Fo-t'u-teng	佛圖澄
Fu Chien	苻堅

fu-jen	伏忍
Han	漢
Ho-t'u	河圖
hoguk pulgyo	護國佛教
Hou Ching	侯景
hsi	西
hsi-chung-hsing	習種性
Hsi-ming ssu	西明寺
Hsi-shou	喜受
hsi-ti	悉地
hsia	夏
hsia chih li	夏之禮
hsiang	相
hsiang-mao	像貌
Hsiao-tsung	孝宗
Hsiao-wen	孝文
Hsieh Ling-yün	謝靈運
hsien	賢
hsien-ch'ien	現前
Hsien-tsung	憲宗
hsin-jen	信忍
hsin-shih chih shen-pen	心識之神本
hsing	形
hsing	性
hsing-chieh	行解
hsing-chung-hsing	性種性
Hsing-hui	行慧
hsing shih	行時
hsiu pai-fa ming-men	修百法明門
hsiu-tao	修道
Hsüan-tsung	玄宗
hsün-jen	順忍
hu	胡
hu	護
hu-fo-kuo	護佛果
hu-kuo	護國
hu-kuo-chu	護國珠
hu-mo (homa/goma)	護摩

hu shih-ti hsing	護 十 地 行
hua	華
hua	化
hua-fo	化 佛
hua-lo-t'ien	化 樂 天
hua-shen	化 身
hua shen-tsu	化 神 足
Hua Yang	華 陽
Hua-yen	華 嚴
huan-chao	還 照
huan-hsi (ti)	歡 喜 (地)
Huan Hsüan	桓 玄
Huan Pin	宦 彬
huang po	皇 伯
hui-hsiang (hsin)	迴 向 (心)
hui-hsing	慧 星
Hui-kuo	惠 果
hui-kuang	慧 光
Hui-k'uang	慧 曠
Hui-lang	惠 朗
Hui-shao	慧 曉
Hui-ssu	慧 思
Hui-yüan	慧 遠
Hyech'o (Hui-ch'ao)	惠 超
Hyeil (Hui-i)	惠 一
Hyonch'o (Hsüan-ch'ao)	玄 超
Iryon	一 然
i	義
i-ch'ieh chih	一 切 智
i-ch'ieh fa ch'ieh ju yeh	一 切 法 且 如 也
I-ching	易 經
I-ching	義 淨
I-hsing	一 行
i-k'ou t'ung-yin	異 口 同 音
i-kuei	儀 軌
i pan	已 辦
i pien	已 辯
i-yü	夷 語

jen[a]	忍
jen[b]	仁
jen[c]	人
jen[b] che	仁 者
jen[b]-che jen yeh	仁 者 忍 也
jen[c]-huo	人 火
jen[a] po-lo-mi	忍 波 羅 蜜
jen[b]-wang	仁 王
jen[c]-wang	人 王
ju yu ju wu	如 有 如 無
Jokei	長 慶
ju	如
ju-i-chu	如 意 珠
ju-lai	如 來
ju-lai chia	如 來 家
ju-lai-tsang	如 來 藏
jung	戎
jung hua pu tsa	戎 華 不 雜
k'ai-fu	開 府
K'ai Wu	蓋 吳
K'ai-yüan	開 元
Kakuban	覺 鑁
kan-hui	乾 慧
K'ang-seng-hui	康 僧 會
Kao-tsu	高 祖
k'ao	考
ko-i	格 義
Ko Shu-han	哥 舒 翰
K'ou Ch'ien-chih	寇 謙 志
Koyasan	高 野 山
kuan	觀
kuan-chao-chih	觀 照 智
kuan-ting	灌 頂
Kuan-ting	灌 頂
kuang-hua	廣 化
Kuang-ming	光 明
Kuang-tse ssu	光 宅 寺
Kuei-chu	貴 筑
kuei-hsing	鬼 星

kuei-huo	鬼 火
Kūkai	空 海
k'un	坤
kung-yung	攻 用
k'ung-ti	空 地
kuo	國
kuo-shih	國 師
kuo-yü	國 語
Lei-tien-hou	雷 電 吼
Li-ch'en	離 塵
li-ch'un	立 春
Li Heng	李 恒
Li Kua	李 适
li-kou	離 垢
Li Lung-chi	李 隆 基
li-shih chih fa	理 事 之 法
Li Shih-min	李 世 民
li-ta	離 達
Li Wu	李 無
Li Yü	李 豫
Li Yüan	李 淵
Liang	梁
Liang-pi	良 賁
Lien-hua sheng	蓮 華 勝
Lien-hua shou	蓮 華 手
ling-pao	靈 寶
Ling-wu	靈 武
Ling-yao ssu	靈 曜 寺
liu-chieh	六 界
liu-ch'ü	六 趣
Lo-shu	洛 書
Lo-yang	洛 陽
lou	漏
lu	律
lun-hsing	輪 星
lun shen	輪 身
lung-huo	龍 火
Lung-men	龍 門
lung-pao shen-wang	龍 寶 神 王

Lung-wang-hou	龍王吼
man-hsing	濕星
mao-lun	毛輪
mi-chiao	密教
miao-chüeh hsing	妙覺性
Miao-in	妙因
mieh	滅
Ming	明
ming-hui	明慧
Ming-t'ang	明堂
Ming-tsung	明宗
ming-wang (Jap. myōō)	明王
mo-fa	末法
nan-sheng	難勝
nan-ting	難頂
nei-hu	內護
nei tao-ch'ang	內道場
nei wai hu	內外護
neng-jen	能忍
Ninnōkyō	仁王經
Ojin (Wu-chen)	悟真
o-kuei	惡鬼
o-lung	惡龍
pan-chiao	拌教
Pan-tsu	斑足
pao-shen	報身
Pao-sheng	寶勝
Pao-ssu-wei	寶思惟
pen-chüeh-hsing	本覺性
pen-tsun	本尊
p'i-kuei-chu	辟鬼珠
pien-chao ju-lai	徧照如來
pien shen-tsu	變神足
pien-wen	變文
ping nu wei pi-ch'iu shou pieh-ch'ing fa	兵奴為比丘受別請法
p'ing-teng	平等
p'ing-teng chüeh	平等覺
po-jo-po-lo-mi (to)	般若波羅蜜(多)
pu-kung fa	不共法

Pu-k'ung (chin-kang)	不空(金剛)
Pulga Saui (Pu-k'e-ssu-i)	不可思議
pu-shih	不實
pu-t'ui-chuan	不退轉
Pu-tung (Fudo/Acala)	不動
P'u-hsien	普賢
P'u-ku Huai-en	僕固懷恩
P'u-ming	普明
p'u-sa	菩薩
p'u-ti fen-fa	菩提分法
Saicho	最澄
Sai-huang	塞黄
san-chia	三假
san-mi	三密
san-ti san-mei	三諦三昧
se-ti	色諦
seng-chi-hu	僧祇户
seng-t'ung	僧統
Seng-yu	僧祐
sha-men t'ung	沙門統
shan-chüeh	善覺
shan-hui	善慧
Shan-shih	善施
shan-ti	善地
Shan-wu-wei	善無畏
Shan-yüeh	善月
Shang-ch'ing	上清
shao-fen hua	少分化
she	捨
she-ch'eng	舍成
she-shou	攝受
shen-fu	神符
shen-tsu	神足
sheng-hui	勝慧
sheng-i ti	勝義諦
Sheng-shou	勝受
sheng-t'ai	聖胎
sheng-tao	聖道
sheng-wang	聖王

sheng-wei	聖位
shih	施
shih-chien ch'eng-chiu	世間成就
shih chien hsin	十堅心
shih-chih	十止
shih-chu	十住
shih-fu	士夫
shih hsien-kuan	事現觀
shih-hsin	十信
shih-hsing	十行
Shih-hu	施護
shih-shan	十善
shih-shih	施食
shih-ssu jen	十四忍
shih-ti	十地
Shih-tsung	世宗
shih-tzu fen-hsün	獅子奮迅
shih-tzu hou p'u-sa	獅子吼菩薩
Shingon	真言
shou pieh-ch'ing	受別請
shu-huo	木火
shuang-chao	雙照
ssu-ta	四大
su-chih	速疾
su-kuo-kung	肅國公
su-san wang	粟散王
su-shih-ti	俗世諦
Su-tsung	肅宗
Sui	隋
sui-hsing	歲星
Sun Ch'o	孫綽
ta chi-ching miao san-ma-ti	大寂靜妙三摩地
ta-hou p'u-sa	大吼菩薩
ta-hsien (ṛṣi)	大賢
Ta hsing-shan ssu	大興善寺
ta-hung-chiao san-tsang	大弘教三藏
ta-kuang-chih Pu-k'ung san-tsang	大廣智不空三藏
ta-li hou p'u-sa	大力吼菩薩
ta-te	大德

t'a-shou-yung shen	他受用身
T'ai-i	太乙
t'ai-pai-hsing	太白星
T'ai-tsung	太宗
Taimitsu	台密
Tai-tsung	代宗
T'ai-wu	太武
T'ai-yuan	太原
T'an-yao	曇曜
T'ang	唐
Tao-an	道安
tao-ch'ang	道場
tao-chung-hsing	道種性
tao-hsing	刀星
tao-jen t'ung	道人統
te	德
Te-tsung	德宗
t'e-chin	特進
teng-chüeh	等覺
teng-chüeh hsing	等覺性
ti	地
ti	帝
ti-hsien-kuan	諦現觀
ti-i-ti	弟一諦
ti-i-i ti	弟一義諦
ti-i-i-ti san-mei	弟一義諦三昧
Ti-lun	地論
T'ien-chu	天竺
t'ien-hsia	天下
t'ien-hsia chih kung	天下之公
t'ien-hsia wei chia	天下為家
T'ien-lo	天羅
t'ien-lung	天龍
T'ien-t'ai	天台
t'ien-ti-ching	天地鏡
t'ien-tzu	天子
ting-sheng-wang	頂生王
Toji	東寺
Tomitsu	東密

T'o-pa	拓跋
Tsan-ning	贊寧
tse-mieh	擇滅
Tsui Hao	崔浩
tu-wei-na	都維那
Tun-huang	敦煌
T'ung-chih	同治
t'ung-kuan	統官
tzu-hsiang	自相
tzu-hsing-lun shen	自性輪身
tzu-liang	資糧
tzu-shou yung-shen	自受用身
tzu-tsai-t'ien	自在天
Wa-kuan ssu	瓦官寺
wai-hu	外護
wang (king)	王
wang-lai	往來
Wang Wei-hsien	王維賢
wei	味
Wei	魏
wei hui-yu	未會有
wei-na	維那
wei-nu shen	威怒身
Wei Yüan-sung	衛元嵩
wei yung-hu ta sui kuo-t'u	為擁護大隋國土
Wen-ch'eng	文成
wen-tzu	文字
wen-tzu-hsing li	文字性離
Wŏng-ch'ŭk	圓測
wu	無
wu-chieh hsien	五戒賢
wu fen-tuan	無分段
wu hsing	五行
wu-hsüeh che	無學者
wu-hsüeh-tao	無學道
wu jen	五忍
Wu-liang-li-hou	無量力吼
wu-ming hsi	無明習
wu-shang chüeh	無上覺

wu-sheng-jen	無生忍
wu shuo	無說
wu t'ing	無聽
wu-tu-shih	五濁世
wu-wei kung-te	無為功德
Wu-wei-shih-li-hou	無畏十力吼
wu wu ti shih wu	無無諦實無
yang	陽
Yang Kuang	楊廣
yeh	葉
yeh-tzu-tsai	業自在
yen-hui	焰慧
yen-lo hsing	閻羅星
Yen Ying	嚴郢
yin	陰
ying-hua shen	應化身
yirim (I-lin)	義林
yu	有
Yü Ch'ao-en	魚朝恩
yu-hsüeh (che)	有學(者)
yü ping-nu fa teng wu yu i	與兵奴法等無有異
yu-wei kung-te	有為功德
yüan	源
Yüan	元
Yüan-chao	圓照
yüan-chih	圓智
yüan hsien-kuan	緣現觀
yüan-hsing	遠行
yüan-ta	遠達
Yüan Tsai	元載
Yüan-ying	圓瑛
Yüeh-kuang p'u-sa	月光菩薩
Yüeh-kuang t'ung-tzu	月光童子
Yüeh-kuang wang	月光王
Yün-kang	雲岡

Works Cited

Reference Works

Analytic Dictionary of Chinese and Sino-Japanese. Compiled by Bernhard Karlgren. Paris: Librairie Orientaliste Paul Guenther, 1923. Reprint. New York: Dover, 1974.

Buddhist Hybrid Sanskrit Grammar and Dictionary. Vol. 2. *Dictionary*. Compiled by Franklin Edgerton. New Haven: Yale University Press, 1953.

Bukkyō daijiten. Published under the direction of Mochizuki Shinkō. 10 vols. Kyoto: Sekai Seiten Kangyō Kyōkai, 1955.

Daikanwa jiten. Compiled by Morohashi Teisuji. 13 vols. Tokyo: Daishūkan Shoten, 1955–60.

A Dictionary of Chinese Buddhist Terms. Compiled by William E. Soothill and Lewis Hodus. London: Kegan Paul, Trench, Trubner, 1937. Reprint. Delhi: Motilal Banarsidass, 1977.

Encyclopedia of Religion. Edited by Mircea Eliade. New York: Macmillan, 1986.

Fo-hsüeh ta-tz'u-tien. Compiled by Ting Fu-bao. Shanghai: I-hsüeh shu-chu, 1921, 1925. Reprint. Taipei: Hua-yen she, 1956.

Grammatica Serica Recensa. By Bernhard Karlgren. Stockholm: Museum of Far Eastern Antiquities, 1964.

Hōbōgirin: dictionaire encyclopédique du bouddhisme d'après les sources chinoises et japonaises. Edited by Paul Demieville and Jacques May. 6 vols. to date. Tokyo: Maison Franco-Japonaise, 1929– .

Mikkyō daijiten. Compiled and edited by Matsunaga Shōdō. Kyoto: Naigai Press, 1931–33.

The Pāli Text Society's Pāli-English Dictionary. Edited by T. W. Rhys-Davids and William Stede. London: Pāli Text Society, 1921–25. Reprint. New Delhi: Oriental Books Reprint, 1975.

A Pronouncing Dictionary of Chinese Characters in Ancient Chinese, Mandarin and Cantonese. Edited by Chou Fa-kao. Hong Kong: Chinese University of Hong Kong Press, 1979.

A Sanskrit-English Dictionary. Compiled by Monier Monier-Williams. Oxford: Clarendon Press, 1898.

Shingon jiten. By Hatta Yukio. Tokyo: Hirakawa shuppansha, 1985.

Theological Dictionary of the New Testament. Edited by Gerhard Friedrich. Grand Rapids, Mich.: Wm. B. Eerdmans, 1971.

Primary Sources

Chang Chiu-ch'eng (1092–1159). "Chung-yung chieh." *Chang Chuang-yüan Meng-tzu chuan, Ssu-pu tsung-kan*. Shanghai: Commercial Press, 1919–37.

Chu Hsi (1130–1200). "Tsa-hsüeh pien." in *Hui-an hsien-sheng wen-kung wen chi. Ssu-pu pei-yao*. Shanghai: Chung-hua shu-chu, 1927–37.

Hsin-chiao pen sung-shu. Compiled by Shen-yüeh (441–513). Taipei: Ting wen shu chu, 1990.

Jen-wang hu-kuo po-jo-ching. Pu-k'ung (705–74). Printed at Chin-ling, 1871.

Kakuban (1095–1134). *Kōgyōdaishi zenshu*. Tokyo: Kajisekkai shisha, 1910.

Kokuyaku Issaikyō. Tokyo: Daitō shuppansha, 1930– .

Ku-chin t'u-shu chi-ch'eng. Compiled by Ch'en Meng-lei (1651–ca. 1723) et al. 100 vols. Taipei: Wen-hsing shu-tien, 1964.

Liu Hsü (887–946) et al. *Chiu t'ang shu*. Peking: Chung-hua shu-chu, 1975.

San kuan i. In *Wan-tzu hsü-tsang ching*. Chih-i (538–97). Reprint of *Dai-nihon zokuzōkyō*, 148 vols. Hong Kong: Ying yin hsü tsang ching wei yüan hui, 1967– . Vol. 98.

Taishō shinshū daizō-kyō. Takakusu Junjirō and Watanabe Kaigyoku, eds. and comps. 85 vols. Tokyo: Taishō issaikyō kankō-kai, 1924–34. Reprint. Taipei: Hsin-wen feng ch'u-pan she, 1974.

- T 7 *Ta po-nieh-p'an ching* (*Mahāparinirvāṇasūtra*). Translation attributed to Fa-hsien (fl. 399–416).
- T 152 *Liu-tu chi ching*. K'ang Seng-hui (d. 280).
- T 202 *Hsien-yu ching*. Attributed to Hui-chüeh (fl. 445).
- T 222 *Kuang-tsan ching* (*Brilliant Praise Prajñāpāramitā*). Translated by Dharmarakṣa (fl. 265–313).
- T 223 *Mo-ho po-jo-po-lo-mi ching* (*Pañcaviṃśati-sāhasrika-prajñāpāramitā*). Translated by Kumārajīva (350–409).
- T 231 *Sheng-t'ien-wang po-lo-po-lo-mi ching* (*Pravaradeva-rāja-pariprccha*). Translated by Upaśūnya (fl. 538–565).
- T 235 *Chin-kang po-jo-po-lo-mi ching* (*Vajracchedika-prajñāpāramitā*). Translated by Kumārajīva (350–409).
- T 243 *Liu-ch'u ching*. Pu-k'ung (705–774).
- T 245 *Jen-wang hu-kuo po-jo-po-lo-mi-to ching*. Attributed to Kumārajīva (350–409), but written ca. 470–90.
- T 246 *Jen-wang hu-kuo po-jo-po-lo-mi-to ching*. Pu-k'ung (705–74).
- T 273 *Chin-kang san-mei ching*. Anonymous.
- T 278 *Ta fang-kuang fo hua-yen ching* (*Avataṃsaka sūtra*). Buddhabhadra (359–429).
- T 279 *Ta fang-kuang fo hua-yen ching* (*Avataṃsaka sūtra*). Śikṣānanda (652–710).
- T 285 *Chien pei i-ch'ieh chih te ching* (*Daśabhūmikā*). Dharmarakṣa (fl. 265–313).
- T 286 *Shih-chu ching* (*Daśabhūmikā*). Kumārajīva (350–409).
- T 494 *A-nan ch'i-meng ching*. Attributed to T'an wu-lan (ca. 381–95).
- T 663 *Chin-kuang-ming ching* (*Survaṇaprabhāsa*). Translated by Dharmarakṣa (fl. 265–313).
- T 664 *Ho-pu chin-kuang-ming ching* (*Survaṇaprabhāsa*). Translated by Dharmarakṣa (fl. 265–313) and Pao-kuei (ca. 300).
- T 665 *Chin-kuang-ming tsui-sheng wang ching* (*Survaṇaprabhāsa*). I-ching (635–713).
- T 681 *Ta-ch'eng mi-yen ching*. Divākara (fl. 613–688).

T 682 *Ta-ch'eng mi-yen ching*. Pu-k'ung (705–74).
T 848 *Ta p'i-lu-ch'e-na ch'eng fo shen-pien chia-chih ching* (*Mahāvairocanābhisambodhi Sūtra*). Translated by Śubhākarasiṃha (637–735), with aid of I-hsing (683–727).
T 865 *Chin-kang-ting i-ch'ieh ju-lai chen-shih she ta-ch'eng hsien-ti ta chiao-wang ching* (*Sarvatathāgatatattvasaṃgraha*). Translated by Pu-k'ung (705–74).
T 866 *Chin-kang-ting yü-ch'ieh chung lüeh ch'u nien-sung ching* (*Sarvatathāgatatattva-saṃgraha*). Translated by Vajrabodhi (671–741).
T 867 *Chin-kang-feng-lo-ko i-ch'ieh yu-ch'ieh yu-chi ching*. Translated by Vajrabodhi (671–741).
T 869 *Shih-pa-hui chih-kuei*. Pu-k'ung (705–74).
T 873 *Chin-kang-ting lien-hua-pu hsin nien-sung i-kuei*. Pu-k'ung (705–74).
T 882 *Fo shuo i-ch'ieh ju-lai chen-shih she ta-ch'eng hsien ti san-mei ta chiao-wang ching* (*Sarvatathāgatatattvasaṃgraha*). Translated by Shih-hu (Dānapāḷa, fl. 980s).
T 893 *Su-hsi-ti chieh-lo ching* (*Susiddhikara sūtra*). Translated by Śubhākarasiṃha (637–735).
T 900 *Shih-pa kuei yin*. Kūkai (774–835).
T 903 *Tou-pu t'o-lo-ni mu*. Attributed to Pu-k'ung (705–74).
T 930 *Wu-liang-shou ju-lai kuan-hsing kung-yang i-kuei*. Pu-k'ung (705–74).
T 937 *Fo shuo ta-ch'eng sheng wu-liang-shou chüeh-ting kuang-ming wang ju-lai to-lo-ni ching*. Dharmadeva (d. 997).
T 944a *Ta fo-ting ju-lai fang-kuang hsi-tan-tuo po-tan-lo t'o-lo-ni*. Pu-k'ung (705–74).
T 944b *Ta fo ting ta t'o-lo-ni*. Anonymous.
T 950 *P'u-t'i-ch'ang suo shuo i-tzu-ting lun-wang ching*. Pu-k'ung (705–74).
T 951 *I-tzu-ting lun wang ching*. Bodhiruci (fl. 693–727).
T 982 *Tu-sung fo mu ta k'ung-ch'iao ming-wang ching ch'ien*. Pu-k'ung (705–74).
T 989 *Ta-yün-lun ch'ing-yü ching*. Anonymous.
T 990 *Ta-yün ching ch'i-yü t'an-fa*. Pu-k'ung (705–74).
T 994 *Jen-wang hu-kuo po-jo-po-lo-mi-to ching t'o-lo-ni nien-sung i-kuei*. Pu-k'ung (705–74).
T 995 *Jen-wang po-jo nien-sung fa*. Pu-k'ung (705–74).
T 996 *Jen-wang po-jo t'o-lo-ni shih*. Pu-k'ung (705–74).
T 1085 *Kuan-tzu-tsai p'u-sa ju-i-lun nien-sung i-kuei*. Pu-k'ung (705–74).
T 1096 *Pu-k'ung pa-so t'o-lo-ni tzu-tsai wang ch'ou ching* (*Scripture of the Amoghapāśa Dhāraṇī, the Sovereign Lord of Spells*). Ratnacinta (d. 721) and Li Wu (fl. 720s).
T 1097 *Pu-k'ung pa-so t'o-lo-ni tzu-tsai wang ch'ou ching* (*Scripture of the Amoghapāśa Dhāraṇī, the Sovereign Lord of Spells*). Ratnacinta (d. 721).
T 1249 *Pi-sha-men i-kuei*. Attributed to Pu-k'ung (705–74).
T 1313 *Fo shuo chiu-pa yen-k'ou o-kuei to-lo-ni ching*. Pu-k'ung (705–74).
T 1314 *Fo shuo chiu mien-jan o-kuei to-lo-ni shen-ch'ou ching*. Śikṣānanda (652–710).
T 1315 *Shih-chu o-kuei yin-shih chi shui fa*. Pu-k'ung (705–74).
T 1318 *Yü-chieh chi yao chiu A-nan to-lo-ni yen-k'ou kuei-i ching*. Pu-k'ung (705–74).
T 1319 *Yü-chieh chi-yao yen-k'ou shih-shih ch'i-chiao A-nan-to lueh-yu*. Pu-k'ung (705–74).
T 1320 *Yü-chieh chi-yao yen-k'ou shih-shih i*. Anonymous.
T 1484 *Fan-wang ching* (*Brahmajāla sūtra*). Translation attributed to Kumārajīva (350–409).
T 1485 *P'u-sa ying-lo pen-yeh ching* (*Scripture of the Original Acts That Serve as Necklaces for Bodhisattvas*). Attributed to Chu Fo-nien (ca. 365).

T 1509 *Ta chih-tu lun* (*Mahāprajñāpāramitāśāstra*). Kumārajīva (350–409).

T 1579 *Yü-chieh shih-ti lun* (*Yogācārabhūmiśāstra*). Translated by Hsüan-tsang (602–64).

T 1581 *P'u-sa ti chih ching* (*Bodhisattvabhūmi*). Dharmarakṣema (385–433).

T 1582–83 *P'u-sa shan-chieh ching* (*Bodhisattvabhūmi*). Guṇavarman (fl. 367–431).

T 1705 *Jen-wang hu-kuo po-jo ching shu*. Attributed to Chih-i (538–97), but a product of the early T'ang.

T 1706 *Fo-shuo jen-wang hu-kuo p'an-jo-po-lo-mi ching shu*. Shan-yüeh (1150–1241).

T 1707 *Jen-wang po-jo ching shu*. Chi-tsang (549–623).

T 1708 *Jen-wang ching shu*. Wŏng-ch'ŭk (fl. 640–60).

T 1709 *Jen-wang hu-kuo po-jo-po-lo-mi-tuo ching shu*. Liang-pi (717–77).

T 1716 *Fa-hua hsüan-i*. Chih-i (538–97).

T 1777 *Wei-mo ching hsüan shu*. Chih-i (538–97).

T 1796 *Ta-jih ching shu*. Śubhākarasiṃha (637–735) and I-hsing (683–727).

T 1798 *Chin-kang-ting ching ta yü-ch'ieh pi-mi hsin ti fa-men*. Pu-k'ung (705–74).

T 1827 *Pai lun shu*. Chi-tsang (549–623).

T 1911 *Mo-ho chih-kuan*. Chih-i (538–97).

T 1918 *Ssu nien-ch'u*. Attributed to Chih-i (538–97).

T 1929 *Ssu chiao i*. Chih-i (538–97).

T 1934 *Kuo-ch'ing po-lu*. Kuan-ting (561–632).

T 2034 *Li-tai san-pao chi*. Fei Ch'ang-fang (ca. 561–97).

T 2035 *Fo-tsu t'ung-chi*. Chih-p'an (fl. 1258–69).

T 2039 *Samguk yusa*. Iryŏn (1206–89).

T 2055 *Huüan-tsung ch'ao fan ching san-tsang Shan-wu-wei hsing-chuang*. Li Hua (fl. 754).

T 2055 *Shan-wu-wei san-tsang ho-shang pei-ming*. Li Hua (fl. 754).

T 2056 *Ta-pien-cheng kuang-chih pu-k'ung san-tsang hsing-chuang*. Chao Ch'ien (fl. 780s).

T 2059 *Kao-seng chuan*. Hui-chiao (497–554).

T 2060 *Hsü kao-seng chuan*. Tao-hsuan (596–667).

T 2061 *Sung kao-seng chuan*. Tsan-ning (919–1001).

T 2102 *Hung-ming chi*. Seng-yu (445–518).

T 2120 *Tai-tsung-ch'ao ssu-k'ung ta-pien-cheng kuang-chih san-tsang ho-shang piao-chih-chi*. Yüan-chao (d. 800).

T 2122 *Fa-yüan chu-lin*. Tao-shih (d. 683).

T 2145 *Ch'u san-tsang chi-chi*. Seng-yu (445–518).

T 2146 *Chung-ching mu-lu*. Fa-ching (ca. 594).

T 2156 *Ta-t'ang chen-yüan hsu-k'ai-yüan shih-chiao lu*. Yüan-chao (d. 800).

T 2157 *Chen-yüan hsin-ting shih-chiao mu-lu*. Yüan-chao (d. 800).

T 3007 *Bessonzakki*. Shinkaku (fl. 1117–80).

Taishō Iconographic Supplement (*Taisho Zuzō*)

Asabashō. Shōchō (1205–82). T supplement, vol. 9.

Byakuhōkushō. Ryōzen (1258–1341). T supplement, vol. 6.

Kakuzenshō. Kakuzen (1143–1218). T supplement, vol. 4.

Kakuzen hitsu ninnōkyōho. T supplement, vol. 4.

Zuzōshō. Ejo (fl. 1130s). T supplement, vol. 3.

T'ang hui-yao. Wang P'u (922–82). 3 vols. Kiangsu shu-chu, 1884.
Tun-huang pao-tsang. Edited by Huang Yung-wu. Taipei: Hsin-wen-feng ch'u-pan-she, 1981.
Wei jen-wang po-jo ching chiang-ching pien-wen. Pelliot manuscript no. 3808.

Secondary Sources

Alper, Harvey P., ed. *Mantra*. Albany: State University of New York Press, 1989.
Anesaki Masaharu. *History of Japanese Religion with Special Reference to the Social and Moral Life of the Nation*. London: Kegan Paul, Trench, Trübner, 1930. Reprint. Rutland, Vt.: Charles E. Tuttle, 1963.
Aronoff, Arnold. "Contrasting Modes of Textual Classification: The Jātaka Commentary and Its Relationship to the Pāli Canon." Ph.D. diss., University of Chicago, 1982.
Astley-Kristensen, Ian. *The Rishukyō: The Sino-Japanese Tantric Prajñāpāramitā in 150 Verses (Amoghavajra's Version)*. Buddhica Britannica Series Continua 3. Tring, U.K.: Institute of Buddhist Studies, 1991.
———. "Two Sino-Japannese Dhāraṇī Dictionaries." *Temenos* 23 (1987): 131–34.
Bareau, André. *Les sectes bouddhiques du petit véhicule*. Saigon: École française d'Extrême-Orient, 1955.
Beal, Samuel. *A Catena of Buddhist Scriptures from the Chinese*. London: Trübner, 1871. Reprint. Taipei: Ch'eng Wen, 1970.
Bell, Catherine. *Ritual Theory, Ritual Practice*. Oxford: Oxford University Press, 1992.
Benn, Charles David. *The Cavern Mystery Transmission: A Taoist Ordination Rite of A.D. 711*. Honolulu: University of Hawaii Press, 1991.
———. "Taoism as Ideology in the Reign of the Emperor Hsüan-tsung (712–755)." Ph.D. diss., University of Michigan, 1977.
Berger, Patricia. "Preserving the Nation: The Political Uses of Tantric Art in China." In Marsha Weidner, ed., *Latter Days of the Law: Images of Chinese Buddhism, 850–1850*. Honolulu: University of Hawaii Press, 1994.
Beyer, Stephan. *The Buddhist Experience: Sources and Interpretations*. Belmont, Calif.: Wadsworth, 1974.
———. *the Cult of Tārā: Magic and Ritual in Tibet*. Berkeley and Los Angeles: University of California Press, 1973.
Bharati, Agehananda. *The Tantric Tradition*. New York: Rider, 1965.
Bhattacharyya, Benyotosh. *An Introduction to Buddhist Esoterism*. Varanasi: Chowkhambra Sanskrit Series Office, 1964.
Birnbaum, Raoul. "Introduction to the Study of T'ang Buddhist Astrology." *Bulletin: Society for the Study of Chinese Religions* 8 (Fall 1980): 5–19.
———. *Studies on the Mysteries of Mañjuśri: A Group of East Asian Maṇḍalas and Their Traditional Symbolism*. Boulder, Colo.: Society for the Study of Chinese Religions, monograph no. 2, 1983.
Bokenkamp, Steven. "Stages of Transcendence: The *Bhūmi* Concept in Taoist Scripture." In Robert E. Buswell Jr., ed., *Chinese Buddhist Apocrypha*. Honolulu: University of Hawaii Press, 1990.

Boodberg, Peter Alexis. "The Language of the T'o-pa Wei." *Harvard Journal of Asiatic Studies* 1 (1936): 167–85.
———. "The Semasiology of Some Primary Confucian Concepts." In *Selected Works of Peter A. Boodberg*. Compiled by Alvin P. Cohen. Berkeley and Los Angeles: University of California Press, 1979.
Bredon, Juliet, and Igor Mitropanow. *The Moon Year: A Record of Chinese Customs and Festivals*. Shanghai: Kelly Walsh, 1927.
Brough, John. "Thus I Have Heard. . . ." *Bulletin of the School of Oriental and African Studies* 13.2 (1950): 416–26.
Buswell, Robert E., Jr., ed. *Chinese Buddhist Apocrypha*. Honolulu: University of Hawaii Press, 1990.
———. *The Formation of Ch'an Ideology in China and Korea: The Vajrasamādhi-sūtra, A Buddhist Apocryphon*. Princeton: Princeton University Press, 1989.
———. "Introduction: Prolegomena to the Study of Buddhist Apocryphal Scriptures." In *Chinese Buddhist Apocrypha*, pp. 1–30.
Cammann, Schuyler. "Islamic and Indian Magic Squares." In two parts. *History of Religions* 8 (February 1969): 181–209, 271–99.
———. "The Magic Square of Three in Old Chinese Philosophy and Religion." *History of Religions* 1 (August 1961): 37–80.
———. "Old Chinese Magic Squares." *Sinologica* 7 (1962): 14–53.
Caswell, James O. *Written and Unwritten: Buddhist Caves at Yüngang*. Vancouver: University of British Columbia, 1988.
Chan, Wing-tsit. *A Sourcebook in Chinese Philosophy*. Princeton: Princeton University Press, 1969.
Chandra, Lokesh. *The Esoteric Iconography of Japanese Maṇḍalas*. Śatapiṭaka Series no. 92. New Delhi: International Academy of Indian Culture, 1971.
Chandra, Lokesh, and David L. Snellgrove. *Sarva-Tathāgatha-Tattva-Saṅgraha*. Śata-piṭaka Series, vol. 269. New Delhi: Mrs. Sharada Rani, 1981.
Chang, Garma C. C. *The Buddhist Teaching of Totality: The Philosophy of Hwa Yen Buddhism*. University Park: Pennsylvania State University Press, 1974.
Chavannes, E., trans. *Cinq cents contes et apologues extraits du tripiṭaka chinois*. Paris: Adrien-Maisonneuve, 1962.
Ch'en, Kenneth K. S. *Buddhism in China: A Historical Survey*. Princeton: Princeton University Press, 1964.
———. *The Chinese Transformation of Buddhism*. Princeton: Princeton University Press, 1973.
Chou I-liang. "Tantrism in China." *Harvard Journal of Asiatic Studies* 8 (March 1945): 241–332.
Cohen, Alvin P. "Coercing the Rain Deities in Ancient China." *History of Religions* 17 (February–May 1978): 244–65.
Cohen, Richard S. "Discontented Categories: Hināyāna and Mahāyāna in Indian Buddhist History." *Journal of the American Academy of Religion* 63.1 (1995): 1–25.
Colpe, Carsten. "Syncretism." *Encyclopedia of Religion*, 14: 218b–227b.
Conze, Edward. *Buddhist Scriptures*. Harmondsworth, England: Penguin Books, 1959.
———. *Buddhist Thought in India: Three Phases of Buddhist Philosophy*. Ann Arbor: University of Michigan Press, 1973.
———. *The Large Sūtra on Perfect Wisdom*. Berkeley and Los Angeles: University of California Press, 1975.

———, trans. *The Short Prajñāpāramitā Texts*. London: Luzac, 1973.
Conze, Edward, I. B. Horner, D. Snellgrove, and A. Waley. *Buddhist Texts Through the Ages*. Oxford: Bruno Cassirer, 1954. Reprint. New York: Harper & Row, Harper Torchbooks, 1964.
Cook, Francis. *Hua-yen Buddhism: The Jewel Net of Indra*. University Park: Pennsylvania State University Press, 1977.
———, trans. *The Buddha-carita of Aśvaghoṣa*. In Cowell, ed., *Buddhist Mahāyāna Texts*. New York: Dover, 1969.
Cowell, E. B., ed. *The Jātaka: or Stories of the Buddha's Former Births*, 6 vols. and index. London: Pāli Text Society, 1895–1913. Reprinted in 3 vols. London: Luzac, 1969.
Crease, Robert P., and Charles C. Mann. "How the Universe Works." *The Atlantic Monthly*, August 1984, pp. 66–93.
Dasgupta, Shasi Bushan. *An Introduction to Tantric Buddhism*. Calcutta: Calcutta University Press, 1958. Reprint. Berkeley, Shambhala, 1974.
Davidson, Ronald M. "An Introduction to the Standards of Scriptural Authenticity in Indian Buddhism." In Buswell, *Chinese Buddhist Apocrypha*, pp. 291–325.
Dayal, Har. *The Bodhisattva Doctrine in Buddhist Sanskrit Literature*. London: Routledge & Kegan Paul, 1932. Reprint. Delhi: Motilal Banarsidass, 1970.
Demieville, Paul. "Byō." In *Hōbōgirin*, 3:224b–270a.
Derrida, Jacques. *Of Grammatology*. Translated by Gayatri C. Spivak. Baltimore: Johns Hopkins University Press, 1991.
———. "Structure, Sign, and Play in the Discourse of the Human Sciences." In Hazard Adams and Leroy Searle, eds., *Critical Theory Since 1965*. Tallahassee: Florida State University Press, 1986.
DeVisser, M. W. *Ancient Buddhism in Japan: Sūtras and Ceremonies in Use in the Seventh and Eighth Centuries A.D. and Their History in Later Times*. 2 vols. Leiden: E. J. Brill, 1935.
Donner, Neal, and Daniel B. Stevenson. *The Great Calming and Contemplation: A Study and Annotated Translation of the First Chapter of Chih-i's Mo-ho chih-kuan*. Honolulu: University of Hawaii Press, 1993.
Douglas, Mary. *Natural Symbols: Explorations in Cosmology*. New York: Vintage Books, 1973.
———. "The Social Control of Cognition: Some Factors in Joke Perception." *Man*, n.s., 3.3 (1968): 361–76.
Dumont, Louis. "The Conception of Kingship in Ancient India." *Contributions to Indian Sociology* 6 (1962): 48–77.
Duquenne, Robert. "Daigensui (myōō)." In *Hōbōgirin*, 6:610a–640b.
———. "Daitoku myōō." *Hōbōgirin*, 6:652–70.
Durkheim, Emile. *The Rules of Sociological Method*. Translated by S. Solovay and J. Mueller. New York: The Free Press, 1938.
Durt, Hubert. "The Dating of the Historical Buddha (Part I)." In Heinz Bechert, ed., *Symposien zur Buddhismusforschung*, 4:1. Göttingen: Vandenhoeck & Ruprecht, 1991.
———. "Daibucchō." In *Hōbōgirin*, 6:596b–598a.
Eastman, Kenneth. "The Eighteen Tantras of the Vajraśekhara/Māyājāla." Paper presented to the 26th International Conference of Orientalists in Japan. Tokyo, 1981. Resume in *Transactions of the International Conference of Orientalists in Japan* 26 (1981): 95–96.
———. "Mahāyoga Texts at Tun-huang." *Bulletin of the Institute of Cultural Studies at Ryukoku University* 22 (1983): 42–60.
Eberhard, Wolfram. *A History of China*. 3d ed. Berkeley and Los Angeles: University of California Press, 1977.

Eliade, Mircea. *A History of Religious Ideas*. Vol. 2, *From Gautama Buddha to the Triumph of Christianity*. Translated by Willard R. Trask. Chicago: University of Chicago Press, 1982.

———. *The Myth of the Eternal Return*. Translated by Willard R. Trask. New York: Pantheon, 1954. Reprinted with new preface as *Cosmos and History*. New York: Harper Torchbooks, 1959.

———. *The Sacred and the Profane: The Nature of Religion*. Translated by Willard R. Trask. New York: Harcourt, Brace & World, 1959.

———. *Shamanism: Archaic Techniques of Ecstacy*. Translated by Willard R. Trask. Bollingen Series no. 76. New York: Pantheon, 1964. Reprint. Princeton: Princeton University Press, 1972.

———. "Spirit, Light, and Seed." *History of Religions* 11 (August 1971): 1–30.

———. *The Two and The One*. Translated by J. M. Cohen. London: Harvill Press, 1965. Also published as *Mephistopheles and the Androgyne: Studies in Religious Myth and Symbol* (New York: Harper & Row, 1965; reprint, Chicago: University of Chicago Press, Phoenix Books, 1979).

———. *Yoga: Immortality and Freedom*. Translated by Willard R. Trask. 2d edition enlarged. Bollingen Series no. 56. Princeton: Princeton University Press, 1970.

Emmerick, R. E., trans. *The Sūtra of the Golden Light: Being a Translation of the Survaṇabhāsottamasūtra*. Sacred Books of the Buddhists, vol. 27. London: Luzac, 1970.

Falk, Maryla. *Nāma-rūpa and Dharma-rūpa: Origins and Aspects of an Ancient Indian Conception*. Calcutta: University of Calcutta, 1943.

Farquhar, David M. "Emperor as Bodhisattva in the Governance of the Ch'ing Empire." *Harvard Journal of Asiatic Studies* 38.1 (1978): 5–34.

Faure, Bernard. "Quand l'habit fait le moine: The Symbolism of the *Kāṣāya* in Ch'an/Zen Buddhism." *Cahiers d'extrême-asie* 8 (1995): 335–67.

———. *The Rhetoric of Immediacy: A Cultural Critique of Chan/Zen Buddhism*. Princeton: Princeton University Press, 1991.

Fischoff, Ephraim, trans. *The Sociology of Religion*. Boston: Beacon Press, 1964.

Fisher, Carney T. "The Great Ritual Controversy in the Age of Ming Shih-tsung." *Bulletin: Society for the Study of Chinese Religions* 7 (Fall 1979): 71–87.

Fontein, Jan. *The Pilgrimage of Sudhana: A Study of the Gandhavyūha Illustrations in China, Japan, and Java*. The Hague: Mouton, 1967.

Forte, Antonino. "The Activities in China of the Tantric Master Manicintana (Pao-ssu-wei: ?–721 A.D.) from Kashmir and His Northern India Collaborator's." *East and West*, n.s., 34, nos. 1–3 (September 1984): 301–45.

———. *Mingtang and Buddhist Utopias in the History of the Astronomical Clock: The Tower, Statue, and Armillary Sphere Constructed by Empress Wu*. Paris: École Française d'Extrême-Orient, 1988.

———. *Political Propaganda and Ideology in China at the End of the Seventh Century*. Naples: Istituto Universitario Orientale, 1976.

Francis, H. T., and E. B. Cowell, eds. *The Jātaka*. London: Luzac, 1969.

Frankfort, H., J. A. Wilson, T. Jacobson, and W. I. Irwin. *The Intellectual Adventure of Ancient Man: An Essay on Speculative Thought in the Ancient Near East*. Chicago: University of Chicago Press, 1948.

Frazer, James G. *The Golden Bough*. Abridged edition by Theodor H. Gaster as *The New Golden Bough: A New Abridgement of Sir James Frazer's Classic Work*. New York: Criterion Books, 1959.

Freud, Sigmund. "Wit and Its Relations to the Unconscious." In *The Basic Writings of Sigmund Freud*, trans. and ed. A. A. Brill. New York: Modern Library, 1938.
Frye, Stanley. *The Sūtra of the Wise and the Foolish*. Dharamsala: Library of Tibetan Works and Archives, 1981.
Fun Yu-lan. *A History of Chinese Philosophy*. 2 vols. Translated by Dirk Bodde. Princeton: Princeton University Press, 1953.
Gadjin, Nagao. "On the Theory of the Buddha-Body." *The Eastern Buddhist* 6 (May 1973): 25–53.
Geertz, Clifford. "Religion as a Cultural System." In William A. Lessa and Evon Z. Vogt, eds., *Comparative Religion: An Anthropological Approach*. 3d ed. New York: Harper & Row, 1972.
Gernet, Jacques. *Buddhism in Chinese Society: An Economic History from the Fifth to the Tenth Centuries*. Translated by Franciscus Verellen. New York: Columbia University Press, 1995.
Gibson, Todd. "Inner Asian Contributions to the Vajrayāna." *Indo-Iranian Journal* 38 (1995): 1–21.
Gimello, Robert M. "Chih-yen (602–668) and the Foundations of Hua-Yen Buddhism." Ph.D. diss., Columbia University, 1976.
———. "Random Reflections on the 'Sinification' of Buddhism." *Bulletin of the Society for the Study of Chinese Religions*, no. 5 (Spring 1978): 52–89.
Gokale, Balakrishna G. "Early Buddhist Kingship." *Journal of Asian Studies* 26.1 (1966): 15–22.
Gomez, Luis. "The Bodhisattva as Wonder Worker." In Lewis Lancaster, ed., *Prajñāpāramitā and Related Systems: Studies in Honor of Edward Conze*. Berkeley Buddhist Studies Series no. 1. Berkeley: Institute of Buddhist Studies, 1977.
Gonda, Jan. *Ancient Indian Kingship from the Religious Point of View*. Leiden: E. J. Brill, 1966.
Grafton, Anthony. *Forgers and Critics: Creativity and Duplicity in Western Scholarship*. Princeton: Princeton University Press, 1990.
Granet, Marcel. *La pensée chinoise*. Paris: Éditions Albin Michel, 1934. Reprint. 1968.
Gregory, Peter N., ed. *Sudden and Gradual: Approaches to Enlightenment in Chinese Thought*. Honolulu: University of Hawaii Press, 1987.
———. *Tsung-mi and the Sinification of Buddhism*. Princeton: Princeton University Press, 1991.
Griffiths, Paul J. *On Being Mindless: Buddhist Meditation and the Mind-Body Problem*. La Salle, Ill.: Open Court, 1986.
Griffiths, Paul J., Noriaki Hakamaya, John P. Keenan, and Paul L. Swanson. *The Realm of Awakening: Chapter Ten of Asaṅga's Mahāyānasaṅgraha*. New York and Oxford: Oxford University Press, 1989.
Groner, Paul. *Saichō: The Establishment of the Japanese Tendai School*. Berkeley: Berkeley Buddhist Studies Series, 1984.
Guenther, Herbert. *Yuganaddha: The Tantric View of Life*. 2d ed. Varanasi: Chowkhamba Sanskrit Series, 1964.
Guillen, Michael. *Bridges to Infinity: The Human Side of Mathematics*. Los Angeles: Jeremy P. Tarcher, 1983.
Gupta, Sanjukta. "Tantric Sādhana: Pūja." In Sanjukta Gupta, Dirk Jan Hoens, and Teun Goudriaan, eds., *Hindu Tantrism*. Leiden: E. J. Brill, 1979.
Hakeda, Yoshito S., trans. and comm. *The Awakening of Faith*. New York: Columbia University Press, 1967.

———. *Kūkai: Major Works*. Records of Civilization, Sources and Studies, vol. 87. New York: Columbia University Press, 1972.

Hall, David L., and Roger T. Ames. *Thinking Through Confucius*. Albany: State University of New York Press, 1987.

Hawking, Steven. "Is the End in Sight for Theoretical Physics?" In *Black Holes and Baby Universes and Other Essays*. New York: Bantam Books, 1994.

Hayashiya Tomojirō. *Kyōroku kenkyū*. Tokyo: Iwanami Shoten, 1941.

Hayes, Glen. "Shapes for the Soul: A Study of Body Symbolism in the Vaiṣṇava-Sahajiyā Tradition of Medieval Bengal." Ph.D. diss., University of Chicago, 1985.

Heesterman, Johannes C. *The Ancient India Royal Consecration*. The Hague: Mouton, 1957.

———. *The Broken World of Sacrifice: An Essay in Ancient Indian Ritual*. Chicago: University of Chicago Press, 1993.

———. *The Inner Conflict of Tradition: Essays in Indian Ritual, Kingship, and Society*. Chicago: University of Chicago Press, 1985.

Henderson, John B. *The Development and Decline of Chinese Cosmology*. New York: Columbia University Press, 1984.

Hocart, A. M. *Kingship*. Oxford: Oxford University Press, 1927. Reprint. 1969.

Hofstader, Douglas R. *Gödel, Escher, Bach: An Eternal Golden Braid*. New York: Basic Books, 1979. Reprint. New York: Vintage Books, 1980.

Holt, John Clifford. *Buddha in the Crown: Avalokiteśvara in the Buddhist Traditions of Śri Lanka*. New York: Oxford University Press, 1991.

Hookham, S. K. *The Buddha Within: Tathāgatagarbha Doctrine According to the Shentong Interpretation of the Ratnagotravibhāga*. Albany: State University of New York Press, 1991.

Hopkins, Jeffrey. *The Great Exposition of Secret Mantra: The Yoga of Tibet*. London: George Allen & Unwin, 1981.

Horiuchi, K., ed. *Tattvasaṃgraha-Sūtra*. Kōyasan: Kōyasan University Press, 1968–70.

Hsü, Dau-lin. "Crime and Cosmic Order." *Harvard Journal of Asiatic Studies* 30 (1970): 111–25.

Hume, Robert Ernest, trans. *The Thirteen Principal Upanishads*. 2d rev. ed. Oxford: Oxford University Press, 1931. Reprint. 1971.

Huntington, C. W., Jr., and Geshe Namgyal Wangchen. *The Emptiness of Emptiness: An Introduction to Early Indian Mādhyamika*. Honolulu: University of Hawaii Press, 1989.

Hurvitz, Leon. *Chih-I (538–597): An Introduction to the Life and Ideas of a Chinese Buddhist Monk*. *Mélanges chinois et bouddhiques* (Brussels) 12 (1960–62).

———, trans. *The Scripture of the Lotus Blossom of the Fine Dharma*. New York: Columbia University Press, 1976.

———, trans. *Wei Shou: Treatise on Buddhism and Taoism: An English Translation of the Original Chinese Text of "Wei-shu" CXIV and the Japanese Annotations of Tsukamoto Zenryū*. Kyoto: Jimbungaku kenkyū shu, 1955.

Inden, Ronald. "Lordship and Caste in Hindu Discourse." In Adurey Cantlie and Richard Burghart, eds., *Indian Religion*. London: Curzon Press; New York: St. Martin's Press, 1985.

Iwazaki, Hideo. "Fukusanzo to shuso tenno." *Mikkyō gakku kenkyū* 18 (1987): 112–29.

———. "Pu-k'ung and Ko Shu-han." *Journal of Indian and Buddhist Studies* (*Indogaku bukkyōgaku kenkyū*) 34 (March 1986): 514–17.

Iyanaga Nobumi. "Daijizaiten." In *Hōbōgirin*, 6:713–65.

———. "Récits de la soumission de Maheśvara par Trailokyavijaya d'après les sources Chinoises et Japonaises." In Michel Strickmann, ed., *Tantric and Taoist Studies in Honor of R. A. Stein*, vol. 3. *Mélanges Chinoises et Bouddhiques* (Brussels) 22 (1985): 633–745.

Jan Yün-hua, ed. and trans. *A Chronicle of Buddhism in China, 581–960 A.D.* (Translations from the Monk Chih-p'an's *Fo-tsu t'ung-chi*). Santiniketan: Visva-Bharati Research Publications, 1966.

———. "Hui-ch'ao and His Works: A Reassessment." *The Indo-Asian Culture* (New Delhi) 12 (January 1964): 177–90.

Jones, J. J., trans. *Mahāvastu*. 3 vols. London: Luzac, 1949.

Kalinowski, Marc. "La transmission du dispositif des neuf palais sous les six-dynasties." In Michel Strickmann, ed., *Tantric and Taoist Studies*, vol. 3. *Mélanges chinoises et bouddhiques* (Brussels) 22 (1985): 773–811.

Kaltenmark, Max. "Ling-Pao: note sur un terme du taoisme religieux." *Mélanges publies par l'institut des hautes études chinoises* (Brussels) 2 (1960): 559–88.

Katz, Nathan. *Buddhist Images of Human Perfection*. Delhi: Motilal Barnasidass, 1982.

Kawamura, L. S., ed. and trans. *Mādhyamika and Yogācāra: A Study of Mahāyāna Philosophies*. Albany: State University of New York Press, 1991.

Keenan, John. "Pure Land Systematics in India: The *Buddhabhūmi Sūtra* and the *Trikāya* Doctrine." *Pacific World*, n.s., 3 (Fall 1987): 29–35.

Kim, Jong Myung. "Chajang (fl. 636–650) and 'Buddhism as National Protector' in Korea: A Reconsideration." In Henrik H. Sørensen, ed., *Religions in Traditional Korea*. SBS Monographs no. 3. Copenhagen: Seminar for Buddhist Studies, 1995.

Kumura, Kunikazu. "Differences in the Doctrines of the Various Commentaries of the *Ninnōkyō*." *Indogaku bukkyōgaku kenkyū* 29 (March 1981): 120–21.

King, Sallie B. *Buddha Nature*. Albany: State University of New York Press, 1991.

Kirfel, Willibald. *Kosmographie de Inder*. Bonn: K. Schroeder, 1920.

Kitagawa, Joseph M. *Religion in Japanese History*. New York: Columbia University Press, 1966.

Kiyota, Minoru. *Shingon Buddhism*. Tokyo and Los Angeles: Buddhist Books International, 1978.

Kloetzli, Randy. *Buddhist Cosmology: From Single World System to Pure Land: Science and Theology in the Images of Motion and Light*. Delhi: Motilal Banarsidass, 1983.

Kloppenborg, Ria. *The Paccekabuddha: A Buddhist Ascetic*. Leiden: E. J. Brill, 1974.

Kroll, Paul. "Basic Data on Reign Dates and Local Government." *T'ang Studies*, no. 5 (1987): 95–104.

Lal, P., trans. *The Dhammapada*. New York: Farrar, Strauss & Giroux, 1967.

Lamotte, Étienne. *Histoire du bouddhisme indien des origines à l'ere Śaka*. Louvain: Bibliothèque du Muséon, 1958. Reprint. Louvain: Institut Orientaliste, 1976.

———, trans. and annot. *Traité de la grande vertue de la sagesse de Nāgārjuna* (*Mahāprajñāpāramitā-śāstra*). 3 vols. vols. 1 and 2, Bibliothèque du Muséon, no. 18. Vol. 3, Publications de l'Institut Orientaliste, no. 2. Louvain: Bureaux du Muséon, 1944–70.

La Vallée Poussin, Louis de. "Comogony and Cosmology (Buddhist)." In James Hastings, ed., *Encyclopedia of Religion and Ethics*. 13 vols. Edinburgh: T & T Clark, 1908–27.

———, trans. and annot. *L'Abhidarmakośa de Vasubandhu*. 3 vols. Paris: Paul Geuthner, 1923–25.

Legge, James, trans. *Confucius*. 1893. Reprint. New York: Dover, 1971.

———, trans. *The Book of Poetry: Chinese Text with English Translation*. China: The Commercial Press, n.d.

———, trans. *The Works of Mencius*. New York: Dover, 1970.

Legge, James, and Clae Waltham. "The Counsels of the Great Yü." In *Shu Ching: Book of History, A Modernized Edition of the Translations of James Leggee*. London: George Allen & Unwin, 1972.

Lessing, Ferdinand. "Skizze Des Ritus: Speisung Der Hunger-Geister." In Herbert Franke, ed., *Studia Sino-Altaica: Festschrift Für Haenisch Zum 80 Geburstag*. Wiesbaden: Franz Steiner Verlag, 1961.

Levinas, Emmanuel. *Totality and Infinity: An Essay on Exteriority*. Translated by Alphonso Lingis. Pittsburgh: Duquesne University Press, 1969.

Lévi-Strauss, Claude. *The Savage Mind*. The Nature of the Human Series. London: George Weidenfeld & Nicolson, 1966. Reprint. Chicago: University of Chicago Press, 1969.

Levy, Howard. *Harem Favorites of an Illustrious Celestial*. T'aichung: Chung-t'ai, 1958.

Lewis, Mark. "The Suppression of the Three Stages Sect: Apocrypha as a Political Issue." In Robert E. Buswell, ed., *Chinese Buddhist Apocrypha*. Honolulu: University of Hawaii Press, 1990.

Li Chi. "The Changing Concept of the Recluse in Chinese Literature." *Harvard Journal of Asiatic Studies* 24 (1962–63): 234–47.

Liebenthal, Walter. *Chao Lun: The Treatises of Seng-chao*, 2d rev. ed. Hong Kong: Hong Kong University Press, 1968.

Lincoln, Bruce. *Discourse and the Construction of Society: Comparative Studies of Myth, Ritual, and Classification*. New York: Oxford University Press, 1989.

Lombard-Salmon, Caludine. "Survivance d'un rite bouddhique à Java: La cérémonie du *p'u-du*." *Bulletin de l'École Française d'Extrême-Orient* 67 (1975): 457–86.

Lopez, Donald S., Jr. *Buddhism in Practice*. Princeton: Princeton University Press, 1995.

———, ed. *Buddhist Hermeneutics*. Honolulu: University of Hawaii Press, 1988.

L'Orange, H. P. "Expressions of Cosmic Kingship in the Ancient World." In *The Sacral Kingship*, pp. 481–92.

MacQueen, Graeme. "The Conflict Between External and Internal Mastery: An Analysis of the *Khāntivadi Jātaka*." *History of Religion* 20 (February 1981): 242–52.

Mair, Victor H. "Buddhism and the Rise of the Written Vernacular in East Asia: The Making of National Languages." *Journal of Asian Studies* 53.3 (1994): 707–51.

———, ed. *The Columbia Anthology of Traditional Chinese Literature*. New York: Columbia University Press, 1994.

———, trans. *Tao Te Ching: The Classic Book of Integrity and the Way*. New York: Bantam Books, 1990.

Major, John S. "The Five Phases, Magic Squares, and Schematic Cosmography." In Henry Rosemont Jr., ed., *Explorations in Early Chinese Cosmology*. Chico, Calif.: Scholars Press, 1984.

Makita Tairyō. *Gikyō kenkyū*. Kyoto: Kyōto daigaku jinbun kagaku kenkyūjo, 1976.

Malandra, Geri H. *Unfolding a Maṇḍala: The Buddhist Cave Temples at Ellora*. Albany: State University of New York Press, 1993.

Mammitzsch, Ulrich. *Evolution of the Garbhadhātu Maṇḍala*. New Delhi: Aditya, 1991.

Maspero, Henri. "Le Ming-Tang et la crise religieuse chinoise avant les Han." *Mélanges chinois et bouddhiques* (Brussels) 9 (1951): 1–71.

Mather, Richard B. "K'ou Ch'ien-chih and the Taoist Theocracy at the Northern Wei Court, 425–451." In Anna Seidel and Holmes Welch, eds., *Facets of Taoism: Essays in Chinese Religion*. New Haven: Yale University Press, 1979.

Matsunaga Yūkei. *Mikkyōkyōtenseiritsu shiron*. Kyoto: Hōzōkan, 1980.

———. *Mikkyō no reikishi*. Kyoto: Heiraku-ji shoten, 1969.

———. "Tantric Buddhism and Shingon Buddhism." *The Eastern Buddhist* 2 (November 1969): 1–14.

May, Jacques. "Chingo kokka." In *Hōbōgirin*, 4:322–27.

Mills, D. E. *A Collection of Tales from Uji: A Study and Translation of Uji Shūi Monogatari*. Cambridge: Cambridge University Press, 1970.

Misaki, R. "On the Thought of Susiddhi in the Esoteric Buddhism of Late T'ang Dynasty." In *Studies of Esoteric Buddhism and Tantrism in Commemoration of the 1,150th Anniversary of the Founding of Kōyasan*. Kōyasan: Kōyasan University Press, 1965.

Müller, Wilhelm Kuno. "Shingon-Mysticism: Śubhakarasiṃha and I-hsing's Commentary to the Mahāvairocana-Sūtra, Chapter One, An Annotated Translation." Ph.D. diss., University of California, Los Angeles, 1976.

Munro, Donald J. *The Concept of Man in Early China*. Stanford: Stanford University Press, 1969.

Murti, T.R.V. *The Central Philosophy of Buddhism*. London: Allen & Unwin, 1955.

Mus, Paul. *Barabudur: Esquisse d'une histoire du bouddhisme fondée sur la critique archéologique des texts*, 2 vols. Hanoi: Imprimerie d'Extrême-Orient, 1935. Reprint, 2 vols. in 1. New York: Arno Press, 1978.

———. "Le Bouddha paré: Son origine Indienne." *Bulletin de l'École Française d'Extrême Orient* 28 (1926).

Nadeau, Randall. Review of *Chinese Buddhist Apocrypha*. *Journal of Chinese Religions* 20 (Fall 1992): 230–32.

Nagao, Gadjin. "On the Theory of the Buddha-Body." *The Eastern Buddhist* 6 (May 1973): 25–53.

Nakano Genzan. *Fudō myōō zō*. *Nippon no bijutsu* 3, no. 238 (March 1987).

Nattier, Jan J. "The Candragarbha-sūtra in Central and East Asia: Studies in Buddhist Prophecy of Decline." Ph.D. diss., Harvard University, 1988.

———. *Once Upon a Future Time: Studies in a Buddhist Prophecy of Decline*. Berkeley: Asian Humanities Press, 1991.

Nattier, Jan J., and Charles S. Prebish. "Mahāsāṃghikā Origins: The Beginnings of Buddhist Sectarianism." *History of Religions* 16 (February 1977): 237–72.

Needham, Rodney. *Reconnaissances*. Toronto: University of Toronto Press, 1980.

Newman, John R. "The Outer Wheel of Time: Vajrayāna Buddhist Cosmology in the Kālacakra Tantra." Ph.D. diss., University of Wisconsin, 1987.

O'Flaherty, Wendy Donniger. *Dreams, Illusion, and Other Realities*. Chicago: University of Chicago Press, 1984.

Ōmura, Seigai. *Mikkyō-hattatsu-shi*. 5 vols. 1918. Reprint. Tokyo: Kokusho Kankokai, 1972.

Orlando, Raffaello. "A Study of Chinese Documents Concerning the Life of the Tantric Buddhist Patriarch Amoghavajra (A. D. 705–774)." Ph.D. diss. Princeton University, 1981.

Orzech, Charles D. "A Buddhist Image of (Im)Perfect Rule in Fifth-Century China." *Cahiers d'extrême-asie* 8 *Memorial Anna Seidel I* (1995): 139–53.

———. "Answering Difficult Questions." *History of Religions* 24.3 (1985): 282–84.

———. "Cosmology in Action: Recursive Cosmology, Soteriology, and Authority in *Chen-yen* Buddhism with Special Reference to the Monk Pu-k'ung." Ph.D. diss., University of Chicago, 1986.

———. "Esoteric Buddhism and the *Shishi* in China." In Henrik H. Sørensen, ed., *The Esoteric Buddhist Tradition*. Selected Papers From the 1989 SBS Conference. SBS Monographs no. 2. (Copenhagen and Århus: Seminar for Buddhist Studies 1994): 51–72.

———. "Mahāvairocana." In Mircca Eliade, ed., *Encyclopedia of Religion*, 9:126a–128b. New York: Macmillan, 1987.

———. "Seeing *Chen-yen* Buddhism: Traditional Scholarship and the Vajrayāna in China." *History of Religions* 29.2 (1989): 87–114.
———. "Puns on the Humane King: Analogy and Application in an East Asian Apocryphon." *Journal of the American Oriental Society* 109.1 (1989): 17–24.
———. "Reality Words." *History of Religions* 30.2 (1990): 213–15.
———, trans. "The Legend of the Iron Stūpa." In Lopez, *Buddhism in Practice*, pp. 314–17.
———, trans. "Saving the Burning-Mouth Hungry Ghost." In Donald S. Lopez, Jr., ed., *Religions of China in Practice*. Princeton: Princeton University Press, 1996.
———, trans. "The Scripture on Perfect Wisdom for Humane Kings Who Wish to Protect Their States." In *Religions of China in Practice*.
Osabe Kazuo. *Ichigyōzenji no kenkyū*. Kobe: Kōbe shōka daigaku gakujutsu kenkyūkai, 1963.
———. "On the Two Schools of Garbhodbhava Esoteric Buddhism in the Latter Period of the T'ang Dynasty and the Method of the Three Siddhis." In *Studies of Esoteric Buddhism and Tantrism in Commemoration of the 1,150th Anniversary of the Founding of Kōyasan*. Kōyasan: Kōyasan University Press, 1965.
———. *Tōdai mikkyōshi zakkō*. Kobe: Kōbe shōka daigaku gakujutsu kenkyūkai, 1971.
———. *Tō Sō mikkyōshi ronko*. Kyoto, 1982.
Pang, Duane. "The *P'u-tu* Ritual." In Michael Saso and David Chappell, eds., *Buddhist and Taoist Studies* 1. Honolulu: University of Hawaii Press, 1977.
Paper, Jordan. *The Spirits Are Drunk: Comparative Approaches to Chinese Religion*. Albany: State University of New York Press, 1995.
Paul, Diana. *Philosophy of Mind in Sixth-Century China: Paramārtha's Evolution of Consciousness*. Stanford: Stanford University Press, 1984.
Payne, Richard K. "Feeding the Gods: The Shingon Fire Ritual." Ph.D. diss., Graduate Theological Union, University of California, Berkeley, 1985.
———. *The Tantric Ritual of Japan: Feeding the Gods: The Shingon Fire Ritual*. New Delhi: Aditya, 1991.
Pepper, Stephen C. *World Hypotheses: A Study in Evidence*. Berkeley and Los Angeles: University of California Press, 1966.
Perrin, Norman. *The New Testament: An Introduction*. New York: Harcourt Brace Jovanovich, 1974.
Peterson, C. A. "Court and Province in Mid- and Late T'ang." *The Cambridge History of China*, vol. 3, pt. 1. Cambridge: Cambridge University Press, 1979.
Plaks, Andrew. *Archetype and Allegory in the Dream of the Red Chamber*. Princeton: Princeton University Press, 1976.
Poundstone, William. *The Recursive Universe: Cosmic Complexity and the Limits of Scientific Knowledge*. Chicago: Contemporary Books, 1985.
Przyluski, Jean. *The Legend of the Emperor Aśoka in Indian and Chinese Texts*. Translated by Dilip Kumar Biswas. Calcutta: Firma K. L. Mukhopadhyay, 1967.
———. "Les Vidyārāja: Contribution à l'histoire de la magie dans les sects mahāyānistes." *Bulletin d'École Française d'Extrême-Orient* 23 (1923) [Hanoi, 1924]: 301–18.
Pulleyblank, Edwin G. *The Background of the Rebellion of An Lu-shan*. London: Oxford University Press, 1955.
———. *Lexicon of Reconstructed Pronunciation in Early Middle Chinese, Late Middle Chinese, and Early Mandarin*. Vancouver: University of British Columbia Press, 1991.
———. *Middle Chinese: A Study in Historical Phonology*. Vancouver: University of British Columbia Press, 1984.

———. "The Reconstruction of Han Dynasty Chinese." *Journal of the American Oriental Society* 105.2 (1985): 303–8.
Rambach, Pierre. *The Secret Message of Tantric Buddhism*. Translated by Barbara Bray. New York: Rizzoli International Publications, 1979.
Rambelli, Fabio. "Re-inscribing *Maṇḍala*: Semiotic Operations on a Word and Its Object." In *Studies in Central and East Asian Religions*, vol. 4. Copenhagen and Århus: Seminar for Buddhist Studies, 1991.
Read, John. *Prelude to Chemistry: An Outline of Alchemy, Its Literature and Relationships*. Kila, Mon.: Kessinger, 1992.
Reichel-Dolmatoff, Gerardo. *Amazonian Cosmos: The Sexual and Religious Symbolism of the Tukano Indians*. Chicago: University of Chicago Press, 1971.
Reischauer, Edwin O. *Ennin's Diary: The Record of a Pilgrimage to China in Search of the Law*. New York: The Ronald Press, 1955.
Reynolds, Frank E. "Multiple Cosmogonies and Ethics: The Case of Theravāda Buddhism." In Robin W. Lovin and Frank E. Reynolds, eds., *Cosmogony and Ethical Order: New Studies in Comparative Ethics*. Chicago: University of Chicago Press, 1985.
———. "The Several Bodies of the Buddha: Reflections on a Neglected Aspect of the Theravāda Tradition." *History of Religions* 16 (May 1977): 374–89.
Reynolds, Frank E., and Mani B. Reynolds, trans. and comm. *Three Worlds According to King Ruang: A Thai Buddhist Cosmology*. Berkeley: Institute of Buddhist Studies, 1982.
Rhi Khiyong. "*Inwang panya-kyŏng* kwa hoguk pulgyo." In *Han'guk Pulgyo yŏn'gu*. Seoul: Han'guk Pulgyo Yon'guwŏn, 1982.
Rhys-Davids, T. W., trans. *Dialogues of the Buddha*. 3 vols. Sacred Books of the Buddhists, nos. 2–4. London: Pāli Text Society, 1899–1921.
———, trans. *The Mahā-parinibbāna Suttanta*. In *Buddhist Suttas*. New York: Dover, 1969.
Richards, John F., ed. *Kingship and Authority in South Asia*. South Asia Publications Series 3. Madison: University of Wisconsin Press, 1978.
Robinson, Richard. *Early Mādhyamika in India and China*. Madison: University of Wisconsin Press, 1967.
Rogers, Michael C. *The Chronicle of Fu Chien: A Case of Exemplar History*. Berkeley and Los Angeles: University of California Press, 1968.
Rorty, Richard. *Contingency, Irony, and Solidarity*. Cambridge: Cambridge University Press, 1989.
———. *Essays on Heidegger and Others*. Philosophical Papers Volume 2. Cambridge: Cambridge University Press, 1991.
Rosemont, Henry, ed. *Explorations in Early Chinese Cosmology*. Chico. Calif.: Scholars Press, 1984.
Rowel, Teresina. "The Background and Early Use of the Buddha-Kṣetra Concept." *Eastern Buddhist* 6 (1933): 199–246, 379–431; 7 (1936): 131–76.
Ruegg, David Seyfort. *La Théorie du Tathāgatagarbha et du Gotra: Études sur la soteriologie et la gnoseology du bouddhisme*. Paris: École Française d'Extrême-Orient, 1969.
The Sacral Kingship: Contributions to the Central Theme of the Eighth International Congress for the History of Religions. Leiden: E. J. Brill, 1959.
Said, Edward, W. *Beginnings: Intention and Method*. New York: Basic Books, 1975.
———. *The World, the Text, and the Critic*. Cambridge: Harvard University Press, 1983.
Sanford, James H. Review of Yamasaki Taikō, *Shingon: Japanese Esoteric Buddhism*, trans. Richard Petersen and Cynthia Petersen (Boston: Shambhala, 1988). *Monumenta Nipponica* 44 (Autumn 1989): 383–85.

Sangren, P. Steven. *History and Magical Power in a Chinese Community*. Stanford: Stanford University Press, 1987.

Sankalia, H. D. *The University of Nālandā*. 2d. revised edition. Madras: B. G. Paul, 1934. Reprint. Delhi: Oriental Publishers 1972.

Sargent, Galen E. "Tan-yao and His Times." *Monumenta Serica* 16 (1957): 363–96.

Saso, Michael. *The Teachings of Taoist Master Chuang*. New Haven: Yale University Press, 1978.

———. "What Is the *Ho-t'u?*" *History of Religions* 17 (February–May 1978): 399–416.

Satō Tetsui. *Tendai daishi no kenkyū*. Kyoto: Hyakkaen, 1961.

———. *Zoku tendai daishi no kenkyū*. Kyoto: Hyakkaen, 1981.

Schafer, Edward H. *Mao Shan in T'ang Times*. Society for the Study of Chinese Religions. Monograph 1, 1980.

———. *Pacing the Void: T'ang Cults of the Stars*. Berkeley and Los Angeles: University of California Press, 1977.

Schipper, Kristofer. *The Taoist Body*. Translated by Karen C. Duval. Berkeley and Los Angeles: University of California Press, 1993.

Schopen, Gregory. "Archaeology and Protestant Presuppositions in the Study of Indian Buddhism." *History of Religions* 31.1 (1991): 1–23.

———. "Monks and the Relic Cult in the *Mahāparinibbānasutta:* An Old Misunderstanding in Regard to Monastic Buddhism." In Koichi Shinohara and Gregory Schopen, eds. *From Benares to Beijing: Essays on Buddhism and Chinese Religions*. Oakville, Ontario: Mosaic Press, 1991.

Seidel, Anna K. "The Image of the Perfect Ruler in Early Taoist Messianism: Lao-Tzu and Li Hung." *History of Religions* 9 (November 1969, February 1970): 216–47.

———. "Imperial Treasures and Taoist Sacraments: Taoist Roots in the Apocrypha." In Michel Strickmann, ed., *Tantric and Taoist Studies in Honor of R. A. Stein*, vol. 2. *Mélanges chinoise et bouddhiques* (Brussels) 21 (1983): 291–371.

Shastri, D. A. Nilakanta. "Śrī Vijaya." *Bulletin de l'École Française d'Extrême-Orient* 40 (1940): 239–313.

Shuchi-in Daigaku Mikkyō gakki, ed. *Mikkyō-kankei-bunken-mokuroku*. Kyoto: Dōshisha shuppan, 1986.

Smart, Ninian. *Worldviews: Crosscultural Explorations of Human Beliefs*. 2d ed. Englewood Cliffs, N.J.: Prentice Hall, 1995.

Smith, Barbara Herrnstein. "Contingencies of Value." In Robert Von Hallberg, ed., *Canons*. Chicago: University of Chicago Press, 1984.

Snellgrove, David L. *Buddhist Himalaya: Travels and Studies in Quest of the Origins and Nature of Tibetan Religion*. New York: Philosophical Library; Oxford: Bruno Cassirer, 1957.

———. *Indo-Tibetan Buddhism: Indian Buddhists and Their Tibetan Successors*. 2 vols. Boston: Shambala, 1987.

———. "The Notion of Divine Kingship in Tantric Buddhism." In *The Sacral Kingship: Contributions to the Central Theme of the Eighth International Congress for the History of Religions*. Leiden: E. J. Brill, 1959.

Snodgrass, Adrian. *The Matrix and Diamond World Maṇḍalas in Shingon Buddhism*. 2 vols. New Delhi: Aditya, 1988.

Soothill, W. E. *The Hall of Light: A Study of Early Chinese Kingship*. Edited by Lady Hosie and G. F. Hudson. London: Lutterworth Press, 1951.

Sørensen, Henrik H. "A Bibliographical Survey of Buddhist Ritual Texts from Korea." *Cahiers d'Extrême-Asie* 6 (1991–92): 159–200.

———. "Esoteric Buddhism in Korea." In Sørensen, ed., *The Esoteric Buddhist Tradition*, SBS Monographs no. 2. Copenhagen and Århus: Seminar for Buddhist Studies, 1994.

Spiro, Melford. *Buddhism and Society: A Great Tradition and Its Burmese Vicissitudes*. New York: Harper & Row, 1970.

Sprung, Mervyn, ed. *The Problem of Two Truths in Buddhism and Vedanta*. Dordrecht, Holland: D. Reidel, 1973.

Staal, Fritz. "Ritual Syntax." In M. Nagatomi et al., eds., *Sanskrit and Indian Studies*. Dordrecht: D. Reidel, 1980.

Stablein, William. "A Descriptive Analysis of the Content of Nepalese Buddhist *Pūjas* as a Medical-Cultural System with References to Tibetan Parallels." In Agehananda Bharati, ed., *In the Realm of the Extra-Human: Ideas and Actions*. The Hague: Mouton, 1976.

———. "Tantric Medicine and Ritual Blessings." *The Tibetan Journal* 1 (1976): 55–69.

Stcherbatsky, Th. *Buddhist Logic*. Leningrad: Academy of Sciences of the U.S.S.R., ca. 1930. Reprint. New York: Dover, 1962.

———. *The Central Conception of Buddhism and the Meaning of the Word "Dharma."* London: Royal Asiatic Society, 1923. Reprint. Delhi: Motilal Banarsidass, 1974.

Stein, Rolf. "Nouveaux problèms du tantrisme Sino-Japanais." *Annuaire du Collège de France* (1975): 479–88.

———. "Quelques problèms du tantrisme chinoise." *Annuaire du Collège de France* (1974): 497–508.

Streng, Fredrick J. *Emptiness: A Study in Religious Meaning*. New York: Abingdon Press, 1967.

Strickmann, Michel. "*Homa* in East Asia." In Fritz Staal, ed., *Agni*. 2 vols. Berkeley and Los Angeles: University of California Press, 1982.

———. "The Mao-shan Revelations: Taoism and the Aristocracy." *T'oung Pao* 63 (1977): 1–64.

———. "On the Alchemy of T'ao-hung-ching." In Holmes Welch and Anna Seidel, eds., *Facets of Taoism*. New Haven: Yale University Press, 1979.

Strong, John S. *The Experience of Buddhism: Sources and Interpretations*. Belmont, Calif.: Wadsworth, 1995.

———. "Gandhakuṭī: The Perfumed Chamber of the Buddha." *History of Religions* 16 (1977): 390–406.

———. *The Legend of King Aśoka: A Study and Translation of the Aśokāvadāna*. Princeton: Princeton University Press, 1983.

———. "Making Merit in the *Aśokāvadāna:* A Study of Buddhist Acts of Offering in the Post Parinirvana Age." Ph.D. diss., University of Chicago, 1977.

———. "The Transforming Gift: An Analysis of Devotional Acts of Offering in Buddhist *Avadāna* Literature." *History of Religions* 18 (February 1979): 221–37.

Suzuki, Daisetz Teitaro, trans. *The Laṅkāvatāra Sūtra*. London: Routledge & Kegan Paul, 1932. Reprint. Boulder: Prajna Press, 1978.

———. *On Indian Mahāyāna Buddhism*. Edited by Edward Conze. New York: Harper & Row, 1968.

———. *Studies in the Laṅkāvatāra Sūtra*. London: Routledge & Kegan Paul, 1930. Reprint. Boulder: Prajna Press, 1981.

Swanson, Paul L. *Foundations of T'ien-t'ai Philosophy: The Flowering of the Two Truths Theory in Chinese Buddhism*. Berkeley: Asian Humanities Press, 1989.

Swearer, Donald K. "Control and Freedom: The Structure of Buddhist Meditation in the Pāli Suttas." *Philosophy East and West* 23 (December 1973): 435–55.

Tajima Ryūjun. *Les deux grandes maṇḍalas et la doctrine d'esoterism Shingon*. Bulletin de la Maison Franco-Japonaise, n.s., vol. 6. Paris: Presses Universitaires de France, 1959.

———. *Étude sur le Mahāvairocana-Sūtra* (*Dainichikyō*). Librairie d'Amerique et d'Orient. Paris: Adrien Maisonneuvre, 1936.

Takakusu Junjirō. *The Essentials of Buddhist Philosophy*. Honolulu: University of Hawaii, 1947. Reprint. Delhi: Motilal Banarsidass, 1978.

Takasaki Jikido. *A Study on the Ratnagotravibhāga (Uttaratantra): Being a Treatise on the Tathāgatagarbha Theory of Mahāyāna Buddhism*. Rome: Istituto Italiano per il Medio ed Estremo Oriente, 1966.

Tambiah, Stanley J. *World Conqueror and World Renouncer*. New York: Cambridge University Press, 1976.

Tamura Enchō, "Early Buddhism in Japan." *Studies in History* (Fukuoka, Japan) 13 (1971): 1–89.

Tanaka, Kenneth. *The Dawn of Pure Land Buddhist Doctrine: Ching-ying Hui-yüan's Commentary on the Visualization Sūtra*. Albany: State University of New York Press, 1990.

Tanaka, Ryōsho. "Tōdai ni okeru zen to mikkyō to no kōshō." *Nipponbunkkyōgakkai nempō* 40 (1975): 109–24.

T'ang Yung-t'ung. *Han wei liang chin nan-pei ch'ao fo-chiao shih*. 2 vols. Beijing: Chung-hua shu-chü, 1983.

———. "On Ko-yi, the Earliest Method by Which Indian Buddhism and Chinese Thought Were Synthesized." In W. R. Inge et al., eds., *Radhakrishnana: Comparative Studies in Philosophy*. London: Allen & Unwin, 1951.

Taylor, Mark C. *Altarity*. Chicago: University of Chicago Press, 1987.

Taylor, Richard. "A Reformulation of the Argument for Contingency." In Keith E. Yandell, ed., *God, Man, and Religion: Readings in the Philosophy of Religion*. New York: McGraw-Hill, 1973.

Teiser, Stephen F. *The Ghost Festival in Medieval China*. Princeton: Princeton University Press, 1988.

———. *The Scripture on the Ten Kings and the Making of Purgatory in Medieval Chinese Buddhism*. Honolulu: University of Hawaii Press, 1994.

———. "T'ang Buddhist Encyclopedias: An Introduction to *Fa-yüan chu-lin* and *Chu-ching yao-chi*." *T'ang Studies* 3 (1985): 109–28.

Thurman, Robert A. F. *The Holy Teaching of Vimalakīrti: A Mahāyāna Scripture*. University Park: Pennsylvania State University Press, 1976.

Toganoo Shōun. *Himitsu bukkyō-shi*. Kyoto: Naigai Press, 1933.

———. *Mandara no Kenkyū*. Kōyasan: Kōyasan daigaku, 1927. Reprinted in *Toganoo zenshū*, vol. 4. Kyoto, 1959.

Tokuno, Kyoko. "The Evaluation of Indigenous Scriptures in Chinese Buddhist Bibliographical Catalogues." In Buswell, *Chinese Buddhist Apocrypha*, pp. 31–74.

Ts'en, Chung-mien. "The T'ang System of Bureaucratic Titles and Grades." Translated by P. A. Herbert. *Tang Studies* 5 (1985): 25–31.

Tsukamoto Zenryū. *Shina bukkyōshi kenkyū, hokugi-hen*. Tokyo: Kōbundō, 1942.

Tucci, Giuseppe. "Gyantse ed I suoi Monasteri, Part I: Descrizione Generale dei Tempi." In *Indo-Tibetica*, vol. 4. Rome: Accademia d'Italia, 1941.

———. *Tibetan Painted Scrolls*. Translated by Virginia Vacca. 2 vols. Rome: Libreria Dello Stato, 1949.

Tu Wei-ming. *Humanity and Self-Cultivation: Essays in Confucian Thought*. Berkeley: Asian Humanities Press, 1979.

Twitchett, Denis. "Hsüan-tsung (reign 712–56)." In *The Cambridge History of China*, vol. 3, part 1. Cambridge: Cambridge University Press, 1979.

———. "Lu Chih (754–805): Imperial Advisor and Court Official." In Denis Twitchett and Arthur Wright, eds., *Confucian Personalities*. Stanford: Stanford University Press, 1962.

———. ed. *The Cambridge History of China*. 14 volumes projected. Vol. 3, *Sui and T'ang China, 589–906*. Cambridge: Cambridge University Press, 1979.

Twitchett, Denis, and Arthur F. Wright, eds. *Perspectives on the T'ang*. New Haven: Yale University Press, 1973.

Ullmann, Walter. *A History of Political Thought: The Middle Ages*. Baltimore: Penguin Books, 1970.

Van der Leeuw, G. *Religion in Essence and Manifestation: A Study in Phenomenology*. 2 vols. Translated by J. E. Turner. New York: Harper & Row, 1963.

Van Gulik, R. H. *Siddham: An Essay on the History off Sanskrit Studies in China and Japan*. Sarasvati Vihara Series, vol. 36. Nagpur: International Academy of Indian Culture, 1956.

Wach, Joachim. *The Comparative Study of Religions*. Edited by Joseph M. Kitagawa. New York: Columbia University Press, 1958.

Waldrop, M. Mitchell. *Complexity: The Emerging Science at the Edge of Order and Chaos*. New York: Touchstone, 1992.

Waley, Arthur, trans. *Ballads and Stories from Tun-huang: An Anthology*. London: George Allen & Unwin, 1960.

Wang, Chung-lo. *Wei chin nan-pei ch'ao sui ch'u t'ang shih*. Shanghai: Jen-min ch'u-pan-she, 1979.

Wang, Gungwu. "Early Ming Relations with Southeast Asia: A Background Essay." In John King Fairback, ed., *The Chinese World Order: Traditional China's Foreign Relations*. Cambridge: Harvard University Press, 1968.

Wang Wen-yin. *Fo-chiao fan-i chih yen-chiu*. Taipei: T'ien hua ch'u-pan shih yeh kung-ssu, 1985.

Wang Yi-t'ung. "Slaves and Other Comparable Social Groups During the Northern Dynasties (386–618)." *Harvard Journal of Asiatic Studies* 16 (1953): 293–364.

Warren, Henry Clarke, trans. *Buddhism in Translations*. Cambridge: Harvard University Press, 1896. Reprint. New York: Atheneum, 1963.

Wayman, Alex. *The Buddhist Tantras: Light on Indo-Tibetan Esoterism*. New York: Samuel Weiser, 1973.

———. "Reflections on the Theory of Barabudur as Mandala." In H. W. Woodward Jr. and Luis O. Gomez, eds., *Barabudur: History and Significance of a Buddhist Monument*. Berkeley Buddhist Studies Series 2. Berkeley: The Institute of Buddhist Studies, 1979.

Wayman, Alex, and Hideko Wayman, trans. and intro. *The Lion's Roar of Queen Śrīmālā*. New York: Columbia University Press, 1974.

Weber, Max. *From Max Weber: Essays in Sociology*. Translated and edited by H. H. Gerth and C. Wright Mills. New York: Oxford University Press, 1958.

———. *Max Weber on Charisma and Institution Building*. Edited by S. N. Eisenstadt. The Heritage of Sociology Series. Chicago: University of Chicago Press, 1968.

———. *The Sociology of Religion*. Translated by Ephraim Fischoff. Boston: Beacon Press, 1963.

Wechsler, Howard J. *Offerings of Jade and Silk: Ritual and Symbol in the Legitimation of the T'ang Dynasty*. New Haven: Yale University Press, 1985.

Weinstein, Stanley. "The Beginnings of Esoteric Buddhism in Japan: The Neglected Tendai Tradition." *Journal of Asian Studies* 34.1 (1974): 177–91.

———. *Buddhism Under the T'ang*. Cambridge: Cambridge University Press, 1987.

Welch, Holmes. "Dharma Scrolls and the Succession of Abbots in Chinese Monasteries." *T'oung Pao* 50 (1963): 93–149.

———. *The Practice of Chinese Buddhism, 1900–1950*. Cambridge: Harvard University Press, 1967.

Werblowsky, R. J. Zwi, and C. Juoco Bleeker, eds. *Types of Redemption: Contributions to the Theme of the Study-Conference Held at Jerusalem 14th to 19th July 1968*. Leiden: E. J. Brill, 1970.

Wheatley, Paul. *The Pivot of the Four Quarters: A Preliminary Enquiry into the Origins and Character of the Ancient Chinese City*. Chicago: Aldine, 1971.

Wilson, Thomas A. *Genealogy of the Way: The Construction and Uses of the Confucian Tradition in Late Imperial China*. Stanford: Stanford University Press, 1995.

Wright, Arthur. "Fo-T'u-Teng: A Biography." *Harvard Journal of Asiatic Studies* 11 (1948): 321–71.

Yamamoto Chikyo. *Introduction to the Maṇḍala*. Kyoto, 1980.

———. *Mahāvairocana Sūtra*. Delhi: International Academy of Indian Culture and Aditya Prakashan, 1990.

Yamamoto Kōshō. *The Mahāyāna Parinirvāṇa Sūtra*. 3 vols. Ube, Japan: Karinbunko, 1973–75.

Yamasaki, Taikō. *Shingon: Japanese Esoteric Buddhism*. Boston and London: Shambala, 1988.

Yamazaki, Hiroshi. *Zui tō bukkyōshi no kenkyū*. Kyoto: Hōzōkan 1967.

Yang, Han-sung, Jan Yün-hua, Iida Shotaro, and Lawrence W. Preston, trans. and eds. *The Hye-Ch'o Diary: Memoir of the Pilgrimage to the Five Regions of India*. Religions of Asia Series 2. Seoul: UNESCO Collection of Representative Works, 1984.

Yoritomi Motohiro. *Chūgoku mikkyō no kenkyū*. Tokyo: Daito shuppansha, 1979.

Yoshioka Yoshitoyo. *Dōkyō to bukkyō*. Vol. 1. Tokyo: Nihon gakujutsu shinkōkai, 1959.

Yüan-ying. *Jen-wang hu-kuo ching chiang-i*. Taipei: Wen-shu ch'u-pan-she, 1989.

Zürcher, E. *The Buddhist Conquest of China: The Spread and Adaptation of Buddhism in Early Medieval China*. 2 vols. Sinica Leidensia 11. Leiden: E. J. Brill, 1972.

———. "Late Han Vernacular Elements in the Earliest Buddhist Translations." *Journal of the Chinese Language Teachers' Association* 12.3 (1977): 177–203.

———. "A New Look at the Earliest Chinese Buddhist Texts." In Koichi Shimohara and Gregory Schopen, eds., *From Benares to Beijing: Essays on Buddhism and Chinese Religion in Honor of Professor Jan Yün-hua*. Oakville, Ontario: Mosaic Press, 1991.

———. "Prince Moonlight: Messianism and Eschatology in Early Medieval Chinese Buddhism." *T'oung Pao* 68 (1982): 1–59.

Index